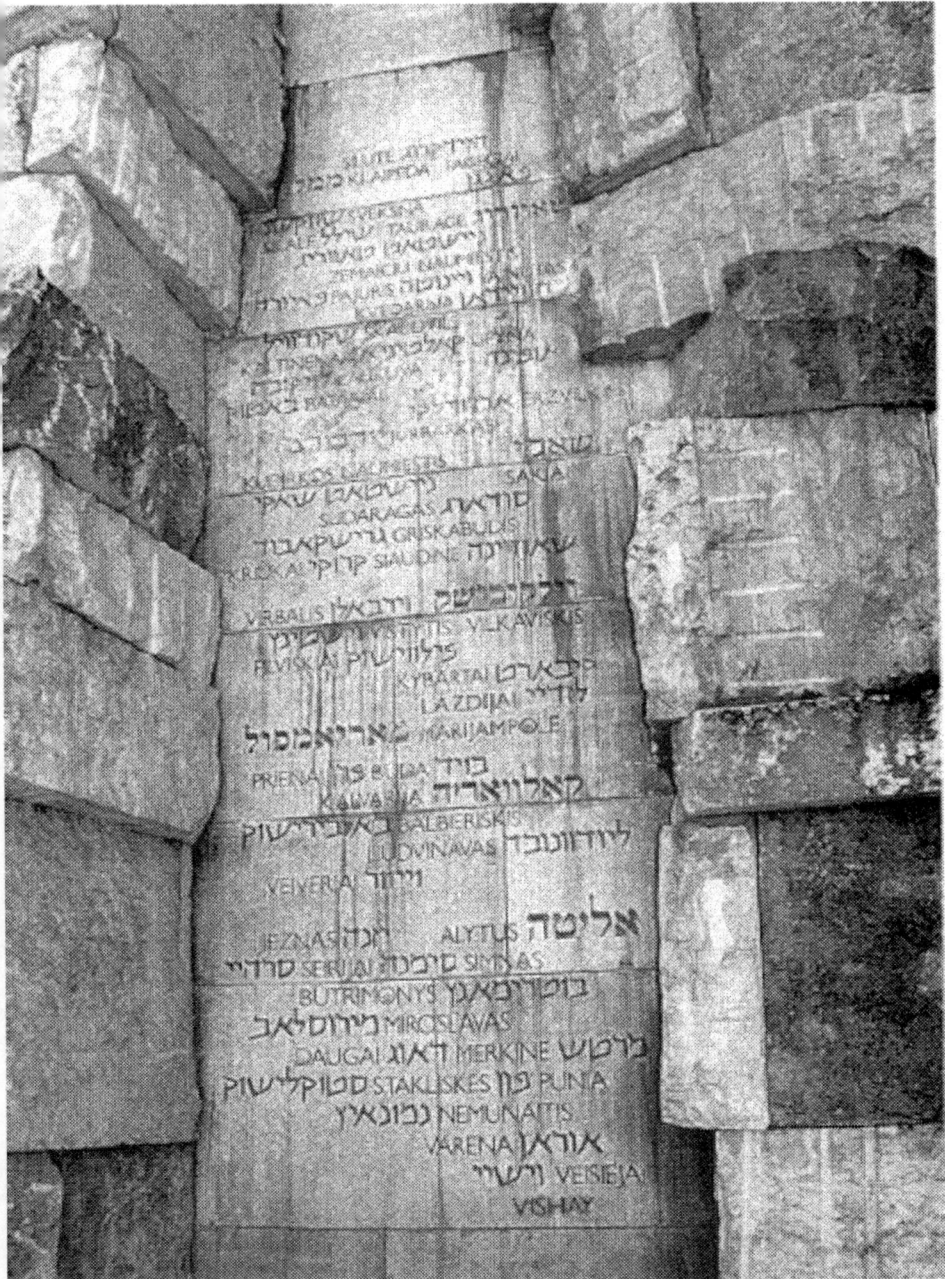

The wall bearing the names of many of the 31 towns in the "Valley of the Communities" in Yad Vashem in Jerusalem.

Preserving Our Litvak Heritage

A History of 31 Jewish Communities in Lithuania

by Josef Rosin

Introduction by Professor Dov Levin

Edited by Joel Alpert

Published by JewishGen, Inc. League City, Texas
An Affiliate of
The Museum of Jewish Heritage
A Living Memorial to the Holocaust

Preserving Our Litvak Heritage

A History of
31 Jewish Communities
in Lithuania

By Josef Rosin

Edited by Joel Alpert

JewishGen, Inc., League City, Texas

Library of Congress Control Number (LCCN): 2005920980
ISBN: 0-9764759-0-1 (hard cover: 738 pages, alk. paper)

Cover photograph of the Synagogue of Vilkaviskis (Vilkovishk) by Balys Buracas. Requests for higher resolution images should be made to Professor Antanas Buracas: anbura@lrs.lt

This book is dedicated to the

Memory of

My Father Yehudah-Leib Rosin,
My Mother Hayah nee Leibovitz
and
My little sister Tekhiyah

Who were murdered by the Nazis and their
Lithuanian helpers

Latvia

Belarus

Russia

Poland

* Tauragnai

* Utena

* Birzai

* Zeimelis

* Panevezys

* VILNIUS

* Kaisiadorys

* Stakliskes

* Seta

* KAUNAS

* Lygumai

* Prienai

* Alytus

* Varena

* Merkine

* Pilviskiai

* Marijampole

* Seirijai

* Telsiai

* Vilkaviskis

* Jurbarkas

* Sakiai

* Zemaiciu Naumiestis

* Taurage

* Sudargas

* Kudirkos Naumiestis

* Kybartai

* Virbalis

* Lazdijai

* Veisiejai

* Kapciamiestis

* Salantai

* Klaipeda

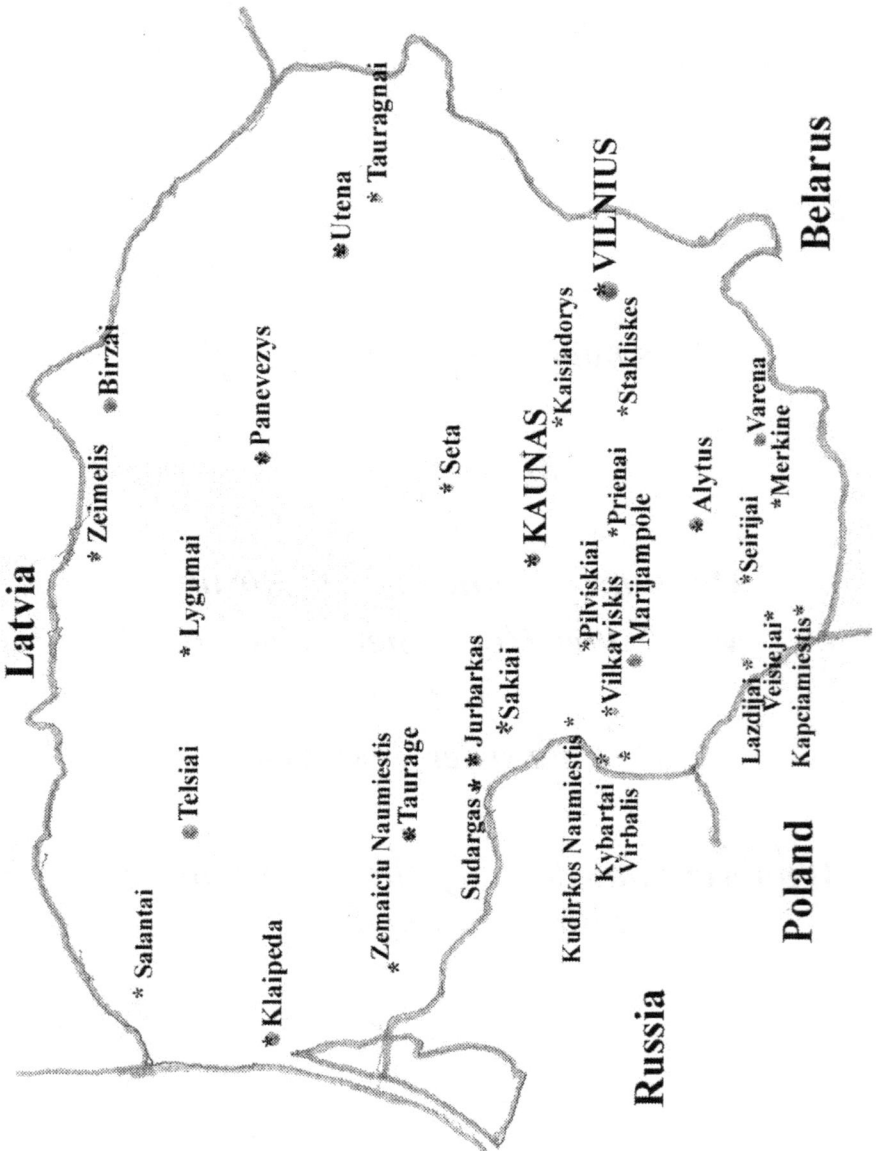

Map of Lithuania
The 31 towns in this book.

Table of Contents

This book is a compilation of the history of 31 towns of Lithuania. In order to fully appreciate and understand the history of each individual town, the reader is urged to first read the **Introduction**, written by the eminent scholar of Lithuanian Jewish History, Professor Dov Levin, retired chair of the Department of Oral History at the Hebrew University, Jerusalem. Both Dr. Dov Levin and the author, Josef Rosin are themselves natives of Lithuania, were raised in the Lithuanian Jewish community and therefore are entitled to be called "Litvaks," which they both proudly wear. They both grew up in Lithuania, Levin in Kovno and Rosin in Kibart, until the start of World War II. They met in the Kovno Ghetto where they were active in the Anti-Nazi underground and later in the forests of Lithuania as Partisan fighters against the German and Lithuanian Nazis. Both men, now retired, have devoted many years collecting and assembling information on Litvak history. In 1996 Yad VaShem published their work, Pinkas Hakehilot. Lita in Hebrew (Encyclopedia of the Jewish Communities in Lithuania); it is a monumental work of over 750 oversize pages detailing the specific history of over 500 Litvak towns. Professor Levin is the editor and Josef Rosin, who wrote about 80% of the entries, is the assistant editor. Unfortunately this significant work is not accessible to the English reading public because it is written Hebrew. Fortunately, however, the introduction of that book has been translated and presented as the book, The Litvaks - A Short History of the Jews of Lithuania, by Professor Dov Levin, published in English in 2000 by Yad VaShem.

This current book now provides an even more detailed account of the 31 communities than presented in Pinkas Hakehilot. Lita (Encyclopedia of the Jewish Communities in Lithuania), as the author is now able to elaborate and offer details that could not be included it due to space limitations. Further Josef Rosin mined the memories and photograph albums of many residents of these towns now living in Israel and elsewhere, to present an even more comprehensive picture of these communities. It must be mentioned that Josef Rosin has accomplished this task in good time, because, today, in 2004, those survivors who were young adults in 1941 are now past their 80th birthday. As I have discovered, the younger generation is finally starting to search for their history as it existed in their Litvak past, and so we are all fortunate that the author Josef Rosin has compiled this book through his thorough research.

It is my honor and pleasure to have been able to work with Josef Rosin and Professor Dov Levin and help bring this book to the English reading public.

Joel Alpert, Editor
Erev Succot, 5765, September 2004

INTRODUCTION

By Professor Dov Levin, Hebrew University

(*) Identifies towns that appear in this book

The Jewish population of Lithuania, which on the eve of the Shoah numbered approximately a quarter of a million souls including Vilna region and the refugees from Poland, (although only around 0.9% of world Jewry during the twenty years of Independent Lithuania), had been recognized for a long time as a specific religious-cultural unit in comparison to neighboring Jewish centers of Poland, Belarus and Ukraine. Lithuanian Jews were distinguished by their intellectual and rational attitude. Not in vain, the Lithuanian Jews were nicknamed not only *"Litvak",* but also *"Tseilem Kop"* ("Cross Head"), suggesting that the Lithuanian Jew would be ready to strike out vertically and horizontally (like the form of a cross, God forbid) in order to achieve his goal, or alternatively to cross check his findings in order to reach the absolute truth.

These attributes and others had implications not only in daily life, but they resulted in various phenomena, currents and systems in the social-cultural strata, such as the reservation of the majority of Lithuanian Jews about "False Messiahs", their opposition to "Hasiduth" (Chassidism), their diligence for studying Torah in the Synagogues (Batei Midrash) as well in the "Yeshivoth Ketanoth" (Junior Yeshivoth) and all the more so in the "Great Yeshivoth." Jewish Lithuania was famous for its great Yeshivoth of Slabodka*, Telzh*, Ponivezh* and Kelem, where hundreds of foreign students also studied. The Salant* community was also well known, because it was from here that the "Musar" (Ethics) movement began and spread (Rabbi Yisrael Salanter), whose principles were based on the idea of intellectual activity and knowledge in order to correct and improve the behavior of the individual. Lithuanian Jewry was also known for fostering the "Hibath Zion" movement, and later by practically adopting the Zionist idea, and at the same time an almost simultaneous openness to the challenge of the "Haskalah" (Enlightenment Movement), whether in Yiddish, Hebrew, Russian or German.

From the historical review above, it seems that these impressive attributes and achievements, as well as the special character of Lithuanian Jewry within the Jewish world, developed alongside prolonged struggles for their economic and civil rights among the majority ethnic Lithuanian population amongst whom they lived, and this in spite of frequent changes of rulers.

The first settlement of Jews in the Great Lithuanian Princedom, also named *Magnus Ducatus Lithuaniae,* began in the fourteenth century by invitation of the Grand Dukes Gediminas and Vytautas (Witold). In 1388, one year after the Christian-Catholic religion was introduced all over Lithuania, the latter also granted the Jews a preferred civil status and incomparable bills of rights in many different spheres, such as protecting their bodies and property; freedom to maintain their religious rituals; significant alleviation in the field of commerce, and money lending - this being permitted in relation to Christians. There was a particular regulation to protect Jews against blood libels. But in 1495 (only three years after the expulsion of Spanish Jewry) Grand Duke Alexander expelled all Jews - then numbering more than 6,000 people - from Lithuania and confiscated their property. Eight years later, when he was also elected King of Poland (according to the joint rule of these two countries); he allowed Lithuanian Jews to return to their homes and gave them back part of their property. Most of the privileges from the time of Vytautas were left intact, even after this event, and for a long period they were of some importance in preserving the legal, civil and economic status of the Jews.

This situation often caused envy among the Christian townspeople, mostly Germans, who were organized in merchant and artisan unions (*cechy*) and who for a long time had enjoyed the "Magdeburg Rights" (according to the precedent granted to merchants in the town of Magdeburg in Germany) and now perceived the Jews as competitors who had to be fought. For example they managed to cause an edict to be proclaimed (*De non tolerandis Judaeis*) according to which it was forbidden for Jews to settle in Vilna and to trade there. In the course of time this interdict lost it significance, however insults to Jews by urban Christians, including students of theological seminars in this town and others, continued for hundreds of years.

This was not the situation of the Jewish population in the northwestern region of the Lithuanian Dukedom, called *Zemaitija* or *Samogitia* (the Jews called it *Zamut*). In contrast to the eastern and southeastern parts of the Dukedom, most of this region was settled by ethnic Lithuanian tribes who in contrast to most of their brethren, accepted the Christian-Catholic religion relatively late (1413) and had not yet been infected by Judo phobia with a religious background.

The first Jewish settlers in Zamut were involved in the business of customs and tax collection. A further wave settled in this region as a result of the expulsion of Jews from Vilna (1527) and Memel* (1567). At this time there were already Jewish settlements in Zamut, such as Utyan*, Birzh*, Zhager, Yurburg*, Palongen, Pokroy, Keidan, Kelem, Shadeve and others.

A considerable advance in the condition of the Jewish population and in the relationship between Jews and the entire population transpired during the period of the actual unification of the Great Lithuanian Dukedom with Poland within the framework of the "Polish Republic" *Rzeczpospolita* (1569-1795).

At this time and for many decades later, feudalism reigned in Lithuania. Most of the population continued to make their living from agriculture as before, from breeding cattle and poultry, from fishing in rivers and lakes and from harvesting trees. A few, mainly Jews, were peddlers, and even fewer Jews dealt with import and export of agricultural products. Very few Jews (generally those close to the establishment) were granted the privilege to lease the collection of levies. With the improvement of roads and sailing routes on the rivers - most of the latter flowed into the Baltic Sea – there was a gradual increase of internal commercial activity, especially the export of timber, flax, grains, poultry, cattle, milk products etc. As a result taverns and storehouses were established near the crossroads and in river ports that developed into villages and towns, where many Jewish artisans and merchants settled. Until the eighteenth century in the area of ethnic Lithuania, recognition as a town was granted to 83 settlements and rights for commercial activity to 87 settlements. In fact there was no big difference between a small and a big town.

An additional factor for Jews becoming firmly established in the economic sphere was the significant growth of the number of Jews who were employed by nobles and estate owners in managing their estates, and also in the leasing of barrooms and taverns in rural areas. As a result, the Jewish bartender or manager was exposed to hostile attitudes from the rural population, who regarded him as an agent of the noblemen who wished to exploit them.

Although most ethnic Lithuanians were already Christians, the belief in devils and ghosts had not yet disappeared, and now the "Jew" replaced these evil symbols. It was not difficult for the Lithuanians to believe in the veracity of the "Blood Libels", a phenomenon that continued to exist until recently.

Despite this, West Lithuania, and in particular the Zamut region, became a relatively safe haven for thousands of Jewish refugees who survived the Period of Tribulation (1648-1667) which started with the mutiny of the Cossacks headed by Bogdan Khmielnitsky and ended with the occupation of Vilna by the Russian army. In addition to the refugees, the "Black Plague" ravaged the population of the region, causing many casualties.

"*Va'ad Medinath Lita*" (The Lithuanian Jewish Council) played an important role in maintaining good relations between the general population and the Jews, as well as between the Jews themselves. This was a quasi-autonomous authority of the union of Jewish communities in the Polish Republic *Rzeczpospolita*. During 138 years (1623-1761), this authority effectively and honorably represented the day-to-day interests of about 160,000 Jews in the Lithuanian Dukedom vis-à-vis the rulers, and also managed to protect their physical safety and dignity against hostile elements in the Christian population. After the "Va'ad" was organized, the communities of the "Ethnic Lithuania" region were included in an administrative unit called "Galil Zamut." Later it was called "Medinath Zamut" which included several sub-units like "Galil Birzh"* and others.

Far reaching changes in the legal and civil status of the Jews occurred during the third division of Poland in 1795, when most of Lithuania was annexed to Russia and became known as "The North-Western Zone", thereby becoming an integral part of the entire administration of the Russian empire. In addition to the provinces (Gubernias), Vilna in the northeast and Grodno in the south, the provinces of Kovno in the northwest and Suwalk in the southwest were also added. These latter two provinces of Kovno and Suwalk included Kibart* and the other 30 Jewish communities which are covered in this book.

At the end of the 18th century there were several areas in this region where half of the population was Jewish and in a few even a decisive majority. In urban settlements, Jews usually tended to concentrate in a defined area, like a Jewish quarter, sometimes called "*The Jews' Street*." The other Jews who were scattered or outside this area were strongly linked to and remained in close contact with the Jews living in the Jewish quarter.

As in other areas in western Russia at this time, this region was also proclaimed as belonging to the "*Tehum HaMoshav HaYehudi*" (The Jewish Pale of Settlement) where many restrictive edicts and harsh limitations were imposed on the Jewish population, causing great hardship that continued almost until World War I.

At the same time the government was troubled by the isolation of the Jews and tried to deal with this problem in different ways, sometimes contradictory to each other. Thus in 1804 Jews were forbidden to live in the villages and sell alcohol to peasants, but as compensation they were allowed to live as peasants on land allocated to them by the government. Schools were opened for Jews, and in Vilna a Beth-Midrash (Seminary) for Rabbis was even allowed. In fact these institutions served as places for the development of a strata of learned men who spoke Russian, which gave them entry into the lower grades of the social and academic establishments. Most Jews who lived in the villages and in the small towns, whose main living was based on contact with peasants and the poor, managed with a minimal knowledge of the Polish and Lithuanian languages. However among the narrow layer of Lithuanian intelligentsia, still loyal to a great extent to the Polish culture and statehood, there were accusations that these Jews were in fact causing the spread of Russian culture on behalf of the ruling class. As a result the Jews found themselves "*between the hammer and the anvil*" in times of war, as during the invasion of Lithuania by Napoleon in 1812. Some of them, favorably impressed by their contacts with French officers, supported the provisional authority established by the French army and even helped to provide information, but the majority remained patriotic to "Mother Russia." The Jews were thrown into even more critical situations during the Polish uprisings against Russian rule in 1831 and in 1863: as on the one hand they were suspected of sympathy with the rulers and some of them were murdered, whereas on the other hand there were the Cossacks, who had been sent by the rulers against the Poles, who abused the Jews after expelling the rebels.

During the revolutionary events against the rule of the Czar in 1905, progressive circles amongst Lithuanian Jews expressed their support for the Lithuanians, requesting national autonomy in ethnic Lithuanian regions i.e. in most of the areas of the Vilna and Kovno Gubernias and in particular in the areas of the Nieman (Nemunas) and Vilija (Neris) river basins.

In view of the elections to the all-Russian parliament (Duma) that took place in the years 1906-1917, preliminary agreements for collaboration between Jews and Lithuanians were arranged, and as a result three Jewish delegates were elected from the Kovno and Vilna Gubernias. At approximately the same time the local branch of the social democratic party in Lithuania published a proclamation in Lithuanian, denouncing pogroms against Jews in these Gubernias.

INTRODUCTION

At the beginning of World War I there were severe assaults against Jews organized by the Russian army in several towns in Lithuania, among them Kuziai, on the pretext that they supplied information to the German army. Even after the libel was strongly refuted by a committee on behalf of the Duma, the military authorities did not retract this accusation. Furthermore, in the summer of 1915, before their retreat from the Kovno Gubernia when under pressure by the German army, they exiled 120,000 Jewish citizens deep into Russia.

Strict fulfillment of orders were imposed by the German military administration (Oberost) on Jews as well as on other residents, but their relations to Jews were correct and they even made allowances for their cultural requirements.

This attitude was due to the presence of several Jewish officers in the German army. Also the identity cards issued to Jews were printed in German and Yiddish. For political reasons the Germans did not allow the establishment of an autonomy framework for Jews, despite the intercession of personalities from German Jewry. A deputation of local personalities, including the chairman of the Vilna community Dr. Ya'akov Vigodsky, Rabbi Yisrael-Nisan Kark from Kovno and others, represented Jewish interests. Some of them advocated collaboration with Lithuanian delegates regarding the establishment of an independent Lithuania.

Considerably closer relations between Lithuanian Jewry and Lithuanians could be seen at the end of World War I, when Lithuania was proclaimed an independent state, and being interested in acquiring the support of world Jewry it granted a broad cultural autonomy to the Jewish minority. Despite the massive participation of Jews in the independence war of Lithuania and their empathy in the struggle against the seizure of the Vilna region by the Polish army, many Jews were nevertheless wounded in pogroms by Lithuanian soldiers in Ponevezh*, Vilkomir and other places at this time.

In the short period there after (1920-1925), which can be called "The Golden Era" of Lithuanian Jewry and the peak of its autonomy status, public Jewish issues were managed by local community committees which were supported and guided in their daily functions by central institutions in Kovno, such as: "The Jewish National Council", the highest institution of the autonomy, "The Ministry for Jewish Affairs" etc.

At left: Stamp of the Minister for Jewish affairs.
At right: Stamp of the National Council of the Jews of Lithuania.

The education system in Hebrew and Yiddish serving about 90% of Jewish children and the chain of popular banks (Folksbank) in 85 settlements were some of many achievements of the autonomy period. In most towns branches of Zionist parties and Zionist youth organizations were active.

Between the two World Wars a considerable number of Jews who left Lithuania immigrated to Eretz-Yisrael. Hayim-Nakhman Bialik, when visiting Lithuania and hearing Hebrew spoken in the streets, was so impressed that he called Lithuania "Eretz-Yisrael of the Diaspora."

In contrast to the Zionists, the radical religious camp (Agudath Yisrael) and the Yiddishisht camp (Folkists and Communists) were numerically smaller. Although Hebrew was spoken in educational institutions, in youth organizations and also in a number of houses, their daily language was Yiddish, which was also the language of the six daily newspapers and other publications.

According to the census of 1923, its 156,000 Jews (7.6% of the entire population of Lithuania) were the biggest minority in the state. The Lithuanian majority numbered 1,701,000 souls (84%). Most Lithuanians were peasants, more than half of the Jews dealt with commerce, crafts and industry and the remainder with transportation, liberal professions and agriculture. Two-thirds of the Jews lived in the temporary capital city of Kovno (Vilna and a region around it was annexed to Poland during this period) and in cities such as Ponevezh*, Shavli and Vilkomir, while the rest could be found in 33 smaller cities and in 246 smaller towns and rural villages.

In spite of the high degree of loyalty that Jews showed to Lithuania and their willingness to fulfill their civil obligations to the state, by the end of the 1930s a considerable sector of the Lithuanian public and authorities decided to restrict the economic livelihood of the Jews. A prominent role in a defamation and incitement campaign on this subject was carried out in cities and towns by members of the association of Lithuanian merchants and artisans - *Verslininkai*. In their journal '*Verslas*' they even advocated the prohibition of the employment of Lithuanian women by Jews.

At the same time the number of Blood Libel incidents - the so called "use of blood of Christian children for baking Matsoth" – increased. There were an increasing number of events where Jews were physically attacked on different occasions: students in Kovno university, by-passers in the streets, and others. Judging from the fact that specific attacks (such as shattering windows in synagogues and setting fire to wooden Jewish houses) were carried out in several villages at the same time, one can conclude that they were organized country-wide. It eventually became clear that some of the nationalist circles who favored these actions, had close contacts with various circles in neighboring Nazi Germany, in spite of the fact that Germany at about the same time (March 1939) annexed the Lithuanian port Klaipeda* (Memel), where Jewish residents escaped "by the skin of their teeth."

This situation as well as the economic depression during this period which affected the Jewish sector in particular, strengthened left wing political circles amongst the Jews. Due to international tensions and an atmosphere of impending war, the possibilities of immigration to America, South Africa and Eretz-Yisrael were restricted.

With the return of Vilna and its region to Lithuania at the beginning of World War II, the number of Jews (including war refugees from Poland) increased to 250,000. Despite the difficult situation, Lithuanian Jews came to the assistance of refugees from Poland, and also showed a warm and generous attitude to Vilna Jews, with whom contact was renewed after a total severance of 19 years. This process stopped to a great extent on June 15th 1940 as a result of the takeover of all Lithuania by the Red Army and the application of Soviet-Communist rule with all that this implied. Despite the misgivings and reservations of many Jews, mainly from the Zionist sector and business owners, the new regime was accepted positively, particularly when the alternative was, according to the opinion of most people, which Nazi Germany could have taken over instead.

In spite of the fact that Soviet rule in Lithuania lasted for only one year, the Jews experienced severe changes in their social and economic position. Due to "Sovietization" they were harmed by the nationalization of the commercial (83%) and industrial (57%) sectors; by the elimination of the Hebrew education system and the religious institutions - the pride of Lithuanian Jewry; by reduction of the Yiddish press, and the closing of all public and political organizations, except those connected to the Communist party. A section of Jewish youth, particularly former members of Zionist youth organizations and Hebrew educational institutions, organized secret underground circles, where they maintained intellectual and social activities in Hebrew in a national spirit.

During this year the Soviet government imprisoned several Jewish leaders, local Zionist activists and also merchants. All of them were exiled to Siberia and to other remote places in the Soviet Union. Others who were destined for the same fate, but had meanwhile been overlooked for some reason, changed their addresses. In spite of the fact that Soviet rule had caused obvious suffering to the Jewish population, the Lithuanians blamed them for the loss of their independence, calling for revenge in due course. Meanwhile the Lithuanian national underground (L.A.F.) strengthened its secret contacts with Nazi Germany and the persecution of Jews, preparing for an uprising against Soviet rule in expectation of an invasion by Nazi Germany. And indeed, already during the first days of war between Germany and the Soviet Union in June 1941, many Jews were murdered with bestial cruelty by their Lithuanian neighbors. Only a small number managed to escape to the Soviet Union, where some of them were privileged to fight in the ranks of the Lithuanian Division of the Red Army against the Nazi German army.

Since the German army managed to overrun Lithuania in a matter of a few days, the majority of Lithuanian Jews remained under Nazi occupation, whilst the hostile Lithuanian population continued ever more actively to perpetrate bloody pogroms, rapes and robberies against their Jewish neighbors. Thousands of Jews from all over Lithuania were imprisoned in jails and in various other localities which later on would serve as mass murder sites, according to <u>a precise German plan which was executed with great enthusiasm by the Lithuanian military and policeman as well as local volunteers.</u> The "Organized Murder" units would appear in villages where Jews lived, usually after the first pogroms. The scared and already plundered Jews were brutally concentrated into synagogues, in market places, in isolated farms or in other buildings. From there they were led, first the men and after that the women and children, to the mass murder sites. There they were forced, whilst being beating and suffering other cruelties, to hand over jewelry and any other valuables they carried with them, to undress and to go down into the pits which had been prepared beforehand, where they were murdered immediately with guns and machine-guns. The wounded and the still alive were buried together with the dead in mass graves. Their clothes and property were plundered by the murderers and local residents.

About 40,000 Jews who survived the mass murders of summer and autumn 1941 and who were destined to serve as a temporary labor force for the German war effort, were imprisoned in ghettos: Vilna, Kovno, Shavli, Shventsian and in several labor camps in east Lithuania. Even at the time of forced labor, organized murders, called "Actions", were carried out as well as cruel deportations to regions outside Lithuania. With the Soviet-German front drawing nearer at the end of 1943 and in the first half of 1944, the Ghettos and labor camps were liquidated and their remnants transferred to concentration camps in Estonia and Germany. When the Red Army returned to Lithuania in the second half of 1944, there were then about 2,000 Jews in Soviet partisan units and the same number in various and odd hiding places which had not been discovered during the liquidation of the Ghettos and the camps. There were also those who had found shelter with non-Jews, mostly residents of villages far from the central towns of Lithuania. If one adds the number of Lithuanian Jewry survivors to those who escaped or were exiled to Russia, and those who survived the concentration camps in Germany, Estonia and elsewhere, it would seem that the enormous number of victims of the "Shoah" in Lithuania reached <u>94% of the 220,000 Jewish residents who happened to be under Nazi occupation: the greatest percentage in all of Europe! It is not surprising that most of the remnants of the "Shoah" left Lithuanian's blood soaked earth.</u> A considerable number of them immigrated to Eretz-Yisrael.

In spite of the fact that the Kibart* community was relatively new compared to most other Jewish communities in Lithuania which had existed for hundreds of years, nevertheless during the second half of the twentieth century, the period discussed in this book, the differences between Kibart and other communities of the same size in this region became blurred. This tendency continued to some degree even after the political-social reversal that took place after the entrance of the Red Army into Lithuania on the 15th of June 1940.

Actually as a result of this invasion the anti-Semitic phenomena mentioned above was arrested, but nevertheless many of Kibart's Jews whose shops and enterprises were nationalized during the "Sovietization" were victimized economically and socially. Many other Jews were also harmed, in particular supporters and activists of the Zionist camp whose organizations were closed by the new authorities. In contrast to previous conditions, during this period it was possible for every Jew to integrate into every job in the government and into municipal institutions, but activists and friends of the leftist camp were preferred.

Shortly before the Nazi Germany invasion, several Kibart Jews were detained and exiled to Siberia for political and economic reasons.

With the German invasion into Lithuania on the 22nd of June 1941, a local government comprising Lithuanian nationalists was established in Kibart. They cooperated with the German authorities on the entire issue regarding the annihilation of their local Jewish neighbors and those from adjoining towns. This 'action' was executed in two phases: on the 6th of July 1941 (11th of Tamuz 5701) and on the 11th of September of the same year (19th of Elul 5701). Since then the Kibart Jewish community ceased to exist. A few survivors settled in Israel.

Sixty three years after the complete destruction of this community, one of its survivors, the Engineer Josef Rosin, decided to memorialize his family and community by producing this scholarly work and erecting this "appropriate monument" for his family and community, and also for thirty additional communities, about half of them near Kibart. In contrast to this "young" community that had been established in the middle of the 19th century, most of the other thirty communities were founded in the 17th century (like Yurburg*, Virbaln*), or in the 18th century (Ponevezh*, Telzh*). Only a few, such as Pren*, Meretch*, and Vilkovishk*, were established earlier.

With regard to these and other differences concerning the seniority and size of the surveyed communities and in order to compare the complex material presented equally, the author, correctly, as was done in the Hebrew book, "Pinkas Kehilot Lita" (The Encyclopedia of the Jewish Communities In Lithuania), presented the material of every community surveyed according to the three main periods in which they grew and developed during their existence: 1) from the settlement of the first Jews till after World War I; 2) their condition during the period of independent Lithuania between the two world wars; 3) their history during World War II and in particular under Nazi rule and their almost absolute (94%!) extermination by the perpetrators and their local neighbors and also the fate of the few survivors to date.

There are people who describe the history of Lithuanian Jewry from its flourishing beginning till its bitter and tragic end with the caption: "From zenith to nadir" or literally: "From highest pinnacle to lowest depth."

This definition also applies to all the 31 communities that appear in the book under discussion. Furthermore, a graphic picture of their impressive growth at the end of period 1), their shrinking in period 2) and their absolute destruction in period 3) are given in the two tables below.

Table 1 includes data of the Jewish population according to three censi (1847, 1855/57, 1897) taken in Lithuania during the 19ᵗʰ century, then under Czarist Russian rule. In addition to the absolute growth of the number of Jews in almost all of the 31 towns, they were the absolute majority in 18 of these centers by the end of the century, and this despite the large emigration of Lithuanian Jews to overseas countries during this period.

Table 1 Jewish Population According to Censi of 1847, 1855, 1857, 1897

Town	1847	%	1855-7	%	1897	%	Remarks
Alite	262 (V)	---	---	---	753 (V)	37	(V) Vilna Gubernia
					481 (S)	33	(S) Suwalk Gubernia
Aran	158	---	---	---	1,473	56	
Birzh	1,685	---	---	---	2,510	56	
Koshedar	---	---	---	---	317	38	
Kopcheve	---	---	---	---	528	40	
Kibart	---	---	---	---	533	45	
Lazdey	---	---	1,546	60	1,439	57	
Ligum	---	---	350*	---	482	60	*1876
Mariampol	---	---	2,853	82	3,268	48	
Memel	---	---	289	---	936*	---	*1895 Prussian rule
Meretch	1,565	---	---	---	1,900	74	
Naishtot	1,671	53	---	---	2,091	45	
Naishtot-Tav.	---	---	---	---	1,438	59	
Ponevezh	---	---	3,566	60	6,627	51	
Pilvishok	---	---	976	62	1,242	53	
Pren	---	---	1,479	64	1,190	48	
Salant	999	---	---	---	1,106	45	
Shaki	---	---	1,473	83	1,638	74	
Shat	802	---	---	---	1,135	68	
Serey	---	---	1,492	70	1,614	60	
Stoklishok	443	33	---	---	808	37	
Sudarg	---	---	627	91	~ 600	---	
Tavrig	410	---	---	---	3,634	55	
Taragin	---	---	---	---	596	56	
Telzh	---	---	3,209	61	3.088	51	In 1797--1,650-66%
Utyan	1,416	---	---	---	2,405	74	
Vilkovishk	---	---	4,559	83	3,480	60	
Verzhbelov	---	---	---	---	1,219	37	In 1886--1,253-50%
Vishey	---	---	---	---	974	63	
Yurburg	2,527	---	---	---	2,350	31	In 1766--2,333
Zheiml	753	---	---	---	679	54	
Total:	**12,691**		**22,419**		**52,534**		
Over 50% of Population		**1**		**10**		**17**	

Table 2 shows data of the Jewish population in all the 31 towns during the period of independent Lithuania according to the census of 1923. It would seem that their numbers had decreased to a noticeable degree in most of the towns. Only in 7 towns the Jewish population increased to some extent. In spite of administrative manipulations by the authorities, the Jews retained their majority in only 4 towns (Meretch, Shaki, Shat, Utyan).

There is no doubt that the diminishing numbers of Lithuanian Jews was a result of the increasingly hostile attitude to Jews in the Lithuanian provinces. Not for nothing did people relate to this phenomenon as a bad omen in view of the impending slaughter, when Jews were executed in Lithuanian towns in the summer of 1941 long before the first German soldier appeared, often by their fellow townspeople.

A laconic but very reliable expression of what happened from then until the end of 1945 when Lithuania was liberated from the various murderers of the Jews, is given in the last column (from the right) in Table 2, where the conventional arithmetic symbol "Zero" is scattered over most of the table, meaning 100% of the Jews were murdered!

The reader of this book will understand the considerable differences between relatively large communities where there were several thousand Jews in the period of independent Lithuania (like Memel* or Mariampol*), and tiny communities which numbered only several hundreds (like Kopcheve* or Sudarg*). Regarding the religious and cultural aspects three eminent communities should be recalled: Ponevezh*, Telzh* and Salant*, already mentioned before. Although "Hasiduth" (Hassidism) was not accepted by most of Lithuanian Jewry, there were at least two communities mentioned in this book (Utyan* and Birzh*), where congregations of "Hasidim" and "Mithnagdim" existed peacefully side-by-side.

The basic way of life of the communities reviewed in this book shows community life directed first of all to fulfilling religious commandments, e.g. "Hevroth Kadisha" (burial society), cemeteries, synagogues and different "Minyanim." In bigger communities there were prayer houses for groups of worshipers of the same profession, such as artisans, merchants, shop owners, synagogue beadles etc. Special institutions for studying "Torah" were established: Batei Midrash for adults, "Hadarim" for children and "Yeshivoth Ketanoth" (small Yashivas) for youngsters. In most of the communities various groups of volunteers, acting under different names, worked in welfare organizations, among them "Bikur Holim" - for medical help and hospitalization; "Linath Hatsedek" – to support the poor and sick and to supply free medicines; "Gemiluth Hesed" - providing small interest free loans to the needy; "Zokhrei Petirath Neshamah" - commemoration of the deceased, etc.

Several communities established "Volunteer Fire Brigades." These brigades, on more than one occasion, fulfilled an effective role in protecting Jewish communities in times of pogroms and riots. Here it must be noted that almost

Table 2 Jewish Population of all 31 Towns during the Period of Independent Lithuania, according to the census of 1923

Yiddish Name of Town	Jewish Pop. 1923 *1926	% of Total Pop.	1945	After 1945
Alite	1,715	27%	0	+
Aran	399	---	0	
Birzh	1,807	34%	0	
Koshedar	596	31%	0	
Kopcheve	187	22%	0	
Kibart	1,341	21%	0	+
Lazdey	1,141	48%	0	
Ligum	240	32%	0	
Mariampol	2,545	27%	0	
Memel	* 4,500	13%		751 in 1959 (0.8% of total population) +
Meretch	1,400	66%	0	
Naishtot	901	32%	0	
Naishtot-Tavrig	664	37%	#	
Ponevezh	6,845	36%		221 in 1959 66 in 1989 +
Pilvishok	909	38%	0	
Pren	954	29%	0	
Shaki	1,267	62%	0	
Salant	670	40%	0	
Serey	880	47%	0	
Shat	440	50%	0	
Stoklishok	391	22%	0	
Sudarg	?	?	0	
Tavrig	1,777	32%		14 in 1970 8 in 1989
Taragin	477	48%	0	
Telzh	1,545	33%		70 in 1970 23 in 1989
Utyan	2,485	51%		28 in 1970 9 in 1989 +
Vishey	516	40%	0	
Vilkovishk	3,206	44%	2	
Virbaln	1,233	31%	0	+
Yurburg	1,887	43%		14 in 1970 +
Zheiml	378	31%	0	

The Berelovitz family returned home and 3 members of the family were murdered by Lithuanians.

Total 38,796

(*)In 1923 was performed the first census in independent Lithuania

(**) In January 1945 all Lithuania was liberated from the Nazis.

(+) Jewish population increased compared to the census of 1897 in all the other towns - decreased

every town in Lithuania suffered from one or more fires. Since most houses and synagogues were built of wood, most of the Jewish population became homeless. In such cases, the community Rabbis would publicize the disaster by way of letters, messengers and later also in the Jewish press in Hebrew and in Yiddish, asking for help from near and far communities. On the whole help arrived as requested, and similar methods were adopted for other disasters, i.e. epidemics.

It is worthwhile mentioning here that even before this monumental project was presented to us comprising a document of over 700 pages, Josef Rosin managed to publish, in Hebrew, the monograph "Kibart" published in Haifa in 1988 by the "Association of Former Kibart Citizens." In 2003 an updated and extended edition of this book was published, which is included in this presentation.

I myself was privileged to have known Josef Rosin for more than sixty years, actually since 1943 in the Kovno ghetto, when we were partners in social and cultural activities in the underground organization of survivors of the Zionist-Socialist youth organization "HaShomer HaTsair." Already then he was outstanding with his knowledge of different subjects and his moderate and balanced point of view in internal discussions. In particular he caused us happiness even in the depressive atmosphere of the ghetto, when he would play his wonderful music with his "Garmoshka" (Mouth organ). Later the sounds of his music also gave us pleasure in the heavily forested partisan woods of eastern Lithuania, when we were privileged to be partners of the fighters against the German Nazis and their local helpers. This pleasant tradition continued, when in October 1945 we happened to be together on an Italian fishing vessel, which transported 171 illegal Shoah survivors to Eretz-Yisrael. During these seven very difficult and trying days on board ship, he was given the job of allocating the scarce amount of drinking water provided for the passengers. (It is doubtful that he then foresaw that about half a dozen years later he would hold the position of a department head in *TAHAL-Water Planning for Israel*).

We arrived safely in Eretz-Yisrael, having evaded capture by the British police as illegal immigrants, where both of us joined Kibbutz Beith-Zera in the Jordan valley, and where we worked for some time in the banana plantations. Even after he went to study at the Technion in Haifa and I at the Hebrew University in Jerusalem, we would meet at least once a year with the remnants of our friends who had shared our ideas and also the fate of the Kovno ghetto, while we, and our families would again enjoy the sounds of his mouth organ.

In due course we came to cooperate even more positively on this scientific-literary level too. This happened at the beginning of the nineties, when I was elected by the directorate of "Yad Vashem" to serve as chief editor with the task of planning all the stages and prepare all the required material for publishing the book "Pinkas Kehilot Lita."

Knowing well his involvement and expertise concerning the way of life of Lithuanian Jewry, and also his accuracy when writing, it was natural to approach Josef Rosin first to take on the assignment of assistant editor. I am glad to state that from then on until the publication of the first edition of the "Pinkas" in 1996, we were blessed with productive and beneficial working relations, the result of which is, even if indirectly, the content and standard of the book in front of us.

I wish to praise him for his great efforts in obtaining documentary and photographic evidence from many places in the world, in order to enrich the visual and historic dimensions of the people and the main events referred to in this book.

The author also deserves appreciation for his care in including with awesome reverence most of the names of his hometown's Jews. In view of the terrible tragedy that the Jewish people experienced, it is essential, in my opinion, to repeatedly mention the Jewish names of villages and even more so the names of Jews, particularly those who did not leave descendant or relatives. May we hope that, in this way, their names, at least, will not be lost.

Finally it is appropriate to mark with gratitude and appreciation the professional work of the outstanding American-born Litvak - our mutual friend Mr. Joel Alpert – who invested much energy in preparing this book with all its components and appendices that also have great historical value and human importance. Consequently we are speaking about an *"Act of true kindness"* (*Hesed shel Emeth*) for the hundreds of Kibart people and the other thirty Jewish communities that were destroyed, never to rise again.

Jerusalem, Eve of Shoah Remembrance Day 5764
Professor Dov Levin, The Hebrew University, Jerusalem

The Author, Josef Rosin, About Himself

I am a native of Kybartai (Lithuania). I was born on January 24, 1922 to Hayah (nee Leibovitz) from Marijampole and Yehudah Leib Rosin from Sudargas (Lithuania). They were the owners of a paper and stationary shop in Kibart (the Yiddish name of the town).

I received my elementary and high school education in Kibart, Virbalis and Marijampole. During the years 1939 to 1941 I was a student at the Civil Engineering Faculty of the Kovno (Kaunas) University.

I left my home for the last time on Friday, June 20, 1941, just two days before the German invasion into the USSR began. My parents and my sister stayed in Kibart and were murdered together with all the Jews of the town in July of the same year. I was in the Kovno Ghetto for more than two and a half years until the beginning of February 1944 when I escaped into the woods (first into the Rudniki forests and later into the Naliboki forests in Belarus). I remained there until the liberation by the Red Army. In August 1944 I returned to Kovno. At the end of March 1945, I joined a group of young Lithuanian Jews who determined that we should leave Europe and make our way to *Eretz Yisrael*; we became part of the movement that became known as the *"Brikha" (Flight)* movement. I left Lithuania and after the tribulations of the illegal travel through Poland, Slovakia, Rumania, Hungary, Austria and Italy, I arrived in *Eretz Yisrael* on October 24, 1945 on a ship of *"Ma'apilim" (Illegal Immigrants)*. During the stay in Rumania I married Peninah (nee Cypkewitz) from Wloclawek, who had made a similarly difficult journey from Poland.

We lived in Kibbutz Beith-Zera in the Jordan Valley for nine months In the autumn of 1946 we left the Kibbutz and moved to Haifa, with the aim of continuing my studies at the Civil Engineering Faculty of the Technion. I was accepted in the second course (as a second year student) and after a further year delay because of the War of Independence, I completed my studies in 1950 with the degree of Engineer. In 1958 I received my M.Sc. in Agricultural Engineering from the Technion.

During the War of Independence I served in the Air Force in the Aerial Photography Unit and was discharged with the rank of Staff Sergeant. I served in the Army Reserves until the age of 54.

During the years 1950-1952 I worked at the Water Department of the Ministry of Agriculture and with the establishment of "Water Planning for Israel" (Tahal), I joined this firm, where I worked until my retirement on the first of April 1987. For more than twenty years I held the position of Head of the Drainage and Development Department of that firm.

In 1989, I published my "Memoirs" in Hebrew and in 1994 in English.

During the years 1987 through 1994 I wrote many entries for the Hebrew book *Encyclopedia of the Jewish Communities in Lithuania (Pinkas Hakehilot-Lita)* and participated in publishing this book as the Assistant Editor. This book was published by Yad Vashem in 1996, edited by Dov Levin.

In 2001 and 2002 I acted as the assistant editor for the publication of the Memorial Book of the Jewish Community of Yurburg, Lithuania - Translation and Update.

I have a married son and a married daughter and four grandchildren.

****

The book I am presenting here contains "The Remembrance Book" about my hometown Kybartai (Kibart) as well as thirty articles on Jewish communities in Lithuania. About half of the articles are about towns in the Suvalkija region (the region on the left side of the Nemunas river) (Marijampole (Mariampol), Vilkaviskis (Vilkovishk), Sakiai (Shaki) etc.), that included my home town Kibart (Kybartai). The others I chose because they had larger Jewish communities (Telsiai (Telzh), Klaipeda (Memel), Taurage (Tavrig) etc.), or according to the request of people who originated from these towns (Salantai (Salant), Lygumai (Ligum), Seta (Shat) etc.)

I wrote these articles in English; nearly all of them were edited by Sarah and Mordehai Kopfstein, Haifa, Israel.

The articles on Alytus (Alite), Kudirkos Naumiestis (Naishtot), Marijamole (Marijampol), Panevezys (Ponevezh), Salantai (Salant), Virbalis (Verzhbelov) were edited by my cousin Fania Hilelson-Jivotovsky, Montreal, Canada.

The article on Seta (Shat) was edited by Joe Woolf, Ilaniyah, Israel.

The pictures included in the articles come from various sources: many of them were sent to me, at my request, by people from the relevant towns, living in Israel or abroad. Their names are printed beneath the pictures. Other sources are the four volumes of *Yahaduth Lita* published by "The Association of Lithuanian Jews in Israel", Tel-Aviv, and Yahaduth Lita by way of *"Mosad HaRav Kook"*, Jerusalem. Pictures of the massacre sites and the monuments erected on them were taken mostly from The Book of Sorrow, Vilnius 1997.

Common sources used in most of the articles were:

Yad-Vashem Archives, Jerusalem.

Central Zionist Archives, Jerusalem: 55/1788; 55/1701; 13/15/131; Z-4/2548.

YIVO, NY-Lithuanian Communities Collection.

Kamzon Y.D. Yahaduth Lita, (Hebrew) Mossad HaRav Kook, Jerusalem 1959.

Yahaduth Lita, (Hebrew) Tel-Aviv, 1960-1984, Volumes 1-4.

Cohen Berl,. Shtet, Shtetlach un Dorfishe Yishuvim in Lite biz 1918 (Towns, Small Towns and Rural Settlements in Lithuania till 1918) (Yiddish) New York 1992.

Pinkas haKehiloth Lita (Encyclopedia of Jewish Settlements in Lithuania) (Hebrew), Editor: Dov Levin, Assistant editor: Josef Rosin, Yad Vashem. Jerusalem 1996.

Masines Zudynes Lietuvoje (Mass Murder in Lithuania) vol. 1-2, Vilnius 1941-1944 (Lithuanian).

About the Author

The Book of Sorrow, (Hebrew, Yiddish, English, Lithuanian), Vilnius 1997.

The Lithuanians Encyclopedia, Boston 1953-1965 (Lithuanian).

The Small Lithuanian Encyclopedia, Vilnius 1966-1971 (Lithuanian).

From Beginning to End (The History of HaShomer HaTsair Movement in Lithuania) (Hebrew).

HaMeilitz (St. Petersburg) (Hebrew).

Dos Vort, Kovno (Yiddish).

Folksblat, Kovno (Yiddish).

Di Yiddishe Shtime, Kovno (Yiddish).

Particulars of each town are printed at the end of each article.

Acknowledgments

Many thanks to my relative and friend Joel Alpert for initiating, compiling, proof-reading, editing and publishing this book.

To my good friend Professor Dov Levin for his encouragement and advice.

To my friends Sarah and Mordehai Kopfstein who edited my poor English in most of the articles.

To Peninah, my beloved wife for almost sixty years, for her wise and sensitive remarks.

To my cousin Fania Hilelson-Jivotovsky for editing the English in some of my articles.

To the JewishGen organization for their willingness to publish this book and specifically Carol Skydell for her enthusiastic cooperation and participation in this effort.

To all the people from different towns in Lithuania living in Israel or abroad, who so willingly sent me pictures from their albums and in most cases identified the persons appearing in them.

J. R.

Remarks:

All the Yiddish and Hebrew names were transliterated anew according to the rules issued by YIVO for this purpose.

Notes to the Reader:

Dates in the book are written according to the European standard, as day-month-year, so that, for example, "Dec. 15, 1955" would be abbreviated as "15.12.55."

Because of technical difficulties the Lithuanian names of the towns and places are printed without the particular Lithuanian letters and symbols.

Glossary of Non-English words used this Book

Agadah-Homiletic passages in Rabbinic literature

Agudath-Yisrael-Orthodox anti-Zionist organization

Aliyah (Ascent)-Immigration to Israel

Aron Kodesh-The Holly Arc in the Synagogue

Ashkenazi-Jew from Central or Eastern Europe, America.

Benei-Akiva-Religious Zionist Youth organization

Berith-Milah- Circumcision

Beth-Midrash-A Synagogue for praying and studying the Torah

Bikur-Holim-Welfare society for helping the Ill

Beitar (Brith Yosef Trumpeldor)-The Revisionist youth organization

Bimah-Platform, mostly in the middle of the Synagogue, for reading the Torah

Bund-Jewish anti-Zionist workers organization

Eretz-Yisrael-The Land of Yisrael

Ezrah (Help)-welfare society who took over the functions of the Community Committees after their liquidation in many communities

Gabai-Manager of a Synagogue

Gemara-Talmud

Gemiluth Khesed--Small loans without interest to the poor

Gordonia-Zionist Socialist youth organization

Grosmanists-Jewish State Party led by Meir Grosman

Gubernia (Russian)-Province

HeKhalutz (Pioneer)- Organization with the goal of enabling its members to move to Eretz-Yisrael after undergoing a serious course of training particularly in agriculture

Hakhnasath Kalah-Welfare society for helping poor brides to get married

Hakhnasath Orkhim-Welfare society for accommodating visitors passing through

Halakhah-Legal part of Jewish traditional literature

HaNoar HaZioni-The youth organization of the General Zionist party

HaPoel-the sport organization of the Z.S. party

HaShomer-HaTsair-leftist Zionist youth organization. In Lithuania its official name was: "The Young Guard Organization of Hebrew Scouts"

Hitakhduth- Federation of several Zionist Socialist parties

Humash-First Five Books of the Bible (Pentateuch)

Kadish-Liturgical doxology said by the mourner

Kahal-Assembly

Karaite-member of Jewish sect originating in the eighth century, which rejects the Oral Law

Khalah, Halah-Loaf of bread made of white flour, prepared specially for Shabbat

Khevrah-Kadisha-Burial Society

Kheder (Pl. Hadarim)-Religious Elementary School

Kheder Metukan-Improved Kheder in which also secular subjects were taught

Khupah-Marriage ceremony

Keren Kayemeth Le'Yisrael (KKL)-The Jewish National Fund. Its goals were buying land, planting groves and other reclamation works in Eretz-Yisrael

Keren Tel-Hai-The fund of the Revisionists after they split from the Zionist Organization

Keren Ha'Yesod-Jewish Foundation Fund

Khibath Zion-(Love of Zion)-a 19th century movement to build up the Land of Yisrael before the establishment of the Zionist organization

Khovevei Zion-Members of the above mentioned movement

Khasidim-a sect in Judaism founded by Rabbi Yisrael Ba'al Shem Tov

Khevrah-Society

Kibutz Hakhsharah-Training Kibutz for the Halutsim before their Aliyah to Eretz Yisrael

Klois-a small prayer room

Lekhem Aniyim-Welfare society for supplying bread to the poor

Magdeburg Rights-the Constitution of Magdeburg was an example of almost full autonomy for many towns in eastern Europe

Magen David-The Shield of David-The National emblem of the Jewish people

Maoth-Money

Maoth Khitim-Charity Fund for the poor for buying flour for Matsoth

Matsah, Pl. Matsoth-Unleavened bread for Passover

Melamed, Pl. Melamdim-Teacher in a Kheder

Meshulakh-Emissary for collecting money for different institutions in Eretz-Yisrael

Mikveh-Ritual bath

Minyan, Pl. Minyanim-Ten adult male Jews, the minimum for congregational prayer

Mishnah-Collection of Oral Laws compiled by Rabbi Yehudah haNasi, which forms the basis of the Talmud

Mithnagdim-Opponents to Hasidim

Mizrahi-Religious Zionist party

Mohel-Circumciser

Moshav Zekeinim-Home for the Aged

Linath HaTsedek-Welfare society for helping the ill

Oleh, Pl. Olim (Ascending)-Immigrant to Israel

Olim LaTorah-called up to the reading of the bible in the Synagogue

ORT Chain-International organization for spreading vocational education to the Jews

OZE-(Initials of the Russian name)-International organization for improving the public and personal hygiene of the Jewish population, in particular of the school children

Pinkas-Notebook, Register

Pesakh-Passover

Poalei Zion (Workers of Zion)-Socialist workers party

Poale Zion-Smol (Workers of Zion-left)-Radical leftist party, was forbidden

Rosh Yeshivah-Head of a Yeshivah

Sepharadi-Jew of Spanish stock

Shamash-Synagogue beadle

Shas-Abbreviation of Shisha Sidrei Mishnah-The six books of the Mishnah

Shekhitah-Ritual slaughtering

Shekel, Shekalim-the membership card of the Zionist organization that granted the privilege to vote at the Zionist Congresses

Shokhet, Pl. Shokhtim-Ritual slaughterer-s

Shtibl, Pl. Shtiblakh-Small prayer room for people of the same profession

Shul-Synagogue

Shulhoif-The backyard of the Synagogue

Shulkhan Arukh (The prepared table)-authoritative code of Jewish laws, written by Yoseph Caro (1488-1575)

Sidur-Prayer book

Somekh Noflim-Loans without interest for people who lost their business or property

Suvalkija -the Region of Lithuania on the left side of the Nemunas (Nieman) river

Talmud Torah-Religious school

Tarbuth Chain (Culture)-Zionist Hebrew chain of elementary schools

Tehilim-Psalms

Tifereth Bakhurim-Orthodox boys organization

Tomkhei Tsedakah-Charity

Tsedakah Gedolah-Charity

Va'ad-Committee

Va'ad Kehilah-Community committee

Va'ad Medinath Lita- Autonomous organization for Jewish communities in Lithuania (1623-1764)

Verslas-Lithuanian Merchants Association

WIZO-Women International Zionist Organization

Yavneh Chain-Religious Zionist Hebrew schools

Yeshivah, Pl. Yeshivoth-Talmudic college

Yeshivah Ketanah-Elementary Yeshivah for young pupils

Yiddishist-Ideological fan of Yiddish

Z.S. - Zionist Socialist Party

Z.Z. - Tseirei Zion Party--Young Zionists

Town names in Lithuanian and Yiddish and Locations

Lithuanian Name (Yiddish Name) Other Common Spellings (Lat/Long)
Alytus - (Alite) --- Olita, Alitus 54°24' / 24°03'
Biržai – (Birzh) -— Birzhi, Birzhay, Birże, Birsen, 56°12' / 24°45'
Jurbarkas (Yurburg)--- Jurbork, Georgenburg 55°04' / 22°46'
Kaišiadorys (Koshedar) --- Kaišedorys, Koshedary, Kayshyadoris,
Kasheydarys, 54°52' / 24°27
Kapčiamiestis (Kopcheve) --- Kopciowo, Kapchyamiyestis, Koptchevo,
Koptsiva 54°00' / 23°39'
Klaipėda (Memel) --- Memel, Klaypeda, Kłajpeda 55°43' / 21°07'
Kudirkos Naumiestis (Naishtot) --- Władysławow, Šakių Naumiestis, 54°46'
/ 22°53'
Kybartai (Kibart) --- Kibartay, Kibarty 54°39' / 22°45'
Lazdijai (Lazdey),--- Lożdzieje, Lazdiyay 54°14' / 23°31'
Lygumai (Ligum) ---, Ligumay 56°00' / 23°39'
Marijampolė (Mariampol) --- Starapolë, Pašešupiai, Mariyampole,
Kapsukas 54°34' / 23°21'
Merkinė (Meretch) --- Merkinës, Merecz , Mertsh 54°10' / 24°10'
Panevėžys (Ponevezh)--- Panevezhis, Poniewiesh, Panevezhi 55°44' / 24°21'
Pilviškiai (Pilvishok) --- Pil'vishki, Pilwiszki, Pil'vishkyay 54°43' / 23°13'
Prienai (Pren) ---Prenay, Priyenay, Preny 54°38' / 23°57'
Šakiai (Shaki) --- Szaki, Shakyay, Shaki, 54°57' / 23°03'
Salantai (Salant) --- Skilándžiai, Salanty, Salantay 56°04' / 21°34'
Seirijai (Serey) --- Seyriyay, Serze, Sereje, 54°14' / 23°49'
Šėta (Shat) ---Szaty, Sheta, Shaty, 55°17' / 24°15'
Stakliškės (Stoklishok) --- Staklishkes, Stokliszki, Stoklishki, 54°36' / 24°19'
Sudargas (Sudarg) ---- Sudergas, Sudargis, Sudargi 55°03' / 22°38'
Tauragė (Tavrig) -— Taurogi, Tauroggen, Taurogen, 55°15' / 22°17'
Tauragnai (Taragin) --- Tauraginai, Tauroginie, Tauragunay, Tauraginos
55°27' / 25°49'
Telšiai (Telz) ---Telsze, Telshyay, Telshi, Telshay, Telsche 55°59' / 22°15'
Utena (Utyan) --- Uzjany, Utyana, Uciany, Uciana 55°30' / 25°36'
Varėna (Aran) --- Orany, Oran, Aran, Warna 54°13' / 24°34'
Veisiejai (Vishey) --- Wiejsieje, Viesee, Veisėjai, Vishaya 54°06' / 23°42
Vilkaviškis (Vilkovishk) --- Vilkavishkis, Wyłkowyszki, 54°39' / 23°02'
Virbalis (Virbaln) --- Wirballen, Wierzbołowo, Verzhbelov, 54°38' / 22°49
Žeimelis (Zheimel) --- Zheymelis, Zheyme, Žeimys, Zemel, Zieme
56°17' / 24°00'
Žemaičių Naumiestis (Naishtot Tavrig) --- Zhemaychyu-Naumestis, Nowe
Miasto, Taurages Naumiestis , 55°22' / 21°42'

Alytus (Alite)

Alite (as it was called in Yiddish) is located in the southwestern part of Lithuania on the shores of the Nieman (Nemunas) river, about 360 km from its estuary into the Kurish Gulf (Kursiu Marios), the Bay of the Baltic Sea and about 60 km south of Kaunas (Kovno).

The town was built on both sides of the river, and a bridge linked both parts. In documents of the fourteenth century Alite was already mentioned as a village. In 1377 the German Crusader Order conquered Alite, murdered a part of its population and destroyed tens of villages in the vicinity. In 1392 large battles between the Germans and the Poles broke out in the area.

In 1581 Alite obtained the rights of a town (Magdeburg rights). In 1775 the regional courts from Troki (Trakai) and Meretch (Merkine) were transferred to Alite, an event which contributed to its development and to the increase of its population. The "Hansa" merchants who arranged storehouses with salt on the shores of the river would also pass through Alite.

Until 1795 Alite was part of the Polish-Lithuanian Kingdom, when the third division of Poland by the three superpowers of those times - Russia, Prussia and Austria - caused Lithuania to become partly Russian and partly Prussian. The part of the state which lay on the left side of the Nieman river (Nemunas) was handed over to Prussia while the other part became a part of Russia. So the right side of Alite (Alite1) was ruled by Russia and the left side (Alite2)-by Prussia who ruled there during the years 1795-1807.

After Napoleon defeated Prussia and according to the Tilzit agreement of July 1807, Polish territories occupied by Prussia were transferred to what became known as the "The Great Dukedom of Warsaw", which was established at that time. The King of Saxony, Friedrich-August, was appointed duke, and the Napoleonic code now became the constitution of the dukedom, according to which everybody was equal before the law, except for the Jews who were not granted any civil rights.

During the years 1807-1813, Alite 2 belonged to the "Great Dukedom of Warsaw" and was part of the Bialystok district. The Napoleonic Code was then introduced in this region, remaining in effect even during the Lithuanian period.

In 1915 all Lithuania was annexed to Russia including Alite, but Alite1 was included in Vilna Gubernia and Alite2 - in Suwalk Gubernia. In 1856 Alite2 had 619 inhabitants and of them 285 were Jews. In 1886 there were 843 inhabitants in Alite2 and 926 in Alite1.

Because of these circumstances both parts of the town developed in a different way. The western part (Alite2) developed considerably more than Alite1, especially in the nineteenth century when the Russians constructed fortifications and barracks in the vicinity of Alite 2, paved roads to Kalvarija, Sejny and Daugai and built a railroad through Simnas to Suwalk connecting with the railroad network of Russia.

In 1909 as a result of a great fire most of the town's houses burnt down. During World War I Alite was not damaged.

In the years of independent Lithuania (1918-1940) both parts of Alite were united into one district town. The railroad to Vilna and Suwalk were cut off after Poland occupied the Vilna region. Instead the Lithuanian government built a railroad from Alite through Marijampole that connected at Kazlu-Ruda to the main line Kaunas- Virbalis (Kybartai). All the governmental and educational institutions were located in the western part of the town (Alite2).

At the end of 1939, according to the agreement between the USSR and Lithuania, Vilna and its region were returned to Lithuania, and the USSR established four military bases in this state one of which was in Alite.

In June 1940, after Lithuania became a Soviet Republic, the Soviets started to construct an underground airfield and positions for heavy guns near Alite.

During the Nazi rule, 1941-1944, the Germans and their Lithuanian collaborators murdered tens of thousands Soviet war prisoners and thousands civilians, among them all the Jewish population of Alite and the surrounding towns.

The Jewish Settlement till after World War I

The Jewish community of Alite was one of the oldest in Lithuania. A few Jews lived there since the times of the Great Prince Vytautas (1335?-1430). A more or less organized community began in the sixteenth century.

At the Jewish cemetery of east Alite (Alite1) tombstones dating back to the sixteenth century were found. A "Pinkas" (Notebook) of the "Khevrah Kadisha" from 1755, where the preface was copied from an older "Pinkas", was preserved by the community. The oldest tombstone at the Alite2 cemetery could be traced back to 1852.

According to a list of taxpayers of 1765 there were 360 Jews who paid Head Taxes. In 1847 their number decreased to 262. In 1897 there were 482 Jews in town, 33.6% of the total population.

The Jews of Alite made their living from small commerce, barrooms and providing services to the many soldiers that were stationed in the barracks in the vicinity. Several Jewish families had large farms and made their living from agriculture.

In 1886 a fire destroyed 30 houses in Alite1. On May 12, 1890 a great fire destroyed almost all Jewish houses in town, and hundreds of families were left without a shelter. A big fire occurred also in 1909.

With the breakout of World War I the Jews of west Alite (Alite2) were ordered to leave the town. until April 8, 1915. They were allowed to take with them only enough to fill a cart. They crossed the river into Alite1 where the expulsion order was not in effect. During the German occupation (1915-1918) the Jews returned to their homes and businesses.

Tombstones from 1902 and 1896 at Alite 1 cemetery

Photographed by Sa'adyah Bahat in 1997

The Jewish School with the Teacher Milman 1915?

Picture supplied by Ruth Ben-David

On the list of donors contributing for the settlement of Eretz-Yisrael in 1900 the names of 18 Jews from Alite were mentioned. *(See Appendix 1).*

Among the Rabbis who served in Alite during this period were: Hayim-Nathan Levin (1825-1897), Yosef-Yakov Rosenberg who served there for 40 years (-?-1922), Betsalel Levin, Yitzhak-Noakh Levinbuk (died in 1901 at the age of 48), his son Reuven Levinbuk, Joel Zalkind (1839-?).

During the Period of Independent Lithuania (1918-1940)
Society and Economy

The Jewish community of Alite was one of the pioneer communities organizing its life according to the Autonomy Law regarding the minorities issued by the new Lithuanian government. In July 1919 a Community Committee of 11 members was elected in town. There were then 1,100 Jewish men in Alite, 425 among them had voting rights and 358 actually voted. 3 Orthodox, 3 Zionists, 3 Workers and 2 Mizrakhi members were elected to the Committee. The first chairman was Hayim Kretchmer, a Z"S activist (in 1934 he immigrated to Eretz-Yisrael). The Committee was active in all fields of Jewish life until annulment of Autonomy at the end of 1925.

According to the first government census of 1923 there were 6,322 people in Alite, and 1,715 among them were Jews (27%).

In the elections for the Municipality Council of 1931 four Jews were elected: Nakhum Bernstein, Strelitz, Lifshitz, Nakhum Beirakh. In the elections of 1934, among 12 elected Council members only 3 were Jews: M. Bokshitsky, Sh. Beiral and N. Monosovsky.

In 1935 there were about 8,000 inhabitants in Alite, mostly Lithuanians. Many were employed by the District offices. That year there were 1,400 Jews in town, but during the period not one Jewish person was employed by the District or Municipality offices.

The Jews of Alite made their living from commerce, light industry, crafts and agriculture. According to the government survey of 1931 there were 94 businesses in Alite, 76 were owned by Jews (81%).

Due to the Government's agrarian reform the lands of Jewish farm owners were taken away, and only a few continued to grow vegetables and tend orchards. Many Jews were suppliers for the army stationed in town. Fresh air, pine forests and the Nieman River attracted holiday guests in summer which added to the income of many Jewish families in town.

The Minister for Jewish Affairs in Lithuania Dr. Shimshon Rozenbaum (2) on a visit to Alite 1924. (1) Leib Gorfinkel, (3) Adv. Mendel Bokshitsky

The Main Street (Vilnius) in Alite 2 where many Jewish houses stood

6 Alite

The distribution according to type of business is given in the table below:

Type of the business	Total	Owned by Jews
Groceries	3	3
Grain	7	7
Butcher's shops and Cattle Trade	10	4
Restaurants and Taverns	10	8
Food Products	11	11
Beverages	1	1
Textile Products and Furs	13	10
Leather and Shoes	7	7
Medicine and Cosmetics	6	2
Watches, Jewels and Optics	2	2
Tools and Steel Products	7	7
Building Materials and Timber	1	1
Heating Materials	4	4
Stationary and Books	4	2
Miscellaneous	8	7

According to the same survey there were 51 factories in Alite and of them 24 were owned by Jewish (47%), as can be seen in the following table:

Type of the Factory	Total	Jewish owned
Metal Workshops, Tin, Power Plants	6	3
Headstones, Bricks	1	1
Chemical Industry: Spirits, Soaps	3	1
Textile: Wool, Flax, Knitting	4	4
Timber and Furniture	6	3
Paper Industry: Printing Press	2	2
Beverage. Cigarettes	17	1
Dresses, Footwear	9	7
Leather Industry: Production, Cobbling	1	1
Others	2	1

In 1937 there were 61 Jewish artisans in Alite: 9 tailors, 8 bakers, 8 butchers, 6 hatters, 5 carpenters, 4 tinsmiths, 4 barbers, 2 blacksmiths, 2 shoemakers, 2 painters, 1 oven builder, 1 glazier, 1 bookbinder, 1 locksmith, 1 cord maker, 1 corset maker, 1 photographer, 1 watchmaker, 1 tailor, 1 laundry worker and 1 other worker.

Parts of the governmental Survey of Shops in Alytus District in 1931

Restaurants

ALYTAUS APSKR.
Chasanavičienė R., Alytus,, Juozapavičiaus g.
Janulevičius, Alytus.
Kovalskienė B., Nemaniūnai.
Mankovičius J., Jeznas, Rinkos a.
Racas I., Seirijai.
Stauskaitė J. ,Birštonas.
Svedkauskas K., Miroslavas.
Sulcaitė P., Seirijai, Skalos g. 21.

Iron and Iron Products

ALYTAUS APSKR.
Aminodovas E., Seirijai.
Černevičienė Ch., Alytus.
Černevičius S., Alytus, Turgaus gt.
Farbšteinas Šmuelis, Seirijai.
Gardonas Leiba, Butrimonys.
Glazmanicnė S., Alytus, Vilniaus gt. 21.
Maršakas Mordchelis, Simnas, Didžioji g.
Levinas N., Alytus.
Liubelskienė Rochė, Butrimonys.
Poliakas Samuelis, Seirijai.
Ptašnikas Sepėlis, Butrimonys.
Prusskienė Kunė, Seirijai.
Putianskienė Rachilė, Butrimonys.
Rubinas Salcas, Daugai.
Ščerbakovas Mordchelis, Simnas.
Verbalskis Simelis, Simnas, Didžioji g. 30 Nr.
Zilbermanas Mauka, Daugai.
Židikaneris Samuelis, Alytus.

Sewing Workshop

ALYTAUS APSKR.
Cirelšteinas Joselis, Merkinė.
Kapčiūnas Juozas, Alytus, Stoties g. 12.

Cosmetics

ALYTAUS APSKR.
Cofnasas Iliašas, Butrimonys.
Finienė Feiga, Butrimonys.
Jodeiršis Jonas, Butrimonys.
Kapanecdckas Isakas, Alytus, Vilniaus. 13.
Sarachanas Michelis, Alytus, Vilniaus g. 26.

Leather Factories

ALYTAUS APSKR.
Abramavičius I., Alytus, Juozapaičio g. 21.
Garbarskis Iršas, Seirijai.
Koževnikas Aizikas, Merkinė.

Banks (Folksbank Branches)

ALYTAUS APSKR.
Lietuvos Banko Skyrius, Alytus.
Alytaus Ūkininkų Smulk. Kred. D-ja.
Alytaus Taupm. ir Kredito D-ja.
Alytaus Žydų Liaudies Bankas.
Antnemunio Lenkų Smulk. Kred. D-ja.
Butrimonių Žydų Liaudies Bankas.
Daugų Žydų Liaudies Bankas.
Jezno Smulkaus Kred. D-ja.
Metelių Smulkaus Kred. D-ja.
Merkinės Smulk. Kred. D-ja.
Merkinės Žydų Liaudies Bankas.
Miroslavo Valst. Taupm. Skolin. Kasa.
Pivašiunų Lenkų Smulk. Kred. D-ja.
Seirijų Žydų Liaudies Bankas.

Transportation Means

ALYTAUS APSKR.
Kameneckis Josifas, Simnas.
Redakas Abromas, Merkinė, Bingelių g. 26.

(The Survey of the shops)

The Jewish Folksbank had two branches in both parts of the town and played an important role in the town's economic life. In 1925 in Alite-1 the bank had 213 members and in Alite2 - 144 members. In 1927 the eastern branch (Alite1) had 161 members and the western branch - 364 members. There was a private bank as well owned by Yosef Marshak.

In the middle of the thirties the economic situation of Alite Jews started to decline due to the open propaganda of the Lithuanian Merchant Association-Verslas- propagating against buying at Jewish stores. To achieve their goal the Lithuanians established consumer cooperatives (Lietukis). As a result of this propaganda anti-Jewish outburst began to occur in many places. In April 1932, 21 tombstones at the Jewish cemetery were desecrated in Alite.

According to the information of telephone book list of 1939, there were 130 telephone owners in Alite and among them 50 were Jews.

Education and Culture

The Jewish children of Alite had the opportunity to choose a suitable school among the several the town had to offer: Hebrew elementary school that was affiliated with the "Tarbuth" chain; Hebrew pro-gymnasium; a vocational school of the "ORT" chain; several "Khadarim" (Chadar) and a "Yeshivah". The town had a library with Hebrew and Yiddish books.

The Hebrew School 1937

Many of Alite, teenagers studied at the Hebrew High School (Hareali) in Kovno thanks to scholarships granted by a Jew, a native of Alite Azriel-Mordehai Tcheis who lived in the USA. He also donated funds to build this High School. Many Jewish boys and girls studied at the governmental High School in town where tuition fees were only token (150 Lit. per year=$25).

A group of Jewish girls on the shore of the Nieman

Picture supplied by Ruth Ben David

Sitting from right: Eva Alperin (died during escape to Russia), **Sheine Halperin** (murdered in the Holocaust), **Devorah Katzovitz** (in Israel),

Standing from right: Hayah Katzovitz (in Israel), **Mere Berlinsky** (not known)

There was a drama circle performing Yiddish plays in town from time to time. Jewish theaters from Kovno would also visit Alite occasionally. In 1927 "The Jewish Theater Studio" performed the well-known play of Shalom-Aleikhem "The Great Win". During this period there were two cinema theaters in town, both Jewish owned and contributing to cultural life.

In 1935 22 families of Alite subscribed to the "Jewish Encyclopedia" which started publication in Paris in Yiddish. Among the subscribers there were several mixed families in which the husband was Christian and the wife Jewish (Dr.Stepanov, Petrov etc.) and also a German family (Kesting) which converted to Judaism.

Jewish youth rowing on the Nieman River
Picture supplied by Ruth Ben-David

A group of youth in the 1930s
The third from right: Sheine Helperin, the fourth: Hayah Katsovitz

A group of youth
Below: Sheine Helperin, over her: Hayah Katsovitz
From right: Benjamin Latskovitz, Kliatchko, Aba Zakhupinsky

A Group of "HaShomer-HaTsair" 1933

Zionist and other Activities

All Zionist parties had their supporters in Alite. The Z"S (Zionist Socialist) party was very active. The party members managed to acquire seats in the directorate of "The United Professional Society" which united workers and petty clerks. This could be attributed to the Zionist Socialist's success to interest the Jewish workers in professional activity.

Fundraising for KKL (Keren Kayemeth LeYisrael - The Jewish National Fund) was organized from time to time. Donations for KKL were also made on occasion by the "Olim LaTorah" in the synagogue.

There was also a branch of WIZO (Women's International Zionist Organization), headed by Mrs Dr. Kovarsky. WIZO would arrange lectures on different subjects in the afternoon hours in the Hebrew pro gymnasium; the topics ranged from Zionism, the Arab question etc.

Picture supplied by Ruth Ben David

"HeKhalutz" Branch of Alite 1934

Sitting in the first line from right: **Aba Zakhopinsky, Sarah-Gita Finkelstein, (----- ?).**

Second line from right: **(third) the dentist, (fifth) Hayim Kretchmer, (seventh) Virshov.**

Third line from right: **(third) Osherovsky, (fourth) Hayah Katsovitz.**

Fourth line from right: **(first) Leib Veisenberg from Kibbutz Amir**

In the table below we can see how Alite Zionists voted for the different parties at six Zionist Congresses:

Cong Nr	Year	Tot Shek	Total Votes	Labor Party Z"S	Z"Z	Rev	Gen Zion A	B	Gros	Miz
14	1925	120	----	----	----	--	----	----	----	----
15	1927	139	107	21	---	59	18	----	----	9
16	1929	411	292	87	9	144	45	----	----	7
17	1931	472	415	167	4	205	27	----	----	12
18	1933	719	682	393		211	30	----	19	29
19	1935	770	722	434		--	4	75	135	74

Key: Cong No. = Congress Number, Tot Shek = Total Shkalim, Rev = Revisionists, Gen Zion = General Zionists, Gros = Grosmanists, Miz = Mizrakhi

The Zionist youth organizations active in Alite were "Gordonia" with 30-40 members, "HaShomer HaTzair" and "Beitar". Sports activities were organized by the local branch of "Maccabi" with its 74 members. There was a "Kibbutz Hakhsharah" (Training Kibbutz) affiliated with the "HeKhalutz" and a training center of "Brith HaKanaim"-the youth organization of the Grosmanists. Many of the trainees of these organizations immigrated to Eretz-Yisrael.

Picture supplied by Sa'adyah Bahat

Adv. M. Bokshitsky as the commander of the Volunteer Fire Brigade 1931-1932

There was a "Volunteer Fire Brigade" in Alite with Jews and Lithuanians working as volunteers headed by Adv. Mendel Bokshitzky who was also the initiator of the group.

Religion and Welfare

Although according to its administrative status Alite was one town, the Jews of Alite maintained two different communities. Each community had its own synagogue and its own Rabbi. Several welfare institutions, such as "Gemiluth Khesed", were separated in both parts of the town.

The "Beth-Midrash" building of Alite 2 still exists and is presently used as a storehouse for salt. (see picture below).

Picture taken by Sa'adyah Bahat (Bokshitzky) in 1997
Note Magen David above door
The "Beth-Midrash"

Here was the "Beth-Midrash" in Yiddish and Lithuanian

The Rabbis who served during the last years of the community's existence were:

Aharon Milevsky,

Nakhman Koloditzky (in Alite2),

Yehudah Yablonsky (in Alite1), and

Betsalel Levin.

The last two were murdered together with their communities in 1941.

During World War II and Afterwards

World War II started with the German invasion of Poland September 1, 1939, and its consequences for Lithuanian Jews in general and Alite's Jews in particular were felt several months later.

In agreement with the Ribbentrop-Molotov treaty on the division of occupied Poland, the Russians occupied the Suwalk region, but after delineation of exact borders between Russia and Germany the Suwalk region fell into German hands. The retreating Russians allowed anyone who wanted to join them to move into their occupied territory, and indeed many young people left the area together with the Russians. The Germans drove the remaining Jews out of their homes in Suwalk and its vicinity, robbed them of their possessions, then directed them to the Lithuanian border, where they were left in dire poverty. The Lithuanians did not allow them to enter Lithuania and the Germans did not allow them to return. Thus they stayed in this swampy area in cold and rain for several weeks, until Jewish youths from the border villages smuggled them into Lithuania by various routes, with much risk to themselves. Altogether about 2,400 refugees passed through the border or infiltrated on their own, and were then dispersed in the "Suwalkia" region including Alite.

In June 1940 Lithuania was annexed to the Soviet Union and became a Soviet Republic. Following new rules, the majority of the factories and shops belonging to the Jews of Alite were nationalized and commissars were appointed to manage them. All the Zionist parties and youth organizations were disbanded, several of the activists were detained and Hebrew educational institutions were closed. The Hebrew school changed into a Yiddish one and on the occasion of the October celebrations in 1940 a festive rally for the parents of the students was arranged in the school. A choir and a ballet under the guidance of the teachers Saulitzky and Rabinovitz, a play "For Peace" under guidance of the teacher Slutzky and poetry recitals under guidance of the teacher Elperin were organized at the school.

Supply of goods decreased and, as a result, prices soared. The middle class, mostly Jewish, bore most of the brunt, and the standard of living dropped gradually. At the beginning of June several Jewish families whose enterprises were nationalized were exiled deep into Russia.

On Thursday June 19, 1941, it became clear that the war was approaching. Units of the Red Army with many tanks stationed in Alite2 started to move eastwards across the bridge to Alite1 and the Soviet officers sent their families home to Russia.

On June 22, 1941 World War II began. At dawn of that day Alite was bombed by the German air force. The centers of both parts of the town were destroyed and many Jews were killed. The German army entered Alite2 in the evening of the same day. Heavy battles between the attacking Germans and the Red Army who tried to stop the invasion lasted until Tuesday, the 24th of that month, . On that day the Russian resistance collapsed and the Germans moved forward. The airfield in Alite1 was captured by German parachutists prior to the battle. Only a few Jews managed to escape with the retreating Red Army to Russia.

After two Germans were killed near the flour mill of Marshak, 42 Jewish men and also Lithuanians were murdered near their houses, the owner of the mill among them. The murdered Jews were buried in their back yards.

When the battles moved eastward, the Jews who tried to escape, returned to town, but found their houses looted and destroyed. At that time order in town was maintained by the German "Field Gendarmerie", but the Lithuanian nationalists complained to the German Town Major that the "Gendarmerie" doesn't allow them to handle the Communists and the Jews without restrictions. In the memorandum they wrote that they take upon themselves to "cleanse" the area from "undesirable elements" in ten days. Their wish indeed was granted. Several hundreds Jews were taken from their homes, transported to Suwalk and murdered. Several dozen Jews were concentrated in one of the synagogues in town and the building and its inhabitants were set on fire. After the Gestapo arrived in Alite the remaining Jews were crowded in a Ghetto set up on a few streets in the poor district of the town.

Following a German order a "Juden Rat" was appointed: Adv. Halperin, Adv. Salansky and Kopl Nemunaitzky. They were called to the Municipality to be informed of restrictive clauses concerning Jews: the ban included restriction from walking on the sidewalks, and from being on the street after 8 o'clock in the evening. The order was for all Jews, men and women ages 14 to 50 to wear a yellow patch in the front and in the back and to present themselves to the German Kommandantur" or to the Municipality at 7 o'clock every morning. The Jews of the Ghetto tried to organize for the sake of mere survival, but frequent arrests, abuse and murders didn't make the existence of any organization possible.

In the middle of August 1941 the Soviet war prisoners, who were imprisoned in camps nearby, were ordered to dig big trenches in the Vidzgiris forest. The Jews from Alite and the neighboring towns were cruelly murdered in these trenches by armed Lithuanians. After the war a few of these murderers were caught and sentenced. The shocking stories they told their investigators implied a willingness to kill Jews with cruelty.

According to German sources, between the 13th of August and the 9th of September 1941 in the Vidzgiris forest 1,137 Jews, men, women and children were murdered. According to an unconfirmed source Jews from Czechoslovakia were murdered at the same site, as well as tens of thousands of Soviet civilians and war prisoners.

Only two Jewish girls survived, Belkin and Hayah Kaplan, thanks to the help of two Lithuanians who took care of them through the years of the Nazi occupation. There were two more Lithuanians who helped Jews: a woman who was sent to jail for what she had done and a peasant who lost his mind because of the torture he suffered in jail. Their names are preserved in the archives of Yad Vashem.

The list of mass graves in the book "Mass Murders in Lithuania. 1941-1944" part 2, includes three mass graves:

1) The place: Alytus, corner of Leliju and Vilna streets; on June 23, 1941; 42 men murdered.

2) The place: Vidzgiris forest at the south-eastern suburb of the town, on the left bank of the river; between May 1943 and June 1944; 60.000-70.000 men, women and children murdered (most likely Jews brought from the eastern parts of the USSR)

3) The place: the forest of Alytus at the eastern suburbs of the town, near the barracks; between July 1941 until April 1943, 35,000 people murdered (most likely Soviet war prisoners)

After the war the graves were not cared for and at night some people would come to loot the graves looking for "treasures". On the request of Jewish survivors of Alite, authorities built a monument in 1959 where inscriptions in Russian and Lithuanian stated: "Soviet citizens and war prisoners, victims of the Hitlerist murderers are buried here". The monument is still there, but the plaque with the inscription was removed.

The monument beside the path to the graves with the inscription in Yiddish and Lithuanian: "Stop and think over, this earth is saturated with blood of innocent people"

On March 19, 1993 a new metal monument was inaugurated in the Vidzgiris forest in the shape of a broken "Magen-David" (see next page). The nine huge graves in which the bones of the murdered Jews were buried, were covered with a round black cover and on it there is a white pyramid. Near the path that leads to the hill a memorial plaque was erected that tells the story of the massacre in Yiddish and Lithuanian: **"Here, in this place, the Nazis and their local helpers, in the years 1941-1944, murdered tens of thousands of Jews-children, women, men and old people, most of them from other countries. Let their memory last forever"**. The architect of the site was Mrs. R. Vasiliauskiene and the sculptor - A. Smilingis

A broken Magen-David stands as a monument on the hill of the remembrance site

The graves with black round covers and white pyramids

Alite 21

The wall bearing the name of Alite in "The Valley of the Communities" in Yad Vashem, Jerusalem

The Jewish cemetery of Alite2 was destroyed and nothing was left of it. In Alite1 the old Jewish cemetery was fenced in at the beginning of the 1990s and on the two pillars of the entrance gate two plaques were installed with inscriptions in Yiddish: **"The Alite Jewish cemetery, sacred is the memory of the dead"** and in Lithuanian: **Alytus eternal resting place for the Jews, may the remains of the dead rest in peace".**

דער אליטער ירישער
בית עולם
הייליק איז דער אנדענק
פון די פארשטארבענע

The inscription on the tablet of the entrance gate in Yiddish

ALYTAUS ŽYDŲ
AMŽINO POILSIO VIETA
ŠVENTA RAMYBĖ
MIRUSIŲJŲ PALAIKAMS

The inscription on the tablet of the entrance gate in Lithuanian

Picture taken and supplied by Sa'adya Bahat

Remaining tombstones at the Jewish cemetery in Alite 1, in 1997

Appendix 1 List of Donors from 1900 for the Settlement of Eretz-Yisrael

Dr. Sh. Rabinovitz

Yisrael-Mosheh Remigolsky

Hayim-Mosheh Levinson

Tsevi Finkelstein

Aharon Yurshevitz

Kopel Karzmer

Yisrael-Hayim Glazman

Zalman Blumental

Betsalel Tsernevitz

Hayim-Gedalyah Stolarsky

Mordehai Bokshitsky

Yakov Nimanitzky

Yosef Kubishsky

Yakov Ramirovsky

Yakov Mines

Lipman Dubiavsky

Shrlomoh Beiral

Hayim-Zelig Zelihov

Appendix 2   Partial List of Personalities Born in Alite

Prof. Heinrich Otz (1859-?), published a book in German about the research on The Bible, Berlin 1911

Rabbi David Rapaport (1860-1927), from 1926 the first Rabbi of Kefar-Saba in Eretz-Yisrael

Azriel-Mordehai Tcheis (1874-1939), from 1888 in Manchester USA, philanthropist who donated the means for the building of the Hebrew High School (Hareali) in Kovno, granted scholarships to youngsters born in Alyte and vicinity for high education in the Kovno University and abroad.

Hayim Pekeris (Peker) (1908-), Prof. of Applied Mathematics in the Weitzman Institute, member of the Academies of Science in USA and Israel, laureate of the Rothchild Prize and the Israel Prize in mathematics in 1980.

Yosef Glazman (1912-1943), the last commissioner of "Betar" in Lithuania, commander of the partisans of Ghetto Vilna, fell in battle with the Nazis.

Yisrael Habas (1868-?), from 1907 in Eretz-Yisrael, established and directed the religious weekly "Hayesod, among the buyers of the lands of Benei-Brak.

Beraha Habas (1900-?), daughter of Yisrael, in the years 1935-1953 member of the editorial board of the daily newspaper "Davar", published 30 books on personalities and events of the history of the Jewish settlement in Eretz-Yisrael

David Umru (Latzkovitz), poet, writer and journalist, published his works in the Yiddish press in Lithuania, perished in Vilna in 1941.

Shemuel Matis (1914-1941), published poems, stories and literary articles in the Yiddish press in Lithuania and Argentina, perished at his attempt to flee from Kovno in 1941.

Adv. Mendel Bokshitsky (1899-1941), an active public worker, member of the Municipality Council, chief of the "Volunteer Fire Brigade", active General Zionist. murdered in Ghetto Vilna.

Bibliography

Yad-Vashem Archives: M-1/E-2215/2314; M-11/34; 0-53/21; 0-3/369

Koniukhovsky Collection 0-71, Files 124-127.

JIVO, NY, Collection of the Jewish Communities in Lithuania, Files 75,1376, 1509, 1662.

Yitshak Lifshitz-Lelo Kniah (Without surrender)-through three Ghettos to the Partisan wood, (Hebrew) Jerusalem 1985

Lite, New-York 1951, Volume 1 (Yiddish).

From the Beginning to the End - The Book of the History of "HaShomer HaTzair" in Lithuania (Hebrew), Tel-Aviv 1986.

Dos Vort, Kovno (Yiddish): 11.11.1934.

Folksblat, Kovno (Yiddish): 4.6.1935; 19.7.1935; 21.7.1935; 19.11.1940.

Di Yiddishe Shtime (The Yiddish Voice) Kovno (Yiddish): 18.8.1919; 19.6.1931; 25.4.1932; 7.3.1937.

Yiddisher Hantverker (Jewish Artisan) Kovno, (Yiddish): Nr.3, 1938.

HaMeilitz (St. Petersburg) (Hebrew): 10.6.1890, 22.1.1901

Naujienos (Chicago)-11.6.1949

Family History Library, Europe Film Area, Lithuania, Alytus Civil Registration, Microfilm Nr. 0747740 Item B, Salt Lake City, Utah

Biržai (Birzh)

Birzh - as it was called in Yiddish - (Birzai - in Lithuanian) is situated in the north-eastern part of Lithuania on the shores of the rivers Apascia (pronounced Apashcha) and Agluona and along Lake Siruinis, surrounded by thick forests, not far from the Latvian border. Four islands exist in these rivers; on one of them a palace was built in the 16th century, where Napoleon rested during his march through Lithuania. Because of the town's spectacular landscape it attracted many vacationers. It is one of the oldest towns in Lithuania and was mentioned in 1415 in some documents.

During the years 1492-1806, Birzh belonged to the family of a noblemen by the name of Radzivil (Radvila in Lithuanian). From time to time the town served as the official residence of the family and they invested in its development. Its location, on one of the main roads from Vilna to Riga, was an important factor in its development. During the rule of Prince Christopher Radzivil the First the town developed rapidly economically, especially after it was granted the Magdeburg Rights of a town in 1589. In 1609 Prince Christopher promulgated municipal laws, erected a building for the municipality and established several welfare institutions. Near the town a big fortress was built with a palace inside. As a result of the influence of the Radzivil family, Birzh became the center of the Reformation in Lithuania. Every week two market days were held in Birzh.

In the 17th century Birzh suffered during the wars with Sweden, and during the Northern War the town was damaged again. At the beginning of the 18th century, after the Northern War and regional religious wars, Birzh lost its importance.

Until 1795 Birzh was part of the Polish-Lithuanian Kingdom, when the third division of Poland by the three superpowers of those times - Russia, Prussia and Austria - caused Lithuania to become partly Russian and partly Prussian. The part of Lithuania which included Birzh fell under Czarist Russian rule, first from 1802 as part of the Vilna province (Gubernia) and from 1843 as part of Ponivezh district in the Kovno province.

At the beginning of Russian rule the Magdeburg Rights were denied and Birzh became a regular small town. In 1806 the town was transferred to Graf Tishkevitz's family who kept it till the 1860s.

In 1812 Napoleon's army passed through the town on its way to Riga and Mikolas Tishkevitz organized a special battalion for its service.

During the Polish rebellions in 1831 and 1863, Birzh took an active part in the insurrection against the Russians and heavy fighting occurred in its surroundings, which caused an interruption in the economic development of the town.

In 1869 the town consisted of 536 houses (2 of stone) and 20 streets. At that time Birzh had 3 workshops for leather production and more than 40 shops, several hundreds of artisans, 3 flour mills, 3 doctors, and at the end of the century there was also a pharmacy. In 1883 a big fire destroyed about 50 houses in town. In 1912 a printing press operated in Birzh.

According to the census of 1897, Birzh then had 4,413 residents - 1,255 Catholics, 581 Protestants and 2,510 (57%) Jews.

During World War I Birzh was occupied by the Germans who ruled there from 1915 till 1918. During the fighting over Birzh several tens of houses were destroyed. The Germans constructed a narrow gauge railway which connected Birzh to Shavli (Siauliai), which influenced the development of the town, but in 1918 a large fire destroyed a great part of the town and most of the Jewish community was ruined.

From December 1918 till May 1919 the town came under Bolshevik rule.

During Lithuanian rule there were two weekly market days - on Mondays and Thursdays - as well as two yearly fairs. A branch of the government bank and four private banks did business in the town.

Birzh was known for its "Music Box" (Katarinka) players, who in summer would travel all over Lithuania and return home for the "Great Holidays".

In 1934 the number of houses in town was 1,039 (of them 347 were constructed with solid materials) and its population rose to about 9,000.

Jewish Settlement till World War I.

Jews began to settle in Birzh in the 16th or at the beginning of the 17th century. Tradition maintains that they came as a result of an invitation from Prince Christopher Radzivil (1547-1603) who wanted to promote local economic development. First a group of "Karaites" settled in Birzh and only later, in the middle of the century, also "Rabbinic" Jews settled there. The prince promised to protect them from their Christian neighbors, but in 1662 the Protestant liberal Prince Boguslav Radzivil, who was generally kind to Jews, submitted to the demands of the Catholic residents of the town and the Jews were expelled.

The "Karaite" community in Birzh was first mentioned in a letter of Khaham (Rabbi) Zerakh ben Nathan in 1625 in connection with a fire that harmed the town. It was a very poor community.

A list from 1669 shows that taxes paid by the Karaites were a third less than those paid in previous years, as a result of the decline in their economic situation. The Karaites lived in specific streets and had their own synagogue and cemetery. The Karaites, like the Jews, suffered from persecution by the rulers and their Christian neighbors. In the 18th century the presence of the Karaite community came to an end and their synagogue was passed on to the rabbinic Jews.

During the pogroms in Poland in 1648-49 and in Lithuania in 1656 Birzh also suffered and there are references to this effect in rabbinic literature at the time. During this period the Jews suffered much from mistreatment by Polish estate owners.

In documents from the years 1663 and 1683, there is mention of Jews who came to settle in town and bought the right to do so. In 1683 the townsmen obtained an official resolution which prohibited Jews from settling in Birzh and to acquire property there, but it seems that later the Jews managed to get this resolution cancelled, and they settled in town and in the nearby settlements again. By the beginning of the 18th century a large and important Jewish community already existed in Birzh which had an officially recognized status. However even then they were not left in peace, suffering from mistreatment by government officials and from church heads, who managed in the years 1700 and 1711 to cancel the civil rights of the local Jews. On the 21st of April 1717 the whole community was deprived of its civil rights and was forced to pay a "Skull Tax" of 1,500 Rubles, in addition to the special tax of 350 Rubles which they had previously undertaken to pay to the Great Hetman of Lithuania.

On the other side of Lake Siruinis, about 2-3 km from the center of town, there was a large area of land called "Birzu Dvaras" (Birzh Estate), which had its own administration, its own law court and its own jail, and on which Jews lived for a hundred years or more. In the protocols of the court from the years 1620-1745 we find the names of many Jews who were sentenced in this court, mainly on charges of unpaid debts. (For a list of these names see **Appendix 2**).

During the years of autonomous organization for Jewish communities in Lithuania (Va'ad Medinath Lita, 1623-1764), Birzh was a district (Galil) administrative center responsible for the communities of Posvol (Pasvalys), Salat (Salociai), Pumpian (Pumpenai) and Pokroi (Pakruojis). The Birzh community was mentioned in regulations in the "Pinkas Medinath Lita" from 1726 concerning a conference in Brisk, and in 1731 with regard to a conference in Telzh on the issue of tax collection.

At that time Birzh Jews tried to settle in Riga, then an important port on the Baltic sea, and the town council imposed a special tax, two Reichstaler, on Jews who came to live there. Prince Radzivil tried to cancel this discrimination, but the town council refused fearing that the cancellation of this special tax would encourage more Jews from Poland and Lithuania to come to Riga.

In 1766 there were 1040 Jews in Birzh. From 1775 the existence of a synagogue in Birzh was mentioned.

A document concerning the Birzh district (Galil) dated 1673 tells about the rescue of a Jewish woman and her children from arrest, by payment of a penalty. It seems that they were arrested due to not having paid taxes or a debt to one of the estate owners. As a result of this episode, "Va'ad Medinath Lita" issued a regulation forbidding the borrowing of money from estate owners or priests unless carried out with the knowledge and agreement of the community, and that women and children should not be held responsible for the payment of a debt. Anyone not abiding by this regulation would face boycott and even be deported from the community, losing the right of residence in this town. The community would not accept any responsibility or obligation to help those who would take such a loan (even one penny).

During the second half of the 18th century, the Birzh community was in debt to the Radzivils and the church. The Galil Council authorized community heads to impose strict bans, even a boycott, on those who did not pay their yearly taxes, or who traveled to other communities or away from the Birzh Galil for the High Holidays. It was customary to go to the big towns for the holidays, thus leaving the small ones without a Minyan. The strict orders included the prohibition of arranging a party, a wedding or a Brith-Milah without the knowledge of the community heads, in order to avoid lavishness and the envy of those of insufficient means (regulations of the third of Adar 5530-1770). In the regulations, arrangements for "Shekhitah" were determined in order to avoid difficulties among the "Shokhtim" (ritual butchers). Other regulations dealt with mourning, and even with the dress the bride may wear on her wedding day. All these regulations, administered by the Birzh Galil, were valid for many generations.

In the month of Adar in 1784, the Birzh community council decided to donate a specific sum for Eretz-Yisrael every year - "until Mashiah (Messiah) arrives" - to be collected by two different funds: one for Eretz-Yisrael (Ma'oth Eretz-Yisrael), the other for Jerusalem (Ma'oth Yerushalayim), with each fund having two supervisors (Gaba'im). First, the money was sent to Gaba'im in Vilna; five months later the va'ad (council) decided to send the donations for Eretz-Yisrael to the Rabbi of Brisk and the money for Jerusalem was to be handed over to a "Meshulakh" (messengers who traveled throughout Jewish communities collecting money for institutions in Jerusalem).

In the old Jewish cemetery in Jerusalem there are at least three headstones of Birzh Jews: Mosheh Tsevi ben Aharon Melamed, who died in 1870; the Rabbi's wife Hayah Libe bath Paltiel, died in 1879; Tsevi ben Avraham, died in 1880.

The "Pinkas haKhevrah Kadisha" of Birzh 1804 shows regulations regarding supporting the poor, how to conduct accounts, and payment of hospitalization fees by the employer for his servants when patients were registered.

In 1847 there were 1685 Jews in Birzh. In July 1893 a large fire caused fifty houses to burn down, the damage being estimated then at 50,000 Ruble.

During this period Birzh Jews made their living mainly from commerce, in particular trading with flax and timber. Others earned a living from crafts, farming, light industry and peddling. There were several workshops for weaving and knitting, where wool from England was processed for export, and the white linen made in Birzh was very famous.

In the years before World War I Jews from Birzh leased milk products from the neighboring farms. Others leased taverns and barrooms. The Jews had good relations with their neighbors, and even when pogroms were rampant in neighboring Russia, the Jews of Birzh and its surroundings did not suffer.

In 1908 local priests established a Polish cooperative which became a strong competitor to the Jewish shop owners. As a result, the small "Gemiluth Hesed" institutions, giving small loans without interest, united in order to improve help for Jewish shop owners.

The history of the rabbinate in Birzh is divided in two periods: during the first period there was one Rabbi only for Birzh, Keidan and Vizhun - Tsevi-Hirsh Hurvitz. The second period started in 1713, when Birzh appointed its own Rabbi - Shalom Zak. Since then many famous rabbis have served in Birzh, mainly of the Zak family. For a partial list of the Rabbis who served in Birzh during all its history see **Appendix 1.**

During World War I the Jewish community of Birzh was destroyed. Many of the Jews emigrated or were exiled by the Russian army to Russia.

The Big Beth-Midrash

During the Period of Independent Lithuania (1918-1940)
Society and Economy

After World War I Birzh remained the district administrative center, but its importance declined as the transport of goods via Birzh to Riga was restricted. Nevertheless the town developed, and the community gradually recovered, when some of the immigrants to Russia, who had been exiled, returned and also Jews from neighboring villages settled there. But the increasing number of Jews did not show up statistically in relation to the total population. Many Lithuanian villagers and government officials also settled in Birzh, yet the proportion of Jews had decreased by the middle of the thirties to only 36%, however 75% of the houses in town were owned by Jews.

The "Klois" of the Shoemakers

The Beth-Midrash of the Shamashim

The Synagogue

The Prayer House of the Khasidim (Chassidim)

The "Moshav Zekeinim" (House for the Aged)

Following the law of autonomies for minorities issued by the new Lithuanian government, the minister for Jewish affairs Dr. Menakhem (Max) Soloveitshik ordered elections to community committees (Va'ad Kehilah) to be held in the summer of 1919. In Birzh a "Va'ad Kehilah" of 15 members was elected: 6 General Zionists; 2 Tseirei Zion; 1 Mizrahi; 1 Akhduth (Agudath Yisrael); 3 Workers; 2 independent. The Va'ad was very active in the years 1920-1924 in Kehilah issues and got substantial administrative, financial and advisory assistance from the Ministry for Jewish Affairs in Kovno.

On the 12th of October 1922 the elections for the first Seimas (Parliament) took place. In Birzh the Jewish votes were divided as follows: the Zionist list got 426 votes, Akhduth-125 and the Democrats-13.

In the elections to the town council which took place in 1931, 9 Lithuanians and 3 Jews - Mordehai Smilg, Eliyahu Fridman and Zalman Vainer - were elected.

During this period many Jews made their living from flax and timber, while others were occupied in crafts, agriculture and peddling. Several Jews from Birzh and vicinity were employed in the two Jewish owned flour mills and in other light industry establishments. The flour mills also supplied a living to many Jewish families from Birzh and its surroundings who came there to grind their grain or to buy flour. The flour produced in these mills was packed in sacks and sold all over Lithuania.

There were also Jewish owned weaving and knitting workshops as well as a flax processing workshop where several Jews were employed.

The 1931 government survey showed that there were then 99 businesses in Birzh, of which 77 were owned by Jews (78%), as detailed, according to type of business in the table below:

Type of the business	Total	Owned by Jews
Groceries	14	12
Grain and flax	4	4
Butcher's shops and Cattle Trade	12	9
Restaurants and Taverns	11	3
Food Products	7	7
Beverages	2	0
Textile Products and Furs	12	11
Leather and Shoes	8	7
Haberdashery and Appliances	4	3
Medicine and Cosmetics	2	1
Watches, Jewels and Optics	3	3
Radio, Bicycles and Electric Equipment	1	1
Tools and Steel Products	5	5
Machinery and Transportation	1	1
Heating Materials	1	1
Stationery and Books	3	2
Miscellaneous	9	7

According to the same survey there were 45 factories in Birzh and of them 28 were Jewish owned (62%), as can be seen in the following table:

Type of the Factory	Total	Jewish Owned
Metal Workshops, Tin, Power Plants	3	2
Chemical Industry: Wine	1	0
Textile: Wool, Flax, Knitting	4	0
Timber and Furniture	5	1
Paper Industry: Printing Press, Binding	1	0
Food: Flour mills, Bakeries	11	7
Dresses, Footwear: Sewing, Hats, Shoes	11	5
Leather Industry: Production, Saddlers	6	11
Barber Shops, Goldsmiths, Photo	3	2

In 1931 there were 80 artisans including 63 Jews (79%): 8 tailors, 8 butchers, 6 wool workers, 6 shoemakers, 4 bakers, 4 wig makers, 2 saddlers, 1 tanner,1 hatter, 1 tinsmith and 22 others. They were organized in the "Union of Jewish Artisans"

At the beginning of the thirties 2 Jewish doctors (out of a total of 3), 2 Jewish lawyers (also 2 non-Jewish) and 2 Jewish engineers (as well as 1 non-Jewish) worked in town.

In the middle of the thirties the economic situation of Birzh Jews began to deteriorate, because of competition from Lithuanian artisans and merchants. Despite the fact that there were 80 Jewish owned shops out of a total 118 in town, the aggressive propaganda from the union of the Lithuanian merchants "Verslas" against buying in Jewish shops had its negative effect on Jewish commerce.

The Jewish Folksbank played an important part in the economic life of Birzh Jews, although its beginning was modest: in 1922 it had 100 members (40 of them got loans totaling 40,000 Mark); by 1927 it already had 326 members and in 1929 there was a similar number - 321.

According to the official phone book of 1930 there were in Birzh 121 phone subscribers and of them 41 Jewish (see **Appendix 4)**

A Street in Birzh

Education and Culture

Jewish children had the choice of studying among the various existing schools: the Hebrew "Tarbuth" school with about 180 pupils (its director for 16 years was Elimelekh Erez); the Yiddish school (1924-1939); the religious "Yavneh" school with about 40 pupils; several "Khadarim", or in the "Yeshivah" which was established in the thirties by the local rabbis Leib Bernshtein together with Benyamin Movsha. There was also a Jewish Kindergarten with about 30 children, active till World War II.

A branch of the Yiddish Culture League operated a library with about 300 books, but with only 40 subscribers. Once the police arrested all the members of the League blaming them for Communist activity, and during the search of the library 25 books were confiscated.

Occasionally Jewish theater companies would come to Birzh to present a show, and sometimes a cultural evening, such as a "Literary Judgment", would take place. Because of the dearth of cultural life people would gather on Shabbat afternoon in the Beith-Midrash for a chat on economic or political issues.

The Hebrew Kindergarten with the teacher Pilvinsky-1939
(Identification by Hayim Giselevitz)

Honored Birzh men with the local Rabbi Yehudah-Leib Bernshtein
Standing from left: Mindlin, ---, Shne'ur Sundelevitz,Tabakin, Yitshak Mas,
---,Ratsemor
Sitting from left: ---, Dorfman, Rabbi Yehudah-Leib Bernshtein, Henkin,-.
(Identification by Hayim Giselevitz)

Zionist and other public activities

Almost all Zionist parties were represented. The table below shows how Birzh Zionists voted for the different parties during the six Zionist Congresses:

Cong No.	Year	Tot Shek	Total Voters	Labor Party Z"S	Z"Z	Rev	Gen A	Zion B	Gros	Miz
14	1925	50	--	--	--	--	--	--	--	--
15	1927	36	34	4	12	2	2	--	--	4
16	1929	71	37	7	16	--	3	--	--	11
17	1931	88	72	5	10	36	9	--	--	12
18	1933	---	337	180		128	25	--	3	1
19	1935	412	397	312		--	42	13	15	15

Key: Cong No. = Congress Number, Tot Shek = Total Shkalim,
Rev = Revisionists, Gen Zion = General Zionists, Gros = Grosmanists,
Miz = Mizrakhi

A group of "HaShomer-HaTsair" members 1929
Standing in first line from right: Khyenke Tabakin; fifth-Bronia Rubin;
Standing in first line from left: second-Shefke Ezrakhovitz;
Kneeling in last line below from left: Hinda Shakhar

(Photo supplied by Sheine Roznikovitz-Pres)

Zionist youth organizations active in Birzh included "HeKhalutz", "HaShomer HaTsair", "Beitar", "Gordonia" had 60 to 70 members, the leaders being Peretz Shek and A.Perl, and "Benei-Akiva". The sports movements were "Maccabi" with about 50 members and a rather less active branch of "HaPo'el".

Many Birzh Jews were members in the local voluntary fire brigade and were well represented in its management, and since it owned three fire engines it was the third in size after Kovno and Shavli.

Religion and Welfare

Most of Birzh Jews were "Mithnagdim" who maintained two "Beth-Midrash" (one was called the Great), there were also one Synagogue, two "Klois" (Prayer houses), one of the shoemakers, the other of the "Shamashim" (caretakers of prayer houses). There were also Khasidim (Chassidim) who had their own prayer house as well as several "Minyanim", among them one of "Habad" and another of "Po'alei Tsedek".

The Jewish welfare institutions included "Gemiluth Khesed" which made small loans without interest; "Linath HaTsedek" (care for the ill), "Moshav Zekeinim" (Home for the aged), 'Maskil el Dal" (delicate support to people who lost their livelihood), "Lekhem Aniyim" (Bread for the Poor).

Group of "HaShomer-HaTsair" members

Standing from right: Gita Vishkin, Esther Gude, Yankelevitz, Sheine Roznikovitz, Bilhah Nakhumovitz, ---.

Sitting in second line from right: ---, Itke Moril, Hinda Shakhar, Nakhum Levitas

Sitting in third line: Tsivyah Vishkin, Zundl Fin.

The "OZE" organization, dealing mainly in preventative medicine amongst Jewish school children, had its clinic in Birzh and also served children from the vicinity.

With the deterioration of the economic situation of Birzh Jews before World War II, the OZE clinic closed down and the Artisan Union stopped its activity. Only the "Moshav-Zekeinim" which in 1935 housed six aged persons, four women and two men, continued its activity. The prayer houses and the welfare institutions continued to function rather poorly.

Relations between Jews and Lithuanians during this period were generally normal, although cold and not close. The Lithuanians lived in their alleys and the Jews in the center of the town. During these years anti-Semitism began to rear its head.

(For a partial list of personalities born in Birzh see **Appendix 3**)

Birzh "Maccabi" 1923?
(Picture supplied by Eti Sherman-Bruskin)

The Sherman Sisters-April 1936.
From left: Yentl (Eti), Feige, Rachel

A Party in Birzh-May 1937

Standing from right: ---, Feige Sherman, Shemuel Ferber, Mosheh Rapeika, Hanah-Sarah Morein, (Aunt of Hanah-Sarah ?), (Mother of Hanah-Sarah ?).

Sitting from right: Shemuel Reznikovitz, Tsivyah Gurvitz, Hanah Bokher, Aryeh Ferber, Levin ?, ---, ---, Itke Bokher, Miriam Liman, Shne'ur Propis, Miriam Ger, Mosheh Tselkovitz, Sarah Sherman

(Picture supplied by Eti Sherman-Bruskin)

During World War II

During Soviet rule (June 1940 to June 1941) some Jewish businesses were nationalized. All Zionist parties and youth organizations and also several community institutions were disbanded. The Hebrew school became a government school, with Yiddish as the teaching language. Three Jewish families (Gendler, Beker, Lifshitz, altogether 16-17 persons) were exiled to Siberia.

On the 1st of September 1939 the German army invaded Poland, occupying the country over a period of several weeks. Many Jewish youths, mostly from Zionist youth organization, managed to infiltrate into Lithuania. The Jewish community took care of the refugees in various ways, one of which was the establishment of "Kibbutsei Hakhsharah," where these young people were accommodated and worked for their living. In 1939 a Kibbutz Hakhsharah (training kibbutz) was established in Birzh for refugees from Poland, which was active till March 1940.

The German army entered Birzh on Thursday the 26th of June 1941, arriving from the north, from Latvia, and found the Lithuanian nationalists already organized, headed by a local lawyer. Persecution of the Jews began on the first day of German entry, the first victim being the doctor, Avraham-Zalman Levin. On a pretext of being asked to visit a sick person, two Lithuanians took him out of his house and one of them shot and killed him. Motl Beder was shot trying to defend Rabbi Bernshtein, who was murdered because he dared to protect his community. The young doctor Aptakin tried to hide in a forest, but Lithuanian nationalists found and murdered him. Advocate Kirshon and his family found asylum with Lithuanians who were considered friends, but who handed the whole family over to the police to be murdered. The local "Shokhet" was tied with his beard to the tail of a horse and then towed through the streets till his death.

One month after the Germans entered Birzh, on the 26th of July 1941, all Jews were ordered to leave their houses and to move to a ghetto which had been established in several shabby alleys around the synagogue and the Beith Midrash. Jewish men continued to be arrested all the time, then taken to the Jewish cemetery and other places in the town or its vicinity, and shot.

On the 8th of August 1941 (15th of Av 5701) the final phase of the murder of Birzh Jews began. On this day men, women and children in groups of 100-200 persons were led to the Astrava forest about 3.5 km north of Birzh, about 1.5 km on the road to Paroveja. There, by the edges of the forest, two pits 20 and 30 meters in length and 2 meters wide had been prepared, having been dug previously by 500 Jewish men who were forced to do this work. The victims were ordered to remove their upper clothes and kneel near the pits, into which they were pushed and shot. Whoever still showed signs of life was shot again with a pistol. The massacre took place from 11 o'clock AM till 7 PM in the evening. A local Lithuanian "with a yellow beard" (Jonas Kairys) excelled in brutality during the massacre. The murderers divided the robbed Jewish property among themselves, only giving expensive items to the Germans, after which they returned to the town singing.

According to the report of the special governmental commission of the 25th of May 1945, the number of the Jewish victims in the two pits, each 2.5 meters deep, was 2,400, amongst them 900 children. In a third pit, a smaller one, the corpses of 90 Lithuanians, also murdered by the Germans, were found. 30 more Jewish victims were found in three pits uncovered in the Jewish cemetery, all victims having been shot in the head. After the war the site was fenced, a monument was erected and on it an inscription in Russian and Lithuanian, saying: "Here are buried 3,000 Soviet citizens who were shot in 1941 by Hitler's Fascists."

At the beginning of the nineties this tablet was changed and a new inscription in Yiddish and Lithuanian says: "In this place Hitler's murderers and their local helpers murdered 2,400 Jews - men, women, children and about 90 Lithuanians, on the 8th of July 1941."

A small number of Jewish youngsters managed to escape to USSR and fought with the Red Army, mainly in the Lithuanian Division. A few survived.

Group of Birzh'er survivors at the site of the graves and monument 1989
From left: ---, Lusia Gutman-Rolnik, Rivkah Roznikovitz-Gutman, Sheine Reznikovitz-Pres, Leah Shapiro, Mira Even, Rivkah Hayat, Tsila Ger, Meir Ger

(Photo supplied by Sheine Roznikovitz-Pres)

The monument with the inscription in Lithuanian-1989
From right : Lusia Gutman-Rolnik, Rivkah Gutman, Sheine Pres

The massacre site with the monument in Astrava forest

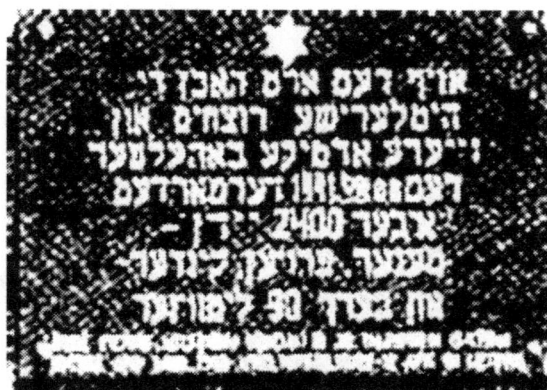

אויף דעם ארט האבן די
היטלעריש רוצחים און
זייערע ארמיקע באהילפער
דעם ... דעם
אצבער 2400 ייד…
מענער פרויען קינדער
און בערך 90 ליטווער

The inscription in Yiddish: "In this place the Hitlerist murderers and their local helpers on the August 8, 1941 murdered more than 2400 Jews-men, women children and about 90 Lithuanians."

The monument with the inscription in Yiddish and Lithuanian

Sources:

Yad-Vashem Archives,: M-1/Q-1233/89, 1460/286; 0-33/1550/1565; 0-53/3,20; 0-57; Testimonies of Elimelekh Erez, Yehudith and Yisrael Lehman, Fruma Sluzhitel

Koniukhovsky collection 0-71. Files 68, 69.

YIVO, NY - Lithuanian Communities Collection, files 122-145.

Oshri-Khurban Lita (Hebrew), pages 46, 204-207.

Lipman M.D. - History of the Jews in Zamut (Hebrew), pages 72-81.

Tabakin Henry-Only Two Remained, Private Edition, Cleveland 1973.

Cohen Berl - Jews in the Radzivil Birzh Principality in the 17th and 18th centuries (Hebrew).

The article I included in the "Anthology of the History of the Jews in Poland", Tel-Aviv 1991, pages 23-44).

Birzh by Rafi Julius - Pinkas haKehiloth. Lita (Encyclopedia of Jewish Settlements in Lithuania) (Hebrew), Editor: Dov Levin, Assistant editor: Josef Rosin, Yad Vashem. Jerusalem 1996.

Dos Vort, Kovno (Yiddish): 26.12.1934, 24.3.1935, 26.3.1935, 28.4.1935.

Folksblat, Kovno (Yiddish): 29.7.1935; 6.7.1939; 13.6.1939.

Di Yiddishe Shtime, Kovno (Yiddish), 2.4.1922.

Der Yiddisher Cooperator (Yiddish) Kovno, Nr. 2-3, 1922.

Tsait (Time) (Yiddish) – Shavl, Nr.28, 4.5.1924.

HaMeilitz (St. Petersburg) (Hebrew): 18.6.1881; 28.11.1884; July 1892;

Nr.153 1893; Nr.59 1894.

YIVO Bleter (Pages), Vol.27, pages 576-578.

Appendix 1 A partial list of Rabbis who served in Birzh

Tsevi-Hirsh haLevi Hurvitz-Rabbi of three communities: Keidan, Vizhun, Birzh. His residence was in Keidan. One of the first rabbis of Birzh. There is his signature on a document in Lublin from 1648.

Yekhezkel Katsenelenboigen-(1668-1749), he would sign as rabbi of Keidan, Birzh and surroundings.

Shalom Zak-(?-1725)

Yisrael ben Shalom Zak, from 1728 in Birzh

Hayim ben Yisrael Zak

Naftali Hertz Klatskin

Shelomoh-Zalman ben Meir Zaksh-(1814-1876)

Azriel ben Gershon-Mendel Ziv

Asher-Nisan ben Yehudah-Leib Levinzon

Pinkhas haCohen Lintop-(1852-1914), rabbi of the Khasidim in Birzh

Eliyahu-Ya'akov-Dov ben Hayim Shor-(1848-1936) from 1932 in Jerusalem

Binyamin Movshe-(1887-1941) the last Rabbi of Birzh, murdered by the Lithuanians;

Yehudah-Leib Bernshtein-(?-1941) the last Rabbi of Birzh, murdered by the Lithuanians.

All above mentioned Rabbis published booklets or books on religious issues.

Appendix 2

List of Jews mentioned in protocols of the Birzh Estate Court (1620-1745)

Aron Yoselevitz, Avram Itselevitz, Itsel Danilevitz, Aron Markovitz, Marek Shlomovitz, Shelomoh Markovitz, Marek Nakhakhovitz, Idel Izakovitz, Mozes Shmerlovitz, Mozes Zalmanovitz, Yisrael Mozeshovitz, Mozes Zundelovitz, Yisrael Izakovitz, Idel Natanovitz, Yisrael Lazarovitz, Hayim Shabshevitz, Rasia Abramotz, Avram Mishnovitz, David Elyashevitz, and wife Lipka, Shakhna Nakhmanovitz, Yozef Hirshevitz and more.

Appendix 3   A partial list of personalities born in Birzh

The well known Rabbis family Klatskin had its roots in Birzh

Yehoshua-Josef Preil-(1858-1896), wrote many articles in the Hebrew press "HaLevanon", "HaMeilitz" and several books. Died in Kovno.

Josef-Elhanan Melamed-(1859-1932), rabbi in different towns of Russia, published several books, immigrated to Eretz-Yisrael and was director of the "Mizrahi" school in Hevron, died in Jerusalem.

Elhanan-Bunem Vaserman–(1876-1941), one of the most famous Yeshivah heads in his generation. Was murdered in the Ninth Fort of Kovno.

Elazar-Meir Preil-(1881-?), rabbi in Manchester, Brooklyn, Trenton and Yeshivah head at the Yeshivah University in New-York. Published articles in the Hebrew religious periodicals "HaPardes", "Sha'arei –Zion" etc.

A.B.Kohen-(1873-?) published his book in English "Memoirs of 85 Years" (1958)

Tsevi Golombok-(1880-1954), since 1903 in England, in 1914 publisher and redactor of his Jewish evening newspaper. In 1918 redactor of his weekly: "Yiddishe Shtime". From 1928 publisher and redactor of the Jewish-English weekly "Jewish Echo" in Glasgow, where he died.

Yitshak-Aharon Berger-(1889-1979), since 1902 in America, published poetry in the Yiddish press of America, died in New-York.

Yosef-Yehudah-Leib Zosnitz-(1837-1910), mathematician and nature sciences researcher, died in New York.

Appendix 4 - Copy of the official phone book of Birzh 1930

Kāla   Biržai

BETYGALA
Raseinlų apskr.

Pt., atv., mok. kvd. 28—35
Ariogala

Janulaitis, P., kunigas-dekanas,
Betygala 2
Valsčiaus valdybos raštinė,
Betygala 3
Vlešas telefonas pasikalbėji-
mams, Pašto įstaiga . . . 4

BIRŠTONAS.
Kauno apskr.

Vasaros metu — pt., atv., kitu laiku
— agt., šv., mok. kvd. 46—43
Nemaniūnai Prienai
. . .

BIRŽAI
Ptt., vtv., mok. kvd. 9—53.
Kaunas   Pasvalys
Pabiržė   Parovėja
Panevėžys   Skaistkalnė (Latv.)
Papilys   Suostas
Vabalninkas.

Alaus bravaras, Rotušės g-vė 18   20
Apskrities ligoninė, vedėjas
d-ras Mikelėnas (10—12), Li-
goninės g-vė 7
Apskrities valdyba, Rinkos gat-
vė 18 53
Apskrities viršininko raštinė,
Rinkos g-vė 18 55
Arešto namai, Pasvalio g-vė 16   71
Bajorūnas, Jonas, provizorius,
Vytauto g-vė 31 50
Balbieris, Juozas, įvairių prekių
ūkio krautuvė, Rinkos g-vė 18   1 40
Beras, Icikas, namų savininkas,
Tilto g-vė 14 80
Berenšteinas, Leiba, žydų rabi-
nas, Tilto g-vė 23 . . . 88
Binkis, Albinas, apskrities ag-
ronomas, Vytauto g-vė 1 . . 1 39
Bocheris, Efroimas, linų pirklys,
Vilniaus g-vė 41 64
Brilis, Šmuelis, linų pirklys Vil-
niaus g-vė 24 4
Broga, Jonas, mok. inspekto-
riaus padėjėjas, Vytauto gat-
vė 1 15
Didžiulis, Vytautas, gamtos mo-
kytojas, Malūno g-vė 18 . . 1 26
„Ekonomija", valcų malūnas,
Rotušės g-vė 16 81

Elektros stotis, Dvaro g-vė 10   65
Ezrachovičius, Aronas, linų pir-
klys, Vytauto g-vė 22 . . . 86
Fridmanas, Leiba, namų savi-
ninkas, Vytauto g-vė 8 . . 82
Fridmanai, brol ai, kolonialių
pfekių parduotuvė, Vytauto
g-vė 26 . . . . 1 13
Gaisrininkų savanorių draugija,
Vytauto g-vė 11 63
Gelažius, P., apskr. veterinari-
jos gydytojas, Prekių g. 10.   13
Geležinkelio stotis 14
Gendleris, Mauša, medžių pre-
kyba, Vytauto g-vė 14 . . 15
Gendleris, Mauša, geležies pre-
kyba, Karaimų g-vė 29 . . 46
Gendleris, Zundelis, benzino
parduotuvė, Vytauto g-vė 20   1 09
Geselevičius, Leiba, linų pirklys,
Radvilų g-vė 1 11
Gimnazija, Vytauto g-vė 31 .   66
Chaltas, Motelis, sėmenų pirk-
lys, Pasvalio g-vė 35 . . . 1 34
Chodašas, Salomonas, manufak-
tūros prekyba, Vytauto gat-
vė 6 45
Jakubėnas, Povilas, d-ras, kun.
superintendentas, Reformatų
g-vė 14 22
Jakubkevičius, Karolis, vežikas,
Dvareckienės g-vė 17 . . 1 43
Jansonas, Hari, linų apdirb. fab.
riko vedėjas, Radvilų g-vė 4   1 51
Jansono, T. įpėd., linų verpyk-
la, karšykla ir valcų malūnas, Malūno g-vė 17 . . . 38
Jegermanaitė, Olga, aptiekos
savininkė, Aptiekos g-vė 1,   32
Ycas, Jonas, profesorius, Šim-
peliškio vienk. 21
Kacas, Binė, žyginių arklių stoties laikytojas, Pasvalio gat-
vė 29 91
Kacas, Icikas, malūno „Ekonomija" akcininkas, Tilto g-vė 8   1 04
Kacas, Šolomas, žyginių arklių
stoties laikytojas, Vytauto
g-vė 1 90
Kacas, Berelis ūkininkas, Vytauto g-vė 21 29
Kairys, K., žemės ūkio mašinų
parduotuvė, Rotušės g-vė 7.   28
Kanelis, Dovydas, liaudies mokytojas, Žemoji g-vė 6 . . 76
Karo komendantūra, Stoties
g-vė 10 8

...anlas, Chalmas, geležies prekybá, Rinkos g-vė 23 . . 99

Rozinkovičius, Jankelis, kailių pirklys, Tilto g-vė 27 . . . 72

Rozmanas, Vladas, apskrities viršininkas, Kilučių g-vė . . 96

Smulkaus kredito bankas, ūkininkų sajungos, Rinkos g. 3 26

Spausuvė ir guminių antspaudų dirbtuvė, Vytauto g-vė 34 . 42

Stefanavičius, Fortunatas, advokatas, Aukštoji g-vė 17 : 37

Šaulių XVIII rinktinės vadas, Aptiekos g-vė 2 52

Šernas, Jonas, valsčiaus viršaitis, Ežero g-vė 18 . . . 1 44

Šiaulių apyg. teismo antstolis Olšauskas, Antanas, Rotušės g-vė 6 36

Sickys, Vilius, ūkininkas, Malūno g-vė 15 . . . . . . 1 24

Tabakinas, Tevelis, Radvilų g-vė 1 . . . . 1 30

Taikos teisėjas, Reformatų g-vė 10 31

Tamulėnas, Motiejus, matininkas, žemės tvarkytojas, Ežero g-vė 17 . . . . . . 1 00

Telegrafas. 23

Teismo tardytojas, Vytauto g-vė 8 . . . . 1 46

Urniežius, Stasys, apskr. felčeris, Lauko g-vė 5 . . . 54

Valiūnas, Juozas, agronomas, inspektorius, Naradavos dv. 91

Valsčiaus valdyba, Vytauto g. 1 61

Variakojis, Petras, agronomas, valcų malūnas ir vilnų karšykla, Astravo dv. . . . 68

Variakojis, Petras, žemės ūkio smulk. kredito banko direktorius, Radvilų km. 1 19

Vasiliauskas, Valtiekus, kino „Žvaigždė" savininkas, Rotušės g-vė 12 40

Viešas telefonas pasikalbėjimams, Pašto įstaiga. . . 8

Verbilugevičius, Liudas, kailių dirbtuvės savinin., Kapų g. 2 92

Zakas, Molsiejus, prisiek. adv. padėjėjas, Vytauto g-vė 21 . 1 49

Zelbovičius, Mendelis, gyvulių ir javų pirklys, Vytauto gatvė 18 85

„Zingerio" siuvamųjų mašinų b-vė, Biržų skyrius, Vytauto g-vė 5 45

Zundelevičius, Hiršas, viešbučio „Metropol" savin., apdr. d-jos „Lietuva", agentas, Vytauto g-vė 26a 1 67

Žemės tvarkytojo raštinė, Reformatų g-vė 7 5

Žemės ūkio draugija, Vytauto g-vė 1 25

Žemė ūkio smulkaus kredito bankas, Tilto g-vė 9 . . 12

Žydų liaudies bankas, Rinkos g-vė 20 38

Žuranskas, Antanas, namų savininkas, Muravanka . . 62

BLYMAČIAI

Klaipėdos apskr.

Gir., vip., mok. kvd., 24—11.

Pėžaičių abon. Nr. 4.

BUBIAI

Šiaulių apskr.

Agt., šv., mok. kvd. 17—32.

Bazilionai Siauliai.

Kurkauskas, Vladas, Mirskiškės dvaras 3

Roppas, Bubiu dvaras 2

Zubovas, Dimitrijus, Bubiu dvaras. 1

BUNDALAI

Šilutės apskr.

Gir., vip., mok. kvd. 26—10

Šakučių abon. Nr. 6.

Appendix 4 - Partial List of Lithuanian Murderers of Jews of Birzai and the Surrounding District

Armonavicius Kazys	Vaskai
Armonavicius Telesforas	Vaskai
Augustinas Vasilius	Nemunelis
Baltulis Petras	Pasvalys
Barkauskas Antanas	Pasvalys
Bavilauskas Vacys	Birzai+
Belte Jonas	Vaskai
Bilauskas Petras	Pasvalys
Bizauskas Juozas	Joniskelis
Blagosciunas	Joniskelis
Blazys Jonas	Valkininkai
Brazinskas Juozas	Joniskelis
Burkus Kazimieras	Pasvalys
Bvelskis Stasys	Vaskai
Bytautas Antanas	Vaskai
Disa	Pumpenai
Dragunas Pranas	Vabalninkai
Drazdauskiene Irena	Joniskelis
Dulevicius	Vaskai
Dziuve	Joniskelis
Eidukonis Kazys	Vabalninkas
Garlauskas Petras	Vaskai
Gintautas Povilas	Vabalninkas
Graziunas	Valkininkai
Gruzauskas Kazys	Pasvalys
Gudas Leonas	Pasvalys
Ignatavicius (Chief of Pol.)	Birzai
Jakeliunas Jonas	Vaskai
Jankauskas Petras	Joniskelis
Janonis Antanas	Valkininkai
Jarasiunas Jonas	Vaskai
Jerasiunas Petras	Joniskelis
Jonilis	Pumpenai
Juraitis Juozas	Joniskelis
Jurevicius Juozas	Joniskelis
Jurgaitis Juozas	Joniskelis
Jurgaitis Petras (Colonel)	Joniskelis

Kairys Jonas	Birzai
Kalkis Jonas	Vabalninkas
Kalkis Petras	Vabalninkas
Kateiva Leonas	Birzai
Kazenas Jonas	Pasvalys
Kaziunas Antanas	Birzai
Keksa Juozas	Joniskelis
Kimbrys Jonas	Joniskelis
Kimbrys Petras	Joniskelis
Kotkevicius Jonas	Joniskelis
Krivickas Jonas	Pasvalys
Krivickas Petras	Pasvalys
Kruopys Povilas	Vaskai
Kubilius Jonas	Pasvalys
Kudirka	Nemunelis
Kunickas	Valkininkai
Labeikis Balys	Pasvalys
Lelis	Pumpenai
Liepa Juozas	Joniskelis
Liukpetris Povilas	Pasvalys
Macelis Jonas	Joniskelis
Macelis Juozas	Joniskelis
Macelis Karolis	Joniskelis
Magelinskas	Vaskai
Misiunas Bolius	Vaskai
Mitka Jonas	Vaskai
Morkunas Jurgis	Pasvalys
Nogentas Ignas	Pasvalys
Pakarna Vladas	Joniskelis
Petraitis	Pumpenai
Petrikenas Antanas	Vabalninkas
Petronis Stasys	Vabalninkas
Radzevicius	Joniskelis
Ridikas Jonas	Joniskelis
Sianciunas	Vabalninkas
Simonaitis Mykolas	Vaskai
Simonavicius Mykolas	Vaskai
Simonis Povilas	Nemunelis

May God punish these cowards. May they and their associates and collaborators and their closest, their descendants and offspring, stand defamed and cursed to all posterity.

Jurbarkas (Yurburg)

Yurburg (Jurbarkas in Lithuanian) is situated on the right hand shore of the Nieman (Nemunas) river where the tributaries Mituva and Imstra converge. The town used to be about 12 km (7.5 miles) to the east of the Prussian border, surrounded by woods. It began as a stronghold of the Knights Order of the Cross in the thirteenth century named Georgenburg or Jurgenburg, but after the border between Lithuania and Germany was defined in 1422, Yurburg became a border town and a customs point. During the thirteenth century the importance of Yurburg increased due to the harvesting of trees in the surrounding woods for commercial purposes, when the logs were floated on the Nieman River to Prussia. Thanks to the ethnic diversity of its inhabitants, its location on a main sailing route - the Nieman - and its proximity to Prussia, Yurburg became a communication and commercial center between east and west. During Russian rule (1795-1915) the town was included in the Kovno Gubernia (province).

As a result of railway construction and road improvement in the region during the nineteenth century, sailing on the Nieman subsided and the growth of Yurburg slowed. The town was taken over by rebels for a short time during the Polish mutiny in 1831, but after the mutiny was repressed by the Tzar, Yurburg returned to its former life.

German culture from across the border influenced the social life greatly and affected the mode of living in town, which also continued to be the case during the period of Lithuania's independence (1918-1940).

Because of its topographic situation and location between the two rivers and the Nieman, the town frequently suffered from floods. In 1862 eighty houses were inundated and their residents rescued themselves by climbing onto the roofs. Yurburg also suffered from fires, the greatest fires being in 1906 when 120 of its houses burnt down.

Jewish Settlement till after World War I

Yurburg was first mentioned in the book of Rabbi Meir ben Gedalyah (1558-1616) from Lublin "Sheloth uTeshuvoth" (Questions and Answers) concerning the case of an "Agunah" (deserted wife) whose husband had been killed in Yurburg. The testimonies of this case were reported in 1593 and 1597. During the period of the autonomous organization of Jewish communities in Lithuania "Va'ad Medinath Lita" (1623-1764), Yurburg was included in the Keidan district, and by 1650 there were already seven Jewish houses in town.

In the middle of the 17th century, some Yurburg's Jews earned their living by renting the right to collect taxes for the government in Yurburg, Birzh and other towns, and this was done under the cover of Christians.

At the beginning of the 18th century the community wanted to replace the officiating Rabbi, but he complained to the authorities and received a " letter of protection " from the king. On the 17th of November 1714 Rabbi Aizik Leizerovitz was mentioned in an official document, but detailed information of Jewish settlement of Yurburg exists only from the year 1766. At this time there were 2,333 Jews in the town who owned a few prayer houses, among them the magnificent wooden Synagogue built in 1790, one of the oldest in Lithuania. There was also a Jewish cemetery, as well as welfare and religious education institutions. In 1862 there were 2,550 Jews in Yurburg.

Flooding in Yurburg
[Courtesy of Jack Cossid]

Yurburg Jews suffered during the Polish mutiny in 1831. A local resident, Reuven Rozenfeld, was hanged by rebels, who blamed him for aiding the Russian rulers. After the mutiny was quelled, a trial of those involved in the hanging took place for many months, among the accused was a Jew named Tuviyah ben Meir Danilevitz. After being imprisoned in Rasein for 13 months, he was acquitted due to lack of evidence.

In 1843 the Czar issued an order stipulating that Jews living in an area within 50 km of the western border of Russia should be transferred to some of the Gubernias (provinces) inside Russia. Yurburg's community was one of 19 communities that refused to obey this order.

Most of Yurburg Jews made their living from the timber trade, floating timber to Germany, commerce, customs commission, transport and shop keeping. In 1865 a branch of one of the largest commercial firms in Germany "Hausman et Lunz" opened in town.

The local garrison was also situated there, providing a living for Jewish merchants. In 1861 Jewish soldiers of the garrison donated money for writing a new "Torah Scroll," which was later brought into the synagogue by the Jewish soldiers, with due festivity. The celebration was attended by respected local people, headed by the commander of the garrison.

At the end of the 1880s a cooperative credit company was established, for which it took three years to receive permission to operate from the authorities.

As a result of the general atmosphere in Yurburg, the "Haskalah" (Enlightenment) movement flourished there among the Jews more than in Zhamut's (Zemaitija region) other communities. This was demonstrated by the cooperation of the community heads in the establishment of a quite modern Talmud-Torah in 1884, where 100 poor children studied, and in addition to religious subjects, Hebrew and grammar, mathematics and Russian were also taught. Members of the management of this institution were: L.Valk, M.H. Kostin and L.Boger, one of the teachers being the famous Hebrew writer Avraham Mapu. Although the school was under the supervision of the government, its financial maintenance was mainly the responsibility of the community. Due to the fact that the 900 Rubles received from the "Meat tax" was not sufficient, the community heads appealed to former Yurburgers in New York, Saint Louis and Rochester in the United States for help. A partial list of donors (who donated from $0.50 to $750) was published in the Hebrew newspaper "HaMeilitz" in July 1889.

The Yurburg Jewish institutions also served smaller Jewish communities in the vicinity, such as Shaudine, Pakelnishok, Gaure. (After World War I there were no more Jews in Pakelnishok).

Exterior of the Old Wooden Synagogue of Yurburg Built in 1790
Photograph courtesy of Balys Buracas (anbura@lrs.lt)

During the years of famine (1869-1872) which affected many parts of Lithuania, Yurburg suffered less and its Jewish residents donated money to needy communities. The fundraisers were Yitshak-Aizik Volberg and Shelomoh Bresloi.

In a list of donors for the Settlement of Eretz-Yisrael dated 1896, names of 20 Yurburg Jews appear (see **Appendix 3**). The fundraisers were Tsevi Fain and Avraham-Yitshak Kopelov.

In the old Jewish cemetery in Jerusalem there is a headstone of Rivkah Gitel bat Mordehai Margalioth from Yurburg. During World War I many of Yurburg's Jews left the town, some returning later.

During Independent Lithuania (1918-1940)

After the establishment of independent Lithuania, Yurburg was included in the Raseiniai district. The number of Jewish residents in Yurburg was smaller than before as some of those who had left did not return and also due to immigration abroad. However, their proportion amongst the whole population increased, as can be seen from the first census performed by the government in 1923. There were 4,409 residents including 1,887 Jews (43%), while in 1897 there were 7,391 residents, of them 2,350 Jews (32%)

Chair of "Eliyahu HaNavi" in the Old Wooden Synagogue - 1927
Courtesy of Ben Craine (Detroit, Michigan, USA)

The Bimah in the Old Synagogue of Yurburg

Photograph courtesy of Balys Buracas (anbura@lrs.lt)

In 1922 the elections for the first Lithuanian Seimas (Parliament) took place, with 774 Utyan Jews participating. 477 voted for the Zionist list, 199 for the Democrats and 98 for the religious list "Akhduth."

According to the autonomy law for minorities issued by the new Lithuanian government, the minister for Jewish affairs, Dr. Max Soloveitshik, ordered elections to be held in the summer of 1919 for community committees in all towns of the state. In Yurburg a committee was only elected five years later, in 1924, after much pressure from the National institutions of Lithuanian Jewry (Va'ad HaAretz). The committee (Va'ad) comprised five members of the Workers list, three Zionist-Merchants, two Religious, two Democrats, one "Tseirei-Zion", one Mizrahi and a representative of the butchers. The committee, which collected taxes as required by law and was in charge of all aspects of community life, was active till the end of 1925 when the autonomy was annulled.

Among the 14 members at the local council (later the municipality) elected in 1924, six were Jews, one of them serving as deputy chairman and another as a member of the management. The elections of 1931 resulted in three Lithuanians, one German and one Russian being elected, as well as five Jews: Z. Levitan, M. Shimonov, Y. Grinberg, Sh. Zundelevitz, Adv. H. Naividel, one of them as deputy chairman. In the elections of 1934, when two Jewish lists were presented, four Jews, four Lithuanians and one German were elected.

At right: stamp of the office of the Minister for Jewish Affairs
At left: stamp of the Jewish National Council in Lithuania

During this period, as previously, Yurburg's Jews made their living from trade with timber, fish, poultry, fruits and eggs that were exported to Germany. Others dealt in crafts, fishing and shipping, a large part of economic activity taking place on weekly market days (Monday and Thursday) and during the 24 annual fairs.

According to the government survey of 1931 there were 75 businesses in Yurburg, 69 being owned by Jews (92%).

The list of traders according to the type of business is given in the table below:

Type of the business	Total	Owned by Jews
Groceries	3	3
Grain and Flax	4	4
Butcher's shops and Cattle Trade	13	9
Restaurants and Taverns	4	2
Food Products	9	9
Beverages	2	2
Textile Products and Furs	13	13
Leather and Shoes	4	4
Haberdashery and Utensils	6	6
Medicine and Cosmetics	3	3
Radio, Bicycles, Sewing Machines	1	1
Tools and Steel Products	5	5
Heating Materials	3	3
Books and Stationary	1	1
Others	4	4

According to the same survey there were 19 light industries in Yurburg, including 18 owned by Jews (95%), as can be seen in the following table:

Type of the Factory	Total	Jewish Owned
Power Plants	1	1
Sawmills and Furniture	2	2
Paper Industry: Printing Press	1	1
Food Industry	8	7
Dresses, Footwear	3	3
Others	4	4

In 1937 there were 93 Jewish artisans: 19 tailors, 12 butchers, 12 bakers, 8 shoemakers, 6 barbers, 5 stitchers, 4 painters, 3 hatters, 3 glaziers, 2 oven builders, 2 locksmiths 2 electricians, 2 watchmakers, 2 jewelers, 2 photographers, 1 tinsmith and 8 others. In 1925 there was also one Jewish doctor and 2 dentists.

The Jewish popular bank (Folksbank), established in 1922, which later had up to 400 members, played an important role in the economic life of Yurburg's Jews. Among the great businesses in town the private bank of the Bernshtein family, the "Export-Handel" company and the shipping companies in the Nieman River, should be mentioned.

By 1939 there were 116 phone owners, 41 of them belonging to Jews.

One of the steamships wharfing in Yurburg

Throughout the ages mutual tolerance existed between the different ethnic groups in Yurburg, and this also continued during Lithuanian rule. However, there were exceptions from time to time, as in 1919, when Yurburg Jews complained to the minister for Jewish affairs in Kovno about a decision by the local authorities that all signs should be in the Lithuanian language only. Previously there had been some signs on Jewish shops in Yiddish or in Hebrew. One of the factors that fostered strong mutual relations was the local branch of the Organization of Jewish Combatants for the Independence of Lithuania, but during the 1930s a significant decline took place in the relations between local Lithuanians, Germans and their Jewish neighbors. It expressed itself by the suppression of Jewish commerce, such as the closing of the "Export-Handel" company, in assaults and in the burning of Jewish property, i.e. the flourmill of the Fainberg family.

Adding to the deterioration of the economic situation of Yurburg's Jews, the lower and middle classes in particular, were the many fires and floods caused by the rising water level in the Nieman due to the melting of the ice in spring.

Yurburg was famous in Lithuania for its Zionist atmosphere and Hebrew culture that dominated it. One of the two public parks was almost officially called "Tel-Aviv," and the Hebrew high school was called "Herzl" after the founder of the Zionist organization. In addition to the old Talmud Torah, which was turned into a modern elementary school, a new Hebrew school of the "Tarbuth" chain was also established. There was a public Yiddish library called after "Mendele Mokher Sefarim" and a Hebrew library named after Y. H. Brener.

The highest grade of the Gymnasium in the first year of its existence (without external students), the teachers - from right; Kaplan (gymnastics), Lifshitz (Natural Science), Mrs. Efrath-Rosenboim (Languages), Tsentkovsky (Tanakh - Bible), Dr. Efrath (Principal, Mathematics) Kosotzky (Literature)

The students - from right: Dartwin, Kobelkovsky, Zevulun Petrikansky, Hannah Fainberg (Feinberg) (x - ?), Shlomovitz; below to the right - Hinda Levinberg, Klara (Clara) Petrikansky

The "Maccabi" sports organization with about 100 members, an urban Kibbutz of HeHalutz named "Patish" and branches of all Zionist parties, were established. There was also much activity by Zionist youth organizations, such as "HaShomer-HaTsair," "Beitar " and "Benei-Akiva"

The "Maccabi" sports organization with about 100 members, an urban Kibbutz of HeHalutz named "Patish" and branches of all Zionist parties, were established.

There was also much activity by Zionist youth organizations, such as "HaShomer-HaTsair," "Beitar " and "Benei-Akiva."

The Leftist-Yiddishist movement, the "Jewish Knowledge Society" and the sports organization the "Jewish Workers Club" were also active among Yurburg's Jews. Communist youth too had their supporters.

Committee members of the Maccabi Organization of Yurburg. Sitting from the right: Rafael Kizel, Berl Levinger, and Avraham Altman. Standing from the right: Yitskhak Rakhtsa, Zevulun Petrikansky (Poran); Elyashev, Miasnik, Yosef Gutman *(emigrated to El Paso, Texas)*.

A group of Beitar Scouts, 1926

The "Va'ad" (board) of Betar.

From left to right: Simkha Rokhtzo, Ark Rickler, Mosheh, Pinki Kopinski and Jack Cossid as the secretary of the organization. December 1, 1937.

The table below shows how Yurburg Zionists voted for the different parties at five Zionist Congresses: (See the key below the table)

Congr Nr.	Year	Total Shkalim	Total Voter	Labor Z"S	Party Z"Z	Rn	GZ A	B	Gm	Mz
15	1927	64	40	29	6	---	5	--	--	---
16	1929	118	44	28	2	11	3	--	--	---
17	1931	53	40	20	10	4	6	--	--	---
18	1933	---	143	101		19	9	--	10	4
19	1935	---	359	257		---	14	40	19	29

GZ = General Zionists Gm =Grosmanists Rn = Revisionists Mz= Mizrachi

During Nazi rule a member of the illegal Communist youth organization named Yekutiel Elyashuv, who had managed to escape to Russia at the beginning of the war, was parachuted in Lithuania. He fell in battle.

For the list of Rabbis who served in Yurburg during the years, see **Appendix 1**. For a partial list of personalities of Yurburg, see **Appendix 2**.

During World War II and Afterwards

World War II broke out on the first of September 1939, when the German army attacked Poland. A German-Soviet agreement of August 23rd 1939 had stipulated that Lithuania would be under German influence, but that same year, in September 1939, Germany and the Soviet Union decided that Lithuania would be under Soviet influence. Accordingly the agreement of October 10th 1939 stipulated that the Soviet Union return Vilna to Lithuania, this ending its occupation by Poland. This included an area of 9000 square kilometers around the town, and Soviet troops were allowed to establish bases all over Lithuania.

On June 15, 1940, Lithuania was forced to establish a regime friendly towards the Soviet Union, and after the new government headed by Justas Paleckis was installed, the Red Army took over Lithuania. President Smetona fled, Lithuanian leaders were exiled to Siberia, and political parties were dissolved. A popular Seimas was elected, 99% of its members being communists, and decided unanimously that Lithuania join the Soviet Union.

The seller of the General Zionist newspaper "Di Yiddishe Shtime"

Following new laws, the majority of factories and shops belonging to Jews of Yurburg were nationalized and commissars were appointed to manage them. Most of the artisans were organized into cooperatives (Artels). Some flats and buildings were confiscated. Some enterprises were turned into government institutions, others into public and communal companies.

After these events the supply of goods decreased and, as a result, prices soared. The middle class, mostly Jewish, bore most of the brunt, and the standard of living dropped gradually.

All Zionist parties and youth organizations were disbanded, the Hebrew "Tarbuth" school was closed, and the Yiddish school which was broadened, became an official Soviet institution. At this time Yurburg numbered about 600 Jewish families.

On the 22nd of June 1941 the war between Germany and the USSR began, the German army entering Yurburg on the same day. Many people connected to the Soviet regime tried to escape, but only a small number managed to board a steamer, which sailed to Kovno. Very few managed to escape to the USSR. **(See also the BA Thesis of Ruta Puisyte from the University of Vilnius "Holocaust in Jurbarkas** " at:

< http://www.shtetlinks.jewishgen.org/Yurburg/bathesis.html>.)

Those Jews who remained in town hid in the bathhouse, but German soldiers discovered them and forced them to return to their homes. Although the Gestapo should have processed Jews from Tilzit, during the first weeks of the occupation the fate of the Jews was in the hands of the local Lithuanian police and its newly appointed head, a teacher in the local high school. The Lithuanians forced Jewish youths to work in various jobs, including cleaning the streets. The Lithuanians also forced Jews to destroy the old and magnificent wooden synagogue (built in 1790) with their own hands, including the "Bimah" and "Eliyahu's Chair" with their splendid ornamental wooden carvings. See the images at the beginning of this article.

During this work, Jews were beaten and mistreated, one example being when a brick was fixed to the town cantor's beard (Alperovitz) and he was thus led through the streets. On Saturday, June 28, 1941, Lithuanian police forced the old Rabbi Hayim-Reuven Rubinshtein as well as Jewish family heads to bring all Torah scrolls and other holy books to the synagogue yard to burn them. The next day policemen made Jews run through the streets in a so-called procession, while a sculpture of Stalin was carried ahead. In front of a curious crowd, Jews were forced to dance and humiliate themselves by declaiming speeches that were dictated to them and similar actions. Several Jewish doctors and learned people were murdered, after having been humiliated and tortured by local Lithuanians.

On the 3rd of July 1941 (7th of Tamuz 5701) German and Lithuanian police detained 322 Jews, whom they led to the Jewish cemetery cruelly beating them on the way, and then shot them one by one near the pits which had previously been dug. One of the victims was the exporter Emil Max, who as a German soldier during World War I, was decorated with an Iron Cross, first degree. He attacked a Gestapo officer, and was shot dead immediately. After the carnage a party for the murderers was arranged in town.

On the 27th of July, 45 elderly Jews were put on carts to be taken to Rasein for a supposedly medical inspection. After a journey of 15 km they were murdered together with the coachmen who transported them and with Jews from neighboring villages. On the first of August, 105 elderly Jewish women were murdered in the same manner. On the 4th of September, 520 women, children and relatives of the 322 men, victims of the carnage of the 3rd of July, were imprisoned for 3 days in the yard of the Jewish school, after which they were transferred to the yard of Motl Levyush which served as a labor camp. At midnight, the 7th of September, these women and their children, who resisted and hit the Lithuanian murderers with their fists and shouted with anger, were led to the Smalininkai grove (seven kilometers from Yurburg), where they were shot with rifles and machine guns, with only a few girls managing to escape. One week later the last 50 Jews, who had been left temporarily in Yurburg for work, were murdered too. Only a few were hidden by peasants.

During the three years of Nazi occupation, several Jews who managed to escape away from the hands of the rulers and also from local residents who were liable to betray them to the police, roamed around in the surroundings of Yurburg and Staki. The Fainshtein brothers, armed with automatic weapons, met a Soviet pilot whose plane had been shot down, and together they acted as a partisan group.

Later on several tens of Jews from the Kovno ghetto and from other places joined this group and in the spring of 1944 they numbered 35-40 armed fighters. From time to time they attacked German vehicles on the roads and punished Lithuanian collaborators. When the frontline approached their base, they were suddenly surrounded by German gendarmerie and after a short fight all fell in battle. From this group only two wounded women and five men (among them the Fainshtein brothers who were absent from the base during the fight) survived. Among Yurburg's Jews those who survived were those who had managed to escape to Russia, those who arrived in the Kovno ghetto and several others who fought with the partisans.

After the war a monument was erected on the mass graves.

In 1991 **"The Book of Remembrance" of Yurburg Jewish Community"** was published in Hebrew and Yiddish, edited by Zevulun Poran (Petrikansky).

The number of Jewish survivors who returned to live in Yurburg decreased, in 1970 there were nine Jews, in 1977 there were four, in 1998 only five, and in 2001 there were none!

In 1991-92 the government cleaned and restored the old Jewish cemetery.

In 2003 **"The Memorial Book for the Jewish Community of Yurburg-Lithuania; Translation and Update"** (English), (Editor and Compiler: Joel Alpert, Assistant editors-Josef Rosin and Fania Hilelson Jivotovsky; NY 2003) was published.

The monument on the mass graves near Kalnenai village. The inscription
in Yiddish says: "In this place the Nazis and their local helpers cruelly
murdered on the 5th of September 1941 500 Jews."

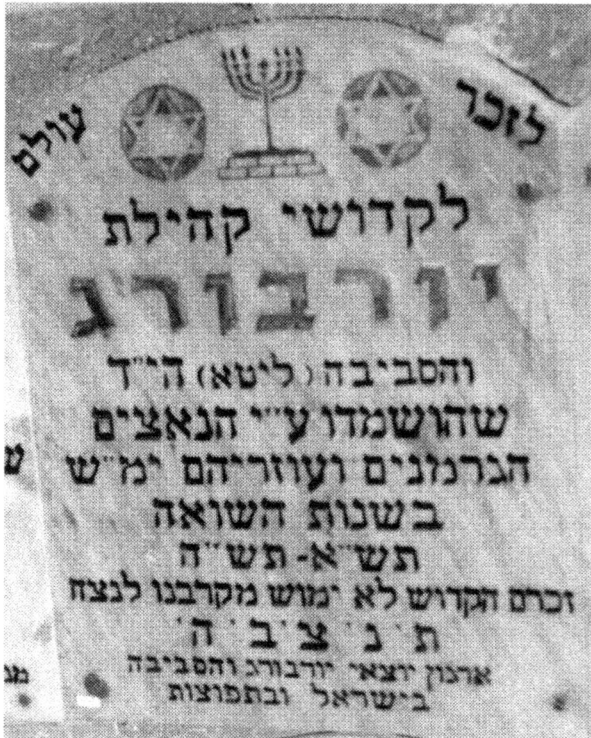

The Memorial Plaque in the Holocaust Cellar in Jerusalem

Sources:

Yad Vashem Archives: M-/Q-1314/133; M-9/15(6); TR-10/40,275 Koniukhovsky Collection 0-71, files 49,50.

Central Zionist Archives-Jerusalem, Z-4/2548; 13/15/131; 55/1788; 55/1701; YIVO, Collection of Lithuanian Communities, New-York, Files 507-509, 1388, 1523.

The Oral History Division of the Institute of Contemporary Jewry, the Hebrew University in Jerusalem, evidence 65/12 of J.Tarshish.

Gotlib, Ohalei Shem, -page 93 (Hebrew).

Kamzon J.D., Yahaduth Lita (Lithuanian Jewry), pages 147-154 (Hebrew), Rabbi Kook Publishing House, Jerusalem 1959.

Levin Sh.- "Lithuanian Jews in the 1831 Uprising"- YIVO Pages.

Poran Zevulun-Sefer haZikaron leKehilath Yurburg-Lita, (Hebrew and Yiddish) Jerusalem 1991.

The Memorial Book for the Jewish Community of Yurburg-Lithuania; Translation and Update (English), Editor and Compiler: Joel Alpert, Assistant editors-Josef Rosin and Fania Hilelson Jivotovsky; NY 2003

Dos Vort -daily newspaper in Yiddish of the Z"S party, Kovno-30.10.1934; 11.11.1934; 12.2.1939.

Di Yiddishe Shtime-daily newspaper in Yiddish of the General Zionists-Kovno, 24.8.1919; 3.9.1919; 4.4.1922; 25.4.1923; 19.10.1924; 23.11.1924; 19.6.1931; 28.8.1931; 5.10.1937.

HaMeilitz, St.Petersburg, (Hebrew), 18.8.1886; 3.1.1889; 19.4.1889; 19.2.1899; 2.7.1893; 6.3.1901.

Folksblat - daily newspaper of the Folkists, Kovno (Yiddish), 7.3.1933; 10.4.1935; 16.7.1935; 21.3.1937; 29.3.1937; 5.10.1937; 20.11.1940.

Funken, Kovno (Yiddish), 8.5.1931.

Di Zeit (Time), Shavl (Yiddish)-5.6.1924; 6.5.1924.

Hamashkif - daily newspaper of the Revisionist party, Tel-Aviv (Hebrew) 22.4.1945.

Forverts -New York (Yiddish)-4.4.1946.

Gimtasis Krastas - (Country of birth) (Lithuanian) 8.9.1988.

Naujienos ,Chicago-(News) (Lithuanian) 8.9.1949.

Sviesa, Jurbarkas, (Light) (Lithuanian) 12.7.1990; 8.8.1990; 11.8.1990.

Valstieciu Laikrastis-(Farmers Newspaper) (Lithuanian) 26.4.1990.

Appendix 1

A list of Rabbis who served in Yurburg

Aizik Leizerovitz - mentioned in an official document in 1714.

Aryeh-Yehudah-Leib - during the18th century.

Yehushua-Zelig Ashkenazi (about 1785-1831), refused to accept a salary because he had a rich father-in-law.

Mosheh haLevi Levinson, from1861 in Yurburg.

Ya'akov-Yosef ben Dov-Ber (1841-1902), from 1888 a Rabbi in New York where he died.

Yehezkel Lifshitz (1862-1932), in Yurburg 1887-1891.

Avraham Dimant (1863-1940), in Yurburg for several tens of years until his death.

Hayim-Reuven Rubinshtein (1888-1941), the last Rabbi of Yurburg, murdered by the Lithuanians.

Most of the above mentioned Rabbis published books on religious matter.

Appendix 2   A partial list of personalities in Yurburg.

Shelomoh Fainberg (1821-1893), philantropist, moved to Kovno in 1857, married Baroness Rosa von Lichtenstein from Vienna, in Koenigsberg from 1866. He received the title of " Councellor of Commerce " from the Czar, and died in Koenigsberg.

Shelomoh Shakhnovitz - author of the book "The Skill of Reading the Torah" (Keidan 1924).

Mendel Shlosberg (1843-??), moved to Lodz, where he participated in the development of the Polish textile industry.

Shelomoh Goldstein (1914-1995), a graduate of the Hebrew high school in Yurburg and a graduate of Rome university in chemical engineering, one of the leaders of "HeHalutz" in Lithuania, was imprisoned in the Kovno ghetto. Lived in Skokie, Illinios (near Chicago) USA, from 1948, a philanthropist who supported many Jewish and Zionist institutions in America and in Israel, among them the Hebrew University in Jerusalem. For many years a member of the Zionist executive.

Zalman and Tuviyah Samet, born in Yurburg in 1857 and 1858, founders and directors of the big firm "Brothers Samet" in Lodz.

William Zorach (1887-1966), sculptor and painter, also painted many pictures on Yurburg. He died in Bath, Maine, U.S.A

Shelomoh ben Yisrael Bresloi, a learned man and philanthropist, donated 500 Rubles for establishing a "Gemiluth Hesed" in town.

Hirsh Noteles, sent a Hebrew poem to the Czar and received a letter of thanks and a golden ring as a memorial gift.

Appendix 3

List of donors for Settlement of Eretz-Yisrael, published in 1896

Gut Leib
Garzon Mordehai
Homler Avraham-Leib
Helberg Shemuel
Hershelevitz Avraham
Yablonsky David-Shelomoh
Yozefer Hayim-Nathan
Yozelit Hayim
Leibovitz Aba
Mendelson Leib
Myakinin Avraham

Segal Ya'akov
Fainberg Gavriel
Pustapedsky A.H.
Kopelov Avraham-Yitshak
Kaplitz Hertz
Rubinovitz Max
Dr. Rabinovitz Tsezar
Rochelson Shimon
Rivkin Dov

The fundraisers were Tsevi Fain and Avraham-Yitshak Kopelov.

Kaišiadorys (Koshedar)

Koshedar (in Yiddish), 24 km southeast of Kovno, developed in the second half of the 19th century when the Kovno-Vilna railway line was constructed and a station was built there. Later, when the Koshedar- Siauliai railway line was built, the town became an important and busy railway junction.

Until 1795 Koshedar was part of the Polish-Lithuanian Kingdom, when the third division of Poland by the three superpowers of those times - Russia, Prussia and Austria - caused Lithuania to become partly Russian or Prussian. The part of Lithuania which included Koshedar fell under the rule of Czarist Russia. From 1802 it was part of the Vilna province (Gubernia) as a county administrative center.

During independent Lithuania (1918-1940) Koshedar continued to be a county administrative center, and as a result of Poland's occupation of Vilna and its region, which included the town Trok (Trakai), Koshedar also served as the administrative center of the Trakai district. During this period the importance of Koshedar decreased because, according to the new border with Poland, the railway connection to Poland and Russia ceased to exist.

Jewish Settlement till World War II

Jews settled in Koshedar while the railway station was being built. The first Jewish families - David Tekatch, Shemuel Morgenshtern, Hayim Strashun and Yakov Khayuth (Khayes) - settled near the station and made their living in timber, while their wives kept hotels, restaurants and bars. Jews who arrived later built their houses in the town itself, some 2 km from the station.

By 1897 there were 833 residents in Koshedar, of them 317 Jews (38%).

About 60 Jewish families, whose economic situation was stable, lived in Koshedar before World War I. They had a Beth-Midrash and employed a Rabbi, a Shokhet and a Mohel. The children studied in a "Kheder Metukan" (Improved Kheder). There was also a library.

Zionism gained support in Koshedar, and at the regional conference of the "Zionist Associations" of the Kovno and Vilna Gubernias, which took place in Vilna in 1898 with the participation of 71 delegates from 51 cities and towns, the delegate from Koshedar was the local Rabbi Tsevi Hurvitz. The list of donors for the settlement of Eretz-Yisrael, published in the Hebrew newspaper "HaMeilitz" in the years 1893-1899, contains 74 names of Koshedar Jews. The fund raisers were Rabbi Tsevi Hurvitz, Mosheh Gelvan and Shelomoh Tekatch. The correspondents for "HaMeilitz" were Yosef Fraker and D.Zak.

After the establishment of independent Lithuania in 1918, and following the autonomy law for minorities issued by the new Lithuanian government, the Minister for Jewish Affairs, Dr. Menakhem (Max) Soloveichik, ordered elections to be held for community committees (Va'ad Kehilah) in the summer of 1919. In Koshedar the elections took place in autumn 1919 and a committee of 9 members was elected: 2 General Zionists, 3 from the artisans, 4 undefined. This committee was active in almost all fields of Jewish life until the end of 1925, after which the autonomy was annulled.

At the elections for the first Lithuanian Seimas (Parliament) in October 1922, the Zionist list in Koshedar received 139 votes, the Democrats - 23 and "Akhduth" - 16.

According to the first census performed by the government in 1923, Koshedar had 1929 residents, of them 596 Jews (31%).

During this period the local Jews made their living from commerce, crafts and light industry. According to the government survey of 1931 there were 20 businesses, including 15 owned by Jews (75%).

Details according to the type of business are given in the table below:

Type of the business	Total	Owned by Jews
Groceries	1	1
Butcher's shops and Cattle Trade	4	1
Restaurants and Taverns	7	6
Beverages	1	1
Textile Products and Furs	2	2
Medicine and Cosmetics	1	1
Radio, Sewing Machines and Electric Equipment	1	1
Timber and Heating Material	1	1
Machines and Transportation	1	0
Miscellaneous	1	1

According to the same survey, Koshedar had 11 light industry factories, 9 of them owned by Jews (82%), as can be seen in the following table:

Type of the Factory	Total	Jewish Owned
Metal Workshops, Power Plants	1	0
Chemical Industry: Lubrication Ointment	1	1
Textile: Wool, Flax, Knitting	1	1
Food: Flour Mills, Bakeries	3	3
Sawmills, Furniture	1	1
Furs, Hats	4	3

By 1937 there were 27 Jewish artisans: 6 tailors, 5 butchers, 3 bakers, 3 barbers, 2 shoemakers, 2 stitchers, 1 glazier, 1 book binder, 1 blacksmith, 1 tinsmith, 1 painter, 1 saddler.

The Jewish Folksbank played an important role in the economic life of Koshedar's Jews. In 1927 it had 170 members, but in the thirties the number of its members decreased to 110. In 1939 there were 64 phones in town, 7 of them belonging to Jews.

The deterioration of Koshedar as a railway junction to Vilna and eastwards and the economic crisis in Lithuania caused many Koshedar Jews to immigrate to America, South Africa and Uruguay. Some immigrated to Eretz-Yisrael. At the end of the thirties only about 60 Jewish families were left in Koshedar, who subsisted mainly from the two weekly market days.

Jewish children, numbering a yearly average of about 40 pupils, studied in the Hebrew school of the "Tarbuth" chain. Several graduates of this school continued their studies in the Hebrew High Schools in Kovno. There was a "Kheder" with 15 boys, and also a Yiddish library of the "Libhober fun Vissen" (Seekers of Knowledge) association.

Many belonged to the Zionist movement, and all Zionist parties had representatives in town, as can be seen from the results of elections to Zionist Congresses in the table below:

Cong No.	Year	Tot Shek	Total Voters	Labor Party Z"S	Z"Z	Rev	Gen. A	Zion B	Gros	Miz
15	1927	21	15	3	3	--	4	--	--	5
16	1929	61	29	4	8	2	11	--	--	4
17	1931	62	31	14	14	1	3	--	--	3
18	1933	---	94	58		27	4	--	--	5
19	1935	147	139	69		--	10	28	9	23

Key: Cong No. = Congress Number, Tot Shek = Total Shekalim,
Rev = Revisionists, Gen Zion = General Zionists, Gros = Grosmanists,
Miz = Mizrakhi

Zionist youth organizations in Koshedar included "HaShomer HaTsair", "Beitar" etc. Sports activities took place in the "Maccabi" branch with about 40 members, while there was also the "Tifereth-Bakhurim" organization for religious boys.

Stamp of the "Tehilim" Society

Koshedar Hebrew Elementary School 1936

Koshedar Jewish Scouts

Religious life in Koshedar concentrated around the Beth-Midrash where lessons were given by the Tehilim society, the Mishnah society and the Shas (Talmud) society.

Among the Rabbis who served in Koshedar were:

Binyamin Meizel (from 1881);

Tsevi-Hirsh Hurvitz (in Koshedar 1890-1902);

Yisrael-Aba Kriger (from 1903);

Shalom-Yitskhak Shtchupak, (served 1922-1929);

Aharon-David Yafe, its last Rabbi (served 1934-1941), was murdered in 1941.

Among the personalities born in Koshedar were:

Morris Gest (Gershonovitz 1881-1942), who immigrated to America at the age of 12. He was an impresario who brought famous artists from Europe to America and cooperated with Reinhardt in the direction of the play "The Miracle";

Rabbi Yosef Kanovitz (1878-?), who served in several towns in Lithuania, and lived in America from 1915, where he served as Rabbi in several cities in New Jersey and New York.

Koshedar "Tifereth Bakhurim" Organization 1938

Studying "Talmud" at the Beth-Midrash

During World War II and Afterwards

In June 1940 Lithuania was annexed to the Soviet Union and became a Soviet Republic. Following new rules, most of the industries owned by Jews were nationalized. A number of Koshedar Jewish shops were nationalized and commissars were appointed to manage them. The supply of goods decreased and, as a result, prices soared. The middle class, mostly Jewish, bore most of the brunt, and the standard of living dropped gradually. All Zionist parties and youth organizations were disbanded and the Hebrew school was closed.

On the 22nd of June 1941 the German army invaded Lithuania, entering Koshedar two days later. Lithuanian nationalists immediately took over the town and began to plot against the Jews. Four Jewish men who were detained during these first days, were taken out of town and disappeared. Shortly afterwards the Lithuanians organized a provocation by hiding eight rifles and a machine-gun in the Beth-Midrash. A "search" resulted, of course, in the discovery of the arms, and thus the Rabbi and the Shokhet were arrested. Both were forced to run through the streets, being abused and hit until the old Rabbi David-Aharon Yafe died.

In the middle of August all Koshedar Jews were imprisoned in a large warehouse, which had been built for storing grain near the railway station during the short Soviet rule. Jewish men from Zhosle (Zasliai) and Zhezhmer (Ziezmariai) were also brought to this warehouse. Apparently none of the imprisoned people escaped, because they did not believe that they were in danger. Every day men and women fit for work were taken to various types of work in the town or with farmers or to excavate peat. Those who stayed in the warehouse were abused and robbed by the Lithuanian guards.

On the 28th of August 1941 (5th of Elul 5701) all Jews from the warehouse were put on trucks and led in the direction of Zhezhmer. At a point five km from Koshedar, near the village of Vladikiskis in Strosiunu forest, all were shot and buried in mass graves. A Lithuanian ranger who hid a Jew with two little children was shot by the Gestapo.

The Lithuanian murderers were the local police chief Peskauskas, Zitkus, Norbotas Vuckauskas and others.

After the war two separate monuments were erected: one on the graves of the men and on it the number 2,200, and the other on the grave of the women and children where the number 1,800 is written. It would appear that Lithuanians and Soviet war prisoners were also buried in these graves.

In 1990 the mass graves were fenced off anew by the local authorities and on one of the graves three big oak-wooden carvings, entitled "Pain", by the sculptor Vidmantas Kapaciunas from Zhezhmer, were erected.

On the fiftieth anniversary of the murders the tablets on the monuments were replaced and on the new ones the following inscriptions in Lithuanian and Yiddish were written: "In this place on the 28th of August 1941, Nazi murderers and their local helpers cruelly tortured and buried alive 2,200 Jews from Ziezmariai, Zasliai and Kaisiadorys". On the other monument the same inscription was written with one change: "...1,800 Jewish women and children...".

The monument and the three wooden carvings on the mass graves of the men at Strosiunu forest.

In May 1943 sixteen young men from Kovno ghetto were brought to Koshedar to construct a camp for about 300 people, who were ordered mainly to excavate peat in the nearby wet fields. Later Jews from Zhezhmer, Zhosly and other towns were brought to the camp.

At the beginning of 1944 an S.D. officer took 12 young men from the camp for a special task, which was later revealed. They were brought to the terrible Fort IX in Kovno to excavate and burn the corpses of the murdered, after 64 men who had previously performed this work had managed to escape on the eve of Christmas 1943. Several men in the camp made contact with partisans in the vicinity and organized a group to escape and join the partisans. On the 11th of April 1944 forty four young men escaped and twenty two of them managed to reach and join the regiment of "Genys" in the Rudniky woods, where they remained until the liberation. After the escape Koshedar camp was dismantled and the 250 Jews were transferred to other camps around Kovno.

The monument on the mass graves of the women and children in Strosiunu forest.

Sources:

Yad-Vashem Archives, M-1/E-332/247. Koniuchovsky Collection 0-71, File 83.

Central Zionist Archives: 55/1788; 55/1701; 13/15/131; Z-4/2548.

JIVO, NY, Collection of the Jewish Communities in Lithuania, Files 717-919, 1542.

Zewie A.Brown, M.A.and Dov Levin, M.A.- The Story of an Underground (Hebrew).

The Resistance of the Jews of Kovno in the Second World War. Yad Vashem, 1962.

From the Beginning to the End - The Book of the History of "HaShomer HaTzair" in Lithuania (Hebrew), Tel-Aviv 1986.

Di Yiddishe Shtime (The Yiddish Voice) Kovno (Yiddish): 26.8.1919.

Naujienos, (News) Chicago, 11.6.1949.

Kaisiadoriu Aidas, (Koshedar Repercussion), 24.8.1991.

Kapčiamiestis (Kopcheve)

Kopcheve - as it called in Yiddish -is located in the southwestern corner of Lithuania, about 8 km from Poland and the same distance from Belarus, in an area full of rivers, lakes and woods. The river Baltoji Ancia and the nearby rivers Juodoji Ancia and Nieda flow through Kopcheve.

The origins of this town can be traced to the middle of the fifteenth century, then a small village, owned by the secretary of the Great Prince Kazimir (1427-1492).

Kopcheve was part of the Polish-Lithuanian Kingdom until 1795, when the third division of Poland by the three superpowers of those times - Russia, Prussia and Austria – resulted in Lithuania becoming partly Russian and partly Prussian. The part of the state which lay on the left side of the Nieman river (Nemunas), including Kopcheve, was handed over to Prussia which ruled during the years 1795-1807. During these years Kopcheve was a county .

After Napoleon defeated Prussia and according to the Tilzit agreement of July 1807, Polish territories occupied by Prussia were transferred to what became known as the "The Great Dukedom of Warsaw", which was established at that time. The King of Saxony, Friedrich-August, was appointed Duke, and the Napoleonic code became the constitution of the Dukedom, according to which everybody was equal before the law, except for Jews who were not granted any civil rights.

During the years 1807-1813, Kopcheve belonged to the "Great Dukedom of Warsaw" and was part of the Bialystok district. The Napoleonic code was then introduced in this region, remaining in effect even during the Lithuanian period.

In 1815, after the defeat of Napoleon, all of Lithuania was annexed to Russia, as a result of which Kopcheve was included in the Augustowa Region (Gubernia), and in 1866 it became a part of the Suwalk Gubernia as a county .

During the years of its existence Kopcheve suffered from many fires.

Being located at the junction of several main roads it was possible for Kopcheve to maintain markets and large fairs.

In 1915 the German army occupied the town and ruled there till 1918 when the independent Lithuanian state was established. In 1919, after fighting the Polish army, Kopcheve remained within the border of Lithuania, but Seiny, the district , was included in Poland. The district institutions, called the Sejny district, were transferred to Lazdey, but the town remained a county for the years of independent Lithuania (1918-1940).

Jewish Settlement till World War II.

Apparently Jews began to settle in Kopcheve at the end of the eighteenth century, making their living from small shops, crafts, as in most of the towns of the Suvalk Gubernia, and also managed to acquire large plots of land and to pursue agriculture.

In 1897 its population was 1,314 people, of them 528 Jews.

Kopcheve was known for its scholars and intellectual people. Jewish children studied in a "Kheder", including "Gemara" (Talmud), as well as Hebrew in its curriculum.

A list of donors who helped Jews suffering from hunger in 1871, mentions a Kopcheve Jew, as published in the Hebrew periodical "HaMagid". A list of donors for "The Settlement of Eretz Yisrael", published in "HaMeilitz" in 1899 and 1903, mentions many Kopcheve Jews. Their representative was Ben-Zion Shimshelevitz. More Kopcheve Jews appear in a list in 1909: B.Shimshelevitz, Leib Kopchovsky, Yitskhak Kopchovsky, Yakov Mentsin, Sh.Goritsky. "Agudath-Israel" had 50 members in 1913, and Rabbi Tsve-Aryeh Luria, B"Z. Shimshelevitz, Nisan Menchinsky served on its committee.

In 1918, after World War I, Lithuania became an independent state, and according to the autonomy law for minorities issued by the new Lithuanian government, the minister for Jewish affairs Dr. Max (Menakhem) Soloveitshik, in the summer of 1919, ordered that elections be held for community committees in all towns of the state, and a committee consisting of five members was also elected in Kopcheve. It was active till the end of 1925 when the autonomy decree was annulled. During its existence the committee collected taxes as required by law, and was in charge of almost all aspects of community life, mainly the registration of births, marriages and deaths.

According to the first census of 1923, there were then 835 people in Kopcheve, of them 187 Jews (22%).

During the period of independent Lithuania (1918-1940), Kopcheve Jews made their living from commerce and crafts, but almost every family had a small plot near their houses on which they grew vegetables and fruits. Three families who owned land and plantations dealt with agriculture (Kopchovsky, Smolsky, Pochtiva). In the thirties Tsevi-Hirsh Kopchovsky was the chairman of a public committee for the re-parcellation of agricultural lands in the county.

According to the 1931 survey of the Lithuanian government, Kopcheve had seven shops, all in Jewish hands: 3 textile, 2 butchers, 1 grocery and 1 pharmacy. According to the same survey there were 2 Jewish owned flour mills, one of them (owned by Miler) powered by water on the river Nieda, which also supplied electricity to the town, as well as 2 mechanical workshops. Grazhevsky had a blacksmith workshop and also a bus which took passengers to Kovno. Miler traded in timber and owned a metal workshop. The butcher Ofchinsky would purchase cattle in the vicinity for his shop.

In 1937 there were 18 Jewish artisans in town: 5 tailors, 4 blacksmiths, 4 butchers, 2 shoemakers, 1 baker, 1 glazier and 1 stitcher.

By 1939 there were 20 telephone owners, one of them Jewish.

During this period Jewish children studied in a private Hebrew elementary school. Several graduates of this school continued their studies in the nearby Hebrew high schools or in Kovno. There was also a library and a dramatic circle.

The Zionist movement with all its parties was quite popular in Kopcheve, as can be seen from election results to Zionist congresses in the table below:

Cong No.	Year	Tot Shek	Total Voters	Labor Party Z"S	Z"Z	Rev	Gen. Zion A	B	Gros	Miz
15	1927	13	13	--	--	--	13	--	--	--
16	1929	27	15	15	--	--	--	--	--	--
17	1931	24	12	1	1	--	10	--	--	--
18	1933	---	42	38		--	4	--	--	--
19	1935	65	59	30		--	26	--	--	3
21	1939	32	31	20			7	--	3	1

Key: Cong No. = Congress Number, Tot Shek = Total Shekalim,

Rev = Revisionists, Gen Zion = General Zionists, Gros = Grosmanists, Miz = Mizrakhi

Among the local Rabbis who served in Kopcheve were:

Avraham-Tsevi-Pinkhas Eliashberg (1864-1943), in Kopcheve 1887-1900;

Tsevi-Aryeh-Leib Luria (1871-?), in Kopcheve 1902-1913;

Meir Stolevitz (1871- ?), from 1942 Rabbi in Jerusalem;

Menakhem-Mendel Sher, in Kopcheve from 1938, murdered in 1941.

Locally born personalities included:

Elkhanan (Eduard) Kalman (1891-1939) the historian;

B"Z. Shimshelevitz, scholar and ardent Zionist, who published articles in "HaOlam", an uncle of the second president of Israel - Yitskhak ben Tsevi;

Dr. Yitskhak Kopchovsky, (born 1922) economist, later to be deputy director and member of the directorate of Bank Leumi LeIsrael.

The Zionist youth organization "Gordonia" with 30 to 40 members was active in Kopcheve.

Picture supplied by Yehudah Fridkovsky

The "Gordonia" branch of Kopcheve 1933

First line above, standing from right: Hofman, Meir Kliuk, Sarah Fridkovsky, Nekhemia Kviatkovsky, Khayah-Liba--?--, Khayah Lev, Iser Lev, Roni Smolsky, Leibke Kviatkovsky, Frida Miler, Yehudah Fridkovsky

Second line from right: Bath-Sheva Otrembsky, (below her-half face) **Leah Fridkovsky,** (fourth) **Nekhama Kliuk,** (the sixth) **Khayah Kviatkovsky, Sarah-Ela Hofman**

Lower line sitting from right: (fourth) **Meir Lantsman,** (seventh) **teacher of the Hebrew school,** (last) **David Otrembsky.**

During World War II and Afterwards.

World War II started with the German invasion of Poland on the 1st of September 1939, and its consequences for Lithuanian Jews in general and Kopcheve Jews in particular were felt several months later.

In accordance with the Ribbentrop-Molotov treaty on the division of occupied Poland, the Russians occupied the Suvalk region, but after delineation of exact borders between Russia and Germany, the Suvalk region fell into German hands. The retreating Russians allowed anyone who wanted to join them to move into their occupied territory, and indeed many young people left the area together with the Russians. The Germans drove the remaining Jews out of their homes in Suvalk and its vicinity, robbed them of their possessions, then directed them to the Lithuanian border, where they were left in dire poverty. The Lithuanians did not allow them to enter Lithuania and the Germans did not allow them to return. Thus they stayed in this swampy area in cold and rain for several weeks, until Jewish youths from the border villages smuggled them into Lithuania by various routes, with much risk to themselves. Altogether about 2,400 refugees passed through the border or infiltrated on their own, and were then dispersed in the "Suvalkiya" region.

In June 1940 Lithuania was annexed to the Soviet Union and became a Soviet Republic. Following new rules, a large Jewish house whose area was more than 220 meters was nationalized and its owners – the Fridkovsky family - forced to leave. All Zionist parties and youth organizations were disbanded and Hebrew educational institutions were closed.

The supply of goods decreased and, as a result, prices soared. The middle class, mostly Jewish, bore most of the brunt of this hardship, and the standard of living dropped gradually.

The German army entered Kopcheve on the first day of the war, June 22nd 1941. Only a few Jews who tried to escape managed to get to Russia and survive. With the entry of the Germans, Lithuanian nationalist gangs started to rampage and to abuse the Jews. Jews' life and property were outside the law and everybody could do with them as they wished. Jews were forced to perform degrading jobs, being humiliated all the time.

(Evidence of Rivkah and Ze'ev Mikhnovsky)

On the fifteenth of September 1941, all Kopcheve Jews were transferred to Lazdey under heavy guard and put into the Katkiske Ghetto, about one and a half km from Lazdey. There the Jews from Lazdey, Rudamin, Vishey, Kopcheve and small settlements of the surroundings had been concentrated. They were placed in army barracks according to families, and the entire area was surrounded by barbed wire and armed Lithuanian guards. Daily task groups were used for work outside the compound.

Initially, each person was given 200 grams of unsalted bread and 300 grams of potatoes. Gradually the rations were cut down, and an epidemic of dysentery broke out. People suffered and starved. Some snuck out and ran to nearby villages where they exchanged personal belonging for food or begged for food. Some relief occurred when some of the local farmers were allowed to engage Jews as workers on their farms, provided that they would return them to the ghetto at night. Those who eat at the farms would give up their share of the food in the ghetto so that others could benefit from it.

The internal arrangements of the work schedule were conducted by the Jewish managed "Arbeits Amt" (Work Office). A special committee to manage all affairs of the ghetto was created from representatives of all the communities, and the Kopcheve pharmacist Astromsky was their leader. He did not do a thing without consulting with Rabbi Gershtein of Lazdey. A Jewish police force was organized in the ghetto but had very little authority.

Every gentile was able to do whatever he pleased with regards to Jews and hardly a day passed without some torture or criminal act. For example, a Lithuanian policeman once took a liking to the boots of Yehoshua Vilensky from Rudamin. He called him over, shot him dead, and took his boots.

One day the ghetto was shocked by the secret news Sheina Idovitz and Golda Katorovsky related upon their return from work on Monday, October 27th. Every day they were taken to the town to work for the German commander. That day, they heard a conversation between the commandant of Mariampol, who screamed at the commandant of Lazdey what a terrible shame it was that his Jews were still alive. The commandant from Lazdey apologized and explained that he needed the Jews who were doing necessary work and many of the essential crafts. The commandant from Mariampol screamed again, "You have to fulfill your task or otherwise you will be sent to the front" where upon the commandant of Lazdey replied, "I am a soldier and a man of war, and you won't scare me with this kind of threat."

The mood in the ghetto was instantaneously electrified. The mention of death shook people and scared them in anticipation of the following day. That night some people escaped from the ghetto and went looking for a hideaway with the farmers or in the fields. A few days later, however, when no special events had occurred, everything returned to normal. They expected that the commandant would continue to protect the Jews under his control. By the end of October, most of the Jews throughout Lithuania had already been murdered, while those of Lazdey were among the very few still left alive.

On Thursday, October 30, 1941, the ghetto was sealed and nobody was taken out to work. They were able to see the murderous Lithuanians walking in the distance with spades in their hands. Upon asking the chief of the police as to the meaning of this scene, he responded nonchalantly, "They are going to dig pits for you. This will take a few days and that is exactly the length of time left for you to be alive." After that explanation, many attempted to run away even though the place was well guarded by armed guards. The following morning, escapees were returned to the camp, some werewounded and some had been murdered, and the chief of police came to calm the Jews. He told them that running away did not make sense since everywhere the German foot walks the Jew gets wiped off the face of the earth. He went on to say that a Jew can never find a hiding place from the bullet marked for him, and that very soon the end would come for all Jews wherever they might be.

The Lithuanians sealed all windows and doors to the barracks with planks and metal bars, and the Jews stayed locked up without water or food. Despite all their efforts, 180 people managed to escape from the barracks during the first two nights.

On Monday, November 3, 1941 (the 13th of Mar Kheshvan, 5702), the Jews were taken naked from the barracks to the pits about 300 meters away from the barracks and about 300 meters west of the forest. About 1600 souls were shot to death. Not one person managed to escape. Although the Germans gave the orders for the "operation", they participated only as observers at the scene of the crime, **the actual executioners were Lithuanians**. A gang of apparently experienced murderers from Mariampol also participated in the executions. This gang seemed experienced because of their previous actions, and later refused the Germans' offer to photograph them in order to "memorialize" their actions. Only in December of 1941 did the first signs of the German's retreat and defeat appear, when the Germans were forced back into winter defensive positions.

Sign on the road saying:

"Place of the mass murders of the Jews in 1941 at Katkishke"

Picture supplied by Ruth ben David

As mentioned earlier, many Jews escaped before the slaughter, some being badly wounded, caught, and brought back to the ghetto. On the day of the slaughter, they were dragged with the other sick and helpless to the pits. Many of the escapees were killed by the farmers. After a while, the Lithuanians stopped murdering the caught escapees and incarcerated them instead. When the number of those caught reached 35, they took them to the mass graves and murdered them there.

Of the entire 180 who escaped, only 6 managed to survive the war: Rivkah (Gershtein) Mikhnovsky and her husband Ze'ev Mikhnovsky, Dov Zef, Miriam Kuleisky and her sisters Gita and Bath-Sheva Koifman - all from Lazdey; Khmilevsky from Vishey; Gedaliah Cohen from Rudamin.

In 1944 and 1945, the Soviets recaptured Lithuania, Estonia, and Latvia, and which became Soviet republics again. After the war a monument was erected on the mass graves. The tablet on it was changed in the 1990s.

Entrance gate to the site of the mass graves at Katkishke
The monument in the background
Picture taken by Ruth ben David 1994

The Monument at Katkishke
Picture taken by Ruth ben David 1994

The tablet of the Monument at Katkishke.

The inscription in Lithuanian and Yiddish: "At this place the Hitlerist murderers with their local helpers on the 3rd of November 1941 murdered 1535 Jews from Lazdey district, men, women, children."

Fulgentas Luvelis and his daughter Nida-son and granddaughter of the murdered savior of the Fridkovsky sisters at the Jewish cemetery in Kopcheve. Behind them is Yehudah Fridkovsky.

Photo supplied by Yehudah Fridkovsky

The Fridkovsky sisters survived due to the efforts of two Lithuanian peasants, Zharnauskas and **Levulis**. After the German retreat they were murdered by Lithuanian nationalists for saving the Jewish girls. **(See photo on previous page.)**

List of Kopcheve Jews, as compiled by Yehudah Fridkovsky, see **Appendix 1 below.**

Bibliography.

Yad-Vashem Archives, M-33/972.

Koniuchovsky Collection 0-71, Files 131.

JIVO, NY, Collection of the Jewish Communities in Lithuania, File 1444.

Gotlib, Ohalei Shem (Hebrew) page 170.

Dzuku Zinios (Lithuanian) Nr.57, 29.7.1992.

Appendix 1   List of Kopcheve Jews.   *--murdered at Katkishke

Blumental Mordekhai *	house owner
Blumental Ya'akov	died in Israel
Lev	house wife, died in Israel
Lev Iser	printing press owner in Canada
Lev Khayah	house wife, lives in Israel
Vodnitsky Alter *	restaurant owner
Otrembsky David	???
Otrembsky Bath-Sheva	???
Ovchinsky Berl *	blacksmith
Garbarsky Fishke *	shoemaker
Garbarsky Sender *	
----------------------- *	nickname: farber, owner of paint shop
-----------**Khayah-Libe ***	his daughter
-----------**Esther ***	his daughter
-----------**Feivke ***	grain storehouse
-----------**Avraham ***	
-----------**Mosheh-Ber ***	retired
----------------------- *	a Jewish family, shop owners near the church

Yasinsky Mikhael	restaurant owner, died in Israel
Yasinsky Masha	house wife
Yasinsky Ela	son
Yasinsky Leah	daughter
Yasinsky Ronith	daughter , lives in Israel
Yasinsky Leibke	son, lives in Israel
Yasinsky Aharon	driver, died in Israel
Lantsman Mosheh	butcher
Lantsman Aizik	butcher
Smolsky Mosheh *	shokhet
Smolsky Feige *	house wife
Smolsky Ronith	
Pik Aharon *	blachsmith
Pik David *	
Ribak Leib *	
Ribak Shmerke *	
Krinsky Nekhemyah *	
Miler Shelomoh *	workshop and flour mill owner
Miler Mosheh *	son of Shelomoh
Miler Tania	daughter
Miler Frida	daughter
Kviatkovsky Leib *	
Kviatkovsky Nekhemyah *	
Kviatkovsky Khayah *	
Khazanovsky Fruma *	
Khazanovsky Shelomoh	lives abroad
Fridkovsky Leib *	shop owner
Fridkovsky Nisan *	his son-student
Fridkovsky Rivkah *	daughter-shop owner
Fridkovsky Khanah	daughter-abroad
Fridkovsky Stirke	daughter-abroad
Okunevitz Pesakh *	bakery owner
Okunevitz Khayah *	house wife
Okunevitz Ya'akov *	son
Okunevitz Zekharyah *	son

Kopchevsky Tsevi-Hirsh	agrarian (died in 1934)
Kopchevsky Nadia	his wife
Kopchevsky Yitskhak	student, lives in Israel
Fridkovsky Yehudah	shop owner-lives in Israel
Fridkovsky Yosef	died before the war
Fridkovsky Gita	died in Russia
Fridkovsky Asher	died in Israel
Fridkovsky Khyene	lives in Israel
Fridkovsky Sarah	died in Israel
Fridkovsky Ben-Zion	lives in USA
Fridkovsky Leah	lives in Israel
Lantsman Alter *	
Lantsman Meir	
Lantsman Keile	???
Lantsman Esther-Malkah	???
Lantsman Menukhah	???
Lantsman Nekhamah	???
Lantsman Sonia	???
Lantsman Beile	???
Kliuk Meir *	
Kliuk Mery *	shop owner
Kliuk Nekhamah *	
Grazhevsky Shemuel *	blacksmith
Grazhevsky Mosheh *	
Grazhevsky Paike *	
Grazhevsky Khayim	driver- died in Vilna
Hofman Ber-Leib *	tailor
Hofman Shelomo *	
Hofman Leizer	died in Kopcheve after the war
Hofman Sarah-Ela	lives in Vilna
Ovchinsky Hirsh *	bar owner
Sambursky ------*	

Klaipėda (Memel)

Memel is situated on the site where the Kurish Bay (Kursiu marios-in Lithuanian) meets the Baltic Sea and the river flows into the bay. In olden times this site was a port and a civilian settlement, it being here that in 1252 the Livonian Order erected a fortress that secured the strategic axis Riga-Memel-Koenigsberg-Danzig, this route maintaining the connection between the Livonian and Prussian Orders. In the years 1323, 1379 and 1409 the fortress, as well as the settlement, was destroyed by the Lithuanians, who took revenge for the invasions of Lithuania by the Order. In 1540, the town was ravished by a great fire. During the years 1629-1635 Memel was under Swedish rule and from 1701 the town came under Prussian rule. In 1709 the plague caused the death of about 2,000 of its population. In 1722, some 1,900 people resided in the town and another 1,500 in the fortress.

In 1756 the Seven Years War started and the Russian army and its fleet occupied Memel, controlling it from 1757 till 1762. The border with Lithuania was opened and commerce in Memel developed.

During the American revolutionary war with England in the years 1776-83, the need for timber, flax etc. increased and Memel grew fast. In 1782 the town's population numbered 5,500 people and about 800 ships sailed into its harbor annually.

Memel became the capital city of the Prussian Kingdom between the years 1807-1808, but after the defeat of Napoleon in the years 1812-1813 the Russian Army occupied Memel.

In 1853 the road to Tilzit was completed, in 1892 the railway to Kretinga was inaugurated, telephone communication arrived in 1888, and in 1900 the first power plant was built in the town.

After World War I Memel and its region (Gebiet) were cut off from Germany, and in accordance with the Versailles Treaty the Allies (the Entente) ruled this area with a French garrison headed by a French general as from 1919. On January 10, 1923 the Lithuanian army entered Memel and its region, upon which the French garrison left. On February 16, 1923 the Entente representatives approved Lithuanian's sovereignty over Memel and region. The population won an extended autonomy and interior issues were governed by a local Parliament (Landtag) whose resolutions had to be approved by the Lithuanian Governor who was appointed by the President of the Republic. During Lithuanian rule (1923-1939) Memel was the administrative center of the region.

In December 1938, during elections to the local Parliament, the local German Nazis received 26 out of 29 seats, as a result of which the city became in fact a part of the German Reich. On the 22nd of March 1939 the German army entered Memel and the city and region were officially annexed to Germany, the city Memel serving as a base for the German navy during World War II.

On January the 28th 1945, Memel was liberated from Nazi rule by the Red Army. About 28% of its houses were totally destroyed and more than 36% of the others badly damaged. Since then Memel (Klaipeda) and the region is part of Lithuania.

Jewish Settlement till after World War I

Apparently Jews began to settle in Memel in the 15th century, but the first document about a Jewish presence in the city is from 1567. On the 20th of April 1567 Count Albrecht, under the influence of priests, issued an order stating that all Jews had to leave Memel within 21 days, since then and for the next 76 years it being forbidden for Jews to live or even stay overnight in Memel. It was only in 1643, when commerce in the city was developing, did Jewish merchants, who arrived on Fridays in the city and in particular during the short winter days, were allowed to stay over Sabbath, but on Sundays they had to leave. In those days the rules issued in 1613, according to which it was forbidden for a Memel citizen or merchant to have any contact, open or secret, with Jews, because Judaism was opposed to Christianity, were not treated seriously any more, despite the fact that fanatic clergymen were still propagating these orders.

In 1662 Friedrich Wilhelm, the Kurfuerst of Brandenburg, who wanted to expand trade with Memel, granted privileges to several Jews to settle in the city. One of them was a Dutch Jew named Mosheh Jacobson de Jonge (The Young), a commercial genius who settled in Memel in 1664. He developed trade with timber, furs and in particular with salt, organized shipping lines and established a workshop for repairing and building ships. He got permission to employ Jewish workers, among them a ritual slaughterer and a Jewish teacher for his children, and was also allowed to establish a prayer room in his house. After several years Mosheh Jacobson lost all his property as a result of too much speculation with salt and was forced to return to Holland with all his staff.

Jews were banned from Memel for many more years, and were not even allowed to peddle goods there. This ban was proclaimed publicly once a year, and until 1670 announcements to this effect were attached to the municipal building. It was only during the yearly fair, which took place in the summer and lasted 14 days, when Jewish tradesmen were allowed to import merchandise from Lithuania and Russia, such as agricultural products and expensive furs, and to buy German merchandise. Among the buyers were the rich Polish farm owners and Barons from Kurland. During the Crimean war, when Russia was closed on all sides except for the border with Prussia, 14,248 Jews were registered at the fair of 1854.

A special item sold to Russian tradesmen during the fairs were Hebrew books, among them the "Talmud" and rabbinical literature from the times when they were printed in Germany, or from private libraries of German Jews who did not need them anymore. The few Jewish printing presses in Russia as well as the difficulties caused by the censor, created a market for Hebrew books. In 1720 J. M. Friedlander received permission to sell Hebrew books at the fair. After some time a Jewish publisher from Berlin, Avraham Goldberg, opened a bookshop at the fair.

When rabbinical seminaries opened in Germany the need for religious books there increased, and the book trade in Memel stopped. After the Polish rebellion in 1863 and the construction of the railway to Memel, the importance of the fair diminished.

The system of privileges for "protected" Jews (Schutz Juden) was prevalent even during the times of the liberal King Friedrich the Great (1740-1798). When in 1777 the Jewish philosopher Moses Mendelsohn visited Memel on a business matter, he stayed in Koenigsberg, because he did not have permission to remain in Memel overnight. Only at the beginning of the 19th century, did the liberal legislation of Stein-Hardenberg bring about the cancellation of the severe restrictions affecting the Jews who had existed since the middle ages. But several tens of years passed till Prussian Jews began to settle in Memel that was located in a remote corner of the Kingdom and far from the main traffic arteries. In 1815 there were 35 Jews in Memel among a population of about 10,000 people.

Russian Jews, who came to Memel for their businesses, could not settle there because of lack of prayer houses and other religious institutions which were only allowed for Jews who held Prussian citizenship. As time passed, more and more Russian timber merchants would come to Memel before the High Holidays, staying there until January. They would arrive in the city by carts and even by carriages harnessed to horses, bringing with them cooks and ritual slaughterers, but only for poultry, whereas meat, sheep and cattle would be smuggled in from nearby Lithuanian towns.

Ber Cohen with his three sons Yosef, Aharon and Shemuel were the first Jewish family to receive citizenship in Memel, they brought in the first resident slaughterer by the name of Yosel Vald, all of them coming from the Lithuanian town of Tavrig (Taurage). Several years later, Mr. Vald transferred his position to his son-in-law Yeshayah Wohlgemuth, who after some time received rabbinical ordination. Later the sons of Yosel Vald became great flour and timber merchants.

In 1855 there were 289 Jews in Memel, and in 1867 this had risen to 887. Eleven Jewish babies (9 boys and 2 girls) were born in Memel in 1856, and one died. 16 babies were born (7 boys and 9 girls) in 1857, 3 of them died. Before the Jewish cemetery was established in Memel, local Jews would bury their dead in one of the towns in Prussia or, albeit with great difficulty, in one of the Lithuanian towns. The story goes that a Jewish merchant having died suddenly in Memel, was transferred to Lithuania for burial sitting in a carriage dressed in his coat and a pipe in his mouth, and escorts on either side.

In 1858 the Prussian government demanded the unification of the Russian and German communities in Memel. According to a Prussian law dated July 23rd

1847, which granted autonomy to the Jews, every Jew had to belong to the community and pay taxes, which amounted to a certain percent of his income tax and was collected in some cases with the help of the police. Anyone who did not pay income tax, was also exempted from paying taxes to the community. The community was headed by an assembly of representatives of 16 persons that was elected for 6 years. The assembly elected the community committee of 3-5 from its members, who had to be German citizens to run the community's affairs and maintain contact with the government The united community was officially approved on the 9th of May 1862, as were the regulations of the "Hevrah Kadishah". But in fact two different communities continued to exist, Russian Jews and German Jews, and each of them dealt with its own religious and educational issues. Members of the first committee were Dr.Lazar, S.Glazer and Meir Levi, and later on were joined by Moritz Kon and Julius Abelman.

Until 1900 the chairmen of the committee were Dr. Lazar, Julius Hirsch, Dr. Fuerst, J.Levental, S. Borchardt and Leopold Alexander.

In 1875 1,040 Jews resided in Memel.

Although relations between the Jews of Memel and their Christian neighbors were usually normal, Jews were unable to find employment in municipal and commercial institutions. Due to the fact that anti-Semites could not fight against Prussian Jews who had equal rights, they plotted against those Jews who did not possess Prussian citizenship, and in 1880 several of Memel's Jews who did not have Prussian citizenship were expelled from the city. The number of those expelled increased from year to year until 1885, when the government published an order that all foreign citizens had to leave Memel within a short time, before the 15th of October of that same year. Among the people affected by this order were Jews who had lived in Memel for 20 and even 40 years, but had not bothered to request Prussian citizenship in time, although then it was not difficult to obtain it. According to a source, had this order been carried out to the letter, only about 200 Jews would have remained in Memel. The man who was very active in thwarting this harsh decree was the Rabbi of Memel Dr.Yitzhak Ruelf (1834-1902), who contacted many people in Berlin, but only Chancellor Bismark could help. The Rabbi applied to him three times, resulting in a compromise according to which the city commercial institutions would prepare a list of Jewish merchants acting in Memel and these people would be allowed to stay.

Due to the expulsion of part of the Russian citizens from Memel during the years 1880 to 1886 the number of Jews decreased from 1,214 in 1880 to 861 in 1890. About 100 families, Jewish merchants from Lithuania, remained in Memel, and these were amongst the most important people in the city maintaining trade connections with Russia. But the rights of these Jews were restricted and they were under constant supervision by the authorities. About 700 people, men, women and children, were expelled from the districts of Memel and Heidekrug (Silute in Lithuanian), most of them workers and artisans. Many of them could not return to their Russian homeland for various reasons and it became necessary to help them emigrate overseas. In order to carry out this goal, a large sum of money was needed, which was collected from Jews in Germany and other countries.

Memel Jews traded mainly in timber and grains, but many Jewish timber merchants from Minsk, Pinsk, Vohlin, Grodna and Bialystok would also stay in Memel, and although they were only provisional residents, they played an important role in the community.

The old city of Memel with the Friedrich Market (1915).

Mainly Jewish merchants resided in this quarter

When World War I started in 1914 an order was issued that all Jewish Russian citizens be expelled within one week to Ruegen Island in the Baltic Sea. The Jewish community, the local commerce bureau, the Mayor of the city and the Governor of the region, made efforts to mitigate this harsh decree, and as a result any Jew who was able to produce a guarantee and a recommendation from two German citizens showing that he was not a spy, was allowed to stay on in the region. Thus most of the "strangers" were saved from expulsion.

Education and Religion.

The first religious institution established for Memel's Jews was the cemetery, where in 1823 the first Jewish deceased was buried. In the course of time this cemetery was enlarged three times. In 1835, on the initiative and with the management of Mordehai Vazbutzky and Meir Lifshitz, the "Polish" synagogue and the "Mikveh" were built in order to serve the rich timber traders from Poland and Russia who lived in Memel during the autumn months and also during the High Holidays. For forty years the head of this synagogue was S.Blokh, who was also active in the community.

Rabbi Dr.Yitzhak Ruelf, who served in Memel as the rabbi of the German community from 1865-1898, was the initiator and involved in all educational, cultural and welfare activities in the city during those years.

Prior to the establishment of the autonomic community according to Prussian law, Jewish children , mainly those possessing Russian citizenship, studied with "Melamdim" who came from Lithuania. The rich hired a private "Melamed" for their children, the less wealthy hired a "Melamed" for two or three families and the poor sent their children to a "Kheder" which was financed mostly by the community with parents only paying a small sum. Jews started to send their children to public schools only at the start of the 1860s.

In 1879 Rabbi Ruelf established a school for poor children (Armenschule), most of them having no other way of obtaining some education. The committee for helping Russian Jews in Berlin donated 50,000 Mark for maintaining this elementary school, which was recognized by the authorities, where Hebrew and its grammar, German, Mishnah and Talmud were taught. At the beginning many of Memel's Jews related to this school with reservation, since they were worried about the growth of a Jewish Russian proletariat in the city. A suitable building for the school was erected with the help of a large donation by the Baroness von Hirsch from Paris.

In 1898 Rabbi Dr.Y.Ruelf left Memel and Rabbi Dr. Immanuel Carlebach replaced him. Then the community established a " Religious School for Jewish Children" (Israelitische Religions Schule), consisting of two classes for boys and two for girls.

Many rich parents initiated the establishment of a private religious school and were ready to finance it. It had four classes for boys, five for girls and one common preparatory class. In the preparatory class one learnt for one year and in the other classes, for two years. The teachers in the above mentioned schools were: Dr. I. Carlebach (director), Heineman, Dobrovolsky, Berman, Mrs. Carlebach and Mrs. Gitkin. In this school Hebrew, Bible, Mishnah and Gemara was taught. These two schools were under the supervision of the community by way of an education committee whose members were S. Blokh, Moritz Cohen, A. Aizenstadt, Dr. Med. Hurwitz and H. Schlos. Financial issues of this private school were assigned to a funding committee, whose members were Max Berelowitz, Ch. Sher and D.L. Wolfson.

In 1896 "The Kiryath Sefer" society was established in order to provide Memel's assimilated German Jews with knowledge of the literature and history of the Jewish people. Those active in this society were Rabbi Ruelf- chairman, L.Sheinhaus - his deputy, the teacher Arndt and the pharmacist Lichtenstein.

In 1875, when due to immigration of Lithuanian Jews the Jewish population in the city increased, a "Beth-Midrash" was built. The Lithuanian and Russian Jews could not finance this building by themselves, and were therefore helped with funds collected by Rabbi Ruelf among German Jews. In 1886 a third prayer house, the "Synagogue", was erected in Memel for the German Jews, initiated by Rabbi Ruelf, who also collected the money for its construction. During the High Holidays all three prayer houses were full to capacity and it was necessary to rent an additional hall for the overflow audience.

In 1861, Rabbi Yisrael Salanter (Lipkin), who then lived in Memel, established "The Society of Gemara Students" as well as publishing a weekly pamphlet named "Hatvunah" (Wisdom)) in which famous Rabbis published 'Khidushey Torah'(new commentaries). As many as twelve booklets were published, by a Jewish printing press in Memel. In the summer of 1886, the 25th anniversary of this "Society" was celebrated at the Beth haMidrash on the occasion of completing the 3rd cycle of the "Gemara" (Talmud). At this celebration, which lasted for three days, the speakers were Rabbi Gavriel Feinberg from the Lithuanian-Polish community and Rabbi Dr.Yitzhak Ruelf, the representative of "The Society of the Fans of Zion" in Memel. Rabbi Ruelf was a delegate on behalf of Vilna to the second Zionist Congress that took place in Basel in 1898. He was the only western rabbi who opposed the "Protest Rabbiner" (this was a disparaging nickname Dr.Herzl had given to those German rabbis who had prevented the first Zionist Congress from taking place).

The Rabbis of the German Jewish Community were: Dr.Yitzhak Ruelf - who did much to bring Jews from the east closer to Jews from the west, helped Lithuanian and Russian Jews very much during all the disasters and pogroms they experienced and published articles on them in the international press. He was also the editor of the newspaper "Memeler Dampfboot" and published a book on philosophy in five volumes. He died in 1902 in Bonn at the age of 72. Then there were Dr. Immanuel Carlebach, who died in Köln in 1928, Dr.Yitzhak Stein who died in 1915, and Dr.F.Schlesinger.

The Rabbis of the Lithuanian-Polish Jewish community were: Yeshayah Wohlgemuth, who died in Hamburg in 1899 (see Appendix 1); Gavriel Feinberg, who published the books "Be'er Ya'akov" and discussions on "Khoshen Mishpat" and "Yoreh De'ah" (Berlin 5653); Meir Yoselovsky who died in Memel in 1915, and Mordehai Yitzhak Rabinovitz, who served in Memel from 1917 and published many books.

Welfare and Help.

During the 1880s a "Permanent Committee for Helping Russian Jews" was established in Memel, headed by Rabbi Dr. Y. Ruelf, M.Lurie and A.Vitenberg. In the Hebrew newspaper "HaMeilitz", published in St. Petersburg on June 28th 1881, a world wide appeal to Jews was published asking them to send donations to help victims of pogroms that had occurred then in southern Russia. The money collected was sent through the " J.S. Feinberg's Successors - Koenigsberg and Memel" bank for distribution in Kiev.

Nor did these public spirited workers forget the poor, "HaMelitz" from the 22nd of February 1881 reporting that one Sunday a group of respected men of the community gathered and collected 1,500 Mark, as well as dresses and wood for heating for the poor of the city.

Most of the news from Memel published in "HaMeilitz" was written by David Eliezer Tubiansky and A.L.Sheinhaus.

During 1868 to 1869, years of famine in Lithuania, Rabbi Ruelf saved about 30,000 Jews in the Kovno Gubernia from starving, with money he collected in Germany. During a year and a half he transferred 630,000 Mark in weekly payments to 230 settlements in Lithuania, an immense sum in those years.

When Russian Jews were forced to leave Memel in the years 1880-1886, as mentioned above, Rabbi Ruelf arranged a fund raising event, and every family forced to leave received a sum of money for travel expenses and first arrangements, according to the number of its members.

The " Gemiluth Hasidim Society ", which gave interest free loans to the needy, was established in Memel in 1894. 229 donors raised its basic capital, and during the first year of its activity it distributed 133 loans to the tune of 6,529 Mark. There were 10 members on its board of directors (Ehrenrat): Rabbi Dr. Ruelf - chairman, Rabbi Gavriel Feinberg, Dr.B.M.Hanneman, D.L.Wolfson, A.L.Sheinhaus, Sh.H.Bernstein, T.Lieberman, O.Ratner. W.Naftal, M.Gitkin.

The managers of the society were Gershom Millner, L.Hanneman, A.Kaplan, Akiva Pinkus, Ch.L.Shtronin, M.Altschul, the supervisors being of A.Joffe, Yosef Gilis, the brothers Hanneman and the accountants were M.H.Meisels and A.L.Sheinhaus.In 1897 the Memel "Tsedakah Gedolah" society was established whose aim it was to support the poor.

The proximity of Memel to Lithuania enabled many Lithuanian Jews to come there in order to consult the many doctors who were in the city. At the initiative of Rabbi Ruelf, Shaul-Zvi Blokh and Dr.Pindikovsky, a Jewish hospital was built in Memel in 1871, with donations from German Jews and timber merchants from Russia. Some years later this hospital was already too small to accommodate all the patients, and thus in 1896 a big new building was erected surrounded by gardens. It was situated on a high place with a spectacular view. The plot for the building was acquired by the banker Leopold Alexander, using his own money, but the building was erected with the help of additional donors, such as the Baroness Klara von Hirsch from Paris who donated 40,000 Mark and Ya'akov Plaut from Nizza who donated 20.000 Mark. The hospital that had 32 beds, fulfilled its purpose till the liquidation of the community in 1939.

Between the Two World Wars

The French Governor, who ruled the region on behalf of the Entente, cancelled all restrictions that had been imposed upon the Jews, and thus all the Jewish inhabitants of Memel and the region received citizenship. The Governor nominated a committee of four members, two of them Jews, Moritz Altschul and Leon Rostovsky, as well as one German and a French officer as chairman, to deal with requests for citizenship, as a result of which the number of Jews in Memel increased quickly.

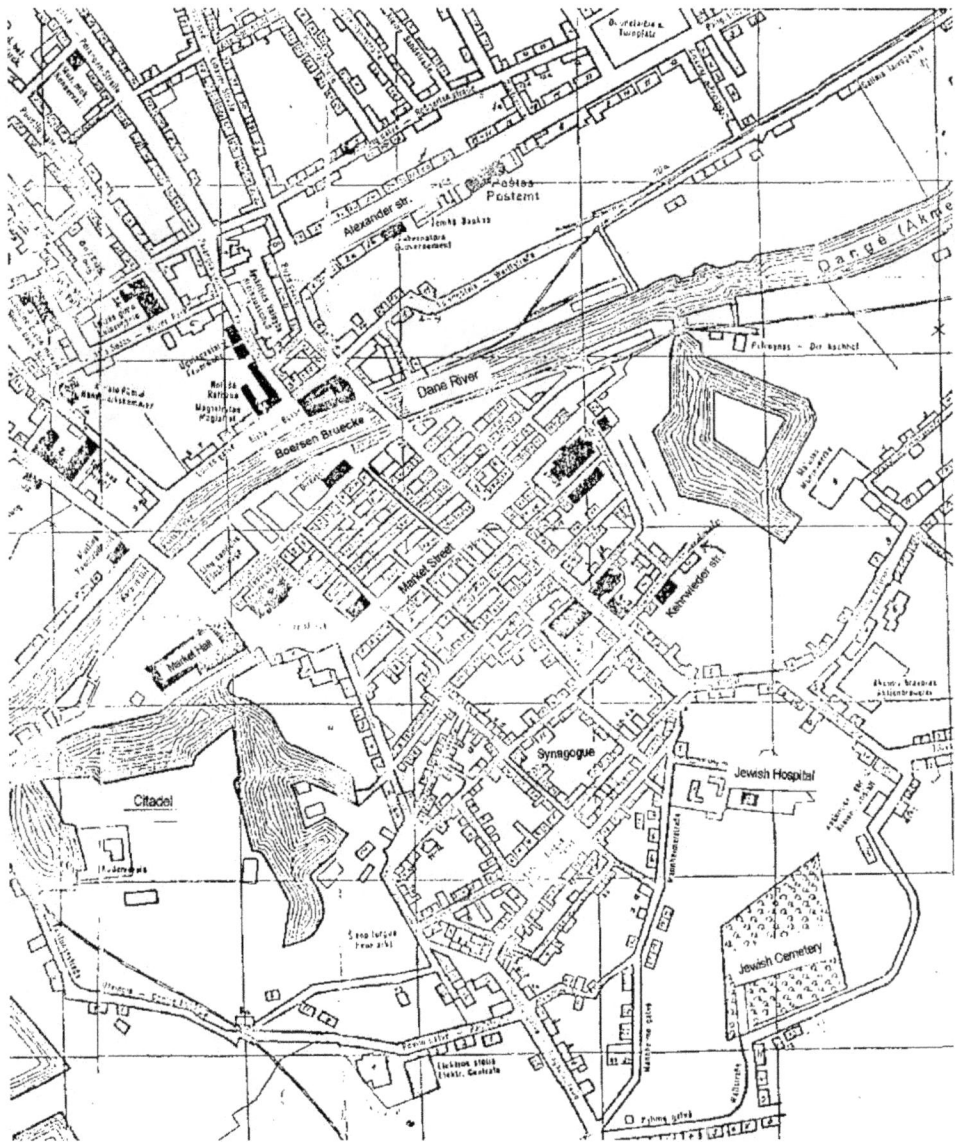

The southern part of Memel where most of the Jewish institutions were located.

The port, the developing commerce, the convenient conditions for developing industry, the possibility to learn a trade and the easing of permission to leave for the west and to Eretz-Yisrael, motivated many Jews to settle in Memel. The Lithuanian Government, having annexed Memel and the region to Lithuania in 1923, was pleased with the increase of the Jewish population, because the Jews together with the Lithuanians reduced the influence of the German majority.

The Klaipeda Port on the Dane River

The number of Jews in Memel in 1910 was 2,000 out of a total population of 21,108 (9%), and by 1928 there were 4,500 Jews, in 1938 - 6,000 Jews (12%) and in 1939 - 7,000 Jews out of a total population of 51,000 (about 14%).

Doctors who held German diplomas moved from Lithuania to Memel and local Jewish lawyers became judges and prosecutors. Among the 21 judges in the city, 7 were Jews and one Jew became a prosecutor, but at the end of 1938 there were only 3 Jewish judges and one Jewish prosecutor left, while their German colleagues plotted against them.

The legal basis for the existence of the Jewish community during this period was still the Prussian law from July 23, 1847 (see above) with additions that the "Directory" approved, i.e. the autonomy laws of the region established on the 28th of July 1924. Officially the "Directory" supervised the activities of the Jewish community, which meant that Rabbis, slaughterers and other employees of the community received their salaries and pensions from the "Directory" similar to the employees of the Christian churches in the region. The "Directory" consisted of 16 members, 8 of whom were elected anew every year, and in 1936 2,000 Jews were registered in the community. Only 900 Jews voted for the "Directory" during the elections of that year, 200 of them voting for the list of "Agudath Yisrael". Memel's Jews were not too active or interested in the activities of the community and this explains the small number of participants in the elections.

Conditions of the Jews of the region were considerably influenced by friction between the Lithuanian ruler and the German population who were in the majority. In 1933, for example, there were 4,510 Lithuanians as opposed to 14,632 Germans in Memel.

When the Nazis came to power in Germany, they began agitating for the region to return to Germany. In 1935 Memel Nazis were convicted of hooliganism, as a result of which the German press wrote that they were victims of a Jewish conspiracy because they were judged by Jewish judges and Jewish prosecutors. In 1937 Nazi youngsters harmed Jewish vacationers in Schwartzort (Juodkrante), a summer resort on the Baltic Sea and the Kurisches Haff. In that same year 10 Jewish students of the School of Commerce and the Pedagogic Institute in Memel suffered from insults and scheming from Lithuanian students. Although the Lithuanians sought to have been interested to oppose such deeds, they were too influenced by Nazi propaganda. During the second half of 1938 the situation of Memel's Jews deteriorated, with Nazis painting swastikas on Jewish shops and even placing bullies outside Jewish shops to prevent buyers from entering. At a gathering of Nazi activists in Memel, they demanded the activation of anti-Jewish "Nuremberg Laws".

In the elections of 1938 for the local Seimas, the Nazis received an absolute majority. The Jews were asked to vote for Lithuanian lists (see poster below).

By the beginning of 1939 half of Memel's Jews had left the city and moved to towns in the western part of Lithuania (Zemaitija), such as Palanga, Kretinga, Jurbarkas, Taurage and to Kaunas. The value of the property the Jews took with them from Memel was estimated at 100 Million Litas (1$ was then 6

Litas). Others sold their property to Germans for low prices, but when it became clear that the city and the region would soon be annexed to Germany, all remaining Memel Jews moved to Lithuania in a panic, leaving their property behind.

Transportation became so crowded and prices soared, causing poor Jews to go by foot to the nearby Lithuanian town of Gargzdai. The Jewish communities helped these refugees to get organized in their new abodes.

In Shavl (Siauliai), Telzh (Telsiai) and Tavrig (Taurage) sick refugees were treated free of charge in the clinics of the "Oze" organization, the children of the refugees were accepted in the schools and high schools. The "Oze" organization supplied food for weak and poor children.

On the 22nd of March 1939 the German army occupied Memel and the region. By that time about 21,000 people had left the city, most of them Lithuanians as well as a small number of Jews, the majority of the latter having left beforehand. The Nazis confiscated private and public Jewish property valued at tens of millions Litas.

On the 14th of April 1939 the last Jews left Memel, some of them without any property.

Society and Economy.

Despite the increasing influence of the Lithuanian Jews, the veteran community of Memel Jews kept its particular character. In an article published in the Yiddish daily newspaper from Kovno "Dos Vort" dated 4th of March 1935 the writer complained that efforts to absorb veteran Memel Jews into Lithuanian Jewish national culture achieved little successes, as German culture had a greater influence on the people. The Jews and even Lithuanians abandoned their cultural values slowly but gradually and assimilated into the German culture in spite of their conflict with Nazism. The veteran Jewish community of Memel still treated Lithuanian Jews, the "Ostjuden", with scorn.

According to the same survey there were 151 industrial enterprises in Memel, 31 of which were owned by Jews (20%). The data is presented in the following table:

Type of Establishment	Total	Owned by Jews
Metal Works, Power Stations, Bricks	20	2
Tiles and Pots	8	0
Chemical Industry, Spirits, Soap	9	3
Textile: Wool, Flax, Knitting	9	4
Sawmills, Furniture	23	9
Printing Presses, Book Binders	8	1
Flour Mills, Bakeries	29	6
Clothing and Footwear, Furs, Hats	11	2
Leather Industry	1	0
Barber Shops, Photographers, Jewelers	33	4

Type of business	Total	Owned by Jews
Groceries	26	9
Grains and Flax	15	9
Butcher shops and Cattle Trade	18	0
Restaurants and Taverns	23	0
Food Products Trade	45	13
Drinks	8	0
Milk and its Products	2	1
Garments, Furs and Textiles	51	26
Leather and Shoes	14	5
Haberdashery and House Utensils	23	9
Tobacco and Cigarettes	3	1
Medicines and Cosmetics	21	1
Watches and Jewels	8	2
Radio, Bicycles, Electrical Equipment	36	5
Tools and Iron Products	28	4
Building Materials, Lumber, Furniture	24	5
Heating Materials	23	8
Machines, Overland Transportation	17	2
Books and Stationary	15	4
Miscellaneous	71	15

Remark: In this survey only family names of owners of businesses were recorded, but not their nationality. Because most businesses were owned by Germans or Jews and because of the similarity of their family names, some inaccuracy could have occurred when determining the nationality of their owners.

Legally the community was a religious organization, but in fact it was a national society that supported the Hebrew kindergarten and school, took part in raising "Bitzaron Ubitachon" funds for Eretz Yisrael etc. Its official name was "The Office of the Hebrew Community" and came under Zionist influence, to the chagrin of "Agudath Yisrael". Its financial condition was sound, because it collected taxes at a rate of 75% of the income tax its members paid. The community owned the cemetery, a bathhouse, the slaughterhouse and the "Synagogue". Isidor (Asher) Hurwitz was the head of the community for many years, and in May 1937 the community celebrated its 75th anniversary.

Memel's Jews developed many businesses and industrial enterprises. According to the government survey of 1931 there were 471 shops and businesses in the city, among them 119 owned by Jews (25%). The breakdown according to type of business is presented in the table above.

According to data of the 1939 "Directory", Memel then had 330 industrial enterprises owned by Jews, which employed 70% of all the German workers.

There were Jewish landowners in the Memel region dealing with agriculture, who were evicted from their lands in 1938.

The Jewish "Folksbank", established in 1925 and which by 1929 had 345 members, played an important role in Memel's economic life, so did the private banks of Konikov, Yavshitz and Zomer.

Education and Culture.

Memel's Jewish children studied in a school where subjects were taught in the German language, and in addition there was also, as from 1927, a Talmud-Torah. On the initiative of Rabbi Dr.Schlesinger who came from Köln in 1933, a Hebrew elementary school and a kindergarten opened in the city despite the objection of veteran Memel Jews and the Yiddishists. 120 pupils studied in the school in 1937 and in the kindergarten there were 40 children. Thanks to the sound financial condition of the community the tuition fees paid by parents were very low. By chance most of the teachers were supporters of the "Mizrahi" party, but the orientation of the school was non-political.

The "Juedischer Kultur Bund" (Jewish Cultural Society) that was a non-political society, which influenced Jewish life in Memel. Because of changes in the composition of the Jewish population, the National-Zionist orientation penetrated into this society too.

Extensive cultural activities took place in "The Society of Hebrew Speakers" and in "The Society for Jewish History and Literature", headed by writer Aryeh-Leon Scheinhaus. He tried to propagate Judaism among broad circles, and for fifty years made efforts to arrange at least six lectures by well known people every winter. It is worthwhile mentioning an incident which occurred in Tilzit and Koenigsberg, when the President of the World Zionist Organization, David Wolfson, was not allowed by the heads of the local Jewish communities to give a lecture on a Zionist theme because they wished to be considered "neutral", but in Memel he gave his lecture on the same subject, arguing that if "we are neutral, we may speak on Zionism as well", this being possible thanks to A.L.Scheinhaus, the head of the Society.

Zionist activity.

A "Kibbutz Hakhshara" (Training Kibbutz) of "Hekhalutz" (pioneer) had already been established at the beginning of the twenties, during the rule of the French Governor, and in 1927 the "Beth Hekhalutz" (House of Hekhalutz) was built with help of donations from wealthy Memel Jews. This was a three storey building equipped with all conveniences, including a kitchen with electric appliances, and it served as an intellectual center of all local Zionists and as a meeting place for members of the "Training Kibbutzim" of the area. In 1925,

Fragments of the governmental survey of shops in Klaipeda (Memel) and its Region in 1931

Grocery shops

Adomeit C., Klaipėda, Kirpėjų g. 4.
Apriaski Gebr., Klaipėda, Aukštoji g. 17.
Baltruschat u. Co, Klaipėda, Laukininkų 41-42.
Betke F. W., Klaipėda, Malūnų pyl. 22a.
Bildau H., Panemunė, Pagėgių aps.
Blells A. I. Nachf. u. Co G. m. b. H., Klaipėda, Kirpėjų g. 4.
Bouchcard B., Klaipėda, Liepojaus g. 24.
Cohn M., Klaipėda, Turgaus g. 35-36.
Frenkler F., Klaipėda, Sauerveino g. 17.
Friedman u. Co, Klaipėda, Teatro g. 1.
Glant I., Klaipėda, Turgaus g. 3-4.
Gronau Gebr., Klaipėda, Laukininkų g. 33-34.
Handelszentrale G. m. b. H., Klaipėda, Liepų g. 12.
Kaiser's Kaffee geschaeft G. m. b. H., Klaipėda, Biržos g. 15-17.
Keiluweit E., Priekulė.
Kon u. Aronson, Klaipėda, Laukininkų 17-18.
Konikoft E., Klaipėda, Bažnyčių g. 5.
Kurschat G., Klaipėda, Naujasis turgus 3.
Laaser u. Neumann, Kurt Scharffetter, Klaipėda, Laukininkų g. 21-22.
Maisels S., Klaipėda, Kepėjų g. 1-2.
Mueschoewsky R. Inh. Klan C., Klaipėda, Turgaus g. 17-18.
Mikuteit A., Šilutė, Tilžės g.
Seidler H., Šilutė, Tilžės g.
Skwar E., Klaipėda, Laukininkų g. 43-47.
Stoch A. u. Co, Klaipėda, Kepėjų g. 22-24.
Schwaz u. Co G. m. b. H., Klaipėda, Laukininkų g. 47.
Schnietz R., Klaipėda, Laukininkų 1a.
Treger F. Nachf., Šilutė, Pr. Joachimo g.
Ulrich R., Klaipėda, Biržos g. 14.
Walker W., Klaipėda, Luizės g. 9-10.
Waller A. Nachf., Šilutė, Senas Turgus 10.
Waren - Einkaufs - Verein A. G., Klaipėda, Puodžių g. 19.

Haberdashery shops

Cohn S. B. u. Eisenstaedt, Klaipėda, Taurgaus g. 46.
Dannemann u. Lewy, Klaipėda, Aukštoji g. 18.
Dieck Šilutė, Turgavietė.
Doerfer J. Nachf, Šilutė.
Elbaum M. Nachf, Klaipėda, Didž. Vandens 30.
Finkelstein S., Smalininkai.
Goerke E., Klaipėda, Liepojaus g. 31.
Gronau Gebr., Klaipėda, Laukininkų g. 33-34.
Gurwitz M., Klaipėda, Biržos g. 14.
Huhn H. Inh. Mattern M., Klaipėda, Biržos 1-4.
Huhn J., Inh. Preiss A., Klaipėda, Tuargaus g. 7-8.
Jordan N., Šilutė, Pr. Joachimo g.
Kuppermann L., Šilutė, Turgavietė.
Lass F. u. Co., Klaipėda, Biržos g. 15-17.
Markuschewitz u. Posen, Klaipėda, Aukštoji g. 11.
Monerings M., Klaipėda, Laukininkų g. 14-15.
Oscherowitz B., Klaipėda, Laukininkų g. 26.
Ofsijowitz B., Šilutė, Turgavietė.
Prokopus A., Klaipėda, Liepojaus g. 30.
Puhn Gebr., Klaipėda, Galvijų turgus 18-19.
Rudat R., Klaipėda, Laukininkų g. 16.
Salzberg A., Klaipėda, Laukininkų g. 26.
Simon J., Klaipėda, Biržos g. 1-4.
Walubat u. Co, Klaipėda, Turgaus g. 48-49.
Wallter R., Klaipėda, Turgaus g. 10.
Zwickies H., Klaipėda, Žvejų g.

Cloth shops

Beer M. Inh. Isaak. L., Priekulė.
Bergmann I., Klaipėda, Perkasų g. 13 - 14.
Brusdeylins A., Klaipėda, Laukininkų g. 11.
Burrack R., Klaipėda, Laukininkų g. 47.
Cohn S. B. u. Eisenstadt, Klaipėda, Turgaus g. 46.
Dehning H. Nachf., Klaipėda, Biržos g. 1 - 4.
Elbaum M. Nachf., Klaipėda, Didž. Vandens g. 30.
Epstein L., Šilutė, Turgavietė.
Fleischmann L., Klaipėda, Didž. Vandens g. 31.
Gidansky L., Klaipėda, Aukštoji gt. 21.
Grasteil R. Inh. Grasteit E., Klaipėda, Laukininkų g. 38.
Gutman J., Klaipėda, Aukštoji g. 22 - 23.
Hanemann F., Inh. Hanemann Sch., Klaipėda, Aukštoji g. 21.
Isaak Gebr., Inh. Isaak N., Saugai, Šilutės apskr.
Kaplan A., Klaipėda, Perkasų g. 6a.
Kuppermann L., Šilutė, Turgavietė.
Lass F. u. Co, Klaipėda, Biržos g. 15 - 17.
Lewin B., Klaipėda, Turgaus g. 3 - 4.
Löwenstein L., Klaipėda, Liepojaus g. 46.
Memeler Textilhandelsgesellschaft Israeilt u. Co, Klaipėda, Skutėjų g. 6 - 9.
Ofsijowitz E., Šilutė, Turgavietė.
Oscherowitz B., Klaipėda, Laukininkų g. 26.
Rudat R., Klaipėda, Laukininkų g. 16.
Salzberg A., Klaipėda, Laukininkų g. 26.
Simon I., Klaipėda, Biržos g. 1 - 4.
Stoljar Sch., Klaipėda, Turgaus g. 39.
Scheer G., Klaipėda, Perkasų g. 5.
Udwin Bebr. u. Aisikowitz, Klaipėda, Aukštoji g. 15.
Quesseleit O., Katyčiai, Pagėgių apskr.
Wabulat C. u. Co, Klaipėda, Turgaus g. 48-49.
Waller R., Klaipėda, Turgaus g. 10.

Timber trade

Ambras D., Šilutė, Pr. Joachimo gt.
„Baltkohl,", Baltische Kohlengesel. m. b. H. Klaipėda, Pietų rag. 6.
Berger R., Šilutė, Tilžės gt.
Betke u. Jouby G. m. b. H., Klaipėda, Biržos gt. 7.
Balticum G. m. b. H., Klaipėda.
Dumont du Voitel Bruno, Klaipėda, Kepėjų gt. 1-2.
Ehmer A. u. Co A. G., Klaipėda, Malūnų gt.
Eilberg A., Klaipėda, Didžioji gt. 2.
Feinbergas Š., Klaipėda.
Freidberg B., Klaipėda. Laivogatvis 1.
Gerlach J. G., Klaipėda, Liepojaus gt. 34.
Jawschitz Gebr., Klaipėda.
Izigsohn H., Klaipėda, Biržos gt. 1-4.
Krause E., Klaipėda, Biržos gt. 15-17.
Kolitz Otto, Šilutė.
Kurschat G., Klaipėda, Naujasis Turgus 3.
Laaser u. Neumann, Kurt Scharffetter, Klaipėda, Laukininkų gt. 21-22.
Leidereite F., Klaipėda, Laivogatvis 1.
Nafthal u. Co, Klaipėda, Liepų gt. 13.
Naftal M., Klaipėda.
Pawlowski M. G. m. b. H., Klaipėda, Liepų 2a.
Raske P., Kalveliai, Klaipėdos kr.
Reiss Gebr., Panemunė, Klaipėdos kr.
Schneider R., Klaipėda, Liepojaus gt. 24.
Schmidt J. C., Klaipėda.
Ulrich F., Šilutė.
Vonberg A., Šilutė, Pr. Joachimo gt.
Walker W., Klaipėda, Luizės gt. 9-10.
Weiner D., Klaipėda, Geležinkelio st.

there were 13 "Agricultural Kibbutzei Hakhsharah" in Jewish and German farms in the Memel region, with about 400 members. The "Beth Hekhalutz" also served as a dwelling for the urban Kibbutz in Memel, which during the thirties numbered about 600 members, of whom about 50 members belonged to "Hashomer Hatzair". There was also an active sanatorium for "Hekhalutz" members. One of the methods to raise funds for these institutions was to publish a "Help Chain" in the movement's periodical, which meant that each donor would call several friends to donate too, each of these would add more donors, so that the numbers of donors were greatly increased. There was also a "Kibbutz Hakhsharah" of "Agudath-Yisrael" also in Memel.

The annexation of Memel and the region to Lithuania strengthened Zionist influence in Memel, a majority of whom became Zionist supporters, and as a result of which the community committee elected were all Zionists. All Zionist parties were represented in Memel. Details of the votes for the Zionist Congresses are given in the following table:

Cong. No.	Year	Total Shek	Total Vote	Labor Party Z"S Z"Z		Rev	Gen. Zionists A B		Gro.	Mizrahi
14	1925	80	--	--	--	--	--	--	--	--
15	1927	103	31	3	3	13	4	--	--	8
16	1929	296	96	16	6	29	18	--	--	27
17*	1931	363	176	41	12	73	27	--	--	23
18	1933	---	858	495		146	152	--	19	46
19	1935	---	1,005	629		---	64	83	66	163

Cong.-Congress; Shek.-Shekalim; Tot. Vote.-Total Voters; Rev.-Revisionists; G.Z.-General Zionists; Gro.-Grosmanists; Miz.-Mizrahi

*the elections took place in the committee's office in Kehrwieder Street.

The Zionist youth organizations working in Memel were "Hashomer HaTzair", "Beitar", "HaNoar HaZioni", "Benei Akiva", "Herzlia", "Young Wizo".

A group of "HaShomer-HaTsair" 1926

Young WIZO in Memel 1934

Jewish youth sports activities took place in branches of "Maccabi" with its 123 members, also "HaPoel" and "Bar Kochva".

Conference of "Hakhsharah Kibbutzim" of Memel Region in 1931

Members of Urban Kibbutz of Memel working at a flax processing plant.

קבוץ עידוני ממלי לפני עליתם
של קבוצת חברים ארציי
27-I-1933

A farewell party for a group of members of the Urban Kibbutz of Memel
before their "Aliyah" (January 1, 1933).

חדר בן-גריון
בבאו לממל

David ben Gurion visiting Memel in 1933

(Ben Gurion can be located above the word "in" of caption above)

Religion and Welfare.

The synagogues that existed World War I continued to serve the people as before.

In the old "Polish" synagogue, some German Jews prayed together with Polish Jews (Ost Juden). The big "Beth Midrash", under the auspices of "Agudath Yisrael", was called "Talmud Verein", and "Agudah" people as well as the Orthodox prayed there. They had their own Rabbi and tried to avoid any contact with the community. The only prayer house belonging to the community (Gemeinde) was the so called "Synagoge", where there were services mainly on the High Holidays, and since it was too small to accommodate all worshippers it was necessary to rent an additional hall for services which both German Jews and Lithuanian Zionists attended. During this period another Synagogue was established named "Ohel Ya'akov", where the Zionists prayed.

The daily Kovno newspaper, " Di Yiddishe Shtime" (The Jewish Voice), dated October 5th 1936, reported that during the last High Holidays all Jewish shops, including those run by owners of mixed marriages, were closed, something that had never happened before Hitler came to power.

The Rabbis who officiated in Memel at this time were: Eliezer Yehudah Rabinovitz, the son of Rabbi Mordehai Yitzhak, who served in Memel from 1920 till 1939, and published articles on religious issues in religious periodicals, also on daily matters in the "Yiddishe Shtime". He was a member of the "Mizrahi" executive, and both he and his wife perished together in the holocaust in Keidainiai. The German Jews were administered by Rabbi Eliezer Halevi Lazarus and later by Dr.Schlesinger. The latter was a cultured man, skilled in Talmud, a scholar of languages, including Hebrew. In 1939 he immigrated to Eretz-Yisrael and became a teacher in the Teachers Seminar in Jerusalem. "Agudath Yisrael", as mentioned before, had their own Rabbi, because Rabbi Rabinovitz was too much of a Zionist.

Those welfare institutions working before World War I continued their activity during this period as well (for example: Maoth Khitim, Tsedakah Gedolah etc.). The "Society of Jewish Women" headed by Mrs.Rosenberg were busy with social help, as was the "Organization of Zionist Women" (WIZO) headed by the ladies August, A.Hazan and Judith Leshem.

Because of the wealth of Memel's community many Lithuanian fundraisers came to collect money there, and only very few returned home with empty pockets.

A partial list of the men who were active in the community is given in Appendix 2 below.

A Jewish family fleeing from Memel on the 21st of March 1939, uniformed Nazis standing by.

During World War II and Afterwards.

The German army invaded Lithuania on the 22nd of June 1941, occupied the whole country in a matter of days, which meant that the refugees from Memel were again under Nazi rule. Their fate was similar to the fate of the Jews of the towns and cities of Lithuania where they had lived for the last two years. Only a few managed to survive those terrible times.

In 1945 Memel (Klaipeda) and its region became a part of Soviet Lithuania and Jews began to settle there again. By 1967 there were about 1,000 Jews in the city, but there was no organized community, no synagogue and no cemetery.

At the end of 1989, when Lithuania began to regain its independence, a crowd incited by Lithuanians attacked a Jewish clerk named A. Lichtenstein and anti Jewish leaflets were distributed in the city. On the 1st of January 1990 Memel's Jews numbered 681 souls out of a total population of 206,400. At that time a branch of "The Society for Jewish Culture", centered in Vilna, and a Sunday School for Jewish children where Hebrew was taught, were established in the city. But many of Memel's Jews were waiting for the opportunity to leave the country.

The old Jewish cemetery had been destroyed during Soviet rule when a radio station with tall antennas was erected in this area. The purpose of this station was to disturb broadcasts from abroad and when leveling the area almost all tombstones were ruined and bones of the dead exposed on the surface. Some of the tombstones were incorporated into the huge concrete blocks that served as a base for the antennas.

On the 10th of May 1991, a funeral for these bones was arranged on the initiative of the "Society for Jewish Culture", also a memorial wall was erected at the site of the old cemetery and several tombstones found at the site were fixed into this wall. The entire area of the former cemetery was converted into a park and a monument was erected with an inscription in Lithuanian, Hebrew and Yiddish saying: "In memory of the Jewish community of Klaipeda which was cruelly annihilated by the Nazis". The architect of this project was S. Manomaitis. (see picture below).

The Memorial wall with fragments of tombstones found on the spot incorporated into it.

A general view of the memorial site

The Lithuanian, Hebrew and Yiddish inscription reads: In memory of the Jewish community of Klaipeda that was cruelly destroyed by the Nazis.

Appendix 1

A picture of Rabbi Yeshaya Wohlgemuth and an appreciation of his personality after his death. "The Jewish Chronicle", London, dated the 6th of January 1899.

RABBI JESAYAH WOHLGEMUTH, OF HAMBURG.

Judaism has lost one of its most learned sons by the death of Rabbi Wohlgemuth. He was for forty years Rabbi in Memel, but left there eighteen years ago to become one of the Klaus Rabbonim in Hamburg. He was a thorough type of the old kind of Rav. His learning was unbounded, and comprised not only a profound knowledge of Hebrew but he was well-acquainted with modern languages and science. His knowledge of English was extraordinary for a man who had never been out of Germany. Quiet and unostentatious, he pursued the even tenor of his way, imparting knowledge to others from the vast store he had gathered up during his long and well spent life. The example he set to his disciples was one of high ideals and nobility of conduct, and he exemplified in his person all the finest attributes of the Jew. Men, such as he, living simple lives, but casting around them good influences, are the true type of the Sages of old. The deceased Rabbi's beautiful life was one long devotion to the sacred task of imparting to others a knowledge of and love for Judaism. All who came under his beneficent teaching had their lives sweetened and their future shaped by his great power for good. His unswerving orthodoxy was accompanied by a toleration for the opinion of others. He was greatly esteemed by such great Rabbonim as Rabbi Yitzchak Elchanan, זצ״ל and Reb Schmuel Mohilever, זצ״ל. He lived to a very great age, being nearly 90, and two years ago he celebrated his diamond wedding. An aged widow, and numerous sons, daughters and grandchildren mourn his loss.

Appendix 2

A partial list of the men active in the Community.

Moritz Altschul - Representative of "Keren haYesod" and a member of the presidium of the Bureau of Commerce in Memel;

Leopold Alexander - Chairman of the community for 20 years;

Isidor (Asher) **Hurwitz** - Chairman of the community, chairman of the Zionist Organization and the patron of the "Khalutzim" in Memel, was murdered in Kretinga;

Ben-Zion Hanneman - A prominent elderly person, a pupil of Rabbi Yisrael Salanter and a distinguished scholar;

Dr.Moritz Hanneman - Head of the Zionists-Socialists, was arrested by the Germans and murdered in jail;

Eliezer Tatz - Teacher and educator, devoted Zionist activist, died in Tel-Aviv in 1945;

Yeshayahu Hanneman - One of the leaders of the religious Jews, murdered together with the Jews from Telzh;

Dr.Herman Jakobson - Chairman of the "Bar Kokhva" sports club, immigrated to South Africa;

Leon Kalenbach - Director of the Jewish Hospital and founder of "Bar-Kokhva";

Avraham Meler - Representative of "Keren Kayemeth leYisrael" in Memel;

Nathan Naftal - Member of the community committee and chairman of "ORT" in Memel, Consul of Portugal, perished in Dachau;

Leon Rostovsky - Chairman of the Board of Directors of the Jewish Hospital, with his financial help a new big wing of the hospital was erected, perished in the Kovno Ghetto;

Yehoshua Rubin - Member of the community committee and an active Zionist, lived in Israel;

Yosef Shulman - Member of the community committee and the Board of Directors of the Jewish Hospital;

Leon (Aryeh) Scheinhaus - Writer and journalist, founder of the "Kiryath Sefer Society" and of the "Hebrew Speakers" Society, one of the editors of the "Memeler Dampfboot" newspaper;

David Wolfson - Herzl's successor as President of the World Zionist Organization, grew up and was educated in Memel.

Feivush Yavschitz - Member of the community committee and chairman of the Zionist organization, died in France;

Appendix 3

Association of Jewish soldiers participants in the liberation of Lithuania. Klaipeda branch.

List of donors for the Yiddish-Lithuanian periodical "Apzvalga", the journal of this Association

Bibliography

Yad-Vashem archives-M-1/21-238,728; 0-4/1,51; 0-33/773,2182,2539; 0-3/1887,3578; 568; TR-2; TR-10/32.

YIVO, Collection of Lithuanian Communities, New-York, Files 1390, 1530, 1677.

Ish Shalom, M.- Besod Khotsvim U'Bonim (Hebrew), Jerusalem 1989.

Mireishith Vead Akharith (From the Beginning to the End), The book "haShomer-haTsair" in Lithuania (Hebrew), Tel-Aviv 1985.

Ruelf I.-The History of the Jews in Memel (German), 1900.

Ruelf Isaak, Meine Reise nach Kovno (German), 1869.

Sheinhaus A.L.-Iden in Memel fun Farzeiten bis jetzt (Jews in Memel from olden times till now) (Yiddish)- YIVO Archives, pages 63778-63786.

Yiddisher Lebn (Yiddish), Kovno-Telsh, 25.1.1924; 26.8.1938.

Amerikaner (Yiddish) New-York, 13.9.1939.

Bulletin of Yita-8.3.1935; 8.4.1935.

Bemisholei Hahinukh (Hebrew), Kovno Nr. 5-6, December 1937.

Dos Vort - daily newspaper in Yiddish of the Z"S party, Kovno 4.3.1935;6.12.1935.

Di Yiddishe Shtime - daily newspaper in Yiddish of the General Zionists-Kovno,

26.2.1928; 22.10.1928; 24.2.1931; 26.5.1936; 25.8.1936; 5.10.1936; 5.5.1937; 6.5.1937; 9.5.1937; 26.5.1937; 15.6.1937; 10.11.1937; 6.7.1939.

Di Zeit (Yiddish) Kovno, 4.12.1933.

HaDoar (Hebrew) New-York, 11 Nissan 5699.

HaMeilitz, Odesa-St.Petersburg, (Hebrew), 30.5.1867; 4.5.1880; 26.10.1880; 22.2.1881; 28.6.1881; 4.10.1881; 6.6.1882; 18.9.1885; 5.10.1885; 15.9.1886; 28.2.1893; 2.12.1895; 30.12.1896.

Vegveizer (Yiddish) Pitsburg, 19.4.1940.

Yerushalaim D'Lita (Yiddish) Vilna, Nr. 2, December 1989.

Volksblat - daily newspaper of the Volkists, Kovno (Yiddish), 21.4.1933; 17.1.1934; 21.5.1936; 14.8.1936; 30.3.1937; 10.11.1938; 24.11.1938; 27.11.1938; 28.11.1938; 2.3.1939; 26.3.1939; 7.5.1939; 4.7.1939; 6.9.1939; 28.11.1939.

Volkshtime (Yiddish), Warsaw, 18.3.1964.

Aufbau (German) New-York, 18.5.1984.

Mazoji Lietuva (Lithuanian) Klaipeda, 8.5.1991.

Vakaru Ekspresas (Lithuanian) Klaipeda,19.2.1991; 21.3.1991; 7.5.1991.

Kudirkos-Naumiestis (Naishtot)

Naishtot - in Yiddish - is situated at the south-western part of Lithuania near the border with East Prussia (now Russia) where the small stream, Shirvinta flows into the Sesupe river. The Shirvinta stream was the border between Lithuania and Prussia and a concrete bridge linked Naishtot with the Prussian town Schirvindt.

Naishtot is listed by the name Novomiasto in documents dating back to the sixteenth century. In 1643 Queen Cecilia Renate granted the town the Magdeburg Rights (Self Rule) and named it Wladislawow - after her husband King Wladislaw the Fourth.

Until 1795 Naishtot was part of the Polish Lithuanian Kingdom. After the third division of Poland by the three superpowers of those times - Russia, Prussia and Austria Lithuania became partly Russian and partly Prussian. The part of the state on the left side of the Nieman River (Nemunas), including Naishtot, was handed over to Prussia, and this town, called then Neustadt was under the Prussian rule from 1795 until 1807. During these years Naishtot was a county administrative center.

After Napoleon defeated Prussia, according to the Tilzit agreement of July 1807, Polish territories occupied by Prussia were transferred to what became known as the "The Great Dukedom of Warsaw", established at that time. The King of Saxony, Friedrich August, was appointed Duke, and the Napoleonic code then became the basis of the constitution of the Dukedom, according to which everybody was equal before the law, except for the Jews who were not granted any civil rights.

During the years 1807-1813, Naishtot belonged to the "Great Dukedom of Warsaw" and was part of the Bialystok district. The Napoleonic code was then introduced in this region, remaining in effect even during the Lithuanian period.

In 1815, after the defeat of Napoleon, all of Lithuania was annexed to Russia. As a result, Naishtot was included in the Augustowa Region (Gubernia), and in 1866 it became a part of the Suwalk Gubernia and a county administrative center.

In 1819 Naishtot was renamed Wladislawow, and it endured till World War I.

In 1835 there were 350 houses in town; 60 of them were built of bricks. That year Naishtot had 4,413 residents, 3,348 Jews among them - (76%). After the big fire of 1865 many brick houses replaced the burnt wooden homes .

Under the Russian rule Naishtot started to grow, and in 1867 the town was declared a district administrative capitol. The reasons for this urban sprawl was due to improved roads and the resulting trade with Germany . With the construction of the new railway connecting St. Petersburg to Berlin in the middle of the 1860s, the importance of Naishtot as a district administrative capitol decreased.

At the beginning of World War I Naishtot passed from one government to another several times. In the spring of 1915 it was occupied by the German army remaining in control of the area until the end of 1918. As a result of fighting more than a quarter of the homes in Naishtot were destroyed.

When the Lithuanian state was established after World War I, the district administrative capitol was moved to Shaki (Sakiai) and the economy of Naishtot suffered. The only governmental institutions left in town were the border guard unit, the border crossing point, customs station and the county court.

In 1934 a memorial was erected in honor of the doctor and poet Vincas Kudirka who was born and buried in Naishtot. He was the author of the Lithuanian anthem. Since that time the town was called Kudirkos Naumiestis. This name was not subject to any changes during the Soviet rule 1940-1941.

In the years 1941-1944 the town was under Nazi rule with all the atrocities and murders characteristic of the regime.

During the struggle for liberation against the Nazis in 1944, a great part of the downtown core was destroyed.

The Jewish Settlement till after World War I

In 1643, when Naishtot was granted the Magdeburg Rights, Christian inhabitants asked the authorities to forbid Jews to live in the town. According to the available data it seems that in the middle of the 17th century Jews had already been living in Naishtot , but according to the inscriptions on the old tombstones at the Jewish cemetery, Jews settled in Naishtot at the beginning of the 18th century. Initially Jews settled around the Synagogue and the Beth-Midrash, and in the quarter near the Sesupe river. The big fire of 1865 caused the destruction of this quarter. Later the Jewish area spread out, and the burnt wooden houses were replaced by brick homes.

During the Prussian rule (1795-1807) the government promised a prize of 1,500 Marks to a person who will be the first to build a solid building in town (the building was not to be built in wood) . The prize was awarded to Yitskhak Abelson, the son of the local Rabbi, Aba Abelson.

In 1797, 429 Jews and 565 Christians lived in town.

In May 1881 a large fire destroyed 200 Jewish and Christian homes and all belongings. A help committee was established who dealt with distribution of the money, food and clothing received from the neighboring Jewish communities and Jewish philanthropists abroad. Thanks to the work of the committee the victims of the fire avoided starvation and helped rebuilt some of the houses. In 1887, another fire destroyed 87 houses and in 1889 in just two weeks two fires broke out and 20 houses were burnt.

In 1871 and in 1893 the town endured a cholera epidemic.

At the end of the 19th century the Jews of Naishtot owned 2 leather processing shops. Before World War I the Naishtot Jews had 4 brush manufacturing plants employing over 100 Jewish workers, 2 soft drink and beer factories, a silk spinning workshop with 40 workers and 60 apprentices. Jewish women worked at the cigarette factory in the neighboring German town of Schirwindt and made knitting products at home. Jews working in trades made a fine living. Among them there were 4 shoemakers, 3 tailors, 2 tinsmiths, 1 cooper, 1 locksmith, a few producers of carts and cabriolets and also roofing specialists and road pavers. Many worked in commerce. Successful merchants among them traded on national and international levels as exporters and contractors. They exported grains, vegetables, fruit and poultry mainly to Germany.

The proximity of the German border was an important factor in the life of Jewish shopkeepers. Germans would come to buy food products in Naishtot lured by cheaper prices. Bringing in different goods from Germany and selling them in Lithuania yielded an additional source of income for many Jews.

Another source of income was smuggling emigrants over the border to Germany. There were cases of fraudulent "smugglers" who would cheat the emigrants by taking away various items belonging to them. In other cases "the smugglers" would keep the migrants in the hostel longer than necessary in order to extort more money. Sometimes the smugglers would set their eyes on a young woman or a nice girl and would detain her longer than necessary. All this aroused indignation in the community and set the community against the "smugglers". However, thousands of Jews who arrived in America with the help of these smugglers remembered them favorably, despite the fact that they had not always been treated fairly.

A few dozen Jewish families in town were agrarians. They owned more than 300 hectares of land and cultivated mostly grains. A part of the Jewish farms were conducted by modern means. Many Naishtot Jews had auxiliary farm facilities beside their houses.

In the same year the "Talmud-Torah" was established in town, and most of the Jewish children studied at the school. Hebrew, Russian and arithmetic were taught at the school as well. In 1887 the school was a solid school with an annual budget of about 1,000 Rubles. There were 4 classes with 4 "Melamdim" (Teachers). Some of the children studied at the Russian school. At the beginning of the nineteenth century, 20 Jewish, 80 Catholic and 50 Protestant students attended the Russian school.

In 1878 a Jewish school, subsidized by the government was open in town. The director of the school was A.Yevarkovsky and one of the teachers was Y.Rozer. These teachers established a library in 1879 where Russian and Hebrew books could be borrowed.

Zionist activity started in Naishtot in 1884 by the "Khovevei Zion" (Lovers of Zion) Society. The main activity of the group was fundraising on behalf of Eretz Yisrael. One of the fundraising activities was the sale of Moshe Montefiore's photographs. In 1899 the Society sent a delegate to the regional conference of the Zionist Societies in Vilna and in 1913 to Druskenik (Druskininkai), and to the regional committee in Suwalk in 1909. The Zionist Society of Naishtot was one of the five Societies of the Suwalk Gubernia with its own delegate, Yitskhak Nisnboim, at the Fifth Zionist congress. In the years 1898,1899 and 1903 the Hebrew newspaper, published in St. Petersburg, "HaMeilitz" printed lists of contributors from Naishtot for the Settlement of Eretz-Yisrael. The fundraisers were Zalman Zubishsky, Eta Rozenberg, Hanah Vistanetsky and Shelomoh Landau.

The Great Synagogue built in 1880

For the Naishtot correspondents who wrote in "HaMeilitz" see **Appendix 4.**

At the old Jewish cemetery in Jerusalem there is a tombstone of a Naishtot man, Rabbi Yosef-Tsevi son of Mosheh HaCohen, who died 1879.

The local "Bund" branch (Anti-Zionist workers organization) struggled for improved working conditions for Jewish workers and also dealt with smuggling revolutionary literature from Germany to Russia. Together with "Poalei-Zion" they organized strikes of the local brush manufacturing workers at the beginning of the twentieth century. One of the first revolutionary organizers in town was the local Yankel-Aba (Apolon) Finkelshtein.

In 1905 the police found a few pistol guns in the "kloiz" and imposed a penalty of 3,000 Ruble on the community.

At the beginning of the 1880s there were many plots organized against Jews, causing migration of Naishtot Jews to America and South-Africa. The Jewish population in town decreased from 2,305 in1908 to 1,600 in1914.

For the Vital Records for Wladislawow of the 19th century see **Appendix 1.**

At the beginning of World War I Naishtot passed from one government to another several times. As a result more than a quarter of the houses in town were destroyed and for several years the town was left deserted in ruins .

During German occupation (1915-1918) about 70% of the Jews returned to town. Living in great poverty, they needed the help of the "The Jewish Aid Committee" in Koenigsberg headed by Dr. Nathan and Dr. Bernard Cohen.

During Independent Lithuania (1918-1940)

(All photos supplied by Braine Rozenblum-Zinger)

On February 16, 1918, the establishment of the Lithuanian State was proclaimed. Consequently the German army withdrew from the area, and life in Naishtot gradually returned to normal.

Following the law of autonomy for minorities, issued by the new Lithuanian government, the minister for Jewish affairs Dr. Menakhem (Max) Soloveitshik ordered elections to community committees (Va'ad Kehilah) to be held in the summer of 1919. In Naishtot, the elections took place in 1919 and a committee of 11 members was elected: 5 were elected from "Poalei-Zion", 2 from General Zionists and 4 from "Agudath Yisrael". This Naishtot committee was one of the first elected in Lithuania.

The committee, active till the end of 1925 when the autonomy was annulled, collected taxes as required by law and was in charge of all aspects of community life.

According to the first census performed by the government in 1923, there were in Naishtot 3,067 people and of them 981 Jews (32 %).

At the elections for the municipality council in 1931, four Jewish members were elected: Shimon Fink, Berl Mitkovsky, Avraham Epshtein and Hirsh Osherovitz. At the elections of 1934, only three Jews were elected.

The Jewish "Folksbank" of Naishtot with 60 members was established in 1920. Its role in the restoration of the post-war Jewish businesses was important, as were loans from the "Joint" organization. In 1927, membership increased to a record 216, but during the 1930s there were only 150 members accounting to 75% of all Jewish families in town. For many years, Z.Tompovsky was the director. One of the more active agencies in town was the branch of "The United Jewish Agrarian Credit Society ".

According to the data provided by the 1931 government survey of business stores in the state, Naishtot had 64 stores, 55 of them owned by Jews (86%).

Division of the stores by type of business is given in the table below:

Type of the business	Total	Owned by Jews
Groceries	6	6
Grains and Flax	6	6
Butchers and Cattle Trade	12	8
Restaurants and Taverns	5	3
Food Products	12	12
Beverages	2	2
Textile Products and Furs	4	4
Leather and Shoes	1	1
Haberdashery and Home Utensils	1	1
Medicine and Cosmetics	2	1
Watches, Jewels and Optics	2	2
Bicycles and Sewing Machines	1	1
Tools and Steel Products	4	4
Heating Materials	4	4
Overland Transportation	1	0
Stationary and Books	1	0

According to the same survey Naishtot had 14 light industry factories, all owned by Jews, as can be seen in the following table:

Type of the Factory	Total	Jewish owned
Metal Workshops, Power Plants	1	1
Chemical Industry: Spirits, Soaps	3	3
Textile: Wool, Flax, Knitting	2	2
Food	1	1
Barber shops, bristle processing, photo shops	7	7

Transfer of regional offices from Naishtot to Shaki caused a deterioration in the economic situation causing many Jews to emigrate abroad.

The big flax processing plant established by the Lithuanian cooperative center-"Lietukis" employed no Jewish workers, except for 3-4 clerks. The bristle industry employed only 10-12 workers. Jewish people working in various trades were represented by 8 bakers, 7 butchers, 4 watchmakers, 3 barbers, 3 hat makers, 2 cobblers and 1 tailor. Several families made their living in the transport business until this type of activity was taken away from Jews in 1936.

One of the Jewish businesses untouched by reforms since before the war was agriculture. 25 families owned an area of 320 hectares and continued to cultivate the land. However, only half of the families were able to make a living in agriculture, while the other half had to seek additional work to supplement their income. There were other Jews who rented land for cultivation .

The concrete bridge on the Shirvinta River (?)

The Nazis took over the rule in Germany in 1933 and in subsequent years, they imposed economic pressure on Lithuania negatively affecting a great number of Naishtot Jews. The border passing with Germany was closed, ultimately resulting in the closure of 24 shops and 2 custom clerk offices. Businesses such as stores, bakeries, and butcher shops, photographer shops and others saw a significant decrease in income attributed largely to the fact that Germans from the other side of the border stopped coming.

In 1935, Naishtot had 193 Jewish families with a total number of population numbering about 750 people.

Their occupations are detailed in the table below:

Occupation or Business	Number of Families	%
Commerce	87	45
Craft	30	15.5
Agriculture	20	10.5
Different professions and Clerks	15	8
Non professional trades	5	2.5
Religious Ministers	5	2.5
Industry	3	1.5
Free professions	3	1.5
Without defined occupation	25	13
Total	**193**	**100**

According to telephone book of 1939 there were 60 subscribers to telephone service, 16 of them were Jews

The market square and the monument of V. Kudirka

Education and Culture

In the 1920s the "Va'ad HaKehila" established and maintained a Kindergarten and an elementary school in which the language of instruction was Yiddish. Later a Hebrew school of the "Tarbuth" branch was established in Naishtot. This school was located in one building together with the Lithuanian school. It was a two-storey building with water supply, sewage and central heating. It was the only building in town boasting such conveniences.

The fifth grade of the Hebrew progymnasium 1925
In the middle the Hebrew teacher Efraim Grinberg

For nine years the Hebrew progymnasium of Naishtot existed. It was established by a former Naishtot Jew named Fain. One of the directors of the school was Dr.Shelomoh Kodesh (he died in 2000 in Israel). After the closure of the gymnasium only a few of Naishtot children studied in Hebrew high schools of the adjacent towns. Several families sent their children to the local "Kheder". Shortly before the Holocaust the local Rabbi opened a "Yeshivah Ketanah", a small yeshiva school for boys.

Pupils of the Hebrew school with teacher Shimberg

First line above from right: Zlata Manheim, Hirsh Rozenblum, Sonia Tsirkman, (seventh) Mosheh Garbarsky

Second line from right: (first) David Rotbart, (third) Miriam Zanditn, (fourth) Berl Polivansky

Third line: Hanah Levinson, teacher Shimberg, Golda Levinson

After World War I, local Jewish youth established a Yiddish library. In 1925 this library was transferred to "Libhober fun Wissen" (Fans of Knowledge) society ultimately accumulating a collection of about 1,100 books. In addition to the library the town boasted an evening school, and was known to organize literature and drama evenings, lectures and a drama group performing plays in Yiddish. The Jewish theaters of Kovno seldom visited Naishtot. Not only was there a Yiddish library but there was also a Hebrew Library, founded by the "Eretz Yisrael HaOvedeth" (Labor party) league. In the middle of the 1930s the "Hekhalutz" and "Sirkin Society" drama group was formed, which on occasion performed a light repertoire of Yiddish plays.

Through the years the majority of Naishtot young people left town settling all over the world bringing the town's cultural activities to a gradual decline. Among the Jewish population, there were only 40 subscribers to the 4 Yiddish daily newspapers published in Kovno

A group of Naishtot youth
From right: Yosef Ziman, Hirsh Rozenblum, Kalman Landau, ----, ----.

Zionist and other activities

The general political leanings among the Jewish population of Naishtot are reflected in the October 1922 elections to the first Lithuanian Seimas (Parliament). The Zionist list got 358 votes, "Akhduth" (Agudath Yisrael)-47 votes and the Democrats-2.

Almost all Zionist parties and youth organizations were represented by town branch organizations. The "HaShomer-HaTsair" branch was established in 1923 and was in operation until 1940 when it was closed by the Soviets. In 1936, this branch had about 50 members. Naishtot also had branches of "Betar", "HeKhalutz" and "Maccabi" with 124 members by the end of the 20-ties.

The results of the elections to 5 Zionist congresses (1927-1935) are presented in the table below:

Cong No.	Year	Tot Shek	Total Voters	Labor Z"S	Party Z'Z	Rev	Gen A	Zion B	Gros	Miz
15	1927	34	23	11	1	--	9	--	--	2
16	1929	51	51	29	2	--	16	--	--	4
17	1931	66	54	17	--	8	22	--	--	7
18	1933	--	245	146		49	22	--	4	24
19	1935	--	335	198		--	4	58	22	53

Key: Cong No. = Congress Number, Tot Shek = Total Shkalim, Rev = Revisionists, Gen Zion = General Zionists, Gros = Grosmanists, Miz = Mizrakhi

The soccer team

Standing from right: (second) Shulman, (third) Yosef Ziman, -----, Yisrael Ziman (?), Yitskhak Zanditn

Second line sitting: ----, ----, Hirsh Rozenblum

Third line: David Rotblat, Khayim Vilonsky, -----.

In 1934, a committee was organized with a mandate to establish a "WIZO" branch in town. A committee of 7 members and one representative of every youth organization organized fundraising for KK"L (Keren Kayemeth LeYisrael - The Jewish National Fund).

Many Jews of Naishtot were members of the "Volunteer Fire Brigade". The administrator of the Brigade was H. Rosenfeld.

Religion and Welfare

The public institutions of the Jewish Community included a magnificent Synagogue, the Beth-Midrash, the "Kloiz", the Bath House and the Mikveh. The community employed a Rabbi, two "Shokhtim" (ritual slaughterers) one of which was also the "Khazan" (Cantor). The list of Rabbis who served in Naishtot is presented in **Appendix 2.**

At the Beth Midrash and the "Kloiz", daily lessons in Talmud were offered by the "Shas" society and in Mishnah by the "Mishnayoth Society". The community also had a "Tehilim" society, "Ein Ya'akov" society, "Menorath HaMaor" society and a "Khevrah Kadisha".

For the lay out of the Jewish institutions in town see map below.

Welfare distribution was organized by "Ezrah" (Help) society, which took over most of the functions of the previous "Va'ad HaKehilah". "Ezrah" owned the building of the "Talmud-Torah", the "Hakhnasath-Orkhim" and the Bath House. Its budget came mainly from donations and from the "Aliyoth LaTorah" contributions. "Linath HaTsedek" and two "Gemiluth Khesed" societies of Naishtot were formed with the help of former Naishtot Jews of South Africa and America. These societies provided financial help to needy families. The "Bikur Kholim" society cared for the sick people. But the decrease of the Jewish population and the worsening of the economic situation halted the activities of the community organizations of Naishtot.

For a partial list of prominent personalities who were born in Naishtot, see **Appendix 3.**

During World War II and Afterwards

World War II started with the German invasion of Poland on September 1, 1939 and its fatal consequences for Lithuanian Jews in general and Naishtot's Jews in particular were to be felt several months later.

In agreement with the Ribbentrop-Molotov treaty on the division of occupied Poland, the Russians occupied the Suwalk region, but after delineation of exact borders between Russia and Germany the Suwalk region fell into German hands. The retreating Russians allowed anyone who wanted to join them to move into their occupied territory, and indeed many young people left the area together with the Russians. The Germans drove the remaining Jews out of their homes in Suwalk and its vicinity, robbed them of their possessions, then directed them to the Lithuanian border, where they were left in dire poverty. The Lithuanians did not allow them to enter Lithuania and the Germans did not allow them to return. Thus, they stayed in this swampy area in cold and rain for several weeks, until Jewish youths from the border villages smuggled them into Lithuania by various routes, with much risk to themselves. Altogether about 2,400 refugees passed through the border or infiltrated on their own, and were then dispersed in the "Suvalkiya" region. Naishtot community was obliged to accommodate and care temporarily for 100 refugees.

In June 1940 Lithuania was annexed to the Soviet Union and became a Soviet Republic. Following new rules, the 3 flour mills and the power station owned by Jews were nationalized. A number of Naishtot Jewish shops were nationalized and commissars were appointed to manage them. Supply of goods decreased and, as a result, prices soared. The middle class, mostly Jewish, bore most of the brunt, and the standard of living dropped gradually.

All the Zionist parties and youth organizations were disbanded and some of the members joined the Comsomol - the Communist Youth Organization. The Hebrew school was closed and in its place a Yiddish school opened.

In the middle of June 1941 several Jewish families were exiled into Russia as "Unreliable Elements", following the nationalization of Jewish businesses, according to rules.

In 1941 before the war there were about 3,300 people in Naishtot, 750 Jews among them.

At dawn on June 22, 1941 the German army entered Naishtot encountering no resistance. The first Jewish victims fell that same day. German soldiers shot David Glodnikov, Mordehai Levinshtein and Iser Grosman. At noon, at the municipality square, in full view of a large public, two Jewish barbers M.Lubovsky and Y.Katz were executed by shooting, after a dead German soldier was found next to their shop.

Naishtot was located on a strip of 25 km near the border with Germany subject to the order of the S.S. Einsatzgruppe Commander F. Stahlecker (he was hanged after the war by the Soviets). According to his order this strip of land had do be handed over to the S.D. from Tilzit with a special assignment to cleanse it from Jews and Communists. The commander of Tilzit S.D. handed over the assignment to the S.D. of Schirwindt who fixed the date for the annihilation of Naishtot Jews.

On June 25th all Jews were ordered to the market square. The Lithuanian mayor informed them that from that day on the Jews would work on different tasks in town: they would dig pits, clean and sweep the streets, repair roads etc. The Jews were immediately engaged to work under the supervision of Lithuanian guards who badly mistreated and humiliated them.

At the beginning of July, after the Jews returned from work, a group of armed Lithuanians led by Germans from Shirwindt, swamped the town and ordered all Jewish men, ages 14 and over to come out to the streets. From there, they were led to the municipality building. Municipality clerks stripped them of their documents, money and other valuables. Then, in groups of 50 they were led to the Jewish cemetery where fresh pits were already dug out by Soviet war prisoners. There, they were shot by both Germans and Lithuanians. Victims were forced to stand on the edge of the pit where they were shot, targeted to fall directly into the pit. The next group of victims before being shot themselves would be forced to drag and push bodies into the pit if a victim failed to fall directly into the pit. A total of 192 men, among them several Lithuanian Communists, were murdered on that fatal day.

The district governor and the mayor were both present at the murder scene. Immediately after the murders these two invited all the participants in the murders to a big party where they thanked the Germans and the Lithuanians for the action. In the days that followed Lithuanian collaborators were still looking for escapees. They caught nine men and murdered them too.

Families of the victims were told that the men were sent to Germany to work . Jewish women had to take over, and were then employed to do the same work as the men before their murder. Specific hours were fixed to buy food and to pump water from the public well.

On August 23rd 1941 women and children were whisked to a makeshift Ghetto in two shabby alleys - the synagogue alley and the bathhouse alley.

On September 16th 1941 (24 of Elul 5701) armed Lithuanians showed up in town forcing all women and children from their homes. All were ordered on to carts and transported the Parazniai forest, about 4 km away from Naishtot. Fresh pits were already dug out. Forcing victims to undress before they were shot, the Lithuanians murdered 650 Jewish women and children. One young woman refused to undress, and a killer cut her dress and stomach open.

Following the annihilation of the Jewish population , the municipality took over Jewish properties and started its allocation. Nasty squabbles began among the Lithuanians during the division process.

One family, Malkah Glik with her 4 children, managed to hide at the farm of Lithuanian peasants and survived.

Bibliography:

Yad-Vashem Archives: Koniukhovsky collection 0-71, Files 149

YIVO NY, Lithuanian Communities Collection, Files1391, 1392

Goldshtein-Golden L. Fun Kovner Ghetto biz Dachau (Form the Kovno Ghetto till Dachau) (Yiddish), New York 1985

Gotlib, Ohalei Shem, page 126

Kodesh Shelomoh, Stories from home (Hebrew), Ashdod 1994

Dos Vort (Yiddish Daily)- Kovno, 11.11.1934, 23.12.1934.

Di Yiddishe Shtime (Daily)- Kovno,17.8.1919, 26.12.1931

HaMeilitz (Hebrew)-St. Petersburg, 23.8.1880, 30.11.1880, 15.3.1881, 21.6.1881, 16.8.1881, 2.8.1881, 6.9.1881, 8.11.1881, 7.3.1882, 14.3.1882, 11.7.1882, 8.8.1882, 24.10.1882, 23.2.1883, 7.5.1883, 17.12.1883, 8.1.1884, 29.5.1884, 4.9.1885, 10.1.1887, 21.2.1887, 31.5.1888, 6.6.1889.

Folksblat (daily) (Yiddish)-Kovno, 13.4.1933, 25.5.1933, 11.8.1935. 19.8.1935, 9.9.1935, 17.9.1935, 19.9.1935, 7.6.1936.

The monument on the mass graves with the inscription in Yiddish and
Lithuanian: Here in this the Hitler murderers with their local helpers
murdered in June 1941, 1000 Jews, men, women, children.

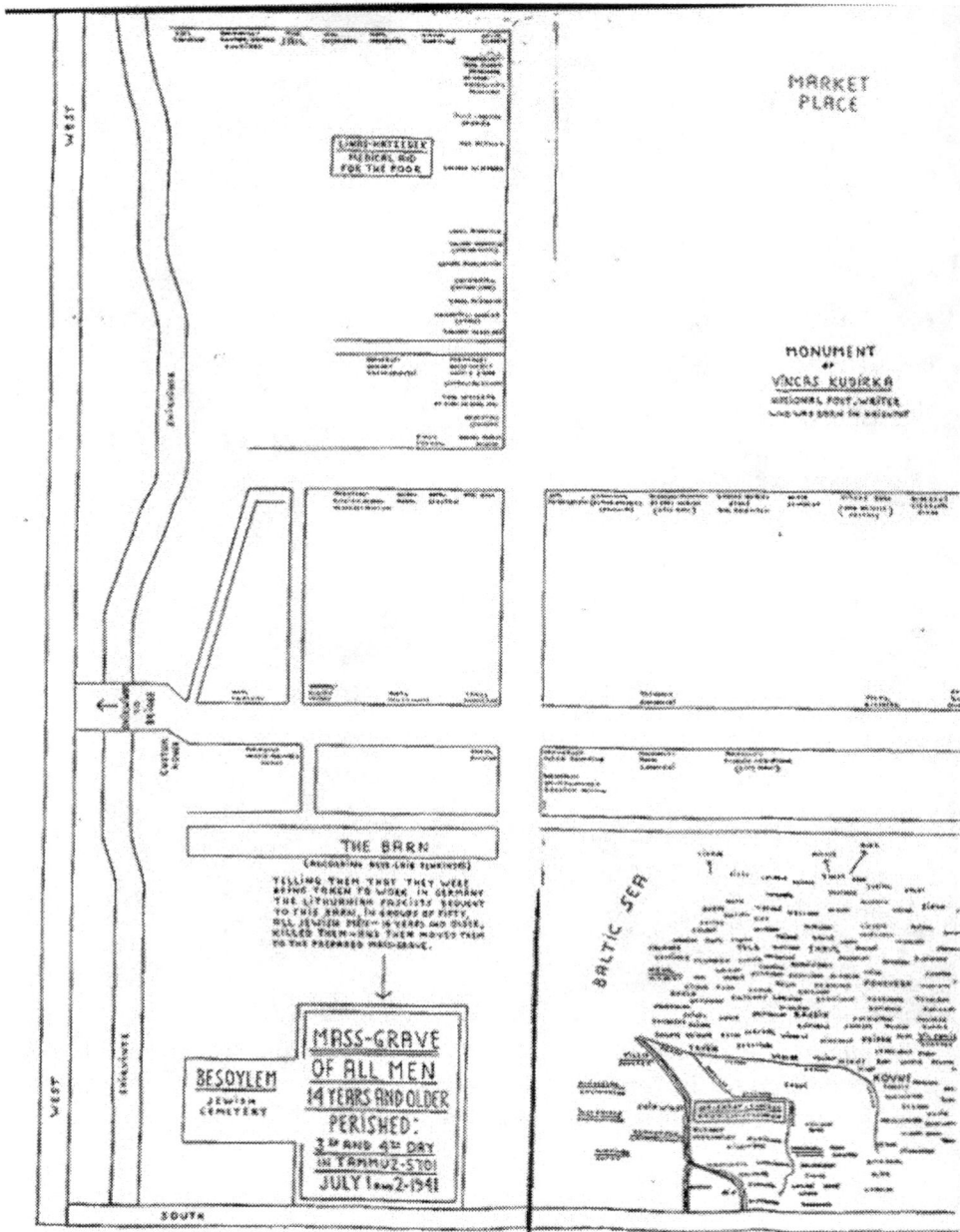

Left half of Naishtot map prepared by Ralph (Yerakhmiel) Goldberg in 1971, Chicago, Illinois, USA.

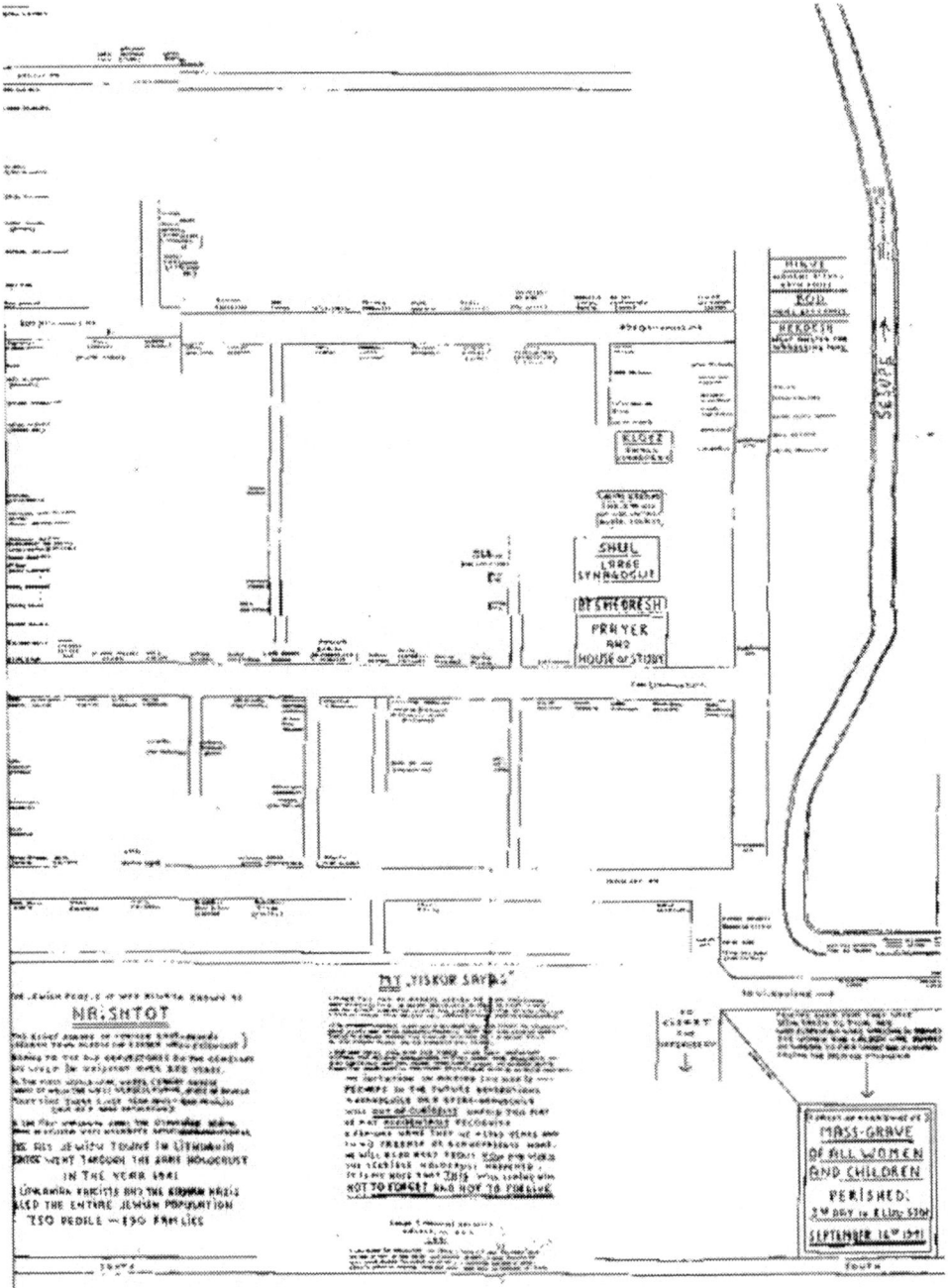

Right half of Naishtot map prepared by Ralph (Yerakhmiel) Goldberg in 1971, Chicago, Illinois, USA.

Appendix 1   PARTIAL VITAL RECORDS FOR VLADISLAVOV
(supplied by Hildy Sanders)

The death record of Rakhama Meyshtovski, 35 years old, daughter of Hilel Bromberg and Khaia;

The birth records of Tamara, Shmul, Beila and the death record of Tamara, children of Mikhel : Meyshtovski and Sora -4 records for 1856- 1865;

-The birth record of Sofa, daughter of Mikhel ben Itsek Meyshtovski and Ester, maiden name Leiman; -The death record of Jankel-Josel, 75 years old, son of Mikhel and Sora; - The birth record of Meier, son of Berel Meyshtovski and Khana;

-The birth records of Khaim, Shloma, Sheina and the death record of Etka, children of Eliash Meyshtovski and Pesha -4 records for 1844 -1864;

-The death record of Eliash ben Eliash Meyshtovski, 59 years old, he left wife Pesha, maiden name Iundelski;

-The marriage record of Khaim Meyshtovski, son of Eliash and Pesh~ and Khana Bartelshtein, daughter of Gersh and Tsypa;

-The birth record of Sheina, daughter of Eliash Meyshtovski and Khana; -The birth record of Feiga, daughter of Eliash Meyshtovski and Tsypa;

-The birth records of Sora and Khaia and the death record of Sofa, daughters of Eliash Meyshtovski and Etka -3 records for 1844 -1846;

-The death record of Estera Meyshtovski, 19 years old, daughter of Nokhim and Leia; -The birth record of Zundel, son of Haushel Meishtovski and Rokha;

-The marriage record of Zundel Meyshtovski (son of Haushel and Rokha) and Sora-Ienta Oppengeim (daughter of Gershon and Tsirlia) and the birth records of their children -Tsypa (birth and death records), Khava-Etel and Tsirlia -5 records for 1861- 1882; Note: in one record surname is Mistovski;

-The birth records of Dvera, Sofa, David and the death records of David and Leizer, children of Ovsei or Govsei Meyshtovski and Khaia -5 records for 1844 -1852;

-The death record of Ovsei Meyshtovski, 50 years old, he left wife Khaia-Rokha and 4 children; -The birth record of Leia, daughter of Hovsei? Meyshtovski and Basha;

-The death record of Estera, 3 years old, daughter of Gersh Meyshtovski and Ienta;

-The death record of Estera, 3 years old, daughter of Iankel Meyshtovski and Rokha; -The birth record of Shmuel, son of Meier-Movsha Meyshtovski and Pesa;

-The death record of Mina-Leia, 6 years old, daughter of Shloma Meyshtovski and Zlata; -The birth and death records of Josel, son of Khaim Meyshtovski and Cherna -2 records;

-The death record of Cherna Meyshtovski, 26 years old, daughter of Leiba Meierovich and Khaia; -The marriage record of Khayin Meyshtovski, son of David and Sora and Estera Mikhalovich, daughter of Gersh and Leia; .

-The marriage record of Tankhel Meyshtovski, son of Abel and Sora, and Basha Grossman, daughter of Kushel and Khena;

-The birth record of Khaia-Mariasha and the death record of Shmul, children of Abel Ben Berel Meyshtovski and Sora -2 records;

-The death record of Nokhim Blokh, 3 years old, son of Abram and Leba;

-The death record of Volf Blokh 42 years old, son of Shimel and Leia;

-The marriage record of Meier Sapiro (son of Khatskel ben Meier and Ienta) and Cherna-Riva Blokh (daughter of Gersh and Sora);

-The birth records of Mirka, Zalman, Volr, Leia, Temka, Nakhrnan and the death records of Zalman, Volf and Leia, children of Shmuel Blokh and Rokha - 9 records for 1846 -1861;

-The marriage record of Gershel? Lurie (son of Meier and Sincea?) and Rokha Blokh daughter- of Shmuel and Ienta.

The marriage record of Volf Grossman (son of Kushel and Khena) and Hinda Meyshtovski (daughter of Abel and Sora);

-The birth records of Shmuila Josel, Khatskel Ovsei and the death records of Shmuila and Orka, sons of Itsek Meyshtovski and Feiga, maiden name Belmon -6 records for 1844 -1869;

-The birth records of Yankel and Khaim and the death record of Iankel, sons of Josel Meyshtovski and Rokha or Rokhama -3 records for 1845- 1848~

-The death record of Berel Meyshtovski, 75 years old, son of Abram and Mariasha;

-The birth record of Khaika-Dobra, daughter of Berel-Abram Meyshtovski;

-The death record of Josel-Mordukh ben Borukh, 80 years old;

-The birth record of Leiba, son of Khaim-Gersh Meyshtovski and Feiga;

-The death record of Iokhevet, daughter of Khaim Meyshtovski and Feiga, maiden name Rotshtein;

-The birth record of Mina, daughter of Kusel-Motel Meyshtovski and Sora-Ienta;

The birth records of Iankel Mina-Leia, Abram-Berka and Tsirlia, children of Shloma-Leizer, Meyshtovski and Zlata, maiden name Vidgerski -4 records for 1864 -1882;

-The birth record of Eliash, son of Itsek Meyshtovski and Perla;

-The death record of Leiba Meyshtovski, 30 years old, son of Mikhel? And Mina;

The birth records of Matla, Shmuila, Rokha and the death records of Josel and Shmuila, children of Leiba Meyshtovski and Tamara- 5 records for 1837-1852;

-The marriage record of Israel Meyshtovski (son of Volf and Pesha) and Rokhama Bromberg (daughter of Hilel and Hinda);

-The death record of Movsha, son of Leiba Meyshtovski and Khaia, 11 years old;

-The birth record of Mina-Ienta and the death record of Riva, daughters of Berko or Berel Meyshtovski and Khava, maiden name Kleperman -2 records;

-The marriage record of Mortkhel-Leiba Roginski (son of Nokhman and Leba) and Khana Meystovski (daughter of Berko and Khava-Ester, maiden name Klein);

-The birth record of Shlioma son of Bentsion Meyshtovski and Khana, maiden name Bartomshtein;

-The death record of Sora Meyshtovski, 45 years old (daughter of Leiser and Feiga Zilberrnan);

-The death record of Khaia Meyshtovski, 57 years old (daughter of Leiba and Freida Abramovich);

-The death record of Eliash-Leiba Meyshtovski, 40 years old, widower;

-The death record of Feiga Meyshtovski, 72 years old, widow;

-The death record of Tsyria Meyshtovski, 80 years old;

-The death record of Gitla Meyshtovski, 70 years old;

-The marriage record of Leiba ben Berel Blekh since Sudargas (son of Berel and Mera, maiden name Bliokh) and Estera bat Leiba Liutinski (daughter of Leiba and Khana, maiden name Liutinski);

-The birth records of Meier, Shimel and Berel, sons of Khonel Blokh and Ester- 3 records for 1845 - 1851;

-The death record of Khonel Blokh, 47 years old;

-The birth records of Khiena, Sora-Leia, Khana, Khonel, Khiena and the death records of Sora and Khan, children of Iankel-Movsha ben Khonel Blokh and Itta, maiden name Sredvigovski or Shedvigovski -7 records for 1857- 1874;

-The birth records of Shmul, Gersh and Iankel, sons of Volf-Shimel Blokh and Gitla bat Vulf -3 records for 1825- 1833;

-The death record of Iz1a Blokh, 58 years old, daughter of Leiba and Pesha;

-The birth records of Khana, Leia, Khiena, Estera-Riva, Nekhama and the death records of Khana and Leia, children of Gersh Blokh and Khaia-Reiza -7 records for 1848- 1864;

-The birth records of Khana-Tsipa, Shimel, Iankel and Leiba, sons of Iankel Blokh and Mera-Golda, maiden name Trepuk -4 records for 1854 -1870;

-The marriage record of Iankel Blokh (son of Volf and Gitla) and Reina Okhron (daughter of Volf and Khaia);

-The death record of Raina Blokh, 26 years old, wife of Iankel;

-The marriage record of Efroim Gelberg (son of Leizer and Dveira) and Etla Blokh, widow (daughter of Movsha and Khana);

-The death record of Riva Blokh, 8 years old, daughter of Girsh and Dvora;

Appendix 2   Partial list of Rabbis who served in Naishtot

Aba Dayan in Naishtot 1740-1752

Menakhem-Nakhum Kharif died 1820

Aba Abelson at the beginning of the 19 th century

Nathan Shtern died 1844

Aryeh-Leib Broido

Eliyahu-Yehudah Daikhes (1816-1856 in Jerusalem)

Betsalel Hacohen in Naishtot 1860-1868, the year of his death

Yisrael-Khayim Daikhes (1851-1937 in Leeds, UK)

Yekhezkel Volpert served in Naishtot for several years after1901

Shemuel Gokhberg (1877-?)

Sender Vilensky

Nekhemyah Fortman born in Naishtot in 1883, murdered together with the community in 1941

Appendix 3
Partial list of prominent personalities born in Naishtot
Yosef Zekharyah Shtern (1831-1904) for 43 years Rabbi in Shavl

Shelomo Pukher (1833-1899) since 1859 state appointed Rabbi in Mitava (Latvia) and since 1893- in Riga. Established a "Talmud-Torah" and a school for girls in Mitava. Teacher of religion for Jewish students in the local high school. Struggled against the Christian "Mission".

Mosheh-Yehoshua Rabinovitz, one of the leading personalities of the Vilna Jewish community at the first half of the 19 th century.

Harry Lois Rozental, born in Naishtot in 1860, educated in Manchester, returned to Naishtot and became a merchant, studied Hebrew and wrote a book "Sod Kedoshim" (Manchester, 1895), explanation about the prophecies of Daniel.

Yeshayahu Volgemut died in1898, for 44 years Rabbi in Memel.

Eliyahu Te'omim Rabbi in Manchester

Aryeh-Leib Blumental Talmudist and mathematician

Gordon Dr. (1874-1943) since1892 in America, exerted significant influence on the Jewish education in USA, died in Minneapolis.

Avraham Hershman (1880-1959) Rabbi in Detroit

Mordehai Bobtelsky (1889-1965) since 1925 Professor of chemistry at the Hebrew University in Jerusalem, one of the first researchers of the Dead Sea, published many research works in English and French scientific publications, died in Jerusalem

Aba-Hilel Silver (1893-1964) reformed Rabbi, one of the leaders of American Jewry

Max Band (1900-1974) known painter, Band studied at the Berlin Academy. He authored "History of Contemporary Art" in 1935. In 1940 he settled in Hollywood and lived there until his death in November 1974. His paintings are exhibited in many museums in USA and Israel.

Tsevi-Hirsh Bernshtein (1846-1907) since 1870 in NY, one of the pioneers of the Yiddish and Hebrew press in America.

Adolf-Mosheh Radin (1848-1909), Rabiner in Kinfin (Prussia), since 1884 in America, very active in helping Jewish immigrants from Russia.

Ya'akov Ter (1861-1935) since 1891 in America, published many plays and historical operettas in Yiddish performed at the Jewish theaters, wrote stories, dramas and anecdotes in the Jewish press in NY.

Yisrael-Iser Goldblum (1863-1925) lived in Paris since 1886, researcher of old Hebrew manuscripts at the great libraries of Europe, published scientific articles on this topics in the Hebrew press, published 2 books, signed his articles with pseudonym YIP"Z.

Herman Bernshtein (1876-1935) since 1893 in America, was for a short time the American ambassador in Albania, establisher and first redactor of the Yiddish daily newspaper "Der Tog", though he himself didn't write in Yiddish, he translated into English many books of Tolstoy, Chekhov, Gorki and others, published a book "The Truth about the Protocols of Zion" proving the lies about the Jewish people.

Shemuel Talpiyoth (1877-1951) since 1894 in Montreal (Canada), one of the founders of Zionist Organization in Canada, published many articles about Judaism, Jewish history etc. in the Yiddish, Hebrew and Jewish-English newspapers.

Shelomo-Yosef Herberg (1884-----) since 1920 in Eretz-Yisrael, published stories and poems in the Hebrew periodicals, translated 40 books since German, Russian and Yiddish into Hebrew, among them books of Gorki, Dostoyevsky and others.

Efrayim Grinberg (1895-1942) teacher and journalist, one of the leaders of the Z"S party in Lithuania, redactor of the daily newspaper "Dos Vort", arrested by the Soviets in 1940, escaped to Russia in 1941 and died there of hunger in 1942.

Kalman Landau (1912---), Chem. Eng., since 1935 in Mexico, published articles about politics, literature and art in the Yiddish press, since 1947 redactor of the local newspaper "Dos Vort".

Tsemakh Feldshtein Dr. (1885-1945) studied in Berlin and Bern History and Philosophy, director of the Hebrew high school in Vilkovishk and since 1922 till1940 director of the "Reali" Hebrew high school in Kovno. Active in the Hebrew and Zionist movement and in the Historic-Ethnographic Society of Lithuanian Jewry. A brilliant orator and journalist. During the Soviet rule (1940-1941) teacher of Russian at the Vilna high school. Active in the cultural life in the Vilna Ghetto. editor of the "Ghetto News". Perished in Dautmergen camp in Germany.

Zalman Lubovsky-Libai Dr., writer and educator, director of the Hebrew high school in Mariampol (till 1935, prior to emigrating to Israel)

Yisrael Ziman, member of the Ruling Council of "HaShomer HaTsair" youth organization in Lithuania, member of Kibbutz "Ma'anith" in Israel, later Head of the department active in searching for missing relatives of the Jewish Agency in Jerusalem. ("HaMador lekhipus kerovim")

Appendix 4   Naishtot correspondents who wrote in "HaMeilitz"

Hayim-Ze'ev Sudavsky,

Alexander Fridman,

Aba Valershtein,

Yosef-Tsevi Valberg,

Shimon-Ze'ev Natelzon,

Yekhiel-Sheftl Rabinovitz

Kybartai (Kibart)

The Book of Remembrance of the Jewish Community of Kibart, Lithuania

Written in Hebrew and translated

into English by Josef Rosin

Edited by Sarah and Mordehai Kopfstein

Originally Published by the Association of former Kibart citizens

Haifa, 1988

The English edition July 1998

Second updated edition July 2003

Remarks to the Kibart Book

Even before my retirement, the idea of commemorating in writing the Jewish Community of my hometown Kibart crystallized in my mind. With the encouragement and help of my long-time friend Dr. (now Prof.) Dov Levin from the History Faculty of the Hebrew University in Jerusalem this idea was realized; for this I thank him profoundly.

I would also like to thank my childhood friends, Peretz Kliatchko and David Shadkhanovitz, who contributed a part of this book and also helped to refresh my memory on different items of life in Kibart.

I also thank the former Kibart natives with whom I have spoken about our common past and those who gave me the photos for this book.

Finally, I would like to thank the members of the executive of the former Kibart natives, David Shadkhanovitz and Zisl Kovensky, who published this book in Hebrew in 1988.

J.R.

Addition to the English translation:

I thank my friends Sarah and Mordehai Kopfstein for their help in translating this book into English.

Remarks to the updated edition:

All the Yiddish and Hebrew names were transliterated anew according to the rules issued by YIVO for this purpose.

There are informative additions and more pictures I managed to gather during the 14 years from the first publication of the Hebrew edition of this book.

Preface

The town Kybartai in Lithuania is situated about 100 km. (62 miles) south-west from Kovno (Kaunas) beside the St. Petersburg-Berlin railway where it crosses the pre-World War II border with East Prussia that was a part of Germany. (*Kibart* is the Yiddish name and will be used throughout the book, whereas the Lithuanian name is *Kybartai* and is the name found on maps and most literature. Kibart is used because this is the name used by the Jewish people, about whom this book is written.)

The history of the Jewish community in Kibart is linked and tightly related to the history of the town itself. The first Jews settled in town with the establishment of the railway station and the customs station on the middle of the 1860s. From then all the changes the town went through were reflected in the life of the Jewish Community.

We can divide the history of the Jewish community in Kibart into the following periods:

A. 1865-1915 - From setting up of the railway station until World War I

B. 1915-1919 - German occupation

C. 1919-1923 - Establishment of the independent Lithuanian State and the increased prosperity of the town

D. 1923-1933 - Ten stable years until the accession of the Nazis in neighboring Germany

E. 1933-1940 - Years of the town's decline

F. 1940-1941 - One year of Soviet rule

G. 1941 - The German Occupation and Destruction of the Jewish community

H. Postscript

J. Appendices

A. 1 8 6 5 - 1 9 1 5

The history of the town and its demographic and economic development

During this period Kibart (Kybartai) was situated on the Russian (Lithuanian) side of the border with Germany (East Prussia). The small stream Liepona - its width was only 4 to 5 meters (about 13 to 16 feet)- was the border between the Empires of Russia and Germany before World War I, and remained the border between Germany and the independent state of Lithuania, which was established after World War I. Kibart did not exist before the construction of the railway from St. Petersburg to the German border, which occurred in about 1865. The site on which Kibart was built was a small village through which the main road to Germany passed. The army of Napoleon used that road during the invasion of Russia. The French soldiers who died in battle were buried in the sand hills about one km from the road.

Kybartai 2004

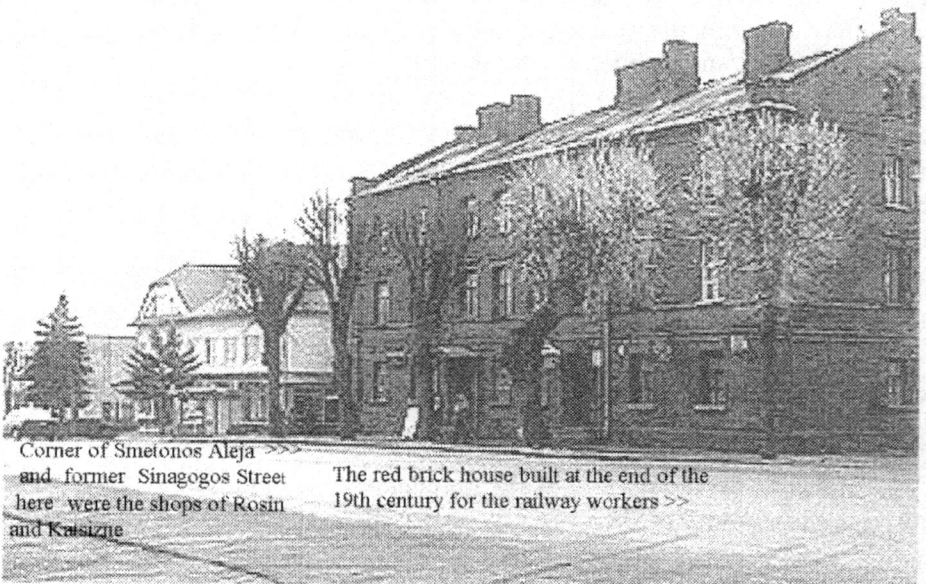

Corner of Smetonos Aleja >>
and former Sinagogos Street
here were the shops of Rosin
and Kalsizie

The red brick house built at the end of the
19th century for the railway workers >>

(Picture taken and supplied by Vytautas Mickevicius)

Corner of Smetonos Aleja and former Sinagogos Street, site of the Rosin Shop

The entire quarter between the former streets Sinagogos, Algimanto and Zydu do not exist anymore. It was destroyed during the retreat of the German army in 1944.

On the left side of the road, near the border, there was a building which served as the stables for the post horses and it also as a station for changing the horses. On the river there was a wooden bridge and on both sides of it were situated the customs station of Russia and Germany. A few farms existed along the right bank of the Liepona and one of them belonged to a farmer named Kybartas and hence the name of the town is derived from his name.

As most of the stations that were built along the railway at some distance from the towns and cities beside which it passed, also the railway station constructed in the Kibart was named Verzhbolova (Virbalis in Lithuanian), after the name of the small town established in the eighteenth century and situated 4.5 km away from this station's site. During the period of independent Lithuania (1918-1940) and until 1965, the station was called Virbalis. Eventually the name of the station was changed to Kybartai.

During the battle of retreat of the German Army in 1944, the luxurious terminal of the station was totally destroyed together with several residences of the town.

The size of the station was out of proportion to the size of Kybartai or Virbalis. It consisted of a large terminal with rooms for passengers, for customs, a luxury restaurant, a water tower, a power station as well as many rail tracks and workshops. In one corner of the station there was a long one story building, which, according to rumors, housed the train of the Russian Czars used for their trips abroad. Near the station there was a public garden called the "Railway Garden," with large trees, paths and benches. In the middle of this garden there was a raised platform with a balcony for an orchestra. At its foot there was a dance floor, which was turned into an ice skating rink in winter. There was also a small building with a primitive bowling alley. Wooden balls of different sizes were used.

Near the station some red brick buildings were built as residences for the railway workers and their families. Different craftsmen started to settle in the town and then shops and pubs opened.

Due to the construction of the Russian railway and its connection to the European network, a large portion of the Russian import and export trade passed through Kibart. As a result there was a great need for customs clerks ("Expediters" as they were called then). Many offices were opened in Eydtkuhnen, the small town on the German side of the border, because there were no suitable buildings in Kibart. Most of the "Expediters" were Jews who came from the border zones of Russia-Austria and Russia-Germany, and also from Poland. When the suitable conditions were created, these people started to settle in Kibart. The border attracted many other people who came to live in Kibart.

All of these people, including the railway workers, needed housing, food etc. So after some years, Kibart grew from a tiny village to a small town, which overtook the older nearby village of Virbalis in the number of its habitants and importance.

Old Rail Station at Kibart - Destroyed in 1944

Border Crossing at Kibart

In 1897 there were in Kibart 1,182 habitants, Lithuanians, Germans and Russians and among them 533 Jews, or 45% of the population.

Five passenger trains passed through the station every day in both directions with hundreds of passengers and two cargo trains with hundreds of rail cars each in which timber, poultry, grain, leather, seeds etc. were exported from Russia to Germany and from Germany were imported machines, chemicals, paints, haberdashery and cloth. To facilitate this process, hundreds of customs clerks, railway and post workers were needed. Tens of the "Expediters" offices with hundreds of clerks and workers were occupied from the morning until the evening in checking and packing all those goods in the packing houses of the customs.

Because of the great importance of the Werzhbolowa station and its customs, the manager of the customs had to be highly educated and with the rank of a general.

The other high officials too, like the engineers and the chemists, required academic education. The required education grade was according to the grade of the position.

A very important position was that of the commander of the gendarmerie in the station. Because of the heavy traffic across the border and because often important people of the kingdom such as ministers, familiars of the king's family and even the Czar himself went through this station, it was important that the commander of the gendarmerie had to be an intelligent and reliable man. People in Kibart remembered the commander Myasoyedow, who was a loyal man and treated decently and equally all the people, regardless of their social or national status.

Before World War I he was suspected of spying for Germany and was sentenced to hanging together with a local Jew named Freidberg. People gossiped that "the Jew was hanged only for balance."

The "Declarants" had a special and respected status. They were clerks in the "Expediters" offices who specialized in the Russian customs laws and knew how to assess the different goods according to the proper paragraph in the law that indicates which the dues were collected. They also knew how to associate with the high officials, to drink together, to play cards and a little "Hutzpah" also didn't harm. The salary of the "Declarants" was not less then those of high officials and reached 150-250 Ruble a month except other incomes. For comparison: a qualified worker earned 25-60 Rubles each month and female workers in socking factories earned 8-10 Rubles.

The first "Declarants" who arrived in Kibart came from the border zones between Russia and Germany and Russia-Austria and also from Poland. Most of them were Jews and experienced. Later young local men joined that profession who with "proper connections" managed to be accepted in an "Expediters" office. The "Declarant" profession was the ambition of many young men.

At the border crossing there was a continuous traffic from six in the morning until nine in the evening. There was also passport and customs inspection.

According to the commercial treaty between Russia and Germany, the habitants of the towns in the border zone like Kibart, Werzhbolowa from the Russian side and Eydtkuhnen from the German side could cross the border with special certificates, buy different goods (up to a limited sum) and return with them to the other side. So Germans from Eydtkuhnen could buy food products in Kibart and cross the border without paying duty on 3.5 kg (8 lb.) of flour, 2.5 kg (5.5 lb.) of meat, eggs, butter, cheese, fruits and vegetables. As a result of this arrangement many shops that sold food products were opened by Jews beside the border. On Tuesdays and Fridays, when markets took place in Kibart, crowds of German women were waiting near the border before it opened in order to get to the market before the Kibart habitants.

In Eydtkuhnen the habitants of Kibart would buy cloth, haberdashery, shoes, imported fruits from the warm lands like citrus fruits, grapes, water melons etc., some for themselves and some to sell.

It's worthwhile to mention two other ways some Jews earned their living: smuggling of goods and "smuggling" of emigrants. The goods on which the duty was very high were passed over the river or through the border passage or by train and sold in Lithuania with great profit. Among those goods were silk cloth, silver and gold watches, different cutlery, etc.

More significant was the role of the smuggling emigrants. At the end of the nineteenth and the beginning of the twentieth century many Russian Jews who lived in the "Tekhum haMoshav" (the special zones were Jews were allowed to live) emigrated to the USA. In order to emigrate legally a passport was needed whose cost not including other expenses was 25 Rubles, the price of half the ship ticket. Many people didn't have the money to pay such a sum or could not get a passport for different reasons, therefore they had to leave Russia illegally. As a result of this, groups of "smugglers" organized along the border who for 5, 6, or 10 Rubles would take the emigrants across the border. They had agents in many towns who would recruit the "clients". Such a group existed also in Kibart, because the conditions there were suitable. The small river Liepona, whose width in some places was not more the 2-3 meters, was watched by the Russian Border Guard and for a bribe of half a Ruble per person to the soldier guarding the border and something to the sergeant who would arrange the guard and something more to the officer in duty, everything became arranged. There were years that every day tens of emigrants would arrive in the town. They were accommodated in private houses or in the villages in the surroundings and when suitable conditions was formed, they would be taken across the border. In Eydtkuhnen they would be collected and accommodated in special hostels or in the barracks of "The Hamburg-America Ship Company". There a doctor would check them for eye diseases or other infectious diseases and the healthy would be transferred by the travel agents through the ports Hamburg, Bremen, Rotterdam and Antwerp and then to America.

But everything not always went well. Because of unforeseen mishaps with the guards, the emigrants would be caught in the fields near the Liepona and be sent back crying by the "etap" to the places where from they came. The "etap" is a Russian word that means transfer of prisoners to their final destination through very many jails on the way. The prisoner would be kept in the jail until more prisoners would be gathered for transferring many to the next jail and so on and so on.

There were also cases in which the "smugglers" would extract fraudulently from the emigrant different things or would keep him in the hostel for more time then needed in order to extort more money from him. Sometimes they would keep in the hostel a young woman or a pretty young woman which the smuggler or one of his helpers found appealing. There were also cases of actual murder. It is known that a trial took place in Germany at the beginning of this century in which a smuggler was sentenced to death for robbing and murdering a Jewish emigrant and his helper sentenced to a long jail term.

Thousands of Jews who arrived to America with the help of these smugglers, remembered them with favor, in spite of the fact that they were not always treated properly.

The Cultural and Social Life until World War I

With the improvement of the economic condition in town, its habitants started to concern themselves with culture and education. In 1910 were in Kibart about 5,000 habitants and among them about 1,000 Jews. The habitants were composed of different nationalities: Russians, Germans, Poles, Lithuanians, Jews and several Tartars. For Russians, Lithuanians and Poles with limited means a school consisting of two classes was opened. Wealthier people sent their children to the high schools in the bigger cities. The Germans in Kibart had an elementary school with Russian as the language of instruction and only the Evangelic faith was taught in German. The Jews had a school with a Jewish teacher for teaching the Russian language. Additionally there were three "khadarim" with "melamdim" (teachers) who taught Hebrew, "Khumash" (Pentateuch) with "Rashi's" commentary and the Bible with the Yiddish explanation. In those "Khadarim" the children learned from early in the morning until evening. Later a few "Improved Khadarim" were added that were more modern and in which several general subjects were taught.

The wealthier Jews and these who wanted to be associated with the intelligentsia and aristocracy sent their children, mainly the girls, to the German schools in Eydtkuhnen. Many Jewish girls studied there and after they became mothers they sent their daughters to the same schools. The German language was then the language of the aristocracy and even new people who came to the town, wanting not to be backward, began to "Germanize"' their Yiddish. The "Declarants," who were a subject of imitation, contributed much to the distribution of the German language. They really needed to use this language in their work at the "Expediters" offices. These who came from Poland with their Polish, didn't want to "lower" themselves to Yiddish and made great efforts to speak German. They came from assimilative circles and all their Judaism amounted to a visit in the synagogue on "Rosh Hashanah" and "Yom Kippur" and in buying "Matsoth" for "Pesakh".

In 1880 the Jewish Community obtained permission to open a Jewish Elementary School, but without any help from the government. "The Association for Spreading Knowledge Among the Jews" supported it with 150 Rubles. The teacher in that school was H. Melamed.

In those years there were no needy people among the habitants of the town, nevertheless a charity existed, "Tsedakah Gedolah," that helped passers by and strangers.

In four lists of donors "For the Hungry in Lithuania" in the years 1872 and 1874 published in the Hebrew newspaper "HaMeilitz", many Kibart Jews are mentioned. At a list published in the Hebrew newspaper "HaMagid" in 1872 there were 36 names of Kibart Jews who donated money for Persian Famine (See Appendix 1)

The fundraisers in Kibart were: Jehoshua-David Fridman, the brothers Grodzensky, Avraham-Yitzhak Goldberg, Tsevi Shidarsky.

In spite of the fact that most of the Jews in Kibart were not devout, there were two places in the town for praying, because of rivalry between two groups.

In "The Central Archives for the History of the Jewish People" in Jerusalem we discovered a document from 1903 (7th of Elul *5663)*, written in Hebrew, concerning a donation of Dov ben Avraham Freidberg and his wife Gitl, for erecting a tablet in the Kibart synagogue. M.Mebel and A.Gasman, artists from Vilna, engraved the "Ten Commandments" on that tablet, including several written sentences from the prayers as well as the prayer for the health of Czar Nikolai, his wife Czarina Alexandra and their children. (See table 20 below).

The Jews didn't have a cemetery in town and they would bury their dead in the nearby town Verzhbolova (Virbalis). Only in 1912 a "Hevrah Kadisha" was established in Kibart and it bought or obtained a parcel for a cemetery outside the town. The initiator and organizer was Yitshak Shraga Khashman. The first tombstones at the Kibart cemetery date from 1912, as friends of the author Dov Shtern and Perets Kliatchko confirmed on their visit there at 1970.

The Catholics and the Lutherans also didn't have churches and cemeteries in Kibart. The Catholics would pray and bury their dead in Vershbolova (Virbalis). The Lutherans did the same, however they had the choice to pray in Eydtkuhnen. Only the Russians had a church and a cemetery in Kibart near the railway station.

In 1905 there were revolutionary events in Russia and their resonance reached Kibart too. In Verzhbolova there were a few hundred Jewish workers in the brush factories who were organized by the "Bund" (Jewish anti-Zionist workers organization). "Poalei Zion," (Zionist workers organization) etc. The Kibart revolutionaries got in touch with those from Verzhbolova and they acted together in bringing in illegal literature from abroad or smuggling out a political emigrant through the border, but their main activity was cultural. It expressed itself in organizing theater performances in Yiddish.

Table 20

עשרת הדברים

I אנכי ה'	VI לא תרצח
II לא יהיה	VII לא תנאף
III לא תשא	VIII לא תגנב
IV זכור את	IX לא תענה
V כבד את	X לא תחמוד

עץ חיים היא למחזיקים בה ותומכיה מאשר

קומו אורו כי בא אורך וכבוד ה' עליך זרח.

הללויה, הללו אל בקדשו הללוהו ברקיע עזו. הללוהו בגבורותיו הללוהו כרב גדלו. הללוהו בתקע שופר הללוהו בנבל וכנור הללוהו בתף ומחול הללוהו במנים ועגב הללוהו בצלצלי שמע הללוהו בצלצלי תרועה כל הנשמה תהלל יה הללויה.

חג השבועות. חג הבכורים.

תורה נביאים וכתובים.

נעשה ע"י [illegible]

[illegible]

[illegible]

תפלה בעד הקיסר יר"ה

הנותן תשועה למלכים וממשלה לנסיכים מלכותו מלכות כל עולמים הפוצה את דוד עבדו מחרב רעה הנותן בים דרך ובמים עזים נתיבה הוא יברך וישמור וינצור ויעזור וירומם ויגדל וינשא למעלה את אדוננו הקיסר ניקולאי [illegible] עם [illegible] הקיסרית [illegible] ירום הודם.

מלך מלכי המלכים ברחמיו יחייהו וישמרהו [illegible] יצילהו [illegible]

מלך מלכי המלכים ברחמיו יתן בלבו ובלב [illegible]

[illegible] בימיו ובימינו תושע יהודה וישראל ישכון לבטח.

ובא לציון גואל וכן יהי רצון ונאמר אמן.

[illegible]

[illegible]

The actors were amateurs and the shows took place in Kibart where a suitable hall and also a public of means existed. The plays were from Yakov Gordin, Shalom Aleikhem, Peretz Hirshbein, David Pinsky and others. The Kibart "aristocracy," who at first didn't attend these plays, got slowly became accustomed to them and even started to enjoy them.

Many Kibart Jews were mentioned in lists of donors for the "Settlement of Eretz-Israel" of the years 1898-1899. The fundraiser was A. Landman.

The Zionist activity in Kibart began before the third Zionist Congress in 1899. In summer of this year a gathering of the Zionist Organizations from the regions (Gubernia) of Lithuania: Kovno, Suwalk, Grodna and Vilna (Kybartai belonged to the Suwalk Gubernia) took place in Vilna. 71 delegates from 51 cities and towns of Lithuania and among them a delegate from Kibart came to this gathering. With the establishment of the "Jewish National Fund" (KKL), the local Zionist organizations began to actively collect for this fund. They distributed the KKL stamps and arranged parties whose income was dedicated for this fund. Many local organizations recorded themselves in "The Golden Book" of the fund as did wealthy people who recorded themselves or their relatives on the occasion of important events in the family. At this time the Blue-White Box of the Fund started to be placed in every Jewish home. The distribution of the KKL stamps to all Russia was organized Shimon Yekhiel Goldberg from Kibart. He was born in 1873 in Kibart, died in 1940 in Tel-Aviv. From 1925 in Eretz-Yisrael, he was the secretary of the known Zionist leader Rabbi Shemuel Mohliver. Goldberg established several settlement companies "Menukhah VeNakhalah", "Ge'ulah" and "Akhvah".

Kibart was apparently one of six towns in Lithuania that voted for the known Zionist activist J. Nisnbaum to be elected as a delegate to the ninth Zionist Congress.

In 1903 Dr. Herzl went to Moscow to meet the Russian Prime Minister Pleve and to explain to him the task of Zionism. On his way back to Vienna he passed through Kibart by train and when the train stopped in Eydtkuhnen, a group of Zionists waited there in order to congratulate him. There was also a photographer from Kibart who wanted to take a picture of Herzl together with the group, but Herzl didn't allow him to do so. At the same year, after the Sixth Zionist Congress, Herzl sent with the known Zionist activist Y.L. Goldberg from Vilna, 25 Rubles to the photographer from Kibart as a compensation for the loss which may have been caused to him.

The famous personalities from this period who were born in Kibart were the painters Yitzhak Levitan and Yakov Mesenblum, the actor and poet Rekhavyahu Mogiluker and the public worker and journalist Avraham Finkelstein.

Y. Mesenblum was born in 1895 and died in 1933 in Kovno. He painted the Jewish milieu on the background of the Lithuanian landscape. His widow, the actress Karnovsky, collected his pictures together, but all were lost together with her in the destruction of the Kovno Ghetto.

R. Mogiluker was born in Kibart in 1913, he was a member of the Hebrew Dramatic Studio in Kovno, from 1946 in Los Angeles, published poems in the Yiddish press in Kovno, Warsaw and Paris, died in Israel.

Statue of Yitzhak Levitan and on a Soviet stamp

(Picture taken and supplied by Vytautas Mickevicius)

Y. Levitan was born in 1860 and at young age moved with his parents to Moscow. He painted more then 1,000 pictures during his life time and was considered as one of the greatest landscape painters of Russia. Most of his pictures are in museums in Russia and a few of them are in "The Israel Museum" in Jerusalem. He died in 1900 from Tuberculosis. In 1977 a statue of Levitan made by the sculptor B. Vysniauskas was erected in a public park in Kibart.

Avraham Finkelstein, from 1923 in Mexico, was a member in the Council of Mexican Jewry, published articles on theater in the Mexican Yiddish press, died in 1964.

B: 1 9 1 5 - 1 9 1 9   Under the German Occupation

At the beginning of the year 1914 Kibart was already in a stable state. At the years before the war a few more exporters of poultry and cattle started businesses in the town, a Bank for mutual aid was established and a branch of the great Russian Bank "Azov-Don" was established in its modern new building.

By 1914 Kibart had a population of about 6,000 inhabitants, including about 1,000 Jews, who enjoyed a relatively high standard of living. All these cultural and economic achievements were destroyed all at once with the beginning of World War I. When the general mobilization was proclaimed in July 1914, many people began to leave the town. Most of Kibart's Russian officials and Jewish population left the town. The war started on a Sunday in August and on Saturday night the last train left the Verzhbolova station. On the same night the bridge over the Liepona River was blown up.

In the town about 2,000 people remained including about 200 Jews, especially the landlords and homeowners. Before the first shot was heard, the remaining people in town started to plunder the property of the runaways and in many cases in order to cover the crime they set fire. So many buildings in the center of the town were burnt.

When fighting in the area began, the town changed hands a few times, and a large part of the town was destroyed.

In the spring of 1915, after the Russian Army under the command of General Renenkampf was defeated near the swamps of Mazuria, he retreated from Prussia and Kibart was occupied by the German army, who remained until the beginning of 1919, when it was handed over to independent Lithuania.

The name of the railway station was changed by the Germans to "Wirballen" and a command post was arranged in the town. The customs warehouses were filled up with munitions and other military equipment and new warehouses were built. The Germans also widened the set of the rails in the station.

During the German occupation some of its former inhabitants returned to Kibart. When in autumn 1915 the Russians evacuated Vilna, more refugees and also other people came to Kibart and began to adjust to the new conditions and look for new occupations, because the border no longer existed and there was no longer any need for the customs clerks as well as many other services. As a result, the economic situation deteriorated.

C: 1 9 1 9 - 1 9 2 3   The years of economic prosperity

On February 16, 1918 the "Taryba," the elected council of Lithuanian personalities headed by Antanas Smetona, proclaimed the establishment of the Lithuanian State. The Germans were still hoping that the "Ober-Ost" region, as they called the territories occupied in the Baltic area, would remain in their hands. Only under the leadership of the "Board of the workers and the sailors" who was established in Germany on November 9, 1918, did the Germans began to evacuate Lithuania.

They sold their buildings and other facilities at half the price. In Kibart they removed all the wire fences from the town and destroyed several buildings they had built during their rule. All Lithuania was evacuated by the Germans by the end of 1919.

At the railway station new signs were hung with the inscription "Virbalis" and it together with the customs house became the greatest in Lithuania. The border between Germany and Lithuania was demarcated along the Liepona river and this small stream became again the border between two countries.

According to the new administrative division Kibart was included in the Vilkaviskis (Vilkovishk) District.

The border was opened then and different merchandise was legally allowed to be imported into Lithuania. The few "Expediters" that were in Eydtkuhnen started anew their activities. With the growth of the import into the country, more and more expediters were added. In Lithuania everybody could be an Expediter, because the duty was charged according to the value of the goods and this simplified the process, so the profession of Declarants was no longer needed.

Because of the great shortage of goods, Lithuania allowed importation of almost everything from Germany. At first the merchants, mostly Jewish, bought goods in nearby Eydtkuhnen. Later on, they travelled to Koenigsberg with suitcases and brought back merchandise by themselves. Then the merchants bought goods all over Germany and the importation increased and the Expediters had much work.

At this time Kibart became an important commercial center and merchants from all over the country started to come to Kibart. They wanted to obtain the goods immediately after the duties were paid and as the goods came out of the packing halls. So many merchants would gather in the town that the only hotel in town (it belonged to a Jewish family, Papir) rented beds by the hour and sometimes people even slept two to a bed.

The devaluation of the German Mark and corresponding the Ost Mark, that was still a legal currency in Lithuania, contributed to the development of the commerce. The goods rose in price from hour to hour and many Jews became rich in the process. In Kibart many shops opened and when the Mark became stable and Lithuania introduced its own currency, the Litas. Kibart had 50 textiles wholesalers, about 15 haberdashery shops, a few leather wholesalers, 5 private banks, 3 public banks, and a government bank, which was established in the building of the former "Azov-Don" bank. The majority of the merchants were Jews. There were also about 50 offices of customs commissioners (expediters) who employed many people. In these years Jews established factories and workshops in Kibart, such as: a factory for shoe wax and tin boxes, for knitting, for weaving, a few sewing workshops for shirts, a sawmill, a flour mill, a factory for oil extraction, two brick factories, and two tea packing workshops. The owners were: Bernshtein, Gamzu, Berniker, Jasven, Alperovich, Shemesh-Gefen, Kushnerzitzky, Ganz, Jurzditsky, Frishman, Frenkel, Kanievsky, Vizhansky, Rubin, Aizenstat and others.

There were in Kibart Jews who exported horses (Rakhlin), poultry and fruit (Kovensky) and a workshop for processing and exporting of linen (Rezvin-Rozenberg).

During these years, when the economic prosperity arrived its peak, many three and four story buildings with all the conveniences were built in the center of the town (the houses of Seinensky, Shadkhanovitz, Kuritsky, Pliskin, Klotnitsky and others). There was then a great demand for flats and shops and all cellars and attics in the town were turned into warehouses. The signs and inscriptions of warehouses were left on many buildings in town for years after they did not exist anymore.

The Jewish "Folksbank" - a credit cooperation - opened a branch in Kibart when the currency was still the Ostmark. Because of the great inflation of the Mark the bank lost all its capital. After that the bank wanted to help the coachmen whose businesses decreased because a bus started to carry passengers from Kibart to Virbalis and back. The bank helped them organize in a cooperative and lent them money to buy several buses. After the business went bad, the bank lost about 25,000 Litas and the cooperative members lost their investments.

In 1921 a branch of "The Jewish Central Bank" opened in Kibart in addition to the branch in Ponevezh and the center in Kovno. During the good times a few tens of clerks worked in this bank and it helped greatly the import and export issues. The activity of the Folksbank then decreased a lot and it moved to Virbalis where only several tens of members left in it.

The great prosperity of Kibart ended, when in January 1923 Lithuania took over the port town of Memel (Klaipeda in Lithuanian) and its zone, situated by the Baltic Sea. The town and the zone belonged to Germany until World War I, after which, according to the Versailles Treaty, it was handed over to the rule of a French High Commissioner with a French garrison. The Lithuanian Government staged an "uprising " and annexed the city and its zone to its state. It's worthwhile to note, that from a geographic sense this zone is indeed part of the Lithuanian state.

The Lithuanian Government was interested for political and also for economic reasons to directed a great part of imports and exports, for economic or political reasons, to the port of Memel-Klaipeda. At the same time the main customs offices were transferred from Kibart to Kovno. As a result, most of the wholesalers and the customs clerks moved to Kovno during several years.

In an announcement that was published on the first of January 1921 in the "Yiddishe Shtime" newspaper on behalf of the "Merchants Association" of Kibart, we can see that there were still 27 cloth and 15 haberdashery shops (including the pharmacy) in town, but most of them moved to Kovno too after a short time (see Table 1).

מעלדונג׳

דער קיבארט. "סוחרים־פארבאנד"

מעלדעט דאמיט דאס פון 1 יאנואר 1921 זיינען אין קיבארט פאראן

פאלגנדע 27 מאנופאקטור ־ און ־ 15 גאלאנטעריי־ פירמעס:

מאנופאקטור:
1) ברוין א. קא׳
2) בלאגאסלאווענסקי ש.
3) ברוידע פסח
4) וויינשטיין געבר.
5) וויינשטיין א. זשעליאנסקי
6) ווידאבליאנסקי א. לעווינסקי
7) זאלצבערג אדאלף
8) זשוקאווסקי
9) טראצקי ב.
10) ידידיה א. בלאך
11) יאכיזון ב.
12) כהן טאכמאן א. אבקעיין
13) לעווין יודל
14) מילין ש.
15) מעראצער ל.
16) מיראז א. גאני׳אנסקי
17) סיינגאנסקי ח.
18) סטאראיאַסקי א. רובינשטיין
19) סטאראיילאנסקי. רעמס א. קא׳
20) ערבשטיין ק.
21) עמינדב א.
22) פאסוויאנסקי געבר.

23) פיר א. שטיין
24) פרידמאן מאצקען סטרעלעץ
25) קאפלאן א. איטקעס
26) רעקארד.
27) שולמייסטער יצחק

גאלאנטעריי:
1) אוליאמפערל געבר.
2) אלפעראויץ געבר.
3) בערנשטיין ש.
4) ווידיש א. שימקאוויץ
5) זיידאק י.
6) חיימאוויץ ר.
7) חאוויץ א. אראנזאן
8) טינאוויץ מ.
9) טילוער. גערשאטאר (אפטייק אנגראם)
10) מענדעלסאהן ל.
11) פליסקין מ.
12) פיין א.
13) קאפלאן געבר.
14) שאטחאנאייץ כ.
15) שאפירא י.

דער פאריין האט אינטער־ נומען א ריי מיטלען צו

פארלייכטערן דעם טראנספארט פון די סחורה

ווי אויך צו פארבילינ די מקחים אויף פאר שידענע ארטיקלען.

פארוואלטונג.

Table 1

They left behind only the signs on the empty shops and the inscriptions on the walls as a reminder of the great prosperity in the town. Then and Kibart returned to its pre-boom days and the living conditions were still quite comfortable.

In 1923 the population of Kibart was 6,300 inhabitants, among them 1,253 Jews. Living conditions were quite comfortable.

The announcement (in Yiddish) in the Jewish press in Lithuania regarding the services of the Central Bank in Kovno and in its branches in Kybart and in Ponevezh

D: 1 9 2 3 - 1 9 3 3   Years of Economic Stability.

After the great boom, during which most of the merchants moved to Kovno, the town entered into a period of ten more or less tranquil years.

The main wide street of Kibart, paved with stones, with large chestnut trees on both sides and a paved sidewalk on one side, which also served as the main road leading to Germany, was called Senapiles Street and later after the name of the President "Smetonos Aleja" (Smetona Avenue). As there were no diplomatic relations with Poland, Lithuania was closed to the East and the South, but in the North the border with Latvia was open, and to the West there was an open border with Germany, so travellers coming from Europe by car had to pass through Kibart. This road, a few kilometers long, was actually the border on one side, whereas on the other side the soccer field and the Jewish cemetery were situated. From there on, there were fields all the way to Virbalis, about 4.5 km distant from Kibart.

Most of the stores were situated along this street, the banks, one cinema called the "Palas," the volunteer fire brigade, 2 pharmacies, one belonging to a Jew, the government elementary school, the German school, a Catholic church, a Pravoslavic church, a Protestant church and also a gas station which was operated by hand. Once a group of motorcycle riders from "Hapo'el" Eretz Israel passed through Kibart and bought gas at this station, which was a big event in Kibart.

Most of the two to four story buildings along the avenue and in the nearby streets were built of brick, some with and some without plaster, but there were no small wooden houses with straw thatched roofs or wooden tiles as could be seen in most Lithuanian towns. Most of Kibart Jews lived in modern houses equipped with running water, sewage systems and electricity, and some houses had central heating. The housing conditions in Kibart were much better than in many other towns in Lithuania with much larger populations.

All the streets at right angles to the avenue faced south, whereas the north side belonged mostly to the railway. One section of the town was situated to the north of the railway station and people had to pass the station to get there.

Life in Kibart was really influenced by the proximity of the German border. The main street of the town stretched to the border crossing, consisting of a wooden bridge over the small stream with customs buildings on either side. These buildings, both on the Lithuanian and German sides, were manned by a policeman and a customs clerk. The police issued certificates to inhabitants of a 5 km zone on both sides of the border, to enable them to cross freely. The German border town of Eydtkuhnen was small, but had four to five story buildings, wide paved streets and nice shops, according to the standards of those times. Many of the merchants, who owned textile, shoe, clothes and other stores, were Jewish (Rubinshtein, Levin, Zilberman and others). Eydtkuhnen had already instituted "White Weeks" and "Seasonal Sales," and the inhabitants of Kibart as well as their friends and relatives from other towns enjoyed these occasions.

Dr. Iviansky was one of several Jewish doctors in Eydtkuhnen who also treated Kibart Jews.

During these years, similar to the times of Russian rule, masses of German women from Eydtkuhnen would come to the market in Kibart, on Tuesdays and Fridays, to buy fresh agricultural produce brought in by peasants from nearby villages. Food products were much cheaper in Lithuania than in Germany and near the border tens of grocery and butcher shops opened up, mostly owned by Jews, who made their living from the Eydtkuhnen inhabitants. There were about twenty Jewish groceries in the town during these years. Kibart and Virbalis Jews would buy dresses, shoes, cloth, cosmetics etc. in Eydtkuhnen. It paid to buy these goods there and to sell them in Lithuania for great profit.

Until the beginning of the Nazi regime in 1933, Kibart Jews bought most of their supplies in Eydtkuhnen, including types of fruit which could not be obtained in Kibart, such as bananas, grapes, water melons, melons etc., and for reasonable prices. The problem was how to cross the border without paying customs' fees, and the method adopted was to take two or three oranges only by hand in a paper bag when crossing the border. New shoes were smeared with shoe polish and not brushed, so they would not look new to the customs clerk. New dresses and cloth would be wrapped around the body under the overcoat, and many other tricks were invented in order to smuggle goods without paying duties.

There were times, during the late twenties, when Jews from Kibart went to the cinema in Eydtkuhnen. Once they even went to a circus show in Stalupeonen, some 20 km from the border.

In 1933, when the Nazis came to power, all this stopped. On the first of April 1933 Nazi guards of the S. A. did not allow people into Jewish stores, and from that day on most of Kibart's Jews did not go to Eydtkuhnen anymore.

Most of Lithuania's main exports were agricultural products, which were sent to Germany, one of the major items being live geese. At the beginning of winter, exporters would bring the geese to a lot in the railway station, and the quacking of geese was heard in town day and night for a month or so. After Hitler had established his rule, he demanded Memel' (Klaipeda) return to Germany. As a means of pressure he cancelled the commercial treaty with Lithuania, so all the geese assigned for export were left without buyers. To solve the problem, the Lithuanian government ordered all its clerks to get a part of their salary in geese, so that the price of geese dropped a lot at the time and people benefited.

The railway station in Kibart reminds one of additional events. All the immigrants (Olim) to Eretz Israel travelled through this station by train. There were years, when a group of "Khalutsim" (Pioneers) passed through Kibart every few weeks, and large crowds of Jews came to see them off. These were happy and exciting events, sometimes even funny. In order to exploit every "Certificate" (Aliyah Permission) issued by the British Mandatory Government to its maximum, every young man married a girl fictitiously, so that each "Certificate" enabled two people to enter Eretz Israel. It often happened that the fictitious couple met in Kibart's station for the first time, the "groom" looking for the "bride" he had never met before by shouting her name.

The Occupations of the Jews in Kibart.

In those years the main occupation of the Jews was commerce, there being shops of haberdashery, grocery, shoes, cloth, paper, books, stationary, meat, iron and tools, household utensils. There were also several small factories such as bookbinding, a shoe polish and tin cans factory, several textile factories, sewing workshops etc. There were many craftsmen: shoemakers, photographers, tailors, fashions, barbers etc. Some were engaged in exporting agricultural products, such as flax, after processing it, and horses for meat. Apart from those there were one cinema owner, two tavern owners, several customs clerks, teachers, bank clerks, two carriages and one taxi owner. The economic life in town concentrated around the Jewish Central Bank and the Jewish Popular Bank. Two especially Jewish occupations existed, one being illegal trading foreign currency and the other "Couriers". Several Jews made a good living by trading with foreign currency, and these "Couriers" were people who travelled by train to Kovno every morning and returned in the evening. They passed on orders from the merchants of Kibart to the wholesalers in Kovno, and then brought the ordered goods back by themselves on the same day. They also sold smuggled merchandise from Germany to the rich merchants in Kovno, and there were seven families who made a rather a poor living from this occupation. In particular the author remember at least one case when the community had to buy the monthly train ticket for one of these couriers, because the man did not have the money to do so.

At left: Stamp of the Minister for Jewish affairs.

At right: Stamp of the National Council of the Jews of Lithuania.

Public and Cultural Life.

Following the law of autonomies for minorities issued by the new Lithuanian government, the minister for Jewish affairs Dr. Menakhem (Max) Soloveitshik ordered elections to community committees (Va'ad Kehilah) to be held in the summer of 1919.

The veteran "Gabaim" of Kibart did not want a "Community Committee" to be elected, since they had enough power of their own. Only after tremendous persuasion was a "Community Committee" elected, most of its members tending to the left. Shortly afterward, this Committee was forced to resign and in the next elections, a Committee was forged with a right wing was elected. Later, in the autumn of 1923 a mixed Committee was elected with a small majority of right wingers, but the left were more active and pushed for establishing an elementary school and social help in town. Towards these elections five lists were presented:

162   Kibart

Fragments of the government Survey of Shops in Vilkaviskis District in 1931

Cloth

VILKAVIŠKIO APSKR.
Blagoslovempienė S., Kybartai, Žydų g. 5.
Berenšteinaitė Chana, Pilviškiai, Turgavietė 2.
Blochas Ch., Kybartai, Sinagogos 7.
Černcvskienė Chanė, Vilkaviškis.
Eisiškis Ch., Vilkaviškis, Gedimino g. 11.
Elsonas Mauša, Pilviškiai, Turgaus g. 9.
Evizonas Miriannas, Virbalis, Vilniaus g. 45.
Fainbergienė Rocha, Vilkaviškis, Turgavietė 14.
Fainbcrgas Ch., Vilkaviškis, Gedimino g. 3.
Feinbcrgas Nochumas, Virbalis, Turgavietė 12.
Finkelšteinienė Ch., Pilviškiai, Turgavietė 16.
Fridmanienė Gitel, Vilkaviškis, Turgavietė.
Fridmanas Vulfas, Pilviškiai, Turgavietė 12.
Garbas Giršas, Virbalis, Vilniaus g. 33.
Geršteinns B., Pilviškiai, Turgavietė 22.
Gitelevičius Icikas, Virbalis, Vilniaus g. 49.
Gochenbergas Samuelis, Virbalis, Vilniaus g. 53.
Goldšteinienė Dvora, Virbalis, Vilniaus g. 44.
Guntorius J., Bartininkai.
Gurvičienė N., Vilkaviškis, Vytauto g. 17.
Chazonas Ovsėjus, Vilkaviškis, Turgavietė 16.
Ironienė D., Vilkaviškis, Turgavietė 1.
Jablonas Fišeliš, Pilviškiai, Turgavietė 3.
Jasvenienė Chaja ir Jasvenas, Kybartai, Senapilės 55.
Kaplannai B. ir G., Vilkaviškis, Vytauto g. 7.
Kaplanienė Iudė, Turgavietė 6.
Laksienė Jochoeda, Vilkaviškis, Turgavietė 20.
Laprunskienė Riva, Vilkaviškis, Kęstučio g. 5.
Levitas E., Kybartai, Vištyčio g. 5.
Lebertavičius Jonas, Gražiškiai.
Lipšicas Abromas, Vilkaviškis, Turgavietė 17.
Miklišauskis Joselis, Vištytis, Bažnyčios g. 13.
Mejerovičius Ošeris, Vilkaviškis, Kęstučio 11.
Milcas S., Kybartai, Senapilės 59.
Olkenickis S., Virbalis, Vilniaus g. 41.
Orlinskis J. D., Virbalis, Turgavietė 12a.
Petrulis V. ir Gelgotas, Vilkaviškis, Gedimino g. 8.
Ryckis A. ir Maknavičius S., Virbalis, Turgavietė 16.
Rubinovienė Dora, Vilkaviškis, Turgavietė 8.
Seinenskis, Kybartai, Senapilės g. 83.
Sluckis Aronas, Vilkaviškis, Turgavietė 7.
Švarcas Ickus, Pilviškiai, Turgavietė 8.
Trikašai Peša ir Aronas, Vilkaviškis, Turgavietė 18.
Vladislavovskienė C., Pilviškiai, Jurkšų g.
Volovickis Simsonas, Vilkaviškis, Kudirkos g. 2.
Zedachienė Rachilė, Vilkaviškis, Vytauto ģ. 13.
Želka Juozas, Gražiškiai.

Textile

„Columbus", *Bernikeris J.*, Kybartai.
„Liucija", *Rusanovienė*, Kybartai.
„Rekord", *Grosbardaitė M.*, Vilkaviškis, Maironio g. 17.

Grocery

VILKAVIŠKIO APSKR.
Arongauzas Mordchelis, Vilkaviškis, Sinagogo g. 5.
Balberiskis Abromas, Vilkaviškis, Vytauto g 25.
Bergneris V., Kybartai, Senapilės g. 99.
Fainbergas. Jakobas, Vilkaviškis, Vytauto g 27.
Geležūnas Juozas, Virbalis, Geležinkelio stc tis.
Ginsburgas J. ir Švarcas, Kybartai, Sinago gos g. 5.
Heimanas Tobijas, Kybartai, Senapilės gt.
Heimanytė Ehana, Virbalis, Vilniaus g. 19.
Jurkšaitis M., Kybartai, Naujakurių g. 54.
Lakovskis Sanderis, Virbalis, Vištyčio g. 19.
Levinsonas Giršas, Vilkaviškis, Kęstučio g. 18
Levinsonas I., Vilkaviškis, V. Kudirkos g. 18
Losmanas ir Grosbardas, Vilkaviškis, Kęstuč g. 30.
Norkeliūnas Vincas, Kybartai, Algimanto g
Okrovskis Judelis, Virbalis, Gedimino g. 31.
Solskiai Br. ir B-vė, Pilviškiai, Turgavietė ?
Šamesas Isakas, Virbalis, Vilniaus g. 11.
Vinkelšteinas Šliomas, Vilkaviškis, Vilniaus g 23.
Volbergas Berelis, Vilkaviškis, Vytauto g. 30

Food Products

Bernšteinas J. ir Malachas, Kybartai, Senapilės g. 83.
Hmiclevskis Hiršas, Vilkaviškis, Basanavičiaus g. 2.
Chaitas Abromas, Vilkaviškis, Prieglaudos g. 12.
Kabanskis J. ir sūnus, Virbalis, Vilniaus g. 39.
Kalvaitis P., Vištytis, Bažnyčios g.
Kopelovičius L., Kybartai.
Kretingė B., Vilkaviškis, Vytauto g. 11.
Liet. Koop. B-vių Sąjungos, Vilkaviškio skyrius, Turgavietės g. 2.
Londonaitė Roza, Vilkaviškis, Kęstučio g. 13.
Londonas Elijašas, Vilkaviškis, Kęstučio g. 15.
Makovskis A., Vilkaviškis, Kęstučio g. 8.
Mikolavičius V., Pilviškiai, Turgavietė.
Pustopedskis Elijašas, Vilkaviškis, Gedimino g. 11.
Sidoravičius Isakas, Vilkaviškis, Gedimino g. 16.
Šulmanienė Chaja, Vilkaviškis, Turgavietė 13.
Veicas A., Vilkaviškis, Algimanto g. 6.
Vištaneckis Mozė, Virbalis, Vilniaus g. 59
Vižanskis Jankelis, Pilviškiai, Jurkšų g. 50.
Volbergas Šeftelis, Vilkaviškis, Turgavietė 16.
Zedakienė Choja, Vilkaviškis, Vytauto g. 13.

Cattle Trade

Bermanas Ch. ir Co, Virbalis.
Goldbergas Volfas, Kybartai, Senapilės gt. 83.
Lerzeris Hansas, Stalupėnai.
Maševskis Hermas, Kybartai, Vydūno gt.
Rachlinai D. T., Kybartai, Senapilės gt. 89.
Raudzinskis Giršas, Virbalis, Sinagogos gt. 4.
Telgendrecheras Mottes, Kybartai, Senapilės gt. 9.
Vichtas M., Pilckolon.

1. **Tseirei-Zion - Hitakhduth**: Shimon Volovitsky, Aba Jaffe, Avraham Kloizner.

2. **Non party**: Mosheh Naihertzig, Shemuel Rakhmil, Sheraga Beker, Kalman Glikson, Aharon Hurvitz, Mosheh-Joseph Alperovitz, Avraham-Aba Zholtok. Craftsmen and parents of the school children: Leikin, Zilin, Shtelman, Mandelblat, Rivlin, Aizenshtat.

3. **Folkists:** Tuviyah Shereshevsky, Shalom Filipovsky, Mosheh Rabinovitz, Shemuel-Mosheh Segal, Yakov Bialostotsky.

4. **Zionists**-Merchants-Retailers: Shimon Goldberg, Aba Yedidya, Yitshak-Shraga Khashman, Michael Shadkhanovitz, Shemuel Maroz, Eliyahu Katz, Meir Leibovitz, Hayim-Nisan Telem, Hayim Seinensky, Mordehai Frenkel, Alexander Gershater, Eliyahu Shvartz, Yakov Rozuk, Lipa Sukenik, A.J. Verzhbelovsky, Reuven Blokh, Dov Perlman, Shimon Miltz, Barukh Fridman, Shabtai Fainzilber, (see Table 2: an invitation issued by the Merchants Association, the Textiles Section of Kibart to it's members, written in Yiddish, to a meeting to discuss the coming elections).

Table 2

Each list was presented with signatures of supporters. It is not known who was elected to the Community Committee, but according to the names of the different sub-committee members one can see that there was reasonable representation of all lists.

Among the sub-committees it is worth mentioning the education sub-committee, which at its first meeting on October 10, 1923 discussed the issue of the school and the library, and it is interesting to note that the protocols of this sub-committee were written in Hebrew. Among its members were Shereshevsky, Goldberg, Rekhmat, Jafe, Leikin, Rakhmil. Shereshevsky was elected chairman and Jafe as secretary, who was then the director of the school.

Another sub-committee was for social help. Its members were Khashman, Volovitzky, Rakhmil, Shereshevsky, Yedidya. Y.Sh.Khashman was elected chairman.

The Community Committee existed until the end of 1925, when the Autonomy for Jews, also for other minorities, was annulled. At the last meeting of the Committee on December 20, 1925 it was decided to appoint four sub-committees who would care for the community's affairs after the annulment of the official committee:

a) The education sub-committee, its members being T.Shereshevsky, Sh.Volovitzky, and M.Leibovitz,

b) The sub-committee for social help whose members were Sh.Rakhmil, M.Shadkhanovitz and Sh. Maroz,

c) A sub-committee on religious affairs including ritual slaughter with the same composition as above, and

d) A sub-committee for the liquidation of the Community Committee, its members being Sh.Volovitzky, M.Rabinovitz and M.Leibovitz. This sub-committee had to settle the main Committee's debts and also to apply to the Jewish faction of the Seimas, asking it what to do with the buildings and archives which belonged to the Committee.

The archives of all the Community Committees were transferred to the "YIVO" Institute in Vilna, and during World War II the Nazis transferred them to Frankfurt in Germany, where they were found after the war, after which they were finally stored in the "YIVO" Institute in New York. This is the source of all the copies in the tables.

In order to illustrate the views of the Jewish public in Kibart one can use the results of the elections to the first Lithuanian Seimas in October 1922. 403 Kibart Jews participated, of whom the Zionist list received 324 votes, "Agudath-Yisrael" (religious) got 47 votes and the Democrats (the Folkists) 32 votes.

In 1924 Kibart was declared a town with self rule, and a municipality was elected consisting of 25 members: 6 Jews, 7 Germans, 1 Russian, 1 Pole, and 10 Lithuanians.

In the 1931 elections 12 members were elected to the municipality: 2 Jews, 4 Germans and 6 Lithuanians. The elections of 1934 resulted in the election of 2 Jews, 3 Germans and 7 Lithuanians, pharmacist Budrevicius being elected Mayor. Among the Jews who officiated as members of the municipality during these years mention should be made of Y.Sh. Khashman, Yurzditzky, Sh Volovitzky, A.Vidomliansky and others.

Elementary Education.

A Jewish school had already been established in Kibart in 1919, which was more like a "Kheder" and was situated in the "Ezrath-Nashim" (Women's Hall) of the Synagogue. For a long time the community did not manage to create a school of reasonable standard for several reasons, among them the proximity of the German border which enabled many Jewish children to go to kindergartens and schools in Eydtkuhnen. The older children would study in the high school in Stalupoenen, a German town about 20 km from Kibart. With the establishment of the Hebrew High School in Virbalis in 1919, wealthy parents with a national conscience sent their children there In that High School which included elementary classes, tuition levels were comparatively high, but there were problems of finding skilled teachers. (see table 6: the protocol, written in Hebrew, of the meeting of the Education Sub-Committee on the 14.10.1923 in which the situation of the school, a building for the school and the library were discussed).

The new sub-committee for education carried out a survey of all children between the ages of 7 to 13 in order to create the possibility of establishing an excellent school in Kibart. Parents were asked where their children were learning at present and whether they would agree to admit them into the Hebrew "Tarbuth" elementary school. 95 children of the above mentioned ages were interviewed, of whom 18 studied in Eydtkuhnen, 13 in the Hebrew High School and the remainder in the existing school or privately. 55 parents agreed to enroll their children into the new school, whereas the remainder answered negatively or did not give a definite answer (see tables 7, 8, 9, 10).

A Hebrew school with 4 classes and 2 preparatory classes was established in Kibart in 1925. Hebrew was taught from the first preparatory class, Lithuanian from the second, but Yiddish, the mother tongue was not taught at all. A.Jafe was the director of the existing school and the teachers were Y. Reznik, M.Rabinovitz and Tsigler for the Lithuanian language. Mr. Jafe resigned and after considering all the candidates, M.Goldoft, a teacher who was also authorized to teach Lithuanian, was appointed director. Together with the establishment of the school, a Jewish kindergarten was opened by the wife of the director of the school, Mrs. Goldoft

Table 6

42793

כאלקטאל... ...שיבת הועדה להכלכה ...
371 - הפרל התירהאת... ד/14 ,1923 ...ר 4 ...
נתתתפ...: מר ...ש..., מר גולדברג, מר ו.נאל... מר ...ה. ו.מר ...

סדר היום

1) בחירת ...ועדות
2) ...ענין בית הספר
3) ...של ...הלה
4) ...ה ...ספ...

---

1. ...נ... את הועדה ...כור א...6. ...ר...ל ...גניר ... ...ה.
2. ...מ... ...פה ...ולא ע..ז ה...ל הה..ל...ל בית בית הספר, ...ר, ...גבו כ... ...נ...ת ... ...מק...ם ה...ל...יא / ה...עת ...יא הקט...ר ...ה..ב ...ל בית הספר ... הו...ל..ק..
3. א... ...ש...ל ...ל... ל... ה...מק...ת ...ל...ם פ...ל...א / ...ל..ה... ה...ל... ...ר... ...ר, ...ה ...ל... ...ספ... ה...א...ג..רית, מר גו...ב...ג ...ן ...ש...ל... ...ר...ת /...ל...א ל... ...ה הא...ור.. כ...ה ....א... ...נ... ...ל... ז... ה...ל... ...ת... בי...ת הס..., א... י..ה ...מ...ת ... ...ל ה...ת ...... א... .: ...ל...ן א...ל ל...א..ו ...ת ...נ ...ה... ...ל ...ל... ה...ה..
4. א... ...ש... ...ל...ה ...ל את ה...ה... /...ו...ה ...הק...ל... ...ל... ...ש...ה ...ה...... לס...ה.

פ...זיצער
סעקרעטאר

Table 7

			10.			1
			7.			2
			13.			3
			7.	3/3		4
			11.			5
			9.			6
			13.			7
			10.			8
			12.			9
			9.			10
			11.			11
			9.			12
			8.			13
			12.			14
			10.			15
			7.			16
			9.	3/3		17
			8.			18
			8.			19
			13.			20
			12.			21
			8.			22
			10.			23
			10.			24
			8.			25
			7.			26
			8.			27
			11.			28
			10.			29

Table 8

מערת הנפטר	שנה	יום פטירה	גיל	שם האם	שם הנפטר ושם אביו	No
			10			30
			8			31
			10			32
			7			33
			11			34
			10			35
			12			36
			9			37
			3			38
			13			39
			10			40
			4			41
			12			42
			12			43
			7			44
			13			45
			10			46
			8			47
						48
			13			49
			12			50
			7			51
			8			52
			12			53
			10			54
			11			55
			9			56
			13			57
			12			58

Table 9

						№.
			10			57
			12			60
			12			61
						62
			11			63
						64
						65
			12			66
			10			67
			8			68
						69
			11			70
						71
			9			72
			12			73
			12			74
			10			75
			12			76
			8			77
			11			78
						79
						80
						81
						82
			11			83
			12			84
			8			85
			12			86
			12			87

Table 10

According to the Lithuanian Education Law each minority had the right to establish a school for its children where the language of instruction was that of that minority. Teachers' salaries were paid by the government, but in this school there were always one or two additional teachers who received their salaries from the Parents' Committee. The school had a complement of about 100 - 150 pupils, and all graduates knew Hebrew well. Every year the school arranged a festivity including a play in Hebrew, which was an important event in the cultural life of the town.

After the first school director Mr. Goldoft emigrated to South Africa, a young teacher, graduate of Hebrew Teachers Seminar in Kovno, Aryeh Varshavsky, was appointed in his stead. He fulfilled his duty successfully until 1940, when Lithuania became a Soviet Republic and Hebrew education was eliminated.

In the table below view the subjects of instruction and the hours per week in class 2 (preparatory) and in class 6 in Kibart "Tarbuth" school:

Subject	Class 2	Class 6
Bible	4 *	6
Hebrew	6	6
Lithuanian	4	6
History	---	2
Geography	2	2
Mathematics	6	6
Nature	---	2
Painting	2	2
Handicraft	3	---
Singing	2	2
Gymnastics	3	2

*According to the Government-only two hoursper week.

Among the teachers of the school there are fond memories of Leah Yablokovsky and Shoshanah Klein. Leah Yablokovsky taught the lower grades for few years, emigrated to Eretz-Israel and continued teaching in Tel-Aviv. Shoshanah Klein, who was a very beautiful woman, married and emigrated to South-Africa. Among the men teachers worth mentioning are Mordehai Lurie, who taught in this school during all its existence; Avraham Vizhansky, Mosheh Leibovitz, Shemuel Matis and others.

Aryeh Varshavsky and Shalom Vidomliansky

It should be pointed out that when money was plentiful in the twenties, the Community was not wise enough to buy a plot of land in order to build a suitable building for the Hebrew school. During all the years of its existence the school rented buildings which were not always suitable, and the Parents Committee had to pay the rent. On the other hand, this Jewish community donated generously to the building of the modern Catholic church, which was built opposite the railway station, as well as to the building of the German church and school built at the other end of the town.

For many years Meir Leibovitz was the chairman of the Parents Committee and Mrs. Dobe Shtern one of its active members.

The Hebrew High School in Virbalis (Written by David Shadkhanovitz).

Most of Kibart's Jewish youths received their high school education in the Hebrew High School in Virbalis; the others studied in the Government High School in Kibart.

In 1918, after the war and with the establishment of the Lithuanian Republic, a group of Jewish men from Virbalis (Leizer Kagansky, Motl Ilenberg, Aryeh Benyakonsky, Yanek and Aba Filipovsky, Asher Uliamperl and others) initiated the establishment of a Jewish High School in Virbalis. In this school the language of instruction of all subjects would be Hebrew with Sephardic pronunciation, as in Eretz-Israel. There were people who did not like the idea of a Hebrew high school and tried to sabotage it, but the pioneers of Hebrew education overcame all obstacles.

The pupils and teachers of the Hebrew elementary school "Tarbuth" 1931

First line from right: A.Khashman,—,Z.Golding, E.Ozerov, H.Jasovsky, F.Saharovitz, B.Sheinzon, —,

Second line: S.Jofe, D.Levin, —, G.Borovik

Third line: E.Kliatchko, Z.Borokhovitz, —, Tsibulsky(?), ---, Y.Skrobiansky, M.Khlamnovitz, the Principal A. Varshavsky, teacher L.Yablokovsky, teacher M.Lurie, Y.Feferman, P.Kliatchko, D.Shtern, H.Borokhovifz, P. Shimkovitz

Fourth line: E.Halperin, —, A.Leibovitz, T.Beker, N.Levin, Magiliuker, B.Borovik, Y.Levin, Margolis(?), Skrobiansky, B.Zilbersky, Kanopke(?), F.Shtern, J.Rosin, H.Bartenshtein, —,

Fifth line: L.Tsikhak, Beirakhovitz, M.Landau, M.Grudzinsky, —, M.Vizhansky, R.Vilensky, Levin, Levin, —, Z.Borovik, -—, -

In Iyar 5679 (1919) pupils were enrolled in the High School and the beginning of the school year on the second of Heshvan 5680 (10.26.1919) was announced. This was actually the second Jewish high school in Lithuania and in the Diaspora, in which the teaching language was Hebrew, the first being in Marijampol. 200 pupils were accepted at the school, which started with only three classes and two preparatory classes. There was also a fourth class, not full and unofficial.

.

The graduation class of the Hebrew "Tarbuth" school 1938

On top the Headmaster Aryeh Varshavsky, to his left the Committee Chairman Meir Leibovitz (the author's uncle).

The arrows on the right side are marking the author's sister (fourth from the bottom) and his cousin (second from the bottom).

The opening of the school was accompanied by many difficulties, social, pedagogical and financial, as it should be remembered that the communities of Kibart and Virbalis had only just began to recover from the disasters they had faced during the war. Most people had a hard life and found it difficult to make a living, and the staff of teachers, the pioneers of Hebrew education, had problems in sorting out the pupils. During the war one part of the Jewish population had scattered all over Russia due to the ruling Tzar's policy of exiling people, and the other part was under German rule. Most of the applicants for acceptance at the school had no knowledge of Hebrew and the level of their general education was somewhere between a Russian school, a "Kheder" and a German school. It was difficult to grade pupils, when youngsters of the same age had such different educational backgrounds.

בפרוגמנסיון העברי בווירבלן

(כאשר מטעם הממשלה הליטאית) הקיים מחדש אייר תרע"ט

▬▬ מ ת ה י ל י ם ה ל ס ו ד י ם ▬▬

ביום א' לסדר נח, כ' חשון תרף 26 לחודש אקטאבר 1919.

בשנות הקבלה תחתלה טוב ד' בראפיה, כ"ח חשרי תרף 22 לחרש אך'
מאבר 1919. בשנה הלמודים התיאה המתחנה נ' מחלקה. רביעית וחמישית. תלמ־
דיב חדשים מתקבלים לשני רבצנות ולחמש המחלקות היסודיות.

ידיעות מפורטות אפשר להשיג בלשכת הפרוגמנסין.

הכתבת:

Vedejui Virbalio Žydų progimnazijos Virbalis Vilkav. apskr.

The biggest problem was the complete lack of textbooks, even in Hebrew subjects. The pedagogical team had doubts about the character of the Hebrew High School, as to whether it should it be according to the "program" of the Russian or of the German schools. After many discussions the teachers rejected all the elements of foreign high schools and a curriculum for the Hebrew High School was drawn up. In addition to the pedagogical problems, the Parents Committee had to solve problems of purchasing even minimal amounts of teaching aids, and above all, a suitable building.

All this required a considerable amount of money, and which was not plentiful in Virbalis in those days. Despite the difficulties, the Jews of the town contributed each according to his ability and a destroyed building was purchased and rebuilt. Several maps were bought, also a microscope, but most of the aids for teaching subjects such as nature, geography and physics were prepared from wood, clay and paper by the pupils themselves. The first director of the school was a native of the small town of Serey (Seirijai), Dr. Ya'akov Rabinson, who had graduated in Warsaw and returned to Lithuania in order to obtain this difficult and pioneering position. (a known lawyer, adviser to the Lithuanian Foreign Ministry before World War II, later the legal adviser of the Israeli delegation to the UN).

Among the first teachers were Avraham Eliyahu Sandler, Mitkovsky, Masha Frenkel, Dudnik, Shilansky, Aharon Frank, Mosheh Frank, Fridman, Reizel Rozenblum (the daughter of A.E.Sandler), Geisinovitz (the father of the well-known Aba Akhimeir), Sambursky, later a professor of mathematics at the Hebrew University in Jerusalem, Ash-Bartana, in due course a teacher of mathematics in the "Rehavya" high school in Jerusalem. Reuven Kaplan was the secretary of the school during all the years of its existence.

Table 11

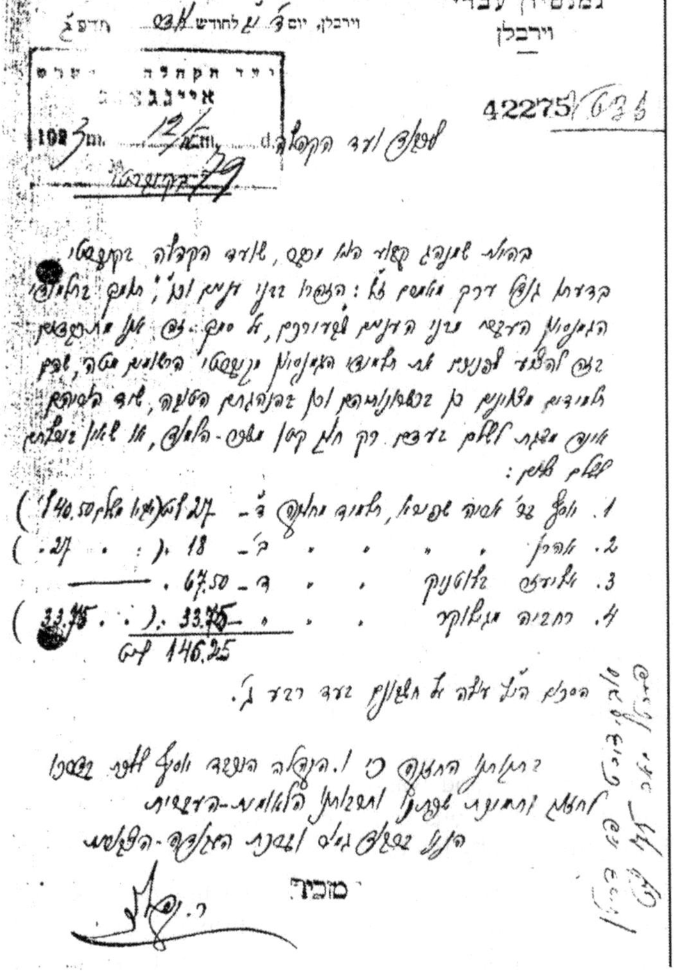
גמנסיון עברי
וירבלן
וירבלן, יום לחודש
42275
מזכיר

One of the tasks of the Hebrew High School education was to educate the youth in the spirit of Zionism and to prepare them for “Aliyah” to Eretz-Israel. Accordingly the subject of Eretz-Israel, settlement, the landscapes of the land and its geography were given high priority by the teachers and were popular with the pupils. Before they knew where Mont Blanc was, they knew about Mount Tabor and the Carmel, and before they heard about the Rhine and the Danube, they knew about the Jordan and the Kishon Rivers. The study of the Bible familiarized them with the history of Eretz-Israel and the love of the land.

Slowly the school emerged from its initial period and became a routine educational and cultural factor. After several years the school was a full high school with eight classes and two preparatory classes, and the first class graduated in 1925.

During the next few years the numbers of pupils grew. They came from the adjacent towns of Vishtinetz (Vistytis), Naishtot (Naumiestis-Kudirka), Shaki (Sakiai) and others. By the end of the twenties and the beginning of the thirties, Kibart's pupils constituted the majority in the school, numbers being not the only important factor, but also the income from their tuition fees, which was the main part of the school's total revenue. (**See Table 11**: a letter from the Virbalis Hebrew High-School dated the 12.4.1923 to the Community Committee of Kibart regarding payment for tuition fees for 4 talented and well- behaved pupils, who's parents can not afford to pay).

Even the Purim and Hanukkah parties, arranged in order to increase the school's financial resources, took place in the hall of the "Palas" cinema in Kibart, because of the more comfortable situation of Kibart Jews.

Due to the growth of the school and the need for improved conditions, the situation of the old buildings having worsened, it was decided to replace them in a suitable modern building. The purchase or the erection of a new building entailed great expenses and of course most of the money was to be found in Kibart. The Kibart members of the Parents Committee wanted to take advantage of this opportunity to buy a suitable building in Kibart and transfer the school to their own town.

During the late twenties the only means of transport between Kibart and Virbalis was by coach and a single bus which belonged to a corpulent German named Tit, who spoke juicy Yiddish like a Jew. The pupils from Kibart would go to Virbalis on the crowded bus, with the older children sitting down and the smaller ones from the preparatory and the first grade sitting on their knees. Despite the crowding the mood was happy and the children enjoyed the trip. During cold winter days Tit's bus was stored away most of the time, as a result of which transportation was by horse-drawn sleds.

The strong desire of Kibart parents to move the high school to Kibart was therefore understandable. In fact it was decided to buy a two story building in Seinensky's yard, where later Alperovitz established a shirt factory, but because of the intense objection of people from Virbalis this decision was not carried out. Their arguments were both historic and economic: a) the high school had been established originally by the people of Virbalis, b) many of Virbalis' Jews had an additional income from accommodating and supplying meals to outside pupils. So it was decided to purchase Sudarsky's building in the main street opposite the public garden and to adapt it to its new purpose. Classrooms were renovated and for the first time rooms for nature studies and physics were available. Central heating, a novelty in those days, was also installed in the building.

In the middle 1920s Director Dr. Rabinson left the school and Mikhael Bramson was nominated to take his place. He was a tall and slender man, a strict disciplinarian, and was thought to be among the foremost teachers of the Lithuanian language. He lived in Kibart with his short and round wife who only spoke Russian. During these years most teachers changed, among them the Bible teacher Mr. Salant who was popular with the pupils. He emigrated to Eretz-Israel and taught for many years in Kibbutz Ein-Harod. Nature study was taught by Mr. Tsimbalist who also immigrate to Eretz-Israel. The Lithuanian language teacher was Mr. Katz, and English was taught by B.Shulgaser who was also an amateur actor and very popular in society. His wife Mrs. Shohat-Shulgaser taught German, was a strict disciplinarian and appeared in class elegantly dressed and made up, which was unusual in those times. Mr. Kizel, a quiet and modest man very popular with his pupils, taught Hebrew and literature in the higher classes. Mr. Lifshitz was the drawing teacher, but because pupils held this subject in low esteem, he suffered quite a lot from them. The teacher of mathematics was Tabakhovitz. and other teachers included Averbukh and Jerushalmi.

In 1934, the high school was closed by the government, and a pro-gymnasium was established instead, with Tabakhovitz as director. A year later he was asked to take over the position of director of the Hebrew High School in Mariampol.

M.Bramson, the former director of the Virbalis High School moved to Kovno and established the Jewish-Lithuanian High School there.

The High School in Virbalis was closed because of lack of pupils in the higher classes and the great deficit in its budget. The pro-gymnasium was a private school and was administered by a specially established company "Haskalah" whose chairman was Mikhael Shadkhanovitz, who often covered its deficits with his own money. This school carried on until Lithuania became a Soviet Republic in the summer of 1940, when the Hebrew Education Net, the pride of Lithuanian Jewry, was abolished.

Social and cultural activity

In 1922 a branch of the "Tarbuth" (Culture) organization, whose slogan was "The people, the Land and the Language of Yisrael" (Am Yisrael, Eretz-Yisrael and Sefath Yisrael), was established in Kibart. The local branch applied to the Community Committee for an allocation of 3,000-4,000 Mark per month for performances of cultural activities " so that the Jewish Torah and its wisdom should not be forgotten". The application was signed by six members of the branch, but only three of them could be deciphered: Sh. Goldberg, L. Rosin (the author's father), H. N. Telem. (see Table 12 below).

The intelligent youths in the town, who had arrived there during the war from the Vilna region, established a Society for the Arts. On their initiative musical concerts with singers, lectures on different subjects and amateur shows took place. In the thirties a Jewish director named Rubin who had relatives in Kibart escaped from Germany and arrived in Kibart.. He staged the show from the Jewish writer J.Gordin "God, Man and the Devil" in which all the actors were local amateurs, and it was tremendously successful.

Table 12

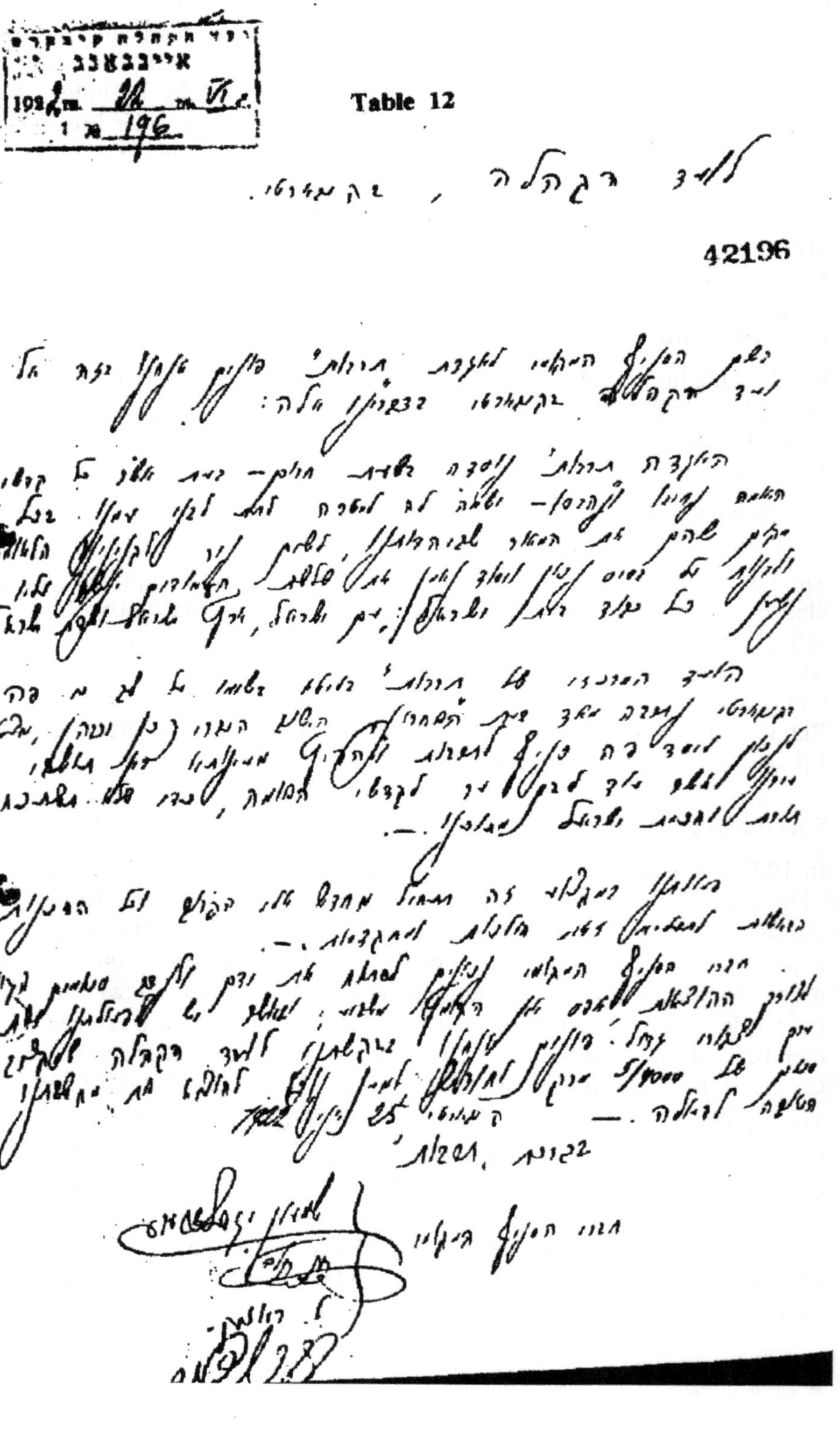
לועד הקהלה, בקיבארטו.

42196

בשם הסניף המקומי להסתדרות "תרבות" הננו פונים בזה אל ועד הקהלה בקיבארטו בבקשה הלזו:

בכבוד, ובשלום

חברי הסניף המקומי

From time to time the Jewish theaters from Kovno and also known Yiddish reciters, like Yosele Kolodny, Hertz Grosbart and others, would bring their shows to Kibart.

The Jewish library received many books in Hebrew and Yiddish. Benjamin Vidomliansky was the librarian most of the time and held this position voluntarily.

There were also experiments in establishing a Jewish club and to open a reading room next to the library, but they failed. People blamed this on the Cafe-Restaurant "Der Russischer Hof" in Eydtkuhnen which played an important role in the history of Kibart's Jews. This Cafe was only several hundred meters from the border, had beautiful halls, a dance band always played, and from time to time performances took place there. Many Jews, mainly the so-called "Golden Youth," would spend their time there. The anti-Semites called this place the "Juden Hof". There was a tale about one of the waiters who once asked when the holiday was coming on which day the Jews are allowed to eat pork. He surely meant of Yom Kippur, when several of Kibart's Jews who did not pray in the synagogue, would go to eat in "Der Russischer Hof".

In the twenties Kibart Jews went to the cinema in Eydtkuhnen, but later two cinemas were opened in Kibart, the "Metropol" and "Palas", and there was no need to go Eydtkuhnen anymore. Once a big circus arrived in Stalupoenen, about twenty kilometers from the border, and many people went to the performances.

Religious affairs

In those years a large synagogue made of red bricks with two floors was built opposite the market square, the second floor serving as the "Ezrath Nashim" (Women's Hall). In the middle of the main hall there was the "Bimah," a podium built of wood with beautiful carvings, whilst on the east wall there was, as usual, the "Aron haKodesh" (The Holy Ark) also built of wood with many engravings. The upper part of the building's walls had high windows made of colored glass, and there were several more rooms serving different needs. Adjacent to the synagogue was another building in which the bathhouse, the "Mikveh" and the library were housed.

The representative of " Keren haYesod" in Kibart was Yehudah Leib Rosin (the author's father), the owner of a stationary shop. The representative of the fund in Lithuania was Eliezer Rosentsveig, who once a year would come to Kibart where a meeting would be organized in his honor, where he would deliver a speech and collect donations for the fund. The actual collection of the money was carried out by Y.L.Rosin, who would transfer the money to the center in Kovno.

"The Keren Kayemeth" (Jewish National Fund) representative in Kibart was Eliyahu Katz, the owner of a grocery shop. Most of the funds were raised by members of the Zionist youth organizations. On Rosh HaShanah eve, Katz would put up notices in both synagogues consisting of white sheets of paper, on which appeared the donors' names with the total sum every donor had given, the amounts of each appeal, and the general total amount of all contributors for the previous year, the letters and the numbers being written by hand in marvelous handwriting. The total sum each donor had contributed was written in red ink and this was, of course, a fact which led to competition among the wealthy of the town, as to who would appear first in the list.

The front wall of the great Synagogue in Sinagogos Street

Vidomliansky Iron Shop
Standing near the shop: Benjamin Vidomliansky in Vistytis street

Zisle Leibovitz (the authors Grandmother)
Rosin stationary shop in Smetonos Aleja

The wedding of the author's parents 1920

Standing from left: Hanah Zalkind, uncle Meir Leibovitz, Mother Hayah, Father Yehudah-Leib Rosin, cousin Hayah Hilelson

Sitting from left: Grandpa Ya'akov Leibovitz, Grandma Zisle Leibovitz,

Grandpa Dov Rosin

The author's family living in Kibart from his Mother's side 1934

Standing from left: cousin Aryeh*, cousin Avraham, the author Josef Rosin

Sitting from left: aunt Sarah*, uncle Meir, Grandma Zisle, Uncle Barukh (Tel Aviv), Mother Hayah*, Father Yehudah-Leib Rosin*

Third line from left: cousin Elyakum*, cousin Tsiporah*, sister Tekhiyah*

(The surname of all the uncles and cousins and of the grandma is Leibovitz)

(*)-murdered by the Lithuanians in July 1941)

Most of Kibart's Jews were not very orthodox, but rather traditional. Except for the Rabbi and the "Shohet" nobody wore a "Kapota" (a long coat) or sported a beard and side locks (Peoth). There were no "Hasidim" and as usual with "Mithnagdim" religious life in town was sedate and tranquil, without the enthusiasm of the "Hasidim". On Saturdays and Holidays the synagogue was almost full with worshipers who had paid for their allotted places for the coming year in advance, before "Rosh HaShanah". On "Rosh HaShanah" and "Yom Kippur" many people, who would not be seen there throughout the year, did come to the synagogue.

There was another smaller synagogue at the other end of town named "Ohel Yitshak," named after Yitshak Sheraga Khashman, its initiator and a member of its committee until his death. Meir Leibowitz (the author's uncle) was their "Ba'al Kore" (the reader of the "Torah" with the proper tune), who fulfilled this duty until his death in 1940.

Until the twenties the Rabbi of Virbalis was also the Rabbi of Kibart. In the spring of 1925 the Community Committee decided to appoint a committee whose task it was to select a Rabbi for Kibart. This committee elected a sub-committee to negotiate with the Rabbi of Virbalis to give up his job in Kibart and also to publish an announcement in the newspapers about a vacancy for a Rabbi in Kibart. The twelve persons in the committee were: Sh.Goldberg, Sh.Davisky, J.Frishman, M.Naihertzig, H.Telem, Sh.Frenkel, Zholtak, Sh.Rakhmil, A.Katz, Y.Khashman, Sh.Maroz.

There were tens of applications from Rabbis all over Lithuania, some of whom the committee interviewed, finally selecting Rabbi Barukh Nahum Ginzburg, one of the founders of the religious education network "Yavneh" and a member of its center.

In the thirties he moved to Janenve (Jonava). Rabbi M.Rabinovitz, a member of the religious Zionist party "Mizrahi," was elected in his place. He died in 1940 during Soviet rule in Lithuania. Neither of these Rabbis interfered too much in the community's affairs. Sheinzon was the cantor in the big synagogue, and the only Shohet (ritual butcher) in town.

Zionist and Public activities.

The Zionist Organization was already active in Kibart during the first Zionist Congresses. After the Balfour Declaration its activities increased and the merchants of Kibart contributed generously to the National Funds. For example, in a 1922 newspaper article it was reported, that an agent of "Keren haYesod" (the fund of the World Zionist Organization) named Dr. Vilensky had raised $6,000 in one evening from the merchants of Kibart. It was known in Lithuania, that if it was necessary to raise funds for Jewish needs, it would start in Kovno the capital, and then continue in Kibart.

When in the beginning of the twenties the "Bank haPoalim" was established in Eretz-Yisrael, many Kibart Jews bought founders' shares in the bank.

A branch of the "WIZO" (Women International Zionist Organization) organization was active in Kibart, its chairwoman being Hayah Rosin, Y.L. Rosin's spouse and the mother of the author of this book, but amongst those active in this branch Mrs. D.Shtern should also be mentioned. The branch arranged such activities as lectures, parties etc., and notices about these activities were displayed in the pharmacy window of Tilzer-Gershater. The biggest and most impressive event of the branch was the "Bazaar" which took place in the middle of the thirties after a festive opening in the hall of the "Palas" cinema. Among other items sold during this "Bazaar" was silver jewelry brought specially from the "Betsalel" art school in Jerusalem.

A group of Kybart youth with their guests at a party

First line from right: Z. Kovensky, A. Levit,----,-, L. Vezhbelovsky, Feldshtein, Akabas, ---

Second line: A. Zarko, Rezvin, sisters Meyer, sisters Bronshtein Y.Filipovsky, L.Arnshtam,

Third line: Berezin, B. Shatenshtein, Y. Kovensky, D. Helershtein,. Muzikant

A group of Kibart youth 1929/1930

Standing from left; ---, Yosef Bartenshtein, ---, ---, Yehudith Borokhovitz, ---, Zisl Kovensky

Sitting from left: Aryeh Shadkhanovitz, Pesha Yasovsky, Ze'ev Sheinzon, Miriam London, Mosheh Borovik

Laying: ---, Shalom Vidomliansky

On June 19, 1932 a parade marking the fiftieth anniversary of the "Khovevei Zion" (The Lovers of Zion) movement and the thirtieth anniversary of the "Keren Kayemeth leYisrael" Fund took place in Kibart. Bicyclists headed the parade, their wheels decorated with blue and white stripes, followed by marching members of "Maccabi" and a band playing. After them came "WIZO" women, and then the uniformed "haShomer-haTsair" members led by Joseph Bartenshtein and Aryeh Shadkhanovitz, and "Beitar" members led by Moshe Khashman. Many Jews joined the parade, which made its way along the main street and from there by bus to the town park in Virbalis, where the celebration ended with speeches, shows and dances.

The central office of "heKhalutz" organization purchased a farm in the vicinity of Kibart, naming it "Kibbush" (conquest), which was the biggest "Hakhsharah" (training) farm in Lithuania, where "Halutsim" (pioneers) candidates for "Aliyah" were trained in agriculture. The Zionist youth of Kibart and Virbalis were in close contact with this farm and supported it as much as possible.

In 1932 an "Urban Kibbutz" was established , consisting of a few tens of "Halutsim" and "Halutsoth". It contained workshops for shoemaking as well as dressmaking and knitting for women and its members also worked in several factories in town, thanks to the unflagging efforts of Zisl Kovensky. The Kibbutz existed until 1936.

The main building of the "HeKhalutz" farm "Kibush" 1925

Halutsim on "Kibush"

Sinagogos street and a part of the market place

The daily Yiddish newspaper "Dos Vort" (Word) of December 17, 1934 published a story about a party which took place in this kibbutz on the occasion of the Aliyah of four girls (Halutsoth) and in honor of Z.Kovensky, who contributed much to the establishment and consolidation of the Kibbutz, and the party opened with a speech by the "heKhalutz" activist Yerakhmiel Voskoboinik. Generally Kovensky's house was the center of Zionist activity in Kibart, and all those delegates of "heKhalutz" and "haShomer-haTsair" from Eretz-Yisrael who came to Kibart, would be accommodated in Kovensky's house. At some time, the "Maon" (Club) of "haShomer-haTsair" was in an empty shop of this house, given to the movement free of charge, the equipment of the "Maccabi" sports organization being stored in Kovensky's storeroom. Contact with the "haShomer-haTsair" movement in Poland, which was much bigger and stronger than in Lithuania, was kept up through Z.Kovensky, who for this purpose rented a post office box in Eydtkuhnen. Material from Warsaw would be sent to this P.O.Box and Z.Kovensky would bring it from there and send it to the leadership of the movement in Kovno. It should be pointed out that until 1938 there were no direct diplomatic relations between Lithuania and Poland, and this was the only way to keep up in touch with the movement in Poland.

The farewell party for Mrs. Vizhansky and Mrs. Shatenshtein to their "Aliyah", arranged by the "WIZO" committee in Kybart 1933.

Sitting from right: Sarah Leibovitz, ____,Vizhansky, Shatenshtein, Hayah Rosin, Bartenshtein, Dobe Shtern, Zisle Leibovitz

Z. Kovensky, who was on good terms with the gendarmes at the border crossing, used to take young "Halutsim" across the border to Eydtkuhnen on their way to Eretz-Israel before recruitment to the Lithuanian Army, fixing the passage for a few hundred Lit.

All "Olim" (emigrants) to Eretz-Yisrael went by train and thus passed through Kibart station, where more people who would also join them, making this a joyful, exciting and sometimes also an amusing event. In order to utilize every "Aliyah Permission" (Certificate) which the British mandatory authorities agreed to grant, every "Halutz" married some girl fictitiously and thus brought her to Eretz-Israel legally too. There were cases when the fictitious couple met at the station in Kibart for the very first time, and sometimes shouts could be heard of someone looking for his "wife" whom he had never met before. There were years, mainly in the thirties, when every few weeks groups of "Halutsim" passed through the Kibart railway station. Lots of Jews would fill the station, and the cylinder shaped hats with a badge on them worn by gendarmes who were at least 1.80 meter tall, could be seen over the heads of the crowd.

Kibart youth at the "Urban Kibbutz" of "heKhalutz". December 1935

First line, from right: Tuviyah Yasovsky, Yerakhmiel Voskoboinik (Khalutz), Benyamin Vidomliansky, Shalom Vidomliansky

Second line: Yisrael Ziman, Mosheh Svirsky, Batyah Slavotzky, Avraham Khashman,

Third line: 3 Khalutzoth

The "haShomer-haTsair" organization started off in Kibart in the early twenties, and many children and youths received their Zionist education in this movement. Because of the semi-fascist rule which existed in Lithuania during most of its independence, this movement was called "The Hebrew Scouts Organization haShomer-haTsair" and to the outside it really appeared as such. The uniforms and the activities were similar to scouts, only in the "Maon" there were discussions about Eretz-Israel, socialism etc., everything according to the age of the members. Among the members of the movement in Kibart who emigrated to Eretz-Israel and of whom some of them joined Kibbutzim there were: Jehudith Borokhovitz-Jaron, Shelomoh Blotnik, Sarah Blotnik-Harari, Joseph Bartenshtein, Hana Staravolsky, Avraham Leibovitz-Ben Yehudah (the author's cousin), Mosheh Melamed, Mosheh Borovik, Shalom Vidomliansky-Shakham and others.

Amongst the leaders of the branch of the movement there was Z.Kovensky, who filled this position for many years, as well as Mosheh Borovik, Joseph Bartenshtein, Avraham Leibovitz, and lastly Yekhiel Feferman who perished in the Holocaust. (**see table 15**: "haShomer - haTsair" membership card of Z.Kovensky, written in Hebrew and Lithuanian).

Table 15

תברת.הסיוע לצופים העברים בליטא
הסתדרות הצופים העברים
„ה ש ו מ ר - ה צ ע י ר"
ההנהגה הראשית

כרטיס   צופה

1) כרטיס זה, מעיד על בעליו, כי נמנה הוא אל
הסתדרות הצופים העברים „השומר-הצעיר" בליטא
2) הכרטיס נותן לצופה את הזכות ללבוש תלבושת
צופים, לשאת סימני צופים ולמלא בפומבי את תפקידיו הצופיים
3) כרטיס זה צריך להמצא תמיד בידי הצופה ובשעת
הצורך על הצופה להראותו אותו
4) אצל כל צופה יכול להיות רק כרטיס אחד
5) אם יאבד כרטיס זה, אין הצופה יכול לקבל
כרטיס אחר כי אם ברשיון מיוחד

Lietuvos Žydu Skautams
REMTI DRAUGIJA
SKAUTŲ ORGANIZACIJA
Vyriausias Štabas.

Skautų   bilietas

Pastabos:

1) Šis bilietas liūdyja, kad jo savininkas
yra Lietuvos Žydu skautų organizacijos narys.
2) Bilietas duoda jo savininkui teisę dė-
vėti skautų uniformą ir ženklus ir viešai eiti
skautu pareigas.
3) Šį bilietą skautas privalo visada turėti
su savimi ir parodyti jį jam reikalaujant.
4) Kiekvienas skautas gauna ir gali turėti tik vieną bilietą.
5) Pametusis šį bilietą gali gauti kitą
tik sulig ypatingu leidimu.

FORM. NR. 2   SP. „LAIMĖ"

Bilieto Nr. 142

Vardas ir pavardė *Zijelis Kovenskis*

Amžius *1909 gimė*

Skyrius *Kybartai*

Skautų pareigas *Vyr. skiltininkes*

Adresas

Bilietas turi galios iki *1932 - XII - 31.*

Draug. Pirmink. *J. Beil.*

Sekretorius *J. Plotnik*

Kaunas: 193* - III - 1.

Skauto(tės) Parašas

כרטיס   № 142

השם ושם המשפחה *בלים*

הקן *קיבארט*   .השכבה *ש*

הגיל *1909*   המדרגה *II*

הבטחה

תפקיד *ראש ק'*

כמה זמן בהסתדרות *10 ח*

התעסקותו

כרטיס זה כחו יפה עד *1932 - XII - 31.*

יושב ראש חברת.העזר *J. Beil*

מזכיר הת"ר

ראש הקן

קובנה: יום *1* לחודש *III*   שנת *1932*

Table 15

Kybart youth with Ya'akov Kovensky who came for a visit from Eretz-Israel, 1935

First line from right: A.Rezvin, Y.Mirbukh, Shatenshtein, B.Vidomliansky, B, Tsikhak

Second line: R.Berniker, M.Khlamnovitz, F.Tilzer, Gershater, A.Shadkhanovitz, Y.Gidansky Sh.Borokhovitz

Third line: S.Frenkel, S.Manheim, ----,. Y.Kovensky, Gershater

Fourth line: Gershater, Sh.Bartenshtein

In 1929 a branch of the "Beitar" movement was established in Kibart. At the peak of its activity the branch had about 40 to 50 members aged 10-18, its activities including scouting, the geography of Eretz-Yisrael, military drill, trips, camping in the woods and also sports activities such as table tennis and football. The heads of the branch were Aryeh Apriyasky (lives in Peru), Zalman Panush (died in Israel) and from 1936 Avraham Rutshtein (exiled to Siberia and died there). From this branch Shemuel Panush, Rivkah Panush-Shemesh, Shemuel Frenkel and Yitzhak Berniker emigrated to Israel.

David Gamzu, the owner of the "Textilia" factory, was among the active "Revisionists" (the right wing Zionist party) in Kibart, and the main sponsor of the party's newspaper "Unzer Moment".

The group "Gesher" of "haShomer-haTzair" in Kybart, 1926

Standing from right: Mordehai Melamed, Aharon Shapira, Ya'akov Kovensky, Eliezer Blotnik, Zisl Kovensky, Shemaya Borokhovitz, Shemuel Abramson, Joseph Shapira.

In the following table one can see how the Kibart Zionists voted at Zionist Congresses in the years 1927-1935, once every two years:

Year	1927	1929	1931	1933	1935
No. of members	107	250	123	------	200
No. of votes	61	90	82	155	165
Zionist Socialists	11	16	9		
Tzeirei Zion	15	19	31		
Labor Party				92	117
Revisionists	4	1	13	31	
General Zionists A	16	30	13	13	15
General Zionists B					6
Grosmanists				1	2
Mizrakhi	15	24	16	18	25

A group of "haShomer-haTzair" members in Kybart 1929-1930

First line from right: S.Yurkansky, Z.Kovensky, H.Toker, Y.Lubotsky, Hofman, J.Borokhovitz,

Second line: Y.Kovensky, M.Melamed, H.Ofseyevitz, Sh.Blotnik, A.Shapira, Pintchuk, Sh.Abramson, M.Svirsky, S. Shapira

Third line: H.Kisetz,---, Magiliuker, Sh.Zarko, M.Linde, A.Katsizne, S.Yebart, E.Blotnik

The sports activities centered around the "Maccabi" branch, which was not a political organization and therefore included members of other movements. This branch had a group for gymnastics, a football team, and in the twenties had 85 members. (see table 16: "Maccabi" membership card of Z. Kovensky).

About 200 people from Lithuania participated in the second "Maccabiya" in Tel-Aviv in 1935 and most of them remained there, which included several young people from Kibart.

Among the activists of "Maccabi"" were Sh.Volovitzky, Dov Sheinzon and others.

The left wing circles in the town, who did not like the Zionist orientation of "Maccabi," established another sports organization "J.S.K.", but it lasted for only one year and closed down in 1926.

Table 16

ŽYDŲ
Sporto ir Gimnastikos Sajunga
MAKABI Lietuvoje
Nario bilietas

כרטיס־חבר

הסתדרות להתעמלות ולספורט
מכב״ בלטא

דפוס א. באק, קובנה.

Narlo mokestis

תשלום המס־ההחדשי לסניף
לשנת 193

יולי־סך	ל.		יאנואר־סך	ל.
הגובה			הגובה	
אוגוסט־סך	ל.		פברואר־סך	ל.
הגובה			הגובה	
ספטמבר־סך	ל.		מרץ־סך	ל.
הגובה			הגובה	
אוקטובר־סך	ל.		אפריל־סך	ל.
הגובה			הגובה	
נובמבר־סך			מאי־סך	
הגובה			הגובה	
דצמבר־סך	ל.		יוני־סך	ל.
הגובה			הגובה	

על הגובה לחתום ולאשר את קבלת המס
מדי חדש בחדשו במשבצתו המיוחדה
חבר שלא שלם שלשת חדשים רצופים
את מס־החדשי יוצא מהסניף.

מלא חובותיך להסתדרותך!

חסתדרות להתעמלות ולספורט
«מכבי» בליטא
(ענף להסתדרות העולמית «מכבי»)

סניף .... נר. 6
שם החבר ....
הגיל ....
משתתף בסקציה: ....

נכנס בסניף «מכבי»
יום ...... לחדש ...... שנת 19.34
בתור חבר ....
(חותם, תוער)

חירינו ...... מזכיר ......

הכרטיס נתן
יום 15 לחדש ...... שנת 19.34

זכור כי את שם «יהודה המכבי» הנך
נושא ישראל — עמך עברית — שפתך וארץ
ישראל — ארצך.

№ ....

Centro Komitetas — ההנהלה המרכזית

Pirmlainhas — יו״ר

Sehretorius — מזכיר

"HaShomer- HaTzair" organization in Kibart, 1932-1933

First row, standing from right: Sarah Jofe, Shifrah Fink, Brahah Sheinzon, Mosheh Khlamnovitz, Moshe Helershtein, Gotlib Borovik

Second row: ---, Joseph Bartenshtein, Yerakhmiel Jofe, Bebka Tsikhak, Mosheh Svirsky

Third row: Sarah Mandelblat, Perelz Kliatchko, Fruma Sakharovitz, Elkhanan Halperin, Dov Shtern, David Shadkhanovitz, Yehiel Feferman, Yitshak Skrobiansky, Grinshtein, Joseph Rosin, Aryeh Leibovitz, Avraham Leibovitz

Fourth row: L.Tsikhak, Tsevi Bromberg, Mendel Vizhansky, ---, ---, Borovik, Ze'ev Sheinzon, --- Rosa Senensky, Rivkah P., B.Borovik

The soccer team of "Maccabi" Kibart 1926-27
(Second from left: Gershonovitz and his son)

HaShomer HaTsair organization in Kibart 1937-1938

First line above from right: Sarah Yofe, ---, Mosheh Khlamnovitz, Emanuel Voltchansky, ---.

Second line: ---, Yafah Froman, Avraham Leibovitz, Yosef Bartenshtein, Esther Ozerov, Dov Shtern,

Yekhiel Feferman, Hayim Borokhovitz, David Levin, Max Vizhansky

Third line: Nehamah Levin, ---, Fruma Sakharovitz, Doba Skrobiansky (?)

Fourth line: ---, Bobe Borovik, Shalom Vidomliansky, Yerakhmiel Yofe, ---, ---, Sarah Mandelblat, Tehiyah Rosin

Fifth line: Miriam Landau. Yente Levin, Margolis (?), last in line- Zalman Epshtein

Sixth line from right: second-Levin, fifth- Yitshak Zakharik. Last-Michael Davidson

A group of Kybart youth 1933-34

First line from right: Yurzditzky, Sh.Borokhovitz, S.Manheim, R.Voltchansky, B.Vidomliansky, A.Shadkhanovitz

Second line: M.Shtern., E.Taburisky, Z.Kovensky, N.Rakhmil, Rog

Third line: M.Dembo, S.Frenkel, Fainzilber, ---, ---, A.Apriyasky

The founding committee of "Maccabi" Kibart, 1924

Sitting from right: Frenkel, ---, Sh.Volovitzky, J.Filipovsky, Beker
Standing: Y.Levit, Jafe, Vald

"Beitar" youth in Kybart. The farewell meeting of A.Apriyasky's departure to Peru and Fima Frenkel's departure to Memel

Second line from right: ---, ——, Tsevi Borokhovitz, Shemuel P., Shemuel Frenkel, ---, Fima Frenkel

Third Line: Zelma Frenkel, Niuta Rakhmil, Avraham Rutshtein, Aryeh Apriyasky, Rivkah P, Shatenshtein, Nehamah Levin

The soccer team of "Maccabi' Kibart 1932

A Kibart youth group 1936

First line from right: Beirakhovitz, Z.Kovensky, Khlamnovitz, A.Shadkhanovitz, B.Vidomliansky, S.Frenkel, Gershater, B.Tsikhak, R.Yasven, N.Rakhmil, R.Berniker, Z.Borokhovitz, A.Borokhovitz, A.Lakovsky, M.Svirsky

Second line: E.Taburisky, Sh.Bartenshtein, ---, Z.Epshtein, E.Halperin

Third line: Gershater, D.Shadkhanovitz, I.Voltchansky, B.Tsikhak, ---,

A group of Kybart youth, 1932

First line, staying from right: Ze'ev Berzdovsky, Hana Sheinzon, Joseph Bartenshtein

Second line: Ze'ev Sheinzon, Sarah Yurkansky, Pesia Yasovsky, Benjamin Vidomliansky

Third line: Shifrah Fink, Jehudith Borokhovitz, Mordehai Borokhovitz, Khyene Berezdovsky

Fourth line: Rivkah P., Rosa Senensky

The "Bar-Mitzvah" party of Mosheh Khlamnovitz 1934

First line from right: Yehiel Feferman, Shemuel P., David Levin, Dov Shtern,Yitshak Skrobiansky, ---,Hadasah Bartenshtein, Frida Shtern, Aya Khashman

Second line: Iser Kahanov, Aryeh Miltz, Yitshak Rabinovitz, ---, Shlomovilz, Mosheh Khlamnovitz, Havivah Khlamnovitz, Peretz Kliatchko, Yitshak Feinzilber, Hayim Borokhovitz, Gotlib Borovik

Third line: Shlomovitz, Mordehai Shtern, ---, ---, ---, Michael Davidson

Fourth line: ---, Yehudah Rabinovitz, ---,

The Voluntary Fire Brigade, with remarkable Jewish participation, should be mentioned. Its station, in the main street near the government elementary school, had a wooden tower five stories high and on it a siren for alarming the volunteers. There was a storeroom with one or two water tanks mounted on a cart, a stand by hand pump activated by four people, also ordinary water containers and long hoses. When a fire broke out the firemen would stop passing carts, untie their horses and harness them to their equipment. This was taken for granted and a common custom.

Shoemaker Tzibulsky was among the Jews who for many years continued to do their duty in the fire brigade, and as such was decorated with many medals of distinction and for some time was even the chief of the brigade. Berniker the manufacturer also held this position for many years.

The Kybart Volunteer Fire Brigade

First line, sitting from right: ---,-, Voltchansky, the mayor Budrevicius, Berniker, the medic Sher

Second line: Tsibulsky, H.Jofe, ---,-, Frenkel---------

Welfare Institutions.

During the German occupation in World War I, many Jewish refugees from Poland arrived in Kibart and by in 1918 a committee to care for them had been established. This committee cared for them very well, enabling some of them to return to their homes or to go on to other destinations, and for others it cared for their livelihood and existence.

Social help was very developed in Kibart, and the Community Committee had a budget of 10,000 to 12,000 Lit per year for this purpose. After this Committee was closed down its functions were transferred to the "Ezrah" institution, which did very well, having among its duties also "Ma'oth Khitim" (help for the poor for Pesakh) and the supply of heating materials for the needy. The chairman of this institution was J. Sh. Khashman for many years.

Over the years the budget for this institution shrunk and by 1935 it was only 5-6 thousand Lit. Taking into account that during the years many rich merchants left and the status of some of the people changed from having been donors to being needy, the activities of the "Ezrah" institution were certainly worthy of their name (Ezrah - help in Hebrew). There were also poor families who moved from other places to Kibart, thinking that that they would be better of living in Kibart, despite the fact that in their former abodes there were many more Jews. Parallel to the "Ezrah" institution was the "Linath-haTsedek" association, whose yearly budget was about 1,500 Lit.

Another association was "Gemiluth Hesed" which granted interest free loans to those in need. Its chairman was Mikhael Shadkhanovitz, who was very active in welfare matters.

The budgets of these institutions were financed from donations and from balls that were organized by local amateurs and sometimes with the help of amateur artists from nearby towns. On February 8, 1930, a ball took place in the hall of "Palas" cinema in Kibart on behalf of the "Ezrah" institution, with different shows performed by youths from Kibart and Virbalis and a band from Vilkavishk.

Another institution working on behalf of health care for children was called "OZE". It began its activities in 1925 with a remarkable budget of 3,500 Lit per year, but ten years later its budget had decreased to only 1,500 Lit, with which they nevertheless did much good work. About 30 children received a glass of fresh milk and a roll every day, weak children received cod liver oil and 10-12 children were sent to a summer resort every summer, two doctors voluntarily practicing preventive medicine and giving medical help. The budget for these activities came from monthly donations of about 50 members, from a one-time fund raising affair and from a yearly ball, the income of which was dedicated to "OZE". Another important action of the Kibart Community at the end of the thirties was to send 10 youngsters to study on its account to the "ORT" vocational schools in Kovno.

Generally Kibart distinguished itself by its generosity not only to local institutions, but "delegates" who came to raise funds for outside institutions did not leave the town empty handed.

In the thirties the Yiddish "General Jewish Encyclopedia" began to be published. There were 10 subscribers in Kibart and compared with much bigger Jewish communities this was a remarkable number.

Another example of the nature of Kibart as a large city was the fact that people addressed each other by their family names - Mr. so and so - and not by a nickname as was common in most of Lithuania. Generally people in Lithuania did not know their neighbors surnames because everybody was called by his nickname, according to the village his grandfather had come from, or by his occupation, or by the name of his mother or grandmother or by a nickname which had been passed on from father to son for generations. Even the Yiddish was a little different in Kibart, the vowels "oi" being pronounced "au" in some words. For example, instead of pronouncing "Boikh" (belly) it was pronounced "Baukh" like in German. The letter "H"' was pronounced correctly and not like in other places "A" or "O" instead. Also the "Sh" and the "S" were correctly pronounced and not like in other places, mainly in north Lithuania, where these two consonants were mixed up and caused many funny misunderstandings.

Kibart today - March 2003, according to information I received lately from there.

The real authorities are in Vilkaviskis, and Kybartai today has only a "seniunas" of a little "seniunija". It is much smaller than "valscius" (county) ."Seniunas" has much less rights, finance and possibilities comparing with pre-war "miesto burmistras"(mayor). This doesn't refer to the new quarters in town built 30-40 years ago.

Only several three story buildings were left in Kybartai after World War II. The town became ugly and dirty -compared with that what can be seen in pre-war pictures.

The town does not enough money for electricity to lighten the streets in the evenings. In 1900 Kybartai already was the first town in Lithuania with municipal electric lighting.

E : 1 9 3 3 -1 9 4 0. The Years of the Town's Decline.

On Saturday, the first of April 1933, Kibart Jews who went to Eydtkuhnen as usual, were surprised to see a uniformed S.A. man in front of each Jewish shop, who prevented them from entering. This was the beginning of the end of German Jews, and for that matter, of East European Jewry too, but on that day people did not as yet imagine to what this would lead and how it would end.

During the following years traffic through this border passage decreased gradually, because most of the Kibart's Jews abstained from going to Eydtkuhnen, very few would cross the border. At the railway station the traffic also decreased a lot, only groups of "Khalutzim' would pass the station from time to time on their way to Eretz-Israel. In the luxurious rooms of the station, once upon a time designated for the Tsars family, the Magistrate's Court was now housed and the only persons frequenting these rooms were those who came to be judged or just curious onlookers.

In the long building near the border where there were at one time 15 shops, only two were left, of all the others only the signs remained. A few carts would pass the border during the day, carrying some goods for processing by those few "Expediters" still in Kibart.

Those merchants whose business was not based on the population of Eydtkuhnen or on smuggling, continued as usual. The same was true of the factories and workshops who produced for the local market.

According to the official 1940 telephone book there were 123 phone subscribers in Kibart, of whom about 36 belonged to state institutions such as the police, border police, customs, courts etc. Of the other 87 subscribers 51 (59%) belonged to Jewish owners of the large shops, the manufacturers and the expediters (see tables 19 and 19a below).

Kybartai

Kirtimai

Vilniaus apskr.

Agentūra. Telefonas.
Vilniaus abon. Nr. 486
Tel. veik. — 1.

Kybartai

Vilkaviškio apskr.

Paštas II eil. Telefonas ir telegrafas.
Taup. valst. kasų skyrius.
Tel. veik. — N.

¢ Abramavičlus, Boris, d-ras, Vilniaus
g-vė 1 65
¢ Alperavičlai, brotlai, akc. b-vė,
galanterijos prekyba ir pirm. Lie-
tuvos baltinių fabrikas, A. Sme-
tonos al. 85 29
¢ Altuteris, Borotis, A. Smetonos alė-
ja 113 35
Arešto namai, Kybartų miesto,
A. Smetonos al. 99 13
Baldomas, Karolis, Gutkalmio dv.. 104
¢ „Baja", baltinių fabrikas, Vilniaus
g-vė 5 69
¢ Berenšteinas, Simonas, fabriko
„Unitas" sav. ir akc. b-vės
„Union Standart" pirmininkas, Al-
gimanto g-vė 6 99
¢ Bernikeris, Jokūbas, A. Smetonos
al. 62 48
¢ Blagoslavenskienė, S., Žydų g-vė 5. 20
Budrevičius, Česlovas, vaistininkas,
A. Smetonos al. 61 78
Budzinskis, Viktoras, Eustachovo
dv. 61
¢ Centnerzverienė, F., A. Smetonos
al. 113 67
¢ Centralnis žydų bankas, Kybartų
skyrius, A. Smetonos al. 93 6
¢ Centralnis žydų bankas, Kybartų
skyrius, buhalterija, A. Smetonos
al. 93 25
¢ Cirutnickis, Maksas, krautuvė,
A. Smetonos al. 48 117
Cepulis, St., kunigas, Kybartų para-
pijos klebonas, Bažnyčios gat-
vė 12 2
Dorbo rūmų kultūros klubas,
A. Smetonos al. 57 115
¢ Daugelsickis, Vulfas, maisto krau-
tuvė, A. Smetonos al. 113 127
Ekspeditorių kambarys, prie Virbe-
lio muitinės 55
¢ Eiperinas, Idelis, pirklys, kolon.
prekyba, A. Smetonos al. 21 ... 82

GERBIAMUS ASMENIS ĮVAIRIOMIS PROGOMIS TINKAMIAUSIA SVEIKINTI — IX — TELEGRAMOMIS

Kybartai

Yeržbolovskis, Aronas, limonado
dirbtuvė, Vištyčio g-vė 6 66
Tėlių sandėlis, sav. B. Račkauskas-118
Yidomitlanskis, Leizeris, geležies ir
dažų prekyba, Vištyčio g-vė 5.. 28
Yirballo geležinkelio stotis 86
Yirballo muitinė:
Viršininkas, kabin. 56
Viršininko St. Naginionio butas.. 111
Pašto siuntinių skyrius, Virballo
geležink. st. 43
Pereinamasis punktas 33
Yineryk, Mėta, Kybartų km. 128
Tetlečių privatinė progimnazija,
A. Smetonos al. 27 97
Žabrickas, Juozas, d-ras, miesto
gydytojas, veneros ligų ambula-
torija, Vydūno g-vė 12 18

TELEFONO ĮSTAIGOSE VISADA TIKRAS LAIKAS, KURIS PAGEIDAUJANTIEMS PRANEŠAMAS TELEFONU

Gaška, Juozas, apylinkės teisėjas, Bažnyčios g-vė 15a 90

Gavėnas, Kostas, Daugėlaičių km. 106

Gelenas ir Samošas, Jonipilvė, A. Smetonos al. 28 19

Geležinkelių multinis agentūra, Virbalio gelež. st. 52

Geležkelių policija, Virbalio gelež. st. 17

Geldūnienė, Anelė, akušerė, Plytinės g-vė 25 77

Gonsas, Dovydas, A. Smetonos al. 60 11

Gimnazija, valstybinė, Bažnyčios g-vė 10 91

Goldbergas, Izakas, A. Smetonos al. 83 40

Goldbergas, Josolis, A. Smetonos al. 62 3

Gramadskis, Liudvikas, šinoptinio ir klimatologinio posto stebėtojas, Šjkėnų dv. 34

Grimienė, Ona, A. Smetonos alėja 17 49

Grinkiškas, Jokūbas, kolon. krautuvė, A. Smetonos al. 83 131

Gurinskas, Jurgis, kunigas, Bažnyčios g-vė 11 102

Jurodickis, Povilas, pirklys, Vydūno g-vė 1 4

Kačiunas, Feisachas, A. Smetonos al. 61 60

Kiliūgas, Albertas, komercijos banko direktorius, Darieus ir Girėno g-vė 17 14

Komercijos bankas, Kybartų skyrius, A. Smetonos al. 97 15

Kovenskis, Abraomas, A. Smetonos al. 113 80

,,Labor'', t-is lietuvoje gelažinių baldų fabrikas, D-ro Šnoiderio g-vė 2 68

Landau, Mauša, A. Smetonos alėja 62 101

Lavitas, Elijas, Sinagogos g-vė 5 46

Lietuvos bankas, Kybartų skyrius, A. Smetonos al. 81:
Direktorius, kabin. 70
Buhalterija 64
Kolūmo kasa, Virbalio gelež. st. 31

Lietuvos darbininkų artelė ,,Darbininkas'', Virbalio gelež. st. 105

Lietuvos ekspedicijos kontora, sav. Eduardas Mešovskis 119

turija, Jašua, dipl. jur., priv. gynėjas, A. Smetonos al. 99 92

Marijampolskienė, I., d-ras, Vydūno g-vė 12 58

Markovskis, Vulfas, d-ras, A. Smetonos al. 99 74

,,Mars'', špizo ir metalo liejykla, sav. Gilžmanas, Gedimino g-vė 21 42

Miesto savivaldybė, A. Smetonos al. 99:
Burmistras 1
Kasline .... (1)

Milcas, Simonas, A. Smetonos alėja 57/59 44

Misturevičius, Pijus, priv. gynėjas, Vilniaus g-vė 5 50

,,Nektaras'', baras, A. Smetonos al. 87 98

Noubacheris, Frydrichas, A. Smetonos al. 11 76

,,Nova'', bagelų ir valdiždžių dirbtuvė, sav. Urbonas, I., Vištyčio g-vė 47 129

Odyniecas, Stanislovas, ekspeditorius, Rambyno g-vė 2 12

Orantienė, Leokadija, akušerė, Gedimino g-vė 22 126

,,Patemonas'', akc. b-vė, pilyline, Virbalio lauke 47

Papočkys, Jurgis, mokytojas, Bažnyčios g-vė 18b 88

Papirienė, C., vicebartis ,,Hotel'', A. Smetonos al. 89 27

Pasienio policija:
Baro viršininkas, Pasienio policijos kordonas 81
I rajono viršininkas, Sakslupio dv. 107
I rajono 2 sargyba, Sionelčių km. 114
II rajono viršininkas, d-ro Šnaiderio g-vė, Liopinaičio namas 7
II rajono I sargyba, Bajorų km. 116
II rajono 2 sargyba 113
III rajono viršininkas, Kybeikių km. 108
III rajono 2 sargyba, Matlaukio km. 109

Paštas, Geležinkelio st.:
Viršininkas, kabin. 63
Raštinė 10
Siuntinių skyrius 84
Registruotos ir paprastos skyriai 110
Telegrafas 23
Viršininko butas 62
Telefono-telegrafo prižiūrėtojas, butas 112

Policijos nuovados raštinė, A. Smetonos al. 81 8

Pradžios mokykla Nr. 1, A. Smetonos aikštė 9

Prapuolenis, Juozas, Bažnyčios g-vė 16a 100

Prenskis, Zacharas, ekspeditorius, A. Smetonos al. 95 73

Rechlinai, br., Vorpučių km., senas dvaras 22

Rachlinas, Boruchas, A. Smetonos al. 62 94

Rachlinas, Isakas, A. Smetonos al. 113 51

Rachilnas, Izraelis, A. Smetonos al. 97 16

Račkauskas, Boruchas, kontora, Vilniaus g-vė 18 120

Račkauskas, Boruchas, pirklys, Vilniaus g-vė 7 55

Reimonas, Robertas, Vilniaus g-vė 1 95

Rezvinas, Evsiejus, pirklys, A. Smetonos al. 93 25

Rudšteinas, Mejeris, auto vežimas, vežlio folksismas, Vilniaus g-vė 12 89

Skardykla, Kybarių miesto, A. Smetonos al. 103

Skrupkus, Stasys, Virbalio pasienio veterinarijos gydytojas, Vištyčio g-vė 11 37

Šapiras, Abraomas, tomšo ūkio produktų prekyba, A. Smetonos al. 60 25

Satchanavičius, Maksas, galanterijos krautuvė, A. Smetonos alėja 83 89

Simbergas, Leiseris, Rambyno g-vė 4 121

Yamulienis, Antanas, Vištyčio gat-vė 26 122

Teismas, Kybarių apylinkės, A. Smetonos al. 93 36

Teismo antstolis, Kybarių apylinkės, A. Smetonos al. 48 21

Tiltaris ir Gerštateckus, naujoji velsinė, A. Smetonos al. 83 35

Ugniagesiai:
Savanorių komanda ....
Virbalio gelažinkelio stoties komanda ....

,,Union Standart'', akc. b-vė, chemiso gamyba, Vilniaus g-vė 12 7

Dzininkų draugija, A. Smetonos al. 3

Dzininkų draugija, urmo sandelis, Algimanto g-vė 6 11

Ūkio bankas, A. Smetonos al. 99 ....

,,Vagos'' artelė, Kybarių skyrius, Miegalio multinė ....

Valsčiaus savivaldybė, A. Smetonos al. 99 ....

Valstybės saugumo policija, Kybarių rajonas, Žeigibio g-vė 13 ....

Valčanskis, Aleksas, Vydūno gat-vė 3 ....

Valčanskis, Aleksas, Vilniaus gat-vė 7 ....

,,Vega'', baltinių dirbtuvė, Vilniaus g-vė 5 ....

Volcas, Abraomas, pirklys, Algimanto g-vė 6 ....

276

In those years the influence of the Lithuanian Merchants Association (Verslas), who propagated the boycott of Jewish shops and to buy only "Lithuanian" (Lithuania for Lithuanians) increased. Slowly but surely this propaganda gained popularity among wider circles and Jewish shops were avoided. As a result not only did many Jewish families leave the town and to look for a livelihood elsewhere, but many young people did so too, in order to find work in Kovno.

In 1937 or 1938 the well known "story" of the geese occurred and this is the time to relate it:

Lithuania's main export items were agricultural products, most of them to Germany, one of the major items being live geese. At the beginning of winter, the exporters would bring the geese to a lot in the railway station. The quacking of the geese was heard day and night during a month or so. The geese or a part of them were transferred across the border by foot and a white throng of geese could be seen flowing along the main street to the border. When Hitler's rule in Germany had become a fact, he demanded that Memel (Klaipeda) and its districts return to German sovereignty. By way of pressure he cancelled the commercial treaty with Lithuania, as a result of which all the geese assigned for export were left without buyers. To solve the problem, the Lithuanian government ordered that all its clerks receive part of their salary in geese. The amount of geese for every clerk was calculated according to his salary. Thus the price of geese greatly decreased and many people enjoyed roast geese and geese schmaltz.

In order to illustrate the image and decline of the town mention is made here of several excerpts from an article written by the writer David Umru which was published in the Yiddish newspaper "Folksblat" in July 1939: "Eydtkuhnen made a living from Kibart and Kibart from Eydtkuhnen." Today both towns have declined in comparison to their living standards in recent times. Kibart is different from all other Lithuanian towns. Not only the grandiose railway station but also the other buildings look similar to a large city. The columns of trees along the sidewalks, the lawns and also the behavior of its people are not provincial. Kibart is imbued with western culture. Even the door frames of the shops are a copy of German examples...

Now there is a struggle with the so-called "German disease." Girls, who not long ago only knew German, opened their mouths and began to speak a fluent Yiddish. Library workers used the opportunity and started to mobilize new subscribers, and if you paid the Lit, so why not to take a book? Then having taken a book, you read a little and even started to feel the taste of it.

The public institutions in Kibart are successful. The activities of the "OZE" and "ORT" organizations are not comparable to that of any other town in Lithuania. Ten youngsters were sent to the "ORT" vocational schools in Kovno financed by the community. Preventive medicine of OZE'" is also on a high level. The only association which is lacking is one which would cause cultural activity to advance to a proper level.

Once there were factories in Kibart. Today there are no factories left, only poverty. About ten men are still "Couriers" who travel to Kovno every day, taking some smuggled goods with them to sell there in order to add some income to their poor livelihood. But in the street poverty is almost unnoticeable. It is well hidden as is appropriate for a town with an outward shine".

In spite of the fact that the situation was deteriorating all the time, it is worthwhile mentioning the help Kibart's Jews gave to refugees from the Suvalk region at the end of 1939.

According to the Ribbentrop-Molotov treaty the Russians occupied the Suvalk region, but after surveying the exact borders according to which Poland was carved up between Russia and Germany, the Suvalk region fell into German hands. The retreating Russians allowed anyone who so wanted to join them and to move into the territory occupied by them, and indeed many young people left this area together with the Russians. The Germans then expelled from their houses those Jews who remained in Suvalk and its vicinity, their property was robbed, after which they were led to the Lithuanian border, where they were left in great poverty. The Lithuanians did not allow them to enter Lithuania and the Germans did not allow them to go back. Thus they stayed there in this swampy area in cold and rain for several weeks, until Jewish youngsters from border villages in Lithuania smuggled them into Lithuania by different routes, with much risk to themselves. Altogether about 2,400 refugees were passed through or infiltrated by themselves, and were then dispersed in the Vilkavishk and Mariampol districts. In Kibart alone 125 refugees were accommodated, among them several tens of "Khalutsim", who got the warm and devoted treatment for which Kibart's Jews were famous.

F: 1 9 4 0 - 1 9 4 1.   Under Soviet Rule.

In June 1940 Lithuania was annexed by the Soviet Union and became a Soviet Republic. The president of the Lithuanian state Smetona together with many of his friends, escaped to Germany via Kibart.

A border guard unit of the Red Army arrived in Kibart and was put up in the buildings of the railway workers at the corner of Vishtinetz (Vistycio) street. Russian soldiers stormed the shops, buying everything they saw. Goods lying in the storerooms without use were brought into the shops and sold for good money.

At the end of July the banks were nationalized and deposits frozen. At first one was allowed to draw 1,000 Ruble per month per family, later this sum were gradually reduced to 250 Ruble. Then those industries for which the following criteria applied were nationalized, i.e. " a factory which employs more than 20 workers or a factory where a minimum of 10 workers are employed, which uses mechanical power and whose products are important for some other factory."

In Kibart most of the Jewish factories were nationalized, commissars installed and appointed as their directors. These were communists who had been freed from jails or those who had been active in the communist underground, among them several local Jews. At the beginning of August commissars were appointed to such shops as Shadkhanovitz, Seinensky and others, whose annual turnover was more than 150,000 Lit.

The owners of the factories and shops became clerks and salesmen in their own enterprises, being responsible to the commissars who kept the keys of the enterprises and kept hold of the cash.

Since they had no managing experience, they were helped by the former owners during the year of Soviet rule before the war.

Russian single officers and officers' families of the border guard were accommodated in private flats in the nicer buildings, where mostly Jewish families were living.

The supply of goods diminished and as a result prices gradually rose. The middle class, mostly Jewish, was badly hurt and its living standard decreased gradually, also wage earners hardly made a living.

During the school year of 1940/41 the Hebrew school became a Jewish school, with Yiddish as the teaching language. Its headmaster A.Varshavsky was dismissed and sent to Kupishok as a teacher, and the school was now directed by teachers Sheine Halperin and Mordehai Lurie. The Zionist Youth Organizations were dispersed and the Comsomol - the Communist Youth Organization - started to mobilize new members. (see Kibart Jewish Kindergarten on the occasion of Chanukah celebration in 1940 in photograph below).

Some "Shaulists" - a nationalist Lithuanian organization of ex- army soldiers - and among them some Zionist activists, were arrested, as were some Jewish traders in foreign currency and also people who had been slandered for different wrong doings.

A tense and fearful atmosphere prevailed and people were afraid of what the morrow would bring. Add to that the rumors, which were spread deliberately, that after the division of Poland between Russia and Germany in accordance with the Ribbentrop-Molotov treaty, Lithuania too would be divided, with Kibart and its environs being annexed by Germany.

According to this treaty all Germans without any exception, who until then lived in Lithuania, were repatriated, and since many Germans lived in Kibart and its surroundings their departure added to the tense atmosphere.

In the middle of June 1941, the authorities started to send families of owners of the nationalized factories, shops and houses, also those suspected of Zionist activity, to exile deep in the USSR. Only a few hours notice was given, during which those doomed to exile had to pack their belongings which were limited in quantity, and were then taken to the freight wagons.

From Kibart Hayim Miltz with his wife and daughter, Michael Shadkhanovitz, his wife and son, Yisrael Rakhlin, his wife, his mother and his little son and daughter, Berniker and his wife and two sons, were exiled.

Broadcasts from the B.B.C. in London about the "Eastern Front" and news about the concentration of the German army along the borders of the USSR, did not have a strong enough impact among Kibart's Jews to make them take their belongings and escape away from the German border as far as possible.

One could possible explain this state of mind by the tense atmosphere and the uncertainty which paralyzed any ability to decide. In addition there was the strong belief in the might of the Red Army which propaganda had managed to be implanted in the minds of most Jews.

(Pictures supplied by Shne'ur Rakhlin-Kopenhagen)
Kibart Jewish Kindergarten-Khanukah 1940
The third from left in the first line above- Shne'ur Rakhlin

G: 1 9 4 1.

German Occupation and Destruction of the Jewish Community.

On June 22, 1941, between 4 and 5 o'clock in the morning, the German army entered Kibart without any real resistance. Only a group of soldiers from the Russian Border Guard fortified themselves in the cellar of the mayor's building and fought to the last man.

The Germans freed all prisoners from jail, among them those accused of resistance to Soviet rule. They immediately started to organize local groups in order to take revenge on the communists and the Jews and also to help the Germans impose order and rehabilitate civilian life. The head of the Lithuanian activists who put themselves under German control was the Doctor Zubrickas, who had arrived in Kibart in 1933, had been active in the Lithuanian nationalist organizations, as a result of which the Soviets had imprisoned him.

During the first days of occupation the German army ruled and did not take any measures against Jews. There were even cases of German authorities helping Jews to get back some property previously robbed by Lithuanians, with Jewish girls serving as interpreters in Eydtkuhnen.

But after several days the Civil Administration was established and one of its first orders was to limit the rights of the Jews. The spokesman of the municipality passed through the streets and with the help of a bell assembled the crowd to read them this order:

1. **Jews are dismissed from their jobs in the municipality and in all other public and economic institutions.**

2. **Jews are forbidden to leave the town or to move to another place without a permit. Jews have to deliver up all weapons and radios in their possessions.**

3. **Jews are forbidden to leave their homes between 6 o'clock in the evening until 6 o'clock in the morning.**

4. **It is forbidden for Jews to have any contact with non-Jews.**

5. **Jews have to prepare yellow patches to be worn on the back and on the front of their garment (at first it was a round patch, later it was changed to a "Magen David").**

The first victims among the Jews were communists who had held positions in local institutions. Great anger was vented on those who had participated in the arrests the Soviet authorities had carried out just before the war. Among the first to be shot was the author's friend from high school Elhanan Halperin, who was a member of the Komsomol.

According to this method, which was, as became clear later on, identical everywhere, all the intelligentsia were detained first and transferred to the Gestapo in Eydtkuhnen. It became known, that when the lawyer Jehoshua

Lurie was detained and transferred to Eydtkuhnen, his wife with their little blond daughter came to the commander of the S.S. and asked him to release her father. He was freed indeed but only for a short time, because a few days later he was murdered together with all the Jewish men of Kibart.

Kibart was situated in a strip 25 km wide from the border with Germany, where Stahlecker had ordered the Gestapo of Tilzit to exterminate all Jews. The head of the Gestapo in Tilzit, Hans Joachim Boehme, contacted the Gestapo and the Border Guard in Eydtkuhnen in order to determine the date and all other details for the murder of the men in Kibart. The execution of this murder was to be an example for the Gestapo man from Eydtkuhnen, Tietz, who was in charge there and who was nominated to execute such murders in the future. (Tietz committed suicide later). The Lithuanian police too was informed about the date of the "operation". Their part was to detain the men, to assemble them and to act as guards, conveyors and executors.

At the beginning of July all Jewish men and youngsters above 16 were taken from their homes and concentrated in a barn in the farm of Baldamas in the village Gudkaimis, about 6 km north of Kibart. There they were ill treated, left without food and water for several days and forced to dig holes in the nearby sand quarry of Peskines.

During the night of Sunday, July 6, 1941, all were shot at the edge of the holes they had dug for themselves, after having been forced to hand over all their belongings and to take off their upper clothing. 185 Jews and 15 Lithuanians, activists under previous Soviet rule, were shot that night. A monument in memory of the victims was erected at the mass graves several years ago. (see picture).

Apparently the only Jew who was in that barn and heard everything, was Benjamin Jasven, the owner of a sewing workshop of men's shirts in Kibart named "BeJa". He managed to hide and 12 days later arrived in the Kovno Ghetto. He managed to survive the 3 years of German rule in Kovno and after the liquidation of the Ghetto he was sent to the concentration camp of Dachau. After he survived Dachau he delivered his testimony to "The Committee for investigation of the crimes of the Nazis and their Lithuanian helpers" in 1947 in Munich.

The head of the Lithuanian gang who took part in the murder was the above mentioned Doctor Zubrickas. Other murderers were the Border Guard policeman Betinas, the policeman Zaganevicius, a German repatriate who returned to Lithuania named Lozovsky, the chief of the police Vailokaitis, the student Budrevicius - the son of the former mayor who was exiled to Siberia, the head of the agricultural society Orintas, and others.

After murdering the men and the youngsters, all women as well as the old and the children were concentrated in the red brick houses which had been emptied from Soviet soldiers. There they stayed for about a month and then all were transported, almost without any belongings, to the Ghetto in Virbalis.

The Ghetto in Virbalis was established in the almost empty streets where the repatriated Germans had lived before. The head of the Ghetto was the only dentist in town, Mrs. Sheine Pauzisky, who used to mix with those Lithuanians who were also her patients and had good connections in the state and municipal institutions.

A special shop was opened in the Ghetto for the supply of food. The shopkeeper was a Lithuanian, an honest man, who took care to supply the required quantities of food to the Ghetto inhabitants.

All young women and children aged 12-16 would go to various types of work in the town and the vicinity. A quasi employment bureau was established in the Ghetto where unemployed people would come to look for work and also peasants from the vicinity who would select women and youngsters for work. Among the employers there were evil and cruel people who treated the women and children very badly, but there were also brave people who maintained relations with the Jews. There were even some who hid 10 Jewish women when the murders began, but of the few women only Bela Mirbukh and her mother from Virbalis survived after hiding for 3 years at the farm of a Lithuanian teacher near the town where Bela worked as an agricultural worker. Bela Rosenberg too, the young daughter of farm owners near the town, survived after being hidden somewhere in the vicinity.

After a short time, one night at the end of July or at the beginning of August, all old women, the sick and all those who were unemployed were taken from the Ghetto and conveyed to the anti-tank trenches, about 2 km north of the town, which the Russians had dug along the German border, where they were shot and buried.

After this "action" the authorities promised that nothing bad would happen to the Jews anymore and according to German methods of deception, the women were told that also their husbands were working in all sorts of jobs nearby. During this time, Lithuanians acquaintances and strangers would come and tell the women that they had seen their men and that they had asked for money, valuables or clothing, which the women would willingly hand over to them. These false requests increased from day to day and the women started to believe, wrongly of course, that maybe there was hope for them to see their beloved ones soon and even to join them. They believed what they wanted to believe and closed their ears to information about murder and extermination, which other women who worked outside told them.

Among the Lithuanian population there were rumors that the end of the rest of the Jews was near, but none came to warn them of this danger. The women lived with the illusion that they would join their husbands soon, baked, cooked and packed parcels. Then came the terrible day, Thursday September 11, 1941, the nineteenth of Elul 5701, when the Lithuanians arrived at night with carts, took all the women and children out to the anti-tank trenches and murdered them there in cold blood.

This was the tragic end of the Jewish Community of Kibart.

In May 1987 the monument in memory of the communities of Kibart (Kibartai), Virbaln (Virbalis) and Pilvishok (Pilvishkis) was unveiled at the cemetery in Holon. Zisl Kovensky, David Shadkhanovitz, Frida Shtern-Rokhman and Berta Seinensky-Sheines initiated and completed this important project on behalf of the former Kibart Community.

The monument at the cemetery of Holon in memoriam of the communities of Pilvishok, Virbaln and Kibart who were murdered in July-August 1941

In 2002 through the initiative of the few remaining former Kibarters a remembrance tablet was fixed at the "Holocaust Cellar" at Mount Zion in Jerusalem. The inscription says: For eternal memory of the martyrs of the communities of Kibart and Virbaln (Lithuania), who were murdered and buried alive by the Nazis and their Lithuanian helpers, may God obliterate their names, the men at the sands of Peskines on 6.7.1941, 11-th of Tamuz 5701, the women and the children at the Vigaines fields on 11.9.1941, 19-th of Elul 5701.

Their sacred memory will never be forgotten.

The remnants of Kibart-Virbaln communities in Israel and in the Diaspora

H: Postscript Written by Peretz Kliatchko, a native of Kibart.

I lived in Kovno after the war and visited Kibart from time to time. I would walk along the streets and alleys and try to imagine the beloved pleasant town in which I had spent my happy childhood. I would stop beside houses and backyards and try to remember the names of the families who had lived in these houses. No Jews lived in Kibart after the war and of those who had lived there when the war began nobody had survived and I did not expect to meet any. I did not even meet Lithuanian acquaintances, because the battle front ended near Vilkavishk and the Germans evacuated the entire population from the front zone, including Kibart, to Germany. Exhausted and battered I would return to Kovno.

In 1960 my friend Dov Shtern, who was born in Kibart, and I went to Kibart in order to look for the mass graves. We knew that the men had been murdered in the sand quarries (Peskines) and so we went there. In nearby single houses nobody knew, or did not want to know, the exact site of the mass graves. The answers we usually received were that these people had been living there only since the war and therefore had no local knowledge, but we were under the impression that they were lying. Then we met a middle aged Lithuanian who asked us what we were looking for, and after we told him he said that he too was looking for the graves of the 15 Lithuanians, communists and activists of the trade unions from Kibart and vicinity, who were murdered together with the 185 Jewish men. He joined us and then he asked the questions. One woman pointed in the right direction saying that it was easy to locate the graves, because the grass on them was much greener than in the fields nearby. We found the place easily; it was not fenced, there were no signs, and cows were grazing in this field. With the exception of the different shades of the color of the grass, it looked like any other field. We stayed there, bowed down, and departed with much pain in our hearts.

Returning to Kovno I wrote a sharp letter of protest to the local authorities, demanding the repair of this terrible injustice. A year later, when we, Dov Shtern and myself, visited this place again we found it fenced off with barbed wire and in the middle there was a wooden sign with an inscription. Cows did not graze there any more.

At the end of the sixties I received information that a trial was to be held in Kovno of one of the criminals who had participated in the mass murder of Kibart's Jews. The trial was to be held in the upper Lithuanian court, *in camera*. The accused was a Lithuanian, the son of a former estate owner, who had hidden all the years until caught recently, but I have unfortunately forgotten his name. It turned out that another murderer, the former policeman Betinas, who had been sentenced to 25 years in prison, had been freed. According to the agreement between Chancellor Adenauer and Secretary Khrushchev all German prisoners, and some Lithuanians too, who did not take an active part in the murder of Soviet citizens, were freed from prisons and camps. Thus, many murderers, against whom there was no legal evidence available that they had actually shot innocent people, were freed. The Lithuanian murderer, who had been in hiding all these years, secretly met with that freed prisoner and concluded that he too was exempt from punishment, but this did not happen. He was detained, investigated, the mass graves were opened up and as a result a charge sheet was prepared and he had to stand trial.

After great efforts I managed to get an entrance permit to the court room. On arrival in court on the day of the trial, I met many old women in the corridor, apparently the wives or relatives of the 15 murdered Lithuanians. As is well known, there were no Jewish witnesses left.

Two soldiers, who took turns every hour, brought the accused into the hall, a tall blond man in his fifties, with fluttering eyes. The court consisted of three judges, a prosecutor and a defender. The prosecutor was a young man with red eyes and a plaster on his nose, apparently the result of a nightly spree. People looked at me in surprise, since apparently my appearance caused some confusion, but nobody asked me anything, because they understood that I had not entered under false pretenses. The judges, the prosecutor and the defense were all Lithuanians, only the soldiers were Russians and they did not understand anything about the trial, because it was conducted entirely in Lithuanian.

After the procedural part, the charge sheet was read, which said that the accused had volunteered to join a group of Lithuanian nationalists who detained all Jewish men in Kibart as well as 15 Lithuanian communists, brought them to a barn near the "Peskines" where they were tortured for a few days, left without any food or drink, and then were shot group by group. I remember that the murderer was asked how it happened that a young person was found amongst the skeletons, because only males above 16 years old were supposed to be killed. He told the court that the 14 year old daughter of the grocery owner Halperin arrived at the barn and did not want to be separated from her father even after she was threatened that she would be killed too, and so she was shot together with all the others. A stethoscope and a pouch embossed with the symbol of the Red Cross was found in the opened graves, "it belonged to the medic Sher" the murderer explained. He gave the court more details, which I have already forgotten.

The women witnesses told the court that the accused, together with several other evildoers, appeared on one night knocking loudly on doors and windows, and after shouting "where are the Bolsheviks?" forced the men to dress quickly, not allowing them to take anything with them. They were seated in carts and taken to the barn, where during the few days that they were kept there, the women were not allowed to approach or to bring them any food. One day a lot of shots were heard from there, during which all the approaches to this place were blocked, and when the women arrived on the next day they found an empty barn and covered graves. They also heard that the clothes of the victims, which they had been forced to remove before being shot, were divided up among the murderers.

The accused claimed that he did not detain people and did not shoot, but that he, armed with a rifle, only transported them in groups to the holes. But the witnesses insisted that he arrested their husbands and one of them even said that his voice still rang in her ears and would never stop. The accused, when replying to the witness, maintained that his voice had changed during the years and she, as a devoted catholic, would surely have to give account of her testimony before a heavenly court and should therefore rethink her testimony. The woman crossed herself trembling and declared fearfully that maybe she was mistaken.

The prosecutor demanded maximum punishment, whereas the defense asked for an acquittal, because the accused had already suffered enough by hiding all these years, there being no proof that he himself had shot people and there was an amnesty for collaboration with the Germans. The speeches of the prosecution and the defense were monotonous as if this were a routine case, instead of being the trial of a murderer of 200 innocent people.

The trial ended with the verdict that the accused was guilty of murder, but taking into consideration that there was no proof that he himself had shot people and that there were no witnesses to this effect, he was sentenced to seven years in prison.

I looked at the murderer's face when sentence was pronounced and saw fear in his eyes on the verdict of guilty of murder, but when he heard the punishment was only seven years in prison his face lit up and he was satisfied. The sentence was final, with no possibility of appeal.

I left the hall confused and hurt, and for several days I could not find peace of mind nor was I able to sleep. Once again I was overcome by all the tragedy of Kibart and could not free myself from these feelings for a long time.

The Testimony of a Murderer.

Vincas Gilinskas was born in 1914 to a wealthy farming family, and attended school for seven grades. In the summer of 1941 he served in the Kybartai police and was one of the participants in the murder of Jews in July 1941, for which he was sentenced. The following is his testimony.

(L.Y.A. (Special Lithuanian Archives) F.K-1. B. 191. P. 69-73)

The Kibart police force consisted of only eight policemen, among them 3 high school students.

In the beginning of July 1941, the chief of police Staugaitis ordered his men to prepare to collect the Jews quickly and bring them to the yard of the police station. The commanders of this action were four uniformed Germans, who spoke Lithuanian well.

When the first group of Jewish men were brought to the pit, one of the high school students shouted "Men, lets try!" Gilinskas did not raise his hand - he did not feel comfortable about it – after all, this was his first time. Nevertheless, getting up courage, he shot two people in the first group. When the second group was forced into the pit, there was a commotion: " I recognized the Jew Milts, who fell at the feet of policeman Vailiukaitis, asking for mercy. I started to shake and kept away from the pit, giving my rifle back to the German, explaining that I have 'some personal needs...'. I refused to take part in the shooting". But after the executions, Gilinskas participated in covering people still living with earth.

Later Gilinskas got to know the real number of victims: " In the chief's office, I accidentally saw a list of the Jewish men with their surnames, and the last number was 116". There were only Jewish surnames on this list, although Lithuanians, Soviet activists, were also shot at this time.

In the autumn of 1941, women and children were murdered. In accordance with the chief's order, Kibart policemen rounded up about 250 women and children, which was not difficult as they all lived in one quarter of the town and the men had already been shot. Vilkovishk police chief Paukstaitis and his men arrived to help. The women and children were transferred to Virbaln on trucks. Gilinskas continues: "When Kibart and Virbaln women who knew each other met, terrible cries, shouts and groans were heard. As a result I became very uneasy, withdrew my hand and went out to town, saying that I had not slept all night and needed to eat. As I left, people had as yet not been shot, but I knew that they were destined to be murdered". After some time Gilinskas returned to the murder site. He was drunk. Somebody gave him a rifle and he shot several times. "I did not know if I had convinced myself or whether somebody was pushing me, but I shot. After that I got two days detention, because of drinking during working time ". After the action the shooters ridiculed Gilinskas for breaking his vow, in addition to which he was transported half alive on a cart lying on bloody garments, and finally he even got some clothes. "Breaking his vow" meant that after the murder of the men in Kibart, Gilinskas had vowed not to shoot people anymore. It is a pity he did not fulfill his vow.

For a partial list of the Lithuanian murderers of Vilkavishk district see Appendix 2.

Written by David Shadkhanovitz, a native of Kibart.

In June 1965, after returning from exile in Russia, I visited Kibart and Virbalis. I wanted to visit the graves of Kibart's martyrs who were murdered by the Nazis and their Lithuanian helpers. With great emotion and a trembling heart I went out in the direction of the Pieskines, where the first 200 victims were murdered. On my way there I tried to ascertain from local inhabitants where the exact place was, but all of them evaded answering, saying that they had been living there only for a short while. A Lithuanian woman from whom I bought flowers, agreed to point out the place of the murder. I found the place in accordance with her description, which was about 2.0-2.5 km eastwards from the railway station along a dust road. I found the graves surrounded by a wooden fence and a sign written in Lithuanian: "Passer by, stop and bow your head for the victims of fascist terror. In this place 200 Soviet citizens are buried, who were shot by German fascists". I placed the flowers there, and with a bowed head said "Kadish".

I returned to Kibart and from there I went to Virbalis in order to visit the graves of the remainder of the Kibart and Virbalis Jews. I knew that these were in the Vigaines, a field about 1.5 km from the town. I remembered this place still from the time of my studies in the Hebrew High School in Virbalis when we went to play soccer and other games. I saw 12 holes /graves, but no fence and no sign could be seen, with cows and horses grazing on the graves. I cried bitterly seeing this terrible sight and recorded it in a photo. I was shocked because of the inhuman attitude of the local authorities who did not care about minimum conditions for remembering the victims. I made my way to the Virbalis local council which was situated in a former Jewish house in the main street, where the only clerk there, a girl, informed me that this issue of commemoration was under the authority of the town mayor, who resided in Kibart. I returned to Kibart, found the office of the mayor and put my case to a clerk, since the mayor himself was not present. He told me that they were aware of the situation, that a monument would be set up soon, and that the area of the graves would be fenced off. Returning to Vilna with a broken heart I sent a letter to the town mayor in Kibart on the same issue, and after some time I received an answer assuring me that a decision had been made to set up a monument that year (1966) and to erect a fence around this place. Three years passed, during which I did not visit the graves again. A week before our Aliyah to Israel (1969), together with my wife and my two daughters, I visited the graves at the "Vigaines" in Virbalis. I brought my young daughters there in order to show them what the Nazi murderers had done to our nation and to our family.

The mass graves near Kibart

The monument on the mass graves near Kibart with the inscriptions in
Yiddish and Lithuanian: "In this place were murdered by the Nazis and
their local helpers the Jews of Kibart-children, women, men and a group
of Lithuanians were shot."

(Among the victims were the author's father and two cousins, Aryeh and
Elyakum Leibovitz)

Monument on the mass graves near Virbalis

The monument established in 1991 on the mass graves near Virbaln where Kibart women and children were murdered.

The inscriptions in Lithuanian and Yiddish on the tables says: "Here was spilled the blood of about 10,000 Jews (Men, Women and Children), Lithuanians, War Prisoners of different nationalities, who were cruelly murdered by the Nazi murderers and their helpers in July and August 1941"

(Among the victims there were the author's mother, sister Tekhiyah, aunt Sarah and girl cousin Tsiporah Leibovitz.)

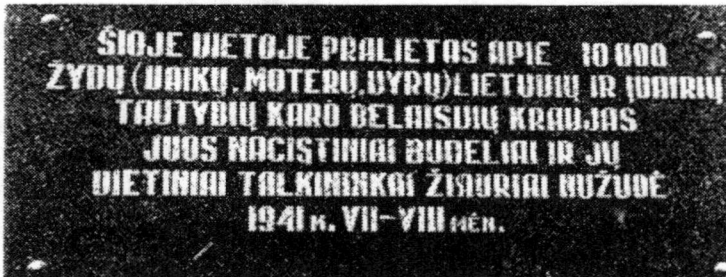

On that visit we found the place fenced off with a chain and there stood a concrete monument more than two meters high. The inscriptions on it, in Lithuanian and Russian, said that in this place Soviet citizens were murdered in 1941 by the Nazi fascists. There was no mention of the fact that at least some of those Soviet citizens were Jews and that their only crime was their Judaism. I found an empty barrel nearby onto which I climbed, and with my small pocket knife I engraved a Magen-David on all four sides of the top of the monument. I heard later from friends who visited the place where Maginei-David could still be seen and were not blurred. I suppose that no one visits this place anymore, and therefore there is no one who could rub out my engraving. (In the 1990s another monument with another inscription was erected as you can see in the photos from there.)

During those two visits to Kibart I was curious to see how the town, where I had spent a happy childhood, would look after the 23 and 27 years that I had not been there and what changes the events of the war had made. I did not expect to meet acquaintances, not Lithuanians and surely no Jews. I only wanted to see the streets and the buildings, each of them a reminder of something my past.

I arrived in Kibart by bus from Virbalis. The entrance to the town along the main street had not changed much. The "Torklerina" stood as before, with a few small changes and the sawmill, which once belonged to Shemesh, continues to work as before. Opposite there stood the former German school and I had no idea which institution was using the building now. Vishtinetz (Vistytis) street was partly ruined and the small houses looked as though they had sunk into the earth. From there on, in the direction of the border, the ruins started. The whole quarter, beginning from our house (Shadkhanovitz), Miltz, Budrevicius, the shop of Rosin and Katsizne and further along in the street of the synagogue the house of Pliskin, the synagogue itself, the house of Veitz, the bathhouse, all were destroyed, with cattle grazing where the buildings had formally been.

In 1969, on my last visit to Kibart, I noticed that on the plot where our house had stood, a large building, designed to be a restaurant, was under construction.

The red brick houses of the railway workers were intact, without any damage, as was the building of the fire brigade, and also the Pravoslav and Catholic churches, which stood there as before.

The grandiose railway station had been razed to the ground, there was nothing left, and in its place a small building had been erected, for selling tickets. The station sign read "Kibartai," not "Virbalis" as for the last 100 years. The "Railway Garden" was ruined too and only some remnants of the bowling alley and a pile of stones where the raised balcony for the orchestra used to be, reminded one of past beauty.

The public park in the main street was not damaged. The houses of the local police and the government bank were ruined, but new similar buildings were being built. Seinensky's house and other buildings towards the border were not damaged, except for some small buildings in the yards which had been burnt. The long Torkler house near the border was undamaged, Lithuanian families lived in the former Jewish shops and in the former custom's building near the border. The wooden bridge over the Liepona stream had apparently been burnt down and a new concrete bridge had been built in its place. Eydtkuhnen was totally destroyed except for the railway station and a few buildings where the shops of Rubinshtein and Zilberman used to be. There was no civilian population in Eydtkuhnen and those few existing houses were defined as a military zone.

To tell the truth I felt some satisfaction that our house and those of the neighbors had been destroyed, but I also felt sorry that many Jewish houses still stood intact, their owners and their tenants having been buried in mass graves, with Lithuanians living in them instead.

Picture taken by Vytautas Mickevicius March 2003

The building of the old government elementary school in Smetonos

Aleja opposite the houses of Shadkhanovitz and Miltz.

A List of Kibart Families according to their Professions.

Grocery shops: Khanes A., Khashman, Epshtein J., Feferman, Fainzilber Sh., Grinshtein, Halperin, Katz E., Katsizne, Kliatchko A., Levin M., Margolis, Maroz Sh., Rotshtein, Shtern A., Shtrasberg, Taburisky, Veitz A., Zilberman A.

Textile shops: Blogoslavensky, Blokh, Ginsburg, Levit, Miltz Sh.

Paper and Stationary shops: Leibovitz M., Rosin Y.L.

Haberdashery: Apriyasky A., Ginsburg, Shadkhanovitz M.

Shoes: Helershtein, Seinensky H.

Tools and Steel Products: Benyakonsky D., Vidomliansky E.

Bakeries: Frenkel, Landsberg, Sakharovitz, Yasovsky J.

Electric Appliances and Bicycles: Khashman Y.

Couriers: Aronovsky, Khashman A., Golding, Kanopke, Levinsky, Mandelblat A., Shtern A.

Exporters: Kovensky, Rakhlin, Rezvin J., Rosenberg

Butchers: Blumberg Z., Fleisher J.

Barbershops: Bernshtein J., Khlamnovitz

Utensils: Miltz H.

Photo shop: Khlamnovitz

Cobblers: Borokhovitz R., Gordon, Levin B., Zakharik

Taverns and Restaurants: Kisetz A., Miltz J., Tomer, Voltchansky

Customs Clerks: Frenkel, Goldberg, Gershonovitz, Gutgold, Prensky, Rachkovsky, Sokolsky, Shereshevsky T.

Hotel: Papir

Watchmaker: Epshtein

Factory Owners: Alperovitz, Aizenshtat, Berniker, Bernshtein Sh., Itskovitz, Frenkel, Frishman J., Gamzu D., Gans, Gefen, Kanievsky, Kushnerzitzky, Rubin, Shemesh, Verzhbolovsky A.,Yasven B., Yurzditzky, Zilberman.

Doctors: Abramovitz, Mariampolsky (couple), Sher A., (medic)

Dentists: Kleinshtein, Pauzisky

Teachers: Halperin Sh, Leibovitz M., Lurie M., Matis Sh.

Lawyers: Bartenshtein, Lurie J.

Pharmacy: Gershater A., Tilzer

Clerks and Bookkeepers: Blumberg, Davidson, Rabinovitz M., Shlomovitz, Trumpiansky, Volovitzky Sh.

Coachmen: Mogiluker, Yofe, Yurkansky.

Shoemakers: Tsibulsky J., Vilensky

Tailor: Abramson

Others: Altshuler, Artchik (the "shamash" in the small Synagogue), Baron (taxi owner), Bromberg, Berezin, Borovik, Khosn, Dalon, Dembo, Davisky, Etelzon, Frenkel T., Feldshtein, Froman, Gruzinsky, Klotnitzky, Kuritzky, Leikin, Landau, Melamed, Moshe-Leib (the "shamash" of the Great Synagogue), Muzikant, Naihertzig, Pliskin, Pilovnik, Rog, Rakhmil, Rakovsky, Segal, Sheinzon (cantor and "shokhet"), Shatenshtein, Shimberg, Staravolsky, Slavotzky Batia, Tsikhak, Tsentnershver, Vrublevsky M., Yomtov, Zilbersky.

Almost all of these families were murdered by the Nazis and their Lithuanian helpers.

Let this List be a Memorial to the Kibart Jewish Community.

Partial list of former Kibart Jews who lived in Israel and in the Diaspora.

Ozerov (Landsberg) Rachel, Ozerov Esther,

Apriyasky Aryeh (Peru), Apriyasky (Valdshtein) Rachel,

Borovik Mosheh,

Bartenshtein Joseph,

Borokhovitz Mordehai (USA), Borokhovitz (Yaron) Judith,

Berniker, Blumberg (Segal) Zina,

Khashman (Taub) Ayah,

Khashman (Gordon) Tovah,

Davidson Michael (USA),

Fainzilber Yitzhak,

Froman (Kagan) Yafah,

Frenkel Shemuel,

Goldberg Rita,

Ginsburg (Fin) Frida,

Kovensky Zisl, Kovensky Jakov, Kovensky (Priman) Shoshanah,

Kliatchko Perl, Kliatchko Miriam, Kliatchko Peretz, Kliatchko Eli (Germany),

Kaplan Yehudah,

Mogiluker (Gotlib) Shoshanah,

Manheim (Langevitz) Sarah,

Rosin Joseph,

Seinensky (Sheines) Berta,

Shadkhanovitz David,

Sheinzon Dov (USA),

Shtern (Kagan) Malkah, Shtern (Rochman) Frida, Shtern Dov,

Taburisky (Borokhovitz) (USA),

Tilzer Frida (USA),

Varshavsky (Bar-Shavit) Aryeh,

Vidomliansky (Shakham) Shalom,

Vizhansky Max, Yasovsky Hana,

Yasovsky Pesia,

Yasven (Veintraub) Roza,

Yofe Gershon, Yofe Yerakhmiel,

After about fifty years it was difficult to recall all the names of Kibart Jews. No doubt that there are errors and oversights in these lists. The little information which it was possible for us to collect, we gathered with all our heart.

Unhappily many of these persons are not with us anymore.

A group of former Kibart Jews at the party on the occasion of publishing the "Kibart Remembrance Book", Tel-Aviv March, 22., 1989
From left: Shemuel Panush, Bela Mirbukh- Upnitsky ,Zisl Kovensky, Josef Rosin, Frida Shtern-Rokhman,-----, Berta Senensky- Shilansky, David Shadkhanovitz

Bibliography.

The Archives of the Jewish Community Committee in Kibart- "YIVO" New-York Files 943-965.

The Archives of Yad Vashem- Jerusalem.

The Jewish Encyclopedia (Russian). St. Petersburg 1908-1913.

Akhsanyah shel Torah (Report of the Hebrew High School in Virbaln 5679-5681), (Hebrew) Berlin Virbaln 1921.

Kibart - Shie Tevik (Tuviyah Shereshevsky), the daily newspaper "Folksblat" (Yiddish) Kovno, November 1935.

The daily newspaper "Dos Vort" (Yiddish), Kovno,11.11.1934; 17.12.1934.

The daily newspaper "Di Yiddishe Shtime" (Yiddish), Kovno.20.1.1924.

The socioeconomic situation of the Jews in Soviet Lithuania, 1940-1941- Dr. Dov Levin.

From the Province - David Umru, "Folksblat" (Yiddish) Kovno, 25.7.1939.

The daily newspaper "Di Yiddishe Shtime" (Yiddish), Kovno.20.1.1924.

The socioeconomic situation of the Jews in Soviet Lithuania, 1940-1941- Dr. Dov Levin.

Appendix 1

Persian Famine Donation List from Kybartai 1872

Surname	Given Name	Comments
BAMASH	Yakov	
BERKOWITZ	Dov	
BLUMGARD	Shalom	from Virbalis
EITZELEWITZ	Yitzchok Leib	from Oshmyany (Ashmine)
ETILZOHN	Calev	
ETILZOHN	Meir	
FLIGELTANG	Yehoshua	
FOKSMAN	Shmuel	
FRANK	Yechiel	
FREINKEL	Tzvi	
FRIEDBERG	Avraham	
FRIEDBERG	Dov	bridegroom
FRIEDBERG	Menachem Aharon	
FRISHMAN	Kopil	
FRISHMAN	Mordechai	
GOLDBERG	Ari Leib	2nd donation
GOLDBERG	Avraham Yitzchok	
GRODZENSKI	Ari	
GRODZENSKI	Gebrider	
GULUS	Michel	
GULUS	Tzvi	
LEWINSHTEIN	Ari Leib	
MANESHEWITZ	Mordechai Zelig	
MARKOWITZ	Pesach	
MOREDECHOWITZ	Note	
PORTAGEZ	Aharon ben Yitzchok	
PORTAGEZ	Yitzchok	father of Aharon
SEGELOWITZ	Moshe	
SENIER	Eli	
SHIDARSKI	Tzvi	
SHLAMSKI	Dovid	
WOLFE	Yakov Leib	
WOLFE	Yitzchok Eli	
WOLTZANSKI	Mordechai	
YERKOWITZ	Eliezer	
ZLATOWSKI	Yitzchok	

Appendix 2
A partial list of murderers from Vilkaviskis district
Excerpt from:

LITHUANIA CRIME & PUNISHMENT
6   JANUARY 1999

PERIODICAL EMPHASIZING THE PROBLEMS INVOLVED IN THE RELATIONS WITH THE LITHUANIAN PEOPLE AND GOVERNMENT

PUBULISHED UNDER THE AUSPICES OF THE ASSOCIATION OF THE LITHIANIAN JEWS IN ISRAEL 1, KING DAVID BLVD. TEL-AVIV, 64953, ISRAEL

Partial List of Lithuanian murderers of the Jews of Vilkaviskis and its district

Ambrasas Vincas	Pilviskiai	Jurgilonas Kostas	Vilkaviskis	Prapuolenis Juozas	Kybartai
Bablevicius Vladas	Virbalis	Jurgsys Antanas	Pilviskiai	Ramanauskas Juozas	Pilviskiai
Baltramonius Viktoris	Vilkaviskis	Jurgsys Stasys	Pilviskiai	Reinys Kazys (Dep.	
Baltusis (Zveijas) Antanas	Pilviskiai	Jurgsys Vladas	Pilviskiai	Chief Dec. Pol.)	Vilkaviskis
Barakauskas Juozas	Pilviskiai	Juskevicius Jonas	Pilviskiai	Strimaitis Petras	Pilviskiai
Barkauskas Jonas	Pilviskiai	Juskevicius Juozas	Pilviskiai	Stura Antanas	Pilviskiai
Brazys Jonas	Vilkaviskis	Juskevicius Vladas	Pilviskiai	Stura Jurgis	Pilviskiai
Breneizeris Juozas	Vilkaviskis	Kalvaitis Juozas	Pilviskiai	Taculauskas Juozas	Vilkaviskis
Bridzius (Chief of Police)	Pilviskiai	Kaminskas Juozas	Vilkaviskis	Totoraitis Antanas	Pilviskiai
Brozis Kazys	Vilkaviskis	Kaminskas Kazys	Pilviskiai	Vailokaitis	Kybartai
Buksnys Jonas	Vilkaviskis	Kilikevicius Jonas	Vilkaviskis	Vaskevicius Antanas	Vilkaviskis
Buragas Pijus	Pilviskiai	Kiskiunas Jonas	Virbalis	Vaskevicius Vincas	Vilkaviskis
Dabrila Pranas	Vilkaviskis	Korgsas Jonas	Vilkaviskis	Velivys Antanas	Vilkaviskis
Dedelis Petras	Vilkaviskis	Letuvnikas Adalus	Vilkaviskis	Vosylius Albinas	Pilviskiai
Delininkaitis Matas		Navickas Justinas	Virbalis	Zaganevicius Kazys	Kybartai
(Chief of Sec. Pol.)	Vilkaviskis	Norkevicius Juozas	Pilviskiai	**May God punish these cowards.**	
Dereskevicius Alfonsas	Virbalis	Okonis Tauberis	Vilkaviskis	**May they and their associates and**	
Janovickas Jonas	Virbalis	Petraitis Viktorus	Vilkaviskis	**collaborators and their closest, their**	
Janovickas Juozas	Virbalis	Povilaitis Justinas	Pilviskiai	**descendants and offspring, stand**	
				defamed and cursed to all posterity.	

Photographs of headstones at Kibart Jewish cemetery taken by Samuel Rachlin and Nancy Lefkowitz, can be viewed on the World Wide Web (WWW):

http://www.shtetlinks.jewishgen.org/kibart/cemetery.html   and
http://www.shtetlinks.jewishgen.org/kibart/cem2.html respectively.

Appendix 3

Two particular letters among many others from people connected with Kibart who found " The Kibart Yizkor Book" on the Internet.

Subject: Kibart Page

From: SamRach@aol.com

Dear Mr.Rosin,

I have read the material on your Kibart site with great interest and noticed that my father's name appears in the pages as one of the Kibart natives. I would like to be on your mailing list and receive whatever relevant material you and other Kibartniks may be in the possession of.

My father, Israel Rachlin, the son of Shneur and Sara Rachlin, was born in Kibart in 1906. As your paper correctly states, he was born into a family of horse exporters, a business that he took over upon his graduation from the University of Leipzig in 1932. He managed the business until the Soviet occupation in 1940. The whole family, my father, my Danish-born mother, grandmother and my two older siblings, were arrested on June 14, 1941 and deported a few days later to Siberia together with the thousands of others thereby escaping the fate of most of the other Kibart Jews who perished in the Holocaust including my father's relatives. My parents passed away recently, my father in October 1998, and my mother just about three months later, in February 1999. They left behind 4 volumes of memoirs, the last appeared on the day my father died, all published in Danish by two leading Danish Publishers. The first volume, **16 Years in Siberia**, has also been published in English by the University of Alabama Press. *All four volumes have descriptions of life in Kibart, a place my father loved and told about all his life.* After the fall of the Soviet Union, my father actually established contact with the city authorities in Kibart and corresponded with the mayor. He also received confirmation that the family house was still standing, and he also received a picture of the house.(I have the exact address in some of the papers my father left behind.) I plan to go to Lithuania this spring or summer to visit the place where my father was born. My grandfather, Shne'ur Rachlin and his brother Eliya, are buried in the Jewish cemetery, but I suspect that nothing is left of that cemetery. In any case, I am planning to go back and see what is left.

Last summer, I revisited my own birthplace in Yakutia [Siberia] and retraced part of the route of my parents' deportation. I went down the Lena river from Yakutsk to Bykov Mys at the Arctic Ocean, where my parents and siblings spent one year. I produced a 90 minutes long TV documentary about this trip and the family history, and it just aired in Denmark 10 days ago. I hope it will eventually be aired in Israel, too.

Just briefly about myself: I am a journalist, working as a foreign correspondent for Danish TV in Moscow and living in Washington DC with my family. This was all for now. I hope you will put me on your list and keep me posted about Kibart matters - as you understand I am an interested Kibartnik descendant.

Sincerely yours,   *Samuel Rachlin*

PS. The English version of my parents' memoirs is **"Sixteen Years in Siberia"** **Memoirs of Rachel and Israel Rachlin,** published by the University of Alabama Press, Tuscaloosa and London. 1988. Library of Congress Cataloging-in Publication Data 1. Rachlin, Rachel 1908- 2. Rachlin, Israel 1906 - 3.Jews-Soviet Union-Siberia-Biography DS135.R95A15813 1988 947'.004924022 86-25096 ISBN 0-8173-0357X.

The name of my recent documentary on Danish TV was **"The Journey Back to Siberia"**. It aired in Denmark on January 18 and 19, 2000.

Kaunas, 17-th of October 2002

Dear Mr.Rosin

Thank you very much for answering my letter.

My previous letter was short - to know you are OK, and to know what language can be used. I am very happy now - that is true...So, for the first - a bit about myself. I was born in March of 1945, in Kybartai (to be true - in a military hospital located in Eitkunai, because there was no hospital in Kybartai at that moment).

I can tell that I was born in Eydtkuhnen, East Prussia - for a joy... I was living in Kybartai till 1962 - when I graduated from Kybartai school (the building of ex-Mittelschule). We lived in Torkleryne, Kestucio str., house of Adomaitis (next to Koltunovas, faced to Grubert's house).

My father Vaclovas was working at the railway station and my mother was keeping around the house at that time.

I graduated from Kaunas Polytechnic institute in 1968 as radio engineer, and was working in a semi-military research institute as designer of radio measurement equipment for 18 years, later - in a cardio-neurologic clinic with medical electronics and computers, now more than 10 years I am working as a computer application manager in a Kaunas heating and power plant.

I am married, have 5 children and 7 grandchildren.

My childhood and youth spent in Kybartai could be very happy - may be this is a reason of my love to this town. I see sunny green banks of summer's Sirvinta in my night dreams, my ears are wet when I leave Kybartai after a short visit. I feel being in exile, a special kind of exile - it isn't forced exile, it isn't physical (I can return to Kybartai for a while at any moment - if I wish), but it is a spiritual exile - it is so hard to live in a city which is foreign to me, and to know I never will live in my lovely town of youth...

I am trying to find and save into computer databases all possible information about Kybartai. What I am searching for most and what I have - next time. I am not a historian or writer, I am only a simple engineer, so there is a rising question: what I'm going to do with all this information? I don't know...

I am still working man, I have many duties, many interesting occupations. I don't know how long God will keep me here, in this world...

The easiest task - to place on a web pages as much info as possible - for a wide access for all people wishing to use it, and I am going to do this.

I'd like to write what I think about you and your work "The Book of Remembrance of the Jewish Community of Kibart." I can't remember when I connected to Internet and made my first search on word "Kybartai" (it was a long time ago - I'd found only 16 matching documents then), but I do remember that feeling of shock what I experienced, when I'd found your work... I laid off away all my works to be done on that day (I had an access to Internet only at my work place then), and was reading, reading... After a reading I was thinking a long long time...

About these young people whose faces I'd saw, about these what aren't (don't exist anymore), about these who are, but will never return...

About that part of Kybartai resident's what we had lost - forever. Lost them, their children and grandchildren. About that, what we lost with never having them living with us.

I had a great desire to write a letter of gratitude to you at the same second when I had finished the reading, but I am writing only now. May be, after the three years had gone...

I wasn't going to write about that material what you collected and published - it goes without saying.

I was going to write only about that, what I'd read "between lines" - it appeared to me that you love that tiny bit of land called "Kybartai", and that it is dear to you no less than it is dear to me...

That we are very similar in this. It was very important to me...

The Lithuanian-Jewish relations after the Holocaust tragedy aren't such as they were before, alas...

Your book excels in tolerance and objectivity, it doesn't bitter old wounds, and after reading of it remains only favor and sympathy to people what could be alive and could live with us - if terrible human mistakes wouldn't be done...

I had printed your book and can show it at any time to anybody and anywhere without doubts and fear. I lay stress once more - your book is most tolerant of all I had seen.

Thank you very very much!

Sincerely,

Vytautas Mickevicius

Appendix 4

List of readable headstones at Kibart Jewish cemetery, 2001

Most of the photos were taken by Nancy Lefkowitz, several by Samuel Rakhlin (S.R.)

See: http://www.shtetlinks.jewishgen.org/kibart/cem2.html
http://www.shtetlinks.jewishgen.org/kibart/cemetery.html

1. Bromberg

2. Blogaslovensky Hayah-Rachel bat Eliezer (S.R.)

3. Filipovsky Rachel-Leah bat Avraham-Mordehai

4. Freidberg Ya'akov ben Azriel-Zelig

5. Frenkel Zelde bat Hayim-Yosef

6. Goldberg Rivkah bat Yosef-Tsevi

7. Grabovsky Avraham-Aharon ben Mosheh

8. Hanas Hanah bat Tsevi

9. Leibovitz Ya'akov ben Meir (The authors grandfather)

10. Rakhlin Eliyahu ben Yehudah (new erected)

11. Rakhlin Shne'ur-Zalman ben Eliyahu (new erected)

12. Shtrasberger Hayah-Liba bat Azriel haLevi Luria (S.R.)

13. Shwartz Hayah-Sarah bat Yehudah-Leib haLevi (S.R.)

14. Shwartz Eliyahu ben Hayim-Aizik (S.R.)

15. Volfovitz Pesakh ben Mordehai

16. Yasven Hayah bat Eliezer

17. YomTov Ya'akov ben Yosef

18. Yoselevitz Mordehai ben Hayim

19. Zlosotsky (?) Ya'akov ben Yitshak

The tomb and tombstone of Ya'akov Leibovitz (the author's grandfather) at the Jewish cemetery in Kibart   *(Photo taken by the author in 1933)*

Condition of same tombstone in 2001   *(Photo by Nancy Lefkowitz)*

Lazdijai (Lazdey)

Lazdey (in Yiddish) is located in the South Western part of Lithuania, at the junction of roads leading to Mariampol (Marijampole) and Alite (Alytus), with several big lakes nearby. Lazdey was established by King Zigmunt II August in 1570, and was granted the Magdeburg Rights in 1579 as well as permission to maintain a weekly market and two yearly fairs.

Until 1795 Lazdey was part of the Polish Lithuanian Kingdom, when the third division of Poland by the three superpowers of those times - Russia, Prussia and Austria – resulted in Lithuania becoming partly Russian and partly Prussian. The part of the state that lay on the left side of the Nieman River (Nemunas), including Lazdey, was handed over to Prussia that ruled there during the years 1795-1807. During these years Lazdey was a county administrative center.

After Napoleon defeated Prussia and according to the Tilzit agreement of July 1807, Polish territories occupied by Prussia were transferred to what became known as the "The Great Dukedom of Warsaw", which was established at that time. The King of Saxony, Friedrich August, was appointed Duke, and the Napoleonic code now became the constitution of the Dukedom, according to which everybody was equal before the law, except for the Jews who were not granted any civil rights.

During the years 1807-1813, Lazdey belonged to the "Great Dukedom of Warsaw" and was part of the Bialystok district. The Napoleonic code was then introduced in this region, remaining in effect even during the Lithuanian period. In 1827 Lazdey had a population of 1,988 people living in 272 houses.

In 1815, after the defeat of Napoleon, all of Lithuania was annexed to Russia, as a result of which Lazdey was included in the Augustowa Province (Gubernia), and in 1866 it became a part of the Suwalk Gubernia as a county administrative center.

During the years of its existence Lazdey suffered from many fires.

In 1915 the German army occupied the town, ruling there till 1918 at which time the independent Lithuanian state was established. In 1919 the Polish army took over in Lazdey, but was expelled after several days. Lazdey remained inside the border of Lithuania, but Sejny, the district administrative center, was included in Poland. The district institutions, which were in what was called the Sejny district, were transferred to Lazdey, but the town remained a county administrative center only for all the years of independent Lithuania (1918-1940). The invasion of the German army in June 1941 caused the demolition of almost all the town.

Jewish Settlement till After World War I.

Jews had already settled in Lazdey by the end of the sixteen's century, but as an organized community they functioned from about 1689 in line with the permission granted by King Jan Sobiesky, and by the middle of the nineteen's century they had grown to 60% of the entire population. They built their houses around the market square and made their living from commerce. As a result of frequent fires many Jewish houses burnt down and their owners needed help from nearby Jewish communities and from Lazdey emigrants in America. In the summer of 1879 about 200 houses were ravished by fire and their owners became homeless. An appeal for help published in the Hebrew newspaper "HaMelitz" of St. Petersburg on the 30th of July of that year brought much help in money and food. It is reported that the Russian district officer obtained a loan of 3,000 Ruble for them, but another version maintains that the Polish squire Mishinsky of the neighboring town Meteliai donated 3,000 Ruble for the Jewish as well as Christian victims of the fire. In 1886 another fire caused the destruction of about 250 Jewish houses as well as the death of an old man and a young woman, after that the authorities prohibited the construction of straw roofs in the center of town. Two years later, in 1888, about 70 houses, which had been left intact during the previous fire, burnt down. In this fire the old synagogue and the "Beth-Midrash" with all its books were destroyed, and a Jewish woman was also a victim. Another large fire occurred in 1910, all these events causing the deterioration of the economic situation of the town's Jews, which in 1887 amounted to about 1,500 souls.

Apart from the usual Jewish occupations, Lazdey was surrounded by Jewish farms and farmers till World War I. Many Jewish families also maintained vegetable gardens behind their houses.

Nevertheless the community in Lazdey was well organized and in 1872, during a great famine in some parts of Lithuania, local Jews donated money for the starving, the collectors being Yehudah Glikman and Meir Simkha Zilberman.

Jewish children studied at "Khadarim" and "Talmud-Torah" and by 1887 there were 14 "Melamdim", 3 private teachers and 14 Judaica studying societies. Among the welfare societies it is worth mentioning "Lekhem Aniyim" (Bread for the Poor) who distributed money to poor families for a scanty subsistence, a "Khevrah Kadisha" (Burial Society) etc.

There were youngsters longing for knowledge and the "Society for distributing knowledge among the Jews" of St. Petersburg sent them books in Russian and Hebrew. The "Khibath Zion" movement had many admirers in town. In 1881 Jews from Lazdey joined the "Yesud HaMa'alah" society, established in Suwalk by Eliezer Mordehai Altshuler with the aim of settling in Eretz Yisrael. One of the members of the second delegation who went to Eretz Yisrael in order to buy land for the society was Mendel Burak from Lazdey, but for various reasons this idea was not carried out. In 1901, for example, there was intense Zionist activity in town, with people buying "Shekalim", a sort of membership card of the Zionist Organization, and donating money for the settlement of Eretz Yisrael

Individual Lazdey Jews left for Eretz Yisrael sometime before the emergence of the "Khibath Zion" movement. In the old cemetery of Jerusalem there are three tombstones of Lazdey Jews: Gershon son of Moshe, died 1910; Reuven son of Yehudah Frid, died 1895; Hayah daughter of Rabbi Yudl Rosh HaGalil, died 1897.

Among the rabbis who served in Lazdey were: Avraham Tsevi ben Meir; Avraham ben Yekhezkel (--?--- 1798), father in law of Yehudah-Leib, son of the "Gaon" from Vilna; Hayim-Yehoshua HaCohen Blumental from 1853 for several years; Yosef-Mosheh Aranzon (1805-1875), died in Chicago; Tsevi-Hirsh Kahana; Yehudah-Leib Ginsburg; Avraham-Eiver Yaffe (1823-1908), in Lazdey 1873-74; his son Yehudah-Leib (1842----?) from 1908 in Lazdey.

On the first of April 1915 Lazdey Jews were exiled into Russia by order of the retreating Russian army. After the war most of them returned home and found that their property had being stolen.

Lazdey covered with snow

During the Period of Independent Lithuania (1918-1940)

After the war the returning Lazdey Jews, who found their property stolen and most of the houses ruined, started to rebuild their lives anew. The conflict between Poland and the new Lithuanian state concerning the sovereignty of Lazdey caused riots against the Jews in town.

According to the autonomy law for minorities, issued by the new Lithuanian government, the minister for Jewish affairs Dr. Max Soloveitshik ordered elections to be held in the summer of 1919 for community committees in all towns of the state. In Lazdey a committee of nine members was elected: eight non-political and one from the Tseirei Zion party. The committee, active till the end of 1925 when the autonomy was annulled, collected taxes as required by law and was in charge of all aspects of community life.

The market square 1937-38

During this period Lazdey Jews made their living from commerce, crafts, agriculture and fishing. According to the government survey of 1931 there were in Lazdey 72 businesses, including 64 owned by Jews (89%).

Details according to the type of business are given in the table below:

Type of the business	Total	Owned by Jews
Groceries	14	13
Grains	6	6
Butcher's shops and Cattle Trade	13	11
Restaurants and Taverns	7	7
Food Products	4	3
Beverages	1	1
Textile Products and Furs	9	9
Leather and Shoes	6	6
Medicine and Cosmetics	1	0
Sewing Machines and Electric Equipment	3	2
Tools and Steel Products	4	4
Timber and Furniture	1	1
Paper, Books and Writing Equipment	1	0
Miscellaneous	2	1

According to the same survey Lazdey had 17 factories, of which 16 were Jewish owned (94%), a power station, 3 flour mills, one shoe factory, one light drinks factory, a workshop for wool combing, 5 bakeries, 2 sewing workshops, 2 mechanical locksmith's workshops.

In 1937 there were 56 Jewish artisans in Lazdey: 9 tailors, 7 shoemakers, 8 butchers, 6 bakers, 6 blacksmiths, 4 barbers, 3 oven builders, 3 carpenters, 2 painters, 2 watchmakers, 1 tinsmith, 1 wool knitter, 1 saddler, 1 stitcher, 1 wood carver, 1 photographer. There were also several porters and carters in town, and about 20 families engaged in agriculture.

During these years the economic situation of Lazdey Jews began to deteriorate because of propaganda by the Lithuanian Merchants Association "Verslas" against buying in Jewish shops and the Lithuanians established cooperatives in order to compete with the Jewish shops. The severance of Lazdey from its natural hinterland after the Polish occupation of the Seiny region, the murder during a robbery of several Jewish farmers who lived in isolated farms in its surroundings, and the transfer in 1935 of the market around which the Jewish shops were located to another place in order 'to improve the look of the town', affected the economic situation of Lazdey's Jews. Most of Jewish youth who could not see their future there, left during these years and moved to Kovno or emigrated abroad.

The Jewish "Folksbank" played an important role in Lazdey's economic life. In 1927 it had 233 members, by 1929 – 262 and in 1933 – 250 members. There was also a branch of "The United Company for Credit to Jewish Agrarians".

In 1922 a large fire caused damage to many Jewish houses in Lazdey. The representative of the "Joint" Association visited Lazdey and approved a loan of half a million Mark, the currency then still valid, for the victims of the fire which was to be divided up by the "Folksbank".

Jewish children received their elementary education in the Hebrew religious "Yavneh" school, with about 200 pupils and 5 teachers. It also ran a library for children. In addition there was also a "Yeshivah" for scores of boys.

Parents who had the financial capacity sent their children to the Hebrew high school in Mariampol, but most of the Jewish youth studied in the local Lithuanian high-school "Ziburys" (Torch), where tuition was minimal. In 1935, for example, 80 Jewish pupils studied in this school.

Among the Zionist Youth Organizations "HaShomer HaTsair" and "Betar" were active, and for some time there were also two "Kibbutsei Hakhsharah" (Training Kibbutzim), one of "HeKhalutz" and the other of the General Zionists.

Sport activities were performed at "Maccabi" (58 members) with its strong football team, "HaPo'el" and for some time also "HaKoakh" who had a string instrument band.

The Jewish volunteer fire brigade which possessed modern fire fighting equipment according to the concepts of those days, had its own building with a hall for shows and also maintained a wind instrument orchestra. The nationalist Lithuanian "Sauliai" society established its own fire brigade and orchestra, threatening to confiscate the Jewish equipment.

The Lithuanian "Ziburys" High School
Picture taken by Ruth ben David (from the Pilitovsky family) 1994

Jewish girls pupils of the "Ziburys" high school 1933
**From left: Frida (Shulamith) Pilitovsky, Sarah (Sonia) Dushnitsky, -
----------, Olga Gurvitz**

Picture supplied by Ruth ben David (from the Pilitovsky family)

Jewish girls pupils of the "Ziburys" high school 1930
Standing from left: Rukhamah Idovitz, Frida Pilitovsky
Sitting from left: Henia Mikhnovsky, Miriam Gail

Picture supplied by Ruth ben David (from the Pilitovsky family)

Lazdey had a public library with about 2,000 books in Hebrew and Yiddish. The Jewish theater from Kovno would come to Lazdey approximately once a year with a Yiddish show. From time to time lectures on different themes, political and literary, were given in town, but this stopped during the latter years. Only the Zionist movement continued its activities, and all Zionist parties had representatives in Lazdey, as can be seen from the results of elections to Zionist Congresses in the table below:

Congr. Nr.	Year	Total Shekalim	Total Voter	Labor Party Z"S	Z"Z	Rev.	G. Z. A	B	G.	Miz.
14	1925	80	---	---	---	--	--	--	--	--
15	1927	39	34	19	10	3	2	--	--	--
16	1929	126	82	42	4	32	3	--	--	1
17	1931	67	60	32	6	15	6	--	--	1
18	1933	---	203	121		62	19	--	1	--
19	1935	---	490	297		--	33	115	11	34

Rev.-Revisionists; G.Z.-General Zionists; G.-Grosmanists; Miz.-Mizrahi

The string orchestra of "HaKoakh" 1930

Picture supplied by Ruth ben David (from the Pilitovsky family)

First line standing from right: Rukhamah Idovitz, Shelomoh Idovitz, Sonia (Sarah) Dushnitsky, Shulamith Pilitovsky

Second line sitting from right: Asher Borovsky, Batiah Prusak, Zerakh Idovitz, Olga Gurvitz, Khayah Hofman, Avraham Garden

Third line sitting from right: Yitshak Opnitsky, Binjamin Starnapolsky

Jewish religious life concentrated around the synagogue, the "Beth-Midrash" (The Shul), several praying rooms called "Klois", and the "Yeshivah". There were groups for studying in the "Talmud –Shas Society", "Mishnah Society" and "Ein Ya'akov", and religious youth was organized within the framework of "Tifereth Bakhurim". The Rabbi during these years was Ya'akov Aryeh HaCohen Gershtein who served in Lazdey for more than 20 years. He was murdered by Lithuanians in 1941.

The welfare institutions included "Lekhem Aniyim" (Bread for the Poor), "Ezrath Kholim" (Help for the Ill), "Gemiluth Khessed" (Loans without Interest) which was affiliated to the "Folksbank", and "Maoth Khitim" (Help for the Needy for Pesakh).

In 1939 there were 123 phone owners in Lazdey, of which 58 were Jews.

The Synagogue and the Yeshivah rebuilt as a youth club 1994
Picture taken by Ruth ben David (from the Pilitovsky family)

The Bath House 1994
Picture taken by Ruth ben David (from the Pilitovsky family)

During World War II and Afterwards

World War II started with the German invasion of Poland on the first of September 1939, and its consequences for Lithuanian Jews in general and Lazdey Jews in particular were felt several months later.

In agreement with the Ribbentrop-Molotov treaty on the division of occupied Poland, the Russians occupied the Suvalk region, but after delineation of exact borders between Russia and Germany the Suvalk region fell into German hands. The retreating Russians allowed anyone who wanted to join them to move into their occupied territory, and indeed many young people left the area together with the Russians. The Germans drove the remaining Jews out of their homes in Suvalk and its vicinity, robbed them of their possessions, then directed them to the Lithuanian border, where they were left in dire poverty. The Lithuanians did not allow them to enter Lithuania and the Germans did not allow them to return. Thus they stayed in this swampy area in cold and rain for several weeks, until Jewish youths from the border villages smuggled them into Lithuania by various routes, with much risk to themselves. Altogether about 2,400 refugees passed through the border or infiltrated on their own, and were then dispersed in the "Suvalkija" region including Lazdey where 150 of them were accommodated.

In June 1940 Lithuania was annexed to the Soviet Union and became a Soviet Republic. Following new rules, the majority of the shops belonging to the Jews of Lazdey were nationalized and commissars were appointed to manage them. Also several Jewish houses whose area was more than 220 meters (about 2000 sq. ft) were nationalized and their owners were forced to leave them. All the Zionist parties and youth organizations were disbanded, several of the activists were detained (the local Betar commander Dzivak and Adv. Bergson) and Hebrew educational institutions were closed. A part of the Jews started to intertwine into the new rule institutions. At the October celebrations in 1940 an amateur troupe ("Artistic Brigade") from Vishey performed in Lazdey the play "Bar Kokhva" of Goldfaden with the accompaniment of a local Jazz band.

The supply of goods decreased and, as a result, prices soared. The middle class, mostly Jewish, bore most of the brunt, and the standard of living dropped gradually. At the beginning of June 5 Jewish families whose enterprises were nationalized were exiled deep into Russia (among them Prusak, Titevsky, Gurvitz).

The tragic fate of the Jewish community of Lazdey during the Nazi rule is further told by Rivkah Gershtein Mikhnovsky and her husband Ze'ev Mikhnovsky and by Gedalyah Cohen. Their story was translated into English by Benjamin Ronn.

"The night before the war between Germany and Russia commenced, the inhabitants of Lazdey were occupied in digging defense trenches. At approximately 3:00 a.m. on June 21, 1941, they noticed red flares that were sent from across the border. Immediately thereafter, a heavy bombardment into Soviet Russian territory (Lithuania) began. German bombs also fell in the center of Lazdey and the houses caught on fire, which spread and consumed most of the Jewish homes.

The German army entered Lazdey on Sunday, June 22 at 10:00 a.m. Terror spread throughout the residents. Thousands fled. Only about forty Jews managed to escape with the Soviets by jumping onto their trucks. The rest escaped to the nearby villages where they hoped to find shelter with the farmers. Most of the farmers did not provide shelter for the Jews, did not allow them into their homes, and even denied them a drink of water. The Jews were often received with shouts of "Go back to Stalin, your father!"

During their escape, bomb fragments injured several of the Jews and some were killed.

On Monday morning, the entire surrounding area calmed down. The German Army had moved forward and the city no longer was on the front. Many of the Jews returned to Lazdey only to be attacked by the local Lithuanians. Noakh Kadushin, a leather worker, was badly beaten, and two Jews were forced to dig a grave for him and to bury him alive.

On the same day that the Jews fled Lazdey, they were joined by other Jews who were still roaming around the countryside, and they all moved toward Serey, which was approximately 5 kilometers away. Serey, however, was also burned to the ground, and there was no room for the wanderers. The Jews of Lazdey continued to roam in the fields near Lazdey until Shabbat, when the Nazis gave an order that all the Jews of Lazdey should return to Lazdey.

On Monday, June 23, 1941, a meeting of 30 members of the Lithuanian intelligentsia took place in Lazdey. They elected a committee that would manage the affairs of the region. They also declared their thanks and appreciation to the German army and Adolf Hitler. On Wednesday, June 25th, the committee decided to place the Jews in two wooden shacks. The shacks were originally erected by the Russians. In effect, the Jews only had one and a half shacks because the wives and children of Russian officers occupied half of one of them.

Many of the Jews were arrested by the Lithuanians and accused of being of Communists. They arrested young men, almost children, claiming that they were members of the "Comsomol" (Young Communist League). Many were arrested without being accused of anything. If a Lithuanian had any grievances or against any of the Jews, he now obtained his revenge. Many of the people who were arrested were Zionist Revisionists and old people as well. All the people who were arrested were moved to Mariampol and were murdered there.

The remaining Jews were condemned to hard labor. They were given the task of clearing up the ruins of the bombed-out houses and many other jobs that would shame them. Those who had land were given permission to live in their own barns and work in their own fields.

One day a German and a fellow named Zarembo, who was from Lazdey but originally of Polish origin, came to the shacks and took out the Rabbi of Lazdey, Rabbi Ya'akov Aryeh HaCohen Gershtein, and started beating him with riding whips. When the members of his family came out to see what was happening to their father, they were also beaten. The Rabbi was later put on a truck and driven away.

The Jews went to the local priest to ask for his help because Rabbi Gershtein served as the local Rabbi for over twenty years and had an excellent reputation among Jews and non-Jews alike. The priest excused himself by saying that he was not able to help the Rabbi at all. The chief of police was also not willing to help. Later in the day, those who were returning from one of the work gangs related that they saw the Rabbi being brought to where they were working. He was forced to carry heavy sacks of cement. While everyone else was allowed to return as usual on the wagons, the Germans mocked him and said, 'Let him walk". Shortly thereafter, the Rabbi returned to the shacks.

The Jews were only allowed to walk in the gutters and were not allowed to step or walk on the sidewalks. Upon seeing a German soldier, a Jew was compelled to remove his hat and bow his head with his face facing the soldier. Only when the German left was he allowed to return his hat and straighten up.

Almost from the first day of the Nazi occupation the Jewish residents were the focus of torture and robbery. Both the Germans and the Lithuanians demanded watches, jewelry, silver, gold, and other valuables under threats of bodily harm. Policemen and Lithuanian thugs would often beat people mercilessly. Every Sunday after the Lithuanians left their church, they would take the Jewish males from the shacks, bring them to the marker square, and would torture them with so called "physical exercise." They would force them to roll in the dirt, hit each other, and perform other stunts to the amusement and pleasure of the spectators. Thugs would attack the Jews and hit them mercilessly. The Lithuanian guards would demand from the Jews that they turn over their money, gold, and valuables to them. They would *force* them to strip and would search their clothes. A significant amount of property was stolen from the Jews in those days.

Rumors about murder and extermination of the Jews in the surrounding areas were reaching Lazdey. In mid-September, the rumor was heard that the Jews of nearby Leipun were murdered. On September 15, the Jews of so Lazdey were ordered to move to the army barracks in the estate of Katkishok (Katkiske) about a kilometer and a half away. They were promised that a ghetto would be set up for them where they would spend the duration of the war. The Jews of Lazdey already knew that the Jews in other cities of Lithuania were almost totally eliminated; therefore, they treated this proposed move with great of suspicion. Some of them went out to explore Katkishok and to find out if there were any pits dug for a mass burial site. The lack of pits eased their to concern only a slightly.

A few hours later, Jews from the nearby communities of Vishey, Kopcheve and Rudamin as well as Jews from the nearby villages were brought to Lazdey. All of them were destined for Katkishok. This fact calmed the Jews somewhat. They thought that the Germans were serious in creating a ghetto. That very same day, all the Jews were moved to Katkishok. They were placed in the army barracks and quartered by family, and the entire area was surrounded by barbed wire and armed Lithuanian guards. Daily work groups were used for work outside the compound.

Initially, they gave each person 200 grams of unsalted bread and 300 grams of potatoes. Gradually the rations were cut down, and an epidemic of dysentery broke out. People suffered and starved. Some snuck out and ran to nearby villages where they exchanged personal belonging for food or begged for food. A certain relief occurred when some of the local farmers were allowed to engage Jews as workers on their farms, provided that they would return them to the ghetto at night. Those who ate at the farms would give up their share of the food in the ghetto so that others could benefit from it.

The internal arrangements of the work schedule were managed by the Jewish *Arbeits Amt* (Work Office). A special committee to manage all the affairs of the ghetto was created from representatives from all of the communities. The pharmacist Astromsky from Kopcheve was their leader. He did not do a thing without consulting with Rabbi Gershtein of Lazdey. A Jewish police force was organized in the ghetto but had very little authority.

Every gentile was able to do whatever he pleased. Hardly a day passed without some torture or criminal act. For example, a Lithuanian policeman once took a liking to the boots of Yehoshua Vilensky from Rudamin. He called him over, shot him dead, and took his boots.

One day the ghetto was shocked by the secret news Sheina Idovitz and Golda Katorovsky related upon their return from work on Monday, October 27th. Every day they were taken to the town to work for the German commander. That day, they heard a conversation between the commandant of Mariampol who screamed at the commandant of Lazdey what a terrible shame it was that his Jews were still alive. The commandant from Lazdey apologized and explained that he needed the Jews who were doing necessary work and many of the essential crafts. The commandant from Mariampol screamed again, "You have to fulfill your task or otherwise you will be sent to the front" whereby the commandant of Lazdey replied, "I am a soldier and a man of war, and you won't scare me with this kind of a threat."

The mood in the ghetto was electrified instantaneously. The mention of the words of death shook the people and scared them in anticipation of the following day. That night some people escaped from the ghetto and went looking for a hideout with the farmers or in the fields. A few days later, however, when no special events had occurred, everything returned to normal. They expected that the commandant would continue to protect the Jews under his control. By the end of October, most of the Jews throughout Lithuania were already murdered, while those of Lazdey were among some of the very few left alive.

On Thursday, October 30, 1941, the ghetto was sealed and nobody was taken out to work. They were able to see that the murderous Lithuanians were walking in the distance with spades in their hands. Upon asking the chief of the police as to the meaning of this scene, he responded nonchalantly, "They are going to dig pits for you. This will take a few days and that is exactly the length of time left for you to be alive." After that explanation, many attempted to run away even though the place was well guarded by armed guards. The following morning, escapees were returned to the camp, some were wounded and some had been murdered, and the chief of police came to calm the Jews. He told them that running away does not make sense since everywhere the German foot is placed the Jew gets wiped off the face of the earth. He went on to say that a Jew can never find a hiding place from the bullet that is marked for him, and that very soon the end will come for all the Jews wherever they might be.

The Lithuanians sealed all windows and doors to the barracks with planks and metal bars. The Jews were locked up without water or food. Despite all their efforts, 180 people managed to escape from the barracks in the first two nights.

On Monday, November 3, 1941 (the 13th of *Mar-Heshvan*, 5702), the Jews were taken naked from the barracks to the dug out pits about 300 meters away from the barracks and about 300 meters west of the forest. About 1600 souls were shot to death there. Not one person managed to escape. Although the Germans gave the orders for the 'operation,' they participated only as the observers at the scene of the crime. **The actual executioners were Lithuanians.** A gang of apparently experienced murderers from Mariampol also participated in the executions. This gang seemed experienced because of their actions and later, that they refused the Germans' offer to photograph them in order to "memorialize" their actions. Only in December of 1941 did the first signs of the German's retreat and defeat appear when the Germans were forced back into winter defensive positions. As mentioned earlier, many escaped before the slaughter. Some were badly wounded, caught, and brought back to the ghetto. On the day of the slaughter, they were dragged with the other sick and helpless to the pits. Many of the escapees were killed by the farmers. After a while, the Lithuanians stopped murdering the caught escapees and incarcerated them instead. When the number of the caught escapees reached 35, they took them to the mass graves and murdered them there.

From the entire 180 who escaped, only 6 survived the war: Rivkah (Gershtein) Mikhnovsky and her husband Ze'ev Mikhnovsky, Dov Zef, Miriam Kuleisky and her sisters Gita and Bath-Sheva Koifman-all from Lazdey; Khmilavsky from Vishey; Gedalyah Cohen from Rudamin.

In 1944 and 1945, the Soviets recaptured Lithuania, Estonia, and Latvia, and they were again made Soviet republics. Seven kilometers from the Polish border, Lazdey was made a Soviet administrative district center in the Lithuanian Soviet Socialist Republic. Suvalk remained in the Bialystok province of Poland.

After the war, Rivkah and her husband Ze'ev Mikhnovsky returned to their native town of Lazdey. There they had a child there, the last known Jew to be born in Lazdey. Shortly afterwards they moved to Eretz-Yisrael and no Jews are known to have lived in Lazdey since. Lazdey's population in 1959 was 3109.

During the war, the tombstones in Lazdey's Jewish cemetery were overturned. Apparently, it was not demolished and built over as the Soviets did to numerous other Jewish cemeteries.

The entrance gate of the Jewish cemetery, the only scraps
Picture taken by Ruth ben David 1994 (from Pilitovsky family)

On the 13th of *Mar-Heshvan* every year, natives of Lazdey living in Israel assemble in the Tel Aviv area for a memorial service in memory of the day of the annihilation of the Jews of Lazdey. After the memorial service, there is usually a friendly get-together. The well-known lawyer and native of Lazdey, Avraham (Golub) Tory, often speaks at these meetings. Each year, however, the attendance decreases as fewer natives of Lazdey remain alive".

The names of the Lithuanians who sheltered them are saved at the archives of Yad-Vashem.

After the war the survivors of the above mentioned towns erected a monument on the mass graves at Katkiske. In 1991 a new monument was erected with the inscription in Lithuanian and Yiddish: **At this place the Hitlerist murderers with their local helpers murdered on the November 3, 1941 1,535 Jews from the Lazdey district, men, women and children.**

According to the survey of Jewish cemeteries in Lithuania performed in 1990, a Jewish cemetery was found at the Lazdey district in the village Bukta.

Sign on the road: The place of the mass murder of the Jews in 1941 at Katkiske

Picture taken by Ruth ben David 1994 (from Pilitovsky family)

Entrance gate to the mass graves and the monument

Picture taken by Ruth ben David 1994 (from Pilitovsky family)

The Monument

Picture taken by Ruth be David 1994 (from Pilitovsky family)

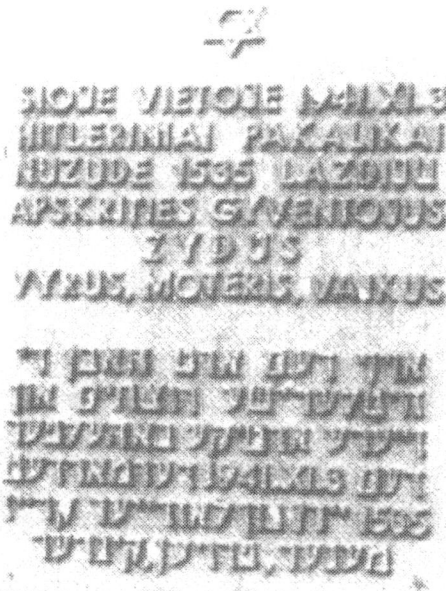

The tablet on the Monument

Bibliography

Yad-Vashem Archives, Koniukhovsky Collection 0-71, Files 131,132

Central Zionist Archives: 55/1788; 55/1701; 13/15/131; Z-4/2548.

JIVO, NY, Collection of the Jewish Communities in Lithuania, Files 517-540, pages 22596-23618

HaMeilitz (St. Petersburg) (Hebrew): 30.7.1879, 16.11.1879, 29.3.1881, 14.7.1884, 9.7.1886, 2.7.1888, 11.12.1893.

Folksblat, Kovno (Yiddish): 23.6.1935, 24.6.1935, 25.7.1939, 17.11.1940.

Di Yiddishe Shtime (The Yiddish Voice) Kovno (Yiddish): 28.12.1920, 22.8.1922, 12.2.1928, 9.8.1932, 22.5.1935.

Der Yiddisher Kooperator –Kovno (Yiddish): Nr.2-3, 1922

Dzuku Zinios (Lithuanian) Nr.55, 22.7.1992

Appendix 1.
List of reporters from Lazdey to the Hebrew periodicals "HaMeilitz" and "HaTsefirah".
In "HaMeilitz": Shmeriah Gisovsky, Tsevi-Aryeh Ginzburg, Avraham-Yitshak Hurvitz, Yosef Meirberger, Shemuel Burak, Zalman-Mordehai Bernshtein.
In "HaTsefirah": Elyakum Levinzon, Yehudah Akhron.

Appendix 2.   Partial list of personalities born in Lazdey.

Yisrael Prais (1869-1942), reporter and writer, from 1890 in USA, pioneer of spreading the "Khibath Zion" ideology among religious Jewish circles in America, published articles in the Hebrew periodicals "HaMeilitz", "HaMagid" and HaTsefirah" and later in the Yiddish press in America. Published many books on Jewish historical themes.
Yosef Akhron (1886- 1943) composer, violinist and teacher. Among his compositions: "Hebrew Tune", 3 concerts for violin, concert for piano and many more.
Shemuel Bortn Sekler (1897-??), immigrated to USA, researcher and inventor.
David Cohen (1901-murdered in 1941), painter.
Yakov fon Idelson, in 1843 Russia's consul in Koenigsberg, despite being an apostate, helped Jews in trouble.
Sarah Dushnitsky-Nishmith-Shner, born in Sejny in 1913, but lived from the age of twelve in Lazdey where she graduated in the Lithuanian high-school. M.A. in Educational Psychology from Vilna University and M.A. in Classic Linguistics from Kovno University. In 1940 headmistress of the Teachers Seminar "Tarbuth" in Vilna. 1942-1944 with the partisans in the Belarus woods, from 1948 in Kibbutz Lokhamei HaGetaoth, writer and researcher of the Holocaust in the "Ghetto Fighters House". Published 2 books for children, many books and stories and many articles mostly on research of the Holocaust.

Appendix 3.   List of Lazdey Jewish families who perished in the Holocaust, according to the streets in which they lived.
(Compiled by Rivkah-nee Gershtein- and Ze'ev Mikhnovsky)

Starishok Street (beginning from the bridge)
1. Ozhekhov Yitskhak
2. Paulan Binyamin
3. Paulan Efraim
4. Paulan Yosl and Payeh
5. Falkovitz Ber-Leib
6. Falkovitz Avraham
7. Grudzin Bertshik
8. Dumbelsky
9. Ribak
10. Sider Yekhezkel
11. Mariampolsky Getsel
12. Matskibutsky Mordehai
13. Punsky
14. Dimant Barukh-Shelomoh
15. Bas Yosef-Heshl
16. Epshtein Mosheh-David
17. Punsky Shemuel
18. ---?--- Tsadok+Pantofel (daughter and husband)
19. Pintshikhovsky (blacksmith)
20. Bergzon Dobrusha and sons
21. Zilonsky Zalman
22. Mariampolsky Barukh
23. Zubritsky
24. Shilingovsky Reuven
25. Prusak Avraham
26. Khoronzitsky
27. Matskibutsky Yerakhmiel
28. Bas Hayim
29. Rabbi Gershtein Ya'akov-Aryeh
30. Man Hayim-Yenkl
31. Goldman Alter
32. Gibralter Shimshon
33. Ribak Yosl-Henakh
34. Einbinder Alter
35. Frank Khloine
36. The sisters Sarah and Heshka (seamstress)
37. Leidman Mosheh
38. Leidman Hayim
39. Bernshtein Alter
40. Man Yitskhak and brother
41. Smolan and wife Feige
42. Gisovsky Leib
43. Subartevitsky Hayim
44. Shats Karpel

The Alley between the Prusak and Khoronzitsky families
45.Shimantshik Elyakum
46.Sveisky Reuven
47.Luksniansky Yeshayahu
48.Katkishky Avraham nad wife Zlate (seamstress)
49.Zef Aba (mortician)
50.Zusman Mendel
51.Lefkutz
52.Kovalsky Yisrael
53.Polazdeisky
54.Yakir (mortician)
55.Yablon
56.Paulan Hayim Itsel
57.Lefkutz
58.Lefkutz Zisel

Starishok Street (continuation from the other side of the bridge)
59.Rindzunsky
60.------------- (the shoemaker from Suvalk)
61.Milikovsky (teacher)
62.Shchupatsky Avraham
63.Vafner Eli (Scriptures copier)
64.Prager Yisrael
65.Prusak Ya'akov
66.Prusak Shalom
67.-------- Meir (tailor)
68.Borovsky
69.Ozhekhov Yisrael
70.Levin Matityahu
71.Groznik Shemuel
72.Gurvitz Tsevi
73.Prusak Shemuel
74.Paulan Hayim Yitskhak
75.Mariampolsky Avraham
76.KantarovskyYa'akov
77.Gorfinkel
78.Kshevitsky-Luksiansky
79.Zeligson
80.Grudzin Reuven
81.Grudzin Gershon
82.Kufran Malka and Kazys (survived thanks to her Lithuanian husband)
83.Grudzin Sarah
84.Prusak Eliyahu
85.Prusak Nekhama
86.Kulitsky Shemuel
87. Levinzon Note
88.Reikher David

Around the Market Square

89.Sider Avraham
90.Shmulkovsky Yosl
91.Finkelshtein Barukh
92.Gilary Eliezer
93.Rozenblum
94.Golub Zerakh
95.Beker Betsalel
96.Smolsky
97.Pilitovsky
98.Kantorovsky-Mikhnovsky
99.Meretsky Asne
100.Lishkov Mordehai
101.Volovitsky Velvl
102.Volovitsky Yosl
103.Kantarovsky Aba
104.Shilibolsky Kune
105.Finkelshtein Shepsl
106.Shilingovsky Shalom
107.Kahanovitz
108.Kalvarisky Yisrael
109.Shishlov Mordehai
110.Aks Yeshayahu
111.Prusak Leibush
112.Khalote Ya'akov
113.Kubelsky (lawyer)
114.Tsimerman
115.Kreingel
116.Kohen Alter
117.Levin
118.Kulesky Bath-Sheva
119.Broide Pesakh
120.Bergson
121.As (barber)
122.Idovitz
123.Milman (teacher)
124.Mirkes

Kovna Street

125.Markus Sime
126.Lipsky
127.Kalir Menakhem (cantor) immigrated to Eretz Yisrael before the war
128.Pilitovsky Yakir
129.Krasnopolsky
130.Baranovsky Hayim-Shimon
131.Krikshtansky brothers
132.Abramovitz Ane
133.Kaufman Shelomoh
134.Soloveitshik

135.Oftshinsky Yosl
136.Prusak Eliyahu
137.Klibansky+Liberman Naftali
138.Hakhnokhi
139.Lefkutz
140.Katsenelenboigen
141.Shapira
142.Voltshansky
143.Khoronzitsky
144.Dzivak Kalman
145.Kohen Ya'akov-Yosl
146.-------- Eli   (poultry merchant)
147.Pintshikhovsky David
148.Rabinovitz Mordehai-Velvl
149.Doberman David
150.Zavatsky Avraham
151.Zavatsky Yitskhak
152.Sokol
153.Sider Leib   (oven builder)
154.Gerdasky Shmerl
155.Getker
156.Levin   (hatter)
157.LevinVelvl
158.Zinger   (tailor)
159.Liubovitz Peshe
160.Prusak Hayim-Yosl
161.Okunevitz Hayim-Mendl
162.Berkman
163.Breitbord
164.Tenenboim Hayim

Seiny Street
165.Titevsky Yeshayahu
166.Kopilovsky David
167.Okunevitz Moshehe
168.Paulan and sons Iser, Aba, Shelomoh, Nakhum and married sister Khayah
169.Lipshtein
170.Paulan Asne
171.Dunsky Avraham   (baker)
172.Dunsky   (bank clerk)
173.Paulan Berl-Zelig
174.Norkin
175.Dushnitsky
176.Lisovsky
177.Paulan Meir
178.Rubinshtein Motl
179.Paulan Mosheh-Mikhel
180.Shilingovsky
181.Yurzditsin Yisrael
182.Brozovsky Shepsl

183.Polazdeisky
184.Sheiman
185.Navisky Iser
186.Paulan David
187.Tsevikler Sarah-Ita
188.Dvorsky Reuven
189.Shtabinsky
190.Mark Hayim
191.Gibralter Barukh
192. Ginzburg   (doctor)
193.Paulan
194.-------- Yosl and family (son in law of Moshehe David Epshtein)
195.Shtabinsky   (rope maker)
196.Prusak Yosef
197.Burak Meir
198.Burak Iser
199.Kovensky Rukhamah
200.Levin-Kovensky

Dumbli Street
201.Rabbi Domovitz
202.Ratshkovsky Iser
203.Katkishky Leib-Iser
204.Rindzhunsky Kopl
205.Shimantshik Binyamin
206.A family of 4 persons, sister of Ane Abramovitz

The estates in the vicinity of Lazdey

207.Roslender	(Sventezeris)
208.Kalvareisky Yosl	(Barova)
209.Kalvareisky Alter	(Barova)
210.Pagirsky	(Barova)
211.Ziman	(Barova)
212.Gishtrovsky Zerakh	(Rali)
213.Gurvitz	(Katkishok)
214.Leben	(Nirovtse)
215.Shapira Mosheh	(Milotshisky)
216.Zef Mosheh	(Bukta)

Lygumai (Ligum)

Ligum (in Yiddish) is situated in the northern-central part of Lithuania, on the left bank of the river Kruoja, about 27 km northeast from the district administrative center Shavl (Siauliai). An estate with the same name is mentioned in historic documents from the fifteenth century. Nearby the estate the village grew mainly in the nineteenth century, from 331 residents in 1841 to 801 residents in 1897, of them 482 Jews (60%).

Until 1795 Ligum was part of the Polish-Lithuanian Kingdom, when the third division of Poland by the three superpowers of those times - Russia, Prussia and Austria - caused Lithuania to become partly Russian or Prussian. The part of Lithuania, which included Ligum fell under the rule of the Czarist Russia (1795-1915). From 1802 it was part of the Vilna province (Gubernia) and from 1843 as part of the Kovno province.

During the period of independent Lithuania (1918-1940) Ligum was a county administrative center in Siauliai district. Police and post offices were stationed in Ligum. In the town there also were several small factories for processing agricultural products, some workshops and shops.

A Wooden Jewish house

The first Jews settled in Ligum in the 18-th century. Until the beginning of the century there were more Jews in Ligum than in Shavl and the Ligum Jewish cemetery served Shavl Jews as well. Ligum Jews made their living from small trade, crafts and peddling. During several tens of years they became the majority in town. At the beginning of the 19-th century there were a "Beth-Midrash", a "Kheder" and other institutions in town.

In 1876 a big fire occurred in Ligum, which burnt down 60 Jewish houses. In 1887 a big fire burnt down 64 Jewish houses including the "Beth-Midrash" and the Synagogue.

The Synagogue in 1999

(Photo taken by Barry Mann 1999)

In the years before World War I many of Ligum Jews immigrated to America, England and South Africa and about 60 families in Ligum remained. In the summer of 1915 all Ligum Jews were expelled to the inner regions of Russia. After the war only 50 families returned to Ligum.

During the period of Independent Lithuania (1918-1940)

Following the autonomy law for minorities, issued by the new Lithuanian government, the Minister for Jewish Affairs, Dr. Menakhem (Max) Soloveitshik, ordered elections to be held for community committees (Va'ad Kehilah) in the summer of 1919. A committee of 5 members was elected in Ligum. This committee was active in almost all fields of Jewish life until the end of 1925.

According to the first census performed by the Government in 1923 there were 753 people in Ligum, of them 240 Jews (32%). During this period most of the Jews made their living from agriculture, craft, peddling and small trade. The weekly market day, which took place on Wednesdays was their main income source. Almost every family maintained an auxiliary farm and owned a milking cow. Several Jews worked at Yosef Perkis' spinning and dying plant.

According to the government survey on shops and factories taken in 1931 in Ligum there were one butcher's shop and one grocery owned by Jews.

In "Khol haMoed Pesakh" 5693 (13.4.1933) a big fire broke out in Ligum which burnt down 87 buildings in the center of the town, while 44 of them were habitations. Many people became roofless and in the press calls for helping the victims of the fire were published. Until World War II most of the houses were rebuilt.

In 1937 there were 6 Jewish craftsmen in town: 2 butchers, 1 tailor, 1 shoemaker, 1 tinsmith and one another.

There was an Hebrew school in Ligum, but because of the low number of pupils it was closed after two years of operation and a number of the children went to the Lithuanian school. The more prosperous families sent their children to the Hebrew schools in Shavl or Kovno. Boys went also to the "Kheder" of Meir the slaughterer, taught in addition to his main profession.

Most of Ligum Jews were fans of the Zionist movement, but there were a small part of the Jewish youth who were active in the Communist underground.

In the table below we can see how Ligum Zionists voted for the different parties at seven Zionist Congresses:

Cong. No.	Year	Total Shekalim	Total Voter	Labor Party Z"S Z"Z		Rev	G.Z. A B		Gr.	Miz.
14	1925	28	--	--	--	--	--	--	--	--
15	1927	14	--	--	--	--	--	--	--	--
16	1929	15	8	--	3	--	2	--	--	3
17	1931	30	23	--	4	1	--	--	--	18
18	1933	--	19	2		8	4	--	--	5
19	1935	--	24	7		--	--	4	--	13
21	1939	32	24	10		--	2	--	Nat Blk 12	

Rev.-Revisionists; G.Z.-General Zionists; Gr.-Grosmanists; Miz.-Mizrahi ;

Nat Blk : National Block

The elections in 1931 took place in the "Zionist Hall" and in 1939 in "Beth Hamidrash".

The relations between the Jews with their Lithuanian neighbors were by and large normal, but sometimes incidents occurred like the desecration of the Jewish cemetery.

The large fire of 1933 caused extensive damage to about 30 Jewish families, of which only 10 were insured, the. In the same time the economic situation of the Jews was harmed because of the strong competition of Lithuanian organizations headed by the Association of the Lithuanian merchants "Verslas". As a result of their harsh situation a large number families needed support from their relatives abroad.

For the partial list of Rabbis who served in Ligum see Appendix 1.

During World War II

In June 1940 Lithuania was annexed by the Soviet Union, becoming a Soviet Republic. The new rule caused many changes in the economic and social life of Ligum. A number of the providers integrated into government economic institutions. The supply of goods decreased and as a result prices soared. The middle class, mostly Jewish, bore most of the brunt, and the standard of living dropped gradually. All Zionist parties and youth organizations were disbanded and a worsening in the relations with the Lithuanians occurred. In this year there were about 120 Jews in Ligum.

On June22, 1941 the German army invaded Lithuania. Many of Ligum Jews tried to escape to Russia on carts and by foot through Dvinsk in Latvia, but arriving to the Latvian border on the 28-th of June, they became aware that the German army preceded them. Consequently they had to return home. In Ligum the Lithuanian nationalists already took over the rule. With the pretext of searching for arms the Lithuanians robbed valuables from Jewish houses. They also detained Jews with the pretext that they were Communists. Among the captives were honored people, merchants etc. All were transferred to Shavl prison and there they were murdered.

As follows is the testimony of a Lithuanian young woman, Julija Butkute, born in 1915, saved in the "Special Lithuanian Archives" LYA. F.K-1.B.198. P. 2-4., on the fate of Ligum Jews:

"Ligum Jews were detained at the end of July and the beginning of September 1941. The detained men were kept in a cellar of some building, and the women were detained in the synagogue. In the night of the 3-rd to the 4-th of September at the Junkaiciai forest the men and young women were shot. The murder began early in the morning at about 6 o'clock. In town we could smell the odor of the gunpowder. After the "action" the participants, among them the chief of Ligum county police Jonas Petraitis, gathered in the town club where refreshments were prepared. Four German officers coming from Siauliai took part in this gathering.

After several days -- another action. 25 carts were provided for transferring the mothers with their children to the murder site. All began early in the morning. The women were relieved that the convoy is going to Zagare, where they and the mature children will have to work. The women put into the carts their few belongings and the carts moved.

In the middle of the day, at 12 o'clock, the action was already finished. The women were led only to the Junkaiciu forest. In town, the carts loaded with the Jewish belongings returned. The garments (of the murdered) and parcels prepared by the Jewish women were stored in a storehouse owned some time ago by a Jew.

For the participants of the "Action" a party in the club with much alcohol was again arranged. The Germans, after taking part in the party for about half an hour, returned to Siauliai.

For a partial list of personalities born in Ligum see Appendix 2

The tablet at the murder site with the inscription:

In this place the Hitler murderers and their local helpers in year 1941 annihilated 250 Jews, men, women, children

(*Photo taken by Barry Mann 1999*)

The monument on the mass grave.

(*Photo taken by Barry Mann 1999*)

Sources:

Yad-Vashem Archives: Koniuchovsky Collection 0-71, Files 109

Kamzon Y.D.-Yahaduth Lita, page 168

Dov Levin - Ligum (Lygumai), Pinkas haKehiloth. Lita (Encyclopedia of Jewish Settlements in Lithuania) (Hebrew), Editor: Dov Levin, Assistant editor: Josef Rosin, Yad Vashem. Jerusalem 1996.

Dos Vort, Kovno (Yiddish): 25.10.1934.

Folksblat, Kovno (Yiddish): 14.4.1933; 19.6.1933

Di Yiddishe Shtime (The Yiddish Voice) Kovno (Yiddish): 23.7.1929; 14.4.1933; 19.4.1933.

Di Tsait (Time) (Yiddish) Kovno, 21.5.1939

Appendix 1   A partial list of Rabbis who served in Ligum

Nakhum Shapira (1818-1902)

Tsevi-Yehudah Rabinovitz, In 1876 was in Ligum, died in the age of 44.

Dov Rabinovitz, till 1887

Mordehai-Yitskhak -Aizik Rabinovitz, (1856-1920), in Ligum   1887-1902, publish several books.

Mosheh Hurvitz, In Ligum since 1907, immigrated to America, published several books.

Yisrael-Nisan Taitz, in Ligum till about 1921.

Yehudah-Leib Laba, the last Rabbi of Ligum, murdered in 1941.

Appendix 2   A partial list of personalities born in Ligum.

Mordehai-Betsalel Shnaider (1865-1941), since 1896 in Vilna where he was the central personality in education and Zionism, wrote research articles on the Hebrew language in the Hebrew periodicals (HaShiloakh, HaTekufah etc.). Published two volumes of his comprehensive book "The theory of the Hebrew language in its historic development" (Vilna, 1939-1940). The third volume was already prepared to print, but the incoming Soviet rulers dissipated the matrixes. He was murdered in Ponar in 1941.

Rafael Rabinovitz (1897- ?), was the director of the Hebrew high school in Rasein (Raseiniai) and later the director of the Hebrew teachers seminar "Tarbuth" in Kovno. Since 1932 in Tel-Aviv where practiced as a lawyer. Was in charge of the publishing the "HaTalmud HaMenukad" (The vowelled Talmud).

Gershon Weitsman, established the first matches factory "Nur" in Eretz-Yisrael in Ako.

Marijampolė (Mariampol)

Mariampol lies on the banks of the Sesupe (Sheshupe) river, one of the tributaries of the Neman, the main river of Lithuania, about 55 km southwest from Kovno (Kaunas). The first people, who settled in this place in the second half of the 17th century, were peasants. In 1736 the village in the area was callled Starapole. Another new village nearby was called Marijampole, the name appearing for the first time in 1756.   Later these two villages were joined under the name Marijampole.

In 1792 King Stanilaw-August granted Mariampol "The Privilege of a Town".

Until 1795 Mariampol was included in the Polish-Lithuanian Kingdom. According to the third division of Poland in the same year by the three superpowers of those times: Russia, Prussia and Austria Lithuania was divided between Russia and Prussia. The part of the state that spread on the left side of the Nieman river (Nemunas) including Mariampol was handed over to Prussia. During the Prussian rule (1795-1807) Mariampol was a district adminstrative center. In 1800 there were 1,178 people living in the town.

During the years 1807-1813 Mariampol belonged to the "Great Dukedom of Warsaw" and was considered as a county administrative center in the Bialystok District. In 1813, after the defeat of Napoleon, whose retreating troops passed through the town, all of Lithuania was annexed to Russia, and Mariampol was included in the Augustowa Province (Gubernia). From 1817 it again became a regional adminstrative capitol. In 1866 Mariampol was included in the Suwalk Gubernia.   The construction of the main road in 1829 from St. Petersburg to Warsaw stretching through Mariampol, spurred the growth of the town.

After the great fire in 1868, many wooden houses burnt down but were replaced by solid houses rebuilt in the town. The municipal town area of the town was enlarged, and a park, later renown for its greatness and beauty, was planted at that time.

In 1827 there were 1,759 people living in Mariampol and among them 1,157 Jews (66%). In 1840 there were 2,992 people and 2,264 among them were Jews (76%).

Mariampol was under Russian rule for a hundred years (1815-1915). In 1915 during World War 1, Mariampol was occupied by the German Army, remaining in the area until the establishment of the New Independent Lithuanian State in 1918.

During the period of independence of Lithuania (1918-1940) Mariampol was a district adminstrative center. The construction of the railroad in 1923 connecting Mariampol to Kazlu-Ruda, a terminal on the main line from Kovno to Kibart (Virbalis) contributed to the town's further development. Thus Mariampol was connected to the Lithuanian railroads.

The Railway Station

During that period many factories were built in town and among them the Sugar Factory, which produced sugar from beets. Many new homes were built then, and the number of inhabitants grew (9,488 people in 1923). Mariampol became one of the most beautiful towns in Lithuania. It was also a cultural center boasting a large number of high schools in the area. During the Russian rule there were three Russian high schools in Mariampol.

In June 1941 the German Army occupied Mariampol and the occupation lasted until 1944. During the retreat the German army destroyed the center of the town, the power station and the sugar factory.

From 1955 until 1990, during the Soviet rule, the town was called Kapsukas (named after the Lithuanian underground communist leader). After Lithuania was set free from the Soviet rule Mariampol revived it's old name.

The Jewish Settlement before World War 1

It seems that Jews started to settle in Mariampol at the beginning of the 17th century. They settled on the left bank of the Sesupe river, in the village Tarputch. Later it became the suburb of Mariampol. In 1766 there were 347 Jews in the village. At that time the first Synagogue was built in the village and was burnt down during World War I.

Jews began to settle on the right bank of the Sesupe river only at the end of the eighteenth century. During the Russian rule there were no restrictions imposed on Jews to settle in the area, therefore in 1850s and 1860s, Jews constituted 80% of the population of Mariampol. In 1856 there were 2,853 Jews out of a total town population of 3,462 (82%). In 1861 there were 3,015 Jews out of a total town population of 3,718 (81%). In 1897 the number of Jews in the town decreased to 3,268 (48%) while the total population grew to 6,737.

The Jews of Mariampol made their living in commerce and crafts. There were also Jewish farm owners who earned their livelihood from agriculture. Jewish merchants exported flax, grains and poultry to Germany.

During the Polish rebellion in 1831 Jews of Mariampol suffered from the rebels. The rebels hanged a wealthy Jewish family and four community leaders.

In summer 1881 a volunteer fire brigade was established in which most members were Jews.

The Jewish children of Mariampol were educated in a "Kheder" where some Russian was taught. Most of the time was devoted to teaching the Bible, some Talmud and the Hebrew language. For some time, at the end of 1890s, a "Revised Kheder" curriculum was created in Mariampol, where Hebrew using the "Ashkenazi pronunciation" was taught by Yekhiel Yekhieltzik (later Yekhieli) who after "Aliyah" (immigration) became the director of the Girls School in Neve-Tsedek in Tel-Aviv.

At the end of the nineteenth century a "Modern Yeshivah" was founded in Mariampol where Talmud, Hebrew, Bible, Russian, German and literature were taught. At that time the teachers were Hayim Joseph Lurie and Hayim Ber Rosenbaum who later taught in the Hebrew High School of the town. There were Jews in Mariampol who were subscribers to the Hebrew periodicals such as "haBoker", "haZeman" and the children's paper "heKhaver".

In the Russian State High School for Boys only a few Jewish boys were enrolled because there was a maximum quota of 10% for Jews. In contrast, at the two private high schools for girls there was no known quota and many Jewish girls were enrolled (one of them was the writer Devorah Baron).

Because of the study of the Bible and the knowledge of Hebrew, most of the Mariampol Jews were supporters of the "Khibath Zion" (Affection for Zion) movement. By 1881 the local Rabbi, Shelomoh-Zalman Gordon, added his "Haskamah"(approval) to the book of Nathan Fridland "Joseph Khen". The book supported settlement of Jews in Eretz-Israel and became a popular book in the Diaspora. A year later Rabbi Gordon's detailed opinion on the Zionist Movement was published in response to attacks coming from a group of Rabbis known as the "Black Lodge".

In 1882 a group of Mariampol Jews joined the association "Yesud haMa'alah" which was organized in Suwalk by the Mariampol native (1844) Eliezer-Mordehai Altshuler and whose task was to settle in Eretz-Israel. For different reasons, including the opposition of the Rabbis "to anticipate events", the task was not fulfilled.

In 1884 twenty-seven pictures of Mosheh Montefiori were sold in Mariampol as a fundraiser for settlement in Eretz-Israel.

At the first Zionist Congress which took place in Basel in 1897 the delegate from Mariampol was Gedalyah Gitelevitz. At several Zionist Congresses afterwards the delegate from Mariampol was Aba-Yitskhak Rozental. He was also the delegate at the second All-Russian Zionist Conference and the representative on behalf of Suwalk Region at the Zionist Conference in 1908.

Rabbi Eliyahu Klatzkin from Mariampol was the delegate at the regional conference of the "Zionist Associations" whose participants gathered in Vilna in 1899.

The numbers of "Shekalim" (like a membership card) that were sold in the year of the fifth Zionist Congress shows the number of members from Mariampol. belonging to the 'Zionist Association". Between the 1.7.1901 and the 1.7.1902 one hundred "Shekalim" were sold in Mariampol. The "Zionist Associations" in Mariampol were called "Benoth Zion" (The Daughters of Zion), "Tekhiyah" (Revival) and "Bar Kokhva", and they were among those who opposed the "Uganda Plan". In 1905 a youth group, under the guidance of Devorah Baron, was organized in Mariampol and was called "Pirkhei Zion" (The Flowers of Zion). Later its name was changed to "Tikvath Zion" (The Hope of Zion).

On the list of donors of 1909 who supported settlement in Eretz-Israel names of hundreds of Jews from Mariampol appear (see Appendix 1). Among the Jews from Mariampol who immigrated to Eretz-Israel at the beginning of the century were: Rachel Solnik (in 1909), later the wife of Yehudah Gorodeisky, one of the founders of Rekhovoth, Yisrael Yablokovsky (1912) and Barukh Leibovitz (in 1911), later Dr. Barukh Ben-Yehudah. (see below).

A branch of the "Bund" (the anti-Zionist workers organization) acted in Mariampol and disrupted the Zionist activities. Among other activities attributed to the " Bund" was the disruption of the Memorial Assembly which took place in the Synagogue in Mariampol on the "Sheloshim" (Thirty days) after the death of Herzl.

Public life concentrated around the three Synagogues in town: the Central Synagogue, the "Hakhnasath Orkhim" Synagogue and the "Beth haMidrash". The ceiling of the central Synagogue was ornate with colored paintings of a tiger, an eagle, a deer and a lion. The Holy Ark was decorated with beautiful wooden carvings.

Until 1870 the Rabbi of Kalvariya (a town about 18 km south-west of Mariampol) was the Rabbi of Mariampol too. The first Rabbi in Mariampol was Hayim Perlmuter-Shereshover (from 1780 till 1820), after him his son-in-law Yehudah-Leib Kharlap officiated. In subsequent years Shelomoh-Zalman Gordon (died in 1879); Yehonathan Eliashberg (from1879 till 1887); Azriel-Aryeh Rakovsky (died in1894); Eliyahu Klatzkin (from1892 till 1910) served as Rabbis.

The Great Synagogue and the "Beth-Midrash"
(Destroyed during the war)

Institutions of assistance in Mariampol were the same as in most other Jewish Communities of Lithuania: "Gemiluth Khesed", "Linath haTsedek", "Somekh Noflim" (from 1876), "Bikur Kholim" (from 1892) with a budget of 1,600 Rubels, a respectable sum in those days, and other organizations.

With the outbreak of World War I the Germans occupied Mariampol, but after the advancement of the Russian army the Germans retreated. When the Russians returned to Mariampol, they blamed the Jews for influencing Germans, and as a punishment the Russian General Renenkampf ordered the Jews, including the Rabbi, to go out to work and repair the roads on Succoth 1915. In 1915 the Germans occupied Mariampol again and ruled there until 1918.

In Mariampol almost every family had a nickname that past from generation to generation. The family names were used only for official occasions

During the period of the independent Lithuania
Public and economic life.

According to the first census in Independent Lithuania in 1923, the number of Jews in Mariampol decreased to 27% of the total population (2,545 Jews of 9,488 people).

Mariampol was one of the first towns in Independent Lithuania in which the Jewish life was organized according to the Autonomy Law regarding minorities. By 1919 the elections to the Community Committee took place. In the elections 935 persons participated and they were 73% of the privileged to vote. 21 persons were elected to the committee: 6 from the "Tseirei Zion" list; 4 from the General Zionists; 2 artisans; 3 from the "Bund" list; 2 from the "Po'alei Zion" list and 4 independents. In the elections of 1921, 17 persons were elected: 2 General

Zionists; 2 from the "Tseirei Zion"; 1 from "Mizrakhi"; 3 artisans; 5 workers and 5 independents. The Committee was active until the beginning of 1926 when the Autonomy was annulled. During the years of its existence the Committee collected taxes according to the law and were in charge of of all areas of community life with the help of many sub-committees: a sub-committee for taxes, for appeal, for the public bath, for education and culture, for the administration and for social help. Among its other activities the Committee cared for Jewish soldiers who served in the infantry regiment of the Lithuanian army stationed in Mariampol and arranged a kosher kitchen for "Pesah" and a traditional "Seder".

The Jews of Mariampol made their living in commerce, industry, craft and agriculture. According to the survey performed by the Lithuanian government in 1931 there were 146 shops in Mariampol and 121 of the shops belonged to Jews (83%) according to the following table:

Kind of Business	Total	Jewish Ownership	%
Groceries	6	6	100
Grains and flax	14	13	93
Butcher's shops and cattle trade	20	16	80
Restaurants and taverns	12	8	67
Food products	9	9	100
Drinks	1	1	100
Textiles and furs	17	16	94
Leather and shoes	12	11	92
Tobacco and cigarettes	1	1	100
Haberdashery and house utensils	13	13	100
Medicines and cosmetics	5	2	40
Watches and jewels	4	3	75
Bicycles and electrical equipment	3	1	33
Tools and iron products	10	8	80
Building materials, lumber, furniture	4	4	100
Heating materials, cattle food	3	3	100
Machines, terrestrial transportation	3	1	33
Books and stationary	3	1*	33
Miscellaneous	6	4	67

* the shop was called "Moriyah" and belonged to Pilvinsky, later another shop opened and was named "Tushiyah" and belonged to Saks.

According to the same survey there were 54 factories in Mariampol, 26 of them (48%) belonged to Jews. The data is presented in the following table:

Type of establishment	Total	Jewish Owners %
Metal works, power stations	6	1	17
Tombstones, bricks	1	1	100
Chemical industry: spirits, soap	4	2	50
Sawmills, furniture	4	2	50
Printing presses, book binders	5	1	20
Food products	21	14	67
Clothing and footwear	9	3	33
Miscellaneous	4	2	50

In 1931 the population was 13,000 people , 35% Jews among them were Jews.

Near Mariampol there were a few farms that belonged (or were leased) to Jewish families who made their living working in agriculture: Vitenberg, Shohat, London, Meklenburg, Goldberg, Z.Levin. In the farm "Ungarina" owned by the Skarisky brothers there was a "Training Institute" (Hakhsharah) organized for "Halutsim" (pioneers) prior to their immigration to Eretz-Israel. There were also Jewish families in the vicinity of Mariampol who worked in agriculture: Dubzhinsky, Beilis, Berkman, Palnitzky, Dembner.

Vytauto Street

In Mariampol there were scores of Jewish artisans. They were organized in "The Association of the Artisans" with a 100 members in 1937/38: 22 tailors, 10 shoemakers, 9 bakers, 8 butchers, 7 hat makers, 7 stitchers, 6 woodworkers, 5 hairdressers, 4 photographers, 3 tinsmiths, 3 electricians, 3 watchmakers, 2 painters, 2 dressmakers, 1 glaziers, 1 blacksmith, 1 jeweler and 1 other. The "Association" had a Loan Fund ("Gemiluth Khesed") and was represented in the religious institutions, in the municipality and in the "Ezrah" committee, where it had 4 delegates.

An important role in the economic life of Mariampol was played by the Jewish Folksbank. In 1927 it had 525 members and in 1935 - about 500. There were also two private banks, one belonged to Amsterdamsky and the other to Waisberg.

There was also a branch of "The United Company for Financial Credit for Jewish Agrarians" in town.

In the middle of the 1930s the economical situation of the Jews in Mariampol started to deteriorate. One of the reasons was the open propaganda led by the Association of the Lithuanian Merchants ("Verslas") against buying in Jewish stores. To achieve their goal they established Consumer Coops which competed with the Jewish commerce. In 1939 there were also physical outbursts against Jews in Mariampol. In those years many Jewish youths immigrated abroad and a part of them immigrated to Eretz-Israel.

According to the official Telephone Book of 1939 there were in Mariampol 297 phone subscribers, among them 85 belonged to Jews (29%).

In 1920 the elections for the first Lithuanian "Seimas' (Parliament) took place. The Jews appeared with one list that represented the Zionists, the "Agudath Yisrael" and the "Folkspartei". Among the elected Jews was the Rabbi of Mariampol Avraham-Dov Popel.

At the elections for the Municipality Council in Mariampol that took place in the twenties, 10 Jews from 32 Council members were elected. In the elections of 1931, 6 Jews from 15 Council members were elected: Leib Bialoblotzky, Yitshak Levin, Leon Stoklitzky, Berl Altshuler and Hayim Rotshtein. In the elections of 1934 only 4 Jews among 15 Council members were elected: Adv. Stoklitzky, Yitshak Levin, Israel Levin and Aba-Yitshak Rosental who resigned and Dr. Rosenfeld took his place. One of the Jewish members acted as the Deputy Mayor.

Education and Culture

During the period discussed above there were two Hebrew elementary schools, one of the "Tarbuth" movement and the other of the "Yavneh" movement , in Mariampol.

**The sixth graduation class of the Hebrew elementary "Tarbuth" school
with the director Sh. Rozin and teacher Kolbzon, 1927**

During all the years the "Tarbuth" school was open it was in very bad
condition caused by unbearable crowding. The Jewish delegates in the
Municipality and the Jewish Deputy Mayor tried to obtained a grant to build a
suitable building for the school, but despite promises it was not carried out. A
Hebrew kindergarten was established as well. For a short time a Yiddish
school existed in town.

The front of the Hebrew Gymnasium

In 1919 a Hebrew high-school was established in Mariampol. This was the first Hebrew High School in the Diaspora and the second after the "Herzeliyah" of Tel-Aviv. Until its closing in 1940, when Lithuania was annexed to the Soviet Union, 19 graduating classes with about 400 graduates completed their studies, prior to many of them immigrating to Eretz-Israel.

Many of the teachers also immigrated to Eretz-Israel and among them there were the two founders and first directors of the school Dr. M.Meir and Dr. A.Loevenhertz (later he became the director of the high-school in Kiryath Motzkin) and both shared their professional experience and contributed to Education in Israel.

In the first 15 years, studies took place in a building which was an officers' club during the German occupation.. Before it became a school it was renovated. In 1934 after stormy public debates the school moved into a new building initially intended as a Home for the Aged. The last director of the school, A.Tabakhovitz was nominated that year. He, together with a team of other teachers, among them veterans Z.Ayerov, A.M.Levin and H.Rosenbaum perished during the Nazi regime.

On the 4th of May 1939 the 20th anniversary of the high-school was joyfully celebrated in the hall of a movie theatre in Mariampol. Delegates from the government, the municipality, as well as the directors of the town's Lithuanian high-schools and naturally all the former students and graduates of the school participated in the festivities. The Railway Authority granted a 50% discount to everybody who traveled to the celebration.

The first conference of the Hebrew High-School teachers in Lithuania took place in 1921 in Mariampol.

The teachers of the Gymnasium

Sitting from left: ---, Dr. Max Meir, ---, ---, Dr. Avraham Loevenhertz, Levin,---, Rosenbaum, Ayerov, ---.

גימנסיון עברי במרימפול.

••••••••

במרימפול נפתח גימנסיון עברי להתלמדים והתלמידות.

ומגמת הגימנסיון לתת לחניכיה השכלה לאומה וכללית, לכל־
הלמודים הכלליים מלמד על פי תכנית הגימנסיאות הקיימת במ־
שמונה מחלקות, יקבע מקום הגן ללמודים העברים בפ־־ דיתבה
ומלאה: דקרקק, תנ״ך, משנה, מטרות ינ רבעונ יהדישה קי־־־
ישראל. בגימנסיון תלמודה השפות, הורית הלין, תשנית רבמנת
רוסית וליטאית והשפה הצפרנית רשות,

לעת עתה נפתחות שנ מחלקות. ליטן כל הלמודים בארבע
המחלקות הראשונות עברית, בחמשת והשטית לפי שנה ריהת,
בצביל יבאים מהביבה תראנ קטוטה פידחית ליבן להם
אבטריה ישון.

שבר הלטור: לבל תלמיד ירלמידת ר. 200

הערתן להוזים שרט ליהם יתר בתלמד אחר בער חטני
ר. 150 ובער השלישי ר. 125

הבחיות מתחילות בכ״ז שבט 28, יאנואר, יצ״ו. 1919

בקשה על שם הרידקטור מהקבלות סייט כ״א שבט
יאואר,

יכתבת מרימפול דוד מאקס מאוד (Dr. Max Mayer) דהוב היאק
היטן מסמר 4 מטן מן.

רמוקעריי ט גישאן קאינא

The announcement on the opening of the Hebrew High-School in 1919 in Mariampol.

The second graduation class 1922-23

The fourth graduation class 1925

The last graduation class, 1940

The teachers sitting from right: Miss Vitenshtein, ---, --- , Miss Smilg, Rosenbaum, the Director Tabakhovitz, Levin, Ayerov, Rutshtein

The pupils standing from right: Aba Vainshtein (later Gefen), David Bruker, Aryeh Leibovitz (the authors cousin), Jehudith Kushner, Miriam Finkelshtein, Sarah Rudberg, Shevakh Levin, Janetta Medalie, Shimon Zupovitz, Zehavah Pilvinsky, Mosheh Strazdansky.

Standing behind from right: Aryeh Nun, Elkhanan Halperin, --- .

The fate of the above listed during and after the war:

All the teachers were murdered except Mr. Rutshtein who managed to escape to Russia. There he was conscripted in the 16th Division (the Lithuanian) of the Red Army. He fell in battle in 1943.

Aba Veinshtein-Gefen survived the Holocaust, is living in Israel and was the Ambassador of Israel to Romania.

Jehudith Kushner escaped to Russia from Vilna, lives in Lithuania, her two daughters live in Israel.

Shevakh Levin was exiled with his family to Siberia two weeks before the war and remained there.

Janetta Medalie escaped to Russia from Vilna where she studied. Lives in Israel.

Zehavah Pilvinsky escaped to Russia from Vilna. Lived in Israel where she died a few years ago.

All the others were murdered in the Holocaust.

There were several Hebrew and Yiddish libraries in Mariampol: at the High-School, at the Zionist-Socialist club, at the "Sirkin" society. The biggest library was at the "Libhober fun Visen" society (Fans of Knowledge). There were about 4,000 books in Yiddish in addition to Lithuanian, Russian and science books. The "Tarbuth" organization arranged evening lessons in Hebrew and Yiddish. In 1922 about 50 people participated in the lessons.

In Mariampol there was a drama circle presenting shows in Yiddish and Hebrew from time to time. The Yiddish theater from Kovno would occasionally visit Mariampol. There were two movie theatres in town which contributed to the cultural life in Mariampol.

In 1934 when young Jewish refugees arrived from Germany, an agricultural school was opened for them in the "Ungarina" farm. Later vocational courses were offered in that farm for Jewish refugees from Germany and Czechoslovakia organized by "Ort"

Zionist and public activity.

During the years of Autonomy there were quite a few workers' organizations in the community, such as " Bund" and "Po'alei Zion Smol". They established the "Kultur Lige" (League of Culture) in town and arranged evening courses for children and adults. Later all that remained of the "Yiddishists" was the "Folkist" (The Populists) movement. They stood for Yiddish and were opposed Zionism. Their medium was the daily newspaper "Volksblat" that was published in Kovno. However, by then the Zionist movement in all its shades had conquered the Jewish public in Mariampol. We can learn about the division of power among different Zionist parties represented in the Mariampol branches by looking at the results of the elections to the Zionist congresses:

Congr. Nr.	Year	Shekalim	Voter	Labor Party		Rev.	G.Z.		Gro	Miz.
				Z"S	Z"Z		A	B		
14	1925	64	--	--	--	--	--	--	--	--
15	1927	289	143	70	8	23	32	--	--	10
16	1929	775	416	150	69	171	69	--	--	6
17	1931*	--	462	210	14	181	47	--	--	10
18	1933	---	834	524		235	47	--	14	14
19	1935	1,706	958	639		--	99	38	102	80

Rev.-Revisionists; G.Z.-General Zionists; Gro.-Grosmanists; Miz.-Mizrahi

*The elections took place in the Synagogue.

A branch of "WIZO" (Women International Zionist Organization) was also organized in Mariampol. In 1938 it had 138 members, and the chairwoman was Mrs. Medalie, the wife of the known doctor in town Hayim Medalie.

The management of "WIZO" Mariampol
Sitting from left: Ayerov, Leikin, Medalie, Rabinovitz, ---
Standing from left: ---, ---, Rabinovitz, Levin

"HaShomer-haTsair" Branch, 1930

"Beitar" Branch, 1933

Among the Zionist youth organizations organized in Mariampol we can find "haShomer -haTsair", "Beitar", "Gordonia" and "heKhalutz". In 1919 the group "Akhvah" from "heKhalutz" Mariampol went to "Hakhsharah" and in 1920 immigrated to Eretz-Israel. Many of the former members of the Zionist youth organizations are presently residing in the Kibbutzim in Israel. In 1934 there was an urban Kibbutz of "heKhalutz" in town. In 1940 the "haShomer-haTsair" movement organized an "Hachsharah" Kibbutz for refugees from Poland in the farm "Mikhalina" near Mariampol. The farm belonged to the Levin family. Due to political changes in Lithuania this Kibbutz existed only for a short time.

Sports activities took place in the branches of "Maccabi" and "Maccabi haTzair" with 125 members. These branches had a soccer team with its own stadium, where groups for gymnastics and athletics were also organized.

Other sports companies were "JAK" (of the Yiddishists), "haPoel" and haKoakh". Youth groups from Mariampol participated in the first and second "Maccabiyah" (in 1932 and 1935) which took place in Tel-Aviv. Many of them remained in Eretz-Israel.

There was also in town "The Association of the former Jewish soldiers" who participated in the struggle for the Lithuanian Independence.

25.II.33 העשרה ...

Tenth anniversary of "Maccabi" Mariampol 1933

Religion and Welfare

The three synagogues, built around one courtyard before World War I, continued to operate during in this period as well. The central Synagogue would be closed in winter, because there was no heating.

The Rabbis who were appointed in this period in Mariampol were: Avraham-Dov Popel who was the Deputy Chairman of the "Nationalrat" (National Committee) of Lithuanian Jews, Chairman of the Association of the Rabbis and a delegate of the Lithuanian Seimas (died in Mariampol in 1923); Avraham-Ze'ev Halevi Heler (from 1923), who was the last Rabbi of Mariampol and perished in the "Shoah". Shelomoh-Pinkhas Butnitzky (died in 1932) was appointed as the "Dayan" (Religious Judge) .

After the liquidation of the Community Committee in the middle of the twenties, all welfare activities were taken over by the "Ezrah" association. Together with "Adath Israel" it helped the poor, raised money for "Maoth Khitim" (money to buy Matzoth for Pesach) and for the "Moshav Zekeinim" and also acted on special welfare issues. The "Association of the former Mariampol Jews in America" sent $200 for "Maoth Khitim" every year and from time to time would send several boxes of second hand clothes for the poor of the town.

The "OZE" organization maintained a clinic for children and a dental clinic. Its main function was health maintenance among Jewish school children. Weak and poor children would be sent to summer camps for convalescence at the expense of the organization.

The "Gemiluth Khesed" society issued loans without interest to needy people. The other welfare societies continued to act as before: "Bikur Kholim", "Linat haTzedek", "Khevrah Kadishah"etc.

Rabbi Avraham-Dov Popel

Among the natives of Mariampol it is worth to mention: the poet Alter Abelson, later a Rabbi and a preacher in Brooklyn; Shemuel-Tsevi Peltin (1831-1897) who was the publisher of the periodical "Israelita" in the Polish Language for 31 years in Warsaw; Mosheh ben Ya'akov Goldshtein who translated the "Hagadah of Pesakh" and the whole "Makhzor" (The prayer book of the Holidays) into the Russian Language; the writer and translator into Hebrew Avraham-Aba Rakovsky; the journalist and writer of Hebrew books for the youth Avraham Frank (1884-Holocaust); the Zionist activists Alexander Goldshtein and Aba-Yitshak Rosental (1875-1948); Moshe-David Heiman, who established the first factory of concrete products in Mariampol; the doctors Prof. Yehoshua Bronshtein and his brother Prof. Aharon Bronshtein; the pedagogue Dr. Barukh ben Yehuda (Leibovitz, 1894-1990), chairman of the Education Department of the "Va'ad Leumi", the first director general of the Education and Culture Ministry in Israel, the director of the "Herzliya" high-school and Holder of the "Israel Award" for Education (1979); Dr. Eliyahu Segal (1891-1963), the first sports doctor in Lithuania, who was very active in "Maccabi" and published many articles on medical subjects in the daily press in Israel; the painter Aryeh-Leib Margushelsky (1914-1982) founder of the high school for painting in Tel-Aviv; Yisrael Biderman (Izis), photographer and writer; the painter Mosheh Rozentalis (born in 1922).

In the period of World War II and Afterwards

It should be mentioned that Mariampol Jews provided help to refugees from the Suwalk region at the end of 1939 in spite of the fact that their own situation was continuously deteriorating. In agreement with the Ribbentrop-Molotov treaty the Russians occupied the Suwalk region, but after delineation of exact borders between Poland, Russia and Germany the Suwalk region fell into German hands. The retreating Russians allowed anyone who wanted to join them to move into the occupied territory, and indeed many young people left the area together with the Russians. The Germans kicked out the Jews remaining in Suwalk and the vicinity from their homes; they were robbed of their possessions, then directed to the Lithuanian border, and left in dire poverty. The Lithuanians did not allow them to enter Lithuania and the Germans did not allow them to go back. Thus they stayed in this swampy area in cold and rain for several weeks, until Jewish youth from the border villages in Lithuania smuggled them into Lithuania by different routes, with much risk to themselves. Altogether about 2,400 refugees passed through or infiltrated on their own, and were then dispersed in the Vilkovishk and Mariampol districts. In Mariampol alone 250 refugees were accommodated, among them tens of "Khalutsim", who got a warm welcome and loyal assistance for which Lithuanian Jews were famous.

In June 1940 Lithuania was annexed to the Soviet Union and became a Soviet Republic. When troops of the Red Army entered Mariampol, many Jews welcomed them joyfully. This agitated some Lithuanians and for three days Lithuanian hoodlums rampaged in the town. In many Jewish houses windows were shattered and many windows of Jewish stores were shattered as well. An eyewitness recounted that the town looked like after a bombing. As a matter of fact, many of the rioters were detained, but they were released after signing a promissory note not to repeat such acts.

Following new rules, the majority of the factories and shops belonging to the Jews of Mariampol were nationalized. All the Zionist parties and youth organizations were dismissed and several of the activists were detained. Hebrew educational institutions were closed. Supply of goods decreased and, as a result, prices soared. The middle class, mostly Jewish, was hit hard, and the standard of living dropped gradually. Several families, the owners of nationalized factories or shops were exiled deep into Russia.

On Sunday, June 22, 1941, at dawn, Mariampol was bombed by the German Army air strike. The center of the town was destroyed. Twenty people, most of them Jews, were killed. Jews left without housing found shelter in Jewish homes that remained unscathed.

The German Army entered Mariampol the next day, on Monday, June 23, 1941, encircling the town and blocking all the roads leading eastwards. Most of the Jews who escaped from town had to return. Many were murdered by Lithuanians who ambushed them. Only a few managed to reach Russia.

The Lithuanians welcomed the Germans with open arms and immediately started actions against Jews. Already on the first days of the occupation Jews were arrested under false pretences. All of the arrested were murdered in a ditch about 4 km from Mariampol in the direction of Vilkavishk (Vilkaviskis).

Jews were forced to go to work every morning: Men were forced to pick up the debris, women had to work in agricultural labor and housekeeping. The elderly, the town's Rabbi Avraham-Ze'ev Heler among them, were forced to sweep the streets.

Avraham Dembner, a native of the suburb Tarputch, returned in 1946 to Mariampol from Russia and was told by former neighbors about a few young men who staged resistance to Germans and their Lithuanian helpers after being pushed to forced labor. Ze'ev Papirnik, a 24 year old man, snatched a riffle from one Lithuanian, shot one of them to death and wounded the other. He was tortured and murdered.

Mendel Agronitzky resisted the murderers who came to take him for work and separated him from his wife and his daughters. He was shot on the spot.

A few young Jewish people, among them the brothers Vilkozhirsky, Palnitzky and Ruzhnitzky were hanged publicly at the market place for resisting the Germans.

On the 15th of July 1941 the governor of Mariampol district published an order according to which:

  1) Jews were forbidden to walk in the following streets: Vytauto, Church, Donelaicio, Petras Armino and Dariaus ir Gireno;

  2) Jews were forbidden to visit beaches, parks, coffee shops, restaurants, libraries and similar places;

  3) Jews were forbidden to purchase food products on the streets, roads, yards and markets. They would be allowed to buy their food in special shops as determined by the mayor, or in the general shops at restricted times

  4) It was forbidden for Jews to use services of non-Jews;

  5) All the Jews, despite sex or age, had to wear a yellow patch on the front and on the back of their garments in the form of a "Magen-David", 8-10 cm in diameter. Every Jew caught without the patch would be put in jail.

One day a group of Jews were brought to the yard of the Synagogues and forced to take out all the Torah Scrolls and Holly books from the Synagogues, pile them up and burn them. Hanan-Musikant - a musician and a "Badkhan" (comedian) at weddings - jumped into the fire to retrieve a Torah Scroll. The Germans snatched it away from him and threw it back into the fire. He suffered a hard beating.

There was also an order to greet every German soldier by taking off the hat and bowing low. One day the former teacher of the Hebrew high-school Ayerov, a very polite and quiet man, but pensive and a little distraught, failed to notice a German soldier and didn't greet him. The German slapped Ayerov and without hesitation he slapped the German back. He was arrested and murdered in jail.

The same month an order was published that the Jews had to leave their houses and gather in the synagogues and a few adjoining buildings. It was easier for the Germans to assault Jews in this crowded area, take them to forced labor and abuse young women at night. From time to time the Germans would choose young strong men for so-called "work" and then they would murder them in places near town.

In August the Germans forced young Jewish men to dig large ditches behind the barracks near the Sheshupe river. The men found out that the ditches were for the Jews. When the young people told their parents about it the parents were so disturbed they were running to try to cancel the order, but they did not succeed.

At the end of the same month Jewish public workers were summoned to the Lithuanian District Governor who informed them that in a short time a large Ghetto would be formed near the cavalry barracks and the adjoining area. To deceive them he promised that, as long as the war continued, Jews would administer their public and economic affairs by themselves.

The Jews packed their belongings, prepared food for a few days and went in a long cavalcade to the barracks. Upon arrival men were separated and forced into crowded stables. On the following days the men were relentlessly abused by an imposition of "Sports exercises", as the Germans called it. Jews from Kazlu-Ruda, Liudvinova and other nearby villages were brought to the barracks. On the 30th of that month Jews from Kalvaria were brought to that same place. In a similar fashion, men from these groups were forced into the crowded stables. Afterwards, they were ordered to join in the "Sports exercises".

On Monday, 9 th of Elul 5611, (1.9.1941), Mariampol Jews, together with the others who were brought there, about 7,000-8,000 Jews and about 1,000 people of other nationalities were murdered. All were buried in 8 ditches that were dug beforehand, each ditch 70 m long, 3 m wide at the top, and 2 m at the bottom. The ditches were near the Sheshupe river, at the right side of the bridge, on the road to Kalvaria. The massacres started at 10 o'clock in the morning and ended at 4 o'clock in the afternoon. The murderers were mostly Lithuanians, among them University and high school students who volunteered for the "job".

The Jewish men were brought to the ditches in groups of 100-200 men, completely naked. They were forced to lie down in the ditches in lines. From above they were shot by machine guns. When the women and children's turn came a tremendous and tumultuous agitation began, while the drunk murderers began pushing victims into ditches, crashing the heads of children with clubs and spades. Because of the tumultuous agitation many of the victims were wounded but not dead, thus they were buried alive. Lithuanian eyewitnesses recounted that most of the victims were deeply depressed, as if in a fog. Other Lithuanians who were brought to the place to cover the graves the next day told that earth under the graves moved for a long time after the massacre.

Following the murders the bandits divided the goods they have looted from the victims and returned to town singing in a drunk fashion and celebrating the whole night.

Two families committed suicide. Dr.David Rosenfeld administered poison to himself, his wife and his daughter. Cantor Lansky also took poison himself, gave poison to his wife and his three children.

After the war the survivors of Mariampol Jewish community placed a tombstone on the site of the graves. In 1992 a new monument was built (see image below)

The site of the mass graves near the military barracks and the Monument at the site. The inscription in Yiddish and Lithuanian says:

"Here blood was spilled of about 8000 Jewish children, women, men and of 1000 people of different nationalities, that the Nazis and their local helpers cruelly murdered in September 1941"

In the same year a monument was erected in Shunsk (Sunskai) forest near Mariampol (see image below).

The site of the mass grave and the monument on it. The inscription in Yiddish and Lithuanian says: "Here blood was spilled of 200 Jews, children, women and men, who were cruelly murdered by the Nazis and their helpers in 1941. Let the memory of the martyrs last forever".

In the same surroundings, in Rudziai grove, another monument was erected (see image below).

The site of the mass grave with the monument. The inscription in Yiddish and Lithuanian reads: "In this place the Hitlerist murderers and their local helpers murdered Jews from Marijampol in July 1941".

In the "Holocaust Cellar" at Mt. Zion in Jerusalem a Memorial Plaque was erected for the Mariampol Community

In 1992 a monument was placed where the Jewish cemetery once was with no trace of it remaining. The inscription on the monument in Hebrew, Yiddish and Lithuanian says that there was a Jewish cemetery in this place.

Bibliography

Yad-Vashem archives: M-9/13(2); M-21/1/357,670;

0-33/03,85,159,282,283,422.

Koniuchovsky Collection 0-71, Files 128, 130; TR-2/2849,2934; TR-10/1096

YIVO,NY, Collection of the Jewish Communities in Lithuania, Files 585-658, pages 103, 922-925, 28, file 1667.

Marijampole -Lithuania (Hebrew, Yiddish, and English) Published by the former Mariampol Jews, Tel-Aviv 1983.

Lite, New-York 1951, volume 1 (Yiddish)

The Jewish Encyclopedia, St. Petersburg 1908-1913, (Russian)

Bemisholei haKhinuch (In the paths of education) Kovno (Hebrew), May 1939, May 1940

HaMeilitz (St. Petersburg) (Hebrew): 20.5.1879; 20.7.1880; 3.8.1880; 7.6.1881; 20.9.1881; 21.4.1884; 22.10.1886; 7.2.1893; 17.9.1893.

Unzer Veg (Zionist-Socialist newspaper) , Kovno (Yiddish): 18.7.1924; 15.8.1924; 18.1.1925; 24.1.1926; 22.9.1926; 27.2.1929.

Neis (News) Kovno (Yiddish): 22.8.1921.

Der Yiddisher Cooperator, Kovno (Yiddish) 1922, Number 2-3

Dos Neie Vort (The new Word), Kovno (Yiddish): 4.5.1934;10.5.1934

Dos Vort, Kovno (Yiddish): 28.9.1934; 31.1.1939; 26.2. 1939; 5.6.1939

Folksblat, Kovno (Yiddish): 21.5.1934; 5.6.1935; 13.6.1935; 19.6.1935; 26.7.1935;

28.10.1936; 9.3.1937; 16.3.1937; 24.9.1937; 25.4.1939; 13.6.1939; 22.6.1939; 13.7.1939; 6.9.1939.

Di Yiddishe Shtime (The Yiddish Voice) Kovno (Yiddish): 5.9.1919; 24.1.1923; 9.3.1928; 20.9.1928; 30.4.1929; 7.6.1929; 12.6.1929; 14.2.1930; 28.3.1930; 7.7.1930; 27.5.1931; 26.6.1931; 1.12.1931; 26.4.1932; 20.5.1932; 22.6.1932; 8.3.1933; 7.3.1937; 4.11.1937; 1.3.1938; 12.1.1939; 24.2.1939; 13.3.1939; 14.3.1939;

Yiddisher Hantverker (Jewish Artisan) Kovno, (Yiddish) 1.11.1938

Merkinė (Meretch)

Meretch (Merkine in Lithuanian) lies in the southeastern part of Lithuania, on the right bank of the river Nemunas, where the river Merkys and the small stream Stange flow into it. It is a very old urban settlement, where by the 14th century a fortress had been built on a hill near the town, the remains of which still exist today, and the area was one of battles between the German Crusader Order, the Lithuanians and the Poles.

In 1387 the Lithuanian Great Duke Vytautas and the Polish King Jagelo (Jogaila) converted its residents to Christianity.

In 1576 King Zigmunt-August granted the town the Magdeburg Rights for self rule. At that time the exact site of the town was determined and four columns were erected at its four corners, two of which apparently still exist.

During the 17th and 18th centuries' wars, Meretch was badly damaged. In 1655 it was occupied by the Russians and totally burnt down. In 1707 Czar Peter the First arrived in Meretch with his army, awaiting the Swedes. The Russians took horses, cattle and food products from the residents and burnt the rest, as a result of which many Meretch residents starved.

During the uprising of the Poles in 1794 led by Koschiusko, Meretch was again burnt down and destroyed by the Russians.

In the 19th century, under Russian rule, the town was included in the Trakai district of the Vilna Gubernia, becoming an important commercial center because of its location at a junction of the important roads Kovno-Grodno and Vilna-Suwalk, and being situated along the waterways of the Nemunas and the Merkys.

In 1869 its population numbered 1,494 residents, and by 1882 - 2,148 residents lived there. The people of the town made their living from agriculture, fishing, mushroom drying and commerce.

In 1915, during World War I, Meretch was occupied by the Germans who ruled there till 1918, at which time the independent Lithuanian State was established. For a short while the town was occupied by the Bolsheviks, but in 1920 the Poles conquered it until they themselves retreated before the Lithuanian army. In the spring of 1921 a great fire broke out, burning down 100 houses and many farm buildings. The American Red Cross supplied the victims with 84 tons of food and garments.

During the period of independent Lithuania (1918-1940) Meretch was part of the Alytus district and a county administrative center. In the 1920s a central water supply system was built and it became one of the first towns of Lithuania to have such an installation. Later the town got electricity from one of its sawmills where a generator was installed.

During the German invasion of the USSR on the 22nd of June 1941 the town was bombed and many buildings damaged. The Nazi rule with its terror and atrocities lasted until June 1944, when the Red Army reconquered Meretch. During the battles the center of the town was badly damaged.

Meretch Jews at forced labor during World War I

Jewish Settlement till after World War I.

Society and Economy.

The beginnings of Jewish settlement in Meretch can apparently be traced back to the 15th century. A document from 1486 states that the Great Duke Kazimir ordered his clerks to demand that Yanka (Ya'akov) Yatskovitz and his sons pay taxes. In documents dating from 1539 Meretch Jews are mentioned in connection with a conflict between a Jew named Koniuk and a Christian who owed him money. Documents from 1551 mention Meretch Jews in connection with their exemption from having to pay the special tax imposed on all urban and rural citizens.

During the years 1768-1772 Jewish workers were employed in excavating the Nemunas river between Meretch and Rumshishok (Rumsiskis), in order to improve its sailing conditions.

Meretch was included in the list of communities which were subordinated to the "Va'ad Medinath Lita" (The committee of the Jewish communities in Lithuania) (1623-1764), and was mentioned in the " ***Pinkas Va'ad HaKehiloth HaRoshiyoth BeMedinath Lita*** " (Notebook of Major Communities in Lithuania) during the years 1623-1761. In 1765 - 444 Jews resided here, and by 1847 the number had increased to 1565 Jewish residents.

The Market Place

The town was built in the form of a circle, the market square being in the center and around it were the Jewish houses with their shops, vegetable and fruit gardens. Behind them were the Christian neighborhoods.

The Jews made their living from commerce and crafts, and Jewish merchants traveled on business to the bigger cities of Suwalk, Grodno and Vilna. Betsalel Manosovsky rented forest plots from the government for the purpose of felling trees, which were then transported on rafts on the Nemunas to Prussia. He also owned a sawmill and employed both Jewish and Christian workers. Jews owned flour mills, a brick factory, a leather factory, a workshop of candles and a few bakeries. Shoemakers, tailors, carpenters and builders could be found amongst the craftsmen.

At the end of the 19th century Meretch Jews settled in agricultural colonies which the Russian government provided free of charge on condition that they cultivate the land. In 1849 such a colony was established in Panasishok (Panosiskes) and ten families from Meretch settled there. Meretch Jews also settled in those colonies which were established in 1847 in Leipun (Leipalingis) and in Dukshna.

In 1884, on "Khol Hamoed" Succoth, a great fire razed 50 Jewish houses. In the Hebrew newspaper "HaMeilitz" of St.Petersburg dated the 20th of October 1884, an appeal for help for the victims of the fire was published, signed by the Rabbi of Meretch, Yehudah haLevi Lifshitz. In 1893 several fires broke out in the town, for which fifteen Jews were accused of arson, but the accusation was withdrawn. In 1897 a cholera epidemic raged through the town.

A bank established by the JCO (Jewish Colonization Organization) in 1907, initiated by Meretch Jews Yosef Ziman, Mendel-Gershon Yanilov and Avraham-Hertz Miler, played an important role in the economic life of the town.

Education and Religion.

Jewish children received their education in the "Kheder", in the "Talmud Torah" and in the government school established in 1853 on the initiative of the local intelligence. There were two classes in the "Kheder" - the first one for learning to read the "Sidur", and the second one where "Gemara" and "Mishnah" were taught. There the children studied till "Bar-Mitzvah", thereafter the talented pupils continued their study in the 'Yeshivoth' of Lida, Volozhin and Slabodka. There were six "Khadarim" for boys and one for girls. In the "Talmud-Torah" mainly "Sidur", "Khumash" and Hebrew were taught, without tuition fees.

In 1860 a Jewish government school was opened with four classes, boys and girls studying together, the teaching language being Russian. One of the teachers was Yosef-Eliezer Epstein, a student of the rabbinical school in Vilna. The pupils of the "Khadarim" were obliged to attend this school for several hours every day to in order to study Russian.

Shortly before World War I a "Yeshivah Ketanah" (a small or elementary Yeshivah) was established, intended for boys of 13 years of age and upwards. The local Rabbi acted as the supervisor of this school.

Meretch boasted three synagogues, which played a central role in the spiritual and cultural life of the town's Jews. The "Shul", the "Klois" and the "Beth Midrash" lay in the same street and everyone of them had its own worshippers. The "Shul" was a beautiful building with an "Aron Kodesh" (Holy Arc) made from carved wood, brass chandeliers hanging from the vaulted ceiling which was painted azure like the sky, with stars set in it. In the "Shul" prayers were held only on Saturdays and holidays. Guest cantors would appear and tickets would be sold for these appearances. The "Klois" was a great and lovely building too. "Gemara" (Talmud) learning took place in the "Beth Midrash". Many societies concerned themselves with adult study of Judaism: Shas, Mishnah, Tehilim, Tifereth Bakhurim and Shulkhan Arukh whose "Pinkas" from the years 1873-1898 was saved.

The "Haskalah" (Enlightenment) movement appeared in Meretch as well and the Jewish "intelligence" read the Hebrew books of Avraham Mapu, Peretz Smolenskin and others with great interest.

Zionist activity had started by the 1880s. In the summer of 1887 David Veiberg, a settler of Rishon LeZion, came to Meretch to visit his parents. He asked the public to donate for the "Khalutzim" in Eretz Israel, to which the public responded positively and donated generously, but the local Rabbi objected. Once, on a Shabbat eve, on seeing proclamations of the "Mizrakhi" party (The religious Zionist party) in the Synagogue, he became very upset and on Shabbat night ripped them to pieces. In spite of this, Zionist activity continued and in 1898 a Zionist Association was founded.

Welfare institutions included "Hakhnasath Orkhim", "Bikur Kholim", "Linath haTsedek" and a ladies' association for social help.

The "Intelligencia" in 1916

There was a "Voluntary Fire Brigade", most of its members being Jews. During the years the heads of this brigade were Yehoshua David Manisovsky, Yisrael Tuviyah Kubitzky, Benjamin Laukenitzky.

During all this period Jews immigrated to South Africa and mainly to America, many of them settling in New York and Boston. In Boston there existed (maybe even now) the "Meretch Relief Association" which supported the community in Lithuania and kept contact with the few Meretch Jews who had immigrated to Eretz Israel.

During World War I the Jews of Meretch remained in town, even absorbing refugees who were expelled from the Kovno Gubernia by the Russians.

The Rabbis who served in Meretch during this period were: Yitshak son of Tsevi in 1835; David Volpe (---1884); Ben-Zion Shternfeld (1835-1914); Yehudah haLevi Lifshitz (1829-1905); Mikhal-David Stupel (1865-1941) also served as head of the Yeshiva and murdered in the Holocaust. The Rabbis earned a modest salary, but in addition had the exclusive yeast selling concession in town. All the women in town, including the Christian ones, would come to the Rabbis to buy yeast.

During the Period of Independent Lithuania (1918-1940).

As a result of the change of rulers, the Germans, the Lithuanians, the Bolsheviks and later the Polish occupation with its anti-semitic atmosphere as well as the big fire of 1921, Jewish economic life was undermined and many families were in danger of starvation. Only due to the help of "The Jewish American Aid Committee" did the Jews of Meretch manage to survive these difficult years. Bread was sold at half the price to those in need and many

A street in Meretch were many Jews lived

received it free of charge; also a kitchen was established which provided free meals for the needy. In these difficult times there were some additional 200 homeless refugees from Poland, which made problems harder. After life became more normal, they left the town. Help for Meretch's Jews also came from the *"YEKOPO"* (Russian initials for Jewish Aid Committee) organization, in which a native of the town, Dr. Kovarsky, was active. Over the next few years the Jewish community recovered and life returned to its normal course, in which commerce, industry and crafts were entirely in Jewish hands.

According to the government survey of 1931 Meretch had 3 Jewish grain merchants, 5 textile shops and 12 various other shops. The Jews also owned 6 flour mills, 2 sawmills, a cloth painting workshop, a soft drinks factory, a leather processing workshop, a brick factory, a candy factory, a sewing workshop, a tinkers' and a locksmiths workshop. In addition there were tailors, seamstresses, stitchers, shoemakers, bakers and others. By 1937, 105 members were registered in the local branch of the "Association of Jewish Artisans ", including 23 tailors, 22 shoemakers, 12 butchers, 9 blacksmiths, 8 bakers, 3 stitchers, 3 leatherworkers, 3 carpenters, 2 watchmakers, 2 barbers, 2 glaziers, 2 oven builders, 2 hatters, one locksmith, one tinker, one painter, one wood engraver, one photographer, one book binder and 6 others, 2 families being farmers.

In order to make the life of the Jewish shop owners more difficult, two Lithuanian consumer co-ops, supported by the government, were set up. Nevertheless, the Wednesday market day was an important source of income for the Jewish shops nearby.

The Jewish Popular Bank (Folksbank), whose basic capital came partly from Jewish American funds, was the center of the town's economic life. In 1927 it had 416 members, but in 1929 only 325. The director of the branch was Mosheh Shumakher, a public worker and one of the leaders of the local "Hitakhduth".

According to the official phone book of 1939, there were 34 telephone owners in Meretch, 12 of them Jewish.

A group of Young Meretch Jews in 1936

First line above, from right: Hayim-Shelomoh Pugatzky, Simhah Kaplan, ____.

Second line from right: Hanah Krivorutzky, Hayah Pugatzky.

Third line from right: Shalom-Yitshak Romanov, Havivah Rudnitzky, Beile Slonimsky, ---Noakh, Yehudah Karpas.

Fourth line: ----Kaplan, Hayah Krikshtansky, Shtishe Amerikansky, Golda Zalutzky.

Fifth line: Aharon Bendenzon, Ya'akov Klibansky.

Education and Culture.

In 1920, before the political situation in Meretch had stabilized, a Yiddish school with two classes was established. Several years later the "Tarbuth" chain set up a school of five classes, with Yiddish as the teaching language as well, and with Hebrew being taught as one of the school's subjects. The school had a library with Hebrew and Yiddish books and in its reading room there were also children's periodicals of the period, such as "Di Grininke Boimalach" (The Green Trees) in Yiddish and "Olami HaKatan" (My Small World) in Hebrew, and others. For the "Hanukah" and "Purim" holidays, pupils would prepare shows, mostly in Hebrew.

The Hebrew Elementary School 1928 or 1930

Throughout the years of its existence the headmaster of this school was Avraham Sidransky, and among the teachers there were Mosheh Ilivitzky, Efraim Yeverovitz, Nadia Milner, Sonia Finan, Shimon Rubinstein, Kalman Vasilisky, Mosheh Pilvinsky and Rabbi David Goldoft.

In addition a school for boys of the religious "Yavneh" stream was active in the town. It was located in the "Ezrath Nashim" of the ' Klois". The teachers were R' Kalman, Aba Beker, Moshe Yehezkel, Milner and others.

There was also a Hebrew kindergarten. Graduates from the schools continued their studies in the Hebrew pro-gymnasium in Alite (Alytus) or in the Hebrew high schools in Kovno and among the graduates there were some who continued on to Kovno University. Very few continued their studies in universities abroad, thanks to the scholarships granted by the philanthropist Azriel Tchais, a native of this district. There were also Meretch youngsters who studied in the Yeshivoth of Telsh and Ponevezh.

The library, which contained about 3,000 Hebrew and Yiddish books, was an important cultural institution, and Motl Miklishansky, a member of the "Poalei Zion Smol" (Leftists Zionist Workers) party, was its director for many years.

Zionist and other Activities.

All Zionist parties were represented in Meretch., and in 1933 a branch of "WIZO" (Women International Zionist Organization) was active as well. The dominant party was the "ZS-Hitakhduth", as can be seen from the election results to the Zionist Congresses:

Cong Nr	Year	Tot Shek	Total Votes	Labor Party Z"S	Z"Z	Rev	Gen Zion A	B	Gros	Miz
14	1925	50	----	----	----	--	----	----	----	----
15	1927	91	79	5	48	1	3	----	----	22
16	1929	203	124	31	67	6	5	----	----	15
17	1931	285	155	58	53	29	4	----	----	11
18	1933	-----	277	219		37	11	----	1	9
19	1935	-----	589	343		--	48	162	----	36

Key: Cong No. = Congress Number, Tot Shek = Total Shkalim,
Rev = Revisionists, Gen Zion = General Zionists, Gros = Grosmanists, Miz = Mizrakhi

The Hebrew Kindergarten 1930

The fourth class of the "Yavneh" school 1932

Standing in the first line above from right the teachers Shimon Rubinstein and Aba Beker.

Activists of "Hitakhduth" 1925

The committee and the activists of KKL (Jewish National Fund) in Meretch on the celebrating the 25th jubilee of the fund 1927

There were fund raising activities for the National Funds - Keren Kayemeth LeYisrael (KKL), Keren HaYesod, also for Labour party funds in Eretz Israel, from which later on Bank HaPoalim developed. The Lithuanian centers of these funds were in Kovno and from there instructions were given for their activities. From time to time evening parties were arranged, the income of which was transferred to the above mentioned funds and sometimes to the local library too. Donations for KKL were given also on the occasion of an "Aliyah LaTorah" at the synagogue.

"Gordonia" in Meretch 1930

Zionist youth organizations were very active in Meretch and most youths belonged to one of them. The first was "Gordonia" with its 70-80 members who were divided into three age groups, with the eldest being affiliated to the local "HeKhalutz" branch.

Many of this group immigrated to Eretz-Israel and joined the "Kibbutzim" Mishmaroth, Givath Brener, Dafnah, Huldah, Yagur and others.

A branch of "HaShomer HaTsair" was established in Meretch in 1928 by several members who had studied in other towns having absorbed the ideology of that movement, and during these years about 250 boys and girls were members of this organization. The adults of "HaShomer HaTsair" who immigrated to Eretz Israel joined the "Kibbutzim" Beth Zera, Amir, Mizra, Kefar Masarik and others.

"HaShomer-HaTzair" Branch in 1930

"Bnei-Akiva"

The adult group of "Hashomer Hatsair" 1933

"HeKhalutz" in Meretch 1931

In addition there were the "Dror", "Bnei Akiva" and "HeKhalutz" organizations, the latter being a federation of all left leaning politically minded youth organizations.

In 1934 an urban Kibbutz of "HeKhalutz" existed, and there was also a branch of Betar.

The "Maccabi" Branch in 1926

Sport activities were performed in the local "Maccabi" branch. It had also a string band.

The String Band of "Maccabi"

Several entire families immigrated to Eretz-Israel, among them the Kreiners in 1924 and the Zimans in 1925. Yosef Ziman was among the founders of "Nakhlath Yitzhak", now part of Tel Aviv, named after Rabbi Yitshak Elkhanan Spector, the famous Rabbi of Kovno.

For many years the members of the "Voluntary Fire Brigade", who were all Jewish, also served as a "Self Defence" group in case of trouble, and its commander was Yehudah Smolnik for a long time. The hangar of the brigade also served as a cinema.

In 1936 the President of the State decorated three Jewish men - B.Kadish, M.Drezner and Sh.Kotnitzky, having fought for the independence of Lithuania during the years 1918-1919, with the medal of independence. At the local Jewish cemetery a modest monument for fallen Jewish soldiers in Lithuania's war of independence was erected.

Religion and Welfare.

The prayer houses that existed before World War I, continued to serve their purpose as before. Rabbi Mikhal David Shtupel, who officiated in Meretch before World War I and was known for his harsh opposition to Zionism, continued to hold his position until he was murdered in the Holocaust. There were no "Hasidim" in Meretch and no children with long "Peoth" could be seen in its streets.

These were its welfare institutions: "Gemiluth Khesed" (from 1928) for loans without interest, "Mathan BeSether", "Bikur Kholim", "Linath HaTsedek", "Ezrah" and "Khevrah Kadisha". The "OZE" organization cared mainly for school children, and also ran a clinic for the public. All Meretch Jews were partly insured for the use of the Jewish hospital in Kovno "Bikur Kholim", and people of means made a regular monthly payment for this purpose. In the winter of 1939-1940 the community took care of the many refugees who had arrived from Poland.

During and After World War II

After the German army occupied Poland in September 1939 and, in accordance with the Ribbentrop-Molotov treaty the Russians occupied the Suvalk region, but after the delineation of exact borders between Poland, Russia and Germany, this region fell into German hands. The retreating Russians allowed anyone who wanted to join them to move into their occupied territory, and indeed many young Jewish people left the area together with the Russians. The Germans expelled the remaining Jews from their homes, robbed them of their possessions, then directed them to the Lithuanian border, where they were left in dire poverty. The Lithuanians did not allow them to enter Lithuania and the

Germans did not allow them back. Thus they stayed in this swampy area in the cold and rain for several weeks, until Jewish youths from the border villages in Lithuania smuggled them into Lithuania by various routes, at much risk to themselves. Young Jews from Meretch, which was close to the border, were active in smuggling many of these Jews into the country and giving them a warm welcome in Meretch as well as loyal assistance, for which Lithuanian Jews were famous. Altogether about 2,400 refugees crossed through or infiltrated on their own, and were then dispersed in Lithuania.

In June 1940 Lithuania was annexed by the Soviet Union and became a Soviet Republic. According to Soviet economic policy some Jewish factories and shops were nationalized and commissars were appointed to run them, the craftsmen being forced to organize into cooperatives. Supply of goods was restricted, as a result of which prices soared, and the middle class, mostly Jewish, was badly hit with its living standard dropping gradually. The Zionist parties and youth organizations were dispersed and some of its members were absorbed in the Comsomol - the Communist Youth Organization. The Hebrew school was closed and in its stead a Yiddish school opened. The headmaster A.Sidransky was dismissed and a teacher called Lurie was appointed in his place. The librarian M.Miklishansky was arrested and four Jewish families - Kabatchnik, Geler, Odientz, Kubitzky - were exiled deep into Russia.

On the 22nd of June 1941 the German army invaded the USSR . Units of the German army encircled Meretch cutting off all roads, so that not one Jew managed to escape from the town, except for a few who at this time were staying in Kovno. German bombing destroyed the center of the town and most of the Jewish families became homeless.

Together with the entry of the Germans into Meretch, the local Lithuanian bullies headed by a teacher of the elementary school, who was also the manager of the "Shaulist" nationalist organization, started to detain Jews, in particular those who were involved in some way in some activity connected to Soviet rule. The first victim was the youngster Hirsh Guzhansky, who was killed by Lithuanians in the center of town, in Kovno Street, with spades they carried, and buried him there.

On the third day of the war, the 24th of June 1941, the detained Jews were led by the Lithuanians to the Jewish cemetery and there were forced to dig a big pit. Among them were Robert Aroliansky, Shalom Goldman, David Vildkin, Shemuel-Dov Pugatzky, Yitshak Kopelman, Dov Kravitz, Menakhem Krikshtansky. Then they were shot and buried in this pit. During that time several Jews were thrown into the Nemunas river and drowned.

After these murders the unrest in town decreased somewhat and many Meretch Jews deluded themselves by thinking that maybe they would now be left alone. Meanwhile news about the terrible murder of Jews in Kovno reached Meretch. Several Meretch Jews whose sons or relatives worked or studied in Kovno, got permission to go there in order to bring them back and a few actually returned home.

After a short while all Jews were ordered to concentrate in a particular site - the yard of the synagogues which became a Ghetto. Women and small children were crowded into the building of the "Klois" and the men into the "Beth Midrash". The Ghetto was encircled with barbed wire, with armed Lithuanians guarding it. Inside the Ghetto a committee was established whose members were the teacher Avraham Sidransky, Betsalel Vainstein and a few others. These committee members tried to develop contacts with the Lithuanians in order to make easier the life in the Ghetto, but all their efforts were of no avail. Every day groups of Jews heavily guarded were taken to various forced labor tasks. From time to time the Germans, helped by Lithuanians, would put together groups of Jewish men for transfer to a labor camp near Alytus, but in fact they were murdered on the way.

At the end of August 1941 Jews were made to dig long trenches beside the fence of the Jewish cemetery. Tension and fear among the Jews increased, but only a few realized the coming danger, the majority deluding themselves by saying that these trenches were meant for military purposes.

On the 7th of September 1941 the Ghetto was surrounded by heavily armed Lithuanians, who made their intentions very clear: "This is your last night, Jews. Tomorrow is your end". On the next day at dawn, on the 8th of September, the Jews were ordered to leave their abodes and to leave everything behind. Almost naked, being hit and cursed, they were led from the Ghetto to the Jewish cemetery and there beside the trenches they were shot and buried. Several young girls who managed to escape from the murder site, were caught later and murdered as well.

According to a German source, on this day 223 men, 355 women and 276 children, totaling 854 Jews, were murdered in Meretch.

Monument on the mass grave of Meretch

SIOJE VIETOJE 1941 METAIS
HITLERINIAI ZMOGZUDZIAI IR
JU VIETINIAI PAGALBININKAI
NUZUDE 1600 ŽYDU -
MOTERU, VAIKU.

אויף דעם ארט האבן ר
ה סלער-שע רוצחים און
ז- יערע ארטיהע באהעלפער
אין 1941 דערמארדעט
1600 יהודן-
פרויען, קינדער

Plaque at the monument on the mass grave of Meretch

After the town was liberated from Nazi rule in the summer of 1944, a native of the town, a girl partisan called Malkah Pugatzky (later Smali), whose entire family had been murdered there, was the first Jew to arrive back in Meretch. At the site of the mass graves human bones and skulls were dispersed over the surface. She gathered them into a pile and applied to the police for help to bury them, but was not granted permission to do so. They hinted that she should leave town fast because her life was in danger.

Only after more survivors returned from the USSR, among them former soldiers of the Lithuanian Division of the Red Army, and after many efforts, did they receive permission from the authorities to erect two monuments on the two graves - one for the men and the other for the women and children. The inscriptions on the monuments were in Lithuanian and Yiddish, and the expenses of erecting the monuments were covered by the survivors.

In 1991 the inscriptions on the monuments were changed as follows: "At this place Hitler's murderers with their local helpers murdered 1,600 Jews - women, children"

In the town the "Beth Midrash" had become a granary, the "Shul" had been turned into a Lithuanian high school and of the "Klois" only the walls were left.

Bibliography.

Yad Vashem Archives: Koniukhovsky Collection 0-71, Files 93.121; 0-3/3925.

YIVO, NY, Collection of Jewish Communities in Lithuania, File 1531.

Pinkas Va'ad HaKehiloth HaRoshiyoth BeMedirath Lita, 5383-5521 (Notebook of Major Communities in Lithuania, 1623-1761).

The First Conference of the Jewish Regional Committee "YeKoPo" for helping the Victims of the War, Vilna, September 1919.

Glen M. Meretch (Yiddish) Lite, New York, Volume 2.

Meretch-A Jewish Town in Lithuania, Editor Uri Shefer (Hebrew), Tel-Aviv 1988.

Gotlib. Ohalei Shem, page 120.

HaMeilitz (St. Petersburg) (Hebrew): 23.8.1880; 9.6.1884; 20.10.1884; 18.11.1885; 16.12.1885; 21.7.1887; 16.2.1891; 11.7.1894.

Der Yiddisher Cooperator, Kovno (Yiddish)1929, Number 10.

Dos Neie Vort (The new Word), Kovno (Yiddish), 2.7.1934.

Dos Vort, Kovno (Yiddish): 17.12.1934; 14.2.1935; 26.11.1935.

Folksblat, Kovno (Yiddish): 10.3.1933.

Di Yiddishe Shtime (The Yiddish Voice) Kovno (Yiddish): 30/12/1920; 24.5.1928; 26.12.1929; 4.7.1930; 15.7.1930. 26.6.1931; 19.8.1931; 4.2.1932; 9.3.1933; 7.9.1933; 7.3.1937; 11.5.1937; 1.3.1938; 17.7.1938; 13.3.1939.

Yiddisher Hantverker (Jewish Artisan) Kovno, (Yiddish) 1.12.1938. Nr 6.

Appendix 1:   A Partial List of Personalities Born in Meretch.

Harry Fishel (1865-1948), philanthropist, donated funds for establishing the "Tarbuth" school in Meretch, established the Harry Fishel Institute in Jerusalem, died in Jerusalem.

Max Leopold Margalith (1866-1932) Professor of Semitic languages and Bible research in American universities, Editor of the new English translation of the Bible.

Rabbi Zalman-Ya'akov Fridman (1865-?), Rabbi in New York and as from 1893 in Boston.

David-Eliyahu Stone (1888-?), from 1906 in America, one of the founders of the Zionist organization in the USA, member of the Zionist Executive, prosecutor in Massachusetts.

Luis Stone (1884-1957) brother of the above, prosecutor in Boston.

Aharon Frenkel (1886-1941), from 1903 in USA, Hebrew-Yiddish reporter and editor, member of the editorial board of "Hayom" and "Hadoar".

David Berezovsky (1896-1941), journalist and writer, lived in Grodno and from there was taken to be murdered in Treblinka.

Menakhem Glen (Glembotzky) D.Ph. (1898-1978) from 1914 in the USA, published articles and books in Yiddish, Hebrew and English: "On the Shores of the Nieman" (Hebrew), Jerusalem 1937; "Rashi - The Popular Teacher" (Yiddish), N.Y.1947 etc.

Ya'akov Glen D.M. (1905-1974) from 1923 in the USA, published articles on medical issues in the Hebrew and Yiddish press in America and a few books in Yiddish about health and diabetics.

Malkah Pugatzky-Senior-Smali (1919-1992), was very active in the autumn of 1939 in absorbing a group of "Gordonia" members, refugees from the Suwalk region, in Meretch and later in Kovno; being in the Kovno Ghetto joined the anti-fascist underground and took 17 Jewish babies out of the Ghetto bringing them to a Lithuanian nursery; joined the partisans in the Rudniky woods; after the liberation of Kovno was one of the founders of the Jewish orphan home in which poor orphans, gathered from Lithuanian families who hid them during Nazi rule, found a warm home; member of the Zionist underground and a contact woman on behalf of the "Brikha" organization with the Zionists in Lithuania, Latvia and Estonia; arrived in Eretz Yisrael in November 1947 after half a year's detention by the British in Cyprus; from 1951 in Kibbutz Kefar Masarik.

Benjamin Kaplan, A.Vitkind, Mordehai-Zvi Hurvitz were reporters of "HaTzefirah";

Benjamin HaCohen, David Zeiberg, Yakobson, Hayim Gadovsky, G.Zeiberg, Hayim-Yitshak Laukalitzky were reporters of "HaMeilitz".

Appendix 2:   Meretch Jews who fought in the War against the Nazis.

In the Red Army.

Odientz Ya'akov	Sloviansky Betsalel
Aroliansky Masha	Segal Tsevi
Babalsky Ze'ev	Pugatzky Gad
Gordon Mosheh	Pugatzky Avraham
Vidovsky Shemuel	Klibansky Ya'akov
Vildikan Katriel	Ragovsky Zerakh
Lis David	Ragovsky Khyene
Lis Shalom	Rozental Barukh
Man Yasha	Smali (Smolnik) Yosef
Sloviansky Aryeh	

In the USA Army.

Slonimsky Yekhiel

Shafransky (Shafner) Aharon

Shafransky (Shafner) Zerakh

In the British Army - The Jewish Brigade from Eretz Yisrael.

Yanilov Ya'akov

Ziman Yitshak

Rabin Ya'akov

Romanov Yehudah

Romanov Yafah (Sheine Leah)

Among the Partisans.

Sloviansky Mosheh

Laukenitzky Yosef

Pugatzky-Smali Malkah

Panevėžys (Ponevezh)

Ponevezh (Panevezys in Lithuanian) stretches on both banks of the Nevezhis (Nevezys) River in north central Lithuania.

Settlers began to settle on the right bank of the river at the beginning of the 16th century, and it was there where the Old City developed. Later the city stretched to the left bank, and the *New City* was built, becoming the administrative center of the Upyte County.

The nearby village Upyte (15 km away) was the administrative center of the area for hundreds of years. In those years, until the beginning of the 18th century, the Nevezys River played an important role allowing ships to sail up to Ponevezh.

In 1661 the "Old City" was granted permission to arrange two market days per week and two large fairs market per year. During the 17th century and at the beginning of the 18th century the city endured invasions of the Swedes. In 1704 the Swedish Army passed through the city, looting the area.

At the end of the 18th century, the landlord of the town, Prince Nikolai Tishkewitz cut down the forest, which divided the town in two. Ponevezh became one united town and the administrative center of the Upyte district.

After the third division of Poland in 1795 by the three superpowers of that time-Russia, Prussia and Austria, this part of Lithuania including Ponevezh was handed over to Russia. During the Russian rule (1795-1915) Ponevezh was included in the Vilna Gubernia (Province) in 1802, and from 1843 in the Kovno Gubernia. Since then the district acquired the name the "Ponevezh district."

During the Polish rebellions in 1831 and 1863 the city suffered damages, and the rebels hanged some innocent Jews.

After the rebellions were crushed, Russification politics increased, and Russians who agreed to settle in the city enjoyed great privileges.

The construction of the railway Dvinsk (Daugavpils)-Ponevezh-Radvilishok (Radviliskis) in 1873 connecting the main rail to Prussia and the construction of the narrow railway from Ponevezh to Utyan (Utena) and Shventzian (Svencionys) promoted development of the city. A few factories were built, contributing to growth of commerce and trade.

By the middle of the 19th century until World War I the population in the city doubled. (5,908 people in 1857, 12,968-in 1797)

In the years 1915-1918 Ponevezh was under German occupation. During the period of Independent Lithuania (1918-1940) Ponevezh was a district administrative center. The city grew and developed becoming the fourth largest city of Lithuania.

The Jewish Settlement Till After World War I

The Karaites

 A Karaite settlement existed in Ponevezh on the right bank of the river since the end of the 14th century, long before Jews started to settle there. The Lithuanian Great Duke Vytautas brought 483 Karaite families to Lithuania from the Crimea. These families were captured in the war, and 153 families of them settled in Ponevezh. The other families settled in Trakai, which later became the center of the Karaites in Lithuania. The Karaite settlement in Ponevezh was mentioned in the customs lists of 1697/98.

During the Polish rule and at the beginning of the Russian rule the Karaites were treated as Jews despite their different language and customs. In 1863 the Russian rule granted them full civil rights. The subsequent years they gradually kept away from the Jews. They intermarried and their community degenerated. During the period of Independent Lithuania only a few dozen Karaite families lived in Ponevezh on the street next to their Synagogue. In 1932 there were 100 Karaites in town. In 1935 the local Karaites were visited by the "Khaham" (Rabbi) from Trakai.

The Karaite Synagogue

The relations between the Karaites and the Jews were generally good. In 1827 heated arguments started between them caused by pressure to send recruits to the Russian Army.

The leaders of the Karaites in Ponevezh in the 18th century were Avraham Kaplonovsky and Avraham ben Mordehai.

Society and Economy

Jews started to settle in Ponevezh on the left bank of the river, apparently, at the beginning of the 18th century. In 1766 there were 254 Jews in town who paid a " per head tax".

They built their houses around the Market Square and in the adjacent area. They developed trade in flour, yeast and flax production and engaged in skilled occupations and small industries with their numbers began to grow fast.

The market square in 1914

In 1847 there were 1,447 Jews in Ponevezh; in 1857 - 3,566 (60% of the population); in 1864 - 3,648 including 70 Karaites (45% of the population); in 1884 there were 15,030 inhabitants in town and among them 7,899 Jews (52%); in 1897 - 6,627 (51% of 13,044 total population).

Most of the Jews were shopkeepers and merchants, but there were also many in skilled occupations such as carpenters, leather workers, milliners, glove makers, saddle makers, tinsmiths, glaziers, knitters, oven builders, watchmakers, dressmakers, laundry washers, porters, cart owners and other workers, who waited every day at the street corner for an employer. There were also men who were employed in seasonal work such as guarding fields in summer or baking Matzot before Pesakh (Passover).

In 1887 a printing house owned by N. Feigenzon opened in Ponevezh, staying in business for many years.

In 1841 there were 18 shoemakers and 16 tailors among other skilled workers in Ponevezh. At the end of the 19th century there were local Jews who leased cattle from Christian farms and produced milk and cheese. There were also different "Religious Officers", Jewish doctors, lawyers, dentists, pharmacists and teachers. Most of them leaned towards assimilation and were adopting the Russian culture. There was also a minority who were close to Jewish affairs; several of them were supporters of the "Bund" (the anti-Zionist workers organization) and others were supporters of the Socialist Zionism.

The main Jewish suburb of this period was the "Slabodka" built in a swampy area where most of the poor lived. Jewish houses built of wood would burn down from time to time in the big fires.

Wooden houses in the suburb (1914)

Between 1750 and 1796 the town burnt seven times. Fires were also registered in the second half of the 19th century. In 1861 almost all Jewish houses burnt down including the "Beth-Midrash". More affluent Polish farmers in the vicinity helped the victims of the fire (Kudrevitz, Bushinsky, Gruzevsky and others).

In May 1881 more than half of the town burnt down. Eight streets with stores, warehouses filled with goods, three Synagogues with rare books - all went up in flames. 2,000 people remained without shelter. The same year in August another fire broke out, and the properties of fifteen families burnt. In October 1882 fifty houses and twenty-five stores filled with goods went up in flames.

In April 1883 another fire broke out and forty houses where 150 families lived and fifteen shops burnt down. About 800 people were left destitute - without clothes and without food.

After every fire desperate calls for help were included in the Hebrew newspaper "haMeilitz" issued in St. Petersburg. The donations had to be sent to the Rabbi of the city Eliyahu-David Rabinovitz. Significant help for the victims was rendered by the "Charity Fund" of Memel headed by Rabbi Dr.Yitshak Rilf.

In spring 1888 moving ice blocks in the river destroyed the bridge over the Nevezys River. A local man-built a ferry, collapsed one day, and all the passengers fell into the water. Three men drowned and among them the rich philanthropist, one of the builders of the Jewish Hospital -Yisrael Kisin and the other, a young man, 35 years old, Tsevi-Hirsh Shayevitz.

In 1883 Russian Authorities did not permit Jews to live in villages of Ponevezh district. About 400 families in the area were forced to move to Ponevezh to other Jewish homes, which were already crowded due to previous fires.

All this had an impact on the economic situation of the Jews. Almost half of them were very poor. In those years, at the beginning of the 1890s, many Jews from Ponevezh immigrated to South Africa. A strong association of former Ponevezh Jews" was active in that country for many years.

Education and Culture

Jewish children were educated mostly in the "Kheder" and in "Talmud-Torah"schools. In 1893 hundreds poor children studied in the Ponevezh Talmud-Torah. Many of them were fed a daily meal by one of the richer families in town.

During all these years general education schools were also open for Jewish children in Ponevezh. In 1853 a government-sponsored school was founded where the known Hebrew poet Y. L. Gordon taught. After his departure from Ponevezh, the teacher Yitshak Romash founded a private school for girls in 1861 where Russian, German, French, Hebrew, arithmetic and embroidery were taught. There was also an elementary school for boys. In 1878 this school closed and an elementary school for Jewish boys opened in its place. In addition to general subjects, Hebrew grammar, the history of the Jewish people, introduction to Jewish religion and some important prayers with Russian translation were taught. 60 boys, most of them very poor, studied in the school. In 1859 the Government as the inspector of the schools in Ponevezh appointed a local Jew P. Stern.

In 1886 a group of educated young men from rich families (Libshtein, Troib, Dembo, Berman, Grosman, Segal, Levnshtein, Drakin) initiated regular fund raising activities to help the poor children in town. The talented children were sent to study Torah and Wisdom while the others were offered to work as apprentices in skilled occupations.

Before the Polish Rebellion in 1863 there were no restrictions for Jewish boys to register at the Russian high school in town. Several outlawed socialist circles and revolutionists engaged in underground activities acted in it and eventually gave rise to the "Bund". After the rebellion Jewish children were forbidden to study in this high school and they had to commute to other towns. In 1889 twenty-nine Jewish children among 289 pupils (10%) studied in the high school in Ponevezh At the teachers' seminar 164 female students were registered, among them 14 Jewish girls (8.5%).

In 1868 the educated elite opened a library in Ponevezh, ignoring the opposition of the fanatic religious circles. In 1900 a young writer opened an advanced school for Hebrew studies and in several months he had 32 students coming from the more affluent families in town. The "Melamdim" became envious and informed the Police that he was spreading socialist theory. After his apartment was searched no charges were filed against him.

In 1910 the following Jewish educational institutions were open in Ponevezh. Among them there was the School for boys with two classes offering a program for vocational skills, a Talmud-Torah and a private school for girls. The school for boys consisting of two classes, the Talmud-Torah and the vocational class could stay open thanks to the support of the philanthropist Tsemakh Broido. The Talmud-Torah elected Tsemakh Broido, David Kisin, Meir Gurion, Shalom Landoi, and Yitshak Dembo to their Board in 1891.

Many learned men acted in Ponevezh, among them the Hebrew poet Y. L. Gordon, who was a teacher in the government-sponsored school during the years 1853-1860, J. Sirkin; J. Romash and others who struggled to provide education for Jewish youth and fought hard against religious fanaticism in town.

Religion and Welfare

The religious life of Ponevezh Jews concentrated around the ten Synagogues and the "Beth-Midrash". In addition there were tens of "Minyanim", "Shtiblakh" and "Kloisim" for different trades people. At the "Shulhoif" (the yard of the Synagogues) there were five prayer houses, among them the old wooden Synagogue that was apparently built in the 18th century. It had a magnificent "Aron Kodesh" and "Bima" and a very special big copper candelabrum. This yard had the "Glikeles Klois" and the "Beth- Midrash" with its famous "Sun Clock".

In 1912 the Yeshiva called "Ponevezh Kibbutz" was founded by Rabbi Yitshak-Ya'akov Rabinovitz (Itsele Ponevezher) supported by the Gavronsky family from Moscow. A special building was built nearby "Glikeles Klois" which accepted only twenty of the most talented men. They received a monthly scholarship from the widow of B. Gavronsky, the daughter of the tea magnate Klonimus - Ze'ev Wissotsky (born in Old-Zhager, Lithuania, 1824-1904) avoiding dependence on public support. Even when the 'Kibbutz" together with all Ponevezh Jews was exiled to Russia in 1915, the students continued to receive their scholarship.

"Di Shul"

Photos taken in June 2002 by Eli Goldstein South Africa

The "Beth-Midrash" with its Sun Clock

The Yeshiva Building
Photos taken in June 2002 by Eli Goldstein South Africa

The Tablet on the Yeshiva
"In this building was in the years 1919-1940 the Ponevezh Yeshivah."

The Synagogue of the "Tehilim" Society

After the Bolshevik revolution in 1917 the "Kibbutz" was dispersed. In 1919 Rabbi Itsele returned to Lithuania, but after a short time he died of Typhus. The "Kibbutz" existed for seven years, and many known Rabbis in the Jewish World were its students.

The Great Synagogue

Among the Rabbis who served in Ponevezh there was Avraham-Abele Yofe (died in 1820), Shaul Shapira (served in Ponevezh 1839-1853), Moshe-Yitshak Segal (died in 1870), Hilel Mileikovsky (died in 1899), a student of Israel Salanter, who was one of the spiritual leaders of the Russian Jewry for fifty years, Eliyahu-David Rabinovitz-Teomim (served in Ponevezh 1871-1891). The above mentioned Yitshak-Ya'akov Rabinovitz, was the head of the "Yeshiva" of Slobodka in Kovno (1889-1894) and the Rabbi of Ponevezh (from 1896 till his death in 1919). Among the rabbis was also Hayim Khveidansky (during World War I), Mosheh-Yitshak Rabin who was the head of the "Yeshiva" and a "Dayan" for forty years (a religious judge, died in 1902), also Avraham-Eliyahu Pumpiansky (1835-1893) was the Official (state) Rabbi in town for twelve years (1860-1872).

Almost all of the Rabbis published books or booklets dealing with religious issues.

In 1886 the Jewish Hospital in Ponevezh opened in a pleasant and spacious building in a beautiful park. The Hospital was built outside the town on a plot that was purchased by the wealthy leaders of the community (M .Z. Kisin; J. Tsemakhovitz and others) for 10,000 Rubles, an enormous sum in those days.

In 1893 a pharmacy serving the Hospital and providing free medication for the poor opened next door. On "Purim" 1888 a big benefit for the Hospital was organized where the popular poet Elyakum Tsunzer read his poems.

The members of the executive of the Hospital were A.Dembo, J.Berlin, M.Shidersky, J.Sapir and Adv. D, Zakheim.

In Ponevezh "Moshav-Zekeinim" (Home for the Old) opened where dozens of old men and women lived.

The welfare institutions in town were: "Bikur Holim"(care for the sick), "Linath haTsedek" (since 1898), "Hevra Kadisha" (in charge of the burials), a Women Society that cared for the old and the orphans, "Hakhnasath Orkhim" where each poor traveller received lodging for three days and six meals, "Hakhnasath Kalah" (care for poor brides), "Somekh Noflim" since 1890, which provided loans not exceeding 100 Rubles without interest, to small shopkeepers.

In 1887 a Kosher Kitchen (*Ma'akhal Kasher*) was established for the Jewish soldiers who served in the local garrison of the Russian Army.

In the summer of 1894 a cholera epidemic hit the town. A special "Help Committee" was organized which spent 1,500 Rubles on poor patients. There was also a free kitchen distributing meals for 150 poor people no matter what their faith. The meals included bread, meat and a side dish. This Committee existed for only three months existing on the donations provided by the philanthropists of the town .

On two lists of contributors for victims of hunger in different Lithuanian towns in 1871 and 1872 names of Ponevezh Jews appear. The treasurer was Ze'ev Volfson.

Zionist and other activities

Jews from Ponevezh immigrated to Eretz-Yisrael yet before the "Khibath Zion" (Fans of Zion) movement was organized. In the old cemetery of Jerusalem there are at least fifteen headstones of Ponevezh Jews, buried during the 1850s and 1860s (see Appendix 1).

In 1867 a few Ponevezh Jews organized a group with the goal to immigrate to Eretz-Yisrael, following news that American Christians were settling in the Land. But only after twenty years they managed to fulfil their aspiration when together with a group from Bialystok they renewed the settlement of Petakh-Tikvah previously abandoned due to a deadly epidemic of malaria.

In the autumn of 1883 six families from Ponevezh immigrated to Eretz-Yisrael and settled on land bought near Jaffa. Among the Ponevezh Jews immigrating to Eretz-Yisrael before World War I were Dov Leibovitz who joined the "**Bylu**"im (**B**eth **Y**a'akov **L**ekhu **ve**Nelkha), Gitel Yudelevitz (in 1870) with with her second husband Yehuda-Leib Hilman and her three sons, Yits'hak-Ya'akov, Mosheh-Leib and Idel -Monish who consequently earned a living engraving inscriptions on tombstones, Eliezer-Elkhanan Shalit who arrived in 1882, settled in Rishon-leZion becoming the first Jew who cultivated olive trees in the land; Rabbi Eliyahu-David Rabinovitz-Teomim, who arrived in 1905 and was elected as the Chief Rabbi of the Ashkenazi Community in Jerusalem; Hayim-Mosheh Fein with his family who was among the first settlers in Metulla. Professor Gideon Mer (1894-1961) arrived in 1913 and became the adjutant of Joseph Trumpeldor in "The Mule Driver Regiment" of the British Army in World War I. He established and ran the Malaria Research Laboratory in Rosh-Pinah and was the Chief Doctor of the Palmakh (the storm troops of the Haganah) and the head of the Preventative Medicine in IDF. He later became the deputy of the Director General of the Health Ministry of the State of Israel.

At the Regional Conference of the Russian Zionists which took place in Vilna in 1899 one of the two delegates from Ponevezh was Rabbi Yitshak-Ya'akov Rabinovitz. At the conference of the Zionist Associations of Vilna and Kovno Gubernias in 1909 a delegate from Ponevezh participated as well.

In the lists of contributors for Eretz-Yisrael published in "haTsefira" in 1895 and in "haMeilitz" in 1899 and 1900 the names of tens of Ponevezh Jews appear. The fundraisers were Salomon, Kisin and Leib Todes.

On the lists of "Agudath-Yisrael" paying members (the religious anti-Zionist organization) in 1913 twenty names of Ponevezh Jews appear (see Append. 2).

After the attempted revolution of 1905 remarkable fighters of the "Bund" came out from the "Slobodka" quarter of Ponevezh. At that time the "Bund" had about 700 members in Ponevezh. Inspired by the "Bund" the brush workers of

Ponevezh and of Vikavishk, Virbaln, Vishtinets (Vistytis) and other places started a strike with the goal to improve their working conditions. They wanted a working day of eight hours and a raise in salaries. Pavel Berman and Joseph-Shelomoh Mil from Ponevezh were among the other founders of the "Bund". Members of this organization were also active in "Self Defence" group fighting against probable pogroms.

Because of the severity of the reaction coming from the Rule against the revolutionaries and because the Jewish youth didn't see any future for themselves, immigration to South Africa and America increased rapidly. According to statistics about 80% of the Jewish youth of Ponevezh emigrated in those years

During World War 1

In 1915 Ponevezh Jews, together with the Jews of the Kovno Gubernia having received 24 hours notice, were exiled deep into Russia. 43 old men and women, who lived in the "Moshav Zekeinim" were brought to the railway station and exiled together with the others. The Jewish inhabitants, who deserted the town became then refugees. The "Slobodka" Jewish quarter burnt down and all the remaining property looted.

Following the occupation of the town by the German army, Jews who managed to avoid exile hiding in the nearby villages and in the Vilna Gubernia, began to return to Ponevezh. The Community Committee renewed its activities on a small scale, due to smaller numbers of Jews in town.

After the Peace Treaty was signed in Brest-Litovsk, the Bolsheviks entered the town, but they didn't stay for a long time. In April 1919 the newly organized Lithuanian Army expelled them. The Lithuanians spread rumors that Jews were fans of the Bolsheviks and the soldiers abused Jews, looted their properties and engaged in murders.

In three years, in 1922, a trial against two Lithuanians who participated in these incidents took place.

During the Period of Independent Lithuania

Society and Economy

The establishment of the Lithuanian state in February 1918 and the promise bythe government to grant civil and national rights to the minorities including Jews, brought about the recovery of economy and social life in Ponevezh; the Jews exiled in 1915 began to return to their home town.

In accordance with the "Autonomy Law for the Minorities," issued by the new Lithuanian Government, a Community Committee of 24 members was elected in 1919: 2 members were elected from the list of Tseirei-Zion; 1-Mizrahi; 9 from "Akhduth"; 2- artisans, 5- workers; 2- non party; 3- non defined.

Elections to the Committee took place in 1921 and in 1923, when 4,812 people had voting rights.

The Committee was active through its various subcommittees in almost all fields of Jewish life from the middle of 1919 until February 1926. A total of 11 subcommittees were established as follows: education and culture, economy, administration, hospital, social help, childcare, religious issues, the cemetery, help for Pesakh etc. There were also 4 temporary subcommittees for election work and other activities.

The funds for the Committee came from taxpayers' money - there were 864 taxpayers - and from indirect payments such as donations for the Orphans' Home, for the Hospital, "Contribution days" etc. Funds were also derived from different services the Committee offered, like: registrations of births, weddings, divorce, deaths etc. The Committee was also supported by the "Jewish National Committee" in Kovno and by natives of Ponevezh who settled in South-Africa (Johannesburg, Kronstadt, Capetown) and in America (NewYork, Chicago, Baltimore, Philadelphia) and organized their local associations in the above mentioned cities.

According to the first census the government carried out in 1923 there were 19,147 people, among them 6,845 Jews (36%): 3,227 males and 3,618 females in Ponevezh.

After the Community Committee was dissolved by the semi-fascist government that took over the rule in Lithuania, all its functions were transferred to the "Knesseth Yisrael Association" that continued to act as its predecessor. It had about 400 members who paid membership fees, but the committee did not have enough money to support the great welfare institutions like the Hospital, the Orphans Home and the Home for the Aged, therefore the Municipality contributed a part of the budget to these institutions.

The chairman of the council of "Knesseth Yisrael" was Dr. Jur. Shemuel Landoi. He was also the chairman of the management of the town's "Folksbank" and the deputy chairman of "The Union of the Jewish Folksbanks in Lithuania". In the elections for the Municipality Council that took place at the beginning of the 1920s, 12 Jews were elected of the 40 members of the Council and among them the above mentioned Dr. Sh. Landoi. He was also the acting delegate to the "Founding Seimas" (Parliament) on behalf of the "Folkspartei". Naftali Fridman (1862-1921), who was also the delegate to the third and fourth "Duma" (The Russian Parliament) in the years 1907-1917 was an elected delegate to the Seimas. Another delegate to the Founding Seimas was Rabbi Yosef-Shelomo Kahaneman, who became the Rabbi of Ponevezh in 1919.

In the elections of 1931 only 7 Jews of 21 members of the Municipality Council were elected (A.Fleisher, A.Riklis, Adv. Shats, Adv. Landoi, Hazan, Ram, Z.Leibovitz). In the elections of 1934, 5 Jews among the 21 members that were elected. In these elections there were 1,576 Jews with voting rights among 6,766 people with voting rights (23%). For many years Avraham Fleisher was the Deputy Mayor.

The Jews of Ponevezh played an important role in the economic life of the town. They were leaders in trade and export of flax and grains and were owners of the great flour-mills ("Yakur", Rubinshtein, Lev and others) that supplied the greater part of the state's total consumption of flour.

It should be mentioned that among the 25 clerks of the State Bank and among the 21 judges and the many court employees there was not a single Jew.

An important role in the economic life of the town was played by the Jewish "Folksbank". It was established before World War I and was called then "The Jewish Credit Bank". The "Folksbank" had 207 members in 1920, in 1927 - 1,123 members and in 1929 - 984 members. Other financial institutions of Ponevezh were "The Jewish Central Bank" that had only two branches, one in Ponevezh and the other in Kibart (Kybartai); "The Commerce Bank"; "Bank for Mutual Credit" and "Bank Elitsur". There was also the branch of "The United Association for Credit for the Jewish Agriculture in Lithuania" with its head office in Kovno. In 1938 the Association of the Small Store Owners established a Credit Fund for its members.

According to the governmental survey of 1931 there were 216 stores in Ponevezh and among them 163 were owned by Jews (75%). The division according to type of business is presented in the table below:

Type of the business	Total	Owned by Jews
Groceries	18	14
Grains and Flax	11	11
Butcher shops and cattle trade	32	21
Restaurants and taverns	19	7
Food Products	22	21
Beverages	4	4
Textile products and Furs	19	18
Leather and Shoes	23	21
Tobacco and Cigarettes	2	1
Haberdashery and Home Utensils	13	12
Medicine and Cosmetics	9	7
Watches, Jewels and Optics	7	4
Radio, Bicycles and Sewing Machines	3	2
Tools and Steel Products	5	4
Building Materials and Furniture	5	2
Timber and Heating Materials	4	4
Vehicles and Transportation	5	1
Stationary and Books	1	0
Miscellaneous	14	9

According to the same survey there were 105 light industry factories and of them 71 owned by Jews (68%). The different businesses are presented in the table below:

Type of Factory	Total	Jewish owned
Metal Workshops, Power Plants	10	4
Headstones, Glass, Bricks	1	0
Chemical Industry: Spirits, Soaps	1	0
Textile: Wool, Flax, Knitting	16	15
Timber Industry: Sawmills, Furniture	4	2
Paper Industry: Printing Presses, Binderies	3	3
Food Industry: Flour Mills, Bakeries	39	26
Dresses, Footwear, Furs ,Hats	26	17
Leather Industry: Production, Cobbling	2	2
Barber Shops, Pig Bristles, Goldsmith	3	2

Except for the merchants and the clerks, many Jews made their living from skilled occupations. In 1937 there were 263 Jewish skilled tradesmen: 70 tailors, 39 shoemakers, 21 butchers, 14 barbers, 14 tinsmiths, 9 bakers, 8 knitters, 8 painters, 8 tailors, 5 oven-builders, 5 glaziers, 5 milliners, 5 carpenters, 5 blacksmiths, 5 cobblers, 4 electricians, 4 corset makers, 4 bookbinders, 4 photographers, 4 watchmakers, 3 furriers, 3 leather workers, 3 dressmakers, 2 wood etchers, 1 printer, 1 locksmith, 1 textile painter and 8 others.

In 1939 there were about 300 members in the "Association of the Jewish Artisans" in Ponevezh. There were also Jews in independent professions but their number decreased during the years. In 1921 there were 15 doctors and of them 11 Jews (73%), in 1932 there were 27 doctors in town and of them 15 Jews (55%). In 1925 there were 12 Jewish dentists, 7 dental practitioners and several lawyers in town.

The drought that occurred in many regions of northern Lithuania in 1928 to 1929 caused many Jewish families to depend on welfare. It also brought on physical attacks on Jews in Ponevezh. There were attacks on Jews in 1927.

The economic crisis of Lithuania at the beginning of the 1930s and the propaganda of the Lithuanian Merchants Association (Verslas) against Jewish stores, hurt many Jewish families badly. The "Verslas" tried to attract clients by issuing "Blue Stamps" (Credit Stamps) and the "Jewish Merchants Association", issued "Green Stamps" in defiance. Jewish Ponevezh was described then as "a poor town rich with institutions".

In 1939 there were 513 telephones in Ponevezh. 92 of them belonged to private Jews and to the Jewish education and welfare institutions.

In 1939 there were 26,653 people in town and of them 6,000 Jews (22%).

Education and Culture

There were three Jewish educational systems in Ponevezh: the Hebrew-Zionist, the Hebrew-Religious and the Yiddishist.

The Hebrew High School opened in 1920 with about 400 students from many towns of the northern part of the country. The school first opened in rented flats, not suitable for the purpose. The knowledge of the students in different subjects and in Hebrew was not substantial. There were no textbooks in Hebrew and no reference books for the teachers. Not all teachers were professionals, and there were the others who had difficulty getting used to the "Sephardic Pronunciation" accepted in Eretz-Yisrael.

There were conflicts between the parents of the students and the teachers, and much energy was wasted in endless meetings.

Only the third director of the High-School Adv. G. Gurevitz (after Dr. Mer and Dr. Rozenberg) managed to bring peace to the school, and it began to develop. Meanwhile an elementary Hebrew school was opened in a third rented flat. After getting annual support from the government and a free plot of land, a fine two story building was built, and in the autumn of 1928 studies at the school began . A very active person in the process of the construction was Zalman Rabinovitz (died in 1933).

The Building of the Hebrew High-School with its Magen David on the top

From 1927 Adv. Gurevitz was the official director, but the actual director was an invited Dr. Arthur Loewenhertz (the first director of the Hebrew High-School in Virbalis) who managed to bring order and strengthen the discipline in school. In 1929 he immigrated to Eretz-Yisrael (he later became the director of the High-School in Kiryath-Motzkin), and Dr.Yisrael Mehlman was the appointed director. In 1935 he and Adv. Gurevitz immigrated to Eretz-Yisrael and A. Leipziger was appointed as director. He managed to build a new wing to the school enlarging its capacity by 40%. It included a reading room, a physics laboratory and a big hall for sports and for different cultural activities. Then the long-planned Hebrew Kindergarten was opened, and so the children could spend 15 years of their lives in that building. From 1930 the Popular University opened in the same building as well.

In the winter of 1931 the national writer and poet **Hayim N. Bialik** visited the High School and this visit became a festive occassion for the whole Jewish community. From time to time, other well-known Hebrew writers visited the school, such as **Nahum Sokolov, Yitshak Lamdan, Zalman Shne'ur** and others.

Nevertheless, the number of students in the High School declined. In 1929 the number of students was 200, and later the school had not more than 180 students, in comparison to the 400 in the first year of enrollment. The reasons for the decline were the establishment of a High School for girls of the religious "Yavneh" network by Rabbi Yosef-Shlomo Kahaneman in 1928, and the propaganda of the Zionist youth organizations to join the "Kibutzei Hachsharah" (Training Kibbutzim) instead of studying for matriculation. Among the youth the idea became popular that the matriculation is not worth much, and that it is better to join a "Kibutz Hachsharah" and immigrate sooner to Eretz-Yisrael.

The "Yavneh" High School was accommodated in a building that was originally built becauseof a donation for a 'Talmud-Torah' by a former Ponevezh Jew from South-Africa. This school competed with the other Hebrew High-School in the quality of teaching and tuition fees which were minimal.

Teachers of the High School in 1935

From right: Zalman Shilansky*, Dr. Yisrael Feld*,-----,Miriam Khatzkel (immigrated to Eretz Israel in 1935), Yasha -Ya'akov Levin (died in Israel),----, Dr.Yitzhak Rozman (immigrated to Eretz-Yisrael in 1935), Yitzhak Shapira*, Yisrael Bekin*, Dr. Yitzhak Mehlman (immigrated to Eretz-Yisrael in 1935), Yitzhak Shreiber (died in Ponevezh in 1938).

Standing from right: Emanuel Sursky*, Shmeriyahu Oretzkin*

***--Murdered in the Holocaust**

The first class of the Hebrew High School graduated in 1924. There were 17 graduating classes of this High School through the years.

In addition to the above mentioned educational institutions in Ponevezh there was a Hebrew elementary school belonging to the "Yavneh" network (Kheder haRav) with 350 students and a Yiddish Elementary school with 150 students, established in 1918.

The Fifth Graduation Class of the Hebrew High School 1928

The Sixth Graduation Class of the Hebrew High School 1929

המחזור התשיעי של הגמנסיון העברי בפוניבז׳

The Ninth Graduation Class of the Hebrew High School 1932

Both schools were housed in wooden buildings with one courtyard and the conditions were inappropriate. In 1930 the Yiddish school moved into a spacious building. The director of this school was L. Glitzman.

Inspite of the efforts of the Jewish members of the Municipality Council, and many promises, the "Yavneh" school remained in a dilapidated wooden building.

Until 1935 a Yiddish pro-gymnasium supported by the Society "Libhober fun Vissen" (Fans of Knowledge) was open for students, but because of its bad financial condition it was closed that year.

Until 1927 an "ORT" vocational school for carpentry acted in Ponevezh. Later different courses were initiated by "ORT", such as a course for fashion design and others.

The library named after the famous writer **Y. L. Peretz** had more than 1,600 books and was the biggest in town. In 1933 the library had 200 subscribers as follows: 35% workers, 20.5% employed people, 14.6% students, 12.9% merchants, 9.2% free professionals and 7.8% unemployed. 56.2% of the subscribers were with incomplete high school education, 24.8% were self educated, 16.2% were students and graduates of high school, 2.8% were university educated.

The eighth (graduation) class on a excursion near the river Sanzhila (a tributary of the Nevezys), summer 1938.

First line from right: Eliezer Aizenbud (near the water)-lives in Israel; Grinberg **; Moshe Yaffe-died in Israel 1979; Teacher Zalman Shilansky**; Liusia Shmutkin** (lying);

Second line: Aryeh Gordon**; Shimon Bekin-died in Israel; Eliyahu Lofert**; Shulamith Pliatzkin**; Chaya Rapaport**.

Third line: Rivka Volk-lives in South Africa; Yocheved Vexler -died in Israel 1997; Devorah Paleyes**.

** Murdered in the Holocaust

After 1929 the "YIVO" association was active in Ponevezh. In 1933 there were 15 subscribers of the "YIVO Bletter" (YIVO Pages). In the middle of the 1920s the "haBima" theater from Tel-Aviv visited the town and the Community Committee arranged a party in honor of the actors. From time to time, Jewish theaters from Kovno visited Ponevezh with performances. The "Hebrew Studio" with its director Mihael Gur from "haBima" performed Molier's play "Skapen Devilries" in Ponevezh. The town also had also a drama Group.

Meeting of the two graduation classes from Ponevezh and Shavl Hebrew High Schools together with the teachers and several public workers 1938, which took place according to the tradition of hundred days before the final examinations.

The account below shows that of the 47 people appearing on the picture, 22 were murdered in the Holocaust, 9 immigrated to Israel, 8 lived in Lithuania and other countries, the fate of 8 being unknown (see below).

(Names and fates of the people appearing on the picture of the two classes above, supplied by Shimon Levit)

 * Murdered in the Holocaust

First line below, from right:
Mrs. Eta Bekin, public worker, wife of the teacher Yisrael Bekin *
Yisrael Bekin, teacher *
Aryeh Gordon, Ponevezh student *
Zalman Shilansky, teacher *
Eliezer Aizenbud, Ponevezh student, lives in Israel
Mihael Bramson, teacher *
Shemuel Shmukler, student, lives in USA
Shmuel Lifshitz, Shavli student, died after the war

Second line from right:
Dr. Ben-Zion-Hayim Aizenbud, teacher *
Mrs. Zila Bernshtein, public worker, **wife of Dr. Aryeh-Leib Bernshtein** *
Tamar Maimin, teacher *

Dr. Aryeh-Leib Bernshtein, public worker *
Mordehai Rudnik, Director of the Hebrew High-School of Shavli *
Dr. Yisrael Feld, teacher *
Mrs. Mina Joffe, mother of the student Moshe Joffe, died in Israel
---------------------, Shavli student, name and fate not known
Ya'akov Mordel, Shavli student, lives in Israel
Liuba Sher, Ponevezh student, survived and lives somewhere abroad
--------------------, Shavli student, name and fate not known

Third line, from right:
Mrs. Braine Aizenbud, public worker *
-------------------------teacher,*
Mrs. Fux, Secretary of the Ponevezh High-School *
-------------------------, student of Shavli, her name and fate not known
Meir Gurion, Ponevezh student, killed in battle 1943
Leah Shpiz, Shavli student, survived
Esther Weis, Shavli student, lives in Israel
----------------, Shavli student , name and fate not known
Shimon Levit, Ponevezh student, lives in Israel
Rivkah Volk, Ponevezh student, lives in South-Africa
Shulamith Pliatzkin, Ponevezh student *
Yoheved Vexler, Ponevezh student, died in 1997 in Israel
Elka Shmutkin, Ponevezh student *
Nehamah Levit, mother of the student Shimon Levit, died in Shavli in 1966
Pesia Markus, Ponevezh student *

Fourth line, from right:
Shmeriyahu Oretzkin, (half face hidden) teacher *
Mitusia Levian, Ponevezh student *
-------------------,Shavli student, name and fate not known
----------------- , Shavli student, name and fate not known
Gershon Feigelman, Ponevezh student *

Fifth line, from right:
Mosheh Jafe, Ponevezh student, died in Israel 1979
Devorah Subotzky, Ponevezh student *
Liuba Vainer, Ponevezh student, lives in Israel
Sarah Bizun, Ponevezh student *
Shimon-Leib Bekin, Ponevezh student, died in Israel 1989
-----------------------, Shavli student, name and fate not known
-----------------------, Shavli student, name and fate not known
Shelomoh Feigenzon, teacher *

Religion and Welfare

After Telzh, Ponevezh was the first stronghold of the orthodox Jewry in Lithuania and its fame as a Torah Study Center spread all over the world. During this period its 15 prayer houses and the "Shulhoif" were the center of religious life of the Community.

Thanks to the efforts of Rabbi Yosef-Shelomoh Kahaneman, a Yeshivah (The Great Yeshiva), one of the greatest in Lithuania, was established in 1919. In 1928 a truly grand Yeshivah building was built thanks to the donation of the local philanthropist D. Rubinshtein. 400 young men studied there. This Yeshivah was recognized as a college and its students were released from military service until the age of 24 (instead of 21). There were also two "Yeshivoth Ktanoth" (Small Yeshivoth): one in the old Beth-Midrash and the other in "Glikeles Klois" headed by Rabbi Shelomoh-Ezra Mer. In one of these Yeshivoth students were given the opportunity to finish four grades of elementary school and also to continue in the fifth and sixth grades to get an official graduation certificate .

מ ו ד ע ה !

בע"ה

הנהלת ישיבה הק' .אהל-תורה' כ.בית-ריובנשטיין', מודיעה כי גם
לשנת הלמודים הבעל"ם. תרצ"ח – צ'ם, תנתן לתלמידים האחרונות ע'
ישיבה הק' לגמור את ד' מחלקות בית-ספר-אתחלתי גם להמשיך עוד הלמודים
הכללים לפי הקורס המלא של מחלקה חמשית ושישית של בית-ספר ולקבל
תעודה רשמית

Rabinni, S. Kaganui, Panevėžys, Ramygalos g-ve 81 № : לבוא

The announcement on the above mentioned privileges. It was not common for the children who studied in a Yeshivah to get general education as in a regular elementary school and even to get an official certificate. These were the privileges print in the attached announcement.

In the Klois of the "Habad Khasidim" Shemuel-Tsevi Lisahn kept the "Shalosh Se'udoth" meal as the tradition from the Lubavicher Rabbi every Shabbath for 32 years.

In the mornings there was a "Kheder" for the Khasidim children in this Klois and in the evenings Shemuel-Dov Cohen would explain the daily page of the Talmud.

From 1919 during all the period of the Independent Lithuania the Rabbi of Ponevezh was Yosef-Shleomoh Kahaneman. In 1940 he immigrated to Eretz-Yisrael and founded the "Ponevezh Yeshivah" in Benei-Brak. Rabbi Yitzhak Rabinovitz was officiated as the Dayan (religious judge).

During the years of World War I, when Ponevezh Jews were exiled into
Russia, the Jewish Hospital was not in operation . In 1919 the hospital renewed
operation in its nice and neat building. It had 85 beds and the head was Dr. Sh.
Mer (died in 1930). This Hospital delivered medical aid to people in the
vicinity and the surroundings.

4625

פאנעוועזש

אידישער שפּיטאל

צו הרר האגאר..ה.. ..צו

192

№ 55

רער פּאנעוועזשער אידישער שפּיטאל. וואס איז איצט שוין איינגעאר־
דרענט מיט אלע כבשורים לויט דעם מיטמער פון גרויסע שפּיטאלען. קען
שוין יעצט אנגעהטען קראנקע אויך מן גאנצען אוטגענעונה. די קראנקע
וועלבע האבען גוטיג אין שפּיטאל היילונג. און קענען עס אין רעוודהיים
אין קלַין שטערטערָעל גיט בעקומען האבען שוין יעצט די טעגליכקַײט צו
בעקוטען דאס בַיי אונו פאר א לפי ערך קליינעם געצאלט.

דער פּרַיז פאר היילען און אויסהאלמען א קראנקען:

מַארק טעגלוך 40
מיט א עקטטרא ציטער 65 מַאלק טעגייך
פַאר נעודינעדיינס 60 מַארק טעגלוך
פַאר אפּעראציאגען

וועָן די קהלות שיקען זיערע אָריסע קראנקע בעזמען מיר גלַייך מיטפּטיקען
געלד.

פַאר אָריסע קראנקס פון די קהלות, וואלכע וועלען זיך זעצען מיט אונו
אין פַערבינדונג בעצַיימענס, זינען מיר בערַיים צו מַאכען א פַארלַייכמונג
אין די פּרַייזען.

**A form which was sent by the Hospital to the Jewish Communities in the
surroundings of Ponevezh detailing the treatment available and the terms
for receiving patients.**

In 1929 the tenth anniversary of the Hospital was celebrated, and all the people
who took part in the establishment of the hospital including the doctors and
other medical staff were photographed together (see below).

The Hebrew text in the image reads: 10 יאריקער יוכל פון פאנעוועזער אידישער שפיטאל / תרע"ט—תרפ"ט / 1919 — 1929

In the middle of the picture Dr. Sh. Mer and Mrs. Dr. A.Mer

The Jewish orphanage entered its own building in 1930. There were on average 75 children. The Home for the Aged housed 30 people. Other welfare institutions were 'Somekh-Noflim" (Gemiluth-Hesed) which granted loans for the needy without interest; "Linath-haTsedek"; a branch of "OZE" organization whose budget was based on minimal member fees and donations from the local "Folksbank". "OZE" maintained a clinic and during the summer vacations would organize summer camps for Jewish children. The "Kneseth- Yisrael" Association would deliver bread and medical care for the poor for free. It also supported the "Yeshivah Ketanah" and supplied breakfast for poor students of the elementary schools.

In 1933 the "Kneseth-Yisrael" Association established the "Jewish Help Committee". The "Khevrah-Kadisha" which usually acted uncommitted, donated a remarkable sum for this task.

Zionist and other activities

All Zionist parties were represented in Ponevezh and some of them had their own club, like "Tseirei-Zion" (Hitakhduth), Z"S (Zionist Socialists) and the Revisionists. There were also remarkable fund raising activities for the Jewish National Funds-Keren Kayemeth and Keren haYesod. Three Yeshivah students were expelled from the Yeshivah because they donated some money ro Keren-Kayemeth.

There was also an active branch of "WIZO" with 135 women members (1938) in town.

Among the Zionist youth organizations in Ponevezh were "haShomer-haTsair" (before was the "Legion", established by Dr. Yosef Kot), "Gordonia" with 80-90 members, Noar Tsofi-Halutsi (Scout-Pioneer Youth), Z"S Youth, Betar with 90 members in 1931 and "Benei-Akiva".

ראשי הלגין הפונביזאי יד חשון תרפה

The leaders of the "Legion" November 15, 1924

These organizations developed intensive Zionist and social activities. They arranged parades in the streets of the town, performed shows and organized literary parties, debates and lectures on Zionist and literary themes. **The spoken language of many of the teenagers was Hebrew, and they spoke Hebrew in school and in the clubs.**

The branch of "heKhalutz" was one of the veteran associations in town. In 1932 a "Kibutz Hakhsharah " was established in Ponevezh with 60 Halutsim (pioneers). In the 1930s two more "Kibutsei Hakhsharah" acted in town: Kibutz :"Khayim" of "HaShomer HaTsa'ir" and an urban Kibutz of "HeKhalutz HaMizrahi".

A group of members of "HaShomer HaTsa'ir" Ponevezh branch with Ya'akov Gotlib and Dr.Gideon Mer coming for a visit from Eretz-Yisrael, 1927

Kibutz "Hayim" 1939
First line above, second from right: Raya Ger;
Second line below, third from left: Eliyahu Levitas
Third line below, third from left: Levi Dror

Members of Kibutz "Hayim" packing flax

Urban Kibutz of "HeKhalutz HaMizrahi" 1933

Many of Ponevezh Jews, in particular youth, immigrated to Eretz-Yisrael and took part in its development and defense. Several of the veterans of Kibbutz Givath-Brener in Israel were Ponevezh natives.

In 1940 a group of the "Kibutz Hakhsharah" of "haShomer-haTsair" from the Soviet-occupied the Polish city Radom, arrived in Ponevezh. They organized a Kibutz and made a living working different jobs and getting support of the "Joint" association. Some of its members survived the Holocaust and arrived in Eretz-Yisrael after the war joining the Kibutz Nir-David in the Beth-Shean valley.

The table below shows how Ponevezh Zionists voted for different parties at six Zionist Congresses:

Cong Nr.	Year	Total Shek.	Total Voters	Labor Party Z"S	Z"Z	Rev.	Gen. Z. A	B	Gro.	Miz.
14	1925	126	--	--	--	--	--	--	--	--
15	1927	163	40	6	14	3	13	--	--	4
16	1929	282	121	46	35	19	14	--	--	9
17	1931	322	278	81	45	119	19	--	--	14
18	1933	---	724	501		49	42	--	88	44
19	1935	---	1,490	764		--	128	115	292	191

Cong.-Congress; Shek.-Shekalim; Rev.-Revisionists; Gen. Z.-General Zionists; Gro.-Grosmanists; Miz.-Mizrahi.

Among the natives of Ponevezh were:

Rabbi Zalman-Pinkhas Kaplan (1840-1921) served in Yezna and Gelvan, the grandson of Avraham, the brother of the Gaon from Vilna;

Mark Dilon (1843-1903) a known lawyer in Russia who was the general secretary of the Senate in St. Petersburg;

David Apoteker (1855-1911), journalist, immigrated in 1888 to America, and published poems in Hebrew and Yiddish;

Miriam Dilon, sculptor, graduate of the Arts Academy in St. Petersburg, whose sculptures were exhibited in all exhibitions of the Academy in Russia and abroad;

Joseph-Shelomoh Mil (John Mil) (1870-1952) one of the founders of the "Bund";

Pavel (Mihael) Berman (1873-1922), Engineer and revolutionary, one of the veterans of the "Bund";

Zakum (1877-1941), Dr. of Physics and Mathematics and famous cellist who played as first cellist and soloist in the Philharmonic Orchestra of Hamburg; murdered in the Kovno Ghetto;

Rabbi Nahum-Barukh Ginzburg (1882-1941) who served in Kibart and Yaneve; murdered in the Holocaust;

William Luis (1884-1939), judge, one of the leaders of the Zionist movement and chairman of the United Appeal in USA;

David Shulman (1897-1962), arrived in Eretz-Yisrael in 1925 and was one of the founders of the Association of Lithuanian Jews and one of the initiators of the housing project for Lithuanian Jews in Ramath-haSharon;

Avraham Kisin (1899-1945), Doctor of Nature Sciences, teacher in the Hebrew Realistic High-School in Kovno, member of the center of the Z"S party, member of the editorial board of "Dos Vort" newspaper, chairman of the Association of the Hebrew teachers in Lithuania and editor of its journal "beMisholei haKhinukh", died in Dachau concentration camp;

David Fram (1903-1988), published poems in Yiddish in Kovno and South-Africa;

Hayim Lazar (Litai) (--1997), partisan in World War II and writer, one of the leaders of Betar in Lithuania, founder of "The Museum of the Combatants and Partisans" in Tel-Aviv;

Yehezkel Koventor- Bentor (1907-1993), member of the leadership of "haShomer-haTzair" in Lithuania, one of the founders of the Ponevezh branch of this movement, active in the administration of "Al haMishmar" newspaper, member of Kibutz Beth-Zera;

Hirsh Osherovitz (1908-1994), writer and poet in Yiddish, lived in Israel from 1971;

Hayim Maltinsky (1910-1986) writer and poet in Yiddish, from 1947 in Birobidzhan, came to Israel in 1973, published poetry and fiction books in Tel-Aviv;

Eliezer Molk (1913-1997) one of the veterans of Kibutz "Mishmar Zevulun" (later Kefar Masarik), secretary of the Council of Haifa Workers during the years 1969 to 1977;

Avraham Riklis (1920-), educator, active in the center of "heChalutz" in Lithuania, member of Kibbutz Ashdoth-Ya'akov";

Prof. Eliezer Aizenbud (1921-) Doctor of Biology, lecturer and researcher at the Veterinary Academy in Kovno, senior researcher at the Vulkani Institute in Beth-Dagan;

Yosef Shein, theater director and actor;

Benjamin Zuskin , famous actor in the USSR.

During World War II and Afterward

World War II actually started on the 1st of September 1939 when the German army attacked Poland. August 23, 1939 the German-Soviet agreement stipulated that Lithuania would be under the German jurisdiction, but that same year, in September 1939, it was decided by Germany and the Soviet Union that Lithuania will become a state under the Soviet jurisdiction. According to this agreement on October 10, 1939 Vilna was returned (from Polish occupation) to Lithuania by the Soviet Union including a 9000 sq. km.

area around the town, and Soviet troops were allowed to establish bases all over Lithuania.

On June 15, 1940 Lithuania was forced to form a regime that was friendly towards the Soviet Union. When the new government was formed, headed by Justas Paleckis, the Red Army took over Lithuania. President Smetona fled, and the Lithuanian leaders were exiled to Siberia. The parties were dismissed. The popular Seimas was "elected," 99% of its members were Communists. The Seimas then unanimously decided that Lithuania would join the Soviet Union.

Following new laws, the majority of the factories and shops belonging to the Jews of Ponevezh were nationalized. Houses larger than 220 square meters, many of them Jewish, were nationalized too. All the Zionist parties and youth organizations were dismissed, and several activists were detained. The "Comsomol" (Communist Youth Organization) started to mobilize youth into its lines.

Hebrew educational institutions were closed and towards the 1940/1941 school year, the main language of instruction at the former Hebrew Schools was Yiddish.

Instead of the three Kindergartens - "Tarbuth", "Yavneh" and the Yiddish one - a united Yiddish Kindergarten was established with 160 children and housed in two buildings. All the Jewish elementary schools were united into two. The High Schools were concentrated in the building of the "Yavneh" high school and about 600 pupils studied there in two shifts. The name of it was "The third governmental gymnasium with instruction language Yiddish". The "Peretz" library moved into a spacious flat on behalf of the "Folkshilf" (Popular Help) and a reading room opened. The building of the Yeshivah was taken by the Russians and its students wandered from place to place. Jewish Communists who emerged from underground activities, got important jobs in the civic sector.

The supply of goods decreased and, as a result, prices soared. The middle class, mostly Jewish, was hit hard, and the standard of living dropped gradually.

At the beginning of June 1941 at least 27 Jews, the owners of nationalized factories and shops and Zionist activists were exiled deep into Russia. The others sat "on their suitcases" and awaited their turn.

The German army entered Ponevezh on the 26th of June 1941, 5 days after the German invasion into the Soviet Union.

Before a single German soldier was seen in town, the Lithuanian nationalist activists started to offend and abuse Jews. Behind these activities there were several people from the Lithuanian intelligencia in town, like the Principal of the high school, the deputy of the district prosecutor, the secretary of the provincial court and others (their names are preserved in the Archives of Yad-Vashem in Jerusalem). They organized the local students who were subsequently involved in the majority of the murders of Ponevezh Jews.

**The building of the former Hebrew High-School without the Magen-David
on the top of it (refer the picture of this same building on page 325 with
Magen-David)**

On the 4th of July 1941 a call to the local Lithuanian population was published
in the periodical "The Liberated Ponevezh Citizen" stating: "help the German
army to clean our forests and groves from Jews, Bolsheviks and other
strangers, including Lithuanian traitors as fast as possible. So your lives and
properties would be saved".

Rumors about a Lithuanian doctor being murdered by Jews were circulated
throughout the town. This signaled the beginning of the pogroms that were to
follow.

The Jews were now required to report daily at various locations throughout the
town from where they would be taken for various work assignments in the
immediate area. One group of young and fit men were taken away and given
the job of digging peat in the countryside. None of them ever returned.

Every day, local Lithuanian policemen would arrange a "show". They would
march groups of Jews through the streets of the town, while continually
beating them with whips and rifle butts. Those whose strength eventually
failed, had to be carried by others who could still walk. These "performances"
would be watched by a large crowd of jeering spectators who would follow
the procession all over the town.

Many Jewish men of all ranges of life were arrested and brought to the local jail where they were cruelly tortured. Every night they would be awoken and forced to crawl around the yard outside on their elbows and knees in the gravel. All the while, the guards would beat them using spiked whips and eventually the wounded prisoners would be bundled on to waiting trucks which took them to either the Kaiserling (Kaizerlingas) (2 km south-east from Ponevezh) or Zalioji (13 km north-east from Ponevezh) forests where they would be murdered by their captors.

At the beginning of July the Jews were ordered to crowd together in a Ghetto that was established in Klaipeda, Krekanava and Tulvicius streets. The deadline for the Jews to relocate to the Ghetto was July 11th at six in the evening. The area was fenced off with barbed wire and Lithuanians from the auxiliary police were stationed as guards around the perimeter. It was announced that those Lithuanians who had vacated their homes in the streets set aside for the Ghetto, would receive the Jews' homes in return. Avraham Riklis and Moshe Levit were selected as the leaders of the Ghetto community. The Ghetto also served as a concentration place for Jews who were transferred from Raguva, Ramygala, Krekenava and other towns.

After the relocation of the Jews to the Ghetto was completed, 70 dignitaries from the Jewish community were taken hostage so as to ensure that no one would attempt to escape from the Ghetto. Among those arrested were Dr. Golombvik, Dr. I.L. Bornshtein and Dr. Hayim Ben Zion Aizenbud. They were thrown in jail and after a short time transferred to military barracks in the Pajuoste forest. They were subsequently murdered and buried in that spot.

Another version about the fate of Dr. Aizenbud is that he was kept in jail and used as a doctor till the final extermination of Ponevezh Jews.

The murder, abuse, humiliation and torture of the Jews in the Ghetto continued unabated. Armed Lithuanians would burst into houses, beat their Jewish occupants and take any household goods they pleased. Lithuanian women who had previously worked in Jewish homes would barge into houses in the Ghetto accompanied by armed guards. They would point out their former Jewish employers and demand money or valuables, which they knew were on the premises at that time.

Terrible atrocities were inflicted on Jews by Lithuanian guards at different workplaces. They broke the arms of the Jews with handles of shovels, while the Jews were forced to deepen a garbage pit. They pushed Jews into a boiling lime pit, they forced Jews to carry barrels of fuel weighing 200 kg each, and accompanied them with humiliating screaming and beatings. All these tortured victims were consequently taken to Pajuoste and murdered there.

At the beginning of August 1941 the Gestapo officer who was in charge of the Ghetto offered the Jewish representative to move to the empty military barracks near Pajuoste. There, as he promised, would be less crowded and they would get land for cultivation and so they could improve their food rations.

On the 24th of August 1941 (1st Elul 5701) the Germans and their Lithuanian accomplices began the final stage of the annihilation of the Jewish community of Ponevezh. The Jews were led from the Ghetto to the execution site at Pajuoste in groups of 200. When they reached the site they were ordered to take off their clothes and to go down on the knees, whereupon the surrounding Lithuanian guards, armed with machine guns and automatic rifles mowed them down with a hail of bullets. As soon as they were shot another group would be brought. Those who refused to go would be dragged by the guards who beat them senseless with their rifle butts.

Children were wrenched from their mothers and thrown alive into the pits. The murderers would often amuse themselves by throwing babies up in the air and shooting them before they landed on the ground. As most of them were drunk, most of their shots missed the targets and many babies were still alive when they fell into the pits. The murderers would lift out those who had survived by their hair and crush their heads with their pistols.

The last group to be brought to the execution site were the patients of the Jewish hospital together with all the medical staff. The doctors and the nurses were still rearing their white overalls when they arrived at the pits. Among them was the famous surgeon Dr. T. Gutman. He encouraged all the team to accept their fate with dignity and ensured them that their deaths would be avenged by future generations. When his turn came, he took of his coat and handed it over to one of the murderers saying: "you will find enough money in this coat to last you for the rest of life. Aim your rifle at my chest and make sure you don't miss".

The massacre continued throughout the day and on into the evening. By the next morning the pits were overflowing with corpses. There were several pits of 100 meters long an 8 pits of 50 meters. The victims' clothes were piled up and the murderers would rummage through the heaps choosing whatever items they liked.

The filling of the graves was done by Soviet prisoners of war. On one occasion they spotted a child who was still alive in one of the pits. They pulled him out and tried to hide him in the nearby bushes, but the Lithuanian guards spotted them and those prisoners involved were given a severe beating. There were some guards who suggested that the child might be allowed to escape but the militia commander insisted that " the child cannot be allowed to get away. Better to kill him and so ensure that there is no one left to avenge the blood of the Jews". He then aimed his pistol at the child and shot him through the head.

By the evening of August 26th 1941 (3rd Elul 5701) the massacre was over and all the pits had been covered.

In an official report of the German murder groups the number of the murdered Jews in Ponevezh are given as follows:

July 21, 1941	70 Jews	(59 men, 11 women)
July 22, 1941	249 Jews	(234 men, 15 women)
Sept. 4, 1941	403 Jews	(362 men, 41 women)
Sept. 8, 1941	500 Jews	(450 men, 50 women)
Sept. 23, 1941	7,523 Jews	(1,312 men, 4,602 women, 1,609 children)
Total	8,745 Jews	

Even after Ponevezh and the surrounding towns' Jews were murdered in August 1941, Jews still were working in the town and at the airport nearby-till summer 1944. Those were Jews brought from Vilna, Shavl, Riga and from Estonia. Among them were Jews who were transferred from the Kovno Ghetto to Riga and Estonia and also Jewish women from Hungary having passed through Auschwitz. All these Jews were transferred to the Shavl Ghetto a short time before its liquidation, and a part of them were transferred to the concentration camps in Germany. Very few survived.

After the war, during the Soviet rule, a monument on the mass graves was erected and on it a Magen-David. This was one of the unique monuments in Lithuania with this symbol on it. The initiator of this monument was Shemuel Feifert from Trashkun. During the war he served in the Lithuanian Division of the Red Army and after returning to Lithuania he devoted himself to the construction of this monument and to getting back Jewish children who were hidden by Lithuanian families and handing them over to Jewish families who were ready to accept them.

In 1948, while looking for a Jewish child in Riteve (Rietavas), he was murdered by Lithuanians.

According to the book published in Vilnius "Mass murder in Lithuania 1941-1944" Vol. II, during the Soviet rule there were mass graves found near Ponevezh at the following sites:

1.Kurganova (Pajuoste) forest - more than 8,000 victims

2.Kaizerling forest - 103 victims, men . women and 48 Lithuanians, members of an underground

3. Zalioji forest- about 4,500 victims, men, women and children.

At the annual meetings of Ponevezh survivors at the Monument on the mass graves at Pajuoste forest. There they would say "Kadish" for their beloved people and of the pure soul of Shemuel Feifert.

The Monument on the mass graves at Pajuoste forest. The inscription in Yiddish and in Russian say: The four mass graves of the Ponevezh Jews who were murdered by the German-Lithuanian Fascists in August 1941.

The Monument at the same site that was added later with an inscription in Lithuanain: "At this place the Hitlerists and their helpers in 1941 August killed about 8000 Jewish children, women and men."

After the war some Jews returned to live in Ponevezh, but during the years most of them left the town; a part immigrated to Israel and maybe to other countries as well. So the numbers were decreasing. In 1959 there were 221 Jews in Ponevezh, in 1989 only 66 left among the population of 41,000.

In 1971 Avraham Levit, a former Ponevezh Jew, brought a small bag with soil from the mass graves to Yad-Vashem in Jerusalem.

The Monument on the mass graves at Zalioji forest. The inscription in Yiddish says: "Here, in this place the Nazi murderers and their helpers in July-September 1941 remorselessly murdered about 3,500 Jews-children, women, men."

"Sacred is the remembrance of these innocent victims."

The inscription in Lithuanian says: "In this place Nazis and their local helpers in 1941 July-September remorselessly murdered about 4,500 people among them 3,500 Jewish children, women and men."

"Let their remembrance be sacred."

In November 1991 a monument was inaugurated at a central square in Ponevezh at the site where the Jewish cemetery was. The cemetery was destroyed during the Nazi rule and the destruction was completed during the Soviet rule. On the monument an inscription is carved: "At this site was the old Jewish cemetery until 1972. Let the remembrance of the dead be sacred".

The monument at the location of the Ghetto

At the end of September 1993, at the corner of Krakenava and Klaipeda streets at a remarkable ceremony, a monument made from granite in the shape of a symbolic gate of the Ghetto, was inaugurated. On the tables of the gate the inscriptions in Lithuanian and Yiddish were carved - **"Here was the Jewish Ghetto from the 7th of July until the 17th of August 1941."** The sculptor of this monument was V. Zigas.

Bibliography

Yad-Vashem archives- M-9/15(6), M-9/13(2), 694/585; M-1E-385/357, 2487/2551, 2261/2280, 1882/1731, 1160/1128; M-1DN-30/1505; M-1/Q-1219/711405/179, 1335/143, 1448/276; M-21/I/171, 272, 764; O-3/2322, 2581; O-15/135, 138; O-18/135; O-22/53; O-33/330, 409; O-53/21;

Koniukhovsky Collection 0-71, files 61, 62, 63

YJIVO, Collection of Lithuanian Communities, New-York, Files 746-823, pages 32705-35633

The Jewish Encyclopedia, St. Petersburg 1908-1913, (Russian), Vol. 5, pages 507-8

Mark Friedman, The Kehilah in Lithuania, 1919-1926: A Study based on Panevezys and Ukmerge (Vilkomir), Soviet Jewish Affairs, 1976, Vol.6 No. 2, pages 83-103 (English)

Osherovitz Hirsh- Main Ponevezh (My Ponevezh) (Yiddish), Tel-Aviv 1975

Gotlib, Ohalei Shem,-page367 (Hebrew)

Dr. B.Aizenbud, The Ponevezh Hebrew Gymnasium, beMisholei haKhinukh (Hebrew), May 1940

HaMeilitz, Odesa-St.Petersburg, (Hebrew), 11.10.1860, 9.3.1871, 4.9.1878, 30.9.1878, 14.9.1880, 31.5.1881, 13.9.1881, 7.11.1882, 9.4.1883, 21.9.1883, 25.1.1884, 15.4.1884, 23.5.1884, 12.12.1884, 14.12.1884, 13.1.1886, 23.2.1888, 23.1.1889, 31.1.1891, 23.1.1898, 1.6.1900, 28.10.1903, 7.11.1994

Unzer Veg, (Journal of Z"S) (Yiddish) Kovno 27.2.1929

Yiddisher Lebn (Yiddish)- Kovno-Telzh, 26.81938, 2.9.1938

Dos Vort -daily newspaper in Yiddish of the Z"S party, Kovno-7.10.1934, 20.10.1934, 24.10.1934, 11.11.1934, 13.11.1934, 15.11.1934, 20.11.1934, 21.2.1935, 7.3.1935, 13.3.1935, 23.6.1935, 12.7.1935, 27.9.1935,20.11.1938, 23.6.1939

Dos Neie Vort (Yiddish), Kovno-2.7.1934, 13.7.1934

Di Yiddishe Shtime-daily newspaper in Yiddish of the General Zionists-Kovno, 7.2.1919, 30.8.1920, 13.10.1920, 15.2.1922, 10.4.1922, 21.3.1923, 22.1.1928, 23.3.1928, 6.5.1928, 4.10.1928, 12.10.1928, 27.6.1928, 27.9.1928, 30.11.1928, 13.1.1929, 20.12.1929, 24.1.1930, 29.1.1930, 28.3.1930, 23.6.1930, 4.7.1930, 4.8.1930, 7.8.1930, 22.1.1931, 3.3.1931, 13.3.1931, 18.3.1931, 19.3.1931, 24.3.1931, 19.6.1931, 21.8.1931, 28.12.1931, 20.5.1932, 21.9.1932, 25.10.1932, 5.1.1933, 15.6.1933, 25.19.1933, 1.11.1933, 29.12.1936, 4.1.1937, 30.3.1937, 10.10.1937, 1.3.1938, 4.3.1938, 23.5.1938, 19.6.1938, 24.6.1938, 29.6.1938, 7.8.1939

Der Yiddisher Kooperator, Kovno (Yiddish), 1929, Nr.8-9

Folksblat- daily newspaper of the Folkists,   Kovno (Yiddish), 24.8.1921, 21.7.1930, 18.1.1933, 20.1.1933, 17.2.1933, 14.6.1933, 29.6.1933, 14.2.1935, 25.2.1935, 21.3.1935, 2.3.1936, 30.3.1936, 27.8.1936, 30.3.1937, 6.4.1937, 16.11.1938, 16.10.1940, 17.10.1940, 29.10.1940,17.11.1940

Funken, Kovno (Yiddish), 29.5.1931

Yerushalaim d'Lita , Vilna (Yiddish), No.11 (25), November 1991; No.1 (49), January 1994

Pilviškiai (Pilvishok)

Pilvishok - as it was called by the Jews - is situated in the southwestern part of Lithuania, where the stream Pilve flows into the river Sesupe, and is near the St.Petersburg-Berlin railway line. In the 16th century a village with that name had already existed there. In 1792 the town was granted the Magdeburg rights.

Until 1795 Pilvishok was part of the Polish Lithuanian Kingdom, but after the third division of Poland by the three superpowers of those times - Russia, Prussia and Austria - Lithuania became partly Russian and partly Prussian. The part of the state on the left side of the Nieman river (Nemunas), including Pilvishok, was handed over to Prussia, and this town, then called Pilwischken, was under Prussian rule from 1795 until 1807, during which it served as a county administrative center. In 1797, its 67 houses were inhabited by 338 people.

After Napoleon defeated Prussia, and in accordance with the Tilzit agreement of July 1807, Polish territories occupied by Prussia were transferred to what became known as the "The Great Dukedom of Warsaw", established at that time. The King of Saxony, Friedrich August, was appointed Duke, and the Napoleonic code became the basis of the constitution of the Dukedom, according to which everybody was equal before the law, except for the Jews who were not granted any civil rights.

During the years 1807-1813, Pilvishok belonged to the "Great Dukedom of Warsaw", being part of the Bialystok district. During these years it was a poor town with 350 inhabitants. The Napoleonic code was then introduced in this region, remaining in effect even during the Lithuanian period.

In 1815, after the defeat of Napoleon, all of Lithuania was annexed to Russia. As a result, Pilvishok was included in the Augustowa Region (Gubernia), being part of the Suwalk Gubernia and a county administrative center in 1866.

In 1827 the population of Pilvishok was 888 persons. In 1862 the railway line from St.Petersburg to Berlin was constructed, as a result of which Pilvishok started to develop. A railway station was built near the town and this enabled the export of agricultural goods, horses and poultry, to Prussia.

Pilvishok suffered from large fires in 1887 and 1906. In February 1915, during World War I, the German army occupied the town. In May of the same year the Russian army bombed the town, causing bilargeg fires. German rule continued till 1918, after which the independent Lithuanian state was established.

During the period of independent Lithuania (1918-1940) Pilvishok was included in the Vilkovishk (Vilkaviskis) district as a county administrative center, continuing to serve as such also during Soviet rule (1940-1941).

On the 23rd of June 1941 the German army entered Pilvishok and ruled there, with all its murders and atrocities, till July 1944, when the Red Army recaptured the town. As a result of the heavy fighting the center of the town was totally ruined.

Jewish Settlement till after World War I

Jews settled in Pilvishok during the second half of the 18th century. They peddled goods in neighboring villages and would return home only for Shabath and holidays. Jewish artisans, such as tailors, a baker, candle makers etc. made a living there, and there were Jews owning shops and taverns, a brick factory, a wool combing workshop and a dyeing plant.

The railway station on the line of St. Petersburg-Berlin and the proximity to the Prussian border (about 30 km) enabled good conditions for trade with Germany. The Jews dealt in exporting grain, flax, horses and poultry, mainly geese which were bought all over Russia and then loaded on to the train in Pilvishok and sent to Germany.

In 1865, 1,568 people lived in Pilvishok, of whom 976 were Jews (62%). Several Pilvishok Jews appear in a list of emigrants from 1869/70: Sarah Gotshtein, M.Skeshevsky, Bialoblotsky.

A few years before the war, Jewish merchants began to import chemical fertilizer and agricultural machines for the nearby farmers, and several Jewish families were farmers themselves.

The great fire of 1887 caused about 300 Jewish families to become impoverished and miserable. The issue of "HaMeilitz" (The Hebrew newspaper published in St.Petersburg) dated 15th of August 1887 and signed by the local Rabbi Ya'akov-Meir Levin, published a moving call asking for help for victims of the fire.

In 1894 robbers attacked a Jewish house and murdered two families. In 1897 there were 2,335 inhabitants in town, of whom 1,242 were Jews.

Jewish children studied as usual in a "Kheder" and in a "Yeshivah Ketanah". The elder ones continued their studies at the Lithuanian "Yeshivoth", like Slobodka and others. In addition there was a group of intellectual people who received books from "The Society for Spreading Knowledge among Russian Jews" in Odessa, to whom Shemuel Levin sent thanks in 1881. In 1883 this group received books and periodicals, such as HaMeilitz" and "HaShakhar", from a similar society in St.Petersburg.

The Zionist idea influenced many houses in Pilvishok and the town's Zionists were very active. Several Zionist youth organizations were active in, such as "Degel Zion" (Flag of Zion), "Ne'aroth Zion" (Girls of Zion), "Benoth Zion" (Daughters of Zion), whose membership was divided up according to their age. The Zionists initiated courses for Yiddish and Hebrew, established a library and organized shows on improvised stages in big barns.

The town's delegate for the regional conference of Russia's Zionists, which took place in Vilna in 1900 with 168 delegates, was David Kopilovitz. A delegate from Pilvishok participated also in the congress of Zionist Societies, which took place in Suwalk in 1913. In the year 1901/02, 47 "Shekalim" were sold in town. (A Shekel-membership card of the Zionist organization gave the member the right to vote for Zionist congresses).

The Synagogue

Beth HaMidrash

In addition to prayers, the activities of different societies studying Judaism took place in the Synagogue and the Beth-Midrash. These included the "Shas (Talmud) Society", the "Mishnah Society", the "Ein Ya'akov Society" and the "Tehilim Society" for common people, coachmen and peddlers. The rabbi of the Talmud Society was Zalman-Dov Rashigolsky, whose wife ran a small grocery to earn their living. Later on he emigrated to America, where he served as Rabbi. He published two books on "Halakha" and "Agadah".

Welfare during this period was dispensed by the "Gemiluth Khasadim" and "Somekh Noflim" societies, who helped the needy with financial support and loans without interest. "Gemiluth Khasadim" was established in 1876 with a capital of 1,500 . It loaned 25 per year, repayable in monthly installments. "Somekh Noflim" gave loans of 15 per year.

Many names of Pilvishok Jews appear in a list of donors for Jewish victims of fires in 1895.

Independent Lithuania (1918-1940).

On February 16, 1918, the Lithuanian State was proclaimed and established. Consequently the German army withdrew from the area, and life in Pilvishok gradually returned to normal.

Following the law of autonomy for minorities, issued by the new Lithuanian government, the minister for Jewish affairs Dr. Menakhem (Max) Soloveitshik ordered elections for community committees (Va'ad Kehilah) to be held in the summer of 1919. In Pilvishok these took place in 1920 and a committee of 11 members was elected: 5 from "Tseirei-Zion", 2 from 'Tseirei Yisrael", 2 from "Agudath Yisrael" and 2 undefined.

The committee collected taxes as required by law and was in charge of all aspects of community life until the end of 1925 when the autonomy was annulled. Of all the employed in 1924 there were only 178 taxpayers, the remainder being miserably poor. According to its protocols for 1921, tens of children received shoes and dresses from this committee.

After the new regime had established itself, Jews began to return to their pre-war businesses, but the situation had changed. The breakaway of Vilna merchants who had enjoyed close commercial relations with Pilvishok merchants, as well as government policy to bypass Jewish merchants, caused deterioration of the economic situation of the Jewish population. Thus many Pilvishok Jews emigrated abroad and the number of the Jews decreased. The remaining Jews made their living from petty commerce, crafts and agriculture, but many of them needed help from their relatives in America.

According to data provided by the 1931 government survey of business stores in the state, Pilvishok had 46 stores, 41 of them owned by Jews (89%). A breakdown of the stores by type of business is given in the table below:

Type of the business	Total	Owned by Jews
Groceries	4	3
Butchers and Cattle Trade	8	7
Restaurants and Taverns	7	7
Food Products	5	5
Beverages	1	1
Textile Products and Furs	8	8
Leather and Shoes	2	2
Medicine and Cosmetics	2	0
Watches, Jewels and Optics	2	2
Tools and Steel Products	2	2
Heating Materials	1	1
Barber shops	4	3

According to the same survey Pilvishok had 6 workshops, 3 of them owned by Jews, these being for cement products, for combing wool and a sewing workshop.

In Pilvishok the biggest factory operated in Lithuania for processing furs which employed 200 workers. It was owned by the local Fridman family.

In 1937, 21 Jewish artisans could be found in Pilvishok: 5 butchers, 4 tailors, 2 tinsmiths, 2 watchmakers, 2 barbers, 1 glazier, 1 hatter, 1 shoemaker, 1 painter, 1 photographer and 1 stitcher.

The Folksbank played an important role in the economy of local Jews, and had 299 members in 1927.

In 1939 there were 53 telephone owners, 19 of them in Jewish homes.

In 1921 a Hebrew school of the "Tarbuth" chain was established in Pilvishok, with about 130 pupils, including "Torah" studies taught by volunteer teachers, in order to prepare the children for the "Small Yeshivoth", which existed in Lithuania. Some of the graduates of the Hebrew school continued their studies at the Hebrew high school in nearby Vilkovishk (12 km. Away). The "Tarbuth" society maintained a library and a dramatic circle.

In 1928 a Hebrew Kindergarten opened in town, with 15 children.

All Zionist parties had their adherents in Pilvishok, but the labor party was the most active, influencing the cultural life in town very much. At the elections for the first Lithuanian Seimas (Parliament) in 1922, 279 persons voted for the Zionist list, for "Akhduth" (Religious)-141, and for the Democrats-2.

Fragments of the governmental Survey of Shops in Vilkaviskis District in 1931

Cloth

VILKAVIŠKIO APSKR.

Blagoslovempienė S., Kybartai, Žydų g. 5.
Berenšteinaitė Chana, Pilviškiai, Turgavietė 2.
Blochas Ch., Kybartai, Sinagogos 7.
Černevskienė Chanė, Vilkaviškis.
Eisiškis Ch., Vilkaviškis, Gedinino g. 11.
Elsonas Mauša, Pilviškiai, Turgaus g. 9.
Evizonas Mirianas, Virbalis, Vilniaus g. 45.
Fainberpienė Rocha, Vilkaviškis, Turgavietė 14.
Fainbergas Ch., Vilkaviškis, Gedimino g. 3.
Feinbergas Nochumas, Virbalis, Turgavietė 12.
Finkelšteinienė Ch., Pilviškiai, Turgavietė 16.
Fridmanienė Gitel, Vilkaviškis, Turgavietė.
Fridmanas Vulfas, Pilviškiai, Turgavietė 12.
Garbas Giršas, Virbalis, Vilniaus g. 33.
Geršteinas B., Pilviškiai, Turgavietė 22.
Gitelevičius Icikas, Virbalis, Vilniaus g. 49.
Gochenbergas Samuelis, Virbalis, Vilniaus g. 53.
Goldšteinienė Dvora, Virbalis, Vilniaus g. 44.
Guntorius J., Bartininkai.
Gurvičienė N., Vilkaviškis, Vytauto g. 17.
Chazonas Ovsėjus, Vilkaviškis, Turgavietė 19.
Ironienė D., Vilkaviškis, Turgavietė 1.
Jablonas Fišelis, Pilviškiai, Turgavietė 3.
Jasvenienė Chaja ir Jasvenas, Kybartai, Senapilės 55.
Kaplanai B. ir G., Vilkaviškis, Vytauto g. 7.
Kaplanienė Iudė, Turgavietė 6.
Laksienė Jochoeda, Vilkaviškis, Turgavietė 20.
Lapranskienė Riva, Vilkaviškis, Kęstučio g. 5.
Levitas E., Kybartai, Vištyčio g. 5.
Lebertavičius Jonas, Gražiškiai.
Lipšicas Abromas, Vilkaviškis, Turgavietė 17.
Miklišanskis Joselis, Vištytis, Bažnyčios g. 13.
Mejerovičius Ošeris, Vilkaviškis, Kęstučio 11.
Milcas S., Kybartai, Senapilės 59.
Olkenickis S., Virbalis, Vilniaus g. 41.
Orlinskis J. D., Virbalis, Turgavietė 12a.

Petrulis V. ir Gelgotas, Vilkaviškis, Gedimino g. 8.
Ryckis A. ir Maknavičius S., Virbalis, Turgavietė 16.
Rubinovienė Dora, Vilkaviškis, Turgavietė 8.
Seinenskis, Kybartai, Senapilės g. 83.
Sluckis Aronas, Vilkaviškis, Turgavietė 7.
Svarcas Ickus, Pilviškiai, Turgavietė 8.
Trikašai Peša ir Aronas, Vilkaviškis, Turgavietė 18.
Vladislavovskienė C., Pilviškiai, Jurkšų g.
Volovickis Simsonas, Vilkaviškis, Kudirkos g. 2.
Zedachienė Rachilė, Vilkaviškis, Vytauto ģ. 13.
Želka Juozas, Gražiškiai.

Grocery

VILKAVIŠKIO APSKR.

Arongauzas Mordchelis, Vilkaviškis, Sinagogos g. 5.
Balberiskis Abromas, Vilkaviškis, Vytauto g. 25.
Bergneris V., Kybartai, Senapilės g. 99.
Fainbergas. Jakobas, Vilkaviškis, Vytauto g. 27.
Geležūnas Juozas, Virbalis, Geležinkelio stotis.
Ginsburgas J. ir Svarcas, Kybartai, Sinagogos g. 5.
Heimanas Tobijas, Kybartai, Senapilės gt.
Heimanytė Ehana, Virbalis, Vilniaus g. 19.
Jurkšaitis M., Kybartai, Naujakurių g. 54.
Lakovskis Sanderis, Virbalis, Vištyčio g. 19.
Levinsonas Giršas, Vilkaviškis, Kęstučio g. 18.
Levinsonas I., Vilkaviškis, V. Kudirkos g. 18.
Losmanas ir Grosbardas, Vilkaviškis, Kęstučio g. 30.
Norkeliūnas Vincas, Kybartai, Algimanto g.
Okrovskis Judelis, Virbalis, Gedimino g. 31.
Solskiai Br. ir B-vė, Pilviškiai, Turgavietė 3.
Šamesas Isakas, Virbalis, Vilniaus g. 11.
Vinkelšteinas Šliomas, Vilkaviškis, Vilniaus g. 23.
Volbergas Berelis, Vilkaviškis, Vytauto g. 30.

Food Products

Bernšteinas J. ir Malachas, Kybartai, Senapilės g. 83.
Hmiclevskis Hiršas, Vilkaviškis, Basanavičiaus g. 2.
Chaitas Abromas, Vilkaviškis, Prieglaudos g. 12.
Kabanskis J. ir sūnus, Virbalis, Vilniaus g. 39.
Kalvaitis P., Vištytis, Bažnyčios g.
Kopelovičius L., Kybartai.
Kretingė B., Vilkaviškis, Vytauto g. 11.
Liet. Koop. B-vių Sąjungos, Vilkaviškio skyrius, Turgavietės g. 2.
Londonaitė Roza, Vilkaviškis, Kęstučio g. 13.
Londonas Elijašas, Vilkaviškis, Kęstučio g. 15.
Makovskis A., Vilkaviškis, Kęstučio g. 8.
Mikolavičius V., Pilviškiai, Turgavietė.
Pustopedskis Elijašas, Vilkaviškis, Gedimino g. 11.
Sidoravičius Isakas, Vilkaviškis, Gedimino g. 16.
Sulmanienė Chaja, Vilkaviškis, Turgavietė 13.
Veicas A., Vilkaviškis, Algimanto g. 6.
Vištaneckis Mozė, Virbalis, Vilniaus g. 59.
Vižanskis Jankelis, Pilviškiai, Jurkšų g. 50.
Volbergas Šeftelis, Vilkaviškis, Turgavietė 16.
Zedakienė Chaja, Vilkaviškis, Vytauto g. 13.

Pilvishok young men at the market square

From left: Yehudah (Julius) Markson, Yashke Goldberg, ------, Eliyahu
Vizhansky * Mosheh Golomb * ,------, Yeshyahu Goldberg *and son *,
Yitskhak Ginzburg *,----.   *-murdered in the Holocaust

Street in Pilvishok-at left the pharmacy

The Hebrew Kindergarten 1935 - 1937

Pilvishok Jewish Scouts 1925-26

Sitting at the middle: Rachel Levin (died in Israel)

Standing at second line from right: Miriam Kopilovitz (Died in Israel)

Pilvishok Jewish Scouts

Standing from left: second-Miriam Kopilovitz, fourth-Pesia Goldenzon (Died in Israel)

Pilvishok Jewish Youth

The results of the elections to 6 Zionist congresses (1925-1935) are presented in the table below:

Cong No.	Year	Total Shekalim	Total Voter	Labor Party Z"S	Z"Z	Rev	G. Z. A	B	Gr.	Miz.
14	1925	46	--	--	--	--	--	--	--	--
15	1927	63	51	7	13	3	19	--	--	9
16	1929	117	48	9	12	9	15	--	--	3
17	1931	---	117	42	25	33	9	--	--	8
18	1933	---	342	244		68	9	--	4	17
19	1935	400	379	277		--	8	43	5	46

Rev.-Revisionists; G. Z.-General Zionists; Gr.-Grosmanists; Miz.-Mizrahi ;

Nat Blk : National Block

The Zionist youth organizations included "Gordonia" with 50-60 members (the activists: Hanah Pantinsky, Miriam Revelman, Devorah), and "HaShomer HaTsair" as from 1920. A conference which established "The Jewish Scouts Organization HaShomer HaTsair of Lithuania" took place on the 16-18th of April 1922, with the participation of 12 delegates from 6 "Gedudim" (regiments), among them 2 delegates from Pilvishok, "Beitar", "HeKhalutz HaTsair" and Z"S (Sirkin Society). Near the town a training Kibbutz named "HaSolel" was established. Its members worked for some time in diverting the river Sesupe as part of a plan to construct a hydroelectric power station. This station was built and supplied electricity for Pilvishok and its vicinity.

The Khalutsim and members of the youth organization who emigrated to Eretz Yisrael were among the founders of Kibbutz Givat Brener and other Kibbutzim.

Sport activities took place at the local branch of "Maccabi", with about 70 members.

In the middle of the 1920s Pilvishok Jews started to rebuild the synagogue which had been ruined during the war, but a sum of $10,000 was needed for its completion, which they were unable to collect. In 1928 a committee of 7 members was elected, headed by the "Shokhet" Avraham-David Axel.

The welfare institutions which existed before the war continued their activities during this period as well. For "Ma'oth Khitim" (Help for Pesakh for the Needy) 400 Litas was collected every year during the twenties. In 1922, according to the request of the "Nationalrat" (The National Council of Lithuanian Jews), several fund raising events were held in Pilvishok to help starving children in Russia.

The rabbis who served in Pilvishok during the years were:

Aharon Volkin (1865-1942), published many books on religious issues, murdered in Pinsk.

Ya'akov-Meir Levin in 1887 already Rabbi in Pilvishok, died in 1906.

Yekhiel-Ya'akov Veinberg (1885-?), was Rosh Yeshivah at Hildesheimer's Beth-Midrash for rabbis in Berlin, published many research works on "Halakha" in Hebrew and German periodicals, later lived in Montreux, where he was a Rosh Yeshivah, died in Lausanne.

Avraham-Aba Reznik (?-1941) Rabbi in Pilvishok since 1924, a devoted Zionist, member of the center of "Mizrakhi" in Lithuania, murdered in 1941.

During and After World War II

World War II started with the German invasion of Poland on September 1st, 1939, and its fatal consequences for Lithuanian Jews in general and Naishtot's Jews in particular were to be felt several months later.

According to the Ribbentrop-Molotov treaty on the division of occupied Poland, the Russians occupied the Suwalk region, but after delineation of exact borders between Russia and Germany the Suwalk region fell into German hands. The retreating Russians allowed anyone who wanted to join them to move into their occupied territory, and indeed many young people left the area together with the Russians. The Germans drove the remaining Jews out of their homes in Suwalk and its vicinity, robbed them of their possessions, then directed them to the Lithuanian border, where they were left in dire poverty. The Lithuanians did not allow them to enter Lithuania and the Germans did not allow them to return. Thus they stayed in this swampy area in cold and rain for several weeks, until Jewish youths from the border villages smuggled them into Lithuania by various routes, with much risk to themselves. Altogether about 2,400 refugees passed through the border or infiltrated on their own, and were then dispersed in the "Suvalkija" region. The Pilvishok community accommodated and cared temporarily for 100 refugees.

In 1939 there were 2,905 people in Pilvishok, including about 700 Jews (24%).

In June 1940 Lithuania was annexed to the Soviet Union and became a Soviet Republic. Following new rules, the bigger Jewish shops and workshops of Pilvishok were nationalized and commissars were appointed to manage them. The supply of goods decreased and, as a result, prices soared. The middle class, mostly Jewish, bore most of the brunt, and the standard of living dropped gradually.

All Zionist parties and youth organizations were disbanded, the Hebrew school was closed, and in its place a Yiddish school opened.

In the middle of June 1941 four Jewish families were exiled into Russia as "Unreliable Elements", following the nationalization of Jewish businesses in accordance with regulations. These were Yekutiel Fridman and his mother Tovah (but they remained in town after the intervention of the workers committee of the fur factory which belonged to the Fridman family, where Mr. Fridman was the specialist in this vocation), Leib Ushpitz and wife Tsilah, Mosheh Markson and wife Freidl, Meir Shimberg and wife Sarah, sons Hirshl and Barukh. Most of them returned to Lithuania several years after the war.

On the 23rd of June 1941, one day after the war between Germany and the USSR began, the German army entered Pilvishok. Immediately the Lithuanian police took over the rule of the town, the commander and his deputy were Germans. On the 28th of June an order was issued for Jews to wear a yellow "Magen David" on their clothes, not to walk on side walks and not to be in the street after 8 PM. It was also forbidden for Jews to buy goods in the market. One day, the prominent Jews of the town headed by Rabbi Avraham Reznik, were made to assemble in the market square, where their beards were cut off and they were forced to do "exercises". In the beginning of July the men were separated from the women and children and concentrated in a barn in Antanavas street, from where the Lithuanians would take them out for hard and humiliating labor. On their way back from work they were forced to go through swamps, to do "exercises" and to crawl for several kilometers. The German commander ordered the erection of a sewing shop and appointed Leibl Zeiberg as chief tailor. He also issued an order prohibiting Lithuanians to enter Jewish houses or to remove anything without his permission. Another order given stated that only men up to 50 and women up to 45 would be taken for work. The commander also forbade "exercises" in the swamps and advised the Jews to create a Jewish committee whose were to contact him in order to defend the Jews. A committee of 4 persons was set up, headed by Yitskhak Ushpitz, with Yisrael-Ber Axel in charge of maintaining order. Among the local Jews there were a few who had escaped from Vilkovishk, among them Rabbi Eliyahu-Aharon Grin.

On August 27th 1941, early in the morning, all men aged 14 to 70 years old were rounded up in the market square, the sick being brought on carts. They were kept under heavy guard by armed Lithuanians, who maltreated them during the day. At 9 o'clock in the evening they were led back to the barn.

The next day, Thursday the 28th, at 3 o'clock before dawn, all men were taken out of the barn. The 10 artisans were sent to the sewing shop, whereas 200 were given spades and told that they were being sent to Germany for digging peat. They were taken to a place about 1.5 km from town and ordered to dig two big pits. After completing the job they were shot by order of the local police commander and buried in the pits they had just dug. On Friday, the 29th of August, 500 men including Jews from neighboring villages and 20 young intellectual women from Pilvishok, were shot too. Among the victims was Dr. Mosheh Dembovsky, a reserve Colonel of the Lithuanian army, who had fought during the Lithuanian independence war. Before he was shot he told the Lithuanian murderers that their crimes would not be forgotten and that the blood of the innocent victims would forever call for revenge, in response to which the Lithuanians cracked his head with the butts of their rifles. All the victims were piled into one of the pits, the other was left empty. The Lithuanians took the valuables of the victims for themselves.

The women and children were left in town, as well as 10 men who worked for the German "Kommandantur", also 30 men who managed to hide, among them Rabbi Reznik and Rabbi Grin who the women hid in a cellar.

On September 14th it was rumored that the next day something was about to happen. 70 women escaped and hid in surrounding villages. On the next day, the 15th of September 1941 (23rd of Elul 5701) the women and children were ordered to leave their houses and for each to take a small parcel with them, having been told that they were going to be transferred to the Kovno Ghetto. They were assembled in the market square, the 10 men who worked for the German "Kommantantur" and the rest of the men were also included. Among them was also the pharmacist Bolnik, who guessed what was going to happen and swallowed the poison he had prepared before. All, including the two Rabbis, were led to the empty pit. While being beaten, they were forced to undress and then they were shot, and the children were thrown into the pit alive. By evening the murderers returned to the town singing the Lithuanian anthem.

Gestapo men, in civilian dress, photographed the Lithuanian murderers at "work".

The names of the Lithuanian murderers are kept in the archives of Yad Vashem.

According to various sources, between 750 to 1,000 people were murdered on that day. A Lithuanian source says that altogether 1,800 people were murdered in Pilvishok.

In order to catch the Jews who had managed to escape and hide, the German commander announced that all those who had hidden could come back and that nothing bad would happen to them. He also promised them food and a quiet working atmosphere. About 70 Jews continued to work at the sewing shop of the German command.

During the night of the 14th of November 1941, 40 Jews were taken to the village of Baidilis, about 4 km from Pilvishok, and were shot there in a forest. 8 people who worked at the fur factory "Tigras" were transferred to the Kovno Ghetto in May 1942. 26 people who found shelter with peasants in the villages survived. One of the survivors, Barukh Reuven Bialoblotsky, was shot by Lithuanians in 1946.

After the war the survivors of Pilvishok and vicinity erected a monument on the mass graves. In 1986 the former Pilvishok Jews in Israel, together with those of Virbaln and Kibart erected a joint monument for these three communities in the Holon cemetery (see below).

Mass graves of Pilvishok Jews near Baltrusiu village, about 4 km North of the town

Pilvishok survivors at an "Azkarah" beside the mass graves
(Photo taken in the 1970s)

The monument at the cemetery of Holon for the communities of
Pilvishok, Kibart and Virbaln

Appendix 1.   A partial list of Personalities born in Pilvishok.

Eliezer-Dov Liberman (1820-1895), poet, writer and researcher, published many poems, articles and researches of the Bible in the Hebrew press. He also wrote several books.

Aryeh-Leib Bialoblotsky (1851-1881) Rabbi.

Aharon-David Markson (1882-1932), in America since 1904, published articles on literature in the Hebrew press in America, translated Mark Twain's book "The Prince and the Pauper" into Hebrew (Warsaw 1923), died in Detroit.

Ya'akov Klibansky (1888-1950), since 1910 in Eretz Yisrael, editor of the "Hed HaKhinukh" journal of the Teachers Organization in Eretz Yisarel.

Shemuel-Shraga Bialoblotsky (1891-   ) researcher of the Talmud, head of the Talmud department in Bar Ilan University in Tel-Aviv.

Hilel Bavli (1893-1961), in America since 1912, Professor of Modern Hebrew Literature at the Jewish Theological Seminar in New-York since 1937, Hebrew poet and writer, published poems and articles in the Hebrew press in Eretz Yisrael, published several poems and books, translated Dickens' book "Oliver Twist" and more.

Correspondents from Pilvishok at "HaMeilitz": Ts.A.Bialoblotsky, Avraham London, Shemuel Levin.

Bibliography:

Yad-Vashem Archives: M-1/E-1237/1203, 1250/1208,1371/1321, 1670/1554. M-33/987; O-33/58; O-3/3680, 3788, 4161.

Koniukhovsky collection 0-71, Files 154, 155, 156.

YIVO, NY, Lithuanian Communities Collection, Files 840-868.

Lite (Yiddish), New-York 1951, volume 1 & 2.

Gotlib, Ohalei Shem, page 151.

Yiddishe Shprakh (Yiddish language), New York 1944, Vol. 4, pages 51-54.

Kli Sharet (Hebrew) Rabbi Avraham-Aba Reznik, Netanyah, 5707 (1947).

Markson Julius, Lisrod (To survive) (Hebrew), Tel-Aviv 1991.

Dos Vort (Yiddish Daily)- Kovno, 3.1.1935, 3.7.1935, 16.1.1939.

Di Yiddishe Shtime (Daily)- Kovno, 29.12.1920, 28.8.1922, 16.8.1928, 17.8.1928, 1.4.1932.

Der Yiddisher Cooperator (Yiddish), Kovno,Nr.12, 1924.

Kovner Tog (Kovno Day) (Yiddish), Kovno, 30.6.1926.

HaMelitz (Hebrew) St. Petersburg, 25.3.1879, 22.3.1881, 29.8.1882, 19.3.1883, 4.6.1883, 6.8.1887, 15.8.1887.

Prienai (Pren)

Pren (as the town was called in Yiddish) is located in the southern part of Lithuania on the shores of the Nieman (Nemunas) river about 30 km south of Kovno and about 100 km away from its estuary into the Kurish Gulf (Kursiu Marios), the bay of the Baltic Sea.

The town was built on both sides of the river, the main part of the town being on the left hand side of the river, with a bridge linking both parts. Pren was mentioned for the first time in 1502, when the Great Duke Alexander handed the town over to Mikhail Gilinsky.

In 1609 Pren received the so called 'Magdeburg' rights of a town, which King Stanislav August ratified in 1791. By 1766 about 1,000 people lived there.

Until 1795 Pren was part of the Polish-Lithuanian Kingdom, when the third division of Poland by the three superpowers of those times - Russia, Prussia and Austria - caused Lithuania to become partly Russian and partly Prussian. The part of the state which lay on the left side of the Nieman river (Nemunas) was handed over to Prussia while the other part became Russian. Prussia ruled there during the years 1795-1807. At the end of the eighteenth century Pren became a county and started to develop. During that time a glass factory and a paper mill, the largest in Lithuania, were established near the town.

After Napoleon defeated Prussia and according to the Tilzit agreement of July1807, Polish territories occupied by Prussia were transferred to what became known as the "The Great Dukedom of Warsaw", which was then established. The king of Saxony, Friedrich-August, was appointed Duke, and the Napoleonic codex now became the constitution of the dukedom, according to which everybody was equal before the law, except for the Jews who were not granted any civil rights.

During the years 1807-1813, Pren belonged to the "Great Dukedom of Warsaw". The Napoleonic Code was then introduced in this region, remaining in effect even during the Lithuanian period.

In 1815, after the defeat of Napoleon in Russia, all of Lithuania was annexed to Russia including Pren, which became part of the Suwalk Gubernia, and the town's development was encouraged. In 1868 a beer brewery was established there, which became famous throughout Lithuania because of the quality of its products. Market days and fairs took place. In 1827 there were 1,972 people in Pren and by 1856 - 2,304, among them 1,479 Jews.

During World War I Pren was under German occupation (1915-1918). During the years of Lithuania's independence (1918-1940) Pren was included in the Marijampole district, continuing to develop and its population increasing. Many light industries and workshops were established. In 1923, according to the first census of the new government, the population had risen to 3,260 people, among them 650 Jews.

Pren in winter 1936-37

At the end of 1939, according to the treaty between Lithuania and the USSR, a Soviet military base was established in Pren. In June 1941, with the invasion of Lithuania by the German army, the retreating Red Army blew up the concrete bridge over the Nieman, but the town itself was not damaged.

From then on until the autumn of 1944 Pren was under German rule, with all its terror and atrocities.

The Jewish Settlement till after World War I

Jewish settlement in Pren began in the seventeenth century. The "Pinkas haKehilah" mentions that the community belonged to the Horodna (Grodno) district of "Va'ad Medinath Lita" (1623-1764) and the district Rabbi was accustomed to visit and arrange the religious issues there. In 1766 there were 597 Jews in town.

During this period Jews made their living mainly from commerce. Most of them had gardens next to their dwellings, and several Jews rented land from estate owners, selling agricultural commodities, mainly milk products.

Young children received their elementary knowledge at the "Kheder", the bigger ones at the "Yeshivah". In the 1880s Pren also had some intellectuals, thirsting for knowledge, but who did not possess the means to purchase secular books. In 1882 the "Society for Propagating Knowledge among Russian Jews" sent 20 books in Hebrew and Russian to Pren and in the Hebrew periodical

"HaMeilitz" of the third of January 1882 a letter of thanks to this Society was published signed by 12 community members: Reuven Aryeh Leib Helman; Reuven Miller; Zelig Fridberg; Hilel Rozengard; Eliyahu Bergman; Avraham Yosef Rudaminsky; Yitskhak Fabil; Shimshon Markovsky (?); Binjamin Volk; Ze'ev Natanzon; Pesakh Mosheh Naftalin; Betsalel Fridberg. Ben-Zion Gorfinkel volunteered to be the librarian.

During the years of famine 1869/71 many Jews left and settled abroad. In a list of immigrants of 1869/70 the names of Pren Jews appear as follows: S.Gelchevsky, Frume Heinson, A.Zavrev, M.Levin, M.Marlutsky, J.Serstver, E.Serstver, S.Katz.

The welfare institutions acting in Pren were: "Lekhem Aniyim" (bread for the poor), who among others collected funds by means of a lottery (1881) operated by Tsevi Haskel and A.Y.Rudaminsky, and "Gemiluth Khesed" , operated for many years by Aharon Rozengard, who financed its activity through donations. Pren Jews also collected money for communities which had suffered from pogroms or fires. In the summer of 1881 Avraham Yosef Rudmansky and Yitskhak Gorfinkel collected 90 Ruble, a considerable sum in those days, from Pren Jews, sending 40 Ruble to the Rabbi of Augustowa whose town had suffered from a fire, and 50 Ruble, through the editorial board of "HaMeilitz", to help victims of pogroms. For a list of donors as published in "HaMeilitz" see **Appendix 1.**

The Pren community itself suffered from a pogrom carried out by Polish youngsters on August 15, 1882. During the pogrom 20 people were wounded defending themselves, amongst them the catholic priest who went to defend the Jews and was wounded in his head. The rioters robbed Jewish shops and houses and many of them were left very poor. On October 17, 1882 a call for help was published in "HaMeilitz" (Nr.38) signed by Aharon Rosengard, Ya'akov Finkelshtein, Eliezer Goldberg and Efrayim Shereshevsky. A fund raising action took place all over Russia and about 1,500 Ruble were collected. Among the main donors were Baron David Ginzburg who donated 400 Ruble, the St.Petersburg Committee 600 Ruble, the Gubernator of Kovno together with Herman Kahan persuaded the Kovno committee to send 150 Ruble, Shaul Hirsh Hurvitz 30 Ruble through the Rabbi of Memel, Rabbi Dr.Rilf, Lurie and Vitenberg from Memel sent 150 Ruble through the Rabbi of Kovno Elkhanan Spektor, Poliakov from Moscow - 50 Ruble, Yehoshua Tseitlin - 25 Ruble through the editorial board of "HaMeilitz" etc.

Eighty rioters were put on trial, which lasted for about two years. It took place in April 1884 at the district court in Marijampole and 48 of the accused received light punishments, 26 of them being released thanks to the amnesty granted by the Tzar. The prosecutor was Khlebnikov, who described the victims' sufferings impressively, and from the Jewish side there were Adv. Kaminsky from Warsaw and Adv. Frank from Kovno, assisted by Dr. Tsevi Cohen.

The Old Synagogue

The Pren synagogue was built in the eighteenth century and the old Beth-Midrash was rebuilt in 1903. There were two more praying houses (Klois), one of Goldberg and the other of Abelson.

In 1883 thirty families from Pren established a society whose aim was settlement in Eretz Yisrael. In the old cemetery of Jerusalem there are two tombstones of Pren Jews: Yerukham-Fishel ben Eliyahu, died 1882 and Mera daughter of Mosheh, died 1890.

In April 1915, during World War I, the Russian military authorities expelled Pren Jews from the town. Some settled in Vilna, but after the German army occupied Pren, they returned home, finding their houses, their praying houses, the ritual bath and the cemetery ruined and robbed. Thirty families needed to be supported by welfare institutions.

During the Period of Independent Lithuania (1918-1940).
(All pictures of this section were supplied by Peninah Binyaminovitz-Levitan)

According to the autonomy law for minorities, issued by the new Lithuanian government Dr. Max Soloveitshik, the minister for Jewish affairs, ordered elections to be held in the summer of 1919 for community committees in all towns of the state. In Pren a committee of eleven members was elected. The committee, active till the end of 1925 when the autonomy was annulled, collected taxes as required by law and was in charge of all aspects of community life through sub-committees.

According to the first census carried out in independent Lithuania in 1923 there were 3,260 people in Pren, 954 of them Jews.

In the 1931 elections to the local municipality council, three Jews were elected: Y.Yonenzon, A.Ginzburg, Sh. Bruk. In the elections of 1934 three Jews were elected again out of nine council members: Rabbi Rubinov, Yonenzon, Ginzburg.

Most of Pren's Jews dealt in commerce, crafts and industry, and 5 families made their living from agriculture.

According to the 1931 survey of the Lithuanian government, Pren had 36 shops, 32 of them in Jewish hands (89%).

Their distribution according to the type of business is given in the table below:

Type of the business	Total	Owned by Jews
Groceries	2	2
Grain	3	3
Butcher's shops and Cattle Trade	8	6
Restaurants and Taverns	3	3
Food Products	4	4
Beverages	1	1
Textile Products and Furs	4	4
Leather and Shoes	1	1
Medicine and Cosmetics	1	0
Radio, Bicycles and Electrical Appliances	1	1
Watches, Jewels and Optics	1	1
Timber and Furniture	3	3
Machines	2	2
Miscellaneous	2	1

In 1934 there were already 3 Jewish sawmills and 2 iron and tool shops.

By 1937 there were 52 Jewish artisans: 11 tailors, 8 butchers, 7 bakers, 6 shoemakers, 4 barbers, 4 stitchers, 2 hatters, 2 glaziers, 2 carpenters, 1 blacksmith, 1 painter, 1 photographer, 1 saddler, 1 watchmaker, 1 dressmaker, also 3 coachmen, 3 porters and 2 drivers.

According to the same survey there were 18 factories, 13 being owned by Jews (72%), as can be seen in the following table:

Type of the Factory	Total	Jewish Owned
Power Plants	1	1
Beer Brewery	1	1
Oil production, Turpentine, Lime	3	1
Wool combing	1	1
Flour mills	4	3
Sawmills	2	2
Furniture	1	0
Beverage	1	1
Footwear	2	1
Leather Industry	2	2

Parts of governmental Survey of Shops in Marijampolė District in 1931

Transportation Means

MARIAMPOLĖS APSKR.
Abeltonas T., Prienai.
Gordonas Nevachas, Prienai, Basanavičiaus
aikšté 4.
Kaukaitis Vladas, Mariampolė, Kęstučio g. 11.
Kronauzas Samuelis ir Kaplanas, Kalvarija.
Leibovičius Isriun, Balbieriškis.
Maslulio V. ir Baltrušaičio J., Mariampolė,
Basanavičiaus aikšté.
Rozentalis Leiba, Balbieriškis, Kauno g. 87.
Vitmozeris Karolis, Mariampolė.

Furniture

MARIAMPOLĖS APSKR.
Baleckis Antanas, Antanavos k., Kazlų - Rū-
dos v.
Cibirka V. ir Co, Kazlų - Rūda.
Dronelis Leopoldas, Prienai.
Grodmanas Chaimas, Mariampolė, Laisvės g.
23.
Kazos L., Kazlų - Rūda.
Kurtinaitis Juozas, Cassavos k., Sasnavos v.
Kvinta Juozas, Kalvarija.
Laukaitis Pijus, Mariampolė, Kęstučio g. 51.
Marijonų Vienuolynas, Mariampolė.

Leather Factories

MARIAMPOLĖS APSKR.
Sakas Aisinas, Kalvarija.
Folenderis Oseris, Liudvinavas.
Gropmanas Solomas, Prienai.
Gurvičius Mocé, Balbieriškis.
Kaminskas M., Prienai.

An important role in Pren's Jews economic life was played the folksbank, which had 219 members in 1927.

During these years the economic situation of the small shop owners and artisans deteriorated due to competition by associations of Lithuanian merchants and artisans, who agitated against buying from Jews. Many families in town needed to be subsidized by relatives in the USA, and most of the youth left the town and emigrated abroad or found work in Kovno. In 1939 there were 100 telephones in Pren, 28 of them were owned by Jews.

During this period a Hebrew school of the "Tarbuth" chain was inaugurated, with about 130 pupils, and next to the school there was a library with about 3,500 books.

Many Jewish children continued their studies at the Lithuanian high school in town.

The first grade of the Lithuanian high school of Pren 1932

Sitting in the first line below, from right: fourth-YisraelGoldband, fifth-Bustanai Rudnik

Third line from right: second-Dorka Gendler, third-Pola (Peninah) Binyaminovitz-Levitan,third from left-Khyene Fugler-Flaxman

Fourth line standing: first from right-Yosef Tsvaig, first from left-Yisrael Tsines, third-Mendel Milshtein

There was also a Yiddish school, and in 1927 a Kindergarten was established, with Zagarnik as teacher. A private library by Ofenshtein, with books in Hebrew and Yiddish, was also inaugurated. For a short time a "Yeshivah Ketanah" was active, directed by fourth class students of the "Telsh Yeshivah", and during the Autonomy there existed a very active "Cultural Youth Society". The local branch of the "Tarbuth" society organized evening courses, with 45 people participating in 1922.

All Zionist parties had their supporters. The table below shows how Pren Zionists voted for the different parties at six Zionist Congresses:

Cong No.	Year	Total Shekalim	Total Voter	Labor Party		Rev	G.Z.		Gr.	Miz.
				Z"S	Z"Z		A	B		
14	1925	40	--	--	--	--	--	--	--	--
15	1927	60	37	5	9	3	2	--	--	18
16	1929	118	44	11	6	4	9	--	--	14
17*	1931	90	80	2	17	32	17	--	--	12
18	1933	--	266	174		66	11	--	5	10
19	1935	--	238	182		--	9	10	4	33

Rev.-Revisionists; G.Z.-General Zionists; Gr.-Grosmanists; Miz.-Mizrahi; Nat Blk : National Block

*Elections took place at the house of the community committee

Jewish pupils from different grades of the high school with the teacher Mr. Kagan who taught them Bible and religion 1934-35

First line below, from right: Cohen--------------------

Second line from right: Dushchansky, Ushpitz, Teacher Kagan, Tsviyah Milshtein, Khayah'le---, standing Abelson ......

Third line from right: Dorka Gendler, Peninah Binyaminovitz, Khyene Fugler, Golda'le, Eta Cohen....

Fourth line from right: Mendel Milshtein, Yisrael Goldband, Roza Katz, Berta Kovensky, ------, Elka Smolensky, Nekhamah Abelson, Mordehai Kovensky

The Zionist Youth Organizations active in Pren were: "Gordonia" with about 50 members (activist M.Ainshtein), "Z"S Youth" about 100 members, "Hakhalutz HaTsair" 35 members, and "Betar" (activists Shilansky and Shtukarevitz families).

In 1933 a branch of "HeKhalutz" was established with nearly 60 members. For some time a small cooperative factory produced candies in order to support the Khalutsim. Sports activities took place at the "Maccabi" branch with its 103 members. Jewish artisans were organized within "The Society of Artisans".

The old wooden synagogue, the Beth Midrash, which had been rebuilt in 1903, was used for lessons on behalf of "The Society for studying Torah", and the "Klois" also served people during this period. The Rabbi and the Shokhet (slaughterer) made their living mainly from the "Shekhitah" fees, this being in addition to the small salary they received. The butchers and the poor objected more then once to the high Shekhitah (ritual butcher) fees, and finally in 1934 a Shekhitah strike broke out.

The oath of the "Oleh" Gurevitz to Eretz-Yisrael in front of the local branch of Betar March 26, 1935

Standing in front: Gershon Raibshtein, Avraham Shtukarevitz, from right: Shemuel Rudnik, Rubinov,Dorka Gendler, Leah Palenbaum, Yosef Tsvaig, Munia Shtukarevitz

Second line: Mendel Milshtein, Yisrael Tsines

A group of Betar members with the "Olim" to Eretz-Yisrael

First line sitting from right: Shemuel Rudnik*,Yisrael Gurevitz*, Asnath Smolensky*, Avraham Shtukarevitz.

Second line: third from right-Mina Finkelshtein, sixth- Palenbaum Leah*.
(*) "Olim - Immigrants to Palestine"

Pren youth on a visit in Birshtan

From right: Shemuel Rudnik, ---, Vartovsky, Gita Fugler, her brother, ---, ---.

Pren youth at the bridge on the Nieman

From right: Yisrael Gurevitz, Elka Smolensky, Asnath Smolensky, Nekhamah Abelson, Mendel Milshtein

For a partial list of the Rabbis who served in Pren during the years see **Appendix 2**.

The welfare institutions in Pren during this period included "Lekhem Aniyim", "Bikur Kholim", "Hakhnasath Kalah", "Hakhnasath Orkhim", "Tsedakah Gedolah", "Linat haTsedek" and "Khevrah Kadisha".

Among the personalities born in Pren were:

Mordehai Rudnik (1893-1941), member of the Z"S (Zionist Socialist) center in Lithuania, director of the Hebrew high school in Shavli, murdered in Ghetto Shavli;

Yosef Gotfarshtein (1903-1980), lived in Paris, writer, journalist and translator, published articles on theater and art in the Jewish press in Kovno and Paris, and also wrote the extensive article "The Folklore of Lithuanian Jews" in "Yahaduth Lita" vol.1, translated into French stories by Y.L.Peretz and others.

During World War II and Afterward

World War II started with the German invasion of Poland on the 1st of September 1939, and its consequences for Lithuanian Jews in general and Pren Jews in particular were felt several months later.

According to the Ribbentrop-Molotov treaty on the division of occupied Poland, the Russians occupied the Suwalk region, but after delineation of exact borders between Russia and Germany the Suwalk region fell into German hands. The retreating Russians allowed anyone who wanted to join them to move into their occupied territory, and indeed many young people left the area together with the Russians. The Germans drove the remaining Jews out of their homes in Suwalk and its vicinity, robbed them of their possessions, then directed them to the Lithuanian border, where they were left in dire poverty. The Lithuanians did not allow them to enter Lithuania and the Germans did not allow them to return. Thus they stayed in this swampy area in cold and rain for several weeks, until Jewish youths from the border villages smuggled them into Lithuania by various routes, with much risk to themselves. Altogether about 2,400 refugees passed through the border or infiltrated on their own, and were then dispersed in the "Suvalkija" region, including Pren.

In June 1940 Lithuania was annexed to the Soviet Union and became a Soviet Republic. Following new rules, the majority of shops and factories belonging to the Jews of Pren were nationalized and commissars were appointed to manage them. Several Jewish houses whose size was more than 220 square meters were nationalized and their owners forced to leave them.

The supply of goods decreased and, as a result, prices soared. The middle class, mostly Jewish, bore most of the brunt, and the standard of living dropped gradually.

All Zionist parties and youth organizations were disbanded, several of the activists were detained (Palenbaum, M.Ainshtein etc.) and Hebrew educational institutions were closed. The Yiddish school, directed by Khmilevsky, remained open.

Some Jews began to join institutions under the new rule. In the middle of October 1940 a Jewish anti-religious meeting took place at the culture club. The meeting opened with a lecture by Reuven Rom "The harm of religion", with Markin, Lundorf, Shor, Lisovsky and Malevsky sitting at the table on the stage. The meeting was addressed by Nathan Rom on behalf of the "Comyug", as well as by Y.Epshtein, the secretary of the local communist party. During celebrations of the "October Revolution" a special party was arranged for Jewish workers. The activists were: Reuven Rom, Sh.Lundorf, Rafael Blum, A.Sheines, Hayim Gordon, Veber.

The German army entered Pren on June 24th 1941. Groups of Lithuanian nationalists immediately organized and took over the rule of the town. They summoned all the Jewish intelligence, pretending they were needed for work. Among them were the director of the school Ya'akov Rainer, the teacher Shelomo Cohen, the long standing Jewish representative in the municipality council Avraham Ginzburg, the secretary of the magistrates court Minah Finkelshtein and others. All were shot by local high school students.

Several Jews were detained instantly, to be accused of being in opposition to the Soviet regime. Some, together with other detainees, were transferred to the jail in Mariampol, whereas others were shot on the spot.

Restrictions against Jews were issued. They were not allowed to have any contact with non-Jews and had to wear a yellow patch on their back and chest. In Pren a special ban was issued, forbidding smoke be seen coming from Jewish chimneys, so that Jews could not have warm meals at home. Meanwhile humiliation, abuse and robbery continued.

On the fourteenth of August 1941 the annihilation machine started to work. Lithuanian auxiliary policemen ordered the Jews to gather in the synagogue and from there transferred them to the barracks the Soviets had started to build. Armed Lithuanians continued to patrol the streets, dragging every Jew they met to the barracks. Inside these barracks the Jews were kept in terrible conditions, without water and food, and without any sanitary facilities.

In addition to Jews from Pren, Jews from Balbirishok (Balbieriskis), Veiver (Veiveriai), 89 Jews from Yezne (Jieznas), some Stoklishok (Stakliskes) Jews and other small villages were also brought to the barracks. Congestion became unbearable and diseases spread.

On August 25 Jewish men were forced to dig big pits behind the barracks at the beast cemetery. One pit was 20 by 4 meters and the other 10 by 4 meters.

On August 26 (the third of Elul 5701) the final stage of the annihilation began. On that day large groups of Jews were led from the barracks to the pits at the beast cemetery. It is impossible to describe the terrible death procession of hundreds of Jews from Pren and its vicinity. The first two groups comprised men only. They had to undress down to their underwear, and thus clad were led to the pits. After them came mixed groups of men, women and children. The old and ill were brought in carts.

They were shot by machine guns next to the pits and then covered with lime, while many were still alive. According to eye witnesses, corpses in the pits still moved hours after the murder.

The site of the mass graves with the monument

People reported that Mrs. Sarah Blum strangled her own two children, explaining that it is better for their mother to kill them, rather than have them fall into the hands of murderers.

It is known that Mordehai Damsky, who spoke Lithuanian well and had close trade relations with Lithuanians, found shelter with a Lithuanian priest. Hearing that the Jews were being led to their death, he left his hideout and joined his community.

The owner of the known "Goldberg's beer brewery", Shakov, hid with his family at the Lithuanian Dr.Brunda, and paid for this with all his property.

The monument

After some time the doctor expelled the family. Shakov and his family, who were left without a penny, tried to hide in a forest, but afraid that they would die there from cold and hunger, handed themselves over to the commandant of the town. All were shot.

Yudl Yonenzon, a rich Jew, gave a Lithuanian "Activist" a large sum of money for hiding him, but after some time he was shot by his so called benefactor.

Only a few of Pren's Jews survived this terrible time: Yosef Podriachik, (one day to be Dr.Yosef Guri of the Hebrew University), Khyene Fugler-Flaxman, Berta Kovensky-Shtapler all managed to escape to Russia, Peninah Binyaminovitz-Levitan who was hidden by a Lithuanian priest (all living now in Israel) and Eliezer Mozes, who happened to be in the Kovno Ghetto and from there managed to join the partisans in Lithuania and Belarus. He died eventually in Kibbutz Kinereth.

According to Soviet sources 1,078 Jews, men, women and children are buried in the mass grave in Pren, on the left shore of the Nieman river.

The Jewish cemetery of Pren was totally destroyed and at its site a monument was erected.

The monument at the site of the destroyed Jewish cemetery with the
inscription in Lithuanian: till the year 1941 were buried (here) Jewish
residents.

Bibliography.

Yad-Vashem archives-M-1/E-1972/1792; M-1/Q-1341/145; TR-2 report 88; O-53/3,21.

Koniukhovsky Collection 0-71; files 120,129.

YIVO, Collection of Lithuanian Communities, New-York, Files 876-901, 1538, 1671

Gotlib, Ohalei Shem,- (Hebrew).

Dos Vort - daily newspaper in Yiddish of the Z"S party, Kovno-10.11.1934; 11.12.1934; 23.12.1934.

Di Yiddishe Shtime - daily newspaper in Yiddish of the General Zionists, Kovno,

26.1.1923; 25.5.1923; 29.5.1928; 31.5.1928; 1.6.1928; 6.6.1928; 7.6.1928.

HaMeilitz, Odessa - St.Petersburg, (Hebrew), 22.2.1881; 5.7.1881; 3.1.1882; 1.8.1882; 22.8.1882; 17.10.1882; 7.11.1882; 5.12.1882; 19.12.1882; 28.3.1884; 19.5.1884; 11.6.1886; 30.10.1887; 3.5.1896.

Folksblat - daily newspaper of the Folkists, Kovno (Yiddish), 4.11.1935; 30.5.1939; 15.10.1940; 19.11.1940.

Yiddisher Hantverker (Jewish artisan) (Yiddish). Kovno, 1.10.1938.

Di Tseit (The Time) - (Yiddish) Kovno, 4.10.1933.

Naujas Gyvenimas (Prienai), 4.9.1991.

Appendix I   **List of donors to Jewish communities which had suffered from pogroms and fires.**

David Aryeh Zilbernik 5 Ruble (Malinova farm owner)
Eliezer Goldberg 5 Ruble
Aharon Rozengard 3 Ruble
Nakhum Aharon Fridberg 3 Ruble
Ya'akov Moshe Goldberg 3 Ruble
Ya'akov Finkelshtein 3 Ruble
Avraham Fridberg 3 Ruble
Yitskhak Akabas 2.5 Ruble (from Mikhalishky village)
Z. Bagransky 3 Ruble
Efraim Shereshevsky 2 Ruble
Avraham Yosef Rudaminsky 2 Ruble
Dov Ziman 2 Ruble (from Rudupe farm)
Yosef Mordekhai Hurvitz 2 Ruble
Neta Langleben & son 2 Ruble
Yosef Finkelshtein 2 Ruble
Mendel Levinzon 2 Ruble
Eliezer & David Yavenzon 2 Ruble
Binjamin Volk & his mother in law Peshe 2 Ruble
Tsvi Hertz & broth. Kaplan 2 Ruble
Yitskhak Gorfinkel 2,13 Ruble
Yitskhak Rubin 1 Ruble
Moshe Leib Hurvitz 1 Ruble
Tsvi Haskel 1 Ruble
Aharon Langleben 1 Ruble
Dov Gershenovitz 1 Ruble
Moshe Panemunsky 1 Ruble
Aryeh Finkelshtein 1 Ruble
Aharon Tsvi Hurvitz 1 Ruble
Duber Finkelshtein 1 Ruble
Ze'ev Goldberg 1 Ruble
Zelig Katz 1 Ruble
Yisrael Bernshtein 1 Ruble
David Leib Zagar 1 Ruble
Sarah Mondshein (widow) 1 Ruble
Pesakh Moshe Naftalin 1 Ruble
Meir Talpiyoth 1 Ruble
Hilel Goldberg 1 Ruble
Eliezer Tamovsky 1 Ruble
Moshe Neta Feinberg 1 Ruble (from Matsin village)
Zogvil Lapulatsky 1 Ruble (from Marsupi village)
Meir Fogler 1 Ruble
Donations of 60 Kop. and less without names.

Appendix II

Partial List of Rabbis who served in Pren

Tsemakh in Pren during the third or fourth quarter of the eighteenth century

Nathan died in 1822

Nakhum-Shraga Revel (1838-1896) - for 12 years in Pren

Yehudah-Leib Rif in Pren 1871-1883

Simkhah-Dov Zilbershtein

Ben-Zion Krenitz born 1858, in 1898 in Pren

Gershon Barishnik

Avraham-Duber Reines, in 1903 was already in Pren, died in 1956 in Jerusalem

Avraham-Ya'akov Neimark, born in 1879, served in Pren 1909-1924, from 1925 member of the Rabbinate of Tel-Aviv, published the book "Eshel Avraham" in 10 volumes which includes innovations and explanations on the "Talmud Bavli" and "Talmud Yerushalmi", received twice the "Rav Kook Award"

Khaim Pun, from 1938 in Pren, murdered in 1941

Šakiai (Shaki)

The town Shaki - this being its Yiddish pronunciation - is situated in the south-western part of Lithuania near the river Siesartis, one of the tributaries of the river Sesupe, about 24 km east of the Prussian border (now part of the Russian), and about 58 km to the west of Kovno. This is one of the oldest settlements of Lithuania, already mentioned in old chronicles of the 14th and 15th centuries on the occasion of a visit of the head of the German crusader order in 1352. Another source maintained that in 1405 German crusaders had already built a wooden fortress in Shaki.

During the second half of the 16th century five families named Sakaiciai lived there and the small village was named after them, which is also mentioned in documents dating from 1599. The town named Sakiai was mentioned for the first time in 1719. In the 18th century it was owned by a family of princes named Chartorisky, one of whose sons, Mikolai, granted the town the rights of a city (the so-called Megdeburg Rights) in 1776.

Until 1795 Shaki was part of the Polish-Lithuanian Kingdom. The same year the third division of Poland by the three superpowers of those times - Russia, Prussia and Austria - caused Lithuania to become partly Russian and partly Prussian. The part of the state which lay on the left side of the Nieman river (Nemunas), including Shaki, was handed over to Prussia who ruled there during the years 1795-1807.

In 1800 there were 574 inhabitants in Shaki, most of them Jews, living in 65 houses.

According to the Tilzit agreement of 1807, Polish territories occupied by Prussia were transferred to what became known as the "The Great Dukedom of Warsaw", which was established at that time. The king of Saxony, Friedrich-August, was appointed duke, and the Napoleonic code became the constitution of the dukedom, according to which everybody was equal before the law, except for the Jews who were not granted any civil rights.

During the years 1807-1813 Shaki belonged to the "Great Dukedom of Warsaw" and was included in the Bialystok district. In 1813, after the defeat of Napoleon, all of Lithuania was annexed to Russia, as a result of which Shaki was included in the Augustowa Province (Gubernia), and in 1866 it became a part of the Suwalk Gubernia.

During Russian rule (1813-1915) the town started to develop, and before World War I about 4,000 people lived there and it became a district administrative capitol. Shaki was surrounded by woods and most of its inhabitants made their living from them.

When the First World War began many of Shaki's inhabitants left the town. In 1915 the town was occupied by the German army, who then erected a barbed wire fence surrounding it. Many men from Shaki were taken to work in Germany, the town suffered from a shortage of food and epidemics broke out.

The Germans left the town in 1919, at which time it was handed over to the newly created independent Lithuanian State, becoming a district administrative capitol, where new streets were built and government institutions established. There were elementary schools, a Catholic High-School, a Regional Court, a Post Office, a regional Hospital, branches of the State and other banks, 3 doctors, 2 dentists, one veterinary surgeon, 2 pharmacies, several tens of shops, several restaurants and pubs, a power station, a workshop for agricultural machines, 3 flour mills, 2 saw mills, a slaughter house, a dairy, a plant for producing bricks and several workshops for processing flax and wool.

In the summer of 1940 Lithuania became a part of the Soviet Union and Shaki continued to serve as a district administrative capitol. On the 22nd of June 1941 the German army invaded Lithuania and Shaki was occupied on the first day of the war, the Germans ruling there till the end of 1944, when the Red Army reconquered Lithuania.

The Jewish Settlement until World War I and Afterwards

Jews had apparently settled in the village Sakaiciai by the beginning of the 18th century, and dealt in timber. In 1765 Prince Chartorisky allowed Jews to settle in Shaki and to open taverns, so that by the middle of the 18th century Jews numbered more than 80% of the total population. In 1856 out of 1,764 residents 1,473 were Jews (83%), in 1862 there were 3,038 Jews (88%) out of a total population of 3,443, and in 1885 - 3,000 Jews (81%) out of a total population of 3,700. The Jews made their living from commerce and crafts, among them small peddlers, carters, horse traders, one blacksmith, two tailors, one watchmaker and of course merchants and shop owners. The Jewish shops were concentrated around the market square in the center of the town, so that every Sunday the peasants from the surroundings would come to pray in the church, bringing with them products for sale and use this opportunity to buy all they needed in the Jewish shops. Several of the Jewish merchants would export agricultural products to Germany, mainly grain. Several Jews were landowners near the town, growing vegetables and fruit, and many families had a plot of land near their houses, on which they would grow vegetables and fruit for their own personal use and even for sale.

We can learn about the public activities of Shaki's Jews during this period from the "Pinkas haKehilah" (The Community Book) from the years 1768-1776, which consisted of 248 pages of which 132 pages were filled out, and according to which the community had seven leaders who also represented it officially. Several sub-committees were responsible for the evaluation of taxes, for education, caring for the "Yeshivoth", for the elementary schools (the "Kheder"), the "Talmud Torah", the maintenance of the community's property, "Tsedakah Gedolah" which dealt with welfare issues and the "Khevrah Kadishah" who cared for the cemetery. There were also committees for the issues of the "Korobka" (meat taxes), for the synagogues and for Eretz Yisrael, for Yeshivoth and their students who were studying in the Holy Cities in Eretz

Yisrael. In a list of donors for the settlement of Eretz Yisrael from 1899 several names of Shaki Jews appeared, the fund raiser being Shimon Shmuelovitz.

During the famine in Lithuania, at the end of the 1860s, the Shaki community received help from the Help Committee in Memel - 30 Ruble.

Later the Jewish community of Shaki became strong enough themselves to donate money to the hungry in Lithuanian towns. There are three lists from 1871 in which names of Shaki donors appear, the fund raisers being Zeev Glasberg, Feivush-Mordehai Shor, Yitshak Segal. There are also two lists of donors from 1872 for the hungry in Lithuania, in which the fund raisers in the first list were Kalman Blokh, Yitshak Epelbaum, and in the second list Z.J.Blumgarten, Yekhiel-Ya'akov Etelzon.

In a list published in Hebrew newspaper "HaMagid" from 1871 and 1872 there are 185 names of Shaki Jews who donated money for the Famine in Persia.

In a list published in the Hebrew newspaper :"HaMeilitz" from the years 1897 and 1898 are 47 names of Shaki Jews who donated money for the Settlement of Eretz-Yisrael (see Jewshgen.Org.- Database-Lithuania-by Jeffrey Maynard)

During those years, matters of marriage and birth, also of Jews, were within the authority of the local Catholic priest. A Jewish couple, before going to the "Khupah" with the Rabbi, was obliged to register with the priest, and children born to Jewish families had also to be registered in the same way.

During the years 1890 to 1894 the Lithuanian writer Dr. Vincas Kudirka, who wrote the text of the Lithuanian anthem, lived in Shaki. He recalled that he could neither find a flat nor patients in the town, because most of its inhabitants were Jews who had their own doctors. Finally he found a place to live in, it being the old house of the local priest, and named the town "The Jews' Fortress " (*Zydpile* in Lithuanian).

The educational institutions where Shaki's Jewish children studied were mainly the traditional ones: the "Kheder" and the "Talmud Torah". In 1869 a government school for Jewish children opened, whose budget was covered mainly by the Jewish community and by a small government grant, extending to 175 Ruble per year. Its teacher was Yavarovsky, who also established the library in town. A letter to "The Society for Spreading Knowledge among the Jews" in St.Petersburg, signed by 12 people from Shaki, was sent asking for support for the library.

In 1877 this school amalgamated with the Evangelic school, 94 out of 126 pupils were Jewish. For many years Avraham Duber HaCohen Aizendorf, who also wrote the Shaki news in the Hebrew newspaper "HaMeilitz" which was published in St.Petersburg, was the inspector of the school on behalf of the government.

In 'Hameilitz" dated the 22nd of June 1880, a letter to the "Society for Spreading Knowledge among the Jews" in St.Petersburg, signed by Shimon Gral from Shaki, acknowledged the 100 Ruble the society had sent to support the school which was in danger of being closed.

At the beginning of the 20th century a "Kheder Metukan" (an improved Kheder) was established in Shaki, where Hebrew and Talmud were taught as well. Religious fanaticism, boorishness and superstitious beliefs still dominated the community, with only a few reading books other than religious ones and very few studying in the Russian High School in Vilkavishk (Vilkaviskis), about 50 kms away. Only one Jewish family in Shaki subscribed to a newspaper. The Jewish youth of Shaki did not see their future in this backward place and many of them emigrated to America, England and South Africa, whilst others moved to other places in Lithuania.

In a list of Shaki immigrants to America in 1869/70 the following names appear: M.Gitelman, Roize Levin, B.Edelman, M.Kahn, S.Shneider.

In Manchester (England) there were already several tens of former Shaki Jews in 1879, who would send 100 Ruble every year for the "Talmud-Torah", the leader of this group being Gershon Shapir.

Some Shaki Jews emigrated to Eretz Yisrael during the second half of the 19th century, probably being elderly people who wanted to die there in order to be close to the place where the "Mashiakh" (Messiah) would come and the revival of the dead would take place. At the old cemetery in Jerusalem there are at least two tombstones with the inscriptions: Basha Reizel daughter of Eliyahu from Shaki 5653 (1893), Ya'akov Tsevi son of Mosheh from Shaki 5655 (1895).

When World War I broke out in 1914 there were about 4,000 Jews in Shaki, but most left the town after the retreating Russian army instigated pogroms against them. Torah scrolls were burnt, Jews were mistreated and Jewish property looted. During the German occupation (1915-1919) some of the refugees returned to the town, others returned after the war.

The Period of Independent Lithuania (1918-1940)

Society and Economy

With the proclamation of the establishment of the Lithuanian state on the 16th of February 1918 and the evacuation of the German army from Shaki at the beginning of 1919, the Jewish community in town started to organize again.

According to the autonomy law regarding minorities in Lithuania, elections for the Jewish community committee in Shaki were held, when 11 members were elected: 1 from the General Zionists list, 2 from Tseirei Zion, 2-Mizrakhi, 6-undefined. The committee acted till the end of 1925, at which time the autonomy was annulled. During the years of its existence the committee collected taxes according to law, sometimes even with the help of the police, and was in charge of all aspects of community life.

According to the first census conducted by the Lithuanian government in 1923 there were then 2,044 people in Shaki, among them 1,267 Jews (62%).

During the 1920s and 1930s, Jews were in the majority in Shaki and played an important role in the economic and municipal life of the town. In the 1920s 7 out of the 12 members of the municipal council were Jews, and in the elections of 1931 5 Jews were elected out of 9 council members (David Rabinov, Leizer Rubinstein, B.Papishker, Feivel Kotler, Sh.Kaspar). In the 1934 elections the Jews still kept their strength in the council, 5 Jewish members being elected: B.Papishker, J.Mosezon, J.Flaxman, M.Fainzilber and L.Rubinstein. The same happened in the elections of 1936 when 5 Jewish members were elected. During those years 4 Jews served alternately as Mayor: Altfeld, Igdelsky, Lubotzky and Ya'akov Flaxman.

Shaki Jews made a living from commerce, crafts, industry and from growing vegetables and trading with them. Market day, every Tuesday and Friday and the fair once in two weeks, played an important role in the economy.

According to the 1931 Lithuanian government survey there were 82 shops in Shaki, of which 68 belonged to Jews (83%), according to the following table:

Kind of Business	Total	Owned by Jews
Groceries	10	9
Grains and Flax	11	11
Butcher Shops and Cattle Trade	7	6
Restaurants and Taverns	7	4
Food Products	9	9
Drinks	2	2
Textiles and Furs	9	7
Leather and Shoes	4	3
Haberdashery and House Utensils	2	2
Medicines and Cosmetics	3	0
Watches and Jewels	2	2
Bicycles and Sewing Machines	1	1
Tools and Iron Products	7	7
Heating Materials	3	3
Overland Transportation	2	2
Books and Stationary	2	0
Miscellaneous	1	0

According to the same survey of the 16 factories and workshops in Shaki, 12 belonged to Jews (75%). The data is presented in the following table:

Type of Establishment	Total	Owned by Jews
Metal Works, Power Stations	2	1
Wool, Coloring, Knitting	4	3
Flour Mills, Bakeries, Candies, Chocolate	3	1
Bristle Processing, Jewelers Photo Shops	7	7

Additionally there were tens of artisans working in their crafts. In 1938 there were still 60 Jewish artisans in Shaki: 12 tailors, 12 butchers, 6 bakers, 6 hairdressers, 5 hatters, 4 stitchers, 2 tinsmiths, 2 shoemakers, 2 painters, 2 watchmakers, 1 oven builder, 1 electrician, 1 book binder, 1 blacksmith, 1 photographer, 1 carpenter and 1 unknown.

The Jewish "Folksbank" occupied a central role in the economic life of the town, and in 1927 had 137 members and by 1932 this had increased to 170 members. During Soviet rule in Lithuania in 1940 the bank was closed down. Among its directors Froman and Lax should be mentioned. There was also a branch of "The United Company for Financial Credit for Jewish Agrarians."

The market square in Shaki (1927). The house opposite belonged to the Anakhovitz family. *Picture supplied by Gita Anakhovitz-Shmulovitz*

In the mid-1930sthe economic situation of Jews in Shaki began to deteriorate, one of the reasons being the open propaganda led by the "Association of Lithuanian Merchants (Verslas)" against buying in Jewish stores. During those years many Jewish youths emigrated to America and South Africa and some of them to Eretz Israel. Because of "Aliyah" (immigration) restrictions only a few managed to immigrate to Eretz Yisrael as "Khalutzim" (pioneers), whilst many moved to other towns in Lithuania. In 1937 a fire burnt down 6 Jewish houses, including flats and shops. (The houses of K.Kelzon, P.Kruk, L.Ushpitz, Goldart etc.).

All this caused the decline of the Jewish population in Shaki, so that by 1939 only about 600 Jews lived there, about 20% of the total population. According to the official telephone book of 1939, Shaki had 60 phone subscribers, 11 of them being Jews (18%).

Education and Culture

The Jewish children of Shaki studied in schools of the "Kheder" type and in the elementary Hebrew school from the "Tarbuth" chain, which had 4 regular and 2 preparatory classes. Hebrew was taught with "Ashkenazi" pronunciation, and 200 to 400 pupils studied simultaneously. Among the teachers were: Yerakhmiel Goldberg, Broido, Kanovitz, Shor, Cohen, Smilg, A.Yerushalmi, the brothers Tsevi and Eliezer Hanin, Shemuel Golbort, Bukhbinder, Varshavsky, Tsevi Vizhansky, Hamer.

The pupils and teachers of the government high school in 1931/32 with 20 Jewish pupils. *Picturse supplied by Bela Marshak-Shadkhanovitz*

The graduation class 1939 with 3 Jewish girls.

Sitting in the first line, from right:fourth-Bela Marshak
sixth-Gita Anachovitz   ninth-Leah Levinstein

(All the three: Bela Marshak-Shadkhanovitz, Eng.Chemistry Gita Anakhovitz-Shmulovitz, Dr. (Medical) Leah Levinstein-Palunsky with their families are living in Israel)

The large Yiddish library sponsored by the society "Libhober fun Vissen" (Lovers of Knowledge) and a smaller Hebrew library played an important cultural role.

Jewish children received their higher education in the government High School in town, with only very few studying in Hebrew high schools in nearby cities.

In 1931/32 20 Jewish pupils studied in the local High School while in 1939/40 only 3 Jewish girls graduated. (See pictures above).

The drama circle in Shaki (1919)

Standing first from right: Mosheh Kopilovitz, next to him Leib-Hirsh Anakhovitz.

Standing first from left: Dr. Sonia Levin-Anakhovitz

Picture supplied by Gita Anakhovitz- Shmulovitz

A local amateur group arranged theatrical plays from time to time, with great success. The Kovno Jewish theater would also visit Shaki sometimes and perform plays in the local cinema hall.

Zionist Activity.

There were branches of most Zionist parties and youth organizations: "Tseirei Zion", Z"S, "HeKhalutz" (from 1922), "HaShomer HaTsair", "HeKhalutz HaTzair" (from 1932), "Betar" and at the beginning of the twenties also "Poalei Zion-Smol" (Leftist Zion workers). This party participated with a separate list in the elections for the "Nationalrat" (The National Committee of Lithuanian Jews) and for the municipalities. Despite the persecutions and arrests of members of this party by the Lithuanian security forces, a member of this party, Yudl Altfeld, was elected Mayor of Shaki.

We can learn about the comparative strength among the different Zionist parties represented in Shaki branches by looking at the election results for Zionist congresses:

Cong No	Year	Total Shek.	Total Voters	Labor Party Z"S Z"Z		Rev	G.Z. A B		Gros	Miz.
14	1925	28	--	--	--	--	--	--	--	--
15	1927	41	40	1	7	3	19	--	--	10
16	1929	94	46	1	6	2	28	--	--	9
17	1931	--	--	--	--	--	--	--	--	--
18	1933	--	289	222		49	13	--	2	3
19	1935	488	462	319		--	78	14	--	41

Shek.-Shekalim; Rev.-Revisionists; G.Z.-General Zionists; Gros.-Grosmanists; Miz.-Mizrahi

At the end of 1934 a combined club of the Z"S party, "HeKhalutz" and HaOved" opened up in Shaki at a festive celebration with the participation of about 100 members and friends of these organizations (see Appendix 1). The main Zionist activities in town took place in this club, and included lectures, shows etc.

There were also fund raising activities for the National Funds: Keren haYesod and Keren Kayemeth (KKL). In December 1934 a new committee of the Keren Kayemeth (KKL) was elected in Shaki : M.Shohet, Z.Oleisky, A.Marshak, Hamer, H.Gefen, Sh.Kruk, Sh.Golbort, M.Vilensky and Z.Mazinter.

An urban Kibbutz Hakhshara (urban training kibbutz) existed, where some members trained in the local agricultural machinery factory.

Sport activities were performed in the local branch of "Maccabi" with its 48 members.

Religion and Welfare

There were two prayer houses in Shaki: the Beth-Midrash where prayers were held every day, and the grandiose Synagogue (Di Shul), famous in Lithuania for its internal ornaments, where prayers were held on Saturdays and Holidays only.

In 1928 a heated controversy erupted between the two Rabbis who served in Shaki - Rabbi Anakhovitz and Rabbi Fridman - on the issue of the "Beth-Midrash", as a result of which the congregation divided into two parties as well. This controversy brought about the intervention of the law enforcement authorities, so that 3 men were detained for 7 days, one man expelled from the town for 6 months, and the prayer houses were closed on and off for some time. The problem was eventually solved after the law officer passed the issue on to the "Association of Lithuanian Rabbis", who decided that a new Rabbi be elected. Later the punishments were annulled.

Among the Rabbis who served in Shaki during the years were: Shemuel Mohliver (in Shaki 1854-1860) one of the pioneers of "Khibath-Zion" (Lovers of Zion) and one of the fathers of religious Zionism; Mosheh-Betsalel Lurie (in Shaki 1868-1875); Zvi Palterovitz; Shimon-Dov Anolik; Yirmiyahu Flensberg (in Shaki 1889 - till his death in 1914); Avraham-Leib Shor (1922-1926); Aharon Fridman (1926 till his death in 1934); Yosef Anakhovitz (died in 1940); Yosef Goldin was murdered in 1941.

Most of these Rabbis published books on religious topics and recommended books written by other Rabbis.

All the customary welfare societies of the Jewish communities in Lithuania were active in Shaki as well.

A welfare volunteer collecting "Khaloth" for Shabath for distributing among the poor (1937)

For a partial list of personalities born in Shaki see Appendix 2.

The Period of World War II and Thereafter

After the German army had occupied Poland in September 1939 and in agreement with the Ribbentrop-Molotov treaty, the Russians occupied the Suvalk region, but after the delineation of exact borders between Poland, Russia and Germany, this region fell into German hands. The retreating Russians allowed anyone who wanted to join them to move into their occupied territory, and indeed many young Jewish people left the area together with the Russians. The Germans expelled the remaining Jews from their homes, robbed them of their possessions, then directed them to the Lithuanian border, where they were left in dire poverty. The Lithuanians did not allow them to enter Lithuania and the Germans did not allow them back. Thus they stayed in this swampy area in cold and rain for several weeks, until Jewish youths from the border villages in Lithuania smuggled them into Lithuania by various routes, at much risk to themselves. Altogether about 2,400 refugees crossed through or infiltrated on their own, and were then dispersed in Lithuania. In Shaki alone 100 refugees were accommodated and given a warm welcome and loyal assistance for which Lithuanian Jews were famous.

In June 1940 Lithuania was annexed to the Soviet Union and became a Soviet Republic. According to Soviet economic policy some factories and 7 Jewish shops were nationalized and commissars were appointed to run them. Supply of goods was restricted, as a result of which prices soared, and the middle class, mostly Jewish, was badly hit with its living standard dropping gradually. The Zionist parties and youth organizations were dispersed and some of its members were absorbed in the Comsomol - the Communist Youth Organization. The Hebrew school was closed and in its stead a Yiddish school opened.

In the middle of June 1941 five Jewish families whose shops had been nationalized, were exiled deep into Russia (Hirshl Rubinstein, Shemuel Rubinstein, Aharon Marshak, Abramovitz, Shemuel Goldoft)

The German army entered Shaki on the first day of war between Germany and the Soviet Union, on the 22nd of June 1941 at 11 o'clock. Many Jews tried to escape eastwards, but only 50 managed to arrive in Russia. Many were killed on the roads and most of the escapees returned home.

With the entry of the Germans, the Lithuanian nationalists took over the rule of the town. They immediately started to plot against the Jews, and every day new orders were published restricting their civil rights: they were forbidden to maintain any contacts with non-Jews, not allowed to walk on the sidewalks or to buy food products from non-Jews, could not visit public institutions, were forced to wear yellow patches on their garments, had to hand over their radios and more. In addition, a curfew was imposed from 6 o'clock in the evening until 6 o'clock in the morning. Later all Jewish men from 15 years of age and up were ordered to present themselves for work, where they were concentrated in a big barn outside the town, near a field where the Jews used to put their cows out to pasture and thus this field was called "the Jewish pasture"

(Zydlaukas). The barn was heavily guarded by armed Lithuanians, and from there groups of men were taken every day to the nearby forest in order to dig long and wide trenches.

On Saturday, the 5th of July 1941 (the 10th of Tamuz 5701), group after group of men was taken out of the barn and led to the trenches. There they were forced to pull off their garments and jump into the trenches. Men who did not hurry to obey the order were pushed into the trench by force. Then all were shot by the Lithuanians.

Some of the victims tried to resist the murderers. Benjamin Rotshild, the son of the old blacksmith Yisrael-Yitshak, when already in the trench, caught the leg of one of the murderers, dragged him into the trench and hit him badly. The Lithuanian friends of the murderer jumped into the trench, killed Benjamin and took out the badly hurt Lithuanian from the trench and transferred him to the Vilkaviskis hospital. The "crazy one of the town" Motele, who tried to escape from the massacre, was also shot by the guards.

After the murder of the men, 40 wealthy women were expelled from their houses. They were then ordered to take all their belongings with them and in particular their valuables. They were brought into the same barn and there were robbed of everything they possessed. They were forced to undress, then led to the trenches and cruelly murdered.

The remaining women were concentrated in the most pitiable alleys of Shaki, which was proclaimed an open Ghetto, because it was not fenced off. Despite this non-Jews were forbidden to bring in any food products, so the women had to look for food elsewhere and thus endanger themselves.

On the first day that the women were concentrated into the Ghetto, Lithuanian youngsters stormed into the Ghetto, chose 6 beautiful young girls and took them out. These girls never came back. This abduction of young women continued later too, they would be kidnapped and disappear.

Saturday, the 13th of September 1941 (21st of Elul 5701), marked the end of the Jewish community of Shaki. On this day all the women and children were put on carts and brought to the barn. From there group after group was led to the trenches, where they were ordered to undress and then pushed into the trenches and shot. Their belongings were loaded on carts, brought into the town and divided among the Lithuanians. Together with the Jews of Shaki, Jews from the neighboring towns of Kruki (Kriukai), Lukshi (Luksiai), Sintovta (Sintautai), Grishkabud (Griskabudis), Sudarg (Sudargas) and others, were also murdered.

Among the victims of Sudarg were the author's aunt Mina Rosin-Hilelson, his cousin Shelomoh Hilelson, his cousin Elka Hilelson-Goldberg, her husband Yehudah Goldberg and their little daughter Leah'le

After the war a monument was erected on the mass graves, with an inscription in Yiddish: "In these mass graves four thousand innocent inhabitants of Shaki and its surroundings were buried in 1941-1944 by German fascists and

Lithuanian bourgeoisie nationalists. Let the bright memory of the perished live for ever in the hearts of all patriots of our homeland".

Entrance gate to the site of the mass graves. The inscription in Yiddish, Lithuanian and Russian says: "At this place the Hitler murderers and their local helpers in 1941-1944 murdered about 4000 Jews, men. Women, children." *Picture supplied by Nathan Gershowitz*

A group of survivors of the Shaki Jewish community on a memorial meeting near the monument at the mass graves at the end of the sixties.

Standing in the first line, from right: Shemuel Bluman, ---, Mrs. Viliosesky, Riva Altfeld, Lila Shlomovitz, Rita Shlomovitz, Gita Anakhovitz-Shmulovitz, Bela Froman, Vilionsky.

Second line, from right:----, ----, Eige Kuperman, Kuperman, Altfeld (half face), ----, Khiene Vilionsky, Betsalel Rotshild, ----(with the hat), Sarah Gershovitz, ----, Nathan Gershovitz, Tuviyah Goldoft, -----, ----, Yonah Iser----.

Third line, from right: Mordehai Kuperman, -----, Roche-Basia Zilber, -----, Zilber, Moti Gershovitz.

Almost all of these people were in the USSR during the war. Many of them died in Lithuania and a part of them in Israel.

Monument in memory of the murdered Jewish community of Shaki erected in the Holon cemetery.

The inscription in Hebrew: "In memory of the martyrs of Shaki Lithuania who perished in the Holocaust in year 5701- 1941."

Memorial day of the men the 10th of Tamuz, of the women and children the 21st of Elul.

In 1959 there were 2,944 people in Shaki, but not one Jew.

Bibliography:

Yad-Vashem Archives: M-1/Q-1791/358; M-1/E-1275/1241; M-9/15(6); Koniukhovsky collection 0-71, Files151, 152, 153.

The Ya'akov Oleisky Book (Hebrew)-published by "ORT" Israel and "The Association of Lithuanian Jews in Israel". Tel-Aviv 1986.

Dos Vort (Yiddish Daily)- Kovno, 11.11.1934, 30.11.1934, 23.12.1934.

Di Yiddishe Shtime (Daily)- Kovno, 30.1.1928, 3.2.1928, 14.3.1928, 26.2.1928, 27.2.1928, 5.6.1928, 26.6.1928, 26.5.1931, 9.9.1937.

HaMeilitz (Hebrew)-St. Petersburg, 20.5.1879, 10.6.1879, 22.6.1880, 1.8.1882, 19.2.1883, 16.3.1883, 16.4.1883, 10.6.1883, 4.12.1886, 8.12.1886.

Yiddisher Hantverker (Yiddish)-Kovno, Nr. 7, 15.12.1938.

Folksblat (daily) (Yiddish)-Kovno,14.2.1935, 1.5.1936, 9.9.1937, 29.10.1940.

Appendix 1.

The festive opening celebration of the club of the Z"S party, "HeKhalutz" and HaOved" (excerpts from a description from the Yiddish daily newspaper "Dos Vort", the 11th of November 1934).

The chairman of the evening was Alter Pakeltzik. Speeches were held by Shakhne Kruk on behalf of the Z"S party, by Shelomoh Shapira on behalf of "haOved", by Tsevi Gefen on behalf of Keren haYesod, by Yisrael Bluman on behalf of "Keren Kayemeth (KKL)", by Havivah Kovensky on behalf of "HaKhalutz HaTsair", by Yosef Ziman on behalf of the Neishtot branch of "HeKhalutz" and by Shifrah and Zusman on behalf of the Kibbutz "HaMetsaref". Mordehai Vilionsky held a speech in which he asked the members of the party to strengthen activities for it and the National Funds.

Appendix 2.   A Partial List of Personalities born in Shaki.

Yitshak-Leib Goldberg (1860-1935), one of the pioneers of "Khovevei Zion" (Lovers of Zion) in Vilna, from 1890 and for 25 years the representative of the "Odessa Committee", delegate on behalf of Vilna to the first Zionist congress, supported the Hebrew press in Russia and in Eretz Yisrael, The Hebrew University in Jerusalem was built on his land.

Boris Goldberg (1866-1921), one of the leaders of the Zionists in Russia, journalist and member of many editorial boards of newspapers in Russia and London, from 1920 in Eretz Yisrael.

Yehudah Fin (1866-1945), workers leader in England and America.

Nakhman-Ber Etelzon (1828-1920), one of the first Jewish journalists in Chicago and New-York, published the first Yiddish newspaper in Chicago in

1870:"Di Israelitishe Presse" with a supplement in Hebrew "Heichal HaIvriyah", later moving it to New York.

Yosef Even-Odem (1907-1962), M.D. son of Rabbi and Senator Yitshak Rubinstein from Vilna, from 1933 in Eretz Yisrael, published many books on Hebrew terminology of medicine and nature.

Aharon Fridman (1855-1932), cantor in Berlin 1882-1932, was awarded a special title by the German authorities.

Yosef-Irving Pascal (1890-?), M.D.,immigrated to America, developed some inventions in Ophthalmology, published a several books on this issue.

Ya'akov Oleisky (1901-1981), agronomist, director of "ORT' in Lithuania and later in Israel, for many years the chairman of "The Association of Lithuanian Jews in Israel"

Hanah Vurtzel (1872-?), from 1902 in America, published poems in the Jewish newspapers "Forverts", "Togeblat", "Morgen Jurnal" etc.

Hayim Saks (1887-1941), journalist, published articles in the Jewish press in Kovno, murdered in 1941.

Aryeh-David Berezovsky, a known cantor.

Ellis Island List of Jewish Residents of Shaki Immigration to the US

Name	Town	Country	Year
Beile Apelbaum	Szaky		1906
Aron Alexandrowitz	Schaki	Russia	1917
Hirsch Alexandrowitz	Schaki	Russia	1917
Lina Alexandrowitz	Schaki	Russia	1917
Pesa Anachovic	Sakiai	Suwalki	1922
Sara Anchovic	Sakiai	Suwalki	1922
Bluma Anachovic	Sakiai	Suwalki	1922
Rochel Blumberg	Schaky		1899
David Bibischkow	Shakin		1902
Nissen Bajoracky	Schaky		1903
Almen Bialistazky	Sakilst...sk		1903
Chiel Berkman	Schaki		1904
Ettel Berkman	Schaki		1904
Feige Bak	Szakz		1905
Ruwen Boyer	Schakz		1907
Herschel Bjrabina	Schakow		1907
Nottel Bernstein	Szaki	Rus.	1908
Samuel Bloch	Schaky	Russia	1909
Schimchov Bloch	Schaki	Russia	1911
Wolf Feldmann	Szakat		1904
Abram Flaksman	Szaky	Russia	1907
Cecil Frumann	Schaki Schuwalk	Russia	1911
Israel Frumann	Schaki Schuwalk	Russia	1911
Mery Filtz	Szaki	Russia	1911
Isaac Frieman	Sakiai	Lithuania	1922
Braine Filz	Saki	Lithuan	1922
Roche Gutstein	Shaky		1903
Salmen Goldman	Saki		1904
Nachmen Gluck	Schaky		1904
Schleime Grigorowitz	Schaki		1905
Perl Grassmann	Sakisch		1906
Schifre Grassmann	Sakisch		1906
Hirsch Glick	Saki	Russia	1906
Abraham Gittle	Szakasg		1906
Chinki Grenberg	Szaka	Russia	1907
Simon Gottn	Szaky		1907
Chaim Ginsberg	Szaki	Russia	1909
Welwel Glasberg	Saki	Russia	1909
Majer Glasberg	Schaky	Russia	1910
Michla Ginzberg	Szaka	Russia	1911
Elia Ginzberg	Szaka	Russia	1911
...rael Ginzberg	Szaka	Russia	1911
Henie Ginzberg	Szaka	Russia	1911
Sarah Glaser	Szaky	Russia	1912

Mase Goldblatt	Szaka	Russia	1913
Bassewe Gordon	Szakot	Russia	1913
Nesche Ginsberg	Saki	Russia	1913
Hirsch Goldman	Schaki	Russia	1913
Taube Glassberg	Schaki	Russia	1914
Ester Glasberg	Szaki	Russia	1914
Lara Glasberg	Szaki	Russia	1914
Basey Gluck	Saki	Lithu.	1922
Sussel Holzmann	Szaky		1904
Herman Holzmann	Schaky		1904
Israel Holzmann	Schaky		1904
Ester Hodes	Schaki	Russia	1910
Schifre Hillelson	Szaki	Russia	1912
Chaim Jacobsohn	Szaki		1905
Elie Jacobson	Sakin	Russia	1910
Jawiel Jacobson	Sakin	Russia	1910
Breine Jacobson	Sakin	Russia	1910
Calmen Jorkshire	Szaki	Russia	1911
Sundel Kahn	Szaki		1904
Beviach Kahn	Szaki		1904
Chatzkel Kasper	Schaky		1905
Feute Klischowski	Schaki		1905
Chane Kurkolowsky	Sakie	Russia	1910
Lemach Keilson	Schaki Suwalk	Russia	1911
Motel Kagan	Schaki	Lithaua	1921
Motel Kogan	Schaki	Lithuanian	1921
Mandel Lichtmann	Schaky		1904
Chaim Lichtmann	Schaki		1905
Jankel Lichtmann	Szaki	Russia	1909
Schachat Leib	Schaki	Russia	1912
Golde Lichtmann	Szaki	Russia	1912
Gitel Lubowsky	Saki	Lithuan.	1922
Efroim Lubowsky	Saki	Lithuan.	1922
Sena Leja Lubowsky	Saki	Lithuan.	1922
Peisel Michan	Szakiw	Russia	1911
Freide Mariner	Saki		1914
Icek Muskin	Sakin	Lithuania	1921
Lipa Muskin	Sakin	Lithuania	1921
Sora Muskin	Sakin	Lithuania	1921
Mottel Niselowicz	Szaki	Russia	1910
Schmul Nemenczik	Schakie Luwalk	Russia	1913
Blune Orlakewitz	Schaky		1904
Chane Orlakwitz	Schaky		1904
Neyer Odes	Szaki	Rus.	1908
Hirsch Odess	Szaki	Russia	1908
Judal Pabisker	Saki		1904
Schmul Papusker	Schaki		1905
Brinl Papusker	Schaki		1905

Riwe Pafisher	Saki	Russia	1909
Sore Pittelman	Schakwa	Russia	1914
Schennel Resenowitz	Schaky		1903
Leib Rosenthal	Schaky		1904
Mnasche Runisn	Schaket		1904
Rebeka Rosen	Schaky		1906
Saml. Rubinstein	Schaky		1906
Sunel Rubinstemizy	Schaky		1906
Rochel Rubinstein	Schaky		1906
Rochel M. Rubinstemizy	Schaky		1906
Chaije Rosen	Schaky		1906
Lea Rubin	Schak		1907
Leib Razowsky	Czak	Russia	1907
Schloime Rothstein	Schaky	Russia	1907
Chaje Rubel	Szakie	Russia	1907
Judel Rubel	Szakie	Russia	1907
Rine Rockmacher	Szaki	Russia	1912
Flzig Sack	Szaky		1904
Mendel Sack	Szaky		1904
Schmed Sack	Szaky		1904
Mendel Silver	Szaki		1904
Simon Serou	Sakier		1904
Chaze Silver	Szako		1904
Berl Sctor	Schaki		1904
Czerne Sack	Szaky		1904
Schemann Siff	Schaky		1904
Pesche Rael Schulgasser	Schaki	Russia	1907
Jacob Sam. Schulgasser	Schaki	Russia	1907
Efroim Starofolsky	Schaki Suwalk	Russia	1911
Rafael Spalter	Schaki	Russia	1912
Schmul Silberman	Schakie Luwalk	Russia	1913
Kasper Schmerl	Schakin	Russia	1913
Hirsch Starapolsky	Schaki	Russia	1913
Chaja Schajewitsch	Schaksty	Lithuania	1921
Schaie Tobolitzki	Saki		1904
Tadeus Toluszno	Schakelu		1907
Sore Wygonesky	Szaki		1904
Jovel Wilanski	Schaki		1904
Benjamin Werblowsky	Schaki	Russia	1908
Wulf Werblowsky	Schaki	Russia	1908
Sadie Werblowsky	Schaki	Russia	1908
Ite Lore Wiliansky	Szaki	Russia	1912
Rochel Welenska	Saki	Russia	1912
Chase Zecberg	Szaki	Russia	1911
Zalman Zelernik	Szakot	Russai	1913
Rochel Zeeberg	Sakiai	Lithuan.	1921

Salantai (Salant)

Salant - as it is called in Yiddish - is located in the northwestern part of Lithuania, about 32 km northeast from the district town Kretinga. The nearest train station was 12 km from Salant. The town was built on both banks of the Salantas River, the main part being on the left bank. A village with the same name was mentioned in historic documents dating back to 1565. In 1746 the King granted permission for four annual town fairs in Salant.

Until 1795 Salant was part of the Polish-Lithuanian Kingdom, when the third division of Poland by the three superpowers of those times - Russia, Prussia and Austria - caused Lithuania to become partly Russian or partly Prussian. The part of Lithuania that included Salant fell under the rule of the Czarist Russian. From 1802 it was part of the Vilna province (Gubernia) and from 1843 as part of the Kovno province.

At the beginning of the 1880s Count Bogdan Oginsky purchased the lands of the town.

During the 19th century and also during the subsequent years of independence in Lithuania (1918-1940) Salant was a county center in the Kretinga district.

The Jewish settlement till after World War I

Jews settled in Salant since the beginning of the 18th century. In 1765 there were 279 Jews in town who paid poll tax. Aged people as well as the poor and the children under ten years of age were released from making payment, therefore it is reasonable to estimate the number of Jews at this date at about 400.

They made their living in crafts and commerce, in particular in flax trade. The market days and the fairs were the source of their livelihood.

During the years of autonomous organization for Jewish communities in Lithuania (Va'ad Medinath Lita, 1623-1764), Salant community belonged to Birzh (Birzai) district.

During the Polish rebellion in 1831 a rich Salant man Eliyahu Gutkin, helped by the local priest, saved 12 Jews from being hanged by the rebels.

In 1843 the Czar issued an order stipulating that Jews living in the area within 50 km of the western border of Russia should be transferred to some of the Gubernias inside Russia. Salant community was one of 19 who refused to obey this order.

In 1847 there were 990 Jews in Salant. In 1880, 300 Jewish families lived in the town. There were 60 Jewish shops in town, 20 flax merchants, a water-driven flourmill, 15 shoemakers, 7 tailors and other artisans, a doctor, a paramedic, and a pharmacist.

After Count Oginsky became the owner of Salant lands in 1885, he wanted to evict the Jews from their homes claiming that the Jews living on his lands were living there illegally. The conflict had to be resolved in court and the verdict was passed in favor of the Jews who stayed on in their homes after paying the claimant a fee of 60 Rubles per house.

Market place in Salant. *Picture supplied by Dr L.J.Herberg*
The white house at right belonged to Zusmanovitz family.

Jewish children studied at the "Kheder" which was usual in those times. In the years 1903-1910 Salant had a "Yeshivah" and five "Khadarim". In 1906 a library was established, considered illegal in those times. The initiators of the project were Hirsh Ulshtein and one of Rabbi Rabinovitz's sons.

One of the promoters of secular education in town was Mordehai-Aharon Ginzburg, who later became the best-known Hebrew writer of Lithuania.

Salant was becoming known in Lithuania and in the Diaspora for its scholars, the "Musar" men (ethics, morality), the rabbis, intellectuals and writers who trace back their roots to the town.

There was an old synagogue in Salant that apparently was built in the first half of the 19th century.

On the list of Salant Jews who paid the membership fee of "Agudath Yisrael" in1913, thirty-two names show up *(see Appendix 2).* The activists were Rabbi Mordehai Rabinovitz, Tsevi Muskat, Mosheh Milner.

In 1907 local public workers managed to form "Loan and Saving Society", despite obstacles caused by the government.

*For list of rabbis who served in Salant see **Appendix 1**.*

Street with peddlers

The "Khibath Zion" (Affection for Zion) movement and later the Zionism movement was well received in Salant, but even before these movements were established, some of Salant Jews immigrated to Eretz-Yisrael.

In 1838 Rabbi Yosef Zundl Salant immigrated to Eretz Yisrael and in 1902 Naftali Amsterdam did. Yitskhak ben Ze'ev Keidansky with his wife settled in Jerusalem at the end of the 1880s. Beinush Salant was one of the seven founders of the "Nakhlath Shivah" quarter in Jerusalem. Dr. Ze'ev-Wolf ben Mosheh Levinzon, a known doctor in Zemaitija region, agreed to run his practice in Jerusalem arriving in 1846 where he worked until his death in 1873.

Mosheh-Yehoshua (Salant), born 1824 in Salant, arrived in Jerusalem in1872. Served as "Shamash" at the Beth Hamidrash of "Batei Makhase" quarter. Died in 1903 and was buried on Mount of Olives cemetery. He had four daughters and one son.

One daughter and the son immigrated to America in 1912-13 the others lived and died in Jerusalem. (**Appendix 6** contains a Partial list of Salant Jews who immigrated to America in the years 1905-1921)

At the old Jewish cemetery in Jerusalem there are 7 headstones of Salant Jews who passed away at the end of the 19th century:

> Yosef-Zundl ben Binyamin-Beinush, immigrated in 1838 where he died in 1867 at the age of 81.
>
> Rachel-Rivkah bath Tsevi (wife of Rabbi Yosef Zundl), died in 1856,
>
> Tsivyah bath Yosef Zundl, died in 1881,
>
> Mosheh ben Yitskhak Izik, died in1873,
>
> Rachel from Salant, wife of Asher from Shad died in 1875,
>
> Hode-Gite bath Yonah, died in 1884,
>
> Binyamn-Beinush ben Rabbi Shemuel from Salant, died in 1900.

At the Hebrew newspaper "HaMeilitz" dating back to the years 1894-1901 there are 100 names of Salant Jews who donated money for the settlement of Eretz Yisrael *(see Database at Jewishgen.Org, compiled by Jeffrey Maynard)*. The fundraisers were Yomtov Lipman and D.Vazbutzky.

In anticipation of the fifth Zionist Congress that took place in 1902, 50 "Shekalim" were sold in town. The list of members supporting Jewish agrarians in Eretz Yisrael and Syria in 1896 the following names of Salant Jews appear: Yosef Urdang, Hayim Gitkin, Lipman Ziv, Ben-Zion Cohen, Tsevi Cohen, Yehoshua Shwartz, David and Zalman Vazbutsky.

The Hebrew newspaper, "HaMagid," Number. 17 dating back to 1872, lists 80 names of Salant Jews who donated money for the destitute Jews in Lithuania. *(see Database Jewishgen.Org)*

In 1915, at World War I, the Russian army exiled Salant Jews and most of the Jews of the Kovno Gubernia, deep into Russia.

For a partial list of famous persons born in Salant see Appendix 5.

The Synagogue -"Di Shul"
Photo taken by Meir Olstein, supplied by Eli Goldstein

The "Aron Kodesh"

During Independent Lithuania (1918-1940)

According to the first census performed by the new Lithuanian government in 1923 there were 1,677 residents in Salant, of them 670 were Jews (40%).

During this period Salant Jews made their living, as was quite usual, in commerce and crafts.

The 1931 government survey showed that there were 42 businesses in Salant at that time, 38 of the businesses were owned by Jews (90%). Distribution according to type of business is given in the table below:

Type of the business	Total	Owned by Jews
Groceries	10	9
Grain and Flax	5	5
Butcher's shops and Cattle Trade	4	3
Restaurants and Taverns	2	2
Food Products	4	4
Textile Products and Furs	5	5
Leather and Shoes	4	4
Haberdashery and Appliances	1	1
Medicine and Cosmetics	2	1
Watches, Jewels and Optics	1	1
Radio, Sewing machines	1	0
Tools and Steel products	3	3

According to the same survey there were 2 flourmills and a leather factory owned by Jews in Salant. There was also a Jewish venture in production of wax candles named "Electra".

From Irwin Sagenkahn's diary on his trip to Salant in June 1996:

"Our next stop was to try to locate the old Salant synagogue (see above photo), now a cultural museum. When we got there, the main room was used as a temporary exhibit as a zoo. Again, we took pictures of the inside and outside of the old synagogue. This apparently was also the location of the old town square".

In 1937, Jews were engaged in 18 different trades in town: 6 butchers, 4 stitchers, 2 shoemakers, 2 barbers, 1 tailor, 1 baker, 1 tinsmith, 1 watchmaker. There was also one Jewish doctor and a Jewish dentist who was a woman.

The Jewish "Folksbank", which had 126 members in 1927, contributed significantly to the economic life of the town. Two weekly market days were very important in the lives of Salant Jews.

As mentioned above, Salant was a county administrative center. However, only one Jewish delegate represented the community at the county council in 1935.

Since the middle of the 1930s the numbers of Salant Jews declined. The economic crisis in Lithuania as well as the open propaganda of the Lithuanian merchants association "Verslas" against Jewish shops were the reasons Jews began to search for a future elsewhere. The great fire of 1926 destroyed almost half of the town and resulted in many of Salant Jews immigrating to South Africa, America and Eretz-Yisrael. This fire destroyed the Beth-Midrash, 2 Kloises, the Folksbank and the school. 151 families were left homeless and poverty-stricken. In Kovno an assistance committee to help the victims of the fire was organized.

In 1939 there were 24 telephone lines in town, 9 of them belonged to Jews.

After the big fire of 1926

Salant Jewish children studied at the Hebrew elementary school of the "Tarbuth" chain, and in the afternoons religious subjects were taught at the "Talmud-Torah". There was also the private Salant Hebrew Kindergarten.

The old Jewish library became an official institution by then and was named after the writer Y.L.Peretz. It had about 1,600 books in Hebrew and Yiddish. The school had a special library for children.

Many of Salant Jews belonged to the Zionist movement, and all the Zionist parties in town had their followers. All these years fundraising activities were organized for the National Funds.

The table below shows how Salant Zionists voted for the different parties at five Zionist Congresses:

Congr. Nr.	Year	Total Shek.	Total Voters	Labor Party		Rev	G.Z.		Gro	Miz.
				Z"S	Z"Z		A	B		
14	1925	60	--	--	--	--	--	--	--	--
16	1929	80	45	18	6	--	11	--	--	10
17	1931	30	23	8	2	1	7	--	--	5
18	1933	---	122	72		26	17	--	--	7
19	1935	---	200	134		--	22	24	--	20

Shek-.Shekalim;   Rev.-Revisionists;   G.Z.-General   Zionists;   Gro.- Grosmanists; Miz.-Mizrahi

"Mizrakhi", "Agudath Yisrael", "Tseirei Zion", "Sirkin" (Z"S) and "Betar" had their branches in the town as well. During the years 1932-35 a "Kibbutz Hakhsharah" (Training Kibbutz) of "HeKhalutz" acted in town.

Salant Hebrew school 1929-30 (*Picture supplied by Elkhanan Minster*)

First line, sitting from left: Leah Sher, Leah Kitayevitz, Hanah Hokhman*, Minah Khi*, Hanah Elsha*, Minah Plotnik*, teacher Molk, teacher Hayah-Henah Ziv, Dinah Yofe, Ela Zik, Braine Yakh, Elkhanan Minster*

Second line, from left: Motl Gordon, Hanah Molk, Devorah Kaplan*, Hayah Levit, Eta Zinger, Roza Yofe, Devorah Abramson, Velve Yankelovitz, Shneur Zaks, Itse-Motl Sher, Avraham Zaks

Third line, from left: Motl-Berl Shmukler, Leizer Zik, Lipe Sandler*, Mendel Hirzon, Mule Khi, Gute Yofe, Freide Gordon, Freide Rabin, Hinde Zaks, Devorah Yofe, Rachel Shulman*, Yente Shakht*

(*) living in Israel, all others perished in the Holocaust

Fourth class of Salant school 1934-35

Picture supplied by Elkhanan Minster

First line below, from left: Shemuel Khi, Nekhamah Flink, Rachel Levin, Sheine Kitayevitz*

Second line from left: Velvel Leibzon, Yisrael Levin, representative of the Education Ministry, teacher Shereshevsky, teacher?, Ben-Zion Khi

Salant Zionist activists with "Khalutsim" from the local "Kibutz Hakhsharah" 1932-35 *Picture supplied by Leah Sher-Grodnik*

Kneeling from left: Hinde Zaks, Freide Rabin, Freide Gordon, Khalutz ?

Second line standing from left: Hanah Hokhman*, Ela Zik, Feige Zaks, Freide Zaks, Khalutz?, Khalutsa ?, Leah Sher*, Lipe Sandler

Third line: Esther Yofe, Roza Yofe, Dinah Yofe

Young Ladies of Salant 1936

Picture supplied by Leah Sher-Grodnik

From left: Yentel Shakht, Leah Sher, Leah Sher*, Rachel Levy

The Levy family 1930
First line lying from left: Freide Levy, Toibe Sher-Levy, Pesia Levy,
Second line from left: Zuske Levy, Rivkah Levy, Nakhman Levy

Standing from left: Benjamin Khaitovsky, Yonah Markovitz
Kneeling: Etka Rib, Yitskhak?

Picture supplied by Leah Sher-Grodnik

Below is an extract of a letter written by Louis Singer on his impressions visiting Salant in April 1937:

> "I haven't yet told you of the town itself. It consists of a main street about 4 blocks long, 2 parallel streets, one on each side of it at a higher and lower level and 3 intersecting streets. The little river is in the valley below. A very pretty looking village as you approach the valley and river from the east but as you get into the main street, a picture of squalor and ugliness. There are two story buildings stone or wood, all stores in the main block with residences upstairs but all small. Street was quite wide, no sidewalk or paving. No streetlights, no sewers, no running water, no electricity. Women with rakes picking up manure from the streets... Worst of all--believe this or not--women picking up the human manure in the back yards...The gardens and fields are fertilized with this excreta and it can be seen everywhere and smelled. They think nothing of it, it has been the custom of centuries. The bread is as black as a Salant night and looks like the soil from which the flowers grew..."

There was also a presence of religious organizations, such as "Tifereth Bakhurim" for boys and "Beth Ya'akov" for girls. Sports were practiced at the "Maccabi" branch, where on average 58 members participated.

Until the great fire of 1926, the old synagogue, the Beth Midrash and the two "Kloises", served as the center of religious life in Salant.   These buildings were used not only as prayer houses but were actually centers for different groups interested in studying the "Torah".

Among its welfare institutions the town had "Hakhnasath Kalah", "Linath HaTsedek", and a women's society for helping the needy. The Rabbi took care of medical treatment for the poor. He would endorse the visits to the local doctor and would buy medication using the "Korobka" funds (tax money raised through slaughtering).

For the list of Rabbis who were appointed in Salant see Appendix 1

During World War II and Afterward

In June 1940 Lithuania was annexed to the Soviet Union, becoming a Soviet Republic. Following new rules, several shops belonging to the Jews of Salant were nationalized (Davidov, Movshovitz, Florentz), and commissars were appointed to manage them. All Zionist parties and youth organizations were dismissed. Hebrew educational institutions were closed, and the Hebrew school changed into a Yiddish one.

Supply of goods decreased and, as a result, prices soared. The middle class, mostly Jewish, bore most of the brunt, and the standard of living dropped gradually.

The German army entered Salant on the first day of the war with the Soviet Union, on June 22, 1941. That day the Salant Jews who tried to escape to Russia or to hide in Lithuanian villages, were forced to return to their homes, due to a new order forbidding non-Jews to take in Jews. A number of the runaways were killed on the roads. Only a few managed to reach Russia.

The new rulers, helped by the auxiliary Lithuanian police enacted immediately following the events, ordered all Jewish men to exit their houses and sit on the sidewalks with their feet towards the road. The Lithuanian policeman circled around the sitting men and robbed their money and valuables. Then the men were made to run through the streets of the town, and then get up having fallen down while being whipped they were forced to stand and continue running. The Lithuanian public watching along the streets cheered the policemen on their actions. A few days later, at the end of the month, the Lithuanians burnt the books they confiscated from Jewish homes and prayer houses.

On the first of July 1941 all the Jews were ordered to leave their homes and gather in the synagogue with their money and valuables.

The Lithuanian public watching the Jews leave their homes applauded and immediately burst into the abandoned houses looting all that was left.

The Germans placed big baskets at the synagogue and forced the Jews to throw in their money and valuables. Heavy guard of Lithuanian auxiliary police surrounded the building. Every night ten men would be called out and shot following horrible abusive treatment.

At the beginning of July 150 young women were forced out of the synagogue and sent to Shalin (Salynas) farm to work in agriculture. A number of them were sent to work in the fields of Lithuanian peasants. After four weeks of work at the peasants' farms an order was issued to bring the Jews back to the synagogue. On the 12th of September these young women were taken to a field where pits were dug out beforehand. They were all shot and buried. Only one (Bathyah Abelman Yankelevitz) managed to escape and hide at the peasant's she worked before. He hid her till the liberation.

On the 10th of July all the men who were at the synagogue were taken to the river where they were shot and buried in mass graves on the riverbank. Only two, Dr. Yitskhak Perlis and Ze'ev Shindle couldn't take the abuse and committed suicide.

On the 20th of July (25 th of Tamuz 5701) the remaining women and children were skirted to the remote end of the village Shateik (Sateikiai) where they were shot and buried. According to the name list compiled by Salant survivors, 440 Jewish men, women and children were murdered.

Another mass grave was found near the village Shalin, where the 150 young women worked in agriculture.

The Monument on the Mass Grave beside the Jewish Cemetery of Salant. The inscription on the tablet in Yiddish and Lithuanian says: "At this place the Hitlerist murderers and their helpers in 1941 murdered 405 Jews, men, women, children."

Monument on mass grave near Shalin

According to Soviet sources two mass graves were uncovered near Salant: one at the Jewish cemetery where 440 corpses were found, time of murder-July 1941; the second, at the Shateik grove, about 3 km from the village and 8 km from Salant, where 100 corpses of women and children were found, time of murder-July-August 1941.

The Monument on the Mass Grave at Shateik Grove

The inscription on the tablet in Yiddish and Lithuanian says: At this place the Hitlerist murderers and their local helpers in July 1941 murdered 100 Jews Men, women, children.

The wooden totem pole near the Jewish cemetery made by sculptor Bunka with the inscription in Lithuanian: "To the 405 Jews murdered in June 1941 in Salant, in Hebrew - Shema Yisrael."

The monument with the inscription in Lithuanian and Yiddish: "The old Jewish cemetery, sacred is the memory of the dead."

Below are the descriptions of the old Jewish cemetery of Salant by Mr.
Irwin Sagenkahn who visited it in 1993 and 1996:

June 1993

*Following the dirt path that some sort of vehicle had made we continued
through the field for about 100 yards to* **where a fairly new granite monument**
had been erected. And there it was, the old Jewish cemetery at Salantai.

*To our right, a portion of the old cemetery wall remained. There were a
number of monuments, maybe 30 in all, six wide and five deep, standing like
soldiers in formation. Some of the monuments looked like large pieces of
fieldstone with no markings at all. That area was at the top of what might be
described as a rolling hill. As I looked at the meadow beyond, it looked just
like the meadow in the picture I had of my paternal grandfather's monument
(Shemuel Sagenkahn) taken some 70 years earlier.*

*Of the 30 odd monuments erected in this fashion, not more than six had
inscriptions which were halfway legible. I sprayed some shaving cream I had
with me to highlight the inscription on one of the monuments and took a
picture of it. Egle,* **(the Lithuanian guide)** *in the meantime, explored another
area 50 to 100 yards down a slight incline and told us she found more
tombstones. ~ I had given her the picture of my grandfather's stone which had
a wreath at the top. We were all look1ng for a stone with that type of wreath at
the top. We were walking through weeds which were knee high and which had
heavy shrubbery growth. I suspect the orderly arrangement of the tombstones
at the front of the cemetery had been put there within the past few years. I
assume those stones were unearthed in the gully area where we found some
other monuments. These were sort of scattered in a haphazard arrangement. I
am only guessing, but it would appear to me the cemetery was at one time
desecrated and the stones were all thrown in the gully area where Egle had
located some of the monuments. Maybe some of these monuments were then
arranged at the front of .the cemetery for the dedication of the new memorial.*

*Egle had called to us that she had found a stone with the same type of wreath
at the top. Unfortunately, it was not my grandfather's stone. But I sprayed the
shaving cream and took a picture of the highlighted engravers. There were
other scattered monuments in that area, some slightly overgrown with brush
and weeds. That lower section looked exactly like the' location of my
grandfather's gravesite. I took some other pictures of other stones, but most
unreadable. I was disappointed that I was not able to catalogue those stones
that could be read if we had the time to highlight the engravings. Time was
passing by rather quickly and we wanted to talk to somebody who might
remember my father's family. That new memorial at the front of this
overgrown- cemetery had been erected within the past two years. There was
also a* **large totem pole wooden sculpture at least 12 feet high erected in the
cemetery dedicated to the 405 Jewish souls murdered in 1941.**

June 1996

When we arrived at the outskirts of Salant, we had pictures taken by the sign that said 'Salantai'. We decided to visit the Jewish cemetery first since I had remembered its general location. We only had to stop once and ask a woman who was standing at the side of the road. She gave us directions but wanted to know if we were interested in buying her goat.

When we arrived at the cemetery, nothing much had changed in the past three years. The only change was the weed and underbrush growth. Many of the weeds were three feet high or higher. It appeared that some of the tombstones in a gully location were embedded in the ground. I sprayed some shaving cream on two of the stones in an effort to highlight the inscriptions and I took some pictures of these stones.

Avraham Aba ben Betsalel haLevi

Esther-Etl bath Arieh-Leib wife of Avraham-Abali

Died 11 1900

Grunia bath Nathan, died 08 1923

Rachel Heiman bath Yosef, died 01 1897

Sources:

Yad-Vashem Archives: M-33/979; 0-3/1890, 2582, 3548

Gotlib, Ohalei Shem, page 363

HaMeilitz (St. Petersburg) (Hebrew): 5.12.1882, 7.5.1883, 10.8.1883, 27.11.1885, 21.10.1887, 6.6.1888

Dos Vort, Kovno (Yiddish): 23.9.1935

Folksblat, Kovno (Yiddish): 7.8.1935

Unzer Veg (Our way) (Yiddish), Kovno, 2.7.1925

Kovner Tog (Day of Kovno) (Yiddish), 17.6.1926, 18.6.1926

Appendix 1   Partial list of Rabbis who served in Salant

Tsevi Hirsh Broide, for many years he was head of the rabbinical court in Salant. He lived several decades in Jerusalem, where he died in 1865. He used to teach standing up and remained ill with sick legs. He had a great influence upon Rabbi Yisrael Salanter who was his pupil.

Yitskhak Katznelenbogen (1809-1891).

Yehoshua ben Eliyahu Salanter fought against Khasidism together with Leibele Shapiro, Rabbi from Kovno (died in 1853). He was a Rabbi here at the beginning of the 19th century.

Hillel Mileikowski (1819-1899) was the Rabbi in Salant for many years. Reb Hillel was very active in protecting the political interests of Jews in Russia. In 1894, he was a member of the Rabbi's committee, which the Russian Government engaged in handling the status of the Russian Jewry.

Gavriel Fainberg (1825-?), Rabbi in Salant twelve years, died in Memel.

Yosef ben Mosheh Yafe (1846-1897), after Salant from 1893 Rabbi in Manchester (England), where he died.

Meir Altas ben David (1848-1926) was the Yeshiva Head in Telz, in Salant till 1899.

Avraham Aharon Burshtein ben Yehoshua Blumenthal (1867-1926) in Salant from 1900. In the First World War Rabbi in Russia, Rabbi in Bogorodsker Yeshivah and under the Soviets, Rabbi in Cherkas. In 1919 he returned to be a Rabbi in Tavrig. In 1924 he became Rabbi in **Rabbi Cook's**, "Merkaz Harav" Yeshivah in Jerusalem where he died in November 1926.

Mordehai Yitskhak Rabinowitz (1856-1920), 1902-1916 in Salant from 1917, in Memel where he died in June of 1920.

Mosheh-Yonah Viner (?-1941), perished in the Shoah

Meir-Tsevi Klotz (1884-1941) was the last Rabbi, perished in the Shoah.

Almost all Rabbis published books on Torah or Talmud discussions.

Appendix 2

List of membership fee payers in "Agudath Yisrael" 1913

Nakhum Yankelevitz,   Shemuel-David Yoselevitz,   Zalman Melamed,
Yom Tov Lipman-Ziv,   Aba Zilber,   Yitskhak-Leib Yofe,
Nekhemyah Gitkin,   Shemuel Tsiz,   David Davidov,
Bendet Zegerman,   Mosheh Plotnik,   Tuviyah Kangiser,
Yekhezkel-Meir Berman,   Alter Dines,   Shelomoh Vainer,
Duber Zagen (?),   Elkhanan Zagenkhan,   Refael-Tsevi
Nathan-Yakov Berkovitz,   Meir Gerb,   Movshovitz,
Avraham-Mordehai Alsha (?), Zalman Taits,   Shelomoh Kaplan.
Tsevi-Hirsh Grinker,   Mosheh Fritsl,
Yitskhak Patsinke,   Yehudah-Leib Heiman,
Azriel Zaks,   Shaul Movshovitz,

Appendix 5

Partial list of personalities born in Salant

Nakhum Yudelevitz (1862-?), wealthy man and public worker, was the representative of the Odessa committee of "Khibath Zion" movement, delegate to four Zionist congresses (7, 10, 11, 13), since 1921 in Riga and since 1933 in Eretz Yisrael, one of the founders of the glass factory "Gavish", died in Tel Aviv.

Ya'akov Berman (1878-?), studied at the Telz Yeshivah, one of the leaders of the "Mizrakhi" party, delegate to the 12th 13th and 14th Zionist congresses, published articles in the Jewish press. Since 1921 in Eretz-Yisrael, was Deputy Director of the Education Department and Principal Supervisor of the "Mizrakhi" education chain. Director of a Religious-Pedagogic institution in Rekhovoth.

Rabbi Yehudah Asher Ginsburg (1760-1823) was the father of Mordehai Aharon Ginsburg. One of the famous scholars in Vilna and Hebrew writers. He left a manuscript as a composition of grammar and algebra.

Rabbi Yosef Zundel Salanter born in 1786 in Salant, one of the founders of "Muser Shita" (Ethics-on relations between people). Teacher of Yisrael Salanter. Reb Yosef Zundel was a pupil of Rabbi Akiva Eiger and Rabbi Hayim Wolozhiner. Father- in-law of Rabbi Shemuel Salanter. He refused to be in the Rabbinate. Except for a few hours of merchandising, he studied Torah. He wore simple clothes and conducted himself in a most modest way. Many stories were told about his modest behavior. In 1838 Yosef Zundel emigrated to Jerusalem Israel, where he was a teacher for 3 years, then gave his job over to his son-in-law Shemuel Salant. He helped organize groups to rebuild and improve the synagogue "HaKhurvah". He lived in a small dark room, supporting himself by producing vinegar and was satisfied with some fruit juice. He was fasting, studied Torah, and prayed for redemption. Many people came to him daily asking some. He died of cholera in 1865. His son Yehudah Aryeh Leib and his two daughters were all married in Salant and lived there with their families.

Rabbi Mosheh Aronson was born here in 1805. He served for many years in different towns in Lithuania. In 1862, he became Rabbi at "Adath Yeshurun" in New York. He had an argument and fight for everything that is holy.

It became uncomfortable for him to live in New York, so he moved to Jerusalem Israel, but he died on the way. He died in Chicago, July 1875.

Efraim Cohen born 1829. In 1858 graduated from Rabbinate Seminar in Vilna. He was appointed as an inspector for various Jewish problems. He was called by the Russian Government to join the St. Petersburg Rabbis committee.

Rabbi Naftali Amsterdam one of the best pupils of Yosef Zundel Salanter and Yisrael Salanter born here in 1832. In 1867 he became Rabbi in Helsingfors. From 1876 he was the ritual slaughterer, and assistant to Reb Yitzkhak Blazer in Petersburg. Later he was Rabbi in Yasven and Aleksot. Left the Rabbinate and settled in Kovno, and supported himself by his wife's bakery. In 1902 he immigrated to Jerusalem where he was spreading ideas of the Ethics group. Died in Jerusalem in 1916.

Avraham Aryeh Leib, son of Rabbi Yisrael Salanter born in 1839. Head of Beth Din (Rabbinical court) in Brezna.

Elkhanan Kahan was the representative in Petersburg of Yisrael Salanter and Elinke Kretinger to deliver important news about plans the Russian Government has regarding Jews. He died in 1879.

Dr. Lipman Lipkin son of Yisrael Salanter, born here in 1846 graduated from Universities of Yena and Petersburg, famous mathematician. Died in Petersburg in 1876.

Duber Manishewitz, 1858-1914, manufacturer of famous Matzoth in America.

Luis Lurie born in 1887, lived in Boston, from 1917 he was a docent of Psychiatry at the University of Cincinnati, co-worker of the American Journal of Psychology.

William L. Lawrence one of the inventors of the Atomic Bomb, born here in 1888, left Salant in 1905. His name in Salant was Yehudah Leib Wolf Ziv. His father owned a pharmacy in town.

Yisrael Salanter and **Shemuel Salant** were not born from Salant, but it would be unjust not to mention those two geniuses as they carry the name of Salant and have lived there for many years.

Yisrael Salanter (Lipkin) was born in October 1810 in Zhager. He is the creator of "Ethics System", which put a stamp on the religious Jewry in Lithuania and far beyond its borders. After his marriage with Esther Feiga, daughter of Ya'akov Aizenstein, he lived many years in Salant and was one of a group of great scholars there. They studied in the house of a wealthy man who supported everyone with all necessities. In 1849 he built a Yeshivah in Kovno, which became the center of the Ethics movement. A great literature was developed about Yisrael Salanter and about his preaching group, as this was against the centuries long traditional style of teaching in the Yeshivoth.

He published many books dealing with his "Ethics System". Yisrael died in Koenigsberg in 1903.

Rabbi Shemuel Salant is not a born of Salant. He was born in Bialystok. After his marriage to the daughter of Yosef Zundel, he lived for several years in Salant. He was one of the great scholars who lived and studied in the section of town that the wealthy Reb Eliah, son of Nekhemyah gave them. In 1841 he and his wife immigrated to Jerusalem where he was chosen to be Rabbi by the Ashkenazi community. He died in July 1879.

Ber Folkenson born in Salant 1746. Originally he was a merchant in Lithuania and Prussia. Later in 1772 he graduated in Medicine in Berlin and practiced in Mohilev, Petersburg and Hozenput. He started writing songs in German and in 1772 his book of songs "Poems of Polish Jew" was published. He died in 1781.

Mordehai Aharon Ginzburg born in Salant in 1795. Father of the new Hebrew prose. From 1835 lived in Vilna. There with Shelomoh Zalman Zalkin, he established one of the first modern schools for Jewish students. He published many books and articles in Hebrew. He died in 1846.

Shaul Hurvitz, scholar and writer. He was also a lawyer for 15 years. In his book "Maimonides" he discusses Rambams "Laws of loot and loss" that explains which laws match the laws of the Russian code and which laws do not.

Eliezer Shulman (1837-1904), Hebrew writer and translator. Wrote stories in the Hebrew periodicals "HaShakhar", "HaMeilitz" and others. Translated Victor Hugo's famous book "Les Miserables" into Hebrew (Odessa 1867), wrote monographs about Heine and Berne. He was the first one in Hebrew who researched the Yiddish language and its literature. He died in Kiev where he lived for a long time.

Yosef-Hayim Yafe (1865-1938), since 1892 in New York where he worked in turnery, his book "Gezangen" (Songs) in Yiddish was published in New York on his 70 birthday.

Yitskhak Mirkin (1871-1941), since 1913 he lived in Petakh-Tikvah, later in Jerusalem. Teacher of "Talmud", Psychology and Pedagogic at the "Mizrakhi" seminar in Jerusalem. In 1901 graduated in Philosophy from he Bern University. Published songs, articles and books about educational and philosophical problems. Died in Jerusalem.

Appendix 6   Partial List of Salant Emigrants to America 1905-1921 as recorded at Ellis Island

Below are the "Hebrew" listings for Salant on Stephen Morse's Ellis Island web site. Frequently only Russian and not Hebrew, Russian was listed, so those names are not shown below. Hopefully some of the readers will find their family members here. Use the Internet site below to access the ship records.   *Supplied by Elaine Cohen, Los Angeles*

http://home.pacbell.net/spmorse/ellis/ellisjw.html

Name,   town,   year,   age

Abrahams,Ranye Salanti 1905 30y
Berman,Isidor Salanty 1905 19y
Bonk,Aizik Salanty, Russia 1911 40y
Bunish,Hene Salanten, Russia 1907 24y
Colbin,Reiza Salanty, Lithuan 1921 20y
Colbin,Sare Riwe Salanty, Lithuan 1921 24y
Deutscher,Anna Salanten, Russia 1912 29y
Deutscher,Boris Salanten, Russia 1912 34y
Deutscher,Israel Salanten, Russia 1912 3y
Deutscher,Leo Salanten, Russia 1912 3y
Deutscher,Maria Salanten, Russia 1912 7y
Dimant,Meyer Salanten, Russia 1910 22y
Dowgowsky,Chaim Salanten, Rus. 1908 32y
Fishel,Moses Salanten, Russia 1907 18y
Gerb,Gite Salantz 1903 19y
Heer,Gittel Salantai, Lithuania 1921 41y
Heer,Minna Salantai, Lithuania 1921 15y
Heer,Rochel Salantai, Lithuania 1921 13y
Heymann,Herz Salanty 1907 18y
Hurwitz,Judel Salanten, Russia 1910 21y
Jacob,Mina Salante, Russia 1907 47y
Jakab,Mali Salante, Hungary 1909 8y
Jamis,Ebbe Salanton, Russia 1913 20y
Joschelowitz,Tewje Salanten, Rus. 1908 20y
Joselsan,Moische Salant, Russia 1911 18y
Kaganowski,Isler Clometh, Russia 1906 32y
Kahan,Blume Schalanty 1907 17y
Kahan,Mendel Schalanty 1907 39y
Kahn,Feige Saland 1906 32y
Kahn,Jankel Saland 1906 4y
Kahn,Sore Saland 1906 3y
Katz,Blume Salanty, Russia 1911 17y
Kirsch,Chane Saland 1905 45y
Kirsch,Feiwel Saland 1905 15y
Kirsch,Heisch Solonty 1903 20y
Kirsch,Loser Salanty 1904 45y
Klausner,Abel Salant 1905 17y
Klausner,Elke Salant 1905 24y
Kleimann,Boruch Slonita, Russia 1909 7y

Name,   town,   year,   age

Kleimann,Chajes Slonita, Russia 1909 9y
Kleimann,Rochel Slonita, Rus. 1909 30y
Klein,Lina Salante, Hungary 1909 16y
Kolector,Abrum Sielant 1906 9y
Kolector,Beer Sielant 1906 2y
Kolector,Hennie F. Sielant 1906 10y
Kolector,Rose Sielant 1906 30y
Kolector,Taube Sielant 1906 3y
Kolector,Wolf Sielant 1906 4y
Krawitz,Leiver Schalanty, Rus. 1913 32y
Lessem,Moses Salanten, Russia 1910 27y
Lewin,Sure Gitel Salanten 1904 22y
Lewit,Hinde Salanty, Russia 1910 19y
Lewit,Rochel Salanty, Russia 1910 17y
Lipschutz,Hinda Salant, Rus. 1907 65y

Paul,Beige Salanty, Lith. 1921 17y
Paul,Chaje Salanty, Lith. 1921 22y
Paul,Israel Salanty, Lith. 1921 60y
Paul,Sora Salanty, Lith. 1921 55y
Plung,Cjike Salanton, Russia 1913 18y
Plung,Selik Salanty 1907 19y
Pups,Bine Salantin, Russia 1913 22
Rogolsky,Schloma Salanty, Russia 1911 17y
Sagermann,Leiser Salanten 1905 17y
Sandler,Eide Salanty,Kowno, Rus. 1907 25y
Sandler,Scheine Salanty,Kowno,R 1907 50y
Sayal,Nachem Salantz 1899 19y
Schkolny,Pesse Salanty, Kowno 1908 19y
Schkolny,Sroel Salanty, Kowno 1908 22y
Siew,Leibe Salanten 1905 16y
Simpson,Schmul Salante, Russia 1911 21y
Simsohn,Abe Salanten, Russia 1910 20y
Simson,Zusie Salant, Russia 1907 19y
Slowe,Blines Salantin, Russia 1913 9mo
Slowe,Leie Salantin, Russia 1913 27
Slowe,Moritz Salantin, Russia 1913 36
Slowe,Phane Salantin, Russia 1913 2
Taitz,Mendel Salanty, Lithuan. 1921 17y
Takefman, M... Salantz 1904 4...y

Wolpert, Chine Salanten, Russia 1907 18y

Wolpert, Gerson Salanten, Russia 1907 8y

Wolpert,Gnesche Salanten, Russia 1907 9y

Wolpert,Reise Salanten, Russia 1907 45y

Wolpert,Roche Salanten, Russia 1907

Seirijai (Serey)

I am pleased to acknowledge the assistance of Mr. Alan Cooper from Potomac, Maryland USA (descendant of the Vazbutsky family) in providing me with important material on Serey.

Serey, founded in the 16th century near a farm of that name, is located in the south-eastern part of Lithuania, about 25 km south-west of the district administrative capitol Alytus, surrounded by many lakes. Later this farm was owned by the Polish noble family Radzivil, one of whose sons converted to become a Calvinist and thus Serey became the center of Calvinism in Lithuania at the end of the 16th century. At the end of the 17th century Serey received the rights of a town (The Magdeburg Rights) and later on many German artisans settled there.

Until 1795 Serey was part of the Polish-Lithuanian Kingdom, when the third division of Poland by the three superpowers of those times - Russia, Prussia and Austria – resulted in Lithuania becoming partly Russian and partly Prussian. The part of the state which lay on the left side of the Nieman river (Nemunas), including Serey, was handed over to Prussia which ruled there during the years 1795-1807. During these years Serey declined because of its commercial and economic separation from other towns of Lithuania. In 1797 1,094 people residing in 215 houses lived in Serey.

After Napoleon defeated Prussia and according to the Tilzit agreement of July 1807, Polish territories occupied by Prussia were transferred to what became known as the "The Great Dukedom of Warsaw", which was established at that time. The King of Saxony, Friedrich-August, was appointed Duke, and the Napoleonic code now became the constitution of the Dukedom, according to which everybody was equal before the law, except for the Jews who were not granted any civil rights.

During the years 1807-1813, Serey belonged to the "Great Dukedom of Warsaw" and was part of the Bialystok district. The Napoleonic Codex was then introduced in this region, remaining in effect even during the Lithuanian period. In 1808 Serey had a population of 1,100 people.

In 1815, after the defeat of Napoleon, all of Lithuania was annexed to Russia, as a result of which Serey was included in the Augustowa Province (Gubernia), and in 1866 it became a part of the Suwalk Gubernia as a county administrative center. In 1827 there were already about 2,000 inhabitants in Serey and during this period market days and yearly fairs took place and commerce flourished.

During the period of independent Lithuania (1918-1940) Serey was also a county administrative center. The invasion of the German army in June 1941 caused the demolition of almost all the town.

Jewish Settlement until after World War I.

The first Jews settled in Serey apparently at the beginning of the 18th century. They dealt in commerce, agriculture and fishing. Several Jews were owners of large farms (Garbarsky, Vazbutzky, Nun and Ziman), others traded with grains and made a good living. Many families maintained auxiliary farms near their houses, which they used to grow vegetables.

At the end of the 19th century, when a slowdown plagued the economy, many Jews emigrated abroad (England, USA etc.) In a list of Serey Jews who immigrated to America in 1869-70 there are eleven names (see **Appendix 1**).

In 1856 the total population of Serey was 2,138, of them 1,492 Jews. By 1897 there were 2,664 inhabitants in Serey, including 1,614 Jews.

Most of the houses were single family homes, built of wood with roofs of wooden shingles or straw, causing the inhabitants to live in constant fear of destruction by fire. Indeed in 1900 a big fire caused the decline of the local economy for many years. In 1912 a big fire burnt down almost half the town.

Jewish children usually studied in a "Kheder", in a "Talmud-Torah" school and in "Yeshivoth". In 1887, the "Talmud-Torah" under the supervision of the local Rabbi Yekhezkel Volpert, also taught arithmetic and Russian, in addition to the religious subjects. In 1873 professions were taught in the "Talmud-Torah" and 40 children would come after school hours to learn a craft, Yiddish also being a subject which was taught there. These two things were exceptional in Lithuania of those days. The building of the "Talmud-Torah" school erected by the donation of the local philanthropist Markus Meretsky.

During this year a "Kheder Metukan" (Improved Kheder) in a specially purchased building encircled by a garden, was founded. Fifty pupils, in the four rooms of the school under the instruction of four teachers, studied there and were taught, in addition to Bible and "Gemara", also arithmetic and Russian. The teachers were: J.J.Vishaysky, M.M.Ragolsky, Y.Seinensky.

The Old Synagogue

Intellectually gifted youngsters, who did not have the opportunity or the means to get secular books, received various books from the "Society for Spreading Knowledge among the Jews" in Russia. The Hebrew newspaper "HaMeilitz" dated 28.12.1880, published in St. Petersburg, included a letter of gratitude to this society, signed by Asher-Tsevi Rabinson on behalf of the youngsters.

The "Khibath-Zion" movement started its activity in Serey in the 1880s, but by 1810 the name of Shaul son of Shimon from Serey was among the signatories of a letter from the Rabbis from Eretz-Yisrael to their brothers in Lithuania about donations for Eretz-Yisrael, and for Safed (Tsefath) in particular.

In the old cemetery of Jerusalem there is a tombstone of a Serey Jew: Yehudah-Leib son of Meir HaCohen, died in 1884 (5644).

The Rabbi of Serey, Yitskhak Aizik Volpert, participated as a Serey delegate in the regional conference of Russian Zionists which took place in Vilna in 1899. Serey Jews collected money for the settlement of Eretz Yisrael and on the eve of Yom Kippur 5653 (1893) they collected 50 Rubles, a considerable sum in relation to the number of Jews. The money was transferred to the center of "Khovevei Zion" in Odessa.

In lists of donors from Serey for the settlement of Eretz Yisrael, as published in "HaMeilitz" of the years 1884, 1898, 1899 and 1902, the names of hundreds of Serey Jews are mentioned. The treasurers were Rabbi Yekhezkel Volpert, Yom-Tov Lipman Ziv, Dr.Kabaker, Sh.Z.Vazbutsky, Tsevi Simson and the teacher Refael Volpiansky. In the list of 1902 the names of 77 Serey Jews are mentioned (see Appendix 2), and in another list from 1909 the names of 47 Serey Jews appear (see **Appendix 3**).

The Facade of the Synagogue

The Serey synagogue was already built by 1726. It was a wooden building (see picture) of a specific style and in it a beautiful "Aron Kodesh" (Holy Ark) made from mahogany wood with intricate artistic carvings of lions, deer, rams, grapes, "Shofars", "Etrogim", "Lulavim" and cherubs.

In the synagogue daily studies were maintained by the "Khevrah Shas" (Talmudic Society), "Khevrah Mishnah", "Ein Ya'akov" and the "Tehilim Society".

Upper Stamp Left: Belongs to the Klois of the Holy community of Serey
Lower Stamp Left: The Serey branch of the "ORT" Association
Upper Stamp Right: "HaPoel" Serey
Lower Stamp Right: "Ezrah" (Help) Association of Serey

The community possessed "Pinkasim" (Notebooks) from several societies which dealt with studying "Torah", as from the middle of the 19th century.

The "Klois" was the praying house of the artisans and the poor.

All the community institutions were concentrated in the "Shulhoif" (the synagogue yard): The synagogue, the Klois, the bath, the Mikveh, the "Hakhnasath Orkhim" house (established by Markus Meretsky) and a well.

In a list of Jews paying membership fee to "Agudath Yisrael", the names of 34 Serey Jews are mentioned (see **Appendix 4**).

In 1891 the existing welfare societies were reinforced: "Lekhem Aniyim" (bread for the poor); "Hakhnasath Orkhim" (hospitality for passers by); "Malbish Arumim" (care for clothing the poor). In 1896 the "Linath HaTsedek" society, headed by Rabbi R.Y.Volpert, was established. This society sought to cover all expenses of doctors and medicines for the needy.

The Rabbis who served in Serey during this period were:

Hayim Shimshon Vasertsug - known as the Filipover, lived in Serey approx. between 1840-1850, died in 1865; Yosef Elkhanan HaLevi, 1801-1877, in Serey from 1853 till his death; Gershon Rabinson, served from 1876, died in 1908 in Cleveland; Avraham Tsevi Pinkhas Eliashberg, 1863-1943 in Jerusalem, in Serey 1901-1908, emigrated to Eretz Yisrael in 1929; Yekhezkel Volpert ,in Serey 1880-1900, died in 1910.

The "Gaon", Rabbi Eliyahu from Vilna, lived in Serey for one year, during Prussian rule in the house of Yisrael Berliner a rich man and a scholar. Here he completed his book "Adereth Eliyahu" and was friendly with the local "Tsadik" Hayim "Filipover". Possibly the reason the Vilna Gaon spent time in Serey was that his second son Rabbi Yehudah Leib lived there. Yehudah Leib was the son-in-law of a rabbi of Serey, Rabbi Avraham ben Yekhezkel (of Lazdey). Several sons of Yehudah Leib lived in Serey with their families: Rabbi Yosef Yekhezkel Wilner (1788-1849) and Rabbi Tuviyah Yurbarsky (c.1789-1867). The former is buried in Serey and the latter in Jerusalem. Yehudah Leib is not buried in Serey as he died in 1816 whilst traveling through Naishtot (Then Wladislawow).

There was a story in Serey that the street in which Rabbi Eliyahu resided was never touched by fire during his stay there, despite the many fires in the town. David Gordon, the editor of the first Hebrew weekly newspaper "HaMagid", lived in Serey for six years. This weekly was printed in Prussia (1856-1890) near the Russian border, because of problems with the Russian censor.

For the list of the reporters who wrote for the Hebrew periodicals "HaMeilitz", "HaMagid" and "HaTsefirah" see **Appendix 6**.

Before World War 1 about 1,800 Jews lived in Serey. During the war, on the first of April 1915, the Russians exiled them to Russia.

The Period of Independent Lithuania (1918-1940).

After the war ended half of the exiled Jews returned home to Serey. In accordance with the autonomy law regarding minorities, issued by the new Lithuanian Government, a Community Committee was elected at the beginning of the 1920s. 263 persons voted in the Committee elections in the autumn of 1923, and a Committee of 12 members was elected, headed by Dr.L.Finkel. The Committee was active till the end of 1925 when the autonomy was annulled. During its existence the Committee collected taxes as required by law and was in charge of all aspects of Community life. In 1922, for example, it imposed taxes on 133 people, which were divided into six categories. Fifty eight percent of the income was collected from the first two categories who comprised only 25% of all the assessed.

The budget for the six months 1.6.1922-31.12.1922 was 177,800 Lit (Litas) and was divided up into to the following paragraphs:

46.0% for the Rabbi and the Shohet (Slaughterer). This money did not come from the taxes collected by the Committee.

6.7% for the Committee secretary,

17.0% as a subsidy for the doctor,

17.0% for social assistance,

3.0% for the library,

0.6% for rent and maintenance of the office,

0.6% for the Shamash (janitor),

2.4% as a 10% tax for the "Nationalrat" (The National Committee of Jews in Lithuania),

6.7% unforeseen expenses.

The successor of the Committee was the "Ezrah" Society which took over almost all the functions of the Committee. In Lithuanian it says: Serey Jewish welfare, social help and culture society "Ezrah."

Four Jews were elected to the municipal council in 1924.

Serey Jews made their living from commerce, crafts, light industry, agriculture and fishing. There were also peddlers who earned their living by going to villages in the vicinity, selling, buying and bartering on the spot.

According to the 1931 government survey of shops, Serey had 30 shops, 29 of them owned by Jews (97%).

The breakdown according to the type of business is given in the table below:

Type of the business	Total	Owned by Jews
Groceries	2	2
Grains	3	3
Butcher's shops and Cattle Trade	2	2
Restaurants and Taverns	4	4
Food Products	1	1
Beverages	1	1
Textile Products and Furs	6	6
Leather and Shoes	4	4
Medicine and Cosmetics	1	0
Radio, Bicycles and Electric Equipment	1	1
Tools and Steel Products	4	4
Miscellaneous	1	1

According to the same survey Serey had 19 light industry factories, 11 of them owned by Jews (58%), as can be seen in the following table:

Type of the Factory	Total	Owned by Jews
Metal Workshops, Power Plants	3	2
Headstones, Bricks	1	0
Chemical Industry: Spirits, Soaps	2	1
Textile: Wool, Flax, Knitting	2	2
Sawmills, Furniture	2	0
Food industry	5	3
Dresses, Footwear	2	2
Leather Industry: Production, Cobbling	1	1
Others	1	0

The Tzviling family owned a flour mill, a power station and a metal workshop.

Yitzhak-Hirsh Slavatitzky owned a light drinks and beer factory, Moshe Finkel owned the only hostel in town and also a big spinnery.

Jewish shops were concentrated around the market square and their main income was on market days, which took place twice a week, on Tuesdays and Fridays, and at the 16 yearly fairs. Some shops were close to the Catholic Church and as a result of pressure by the priests most of them were destroyed, the pretext being that in a few years the square would become a public park for the benefit of all. By 1936 only two Jewish shops were still left in the square.

Several Jewish families earned their living from fishing in the Nieman river and in the nearby lakes. In 1937 Serey counted 70 Jewish artisans: 20 shoemakers, 9 butchers, 7 tailors, 6 bakers, 4 oven builders, 4 blacksmiths, 3 hatters, 3 stitchers, 2 glaziers, 3 barbers, 2 locksmiths, 2 watchmakers, 1 knitter, 1 dressmaker, 1 leatherworker, 1 cord maker and 1 photographer.

The Boarding House of M. Finkel

Picture supplied by Alan Cooper

The "Folksbank" played an important role in the economic life of Serey Jews, and had 176 members in 1927. There was also an active branch of "The United Society for Credit for Jewish Agrarians" in town. In 1939 Serey had 30 telephone subscribers, half of them Jews.

As a result of the agrarian reform carried out by the Government, most of the Serey Jewish lands were taken away from their owners, causing many Jews to abandon their participation in agriculture. The "Lithuanian Merchants Association - Verslas" established consumer coops and ran a strong propaganda campaign against buying in Jewish shops. The result was a deterioration of the economic situation of Serey Jews, many left the town emigrating abroad, mostly to America, Mexico and South Africa. Among the youth many immigrated to Eretz Yisrael.

In order to consider the establishment of a school for Jewish children the Committee carried out a survey of children aged 7-14 in 1923:

Age	7:	14 children	Age	11:	19	children
Age	8:	25 children	Age	12:	32	children
Age	9:	21 children	Age	13:	18	children
Age	10:	26 children	Age	14:	10	children

Altogether there were 165 children eligible for an elementary school.

Based on this survey a Hebrew school of the "Tarbuth" chain was established in Serey.

Parts of the governmental Survey of Shops in Alytus District in 1931

Restaurants

ALYTAUS APSKR.
Chasanavičienė R., Alytus,, Juozapavičiaus g.
Janulevičius, Alytus.
Kovalskienė B., Nemaniūnai.
Mankevičius J., Jeznas, Rinkos a.
Rozas I., Seirijai.
Stauskaitė J. ,Birštonas.
Svedkauskas K., Miroslavas.
Sulcaitė P., Seirijai, Skalos g. 21.

Leather Factories

ALYTAUS APSKR.
Abramavičius I., Alytus, Juozapaičio g. 21.
Garbarskis Irsas, Seirijai.
Koževnikas Aizikas, Merkinė.

Iron and Iron Products

ALYTAUS APSKR.
Aminodovas E., Seirijai.
Černevičienė Ch., Alytus.
Černevičius S., Alytus, Turgaus gt.
Farbšteinas Smuelis, Seirijai.
Gardonas Leiba, Butrimonys.
Glazmanienė S., Alytus, Vilniaus gt. 21.
Maršakas Mordchelis, Simnas, Didžioji g.
Levinas N., Alytus.
Liubelskienė Rochė, Butrimonys.
Poliakas Samuelis, Seirijai.
Ptašnikas Sepšelis, Butrimonys.
Prusakienė Kunė, Seirijai.
Putianskienė Rachilė, Butrimonys.
Rubinas Saleas, Daugai.
Ščerbakovas Mordchelis, Simnas.
Verbalskis Simelis, Simnas, Didžioji g. 30 Nr.
Zilbermanas Mauka, Daugai.
Židikaneris Samuelis, Alytus.

Banks (Folksbank Branches)

ALYTAUS APSKR.
Lietuvos Banko Skyrius, Alytus.
Alytaus Ūkininkų Smulk. Kred. D-ja.
Alytaus Taupm. ir Kredito D-ja.
Alytaus Žydų Liaudies Bankas.
Antnemunio Lenkų Smulk. Kred. D-ja.
Butrimonių Žydų Liaudies Bankas.
Daugų Žydų Liaudies Bankas.
Jezno Smulkaus Kred. D-ja.
Metelių Smulkaus Kred. D-ja.
Merkinės Smulk. Kred. D-ja.
Merkinės Žydų Liaudies Bankas.
Miroslavo Valsč. Taupm. Skolin. Kasa.
Pivašiūnų Lenkų Smulk. Kred. D-ja.
Seirijų Žydų Liaudies Bankas.

Sewing Workshop

ALYTAUS APSKR.
Cirelšteinas Joselis, Merkinė.
Kupčiūnas Juozas, Alytus, Stoties g. 12.

Transportation Means

ALYTAUS APSKR.
Kameneckis Josifas, Simnas.
Redakas Abromas, Merkinė, Bingelių g. 26.

Cosmetics

ALYTAUS APSKR.
Cofnasas Iliošas, Butrimonys.
Finienė Feiga, Butrimonys.
Jodvirkis Jonas, Butrimonys.
Kapancedekas Isakas, Alytus, Vilniaus. 13.
Sarachanas Michelis, Alytus, Vilniaus g. 26.

It was located in a three storey house built for that purpose. This building also housed a library with several hundred Hebrew and Yiddish books as well as a reading room where available newspapers were located.

The gymnastic hall of "Maccabi" was also in this building, and the activities of the school were supervised by a parents council.

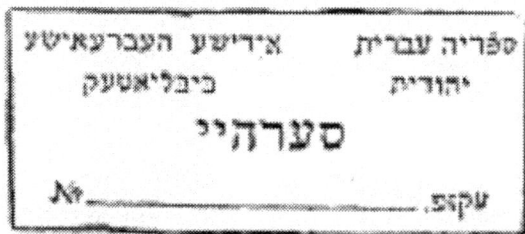

Stamp of the Hebrew and Yiddish Library

There was a "Talmud-Torah" and a government school for carpentry, but only one Jewish boy studied there (in 1936).

Almost all the Zionist parties had adherents in Serey, as can be seen from the results of elections to Zionist Congresses in the table below:

Congr. Nr.	Year	Total Shekalim	Total Voter	Labor Party		Rev.	G. Z.		Gr.	Miz.
				Z"S	Z"Z		A	B		
14	1925	73	---	--	---	--	--	--	--	--
15	1927	61	44	14	4	10	16	--	--	--
16	1929	145	82	30	13	20	19	--	--	--
17	1931	154	154	74	25	43	8	--	--	4
18	1933	---	261	170		75	12	--	1	3
19	1935	---	318	230		--	5	9	47	27

Rev.-Revisionists; G.Z.-General Zionists; Gr.-Grosmanists; Miz-Mizrahi

In addition to the Zionist parties, a branch of "WIZO" (Women International Zionist Organization) with about 50 members was active in town. Also Zionist youth organizations, such as "Gordonia" with about 60-70 members, "HaShomer-HaTsair" and "Betar". The activists of the "Gordonia" branch were: Yekhezkel Berent, Asher Berent, Betsalel Aminadav, Ze'ev Shalkovsky.

Sports activities took place in the branch of "Maccabi" with about 50 members and in the "HaPoel" branch.

Donations for the Jewish National Fund – KKL - were regularly collected and most of the Jewish houses had the KKL Blue Box.

In the 1920s a "Kibbutz Hakhshara" was established on the farm of Nun-Ziman.

In 1934 an "Urban Training Kibbutz" of "HeKhalutz" existed, and there was a Volunteer Fire Brigade, all of whose members were Jewish.

Religious life was concentrated around the old synagogue and the "Klois". The Rabbis who served were Yisrael Goldin (1874-?) in Serey 1909-1924, Eliezer Shchupak, 1877-1939, in Serey 1930-1939, and the last Rabbi was A.Karno.

The welfare societies consisted of "Ezrah", "Bikur-Kholim", "Linath HaTsedek" and others. There was also a "Khevrah Kadisha".

For the partial list of personalities born in Serey see **Appendix 5**.

The Jewish cemetery as photographed by Hana Rosen in August 1998

Picture supplied by Alan Cooper

During World War II and thereafter

World War II started with the German invasion of Poland on September 1, 1939, and its consequences for Lithuanian Jews in general, and Serey's Jews in particular, were felt several months later.

In agreement with the Ribbentrop-Molotov treaty on the division of occupied Poland, the Russians occupied the Suvalk region, but after delineation of exact borders between Russia and Germany the Suvalk region fell into German hands. The retreating Russians allowed anyone who wanted to join them to move into their occupied territory, and indeed many young people left the area together with the Russians. The Germans drove the remaining Jews out of their homes in Suvalk and its vicinity, robbed them of their possessions, then directed them to the Lithuanian border, where they were left in dire poverty.

**The monument at the entrance with the inscription in Yiddish:
"The old Serey cemetery, sacred is the memory of the dead"**

Picture supplied by Alan Cooper

An old tombstone at the cemetery

Picture supplied by Khana Rats-Rabinovitz

**The tombstone of Etil Finkel, daughter of Avraham Ipp, died in
1806**

Picture supplied by Hana Rats-Rabinovitz

The Lithuanians did not allow them to enter Lithuania and the Germans did not allow them to return. Thus they stayed in this swampy area in cold and rain for several weeks, until Jewish youths from the border villages smuggled them into Lithuania by various routes, with much risk to themselves. Altogether about 2,400 refugees passed through the border or infiltrated on their own, and were then dispersed in the "Suvalkija" region. Serey was obliged to absorb 50 refugees.

In June 1940 Lithuania was annexed to the Soviet Union and became a Soviet Republic. Following new rules, several factories and shops belonging to the Jews of Serey were nationalized and commissars were appointed to manage them. All the Zionist parties and youth organizations were disbanded, several of the activists were detained and Hebrew educational institutions were closed.

Supply of goods decreased and, as a result, prices soared. The middle class, mostly Jewish, bore most of the brunt, and the standard of living dropped gradually. At the beginning of June, one Jewish family - four persons of the Tsviling family - whose enterprises were nationalized, were exiled deep into Russia.

On the 24th of June, two days after the beginning of the German invasion, the German army, after heavy bombing, entered Serey, where a large part of the town, mostly Jewish homes, had been destroyed. The victims found shelter on the farm of Yosef Garbarsky, about one kilometer from the town .

The Lithuanians immediately started to persecute and abuse the Jews, and of them, mostly youngsters, were detained as communist suspects, and shot. There was the local physician Dr. Hershl Garbarsky, who was very popular in the town and its vicinity especially among the Lithuanian peasants, for curing the poor and charging no fee, and in addition giving them money to buy the medicines. Lithuanian youngsters called him to a patient, and on his way there they murdered him, throwing his body into the garden near his house. Serey Jews went to his funeral crying and with ominous foreboding regarding the future.

Several days later the Lithuanians detained a large number of Jewish youngsters, leading them in the direction of Alytus for so-called work and murdered them on the way. Zelig Ratchkovsky, a middle aged man, was ordered, together with several Lithuanians, to transport these people on his cart, but he never returned home. The murderers, apparently, did not want him to tell what had happened to his "travelers".

Serey Jews had to perform various types of forced labor, such as repairing roads etc. Every morning they were taken to work, returning home in the evening. They did not suffer from a shortage of food. Rumors about the "good" situation in Serey reached Serey Jews in Kovno by way of a Lithuanian, as a result of which many Jews left their flats there and returned home, after paying much money to Lithuanians who agreed to take them back on horse carts, because this was the only means of transportation allowed for Jews.

The annihilation of Serey Jews apparently took place on the 18th of Elul 5601 (September 10, 1941). All the men were led to the Abreisk grove (Barauciskes) about 3 km south-east from Serey, one km from the road to Leipun (Leipalingis) and there they were shot and buried in pits they had dug themselves as "channels". On the next day the women and children were brought to the same place and were shot. All the Lithuanian dignitaries of Serey, such as the cultured population and the teachers, were present during the murder executed by their own folk.

229 men, 384 women and 340 children, altogether 953 people, are buried in the mass graves.

After the war the few survivors erected a monument on the graves, and in the 1990s the inscription on the monument was replaced by a new one (see photo on next page).

In **Appendix 7** is presented the map of Serey and the list of the Jews in town in 1941.

The Barauciskes grove with the mass graves

The monument on the mass graves

The inscription on the monument in Yiddish and Lithuanian:

"Here was spilled the blood of 953 Jews-children, women, men- who were brutally murdered by the Nazi murderers and their helpers on September 11, 1941."

Appendix 1 (*Hebrew "Het" like "Hanuka" is transliterated as kh*)

Serey Jews who emigrated to America in 1869-70

E.Bergman   R.Levin
A.Bitskovsky   A.Losdoisky
L.Brudzinsky   S.Savsberg
L.Dushvitsky   S.Shalme
A.Katz   G.Trotsky
A.Krepky

Appendix 2

List of donors for the Settlement of Eretz-Yisrael in 1902 as published in "HaMelitz"

Berent Shevakh   Eishovitz Mosheh-Yehudah
Bialostotzky Yehudah-Leib   Epshtein Yonah
Broide Yisrael   Finkel Eliezer-Ze'ev
Bunishky Hayim   Frank Eliezer
Khazan Tsevi   Frank Mosheh
Dolkovsky Eliezer   Garbarsky Eliezer
Eilevitz Aryeh-Leib   Garbarsky Yosef
Eilevitz Nakhum-Meir   Garbovsky Tsevi

Goldberg Ya'akov
Golub Menakhem-Mendel
Gutman Zundl
Gutshtein Aryeh-Leib
Heiman Iser
Horvitz Dov-Ber
Kabaker Yekhezkel
Kabaker Yosef
Kopelman Aryeh-Leib
Lipsky Shemuel-Pesakh
Man Mosheh
Margalioth Yehudah-Leib
Meretzky Eliezer
Meretzky Alter
Miler Ozer
Mishkotz Leib
Mitnik Shemuel
Mordokhovitz Avraham-Yitskhak
Nun Mordehai ben Avraham
Nun Mordehai ben Yehoshua
Nun Avraham
Pinkhovsky Aryeh-Leib
Plotzitzky Aryeh-Leib
Prusak Eliezer
Rabinovitz Mosheh
Rabinovitz Shimon
Ragolsky Meir-Mordehai
Ratchkovsky Yitskhak
Rogovsky Hayim
Rotenberg Yitskhak
Rotzon Shelomoh

Kash Aryeh-Leib
Kalmansky Reuven
Keili Tsvi
Kempnitzky Avraham
Kabaker Hilel
Kabaker Mordehai
Rozenberg Aryeh-Leib
Rozenberg Dov-Ber
Rozental Shemuel-Eliezer
Sandler Alter
Shalkovsky Avraham-Yitskhak
Shalkovsky Shelomoh
Shalkovsky Shemuel-Mosheh
Shmidt Mordehai
Shmidt Yehoshua
Shmidt Yitskhak
Sider Yisrael
Slavatitzky Aba
Slavatitzky Elkhanan
Slavatitzky Yisakhar
Solnitzky Mosheh
Strazh Zelig
Surison Tsevi-Aryeh
Tsirinsky Aryeh-Leib
Tsviling Dov-Ber
Veiser Shemuel
Volpiansky Rafael
Vazbutsky Shelomoh-Zalman
Zef Avraham
Zuskin Tsevi

Appendix 3

List of donors for the Settlement of Eretz-Yisrael in 1909 (47 names) as published in "HaMelitz"

Aronson Benjamin Meir
Bialostotsky Yehudah Leib
Brodov Aryeh Dov
Fagir Noakh
Finkel Eliezer Ze'ev
Frenkel Yosef David
Garbarsky Yosef
Garbarsky Tsevi
Garbarsky Yerukham
Heiman Iser

Hurvitz Ya'akov
Ivri Shelomoh
Iran Alter
Kalmansky Azriel Yitskhak
Kash (?)Aryeh
Kleinzon Hilel
Kopelman Aryeh
Krinsky Mosheh
Kursniansky Avraham
Dr. Linsky Ya'akov

8

448 Serey

Lipsky Shemuel Pinkhas
Miler Menukhah
Nun Mordehai
Pinkovsky Aryeh Leib
Prusak Eliezer
Prusak Yisrael Aharon
Prusak Hayim Yehudah
Ragolsky Meir Mordehai
Ragovsky Hayim
Ratsan Shelomoh
Ratchkovsky Ya'akov
Ratchkovsky Yitskhak
Rozentsveig Yehudah
Rozenberg David

Selsky Aharon
Senevitz Eliezer David
Shalkovsky Shemuel Mosheh
Shalkovsky Dov
Shalkovsky Tsevi
Shmidt Yitskhak
Simson Tsevi Aryeh
Tsviling Dov
Vazbutsky Zalman
Vazbutsky David
Zef Avraham
Zif Eliezer
Ziskin Tsevi

Appendix 4
List of Payers of yearly Membership Fees for "Agudath-Yisrael"

Rabbi Yisrael Goldin
Avraham Zef
Aryeh-Leib Pinkovsky
Aryeh-Leib Avner
Eliezer Meretsky
Aharon Bernet
Eliezer Ritz
Aba Yablonsky
Gershon Heiman
Dov Tsviling
Dov Slavatitsky
Dov-Aharon Brodov
Dov Shklarovsky
Henie Ratz
Ze'ev Shklarovsky
Hayim-Yosef Dunishky
Hayim Shulzinger

Khava Vazbutsky
Yekhezkel Kabaker
Yekhezkel Aminadav
Mordehai Brodovsky
Mordehai Kagan
Menakhem-Mendel "Shatz" and
"Shub" (Khazan and Shokhet)
Yehudah-Leib Kriger
Yisrael Sider
Mosheh Shvartsbord
Mosheh Bogdansky
Etel Ragolsky
Pinkhas-Zelig Strazh
Shemuel Fordshtein
Shabtai Srolovitz
Shelomoh Slavatitsky
Shimon and Tanhum Abelsky.

Appendix 5

Partial List of Personalities born in Serei

Eliezer-Yitskhak Shapira (1835-1915) writer and Hebrew translator, published stories and articles in the Hebrew press.

Paul T. Goodwin (Pesakh Gudansky) (1885-?) from 1907 in the USA, published stories and poems in the Yiddish press:" Freie Arbeiter Shtime" and "Forverts".

Yehoshua Ziman (1898-?) economist, from 1924 in Eretz-Yisrael, published many books in Hebrew on the economy and the settlement of the land.

Henakh (Genrik) Ziman (1910-1987), a son of farm owners, teacher at the Yiddish "Shalom Aleikhem" High School in Kovno and in 1940/41 its headmaster, member of the underground communist party from 1932, escaped to the USSR at the beginning of World War II and was parachuted into the woods of Belarus, organized the Lithuanian Partisan Brigade in the Rudniky woods in 1943 becoming its commander. He was appointed as the editor of the communist newspaper "Tiesa" (Truth) after the liberation of Lithuania and was a strong opponent of Zionism throughout his life.

The Brothers Tankhum, Tsevi and Eliezer Rozentsvaig, educators and Zionist activists.

Rachel Rozentsvaig-Levin (daughter of Eliezer), founder and director of the archives of the "Association of Lithuanian Jews in Israel".

Appendix 6

The Reporters from Serey in the Hebrew periodicals "HaMelitz", "HaTsefirah" and "HaMagid":

> David Robinzon,
>
> Hayim-Yehudah Gazansky,
>
> Aharon-David Meltser,
>
> Eliezer-Yitskhak Shapira,
>
> Y.Weisbrem,
>
> Meir Hurvitz,
>
> Alexander Maimon,
>
> Y.Kalmansky,
>
> Mordehai-Ozer Simansky,
>
> Hayim-Yehudah
>
> HaCohen,
>
> Y,Broido.

Appendix 7 (compiled by Ya'akov Lifshitz)

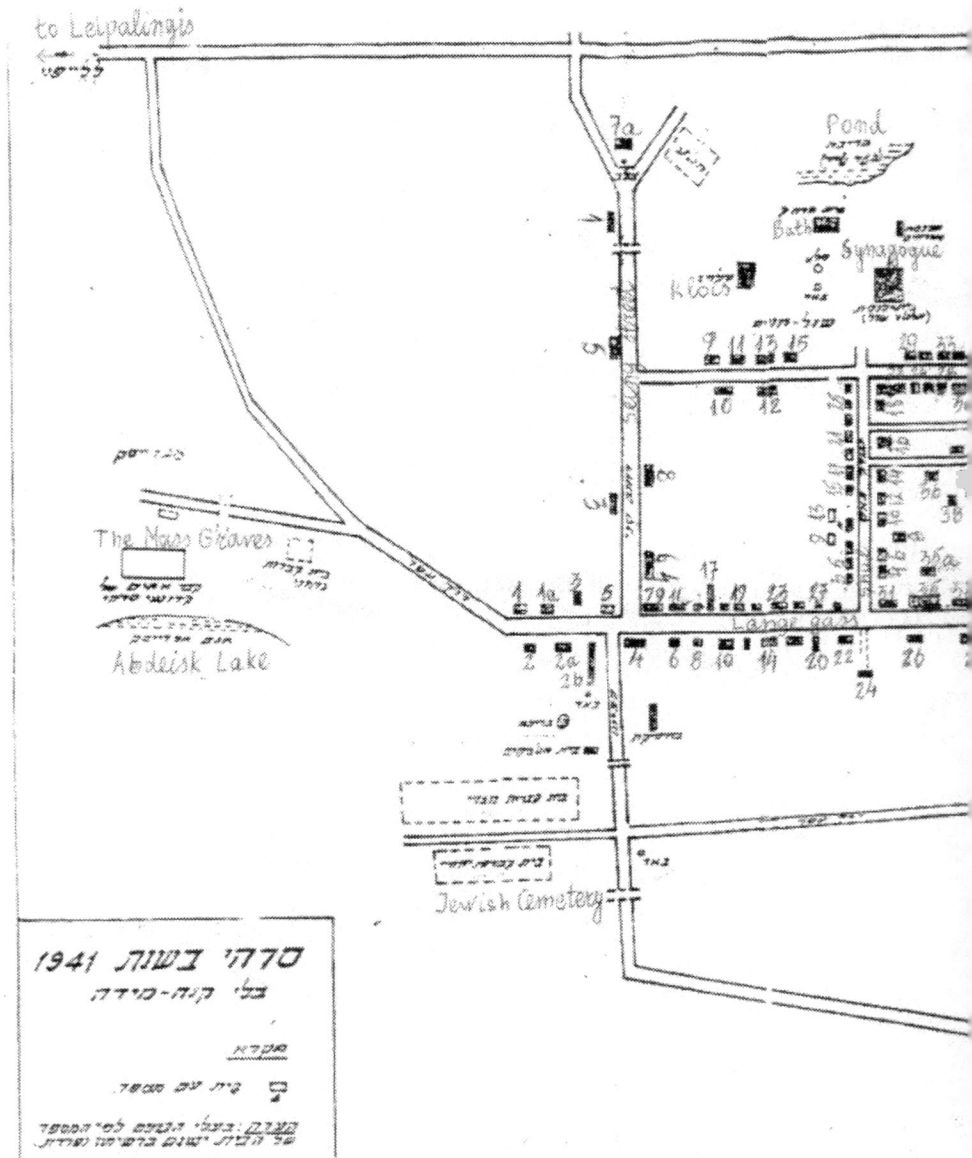

List of Serey Jewish house owners who perished in the Holocaust according to the street in which they lived. The numbers of the list are identical to the numbers of the houses. (see Map)

Serey in 1941
(without scale)

house with its number

Compiled by Ya'akov Lifshitz

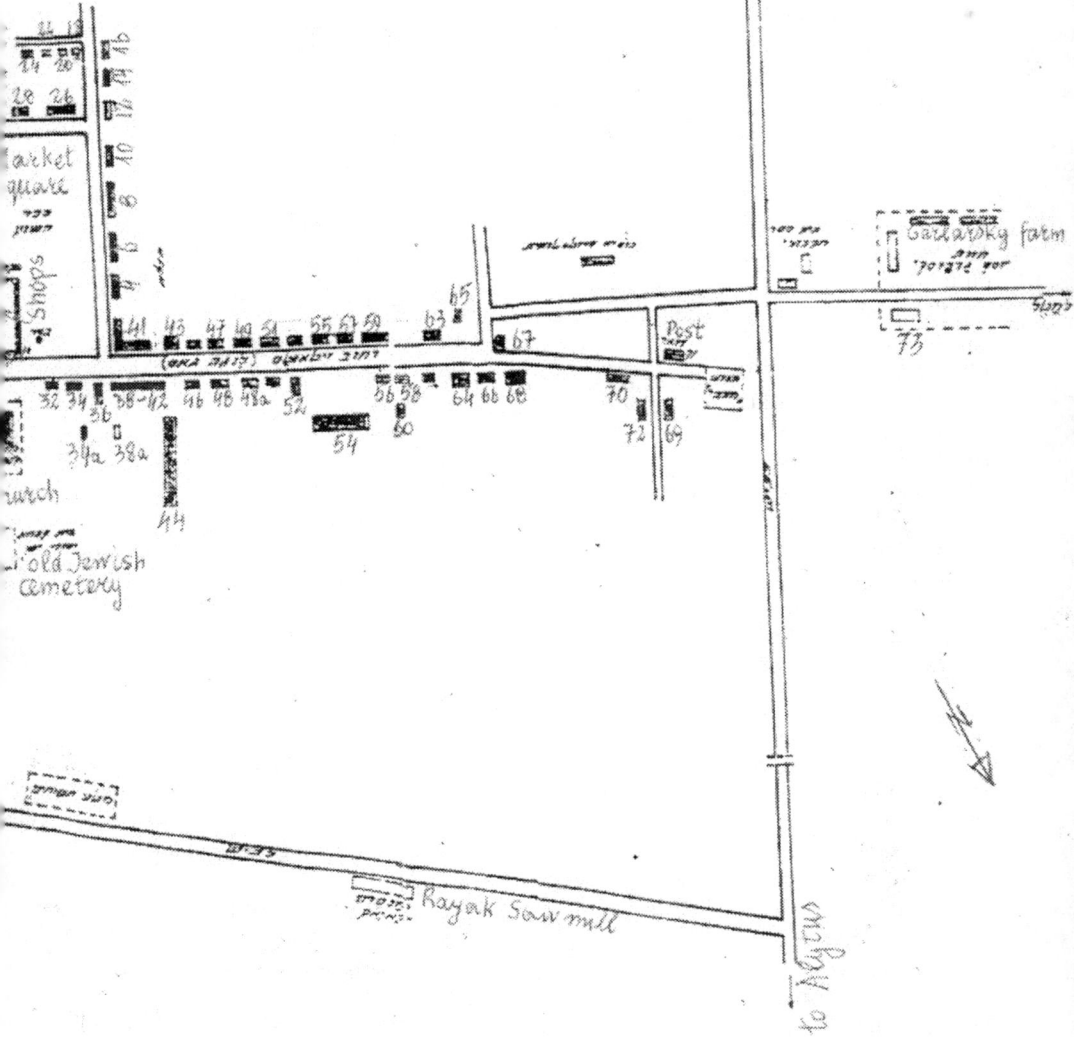

Market Square

Shops

old Jewish Cemetery

Post

Sadaysky farm

Rayak Saw mill

to Aytus

Map supplied by Alan Cooper

Vytauto Street -Di Lange Gass

1. Ya'akov Rats
1a. Zelig Rits
2. Yankel Aron Rubensky
2a. Shemuel Farbshtein
2b. Iron storehouse
3. Leib Kravtsel
4. Yitskhak Tsevi Slavatitsky
his wife Rivkah nee Shulzinger
Basha Slavatitsky
5. Mosheh Levkuts
6. Mosheh Niemchinsky
7. Aharon Eliyahu Zolotovitz
8. Yosef Shklarovsky
9. Gershon Zolotovitz
10. Police
11. Meir Kravtsel
12. Mosheh Leib Radzhunsky (stone building)
Yehoshua Zavatsky
13. --- Gutman
14. Shmuel Rabinovitz
Mosheh Rabinovitz
15. Leib Katsan
16. Yisrael Rudnitsky
17. Yosl Osotstsky (baker)
17a. ---- Khmilevsky (teacher)
18. Yitskhak Rats
19. Shakhne Numeretsky
20. Mordehai Kagan
21. Henia Borovsky (spinster)
Beile Haya Shneider
Yitskhak Kvatkovsky
22. Zundl Vazbutsky
Berl Aronovsky (watchmaker)
23. a family from Kopcheve (former Shulzinger house)
Avraham Pitluk (watchmaker)
24. Rabbi Shchupak
Leizer Aronovsky
25. ---- Gerzon
26. Dvoshe Levin
Nakhum Bogdansky (baker)
27. Leib Shmulkovsky (hatter)
28. Frumah Vazbutsky
Yosef Pinkovsky
29. Gitele Shmulkovsky
30. Catholic church
31. Yerukham Garbarsky
32. Eizer Pinkovsky (two storey brick building)
33. Efraim Streletsky
34. Yeshayahu Lipsky
34a. Hayim Leizer Mordovitsky
35. Berta Finkel (two storey house)
35a. Light drinks and beer factory of Finkel and Slavatitsky
36. David Kovalsky (stone house)
37. Berl Shklarovsky
38. Alter Iran
38a. Yehudah Leib Kriger
39. Libe Kupershmid (stone house)
Shemuel Yenkl Ziskin
Hayim Leib Balbirishky
40. Kune Prusak
41. Eli Aminodov (stone house)
42. Yisrael Aharon Tsviling
43. Yosef Aminodov (two storey brick house)
44. Agricultural machines factory, flour mill and power station (owner Tsviling)
45. Hayim Mende Keili
46. Ya'akov Rachkovsky
Mosheh Rachkovsky
47. Rivkah Prusak
48. Khanah Fridkovsky (brick house)
48a. David Liakht
49. Shemuel Mosheh Shalkovsky
50. Perets Shimkhovsky
51. Asher Borovsky (cord maker)
52. Nakhum Pekarsky
53. ----- Katsan
54. School, Bank, Youth Clubs (two storey house)
55. ----- Gutshtein
56. Zekharyahu Dombelsky (stone house)
57. Itse the blacksmith
58. Yehudah Rozentsvaig
59. Asher Lutsner (brick house)
60. Yisrael Yeglinovitz
---- Potkovitsky (metal worker)
61. Meir Gurvitz
61a. ----- Zalkind (electrician)
62. Ya'akov Kahanovitz (shokhet and khazan)
Shemuel Kotz
Mosheh Bordovsky

63. Barukh Shelomoh Zemiansky
64. Yudl Sandler   (two storey brick house)
    Aharon Prusak
    Magistrate Court
65. Hayim Kriger
66. Ya'akov Sandler
66a. Leib Sandler
67. Nakhum Lapides
68. Shemuel Pinkhas Lipsky   (two storey stone house)
    Spinnery   (owners: Finkel, Slavatitsky, Lipsky)
69. Zelig Miler
70. Hirshl Shalkovsky
    Iser Kravtsel
71. Post office   (stone house)
72. Efraim Kachinsky
73. Yosef Garbarsky
    Dr.Hershl Garbarsky

The Market Square

3. Yudes Zavilevitz
3a. Betsalel Aminodov
4. Shemuel Kalko
5. Sarah Pasernitsky
6. Pesakh Khazan
7. Zelig Rachkovsky
    Meir Ivashkovsky
8. Dr. Leon Finkel
    ---- Ivashkovsky
    Mikhael Hekht
9. Alter Zimlitsky (stone house)
10. Yekhezkel Aminodov
11. Iser Zemiansky
12. Volf Nun
    Rashel Hekht (two storey house)
    Shemuel Goldshmid   (bookkeeper)
    Tsevi Keili
14. ----- Galenty
15. Aharon Berent
16. Azriel   (shoemaker)
17. Shiki Man
18. Nisan   (shoemaker)
19. Pesakh Berent
20. Alter Nervid
21. ---- Palunsky
22. ---- Kolvitsky ??
23. Shemuel Lazevnik
24. ---- Pasernitsky
25. Gedalyahu Mutsiner
26. Not known   (stone house, pharmacy)
27. ----- Liakht
30. Yehudah Leib Bialostotsky (stone house)
32. Mosheh Bogdansky
34. Shaul Rozenberg   (stone house)

Seiny Street

3. Berish Shalkovsky
4. Yosl Kupershmid
5. ----- Krinsky   (black smith)
6. Mosheh Kupershmid
7. Leib Fridkovsky
7a. a family from Meteliai
8. Asher Yershansky
9. ----- Margovitsky
10. Ya'akov Goltz
11. Yenkl Eliyah Kriger
12. Ze'ev Keily
13. ----- Lazevnik
14. ----- Katsinsky

Shul Gass (Synagogue Street)

3. Motl Man
4. Shimon Idelson
4a. Hershl Valtsenboim
5. Henia Shankovsky
6. Itse Leib Aronovsky
7. Leib Keler
8. ---- Gensher
9. Reizl Miler
10. Shimon Rats
11. Ya'akov Miler
12. ---- Kvitkovsky
13. Zelig Miler
14. Shemuel Galinovitz
15. Shimon Pesakhnitsky

16. Avraham Rats
17. Hilel Ostrovsky
18. Yekutiel Kriger (glazier)
19. Alter Man
20. ----- Kvitkovsky
21. Shimon Vazbutsky
22. Mosheh Finkelshtein
23. Iser Rats
24. Hayim Prodovsky
25. Yehudah Miler
26. Yehudah Berent
27. Alter Rumesh
28. Motl Kravtsel

29. Reuven Buk   (bath attendant)
30. Hayim -----   (carpenter)
31. Shepsl Isrolovitz   (baker)
32. Mordehai Blodovsky
33. ----- Bogdansky
34. Yitskhak Sider
35. ---Zherebkovsky
36. Motl Kravtsel
37. Nakhum Rubinsky
38. --------------------- (carpenter)
39. ----- Shvartsbord
40. ----- Brodovsky

Shops at the Market Square

1. Zemlitsky
2. Gurevitz
3. Osotsky
4. Rayak
5. Fire Brigade
6. Berent
7. Gutshtein

8. Rachkovsky
9. ---------------
10. Paliak
11. Bordovsky
12. Purnitsky

Bibliography.

Yad-Vashem Archives: M-1/Q-1333/142; M-33/994

Koniukhovsky Collection 0-71, Files 131.

YIVO, NY, Collection of the Jewish Communities in Lithuania, Files 153, 685-699, 1669.

Morris S. Schulzinger, The Tale of A Litvak. Philosophical Library, New York 1883

HaMeilitz (St. Petersburg) (Hebrew): 10.8.1880; 19.10.1880; 2.11.1880; 28.12.1880; 1.11.1881; 7.8.1883; 22.10.1886; 29.6.1887; 1.10.1887;

Dos Vort, Kovno (Yiddish): 17.12.1934, 20.8.1935.

Folksblat, Kovno (Yiddish): 10.7.1935

Di Yiddishe Shtime (The Yiddish Voice) Kovno (Yiddish): 25.8.1936, 14.4.1938, 29.6.1938.

Naujienos (Chicago)-11.6.1949

Reconstructionist NY, 8.3.1946, page 10-17

Dzuku Zinios (Lithuanian) NR.57,29.7.1992

Šeta (Shat)

(All photos were supplied by Joseph Woolf and Shelomoh Kurliandshik)
Shat (Seta) is situated in the center of Lithuania. A dirt road of about 17 km connected it with the district town Keidan (Kedainiai).

Shat is first mentioned on historical documents during the 17th century. Early in the 18th century it was burnt down during the Swedish invasion. In 1785 the town was granted permission by the ruling king to hold two fairs per year.

Until 1795 Shat was part of the Polish-Lithuanian Kingdom, when the third division of Poland by the three superpowers of those times - Russia, Prussia and Austria - caused Lithuania to become partly Russian and partly Prussian. The part of Lithuania which included Shat fell under czarist Russian rule, firstly as part of the Vilna province (Gubernia) and from 1843 part of the Kovno province. In the 19th century Shat developed at a very fast pace, holding large trade fairs and weekly markets. During this period there were approximately 40 stores, bars, wine distilleries, a factory preparing pelts, flour mills and a drugstore. Towards the end of the Russian rule and the period of Lithuanian independence (1918-1940), Shat was the center of the county in Keidan district. During the autumn of 1915, heavy battles took place between the armies of Germany and Russia in the vicinity of Shat and a fire caused heavy damage in the town. For a short period in 1919, it fell under Bolshevik rule.

Once again in the Second World War the town was burnt down by the Germans. In the years 1941-1944 Shat was under Nazi rule with all its atrocities and murders.

Jewish Settlement until after the First World War

The Jews first settled in Shat at about the middle of the 17th century. It is recorded that the Karaites settled there in 1664 and in the eighteenth century there was a blood libel against a Karaite resident. Shat was one of the few towns in Lithuania where the Karaites lived for many years.

For a number of years at the beginning of the eighteenth century, the Karaite rabbi Joseph ben Yitzhak had lived in Shat, and the last time the Karaite community was mentioned in historical documents was in 1709. In the years 1679-80 there was a blood libel against the Jewish community.

During the period of the autonomous Jewish Council of Lithuania (*Va'ad Medinath Lita*) (1623-1764) Shat was most of the time included in the Keidan Circuit.

Being far from a railway and from a highway it was difficult for Jews of Shat Jews to make a living. They were in trade and crafts and in transport as coachmen. In the nearby villages of Bukantz -Bukonys (10 km away) and Truskava (15 km away) Jews were engaged in farming. In 1847 there were 802 Jews living in Shat.

Kovno Street, on left the house of Kurliandshik family

The town suffered frequently from devastating fires from time to time. In the years 1860 and 1878, 100 homes were burnt down, including the synagogue and *Beit HaMidrash*, and in 1892 again 115 homes were burnt down. The squire Montvila assisted those made homeless by the fires and in 1868-69 also assisted many in the years of drought and hunger. Every year he donated 25 rubles to the fund for *Maoth Khitim* which provided Matzoth for the poor during *Pesakh*. In 1876 he also built a new the house of the *Hakhnasath Orkhim* ("Lodging for Travelers"). In 1889 the new bath was erected.

In 1897, 1640 people lived in town, of them 1135 Jews (69%).

Numerous lists of Jewish residents of Shat, census, revision, candle taxes, box taxes, rabbi electors, etc., including one containing over 1,000 names in the latter half of the nineteenth century are to found in "Lithuanian Archival Documents" in the JewishGen web site (www.JewishGen.org).

Jewish children were depended on their learning at the *Kheder*, until 1898 when a Jewish school was established by the initiative of the Rabbi Yisrael Levin. He rented a large wide house and partitioned the rooms to provide a separate room for each class. He also hired experienced teachers of various subjects, including Hebrew and its grammar, the Bible, etc.

The large *Beit HaMidrash* and the Synagogue were the center of the religious life of the Jews of Shat.

For a list of the Rabbis who served in Shat see **Appendix 1**.

Shat Synagogue 1937

In 1900 the institution *Linath HaTsedek* ("Righteous Lodging") was founded to assist the poor. The same year the Zionist Council was established by Elkhanan-Ya'akov Ritenberg and Betsalel Meitkis the first chairman being Zundel Rubensohn. Of those who donated to assist settlement in *Eretz Yisrael* from the years 1900 to 1903, quite a number of names from Shat are recorded. The fundraisers were A.Y.Wittenberg, Betsalel Hirsch Meitkis and in 1903 a Kurliandshik.

A Street in Shat

The *HaMeilitz* database below lists 32 Shat donors in the years 1898-1900.

The reporters in *HaMeilitz* from Shat were Sh. Rabinovitz and Ya'akov Glik.

At the old Jewish cemetery in Jerusalem a tombstone of a Shater Jew exists: Duber son of Avraham Segal, died in 1871.

The *Bund* (the Anti-Zionist Workers Organization) was organized towards the end of the 19th century followed in 1903 by the *Young Bund*. On the first *yahrzeit* of the mourning for the pogrom at Kishenev, the members of the *Young Bund* climbed onto the *bimah* of the synagogue and prevented the cantor from intoning the prayer for the health of the Tzar.

The Period of Lithuanian Independence (1918-1940)

According to the autonomy law for minorities, issued by the new Lithuanian government, the minister for Jewish affairs Dr. Max Soloveitshik ordered elections to be held during the summer of 1919 for community committees (*Va'ad Kehilah*) in all towns of the state.

According to the regulations, in towns where the Jewish population counted less than 1,000 people, like in Shat, only the chairman of the committee and his deputy were elected. In 1922 the chairman was Ze'ev-Wulf Yofeh, the deputy L.Grinblat and the secretary Hayim Katz. At the end of 1923 the chairman was Yosef Leib Kagan (see an example of the correspondence of the Committee below)

The committee, active till the end of 1925 when the autonomy was annulled, collected taxes as required by law and was in charge of all aspects of community life.

Jewish school children in the 1920s
Standing from left: ----, Rachel Yankelevitz, Sarah Glass, Yokheved Ginsburg
Sitting from left: -----, Leah Isakovitz, Tsiporah Bernshtein, Sarah Bernshtein

According to the first census conducted in 1923 by the Lithuanian government, the population of Shat totaled 877 people and of them 440 (50%) were Jewish.

Shat girls 1930
Standing from left: -------, Tsiporah Bernshtein
Sitting from left: Sarah Bernshtein, Yokheved Ginsburg, Sarah Glass, Leah Isakovitz

Wedding of Basa Vulf and Shemuel Koren in Shat 1930
Top Row from left: fourth-Pesha Vulf, fifth-David Riklis, sixth-Feige Raizman
Second Row: third-Pesha Teper, fifth-Leah (Koren) Rigler,
Third Row: first-Mrs.Teper, fourth-Rachel Vulf, fifth-Oga (Katz) Vulf, sixth-Eli
Vulf, seventh-Khasiah (Koren) Nadel
Fourth Row sitting from left: Sheine Taube (Gordon) Vulf, Shemuel Vulf,
Ya'akov-Hirsh Vulf, child sitting on his lap-Yosef Vulf, the bride Basa Vulf, the
groom Shemuel Koren, Avraham Koren
Fifth Row sitting on ground: fourth-Rachel Riklis

During this period the Jews earned their livelihood from trade, crafts and transport. The weekly market was on Tuesdays and two fairs were held per year, both being important for the livelihood of the Jews of Shat. They would buy agricultural products from the peasants and transport them to Kovno, about 50 km away, where they sold them for higher prices.

According to the census of 1931 conducted by the Lithuanian government, of the 12 stores and other business enterprises of Shat, 9 of them (75%) were Jewish.

Type of Business	Total	Owned by Jews
Butchers and cattle dealers	2	0
Restaurants & inns	3	3
Furs, clothes & textile stores	4	4
Radio, electrical goods & sewing machines	1	1
Iron & steel, tools	1	1
Other	1	0

The same census listed factories for soft drinks, wool combing and felt, all Jewish-owned. The two cousins Hirsh Yofe and Yosef-Leib Kagan owned a limekiln in the nearby village Pilkalnis.

In 1937 there were 37 Jewish craftsmen as follows: 8 tailors, 5 stove and fireplace builders, 3 glaziers, 3 carpenters, 3 blacksmiths, 2 bakers, 2 tinsmiths, 2 butchers, 1 felt-boot manufacturer, 1 knitter, 1 shoemaker, 1 barber, 1 leatherworker, 1 shoe stitcher, 1 other. The Jewish Peoples Bank (*Folksbank*) played an important role in the economy of the town; in 1927 there were 129 depositors. Two years after that there were only 105.

In the mid 1930's the Jewish population decreased and the economic crisis which caused it was due to the boycott and pressures organized by the Lithuanian Merchants Association (Verslas). Those who left sought a livelihood in other places. A large portion of them emigrated to South Africa; some attempted to emigrate to the U.S.A. For many years a "Shatter Association" existed in South Africa and the one in New York was formed in 1909, officially still exists but is inactive.

In 1939 there were 13 telephones in Shat, 7 of them were owned by Jews.

30 Jewish children studied at the Kheder and 70 at the Hebrew elementary school belonging to the *Tarbuth* network. There was also a Jewish library which contained approximately 500 books in Hebrew and Yiddish but very few Jewish residents of Shat used them. There were very little cultural activities, no theater and no cinema, mainly because of the difficulty in reaching Shat, especially during periods of rain. There was no decent road and also no railway line. Electricity was non-existent.

For some time a Jewish soccer team acted in town and a Jewish fire brigade.

Volunteer Fire Brigade about 1925

BACK ROW: 1) Unknown, 2) Meishke Rodblatt, 3) Borke Milner, 4) ? Milner, 5) Ben Zion Ginsburg, 6) Jankele Greenblatt.

SECOND ROW: 7) Abke ?**, 8) Chilke Bloch**, 9) Elke ?, 10) Unknown, 11) Unknown, 12) Jankele Rodblatt, 13) Leibke Milner.

THIRD ROW: 14) Nochke Glick (medic), 15) Feivke Goldman, 16) Chaimke ?, 17) Leibke Kolanchick, 18) Motke Schneid, 19) Unknown from another shtetl, 20) Ziske Kolanchick, 21) Chilke Der Gleser, 22) Judke Katz, 23) Shmulik Kolanchick Kolanchick 24) Chonke ? (signaler).

BOTTOM ROW: 25) Fievke (Der Smid) Aharon, 26) Mishke Glass*, 27) Meike Reis, 28) Hirshel Strauss (commander), 29) Jankele Bloch (deputy commander)*, 30) Saike Milner, 31) Leibke Woolf*.

The Beth Midrash   (*Picture supplied by Ada Green*)

Drinks shop of Glass-Strazh family at Keidan Road

Youth group next to the river Obelis
From left: Sarah Glass, Tuviyah Bernshtein, Leah Isakovitz, Yokheved Ginsburg, ------, Tsiporah Bernshtein, David Rotblat, Sarah Bernshtein, Ben-Zion Ginsburg

The Glass Family in about 1935

Standing from left: Reizel, Hanah-Ella (Glass) Straus, Hershel Straus, Shelomoh-Itsik, Sarah (Glass) Isakson, Leah Glass
Sitting: Rokha-Shula (Shtrom) Glass, Orchik Glass

Of the Jews of Shat who participated in Zionist activities, most belonged to Zionist parties. In 1925 a branch of the Zionist Socialist Party consisting of 10 members was formed. Many activities were organized by the "Grosmanists" and there were a number of Zionist Youth Groups, amongst them *Benei-Akiva* and *HaShomer-HaTsair*. The proportion of members of the various Zionist organizations was influenced by the voting patterns of the Zionist Congresses between the years 1929-1939. The following chart reflects this:

Congr. Nr	Year	Total Shek.	Total Voters	Labor Party		Rev.	G. Z.		Gros	M iz.
				Z"S	Z"Z		A	B		
16	1929	32	--	--	--	--	--	--	--	
17	1931	16	15	2	2	--	8	--	--	3
18	1933	"	25	16		1	6	--	--	2
19	1935	"	125	59		--	1	16	49	--
21	1939	"	29	23		--	1		National Block 5	

Shek.-Shekalim; Rev.-Revisionists; G.Z.-General Zionists; Gros.-Grosmanists; Miz.-Mizrahi

Shat Jewish soccer team
Standing from left: Hayim Mankovitz, a Lithuanian, Shelomoh Kurliandshik, a
Lithuanian, a German,
Barukh Balatin, Aba Teper, Berl Blekher
Sitting from left: Henakh Riklis, Mikhael Yankelevitz, Manes Kurliandshik

The religious life of Shat was centered around the Synagogue, *Beit HaMidrash* and Kloiz (prayer room). Following the resignation in 1935 of the Rabbi Shelomoh Rabinovitz after 30 years service to the community, the town was without a rabbi for some time until the election of Rabbi Elkhanan Vainer, who was the last rabbi of the Shat Jewish Community. Through all the years of the history of Shat, the Jewish Community always had a *Shokhet* (ritual slaughterer). The *Gemiluth Khesed* (charitable loan fund) was also important in the life of the Jewish community in providing interest-free loans to the needy. For a partial list of personalities born in Shat see **Appendix 2**.

Shat Youth Group

Top row from left: Esther Garun, Pesia Vulf, --------, Feigale Raizman
Standing: Manes Kurliandshik, Avraham Garun

The Bernshtein Family
Standing from right: Zalman, Sonia
Second row sitting from right: Sarah Bernshtein Grinblat, her son Arik
Third row from right: Adv. Shimon Bernshtein
From left: Frumah Bernshtein, her daughter Masha.

The Vulf Family
From left: Rachel, Yehudah-Leib, Basa, Eli (in uniform of the Lithuanian army),
-----.

לקדושי קהילת
שאט
(ע"י קיידאן ליטא) הי"ד
שנרצחו הושמדו ונקברו חיים
ע"י הנאצים ועוזריהם
הליטאים ימ"ש בעיר קיידאן
ה אלול תש"א - 41-8-28
זכרם הקדוש לא ימוש מקרבנו לנצח
ת נ צ ב "ה
הוצא ושורד קהילת שאט בישראל ובתפוצות

The Second World War and After

In June 1940 Lithuania was annexed to the Soviet Union and became a Soviet Republic. Following new rules, the majority of the shops belonging to the Jews of Shat were nationalized and commissars were appointed to manage them. Also several Jewish houses whose area was more than 220 square meters were nationalized and their owners forced to vacate them. All the Zionist parties and youth organizations were disbanded and Hebrew educational institutions were closed. Some Jewish youth integrated into the new regime and became members of the *Comyug* (Communist Youth Organization).

In the Yiddish newspaper *Shtraln* ("Rays") of the tenth of August 1940, a report was published by the Shater A. Garun about the festive meeting on the occasion of the integration of Lithuania into the family of the great USSR which took place in Shat on Sunday the fourth of August with the participation of about 3,000 people. There were songs and dances and among others M. Kurliandschik delivered a speech as the secretary of the local *Comyug*, Y. Grinblat in Yiddish on behalf of the peoples committee and Sh. Kurliandschik on behalf of the *Comyug* organization.

Supply of goods decreased and, as a result, prices soared. The middle class, mostly Jewish, bore most of the brunt, and the standard of living dropped gradually. Many families remained without any income. In the middle of June

1941 Shimon Bernshtein and his wife were exiled to Siberia. After 30 years, in 1971 they returned to Vilna where, 2 years later, he passed away.

In 1940 there were about 250 Jews of the total population of 1450 in town.

It should be mentioned that despite all their hardships and poverty, the Jews of Shat never lost their sense of humor, their determination, and their togetherness.

When the German invasion began on Monday 23rd June 1941, local Lithuanians were already armed and on the rampage, and terror spread amongst the Jews. Their fear was great. The younger people tried to escape to the town of Vilkomir, but were intercepted by the armed Lithuanians who poured out of the forests, and brutally forced the young Jews to return to Shat.

On Tuesday morning 24th June, German tanks arrived from the direction of Keidan and were met by large forces of the Russian Army, resulting in a bitter battle. The Jews fled from their homes with nothing but the clothes on their backs. Some of them congregated next to the Jewish cemetery, and some escaped to the estate of Aba Ziv, about 6 km from Shat. Others tried to find refuge with local farmers known to them. Only a score of people remained in the village itself.

The first act of the Germans was to round up Yehoshua Aharon Levi, a respected local Jew. They took him to the Synagogue and ordered him to tear the Torah scrolls. When he refused, they shot and killed him.

The Lithuanian activists, together with the Germans, then went from house to house and forcefully assembled the remaining Jews for hard labor. They were tortured and beaten cruelly. Those Jews who had found shelter amongst known local farmers were forced to leave.

Each day, some Jews returned to their village, but they were killed by the wild mobs.

Old people were dragged out of their homes, tortured and then passed on to the two village madmen, who paraded them through the village, and on to the neighboring village of Vilkalnai, where most of them were murdered.

On the 20th August, the remaining Jews were rounded up, put on trucks and taken to Keidan. At the same time, all those who had hidden on Aba Ziv's estate, including Aba Ziv himself, were also trucked to Keidan. Together with the Jews of Keidan and other villages of the area, (Zeimiai and others) they were held under terrible crowded conditions for thirteen days at the Zirginas, riding school stables.

Except for so called "coffee" they were not fed, the men being taken daily to various forced labor works.

Meanwhile Russian prisoners of war had dug a massive pit on the banks of the Smilga stream.

On the 28th of August they were taken to the pit. The first group of 60 old people were thrown mercilessly into it and fired upon by the Lithuanians with automatic weapons.

Of the next group of 60, some of the Jews of Keidan and Shat resisted, inflicted wounds on some of the murderers and fought until the end.

To avoid any further resistance, the next groups were reduced to 20 victims, for easier control. The last groups were mothers and their children. The mothers and older children were shot and the infants were used as balls by the Lithuanians, being thrown from one to the other and then thrown alive into the pit.

The Russian prisoners were made to throw lime over the bodies, many of them still moving. After the pit was covered, the ground heaved from the mass of victims still being alive. The Germans brought steamrollers to flatten the surface and subdue the victims.

Involved in this massacre were two Lithuanians from Shat (their names are held at the archives of Yad Vashem).

According to the Yaeger Report, a total of 2,076 persons were murdered there; however, the correct figure is bound to be more.

After the war, the few survivors of Keidan and Shat placed a Memorial Stone on the Communal Grave, inscribed in Yiddish, Russian and Lithuanian, which stated: "**Victims of the Fascist Terror**".

In the 1990s the tablet was replaced by a new one with the inscription in Yiddish and Lithuanian: "**Here the Hitler murderers with their local helpers on August 28, 1941 murdered 2076 Jews.**"

The monument on the mass grave in Keidan

From left: Yudel Ronder, Joseph Woolf

The tablet on the monument with the inscription in Yiddish and Lithuanian

The Jewish cemetery was erased during the Nazi rule and the tombstones used by the Lithuanians for building purposes. [Ada Greenblatt's note: according to elderly Lithuanians currently living in Seta, the Jewish cemetery was erased during the Communist rule in 1949 and the tombstones used by the Russians for building purposes]. The photos below show the cemetery as photographed in 1937 and the empty site with the monument as photographed in the nineties.

The Jewish cemetery in 1937

The site of the Jewish cemetery in 1992 with a monument.

The inscription on it in Yiddish and Lithuanian says: "At this place till 1941 was the Jewish cemetery of Shat".

The survivors of Shat Jews were: Haim Burshtein, who managed to join the partisans in the forest near Keidan; the brothers Shelomoh and Manes Kurlandchik, Khaim Mankovitz, Avraham Garun and David Rotblat who escaped to Russia and fought the Nazis in the Lithuanian division of the Red Army. Kh. Mankovitz and Manes Kurliandschik fell in battle.

The following also survived: the sisters Mirah and Liuba Vidutsky, who had successfully escaped from the Kovno Ghetto and remained in hiding.

Leah Aizikovitz and Sarah Grinblat, having been sent to Stutthof concentration camp from Kovno.

Tuviyah Goldberg was another still alive when the Ghetto was emptied.

Fruma Bernshtein, Yehudith Kamod and Rachel Yankelevitz also emerged alive, having been in Russia during the war.

For the list of Shat Jews before World War II, as prepared by Shelomoh Kurliandschik, see Appendix 3.

Bibliography

Yad-Vashem Archives: 0-3/2276; M-33/989; M-1/E-1509/1415; 1700/1569.

Koniukhovsky Collection 0-71, File 40.

YIVO, New York, *Lithuanian Jewish Communities Collection*, File Keidan, pages 44179, 44200, 44201, 44247, 44248.

Shat. Its history and destruction, unpublished article by Shelomoh Kurliandschik.

HaMeilitz (St. Petersburg): 26.8.1887; 13.2.1888; 28.4.1897;12.7.1898; 21.1.1900; 1.8.1903 (Hebrew).

Folksblat, Kovno: 17.7.1935 (Yiddish).

Di Yiddishe Shtime (The Yiddish Voice) Kovno: 18.7.1933 (Yiddish).

Yiddisher Hantverker (Jewish Artisan) Kovno: Nr.3, 1938 (Yiddish).

A group of Jewish soldiers of the Lithuanian Division of the Red Army 1943

First line kneeling from right: Sgt. Shelomoh Kurliandschik, Sgt. Hanan Levin, Corp. Zlate Miller, First Sgt. Reuven Levitan, Fania Ribak. Standing from right: Lt. Yudl Bendet, First Sgt. Zelbovitz, Blekher, Segal, Nadel.

Three Shatter born young men, Sydney Levy (Gaddie), Hymie Schakhman and Joseph Woolf came with the 800 South African volunteers to participate in Israeli's War of Liberation 1948/49.

Appendix 1   Partial list of the Rabbis who served in Shat

Eliyahu ben Yakov Ragoler (1794-1849) who served as rabbi in 1821 and who also established the large yeshiva of Slobodka in Kovno;

Naftali bar Ephraim;

Meir-Mikhel Rabinowitz (1830-1901) who served in Shat for 20 years, author of the book *HaMeir L'Olam*, published in Vilnius, 1903, on the logic system of studying the Torah;

Nahum Shapiro (1818-1902) prodigy of Rabbi Israel Salanter;

Zev-Wolf Avrekh (1845-1922) served in Shat in 1875;

Avraham Druskowitz (served Shat 1897-1902);

Shelomoh-Dov Hacohen Shprintz served in Shat in the 1890's;

Shelomoh son of Meir-Mikhel Rabinovitz (served in Shat from 1903), died 15 July 1933 (15 Tamuz), age 63, as per entry in the metrical register of the Kedainiai Rabbinate, Central Metrical Archives, Vilnius;

Elhanan Wiener, the last Rabbi of Shat, murdered in 1941.

Appendix 2   Partial list of Personalities Born in Shat

Rabbi Yehoshua Rabinovitz (1818-1887), son of Eliyahu Ragoler, from 1847 head of the yeshivah of Kletsk;

Rabbi Mosheh-Yitzhak Rabin (1834-1902) who served for 40 years as the authorized rabbi of Ponevezh and for many years the principal of the famous Ponevezh Yeshiva;

Ben-Zion Shater, head of a Yeshiva in Vilna during the 1880's;

Shemuel ben Meir-Mikhel Rabinovitz, Rabbi in U.S.A., published in *Hatsefirah* complex problems in geometry, died 16 September 1925 (27 Elul 5685).

Mordehai-Manes Monashevitz (1857-1927), an educator and author who founded a well-known school in Liepaja, Latvia, which existed for 38 years. From 1919 in the U.S.A., where he became a school teacher and latterly in New York. From 1870, publisher of poems, essays, Hebrew educational books and plays;

Meir-Yitshak Goldberg (born 1871), Rabbi in Ostrova and Vitebsk;

Ephraim Kaplan (1879-1943) who emigrated to the U.S.A. in 1904, published articles on historical issues and edited *Der Morgen Journal* (The Morning Journal) in New York;

Yb"a Ziv, lived in the second half of the nineteenth century, writer of novels in Yiddish and also poems in Hebrew.

Appendix 3
List of Shat Jews before World War II

Nr.	Surname	Name	Wife	Children	Remarks
1	Beten	Shelomoh	+	2 sons	blacksmith
2	Kurliandschik	Khayim	Masha	Shelomoh, Manes, Hanahh	
3	Milner	Shaye	Sore Etel	Pesia, Volf & grandmother[1]	
4	Garun	Avraham	----------	sister Esther and mother	
5	Yankelevitz	Meir	Rachel	mother	
6	Khases	Leib	+		
7	Grinblat	Lipe	+	daughter and husband[2]	tailor
8	+	--------	Khane-Base[3]	Fradke	
9	Goldshmidt	Manes	Khasi-Beile	Khaya, Keile Rivka, Libe, Tila, Jakob-Mendel and 5 other children	
10	Randman	Chone	Chiene	son Mikhael[4]	from 1938 in USA
11	Vidutsky	Eli	Reizl	Miriam, Liuba, Hanahh, Avraham	
12		Aizik	------	2 daughters	
13		Meir	Sara		carpenter
14	Vulf	Yankel	Sheina-Taube	Elke, Pesia, Shmuel	
15	Goldberg	Markus	Dobre	Tuvia, Nakhman	
16		Khatskel[5]	Hayah		the Shamash
17	Kurlandshik	Shimon	Simche	Aizik, Base, Yente	
18	Strazh	Hirshel	Hanahh		
19	+		+	2 daughters	shoemaker
20		Meike	+		tailor
21	Blekher			Berl, Yekhiel, Ester-Malka, Yankel, Efrayim	
22		Beile		with mother	
23				3 brothers	grain merchants
24	Reznik	Khayim	+	1 daughter	Shokhet
25	Ginsburg	Mendel	+	Yokheved	
26	Bernshtein	Zalman	Sonia		
27	Grinblat	Yankel	Sarah	Aharon, mother-in-law	
28	Burshtein	Itsik	Roza	Khayim, Shimon, Zelda, Leah	
29		Hanah-Rachel		Aba, Bath-Sheva, Pesia	
30	Balatin	Barukh		sister Ita	
31	Aron	Feivel	+	Bela, Kopel	blacksmith
32	Kurliandchik[6]	Leib	+	Mina	
33	Lurie	Alter	Sora	Moshe[7]	
34	Kamod		Beile	Minke	
35	Levin	Aharon	+	Reuven, Shmerl, Moshe	
36	Raizman			Meike, Feigele[8]	
37	Land		Matle	Yitzkhak, Shmuel David	
38	Yankelevitz		Pesia[9]	mother	
39				Yonah, David, 2 sisters	

40	Bernshtein	Yeizel	Toibe	Tuvia, Shimon, Fruma, Tsipora, Sheva, Hanahh	
41	Glass	Aharon	+	Rachel, Leah, Rivkah, Shelomoh, Barukh	
42	Rotblat	David		brother Nathan, father and mother	
43	Riklis	David	Blume	Henakh, Sore[10]	
44	Kidesh	Aba		father and mother	
45	Mankovitz	Khayim		mother Feigel	
46	Tubiansky	Gershon[11]	+		tailor
47	Kagan	Volf	+	Rachel, Avraham	
48	Aizikovitz	Nokhim	Hinde-Gitel	Leah, Rivkah	
49	Sadinsky	Alter		Esther, Golda, father, mother	
50	+		+	daughter	shoemaker
51		Leib			barber
52	Shnaid			Nakhman, Pesakh[12]	
53	Rabinovitz		widow[13]	3 daughters	Rabbi

All together are in this list 195 names. Mr. Shelomoh Kurliandschik estimates that there were may be about 30-40 more Jews in town he couldn't remember. Joe Woolf contends that there were even more. About 94% were murdered.

Notes added by Ada Greenblatt:

[1] Shaye Milner and Sore Etel nee Kurliandschik also had son David Nisan.

[2] Lipe Grinblat's daughter's name was Zelda, the wife of David Schwartz. They had a daughter, Chase, and a son, Chonel. Lipe Grinblat was also the father of Yankel (Nr. 27 above), in addition to another son, Leib, and another daughter (name unknown).

[3] This could be Hanah-Base Vinik, wife of Elias Vinik. If so, they also had a son, David Leib Vinik.

[4] Chone Randman and wife Chiene nee Rogalsky also had daughters Leah and Roche.

[5] There was a Chatzkel Kan and wife Hayah nee Skurkovich (Hayah died in 1936). They had a daughter Feige.

[6] There was a Leib Kurliandschik, wife Feigele nee Shachman, and daughter Hayah.

[7] Alter Lurie and wife Sora nee Altmuner also had children Rachil and Benjamin.

[8] Meike and Feigele Raizman also had sisters Etel, the wife of Hayim Yofe, and Tamara. Their parents, Hayim Leib Raizman and Rochel nee Grinblat, were probably also still living.

[9] There was a Hayim Yankelevich and wife Frume nee Meltzer with daughter Pese.

[10]David Riklis and Blume nee Bank also had son Abram and a daughter Nese, who was married to Hilel Segal.

[11]There was also a Hayim-Leizer Grinblat and wife Roche-Zlate nee Tuviansky with children Hertz Yosel, Gershon, and Shifre-Leah.

[12]There was an Izrael Shnaid and wife Yente nee Kapulnik, with sons Manes and Pesakh.

[13]The widow of Rabbi Shelomoh Rabinovitz was Rochel, daughter of Movsha Meltzer. Her daughters were Sora Sheina, Leah Rasha, and Gitel. She also had a son, Hayim.

Stakliškės (Stoklishok)

Stoklishok (in Yiddish) is located in the southeastern part of Lithuania, surrounded by lakes and woods, about 25 km distance from the Alytus district administrative capitol. The town, first mentioned in historical documents dating from 1521, was a county administrative center during the 16th-18th centuries. In 1759 King August III authorized the town to hold one market day per week and two fairs per year, and in 1795 Stoklishok was granted the Magdeburg rights of self rule.

Until 1795 Stoklishok was part of the Polish-Lithuanian Kingdom, when the third division of Poland by the three superpowers of those times - Russia, Prussia and Austria - caused Lithuania to become partly Russian and partly Prussian. The part of the state which lay on the left side of the Nieman river (Nemunas)) was handed over to Prussia which ruled there during the years 1795-1807, while the other part, including Stoklishok, became Russia.

After the defeat of Napoleon by the Russian army in 1812, all Lithuania including Stoklishok, was annexed to Russia in 1815, first into the Vilna Gubernia and from 1843 into the Kovno Gubernia.

During the 18th century medicinal springs were discovered nearby, but in 1857 the bathhouse burnt down and was never reconstructed, due to the recreation towns Birshtan (Birstonas) and Druskenik (Druskeninkai) having meanwhile replaced it.

During the period of independent Lithuania (1918-1940) Stoklishok was a county administrative center.

Jewish Settlement till World War II

Jews apparently settled in Stoklishok at the beginning of the 18th century. In the middle of the 19th century there were already about 500 Jews, with a Beth Midrash. They made their living from small commerce, fishing, agriculture, timber, and in 1890 the Rabinovitz family established a beer brewery.

In 1847, 1,344 people lived in Stoklishok, among them 443 Jews (33%). By 1897, their numbers had increased to 2,200, including 808 Jews (37%).

In "The All Lithuania Revision List Database" of the Jewishgen Org. Web Site there are 766 records of Stoklishok Jews from the 19th century, copied and transliterated from Lithuanian Archives.

In 1873 a fire burnt down 97 Jewish houses, and in 1893 many Jewish houses were also destroyed by fire. In 1885 peasants from the surrounding villages destroyed a Jewish house which had been built not far from the church.

These events caused the increased emigration of Stoklishok Jews, which had started after the pogroms in Russia at the beginning of 1880, although Stoklishok Jews did not suffer from them.

The Synagogue

In 1887 emigrant families left the town almost every week, and nearly half of Stoklishok's Jews were already in America, causing the closure of the Jewish school which had been established in 1877.

In the middle of the 19th century Jews from Stoklishok had already emigrated to Eretz-Yisrael. In the old Jewish cemetery in Jerusalem at least 2 headstones of Stoklishok Jews can be found, those of Rabbi Ya'akov-Yehudah ben Aryeh, who died in 1862, and of Hinde bath Shelomoh-Zalman, who passed away in 1863.

A list of donors for the "Settlement of Eretz Yisrael" dated 1900 mentions many names of Stoklishok Jews, whose fund raiser was Esther Cohen. A list of donors for Jews in Lithuanian towns who suffered hunger in 1872 also shows several names of Stoklishok Jews.

During the first years of Lithuanian independence (1919-1920), Stoklishok Jews suffered from adverse economic conditions and received help from "YeKoPo" (Committee for Helping Jewish refugees).

According to the autonomy law for minorities, issued by the new Lithuanian government, the minister for Jewish affairs Dr. Max Soloveitshik ordered elections to be held in the summer of 1919 for Community Committees in all towns of the state. In Stoklishok a committee of seven members was elected. This committee collected taxes as required by law and was in charge of most aspects of community life, acting till the end of 1925 when the autonomy was annulled.

According to the first census performed by the government in 1923, Stoklishok had 1,787 residents, amongst them 391 Jews (22%). But the number of Jews diminished, many emigrated to America and South Africa, some of the youth to Eretz-Yisrael, and shortly before World War II only 70 Jewish families were left in Stoklishok.

During this period Stoklishok Jews made their living, as before World War I, from small commerce, crafts and agriculture, there also being several Jewish coachmen. The main income of the local Jews came from the weekly market days and the 6 yearly fairs.

According to the Lithuanian government survey of 1931, there were 11 shops, of which 10 belonged to Jews (91%): 4 horse merchants, 4 textile shops, 1 grocery and 1 shoe shop, as well as a flour mill and a candy factory owned by Jews. In 1937 there were 21 Jewish craftsmen: 6 tailors, 4 shoemakers, 4 butchers, 2 glaziers, 3 blacksmiths, 2 stitchers and 1 baker. In 1939 there were 9 telephone owners in town, of whom 2 were Jewish.

In 1920 a large fire burnt down almost half of Stoklishok's houses including the Jewish school and so that Jewish youths had no place to study. After a year a school was established in an unsuitable building and the Community Committee applied to former Stoklishkers living abroad, mainly in America, appealing in the Yiddish newspaper "Forverts", for help to build a new school in town.

A new school connected to the Hebrew "Tarbuth" chain, was indeed established, in which 50 to 60 pupils studied.

The Hebrew school on the occasion of the 20th anniversary of teacher Pitluk's educational work and of his emigration to America - April 5, 1937

Many of Stoklishok Jews were supporters of the Zionist movement and in elections for Zionist congresses they voted for most of the Zionist parties, as can be seen from the results enumerated in the table below:

Congr.	Year	Total	Total	Labor Party	Re	G.Z.	Gro	Miz.

Nr.		Shek.	Voters	Z"S	Z"Z	v.	A	B		
16	1929	33	32	9	3	3	13	--	--	4
17	1931	33	31	11	9	1	1	--	--	9
18	1933	---	169	125		44	--	--	--	--
19	1935	---	161	149		--	2	1	1	8

Shek-.Shekalim;   Rev.-Revisionists;   G.Z.-General   Zionists;   Gro.-Grosmanists; Miz.-Mizrahi

The Zionist youth organizations active in town were: "HeKhalutz", "Gordonia" (with about 50 members), "HaShomer-HaTsair-Netsakh", "Beitar" and "Sirkin Society' (Z"S Party). The youth society "HaTekhiyah" (Revival) established a library in town and published its own bulletin. Most of the town's youth were active for the National Funds, and on Pesakh eve they would participate in baking "Matsoth" and selling "Maror", while on "Sukoth" eve they would sell "Sekhakh" (Cover) for the "Sukoth". All income from these activities was dedicated to Keren Kayemeth le'Yisrael.

Stoklishok youth at Purim 1934

Sports activities were held in the local "Maccabi" branch which had 50 members. The local fire brigade members were all Jews, volunteers, who were also active, inter alia, in Zionist activities. Many of the young people were in "Kibutzei Hakhsharah" and emigrated to Eretz-Yisrael.

Religious life in town was concentrated around the brick built Synagogue and the old wooden Beth Midrash.

The Bath House

The Rabbis who served in Stoklishok during the years were:

Shelomoh-Reuven Rabinovitz - from 1872;

Yehudah-Idl Hurvitz;

Yeshayah-Zelig Halperin;

Dov-Tsevi Kravitsky - in Stoklishok in 1922, also previous to this date as well as later;

Duber Bergman (1860-1941), who was murdered with his community in Stoklishok in Av 5701 (July 1941).

The writer Yisrael-Ze'ev Kreier (1860-1917) who wrote all his books under the name of Y.Z. Ben-Aryeh was a native of Stoklishok, and became well known among the Jewish public, not only as a teacher and director of a Talmud-Torah in Vilna, but also as the writer of popular science books, and his book "Velt un Veltelakh" (World and small worlds) was published in Vilna in 1894. His book "Ma'ase Ben Aryeh" (Stories of Ben Aryeh) achieved great success and about 50 editions were printed, the 48th edition being issued in Warsaw in 1899. Y.Z. Ben-Aryeh also wrote a book on Hebrew grammar. During World War I he returned to his hometown, where he died in 1919, lonely and forgotten.

A.T.Rabinovitz wrote reports in the Hebrew periodical "HaTsefirah" and Tsevi Barit in "HaMeilitz".

Stoklishok Volunteer Fire Brigade

In Stoklishok there was a "Gemiluth Khesed" society as well as a "Khevrah Kadisha".

A Stamp of the "Gemiluth Khesed" Society

The management of the "Gemiluth Khesed" Society on the occasion of the
emigration of its founder and chairman B. Pitluk to America

Parade of the Jewish Volunteer Fire Brigade

The Jewish cemetery 1935

World War I broke out in August 1914, and in the middle of April 1915, after being defeated in the battles in Tannenberg and in the Mazurian lakes in Prussia, the Russian army began to retreat from Lithuania. In the beginning of May of that year, the commander of the Russian army ordered the exile of all Jews from the Kovno Gubernia into the Poltava and Yekaterinoslav Gubernias, on the pretext that the Jews were friends of the Germans and could be spying for them. For several days 120,000 Jews were exiled in ignominious circumstances, during which they lost almost all their property. On the 10th of May the commander ordered the exile stopped, but hostages were to be taken instead. Stoklishok Jews together with Jews from the other 9 towns benefited from this order and remained in their homes.

During World War II and Afterward

World War II broke out with the German invasion of Poland on the first of September 1939, and its consequences were felt several months later for Lithuanian Jews in general, and especially for Jews of the southern part of the state which bordered on Poland.

In agreement with the Ribbentrop-Molotov treaty on the division of occupied Poland, the Russians occupied the Suvalk region, but after the delineation of exact borders between Russia and Germany the Suvalk region fell into German hands. The retreating Russians allowed anyone who wanted to join them to move into their occupied territory, and indeed many young people left the area together with the Russians. The Germans drove the remaining Jews out of their homes in Suvalk and its vicinity, robbed them of their possessions, then directed them to the Lithuanian border, where they were left in dire poverty, as the Lithuanians did not allow them to enter Lithuania and the Germans did not allow them to return. Thus they stayed in this swampy area in cold and rain for several weeks, until Jewish youths from the towns and villages of this part of the state smuggled them into Lithuania by various routes, with much risk to themselves. Altogether about 2,400 refugees passed through the border or infiltrated on their own, and were then dispersed in the "Suvalkija" region (the part of Lithuania laying on the left side of the Nieman river).

In June 1940 Lithuania was annexed to the Soviet Union and became a Soviet Republic. Following new rules, the majority of the shops belonging to the Jews of Stoklishok were nationalized and commissars were appointed to manage them. All Zionist parties and youth organizations were disbanded and the Hebrew school was closed.

Supply of goods decreased and, as a result, prices soared. The middle class, mostly Jewish, bore most of the brunt, and the standard of living dropped gradually.

At this time there were about 70 Jewish families in the town, consisting of approximately 300 people.

Stoklishok was occupied by the German army several days after the German invasion of the USSR on the 22nd of June 1941. Lithuanian nationalists immediately organized and detained people suspected of supporting the Soviet regime, according to a list of activists from the elections to the Lithuanian Soviet. A Lithuanian police report dated the 5th of July mentions two women who were also detained among these Jews: Golda Heler, a mother of two children, Hayah Iserzon and Barukh Koifman. All those detained were kept in the local prison for a week, after which they were led to the Lilun forest, about 4 km from the town in the direction of Aukstadvaris (Visoki-Dvor), where they were shot and buried in pits dug by Jews who were brought from Stoklishok for this task. They were forbidden, under threat of death, to tell anybody what they had done in the forest, but nevertheless Aizik Kovarsky revealed the secret. Stoklishok Jews did not accept the idea that the pits were intended for them too, as they wanted to believe that they were prepared for Communist activists only.

A list of all Stoklishok Jews was prepared, who had to report in person every day at the local police station, in order to prevent their escape. Pinkhas Kravitz, being the "Juden Aeltester", was appointed as liaison to the authorities, and had to deliver groups of Jews to the authorities everyday for various types of work, such as sweeping the streets, road repairs, cleaning the police station and other public buildings. The request for workers increased every day, until the "Juden Aeltester" was not able to supply anymore, so that one day he disappeared, his fate unknown. After a short time the authorities started to take out small groups of Jews for so called work outside the town, but nobody returned home.

On Shabath, 16.8.1941, larger groups of Jews, sitting in five carts, were moved to Jezne (Jieznas), and in addition to 63 men and 26 women from Jezne itself, were sent to Pren (Prienai), where they were murdered together with local Jews on the 26th of August 1941 (3rd of Elul 5701). On the 7th of September the rest of Stoklishok Jews were put into forty carts and brought to Butrimantz (Butrimonys), where, together with local Jews and those brought from Birshtan (Birstonas) and Pun (Punia), they were crowded into the yard of the local police station.

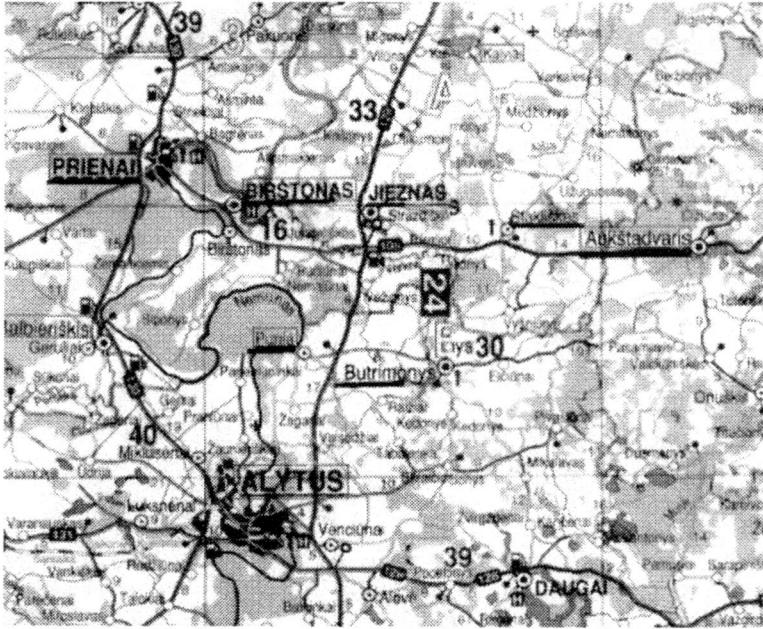

Map of the towns mentioned in this section of the article

On the 9th of September 1941 all were herded into the end of Klidzh street, where two pits had already been dug: one being beside the house of Gudaitis and the other a little further, where people used to obtain sand for repairing roads.

The adults were separated from the children, taken to the edge of the pit and shot. The children were pushed into the pit and then shot, many of them being buried alive. On this Tuesday, the 9th of September 1941 (17th of Elul 5701) 960 adults and 500 children - the Jews of Butrimantz, Stoklishok, Birshtan and Pun - were murdered.

The main murderers were: Kaspirionas, Savitsky, Prashkis, Urbanavicius the miller, the carpenter Sinovskis and others.

Several Stoklishok Jews who tried to hide with Lithuanian peasants were caught and murdered. Only one Jewish girl (Sarah Epshtein) found shelter with a Polish estate owner (Gzhobovsky), later with peasants Josef and Piotr Antonovitz until 1943, when she contacted the partisans in Rudniky forest, joined them and survived.

Five days before the Red Army returned to this area (1944), a group of Jews who had escaped from the Kovno ghetto was caught near Stoklishok and shot, amongst them was Dr. Shelomoh Perlshtein from Stoklishok.

In the list of mass graves which appears in the book "Mass Murder in Lithuania" Vol. 2, those in Butrimantz are mentioned:

1.   The Jewish cemetery - more than 50 victims.

2.   Klidzh (Klydzionys) village, one-half km from the road Butrimantz-Pivasiunai, where on 9.9.1941 the number of murdered Jews came to 740 men, women and children.

Second massacre site of children and old people. Inscription of monument:
"May the Nazi murderers and their collaborators be eternally damned for killing 266 Jews-children and elderly people -in Aug. and Sept. 1941."

Bibliography.

Yad-Vashem Archives 0-3/4215; M-35/58, 159; M-Q-1218/64, 1314/135.

JIVO, NY, Collection of the Jewish Communities in Lithuania, File 1573.

HaMeilitz (St. Petersburg) (Hebrew): 7.6.1885.

Di Yiddishe Shtime (The Yiddish Voice) Kovno (Yiddish): 29.1.1922,

Einikeit, Moscow (Yiddish) 31.8.1944.

Naujienos, Chicago (Lithuanian), 11.6.1949.

The mass grave and the monument in Pren

One of the two massacre sites near the village of Klydzionys where men and women were murdered. The inscription on the monument says: "Blood of 965 innocent Jews from Butrimonys-men and women-flowed here. They were killed by Nazi murderers and their collaborators in August and September 1941".

Sudargas (Sudarg)

The small town of Sudarg (in Yiddish) is situated in the south-western part of Lithuania, in the county of Shaki (Sakiai), on the left bank of the river Nieman (Nemunas) and close to the border with East-Prussia. It lies 9 kilometers (5.4 miles) down-river from the larger town of Jurbarkas (Yurburg or Yurbrik in Yiddish) which lies on the right bank of the Nieman river and can be found on many maps. The town was established during the second half of the sixteenth century, and in 1724 King August the Second granted the town its city rights.

During the third division of Poland in 1795 the territories on the left bank of the river Nieman were given to Prussia and during that period (1795-1807) the above mentioned rights were annulled. From 1807 until 1815 Sudarg was within the boundaries of "The Great Dukedom of Warsaw". At that time people used to say that "when a rooster crowed in Sudarg he was heard in three countries: Poland, Russia and Prussia." After the defeat of Napoleon, Russia took over all the territory of Lithuania and ruled there from 1815 until the First World War. During these years Sudarg was a small town with an growing population: In 1827 there were 373 inhabitants in the town, in 1890 - 900 people and by 1901 about 3,000.

The first Jews probably settled in Sudarg at the end of the eighteenth or at the beginning of the nineteenth century. At that time community institutions were established and for many years the Jews were the majority. In 1856 Sudarg had a population of 689 people, of whom 627 were Jews (91%).

A large forest of about 1,000 hectares (an area of 2 miles by 2 miles) near Sudarg, lying partly in Lithuania and partly in Prussia, was a convenient site for smuggling and many Jews made their living from this activity. There were some people from Sudarg, also including Jews, who would float timber down the Nieman river; in Sudarg these rafts of timber would be disassembled, the logs would be sawed up and loaded onto boats for transportation to Germany. In those days, Sudarg's connection to the world was by way of boats on the Nieman River or by carts in summer and sledges in winter. In spring, when the ice on the Nieman began to break up and the dust roads were full of sludge and mud, the town was practically isolated from the world.

During the period of Independent Lithuania (1918-1940), Sudarg became a forgotten small town, where opportunities to earn a living became ever more difficult. As a result almost all Jewish youths left the town and moved mainly to Kovno (Kaunas) or went abroad and the Jewish population of Sudarg dwindled. The first census in Sudarg undertaken by the Lithuanian government in 1923 showed only 257 people in the town.

During the years before World War I and in the first years of Lithuanian rule many young people from Sudarg emigrated to America (to El Paso and Dallas, Texas and Albuquerque and other parts of New Mexico, and New York City to name a few places) and there raised large families (Rosin-Rosen, Hilelson-Hilson, Guttman, Goodman and others). According to Martin Miller, Joseph

Hillel Goodman (Guttman) from Sudarg helped 47 of his fellow townsmen immigrate to El Paso, Texas in the early part of this century (see below for more information from Martin Miller).

Standing from right: Yits'hak Hilelson, Gershon Hilelson, Leah'le*, her father Yehuda Goldberg *. Sitting from the right: Yits'haks first wife (name unknown)*, Mina Rosin Hilelson *, Elka Hilelson Goldberg (Leah'le's mother)*.   (*) murdered

(The author's aunt and cousins)

The Jews in Sudarg ran a few grocery and haberdashery stores, two taverns, two bakeries, a pharmacy and a wool combing workshop. Others traded illegally in meat, mainly with the Germans on the other side of the border. According to the Jewish Craftsmen Association's survey of 1937 there were then two Jewish tailors, one butcher and one baker in Sudarg.

Throughout the whole period of the presence of a Jewish community in Sudarg, there existed a great synagogue (Di Shul), decorated inside with spectacular wood engravings. This synagogue was used for prayers only in summer, while in winter people would pray in the other synagogue, the "Beth-Midrash," in which there was a stove. Both synagogues were built in the nineteenth century and were made of wood. Among the Rabbis who served in Sudarg were: Tzvi Rom (1844-1886), author of the book "Eretz Hatsevi" (Land of the Deer); Sender Vilensky; and also Regensberg who moved to New York in the 1920s in order to serve there as a Rabbi. In the 1930s J. Cohen served as Rabbi in Sudarg.

The headstones of Devorah-Leah bath Shabtai Rosin and her husband Dov ben Dov Rozin in the Sudarg Jewish Cemetery

In the 1920s there still was a "Heder" in Sudarg, where children learned to read and write, also study some biblical scriptures and a little Hebrew. Later the few Jewish children studied in the Lithuanian school.

The engineer and architect Mosheh Yits'hak Blokh (1893-August, 1942), a native of Sudarg, devoted much of his time to drawing up city plans. He even prepared a plan for excavating a channel from Haifa to the Jordan river, exploiting the difference in height between the Mediterranean and the much lower level of the Jordan in order to produce electric energy. He also had plans for irrigating the Negev.

The British mandatory authorities found his plans interesting, and in 1938 he visited London in order to discuss these with them, but was told that Europe was on the verge of war and that this was not the right time to deal with such plans. He taught painting and drawing in two Hebrew High Schools in Kovno. On the 14th of June 1941 he was arrested by the Russians and sent to a labor camp in the Archangelsk region as a "counter revolutionary", being the chairman of the "Revisionist" (Hatsohar) party in Kovno. He was shot by a guard in August 1942 when he demanded that they stop humiliating prisoners.

Sewing course for Jewish women from Sudarg 1929

Guttmann Berkman family group photo from Sudarg in 1927

The municipality of Be'er Sheva in Israel named a street after Engineer Yits'hak Blokh.

The German Army entered Sudarg on the first day of the war between Germany and the Soviet Union, on the 22nd of June 1941. During the first days after their arrival, the Germans and their Lithuanian collaborators started to plot against the local Jews, which at that time consisted of only about 30 Jewish families. In the beginning of July 1941 the Nazi and their Lithuanian collaborators transferred all men as well as two intellectual young women to Shaki, where they were murdered, together with the local men on the 5th of July 1941 (10th of Tamuz 5701).

The women of Sudarg had sent a Lithuanian peasant to clarify what had happened to their men. The peasant arrived in Shaki just at the time of the murders and was an eye witness to the horror, and on his return to Sudarg he lost his mind. The women and children of Sudarg were murdered on the 6th of July 1941 (11th of Tamuz 5701) in the vicinity of the village of Kidul.

Sources:

YIVO -Collection of the Jewish Communities in Lithuania, File 673, pages 29210-29214

Verbal Evidence by Yits'hak Hilelson (A native of Sudarg)

The biography of Moshe Isaac Blokh by Miriam Blokh-Makhlis, Holon, Israel (1987)

The memorial Book for the Jewish Community of Yurburg-Lithuania; Translation and Update (English), Editor and Compiler: Joel Alpert, Assistant editors-Josef Rosin and Fania Hilelson Jivotovsky; NY 2003

The monument on the mass grave

"In the forest between Kiduliai and Sudargas, Lithuania Hitler's occupation forces took 40 women and 16 children from Sudargas and shot them here. August 11, 1941."

Plaque in Yiddish reads, "In this place Hitler's murderers and their local helpers slaughtered 48 Jews men, women and children on August 12, 1941."

Tauragė (Tavrig)

I am pleased to acknowledge the assistance of Mr. Eliezer Paluksht from Ariel, Israel in providing me with important material on Tavrig.

Tavrig (in Yiddish) is located in the western part of Lithuania in the Zamut (Zemaitija) region near the river Jura, a tributary of the Nieman (Nemunas) River. The town is about 30 kilometers from the border with East Prussia, now the Kaliningrad enclave of Russia, and until World War I was only 7 kilometers from the Memel Gebiet (Region), which was then a part of Germany.

Tavrig was mentioned for the first time in 1507 on the occasion of the building of a church, and appears on a map drawn in 1539 by the Swedish Bishop Olas Magnus (Carta Marina). Since 1567 the town has housed government customs offices.

From 1691 till 1793 the beautiful estate of Tavrig - Tauroggen in German - with its big fields and surrounding woods, belonged to different owners, most of them Germans. According to an agreement at the time, Tavrig was transferred from the Prussian King to the Russians, and in 1846 Czar Nicolai the First gave Tavrig to Prince Vasilshchikov as a present.

After the third division of Poland in 1795 by the three superpowers of that time - Russia, Prussia and Austria - this part of Lithuania including Tavrig was handed over to Russia. During the Russian rule (1795-1915) Tavrig was included in the Vilna Gubernia in 1802, and from 1843 in the Kovno Gubernia. Since then Tavrig was a county administrative center in the Rasein (Raseiniai) district. In 1812 the retreating French army damaged Tavrig when passing through the town.

During the first half of the 19th century trade with Germany developed extensively and large quantities of agricultural products passed through to Germany via the Tavrig customs office, which also handled imported industrial products. For example, in 1855 Tavrig customs processed imported goods from Germany amounting to 9,000,000 Rubles, and exported agricultural products amounting to about 3,000,000 Rubles.

In 1858 Tavrig's commerce increased due to the completion of the Tilzit-Tavrig-St.Petersburg highway and the construction of the railway from St. Petersburg to Warsaw, which was connected to Tavrig by a branch from Kovno (1864). There was also quite a lot of smuggling.

Tavrig had special market days and large fairs. There were two hospitals, a big factory for bricks, one for spirits, a pharmacy and about seventy shops. In 1836 the town suffered a large fire.

Tavrig railway station 1930

In 1915, during World War I, the Germans occupied Tavrig, after most of its houses were bombed. During their rule, which lasted till 1918, they constructed the railway from Shavl (Siauliai) to Tilzit in East Prussia, which passed through Tavrig.

During the period of independent Lithuania (1918-1940), Tavrig became a district administrative capitol. New factories were built and its population continued to increase.

For one year (1940-1941) Tavrig, like all Lithuania, was under Soviet rule.

When the German army occupied Tavrig in June 1941, about 80% of its houses were ruined. The German rule with all its terror continued till autumn 1944.

A Street in Tavrig

During Independent Lithuania (1918-1940)

Society and Economics

After World War I ended and with it the German occupation, Tavrig's exiled Jews began to return. The first census held by the new Lithuanian government in 1923 showed that only half the exiles had returned to the ruined town. (5,470 residents, of them 1,777 Jews-32%).

Following the autonomy law for minorities, issued by the new Lithuanian government, the Minister for Jewish Affairs, Dr. Menakhem (Max) Soloveitshik, ordered elections to be held for Community Committees (Va'ad Kehilah) in the summer of 1919. In Tavrig a Committee of 15 members was elected: 6 neutral men, 4 from "Tseirei-Zion", 1 from the workers list, 4 undefined. This Committee was active in almost all fields of Jewish life until the end of 1925.

With the help of the "Joint" association and the Jewish "Folksbank", Tavrig Jews managed to rebuild their houses and to restore their businesses. Within a short period they again became the exporters of timber, flax and geese to Germany.

In the elections to the first Lithuanian "Seimas" (Parliament) which took place in October 1922, Tavrig Jews voted as follows: the Zionist list - 425 votes, "Akhduth" (Agudath Yisrael) - 160 votes and the Democrats - 9.

In the elections to the Municipal Council, which took place in 1921, 4 Jews were elected in a council of 10 members, and in the elections of 1924, the 18 council members included 7 Jews. As a result of a coalition with the Lithuanian Social Democratic party, a Jew was elected to the post of Deputy Mayor and as representative to the District Council. In 1931, 12 members were elected to the Municipal Council and of them 5 were Jews: Eliyahu Goldberg, Hirsh Berman, Shimon Cohen, Reuven Braude and Ya'akov Fish.

At right: stamp of the office of the Minister for Jewish Affairs
At left: stamp of the Jewish National Council in Lithuania

The restored houses at the market square 1924-25

From right: Epel, Holtsberg (textile), Gitelson, Rabinovitz (wool), Levinson

Picture supplied by Eliezer Paluksht

According to the 1931 government survey, Tavrig had 124 shops, including 101 owned by Jews (81%). Details according to the type of business are given in the table below:

Type of the business	Total	Owned by Jews
Groceries	10	10
Grains and Flax	2	2
Butcher's shops and Cattle Trade	16	8
Restaurants and Taverns	17	12
Food Products	7	6
Beverages	3	3
Textile Products and Furs	14	13
Leather and Shoes	8	7
Haberdashery and Home Utensils	3	3
Medicine and Cosmetics	4	2
Watches, Jewels and Optics	1	1
Tools and Steel Products	9	9
Building Materials and Furniture	1	0
Heating Materials	9	8
Machines, Transportation	2	2
Stationary and Books	3	2
Miscellaneous	15	13

Fragments of the government Survey of Shops in Taurage District

in 1931

Textile

TAURAGĖS APSKR.
Zeltinienė, Tauragė, Vytauto g. 48.

Machines and Transportation

TAURAGĖS APSKR.
Bermanas Hīršas, Tauragė, Turgavietės g. 2.
Rabinavičius Leiba, Tauragė.

Furniture

TAURAGĖS APSKR.
Grėtkis Emilis, Tauragė, Seminarijos g.
Šereševskis J., Tauragė, Šilalės g.
Volfas Lēvas, Tauragė, Respublikos g. 9.

Soap Factories

TAURAGĖS APSKR.
Pagramanskis, Tauragė.

Candies and Chocolate

TAURAGĖS APSKR.
Kvedarienė A., Tauragė, Kęstučio g. 30
Susas, Tauragė, Vytauto g.
Sapyro, Skaudvilė.

Cattle Trade

TAURAGĖS APSKR.
Ceglatas Eugenijus, Šilutė.
Flekseris Beras, Kvėdarna, Lembo km.
Remlingas Arnas, Tauragė.
Švarcmanai Nochum ir Leiba, Tauragė,

According to the same survey, Tavrig had 61 light industry factories, 46 of them owned by Jews (75%), as can be seen in the following table:

Type of the Factory	Total	Jewish Owned
Metal Workshops, Power Plants	1	0
Headstones, Bricks	5	3
Chemical Industry: Spirits, Soaps	1	1
Textile: Wool, Flax, Knitting	7	6
Paper Industry: Printing Presses	1	1
Sawmills, Tar	7	6
Food Products: Mills, Bakeries	25	20
Dresses, Footwear, Furs	8	3
Leather Industry: Production, Cobbling	2	2
Barber Shops and others	4	4

Four Tavrig Jews owned 4 mills: Gitkin-Baikovitz, Yehoshua Cohen, Leib Hirsh, Berelovitz; there was also a candy factory and a sawmill owned by Shereshevsky.

Tavrig Beitar branch

Standing from right: -----, -----, Khavah Leibovitz, Efraim Yezner, ----,
Hayim Yezner (?), Esther Shemesh, -----, -----, Tsevi Levinson, Yerakhmiel
Kablukovsky

Sitting from right: Taibe Leshem, Zalman-Leib Brode, Aizik Levitan,
Netsiv Betar (Commissioner) Eliyahu Glazer, Pinkhas Murinik, -----,
Sitting on the floor: Aharon Bernstein, -----, Yakov Shereshevsky.

Picture supplied by Eliezer Paluksht

In addition to the merchants there were many craftsmen, most of them
organized in a professional society. In 1935 this society had 80 members: 19
tailors, 12 shoemakers, 8 bakers, 5 painters, 5 watchmakers, 5 stitchers, 5
barbers, 3 hatters, 3 butchers, 2 corset makers, 2 glaziers, 2 tinsmiths, 2
photographers, 1 oven builder, 1 electrician, 1 book binder, 1 carpenter, 1
printer, 1 jeweler and 1 other.

There were only two Jewish government clerks in Tavrig, and the
municipality, although 90% of its taxpayers were Jews, did not employ any
Jewish clerks at all. There were almost no Jewish laborers in town, and only in
the big mill were all the employees Jewish. In addition 4 Jewish doctors, 3
dentists, 2 lawyers and 1 midwife worked in the town.

The Jewish Folksbank, which played an important role in the economic life of
the Jewish community, had 234 members in 1927, and 322 members in 1929.
A private bank, director Dr.Vareta, (associate Avraham Epel) added its share
to the economy in town.

The council of Tavrig "HeKhaluts-HaTsair" 1935

Standing from right: Kablukovsky, Khanan Roitman, the ninth Etka Bas. On the floor, first from right Menukhah Itsikovitz

Picture supplied by Miriam Itsikovitz-Zilbersheid

The "Hayim" group of "HeKhaluts-HaTsair" Tavrig 1934

First line standing from right: fourth-Henia Yezner, sixth-Menukhah Itsikovitz. Second line sitting: first-Aharon Brode, third-Miriam Itsikovitz. Beneath lying from right: Matityahu Peshkes

Picture supplied by Miriam Itsikovitz-Zilbersheid

The Itsikovitz Family *(Picture supplied by Eliezer Paluksht)*
Standing from right: Ya'akov, Miriam, Rachel, Tsadok
Sitting: Faivel-Shraga, Menukhah, Freide

In 1939, there were 215 telephone subscribers, of them, 61 were Jews.

The economic situation of the Jewish community began to decline in the middle of the 1930s due to propaganda by the Lithuanian Merchants' Society "Verslas" against buying in Jewish shops. Another factor for this decline was Nazi rule in Germany and the worsening of commercial relations between Lithuania and Germany.

Before the "Pesakh" holiday in March 1935 there was a blood libel in Tavrig. Jews were falsely accused of murdering a Lithuanian baby in order to use his blood for baking "Matsoth". Anti-Semitic proclamations, written in German, were disseminated in town, Jews were beaten in the streets and windows in the Beth Midrash and in Jewish houses were broken. The police detained about 50 people who were suspected of taking part in plotting against the Jews, 30 of them received heavy fines.

Education and Culture

Jewish education in Tavrig was very developed. A Jewish Kindergarten and a modern "Kheder"-"Talmud-Torah" with 120-160 pupils were founded and directed by Lis. The "Kheder" was housed in a special building, built with the help of local philanthropist Leib Baikovitz.

Farewell for Noakh Kopshtein to his "Aliyah" 4.9.1932

Standing from right: Aizik Levitan, Ber Arshinovitz, Hayim Yezner, Yisrael Khatskelevitz, Zalman-Leib Broide, Mendel Itsikovitz

Sitting in the first line from above, from right: Shimon Nudel, ------, Noakh Kopshtein, Shelomoh Seker (?), -------, Reuven Katz

Sitting in the second line from right: ------, ------, ------, Tsevi Levinson, Efraim Yezner-Varpul

Sitting on the floor: Taibe Leshem, -------, ------.

About 200 children studied at the Hebrew school of the "Tarbuth" chain in its own building, which had been erected with the help of the 'Tavrigers" in America. Among the teachers were Lazovsky and Furman.

An additional 200 children studied in the four classes Hebrew pro-gymnasium until 1940, when it was closed under Soviet rule. A former Tavrig Jew in America named Miler donated money for the erection of a modern building for the pro-gymnasium, to be equipped with water supply, sewage and central heating. The inauguration of the building took place in February 1930, its last director being Hayim Mariampolsky. The first director was Efraim Leibzon.

There was a library of the Z"S party founded by Dov Gurevitz, with thousands of books in Yiddish and Hebrew. From time to time the "Lithuanian Government Theater" and "The Jewish Theater" from Kovno would perform in town. There were two cinemas in Tavrig, one of them owned by a Jew.

Sixth class of the Hebrew pro-gymnasium 1931

Standing from right: ------, Sioma Taitelman, Shoshanah Melamed, Miriam Itsikovitz. Sitting in front: teacher H.Mariampolsky

(Picture supplied by Miriam Itsikovitz-Zilbersheid)

During the thirties a private music school was active in the town, whose piano teacher was Miss Roza Palangin. Her class consisted of 22 pupils in 1938, six of them Jewish girls. She immigrated to America in 1940. Her parents were exiled to Komi SSR in June 1941, where they died of hunger in 1943 before aid from America managed to reach them.

Zionist and other activities

All Zionist parties had their adherents in Tavrig. In the table below we can see how Tavrig Zionists voted for the various parties at six Zionist Congresses:

Cong. Nr.	Year	Total Shek.	Total Voter	Labor Party Z"S	Z"Z	Rev.	G.Z. A	B	Gros.	Miz.
14	1925	80	--	--	--	--	--	--	--	
15	1927	136	113	21	35	11	18	--	--	28
16	1929	351	206	25	58	27	25	--	--	71
17	1931	302	254	48	57	42	25	--	--	82
18	1933	775	661	330		50	54	--	83	144
19	1935	1,027	917	348		--	37	61	259	212

Cong.-Congress; Shek.-Shekalim; Rev.-Revisionists; G.Z.-General Zionists; Gros.-Grosmanists; Miz.-Mizrahi

Standing from right: Mina Khi, Eti Cahan, Sarah Vatnik, Tserne Fridman

Sitting: Freide Bender, Dora Epel, teacher H. Mariampolsky, ----, ----.

Sitting on the floor: Levinson, Shemuel Shereshevsky, Noakh Holtsberg

(Picture supplied by Dora Epel-Jofe)

Most Jewish youth in Tavrig belonged to the Zionist youth organizations. There were branches of "HaShomer-HaTsair", "Beitar", "Benei-Akiva", "HeKhalutz", "HeKhalutz-HaTsair", "Netsakh" (Noar Zioni Khalutsi) and others. There was also a branch of the sport organization "Maccabi" with about 58 members.

In 1933 a "Kibbutz Hakhsharah" (Training Kibbutz) "Hakovesh" was organized, most of its members emigrating to Eretz Yisrael, and in the beginning of 1940 there was a Kibbutz Hakhsharah with 60 members of "HeKhalutz" who had escaped from Poland.

Several Jewish youngsters were members of the underground Communist party. The "Tifereth Bakhurim" society, headed by Eliezer-Hilel Hofenstein, was active among the religious youth. There was a branch of the society of Jewish soldiers who had participated in the Lithuanian Independence War (Front Kemfer). This branch had 40 members and it held a significant place in public life, which was also noted by Lithuanian institutions, despite the propaganda of their comrades in arms against buying in Jewish shops.

Religion and Welfare

The religious life of Tavrig Jews was concentrated in four "Batei-Midrash": the great Beth-Midrash, a two storey brick building, the Beth-Midrash "Tifereth-Bakhurim", the Beth-Midrash "Beth-David" and the Beth-Midrash of Baikovitz. There were also two "Kloizim"- the "Shilel Kloiz" and the "Kloiz" in the old town.

For list of Rabbis who served in Tavrig during this period see Appendix 1.

First class of the "Talmud-Torah", farewell from teacher Meirovitz, 1937

Standing from right: Shuster*, Varpul Shelomoh, Galonsky Aharon*, Shkolnik Noakh*, Epshtein Mosheh

Sitting from right: Bulovin*, Genende Dov-Ber*, Teacher Lis*, Teacher Meirovitz, Paluksht Eliezer, Shlekhter Hayim-David*

Sitting on the floor: Shmiltiner*, Baron Tsevi-Hirsh, Peshkes Matityahu*

(*) murdered in the Holocaust in Lithuania

(Picture supplied by Dora Epel-Jofe)

Seventh Graduating Class of Tavrig Hebrew Elementary School 1931

Standing from right: Devorah Varpul, Dora Epel, Mekhanik, Dinah Goldblat, Rivkah Kaplan, Eti Cahan, Ita Levitan.

Sitting: the teachers Fain, Furman, Lazovsky, Zimzon, Naividel

Third line sitting from right: Freide Bender, Gita Kaplan, Shemuel Shereshevsky, Sonia Most, Rachel Gitelson. *Picture supplied by Eliezer Paluksht*

Graduating class of the Hebrew Elementary School 1936-37

First line standing from right: Hirsh Fish, Sarah Birshtansky, Sonia Shlomovitz, Leah Varpul, ---Gurvitz, Rachel Ozer, Zelda Fogelman, Leizerin

Second line standing from right: ----, Henia Borokhovitz, Reize Leizerovitz, ------, Tonia German, Khayah Fridman, Rachel Yezner, Henia Kofman, ------.

The Teachers sitting: Zimzon, Lithuanian language teacher, Lozovsky, Fruma Furman, Furman, Naividel, Fain.

Third line sitting; ----, ----, Devorah Gershon, Hanah Baron, Beile Kaplan, Rivah Kreinovitz, Gershon Volfson.

Sitting on the floor: Frida Shapira, Guta Epshtein, Roza Levit (?), --, ---.

(Picture supplied by Rivah Kreinovitz-Shnaider)

After the liquidation of the community committee at the end of 1925, the "Ezrah" society took over most of its functions. Its possessions included the modern bathhouse with bathtubs and a sauna which had been built with donations from former "Tavrigers" in the USA; the abattoir, also used by non Jewish butchers, its income paying the salaries of the Rabbi and the slaughterers (Shokhtim); the "Khevrah-Kadisha", which also added to the income of the society, its last chairman being Sh. Most.

Additionally there were in Tavrig two "Gemiluth-Khasadim" societies, "Linath-HaTsedek" as well as ladies' societies.

After Rabbi Fridman emigrated to Eretz-Yisrael (see Appendix 1), a controversy erupted with regard to secret elections for the local rabbinate, which were opposed by seven public workers, which included members of the management of the "Ezrah" and the craftsmen societies. These workers were detained by the authorities for several weeks.

(Picture supplied by Dora Epel-Jofe)

Memento of visit of Meir Grosman-leader of the "Grosmanist" party

Sitting in the first line from right: Telem, Krivavnik, Dr.Shapira, M.Grosman, Dr.Vareta, ----, Mrs. Batiah Shereshevsky, Mrs Krivavnik

Sitting in the second line from right: ----, ----, Reuven Katz, Benyaminovitz, Mendel Fridman, Shereshevsky, -------------, Alter Gudel, Adv. Terespolsky, Mrs Rabinovitz, (standing behind them) Salomon Fridman,-----, Leo Epel, -----, Dr. Aronson Libe, ------.

מתכבדים אני בזה להזמין את כבודו ו"ב לבוא לשמחת חג

ה ב ר - מ צ ו ה

של בננו מנחם אליעזר

שתהיה בשבת פ' משפטים כט שבט תרצ"ט (18 II 1939)

רחל ונתן פאלוקסט   מאורגת

The original invitation to the Bar-Mitzvah of Menakhem-Eliezer Paluksht

When Mr. Paluksht arrived in Israel in 1990 he had no Birth Certificate and his Lithuanian surname Palukshtas did not sound Jewish. This invitation, which had been kept by his Israeli relative all these years, solved the problem of the uncertainty of his being a Jew.

For the partial list of personalities born in Tavrig see Appendix 2.

Family group 1935-36
Standing from right: Dr.Yakov Shakhnovitz, his wife Zhenia Epel,
Mrs. Etel Epel, Zheni Fridman, Leo Epel, Avraham Epel
(Picture supplied by Dora Epel-Jofe)

The Leibzon Family - From right: Efraim, Mina, David, Adah
(Picture supplied by Adah Leibzon-Kantorovitz)

During World War II and Afterwards.

World War II started with the German invasion of Poland on the 1st of September 1939, but its consequences for Lithuanian Jews in general and Tavrig Jews in particular had already been felt several months earlier. On the 20th of March 1939, Hitler sent an ultimatum to Lithuania to leave Memel within 24 hours. About 7,000 Jews who lived in Memel and in its region escaped, leaving most of their belongings behind, looking for asylum in the Zemaitija region and in Kovno. Many of them settled in Tavrig, where the Jewish community cared for them.

In June 1940 Lithuania was annexed by the Soviet Union, becoming a Soviet Republic. Following new rules, the majority of factories and shops belonging to Jews in Tavrig were nationalized and commissars were appointed to manage them. All Zionist parties and youth organizations were disbanded, several of the activists were detained, Hebrew educational institutions were closed, and the Hebrew school changed to a Yiddish one (see certificate below that was issued when the pro-gymnasium was already closed).

A hand written certificate signed by the director of the Hebrew private pro-gymnasium Hayim Mariampolsky on June 16th 1940, in which he attests that Paluksht Leizer-Mendel passed the examinations of the third class on the 14th of June 1940.

Those members who were Polish refugees in the "HeKhalutz" "Kibbutz Hakhsharah", were branded as being "unreliable elements" under the new rule and were scattered over several towns in Zemaitija - Kelem, Vilkomir, Yaneve. When Germany invaded Lithuania, about two thirds of them managed to escape to Russia, and after the war about thirty of them came to Israel.

The last class (the third) of the Hebrew pro-gymnasium, June 1940

Standing from right: Gershon Volfson*, Leah Varpul*, Lev Heselkovitz, Rachel Ozer, Hirsh Fish, ----, Shemuel Melamdovitz*, Sonia Shlomovitz.

Sitting from right: Devorah Gershon*, Gita Fridman*, Dora Katsev*, Hene Borokhovitz*, Rivkah Kreinovitz, Hayah Fridman.

Sitting in the second line from above: Rachel Yezner*, Tonia German, Reize Leizerovitz*, teacher Hayim Mariampolsky, Hanah Baron, Beile Kaplan*,

Hene Kofman*.

Lying on the floor, from right: Eliezer Paluksht,----Shuster*.

(*) murdered in the Holocaust (the others are living in Israel or passed away there)

(Picture supplied by Rivkah Kreinovitz-Shnaider)

The supply of goods decreased and as a result prices soared. The middle class, mostly Jewish, bore most of the brunt, and the standard of living dropped gradually. At the beginning of June 1941, 17 Jewish families, altogether about 60 people, who were considered "unreliable elements", were exiled to Komi SSR, the most northern part of European Russia. Some of the exiles began to receive food parcels from former Tavrigers in Baltimore, USA, by the beginning of 1942. Later on almost all the exiles there received parcels from "The Association of Lithuanian Jews" in the USA on a regular basis. This aid helped many families to survive these difficult years.

Members of the Kibbutz Hakhsharah, Tavrig 1940

A list of the exiles appears in Appendix 4.

The German army occupied Tavrig on June 22, 1941, the first day of the war between Germany and the Soviet Union, after bombing the town, when most of its houses were destroyed. About 20 Jews were injured. Residents of the town, including Jews, escaped to nearby villages, others arrived in Shavl and other towns in this region, with only a few managing to reach Russia. After the battles ended, the returning Jews whose houses had been left intact, found that their homes had been looted by their Lithuanian neighbors.

Tavrig was located on a strip of 25 km near the border with Germany subject to the order of the S.S. Einsatzgruppe commander F.Stahlecker (he was hanged after the war by the Soviets). According to his order this strip of land had do be handed over to the Gestapo chief from Tilzit Hans Boehme with a special assignment to cleanse it from Jews and Communists.

At first Jewish life and property were in the hands of the Lithuanian nationalists. Several days later, a Gestapo man named Schwarz arrived in Tavrig and asked the new Mayor Jonas Jurgilas for help to identify Communists. Under orders from the Gestapo, the local police chief F.Mintautas and his policemen detained 300 Jewish men and 25 non-Jewish Communists, some of the latter being released later. The Jewish men were kept in the detention barracks of the 7th Infantry regiment of the former Lithuanian army.

Hans Boehme determined the date of the murder for the 2nd of July 1941 and he himself participated. He let it be known that he wanted to show his men a "sample action", so that they would learn how to behave from now on.

On the 2nd of July 1941 the detainees were brought to the nearby village of Vizbutai (Vizhbutai) where anti-tank ditches had been dug. The Jews were compelled to deepen the ditches and after everything they had was taken away from them, they were forced to kneel at the edge of the ditch with their faces turned towards it. Then the Gestapo men and their Lithuanian helpers shot them in their necks and pushed them into the ditch. Evidence in the Ulm trial showed that Dr. Yafe and dentist Dr. Most were among the murdered.

A second group of 122 Jewish men were murdered on the road to Shilel (Silale) between the 3rd and the 10th of July. The arrest of Jewish men and the abuse of young Jewish women did not stop, and from the first day of the armed Lithuanians' rule there were no limits to their atrocities.

The local Rabbi Levi Shpitz was also abused and shot to death by the Lithuanians after they asked him for a list of Jewish Communists which, of course, he did not have.

During the first days of occupation, a German entered the house of the 80 year old Dr.Y.Shapira and ordered him to dig a pit for burying a dead horse which lay beside his house. The old doctor hesitated, not understanding what he had to do. The German ordered two women, who were called Blind and Most, to dig the pit together with the doctor, upon which he stood the doctor beside the cadaver of the horse and shot him to death, then ordered the women to bury the doctor together with the cadaver of the horse.

Day after day there were arrests, with men and young women being sent to carry out so called work, but nobody returned. They were murdered and buried in mass graves around Tavrig.

The situation of the women and children and the few old men who still survived worsened from day to day. Deserted, orphaned, frightened, starving and helpless they walked aimlessly in the town.

On the 6th of September 1941 the District commander V.Milimas sent a "not to be published" circular (Nr.227) to the Mayor of Tavrig, to the Chairmen of the County Councils and to the police commanders, which contained details of the orders of treatment of the Jews.

The first clause said that the Jews had to be concentrated in one place, and that they must elect a Jewish council by themselves. Any Jew who applies to the authorities had to have the approval of the council. There followed orders of making it compulsory for Jews to wear a yellow "Magen-David" on their clothes; the counting of the imprisoned; a ban on the transfer of property to non-Jews; a ban of walking on sidewalks; Jewish doctors were allowed to care only for Jews; exceptions could be made for the employment of Jewish artisans only where there were no non-Jews who could do the job; Jewish property had to be nationalized and Jews were banned from administering their own property.

Clause 10 of this circular said that Jews could only get the most elementary food products from remains left over after the non-Jewish population had received its needs. This clause also permitted the establishment of a Jewish police to keep order.

The mass graves near Vizbutai village

The Monument on the mass graves near Vizbutai village with the inscription in Yiddish and Lithuanian: "At this place Hitler's murderers and their local helpers murdered 900 Jewish men in 1941 ".

Clause 12 allowed Jews to be sent to work where there was a shortage of non-Jewish workers. Their payment had to be brought to the office of the District Governor, where the workers would receive their wages.

On the same day, September 6, 1941, the police commanders of Tavrig received circular Nr. 228 for transferring Jews into one place.

All the Jews were concentrated into incomplete huts in Vytautas Street, which the Soviet army had started to build as sheds for trucks. The plot was fenced off with barbed wire and guarded by Lithuanian auxiliary police. Every strong woman and grown up child was sent to work. It was forbidden to bring in food. These huts, called a Ghetto, housed Jews in inhuman conditions, hungry and dirty, till the 13th of September. Then they were told to prepare to move to another place, where their conditions would "improve".

On the 16th of September (24 of Elul 5701) trucks arrived to transport all of them to the Tavrig grove, about 6 km northwest of the town, 100-150 meters from the road to Shilel. There they were shot by drunken Lithuanian auxiliary policemen, who excelled in their cruelty. Little babies were shredded in two or their skulls were shattered on trees or rocks and thrown into the pits. A beautiful young girl, Henia Yezner, jumped into the pit alive after the murderers started to molest her.

On this day, 513 old women and children were forced to hand over all the valuables they still owned, to undress down to their underwear, and then they were murdered. One of the Lithuanian murderers, Atkatsaitis, boasted that "he still managed to slap a fat Jewish woman on the bottom".

Several Jews who hid with peasants in the vicinity were caught after a short time, as a result of information given by neighbors.

Only a few Jews were left in Tavrig. Nadel, Nathan Goldberg and Yitshak Shum who worked at the military command, Yisrael Axelrod who worked as a specialist at the sawmill of Shereshevsky. After several weeks they were also murdered. The skilled tanner F.Itzkovitz, his wife and children were left alive for several more months, but after the Germans murdered his family he hanged himself.

According to Soviet sources about 3,000 men, women and children are buried in the mass graves in the Tavrig grove near the village of Antosunija. Near the village of Vizbutai approximately another 900 men and one woman are buried.

In October 1991 a monument on the mass graves at Antosunija, created by the Lithuanian sculptor Bagdonas, was inaugurated at an impressive ceremony. Two plates on top of the monument have inscriptions in Yiddish and Lithuanian: **"At this place Hitler's murderers and their local helpers murdered about 3,000 Jews, men, women and children"**.

On the mass grave in Vizbutai a monument was erected with the following inscription in Yiddish and Lithuanian: **"At this place Hitler's murderers and their local helpers murdered 900 Jewish men in 1941 "**.

After the war a few Jews returned to Tavrig, but their number diminished over the years. **In 1970 14 Jews lived there, in 1979--12 and in 1989--only 8.**

Mass grave and monument at Antosunija

Two plates on top of the monument have inscriptions in Yiddish and Lithuanian: "At this place Hitler's murderers and their local helpers murdered about 3,000 Jews, men, women and children".

A black marble plate was also erected, on which is written: "Their only guilt: they were Jews, whose ancestors lived here in peace for hundreds of years. On this soil they built houses, they were craftsmen, merchants, doctors, and believed in one God. Their memory shall be forever"

Sources:

Yad-Vashem Archives: M-1/E-1738/1619; M-9/8(3), 15(6); M-21/I/661, III/41;

M-33/984, 4043; P-21/2-94; TR-2 report19; TR-10/40, 275, 1096; 0-3/2592, 4043, 6093, 7519; 0-15/634; 0-32-4;

Koniukhovsky collection 0-71. Files 6, 7, 20, 40, 46, 163.

YIVO, NY-Lithuanian Communities Collection, files1386, 1561, 1665.

Galin Hayim, The Kibbutz in Tavrig-Lithuania, History of a Group of Khalutsim from Poland, June 1940 till the end of World War II, (Hebrew), Kiryath-Bialik 1991.

HaMeilitz (St. Petersburg) (Hebrew): 26.4.1881, 7.5.1883, 18.2.1884, 21.3.1884, 24.3.1884, 31.3.1884, 6.6.1884, 18.7.1884, 1.8.1884, 7.11.1884,5.12.1884, 8.12.1884, 14.2.1889, 3.4.1889, 21.12.1896, 15.7.1898,7.7.1901, 13.5.1902.

Dos Vort, Kovno (Yiddish): 26.12.1934, 24.3.1935, 26.3.1935, 28.4.1935.

Folksblat, Kovno (Yiddish): 25.3.1935, 5.6.1935, 17.6.1935, 18.6.1935.

Unzer Veg (Our way) (Yiddish), Kovno, 10.1.1926.

Di Yiddishe Shtime, Kovno (Yiddish), 29.10.1924, 29.5.1928, 21.2.1930, 27.6.1930, 12.5.1931, 19.6.1931, 7.7.1931, 18.3.1932, 28.4.1935, 30.4.1935, 5.5.1935, 15.5.1935, 22.3.1936, 20.3.1938, 23.4.1938, 12.5.1938.

Tauragieciu Balsas (Lithuanian) 2.10.1991.

Gimtasis, Nr. 35, 27 August-2 September, Vilnius, Rimvydas Racenas and Lazaris Palukstas "Zydams nebuvo lengviau" (To the Jews it was not easier).

Appendix 1

A partial list of Rabbis who served in Tavrig

Aryeh-Leib ben Shaul (approx. 1820-1830). As a result of frequent blood libels, decided to study French in order to be able to converse with government officials and estate owners, for which his wife divorced him. It was recorded that on one of these cases he went to Petersburg in order to meet Czar Nikolai the First, but there are no details. Traveling back in carts he became ill and died in Vilna in the spring of 1839, but was buried in Tavrig.

Shimon Zarkhi (born 1788 in Zhezhmer - died 1860 in Jerusalem). During a famine in 1847, Rabbi Zarkhi took an important part in helping the poor. He studied Algebra and Astronomy by himself and also read Latin and Greek books. He arrived in Jerusalem in 1856 where he founded the "Talmud-Torah" "Etz- Hayim".

Mosheh-Yitskhak haLevi Segal, in Tavrig from 1854.

Gershon-Mendel Ziv, in Tavrig 1880-1902.

Yitskhak-Ze'ev Olshwanger (1825 in Plungian-1896 in Petersburg), in Tavrig 1846-1878, was active in the "Khovevei Zion" movement, later Rabbi in Petersburg where he studied sciences, knew Russian and German well.

Avraham-Aharon haCohen Burstein (1867-1926 in Jerusalem). A delegate to the Katowitz conference of "Agudath-Yisrael" in 1912, came to Israel in 1924 and was a teacher at the "Merkaz Harav" yeshivah in Jerusalem till his death.

Yitskhak-Izik Fridman (1874-1944). One of the founders and leaders of the "Mizrakhi" party in Lithuania. Arrived in Israel in 1935 and was the Rabbi of the "Nakhalath-Yitskhak" quarter of Tel-Aviv for nine years. Published many books on religious and Judaic issues.

Levi-Tsevi Shpitz (1887-1941) the last Rabbi of Tavrig, murdered by Lithuanians in July 1941.

Righteous Teachers.

Shelomoh Fridberg (1868); **Barukh-Nathanel Naividel**, born in Tavrig in 1847; **Yosef Gorfinkel; Duber Toiber; David-Shelomoh Epstein;**

Appendix 2

A partial list of personalities born in Tavrig.

Shemuel-Yosef Shereshevsky (1831-died in New York), translated the Bible into Chinese, lived many years in Tokyo.

Iser-Ber Wolf (1844-1935), industrialist, philanthropist and public worker in Kovno.

Menakhem-Dov Dagutsky (1846-?), 1886 Rabbi in Birmingham, 1891-Johannesburg, 1896- Rochester.

David-Teveli Katsenelenboigen (1850-1931), Rabbi in Virbaln, Suwalk, and St. Petersburg, public worker and author of books on Talmudic subjects.

Barukh Rabinovitz (1880-?) Rabbi in Zuhovitz, Vitebsk and from 1926 in Chicago.

Hayim-Fishel Epstein (1874-1942), Chief Rabbi in Dorpat (Latvia) and lecturer at the local university. From 1923 Rabbi in Cleveland, Cincinnati, Brooklyn and St. Louis. Officiated as President of the Orthodox Rabbis Society and published books and articles.

Sh.P.Rabinovitz (1845-1911), writer and translator. Published books on Jewish history in Warsaw and translated "The History of the Jewish People" by Graetz into Hebrew. (8 volumes)

Beinish Epstein (1896-1981). From 1926 in America, published articles in the American Jewish press, in the Warsaw "Moment" and in Hebrew periodicals in Israel.

Y.L. Barukh (Borukhovitz) (1873-1953), writer and translator, from 1926 in Israel, published poems, stories, historic and literary essays in the Hebrew press and translated more than 20 books from Yiddish, English and German into Hebrew. Died in Tel-Aviv.

Dr. Aba Lapin (1863-1940), physician and public worker, chairman of the Historic-Ethnographic Society of Lithuanian Jews and member of the Zionist center.

Dr.Meirovitz famous surgeon, who worked for many years at the Jewish Hospital "Bikur-Kholim" in Kovno.

Reuven Barkath (1905-?), son of Rabbi A.A.Burstein, member of the labor party center in Eretz-Yisrael, member of the directorate of the "Workers Association", Ambassador of Israel to Norway, Chairman of the 7th Knesset".

Yehoshua Avni (Goldberg) one of the first settlers in Herzliyah.

Appendix 4

List of exiled Tavrig Jews to Komi SSR in June 1941.

(supplied by Eliezer Paluksht)

Abramovitz Nakhman* + 4 family members

Aronson Yevsey * + 3 family members

Berman Hirsh + 1 family member

Bernstein Feivel + 0 family members

Berman Orl * + 1 family member

Gudel Albert + 3 family members

Gitkin Yosef + 2 family members

Gitkin Iliya + 1 family member

Hirzon Avraham * + 3 family members

Epel Avraham + 2 family members

Epstein Yisrael * + 4 family members

Fridman Mendel * + 4 family members

Kaplan Yisrael + 2 family members

Palagin Max * + 1 family member

Paluksht Nathan * + 4 family members

Pubzup Gedalyah * + 3 family members

Shereshevsky Herzl + 3 family members

(*) died in exile

Altogether 17 families with 58 people were exiled from Tavrig to Komi SSR.
A few of the family heads were sent to the terrible Reshoty camps in Siberia.

Tauragnai (Taragin)

Taragin is situated in the northeastern part of Lithuania on the shore of Lake Tauragnas about 15 km south east from the district administrative capitol Utyan (Utena). In historical sources from the end of the 16th century Taragin is mentioned as a village and an estate bearing the same name. Later the estate belonged to the noble family Poslovsky. In 1792 regular market days took place in town and several taverns and a workshop produced alcohol acted there.

Until 1795 Taragin was part of the Polish-Lithuanian Kingdom, when the third division of Poland by the three superpowers of those times - Russia, Prussia and Austria - caused Lithuania to become partly Russian and partly Prussian. The part of Lithuania which included Taragin fell under czarist Russian rule, firstly as part of the Vilna province (Gubernia) and from 1843 part of the Kovno province. Taragin was then a county administrative center in the Novo-Alexandrovsk (Zarasai) district with 263 people in 1859. Despite this Taragin was an underdeveloped town. There were in it only 2 public wells and its inhabitants had to carry water in barrels from the lake. During the Lithuanian rule (1918-1940) as well, most of its streets were unpaved and till the second half of the 1930s there was no electricity in town, but it had a natural beautiful view which attracted vacationers.

Jews settled in Taragin in the 18th century. During the next years they established community institutions in center of them the Beth-Midrash and the Kloiz.

They made their living mainly of peddling, commerce, craft and agriculture. The fire of the end of 1893 ruined 50 Jewish houses. Despite the increasing emigration abroad 120 Jewish families still left in town before World War I.

Taragin Jews appear in lists of donors for buying land in Eretz-Yisrael. The collector was Yits'hak Shakhatovitz.

In 1897 there were in Taragin 1,070 citizens of them 596 Jews (56%).

On February 16, 1918, the establishment of the Lithuanian State was proclaimed. Consequently the German army withdrew from the area, and life in Taragin gradually returned to normal.

Following the law of autonomy for minorities, issued by the new Lithuanian government, the minister for Jewish affairs Dr. Menakhem (Max) Soloveitshik ordered elections to Community Committees (Va'ad Kehilah) to be held in the summer of 1919. The elections in Taragin took place in 1922 and Committee of 5 members was elected headed by Yits'hak Rapaport. The Committee, active till the end of 1925 when the autonomy was annulled, was in charge of all aspects of community life.

According to the first census conducted in 1923 by the Lithuanian government, the population of Taragin totaled 999 people and of them 477 (48%) were Jewish.

The economic situation of Taragin's Jews was poor. Also in this period, like before World War I, the main livelihood was small commerce and craft. According to the government survey on shops in the state, performed in 1931, there were in Taragin 7 Jewish owned shops: 3 textile, 1 restaurant, 1 wool combing workshop and 2 weaving work shops. 5 telephones were in town in 1939, but only one of them belonged to the Jewish doctor Leib Romanov.

In 1937 23 Jewish artisans acted in town: 5 tailors, 4 oven builders, 3 knitters, 2 butchers, 2 glaziers, 2 blacksmiths, 1 baker, 1 painter, 1 carpenter and 2 others.

The main economic activity happened at the "Market Day" which took place at Tuesdays. The relations between the Jews and their Christian neighbors were good comparing with other towns.

The Jewish children studied at the elementary school of the religious "Yavneh" chain (about 55 children in average). There acted also a "Kheder" with about 25 boys. The cultural activity in town was very limited. The library which was established by a group of initiative men did not operate for long. Elections for the Zionist Congresses took place in Taragin only in 1935. All 28 voters voted for the Labor party.

A well-known person in town was the benefactor Rachel Menishevitz. The poet Y. L. Gordon wrote a poem about her.

During the years 1940-1941, when Lithuania was a Soviet Republic, most of the Jewish institutions and organizations were dissolved and several of the Jewish shops were nationalized. Along with this, several Jews integrated into the government institutions and into the economy.

With the outbreak of the war between Germany and The Soviet Union, a big unit of the Red Army garrisoned in Taragin and held their position several days after almost all of Lithuania had been captured by the Germans. After the retreat of the relics of this unit, armed Lithuanian nationalists took over the rule in town. During the fight the local church was hit, a fact that increased the aggravation of the population, and found led to attacks and of the local Jews and those who happen to be in Taragin trying to escape to Russia.

The rabbis who served in Taragin were:

Shemuel Albin (1798-1862)

Yosef-Yehoshua Utyaner (----1874)

Eliezer-Tsevi Pines in Taragin since 1875 till 1937, died at the age of 94

Ya'akov Pines son of Eliezer. Last Rabbi of Taragin. Murdered in 1941

The "Yavneh" school

The Old Wooden Synagogue

Rabbi Eliezer-Tsevi Pines

In one night most of the Jewish population was expelled from their homes. They were concentrated into two groups, with more than hundred people in each group. One group was brought to the nearby village Taurapilis and the other group to Lataliai. There they were accommodated in cowsheds and stables and were sent to work at the farms nearby. For food they had to care themselves.

After three days the men were sent to dig pits with the pretext that many killed horses that are laying in the fields have to be buried. During two nights the men armed with spades dug the pits and in the mornings they returned. At the third night they were brought to pits, this time without the spades, were forced to undress, pushed into the pits and shot. The same happened to the other groups. The dead and the wounded were buried together. There were cases when shocked people jumped into the pit before they were shot.

For several days after the murder a guard was posted at the graves. No survivors are known.

The mass graves of Taragin Jews are included in the site of the large mass graves of Utyan and so it was indicated at the memorial monument.

The sculpture "Pain" in front of the entrance gate to the mass graves of the Jews of Utyan and surroundings

(Designer: V. Simonelis)

At the beginning of the 1990s a memorial tablet was fixed at the old Jewish cemetery of Taragin with the inscription in Lithuanian and Yiddish: **"The Old Jewish Cemetery - Blessed is the Memory of the Deceased"**.

Bibliography:

YIVO NY, Lithuanian Communities Collection, Files 459-460

Folksblat (daily) (Yiddish)-Kovno, 23.7.1935

The mass graves and the monument

The tablet of the monument with the inscription in Yiddish and Lithuanian:

"In this place the Hitler murderers and their local helpers at July-August 1941 murdered about 8,000 Jews-men, women, children."

Telšiai (Telz)

Telz, (in Yiddish) one of the oldest towns in Lithuania, is situated in the northwestern part of Lithuania - the Zemaitija region - on the shores of Lake Mastis, and was mentioned in the chronicles of a Crusader Order in 1320. During the second half of the 15th century a royal estate was established there; merchants and artisans began to settle around it. The growing settlement suffered badly during the Swedish invasion in 1710, and two thirds of its population perished from epidemics at that time. In the middle of the 18th century a court was established in Telz, contributing to the development and growth of the town.

Telz was granted the Magdeburg Rights of self rule by King Stanislaw-August in 1791.

Until 1795 Telz was part of the Polish-Lithuanian Kingdom, when the third division of Poland by the three superpowers of those times - Russia, Prussia and Austria - caused Lithuania to become partly Russian and partly Prussian. The part of Lithuania which included Telz fell under Czarist Russian rule, first from 1802 as part of the Vilna Province (Gubernia) as a district administrative center and from 1843 as part of the Kovno Province.

In 1812 Napoleon's retreating army passed through Telz, leaving behind desolation as well as a big gun, which can still be seen in the town park.

The Main Street (about 1916)

The town was damaged during the Polish rebellions of 1831 and 1863. In 1907 a fire lasting two days caused much damage, when the center of the town was burnt down. After some time the town was rebuilt, but brick houses were erected instead of the old wooden houses.

During World War I Telz was occupied by the German army who ruled there from 1915 till 1918, after which the Bolsheviks ruled for a short period.

Until 1931 Telz was the district administrative capitol without the rights of a town, and only then was a municipality elected. The Telz district included the towns of Seda, Zidikai, Skaudvile, Salantai, Kretinga, Plunge, Varniai, Gargzdai.

At the beginning of the 1930s a railway was constructed which connected Telz to the port of Klaipeda as well as to the Lithuanian railway network. This was a dominant factor in the economic development of the town.

Jewish Settlement till after World War 1.

Apparently Jews settled in Telz at the beginning of the 17th century. At the time, during which the "Va'ad Medinath Lita" (1623-1764) was established, the Telz community was a subject of the "Kahal" of the Keidan district.

According to the order of the Russian Senate of the 1st of January 1800, a municipal council was established in Telz, which included three Jewish delegates. In 1804 the Jews were removed from the municipality at the request of the Christian delegates.

2,500 people lived in Telz in 1797, of them 1,650 were Jews (66%).

Telz Jews also suffered from "Blood Libels", one in 1758, the second in 1827. In both cases the so called "accused" were released by the court, but as a result the Jewish population suffered through a period of fear. There were also plots by estate owners who saw the Jews as competitors in producing and selling alcohol, and in 1825 the nobles asked the Tsar to expel the Jews because they "...spread diseases... and threaten to rob and to steal...".

During the Polish rebellion of 1831 Telz Jews suffered both from the rebels and from the Cossacks. A Jew called Monish (Menashe) Lukniker was accused of helping the rebels and was hanged by the Russian rulers.

When the authorities in Telz started to arm the population and to enlist men to fight the rebels, local Jews suggested to the authorities that they should not conscript Jews into the army, as they had no arms and also did not know how to use them. Instead they offered to supply the army with the necessary materials, such as steel, leather, gunpowder etc. to which the authorities agreed, and a document was signed to this effect.

Telz was not spared the years of famine 1869-1872. An assistance committee for Telz Jews, established on behalf of the Gubernator, included the following members: Dr. Mapu, Yehudah-Leib Gordon, the merchants Leib Kantsel (Gordon's father-in-law), and Berman. Later on Izik Rabinovitz and wife, Idel Gordon, Meir Atlas, Yehoshua-Heshl Margalioth, Yitshak Elyashev, Hayim Rabinovitz and his son in law Broide, Rabbiner Khazanovitz, Yeshaya Bai, Shabtai Raseinsky, Aharon Neimark, Gershon Meirovitz were also active. In the Hebrew newspaper "HaMagid" of the years 1872 and 1874, there are lists of Telz Jews who donated money for hunger victims in other Lithuanian towns.

(See list in Jewishgen.Org.- Databases-Lithuania-HaMagid-by Jeffrey Maynard)

In 1870 Telz had 6,481 residents, including 4,399 Jews (68%), and in 1897 there were 6,000 residents and of them 3,088 were Jews (51%).

During the persecutions and pogroms against Jews in the 1880s in Ukraine and other places, the self confidence of Telz Jews was damaged, as a result of which and also because of conscription into the army for a period of six years, many young Jewish men left Telz and immigrated to America, Argentina and South Africa. This wave of immigration lasted till World War I, and during the years 1870-1923 the Jewish population of Telz decreased by 2,854 people. The cholera epidemic of 1893 took many victims, especially among poor Jews, who lived in overcrowded and bad hygienic conditions. The local rabbi, Eliezer Gordon, initiated the establishment of a committee which collected money from the rich in order to supply the sick with medicines, disinfectants and medical help. Around this time the Telz Jewish hospital was established.

The local Jews made their living from commerce, crafts and peddling. In 1841 there were 25 Jewish artisans: 14 tailors, 10 shoemakers and one watchmaker, not counting wandering artisans. Until World War I there was a strong organization of Jewish artisans, which helped its members with loans for buying raw materials and tools. Among the Jewish merchants there were several who had big businesses of grains and flax and made a good living. There were also several textile merchants who imported merchandise from Germany, one of them being Ya'akov Rabinovitz.

The Market Place in Telz 1950

"The Great Yeshivah" was a source of income of many families, who supplied living quarters and food for hundreds of its students. Many families maintained gardens beside their houses as additional income. In the 1880s many Jewish families earned their living while residing in the surrounding villages.

The economic situation of most Telz Jews - the small shop owners, the artisans, the peddlers, the coachmen and the carriers - was difficult. There were also poor people who subsisted on welfare support and some who collected alms by going from house to house.

Telz had four synagogues (Beth-Midrash): the 'great', of the tailors, of the butchers and of the soldiers, where Jewish soldiers would swear the oath of allegiance to the Tsar. The great "Beth Midrash" in particular was impressive because of its dimensions, having beside it a large backyard, the "Shulhoif", where the "Khupah" of wedding couples would be arranged, as well as lamentations during funerals. In addition to prayers, these synagogues were the centers of activities for various societies dealing with "Torah" studies, such as "Talmud", Mishnah", 'Ein Ya'akov" etc.

The Telz "Yeshivah", which had been established in 1880 by three young men (Avreikhim)-Yitshak Ya'akov Openheim, Meir Atlas, Zalman Abel- with the help of a German Jew - Ovadyah Lakhman from Berlin - developed and prospered, and after Rabbi Eliezer Gordon was nominated as its head in 1884, it became the main institution of orthodox education. At the end of 19th century it had about 400 students and was counted as one of the greatest in the world. Next to it there was a preparatory class (Yeshivah Ketanah) for boys aged 10-16.

Amongst the graduates of this "Yeshivah" were rabbis and spiritual leaders of great Jewish communities in the Diaspora and in Israel, such as Rabbi Professor Simchah Asaf, Rabbi Yekhezkel Abramsky, Professor Ben-Zion Dinur, Avraham Hartsfeld, M.Bar-Ilan and others.

The "Yeshivah" Building

(Picture supplied by "The Central Archives of Lithuanian Jews in Israel")

The dormitories of the "Yeshivah" students

(Picture supplied by "The central Archives of Lithuanian Jews in Israel")

The Great Beth Midrash

For a partial list of Rabbis who studied at Telz Yeshivah and their ultimate place of appointment see Appendix 2.

Rabbi Eliezer Gordon and Rabbi Shimon Shkop determined the specific Telz system of instruction, which was accepted in most Yeshivoth of America, where many of their heads were of Lithuanian origin. Rabbi Eliezer Gordon was one of the delegates to the Hamburg Conference in 1909, where the decision was taken to create the "Agudath Israel" party.

In 1910 Rabbi Eliezer Gordon died of a stroke while in London in order to collect money for the Yeshivah. After his death his son-in-law Rabbi Yosef-Leib Blokh (1849-1930) was nominated to be the town's rabbi and head of the Yeshivah. He was considered 'great'; in Torah, resolute in his judgments and one of the most fanatic rabbis of Lithuania. His influence caused the Telz

Yeshivah to become the stronghold of "Mitnagduth" (Anti-Chassidism) and of radical orthodoxy in Israel.

In 1859 a school was established in Telz, its first teachers being Avraham-Simkhah Mapu and Meir Shapira, and in 1866 a school for girls was opened. These two schools were partly financed by the government.

In 1879 Jewish women established a vocational school for girls and nearby a boarding school for girls from poor homes. The head of the founding committee was a rich woman named Feige Lurie who donated the money for maintaining this institution. Poor children studied at "Talmud-Torah" schools and others at institutions of a "Kheder" type, where they learned reading, writing, Bible with "Rashi" commentaries and "Gemara" (Talmud). Two such schools were active till World War I, one run by Shimon Mosheh Viner and the other by Mosheh Fridman.

Rabbi Eliezer Gordon   **Rabbi Yosef Leib Blokh**

Rabbi Shimon Shkop

During the 1880s a Jewish-Russian school for boys and two classes for girls, were established by the poet Yehudah-Leib Gordon (*Yalag*). The orthodox proclaimed war against this school and its headmaster, who answered with his witty pen, but after seven years (1865-1872) in Telz he left the school and the town.

Despite the strong influence of the "Yeshivah", whose directors were against Zionism, there was quite a noticeable activity of "Khibat-Zion" and later of the Zionist movement. In 1889 the "Khovevei Zion" (Fans of Zion) society was already active in Telz, and in 1901-1902 one hundred "Shekalim" were sold. The first activists of this movement in town were Gershon Epshtein and Yosef-Hilel Berman. The Hebrew newspaper "HaMeilitz" of 1898 published three lists of donors aid settlement of Eretz Yisrael, and in 1899 an additional two lists were published. In the same year there were 41 members of the Zionist organization in Telz. In 1898 Telz Zionists were invited to send a delegate to Odessa for electing the Central Committee of "Khovevei Zion".

A delegate from Telz participated in the conference of Zionist societies from Kovno and the Vilna Gubernias, which took place in 1909.

But already before the "Khibat-Zion" movement, Jews from Telz had immigrated to Eretz-Yisrael. In the old Jewish cemetery in Jerusalem there are eight headstones of Telz Jews who died there during the second half of the 19th century:

Hanah, wife of Izik, died 1862;

Leib, son of Ya'akov, died 1863;

Izik Nagar, died 1866;

Ya'akov, son of Benyamin-Ze'ev, died 1868;

Eta-Gishe, wife of Mosheh -Yehoshua, son of Yekhiel, died 1876;

Zlata, daughter of Mosheh, died 1890;

Sheina, daughter of Ya'akov Mendilsh, died 1891;

Avigdor, son of Rabbi Avraham,

Avraham-Yitshak Epelman, born in Telz, came to Eretz-Yisrael in 1883, lived in Jerusalem and made his living from bookbinding.

For a list of correspondents from Telz who wrote in the Hebrew newspapers of these times see Appendix 5.

During Independent Lithuania (1918-1940).

Society and Economy.

On February 16, 1918, the establishment of the Independent Lithuanian State was proclaimed. Consequently the German army withdrew from the area, and life in Telz gradually returned to normal. Telz's Jews, whose number at this period was only half of what it had been before the war, started to reconstruct their businesses and their spiritual life.

According to the first government census of 1923, there were then 4,691 people in Telz, including 1,545 Jews (33%).

Following the law of autonomies for minorities issued by the new Lithuanian government, the minister for Jewish affairs Dr. Menakhem (Max) Soloveitshik ordered elections to community committees (Va'ad Kehilah) to be held in the summer of 1919. In Telz a "Va'ad Kehilah" (Community Committee) of 11 members was elected in 1920, after the "Tseirei Zion" party managed to overcome the opposition of the local Rabbi for collecting taxes for public needs. The committee, active from June 1920 till the end of 1925 when the autonomy law was annulled, collected taxes as required by law and was in charge of all aspects of community life.

In the elections for the municipality council of 1920 and 1931 four Jewish delegates were elected: Dr. Rafael Holtsberg-Etsyon, Mosheh Blokh, Yisrael Kraim, Shalom Talpiyoth (Talpes). In the elections of 1934 only three Jews were elected: Mosheh Blokh, Adv. Broide and Mordehai Levin.

Relations between Jews and Lithuanians were generally correct, but from time to time Jews were attacked as a result of libels. In June 1929 Lithuanian youngsters caused a disturbance and attacked Jews and in autumn 1935 rumors were spread that a Lithuanian girl had been raped, also that a Lithuanian child had been kidnapped by Jews. A frantic crowd attacked the Jews, six were injured, and many windows in Jewish houses were smashed. The police arrested the rioters, who were sentenced to jail. The situation became worse after the Nazis took over in neighboring Germany, and in particular after the annexation of the Memel district to Germany in 1939.

Telz Jews made their living from commerce, crafts and light industry. An additional source of income was the leasing of rooms and the supply of meals to the hundreds of "Yeshivah" students who came from all over Lithuania and from abroad. A few families dealt in agriculture, but the main source of income for shop owners and peddlers were the twice weekly market days.

View of Telz - 1937

The 1931 government survey showed that there were then 78 businesses in Telz, of which 63 were owned by Jews (81%). Their distribution according to type of business is given in the table below:

Type of the business	Total	Owned by Jews
Groceries	7	7
Grain	1	1
Butcher's shops and Cattle Trade	17	12
Restaurants and Taverns	3	1
Food Products	6	5
Beverages	2	2
Textile Products and Furs	17	17
Leather and Shoes	4	4
Haberdashery and Appliances	3	3
Medicine and Cosmetics	4	1
Watches, Jewels and Optics	1	1
Radio, Bicycles and Electric Equipment	1	0
Tools and Steel Products	4	3
Machinery and Transportation	2	1
Heating Materials	2	2
Stationary and Books	1	1
Miscellaneous	3	2

According to the same survey there were 48 factories in Telz and of them 24 were Jewish owned (50%), as can be seen in the following table:

Type of the Factory	Total	Jewish Owned
Metal Workshops, Tin, Power Plants	3	0
Chemical Industry: Spirits, Soaps, Oil	2	1
Textile: Wool, Flax, Knitting	5	2
Timber and Furniture	2	0
Paper Industry: Printing Press	2	1
Food, Flour mills	21	11
Dresses, Footwear	2	2
Barber Shops, Goldsmiths	4	4

In 1922 Jewish artisans reestablished their society with 6 members. In 1937 103 Jewish artisans could be found in town, half of them belonging to their organization, including 14 tailors, 12 shoemakers, 11 butchers, 9 bakers, 6 watchmakers, 6 barbers, 5 stitchers, 5 painters, 4 photographers, 3 glaziers, 3 hatters, 3 corset makers, 3 tinsmiths, 3 dressmakers, 2 oven builders, 2 bookbinders, 2 locksmiths, 1 electrician , 1 blacksmith, 1 cloth dyer, 1 potter and 6 others. The economic situation of most of them was difficult, but the "Gemiluth Khesed" fund of the artisans, established with money from former Telz'ers in America, helped many of them by giving loans without interest. The artisans society signed an agreement with 3 doctors and a pharmacy to provide its members with medical help and medicines at lower prices. On "Chanukah" the society would organize a party, the proceeds of which were used for its activities. With the help of the "HIAS" society the artisans organization would support immigration of artisans abroad.

When Telz was connected to the railway line Shavl-Memel in 1927, the Jewish coachmen and porters lost their living. In 1925 there were 2 Jewish women dentists in town.

From the middle of the 1930s the economic situation of most of Telz Jews deteriorated. The organization of Lithuanian merchants "Verslas", supported by the government, led an open propaganda campaign against buying in Jewish shops. Lithuanian merchants established cooperatives and big modern shops, competing with Jewish artisans and shop owners, slowly supplanting them.

The Jewish Popular Bank (Folksbank), whose director for many years was Mordehai Levin, played an important role in the economic life of Telz's Jews. In 1920 it had 120 members, by 1927 the number had increased to 250 and a year later it had 300 members. There was also a branch of "The United Society for Credit to Jewish Agriculture in Lithuania", which was centered in Kovno.

Telz had 168 phone subscribers in 1939, of them 41 Jewish, including 5 Jewish institutions.

Education and Culture.

Almost the entire education system in Telz was in the hands of the orthodox .

In 1920 a Kindergarten connected to the "Yavneh" chain was established, and from the middle 1930s a Kindergarten belonging to the "WIZO" (Women's International Zionist Organization) was also active. By 1921 there was an elementary school for girls where, in addition to general studies, also prayers, Bible with "Rashi" commentary, Jewish laws etc. were taught, and where 120 girls studied in 1935. In 1920 an "Educational Institute for Boys" opened, where "Gemara" (Talmud) was taught to such an extent that after 4 years of instruction the students could be accepted at the "Mekhinah" (Preparatory class) of the Yeshivah. Girls continued their studies at the Hebrew "Yavneh" High School which had been established in 1921, and was famous all over Lithuania because of its strong religious education and the high standard of its general studies taught there. Rabbis and orthodox Jews of the Zemaitija region sent their daughters to this high school, whose first headmaster was Dr. Levi, followed by Shemuel Tsukerman. For the next 10 years (1923-1933) the headmaster was Dr. Yitskhak Rafael Holtsberg-Etsyon, later the inspector of the government religious education chain in Israel, who died in 1982. Other headmasters were Mrs. Dr. Levitan-Shereshevsky, Dr. Zaltsberg, Shalom Shokhat, Shelomoh Trakhtenberg and Y.Shnaider, the last two murdered in the Holocaust, together with 7 of the 14 teachers who taught at this high school (*See Appendix 6*). During its existence 12 classes graduated from this school, which was disbanded in 1940 when Lithuania became a Soviet republic.

There were biannual courses taught for women teachers from 1923, and from 1928 also an annual pedagogic institution for women teachers granting a matriculation certificate. At this time, a teachers seminary - women and men separately - recognized by the Education Ministry, trained teaching personnel for all the schools of the "Yavneh" chain in Lithuania, pupils studying for 4 years, and altogether 10 classes graduated. Its spiritual director was Avraham Mordehai Vesler (1892-1941), who was murdered in July 1941.

The Hebrew High School "Yavneh"

The second graduation class of the "Yavneh" High School for girls 1927

The one year Hebrew pedagogic institute "Yavneh" Telz, 1929

All these educational institutions were connected to the "Yavneh" chain and were supervised by the town's Rabbi and head of the "Yeshivah" Yosef-Leib Blokh, and after his death in 1930, by his son Avraham-Yitshak Blokh (1890-1941), who inherited his position.

For a partial list of the Rabbis who served in Telz during these years see Appendix 1.

For a partial list of the educational staff of the "Yeshivah" see Appendix 4.

In the years 1920-1927 there was a vocational "ORT" school, where dressmaking was taught, but attempts to establish a school of the popular Zionist "Tarbuth" chain in Telz during all these years failed.

The secular cultural center was the library, housing Hebrew and Yiddish books and where there was also a reading room with newspapers. The "Yeshivah" students would enter the library "sneaking in" order to glance at the books. In the beginning the directorate of the "Yeshivah" were against the reading of secular books, but in time they came to terms with it.

From time to time members of "HeKhalutz", of "The Artisans Organization" and others would promote shows in order to collect money for various public organizations.

The second graduation class of the annual teachers seminar "Yavneh" 1931 - On top of the picture the headmaster Dr. Rafael Holtsberg-Etsyon

The fourth grade of the elementary "Yavneh" school 1938-39 with the headmaster Mentchovsky and teachers Fogelman and Mrs. Golomb

The last picture of the "Yavneh" teacher's seminar in 1940 before it was closed by the Soviets

Sitting from right: Avraham Pozeritz, Nakhum Levin, headmaster Pinkhas Shnaider, Nakhum Sandler, Ya'akov Levin

Standing from right: Yisrael Ardman, Nathan Shkliar, Yavetz, Shpital, Yankelevitz, Tuviyah Ba'al-Shem

Zionist and other public activities.

In spite of the fact that the anti-Zionist religious "Agudath-Yisrael" organization was dominant in Telz, there were many who belonged to the Zionist movement. Almost all Zionist parties were represented in town, including a branch of "WIZO". In the table below we can see how Telz Zionists voted for the different parties during the six Zionist Congresses:

Cong. Nr.	Year	Total Shek.	Total Voter	Labor Party Z"S	Z"Z	Rev.	Gen. Z. A	B	Gros.	Miz.
14	1925	134	--	--	--	--	--	--	--	--
15	1927	87	75	1	44	--	7	--	--	23
16	1929	145	57	3	35	--	7	--	--	12
17	1931	148	113	18	43	26	12	--	--	11
18	1933	---	354	206		83	28	--	2	35
19	1935	473	417	216		--	5	86	3	107

Cong.-Congress; Shek.-Shekalim; Rev.-Revisionists; Gen. Z.-General Zionists;
Gros.-Grosmanists; Miz.-Mizrahi.

Labor party members at the "Keren HaYesod" committee 1934-35

"HaShomer-HaTsair" branch in Telz 1932 with Berl Cohen (First from right), Mosheh Vareyes, Hanah Leibovitz, Hayah Leibovitz, Mikhal Noik and brothers Levin.

Z.S. (Labor) party members

Standing from right: Sason, Eivin, Adv. Sh.Broide, V.Funk, Broide, Grinker, M.Noik

Sitting from right: Leah Kopl, Glaz, Abramovitz, Shepselboim, Borokhovitz

Collections for the National Funds (Keren Kayemeth, Keren HaYesod) were carried out by the local committees of these funds and by members of the Zionist youth organizations: "Tseirei Zion"; "HaShomer HaTsair-N.Ts.Kh. (Noar Tsofi Khalutsi)". The founders were Hanah Sason, Mikhal Noik, Pikele Borokhovitz, Hayah Leibovitz and Hanah Leibovitz; "Betar", founded in 1929 by Leib Tabatshnik, Iske-Yitshak Blokh, Esther Blokh, Eliezer Natanovitz, Noik, Leib Blokh, Meir Yoselevitz; and "Gordonia".

The activists of the Z"S (Zionist -Socialist) party were: Nisan Sason, Are Grinker, Yosl Ba'al Shem, Shepslboim, Hayim Hurvitz, Sheindl Rabinovitz and her husband, Vigodsky and Reuven Katsin.

There were "Kibutzei Hakhsharah" (Training Kibbutzim) of "HeKhalutz" and of the General Zionists. The "Khalutzim" who succeeded in getting a "Certificate" (Aliyah Permission) and immigrated to Eretz-Yisrael, joined Kibbutzim Dafnah, Givath Brener, Yagur and others. In 1933 the "HeKhalutz HaDati" (Religious Khalutz) organization was founded in Telz which established several "Kibutsei Hakhsharah" in Lithuania.

Sport activities were maintained at the "Maccabi" sports organization, which had about 70 members.

HeKhalutz HaDati (Mizrahi) in Telz 1934
In the middle of the second line Tsevi Bernshtein

Athletes of "Maccabi" Telz 1926

A great part of the orthodox population was organized in the "Agudath Yisrael" party and in the "Tseirei Agudath Yisrael" youth organization. These organizations published the monthly "HaNe'eman" (The Trustee) in Hebrew, whose editor was Y.Shemuelovitz from 1925, and the weekly "Der Yiddisher Lebn" (The Jewish Life), in Yiddish. Both were edited in Telz and printed in Kovno.

The periodical "Yiddisher Lebn" (Jewish Life)

Rabbi Kotz from Telz was the chairman of the executive of "Tseirei Agudath Yisrael" in Lithuania. This organization established three "Kibutzei Hakhsharah" in Lithuania and encouraged its members to learn Hebrew and immigrate to Eretz-Yisrael. At their ceremonies they used the blue-white flag.

In 1927 the religious "Tifereth Bakhurim" youth organization was established, the founding committee including: Mosheh Litvak, Yitshak Shmulevitz, Yosef Pogramansky and Mosheh Helfan. In 1929 the organization had 50 members, its spiritual leaders being Rabbi Elkhanan Viner and Rabbi Zalman Dubtsansky. The first members and activists were: Yisrael Khetz, Pesakh Cohen, Mikhael Cohen, the brothers Laikh, Elkhanan Klotz, Mendl Tsvik, Berl Vain.

Until 1920, when it was banned by the government, a branch of the anti-Zionist workers organization "Bund" was active in Telz. The activists were Rivkah Jafe, Motl Maler and others, who also activated a Yiddish elementary school for a short time.

There was a volunteer fire brigade headed by Mosheh Blokh, who was also the founder of the Revisionist party in Telz.

Religion and Welfare.

The four synagogues continued to serve as the center of religious life just as before the war, the same being true of all the societies of learning the "Torah". The great "Beth Midrash" served not only for praying, but also for sermons and speeches of rabbis and public workers, local and outside activists of the Zionist parties. The local rabbi would deliver a sermon to the public twice a year, on "Shabbat Shuvah" (before Yom Kippur) and on "Shabbat HaGadol" (before Pesakh).

In 1921 the "Kolel Rabanim" (quasi-university for rabbis) was established, where students participated in advanced studies in Judaism and Torah, from where important Rabbis in Lithuania and the Diaspora graduated. In 1927 a special building for this institution was erected, and in 1937 a handsome building for the "Mekhinah" (preparatory classes) of the "Yeshivah" was built. The headmasters and teachers of the "Mekhinah" were Avner Okliansky; Pinkhas Helfan, born in Telz in 1898; Mordekhai Katz, later partner in establishing the Telz Yeshivah in Cleveland, Ohio, USA.

In this "Yeshivah", which became larger and stronger in this period and famous all over the Jewish world, discipline was severe, as a result of which many students left. Fanaticism among the orthodox was so strong that in autumn 1938, for example, two respected Rabbis beat a Jewish barber for working on Shabbat, for which they were sentenced in court to four days house arrest.

In 1937, apart from Lithuanian students, the "Yeshivah" had 30 students from Germany, 5 from Hungary, 4 from America, 5 from England, 5 from Latvia, 1 from Africa, 2 from Switzerland, 2 from Belgium, 1 from the Netherlands and 1 from France.

Telz welfare institutions included the hospital with its 16 beds, headed by Dr. Menukhin, "Bikur Kholim", "Linath HaTsedek", "Khevrah Kadisha", "Gemiluth Khesed" (Loan fund -managed all the years voluntarily by Ya'akov David Maizel), "Gemiluth Khesed" of the artisans "Ezrath Poalim", "Gemiluth Khesed" of the Artisans Organization", a popular kitchen and a "Women Society" for supporting the poor and the ill. The "OZE" organization ran a clinic and a summer camp for children from needy families under the direction of Mrs. Rachel Blokh and Mrs. Sonia Rostovsky. In 1939 a building for this camp was inaugurated in a village near Telz, which was named after Dr. Menukhin, who worked voluntarily at "OZE".

In 1939 there were about 2,800 Jews in Telz, about 27% of the total population.

During World War II and Afterwards

World War II started with the German invasion of Poland on the 1st of September 1939, but its consequences for Lithuanian Jews in general and Telz's Jews in particular had already been felt several months earlier. On the 20th of March 1939, Hitler transmitted an ultimatum to Lithuania to leave Memel within 24 hours. About 7,000 Jews who lived in Memel and in its region escaped, leaving most of their belongings behind, looking for asylum in the Zemaitija region and in Kovno. Many of them settled in Telz, where the Jewish community cared for them.

In June 1940 Lithuania was annexed to the Soviet Union, becoming a Soviet Republic. Following new laws, the majority of the factories and shops belonging to the Jews of Telz were nationalized and commissars were appointed to manage them. All Zionist parties and youth organizations were disbanded, several of the activists were detained, Hebrew educational institutions were closed, and the Hebrew school converted into a Yiddish one.

Supply of goods decreased and, as a result, prices soared. The middle class, mostly Jewish, bore most of the brunt, and the standard of living dropped gradually. At the beginning of June 1941 several Jewish families who were considered "unreliable elements" were exiled to Siberia. Among them were at least 2 Zionists with 4 family members (Grisha Volpert, wife Hayah and 2 little daughters) and 2 merchants with 5 family members (Josel and Gavriel Zax), whose enterprises were nationalized

The ending party of the "Gemara Society" at the "Khevrah Kadisha" klois, 1930

The new rulers confiscated the buildings of the "Yeshivah" and the "Mekhinah", and converted them into an elementary Lithuanian school and a storehouse. The residents of Telz were prohibited from renting rooms to "Yeshivah" students on the pretext that the rooms were needed for Red Army soldiers. As a result the students dispersed into five nearby towns (Telz, Trishik, Yelok, Papelan and Shidleve), thereby forcing the teachers to travel from place to place in order to teach them.

Rabbis Mordehai Katz and Eliyahu Meir Blokh left Telz in the autumn of 1940 in order to collect money for the "Yeshivah" and to discuss the possibility of transferring the Yeshivah to another country. They arrived in America in the winter of 1941, together with ten Yeshivah students, who had made the trip through Siberia, Japan and Australia. In this same year a "Yeshivah" opened in Cleveland, Ohio, USA, headed by these two Rabbis.

After the war the Telz-Stone Yeshivah was established near Jerusalem.

When the Jews of Telz became aware that the German army had invaded Lithuania on the 22nd of June 1941, they began to escape to the surrounding villages and to Russia, but very few managed to get there. On the 23rd the town was bombed by the Germans, and on the 26th they entered Telz.

Even before the Germans entered Telz, armed Lithuanians with white stripes on their sleeves took over the town. On Friday, June 27, Telz's Jews were expelled from their houses and directed to the shore of Lake Mastis, having been ordered to leave their houses unlocked. On the shore of the lake they were encircled by armed Lithuanians under German command, which they interpreted to mean that they were going to be murdered or drowned in the lake. The town's Rabbi Blokh consoled them, telling them that they should behave quietly and proudly as Jews behave who are going to die on "Kiddush HaShem" (Sanctification of God). During the night men and women with children were separated from each other, and anyone showing opposition was beaten with rifle butts. The men were left by the lake, whereas the women and children were allowed to return home, where they found their houses emptied of their contents, the doors and windows broken.

The Telz Jewish cemetery

The next day, Shabbat, June 28, armed Lithuanians appeared, expelling the women and children from their houses with beatings, after which they were led to the Rainiai farm, about 4 km from Telz, where they found the men who had been separated from them the night before. A Jew, an American citizen, who had come to visit relatives in Telz, refused to go with them, waving his American passport. He was shot on the spot.

The Jews were held in the open on this farm for several days, and thereafter were imprisoned in stalls full of manure as well as in the barns, men and women being separated. The Lithuanian commander of the camp, Platakis, nominated a Jewish representative committee of seven members, headed by Rabbi Avraham-Yitshak Blokh and his brother Rabbi Zalman Blokh. The other members of the committee were the engineer Tsemakh Ginzburg, Gurvitz and Yitshak Blokh. This committee tried to improve conditions, such as setting up a field kitchen, where rye flour porridge was cooked. In the mornings the prisoners would get 100 grams of black bread, 20 grams of butter and several potatoes. They also got permission to be together with their families.

After eight days the men were taken to work, their first task being to dig up from their graves the corpses of 73 political prisoners who had been imprisoned in Telz prison and had been murdered by Soviet security men before they withdrew. Under the pretext that Jews had taken part in that murder, the Telz men were forced to wash the corpses, to kiss them and lick the decayed wounds. The thirty men who were the victims of this abuse, having been beaten and wounded, were forced later to kneel in the street during the funeral of the murdered. The Catholic Bishop Staugaitis proclaimed the day of the funeral, July 13, as "Holy Sunday", to symbolize victory over Soviet Rule.

All the guards in the camp and in the working places were Lithuanians.

After two weeks an order was issued for the Jews to hand over their money, gold and silver items and other valuables. They were promised through their representatives that everything they handed over would be deposited in the Lithuanian Government Bank till after the war. Each family was allowed to keep 1,000 Rubles. The Jews were warned that anyone not obeying this order would be shot. High school pupils and students, escorted by Lithuanian auxiliary police, came to the camp and robbed the Jews of everything they still possessed, even prams.

On the 14th of July several Germans and Lithuanians appeared in the camp, driving all from the sheds and barns. The women and children were returned to the sheds, but the men up to the age of 15 were forced to run in a circle, fall down and stand up, while Lithuanians armed with sticks stood around, scourging them and hitting them all over their bodies. Many of Telz's residents came to see "the special show" and clapped. Several elderly Jews died there and then, the others, smitten and wounded, were put back into barns.

80 young and strong Jewish men were then taken from there, given shovels and buckets, and led to a nearby grove where pits already existed. They were forced to pump the water out of the pits, then they were shot and thrown into the pits. The shooting was heard at the camp, but the prisoners did not realize what was going on. During the night the Lithuanians came to the camp, demanding 24 men more for work, and after a short while shooting was heard again.

The next day, June 15, 1941 (20th of Tamuz 5701) all men were taken out of the camp, and led, in groups, to the grove and murdered. They were forced to undress and stand on a plank which was put across the pit, and there they were shot. Many fell into the pit unhurt, and thus buried alive. In the afternoon a big rain storm erupted, and the shooting stopped. Those men still alive were ordered to retrieve some garments from the pile, to dress and run to the shacks, where they were concentrated in one of them. Some managed to infiltrate into the women's shack and disguise themselves as women, but the next morning the killing continued, including the disguised men. The rabbis, whose beards were cut off or plucked off together with the skin of their faces, were in the last group.

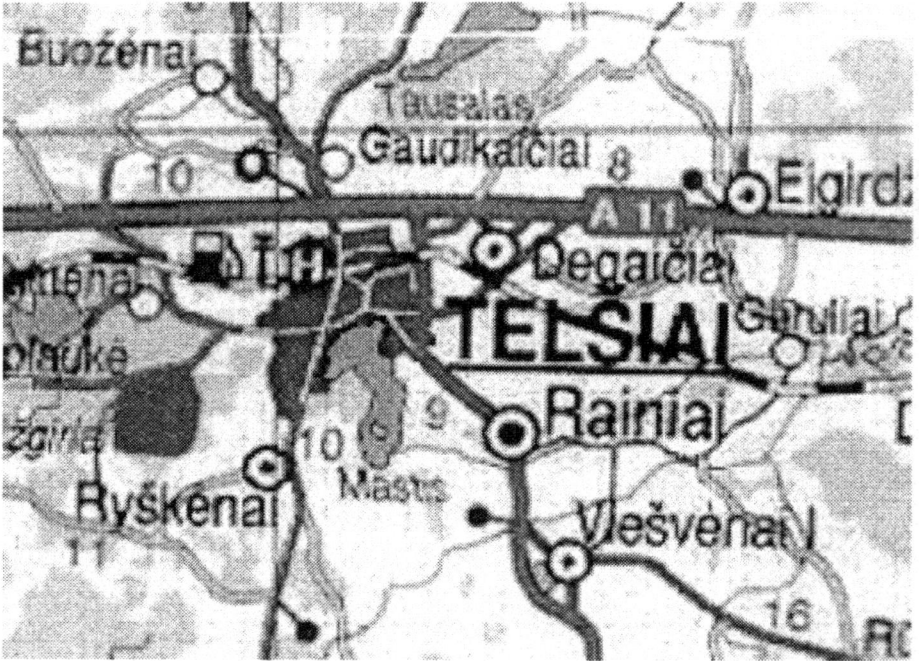

Telz and the nearby murder site

Mass grave sites near the dairy company in Telz

Left: Inscription in Yiddish and Lithuanian: in this place was till 1987 the Telz Jewish cemetery *Pictures taken by Yosef Woolf, Ilaniyah ,Israel, 1996*

Right: Monument on the mass graves at Rainiai

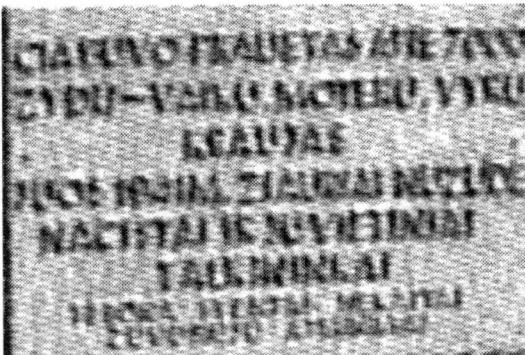

Left: The inscription on the monument above in Lithuanian: "In this place was spilled the blood of about 7000 Jews, children, women, men, who were cruelly murdered by the Nazis and their local collaborators in 1941."

Right: Road sign to the Monument on mass graves at Rainiai killing site

The woods of Rainiai. In this place the blood of 500 innocent Jewish girls and boys was spilled. They were murdered in 1941 by the Nazis butchers and their local collaborators.

Before the shooting the men were forced to take off their clothes, the good clothes being taken by the murderers for themselves and the rest brought to the camp. The women recognized the garments of their husbands and in them even photos of themselves and their children, and a great cry arose. In the nights the Lithuanian guards would burst into the barns and frighten the women, many of whom were raped.

Several days after the murder, the thin layer of soil which covered the corpses at the graves, started to crack and a terrible stench enwrapped the area. This may have been one of the reasons for transferring the women to Geruliai camp, about 10 km from Telz.

On July 22 Lithuanians appeared in Rainiai camp, announcing that in a few hours all women and children would be transferred to the Geruliai camp. Most of these miserable women had to walk on foot, carrying their few belongings to the new camp, with only a few being taken on carts. Before the transfer several SS men with Lithuanians arrived in Rainiai camp and ordered the women to hand over their leather handbags, shoes, boots etc. and also any money they still had.

At the Vishovian (Viesvenai) estate, located about 9 km south-east of Telz, Jews from the following towns were concentrated: Alsiad (Alsedziai), Riteve (Rituva), Vorne (Varniai), Luknik (Luoke), Loikeve (Laukuva), Zharan (Zarenai), Naveran (Navarenai). Here, like in Rainiai, the men were badly beaten and were then murdered on July 15-17. Women and children were also transferred to the Geruliai camp.

This camp had six big shacks where soldiers of the Red Army had been accommodated before, full of lice in the straw, on the ground, and on the walls. The Telz women and children, together with women and children brought from the surrounding towns, altogether about 4,000 people, were crowded into these shacks. The men from these towns had been shot previously at the Rainiai grove and other places. Food was scarce and many women endangered themselves by going to neighboring villages in order to exchange possessions for food. In August 1941 epidemics of typhus and scarlet fever spread. There was no soap and water was in short supply, so many people died. In several cases women and children were taken to the hospital in Telz, but only a few survived.

The law allowed farmers to take Jewish women from the camp for harvesting, because of a shortage of workers, but they had to undertake to keep in touch with the police and return the women immediately on request. Several hundreds of young women were taken by the farmers, their fate depending of the mood of the farmer. There were some who suffered from the farmers who exploited them ruthlessly, but there were also other farmers who treated them more humanly, later even saving some of them after they managed to escape from the ghetto.

Most of the women and children who stayed in Geruliai camp, managed camp life in spite of the hard conditions there, the women's committee attempting to contact the Lithuanian leadership. They approached Bishop Staugaitis to ask his community to show mercy to the women, but he refused. The district commander pacified them, saying that they would not suffer for long, because their end was close. The district doctor Mikulskis, who was close to the Jews and spoke fluent Yiddish, promised to help them. At a meeting of Lithuanians he demanded that the suffering of the women be ended by their quick liquidation.

By the end of August farmers were ordered to return all their women workers to Geruliai. In and around the camp there was a feeling of increased numbers of guards and policemen from neighboring towns.

On Shabbat, August 30th 1941, (7th of Elul 5701), Lithuanian policemen expelled all women and children from the shacks, after having robbed them of their last belongings the night before. The Lithuanians selected about 600 girls and young women from the crowd and led them by foot to Telz. The remaining women were ordered to take off their upper dresses and their shoes and to place them in orderly piles. They were then ordered to form lines, 75 women in a line, and were thus led to the pits which had been prepared near the camp. There they were placed at the brink of the pit and the murderers shot them from behind, the other women standing aside, witnessing the murder of their friends whilst waiting for their turn. Those men who had impersonated women were also among the murdered. Many of the women fell into the pit wounded and were thus buried alive. Children were thrown into the pits alive, the heads of babies being crushed with stones.

Those women and girls who had been brought to Telz were imprisoned in a so-called "Ghetto", which had been established in a shabby alleyway near the lake. Three sides of the Ghetto were encircled by a high wooden fence, with several lines of barbed wire, the fourth side being the lake. There was a gate in the fence, guarded by Lithuanian policemen. Inside the ghetto there were small wooden houses, empty, no furniture and no beds, without windows, doors or stoves. In the middle of the Ghetto was the old Beth Midrash and in the alleyway there was a swamp which had never dried out.

The situation of the women was very difficult. They walked around barefoot, almost naked and were hungry. Some of the garments of the murdered women were brought to the ghetto, the good ones having been taken by the murderers.

Some of the women were taken to work as maid servants in Lithuanian houses where they got some food. Others were allowed to go to the town for several hours in the evenings, in order to beg from door to door for some food. Many were taken for agricultural work by farmers of the surrounding villages. There they were forced to have sexual relations with the farmers. One rich farmer at one of the villages took ten young girls, 14-18 years of age, for work. After the work was finished only five returned to the ghetto, it becoming known later that the other five had been raped and brutally murdered. Most of the farmers used the women for difficult work and treated them with contempt. There were also cases where friendly relations developed between the women and the farmers, some of whom eventually sheltered them when they escaped from the ghetto.

In the ghetto the surviving doctors - Dr. Blat, Dr. Shapira and the dentist Srolovitz - established an improvised clinic. In the terrible ghetto conditions, these doctors tried their best to help the sick women and especially the many women in confinement. All the babies born died after a short time.

On Rosh HaShanah 5702 the women gathered in the old Beth Midrash and a twenty year old woman – Kadishon - volunteered to be the "Sheliakh-Tsibur" (Hazan) for prayers. On "Yom Kippur" too prayers took place and another woman - Goldah Hamerlan - was the "Hazan".

A Lithuanian committee which came to check, as it were, sanitary conditions in the ghetto, disseminated rumors that a typhus epidemic was raging there, as a result of which the local people refused to supply any food to Jewish women, ousting them from the doors of their houses fearing infection.

The autumn of 1941 was cold and the women in the ghetto as well as those who worked in the fields harvesting potatoes, suffered greatly from the cold. From time to time rumors spread that the liquidation of the ghetto was imminent. There were also rumors that conversion to Christianity could save lives, and many young girls approached the local priest asking for conversion. These girls were allowed to leave the ghetto every Sunday in order to go to church.

The monuments on the mass graves near Geruliai

Forest near the village of Viesvenai. One of two adjacent massacre sites

On December 22nd an order was issued to return all the women who worked in the villages to the ghetto. Several peasants brought the women tied up, fearing that they could escape on the way. This was the indication that the end of the ghetto was near. Several hundred women managed to escape from the ghetto over the lake or under the fence.

On the 30th and 31st of December 1941 (9th and 10th of Teveth 5702) the women were taken out from the ghetto and led in groups to the pits beside the Rainiai estate, where they were murdered. Of the women who escaped 64 survived and actually survived to liberation day. Several tens arrived at the Shavli (Siauliai) ghetto, their fate eventually being the same as the other ghetto Jews.

According to Soviet sources there are four mass graves near Telz:

1) In the fields north of the Telz-Plungian railway, where 200 corpses are buried, time of murder - summer 1941

2) Rainiai grove, about 5 km south-east from Telz, date - 30.8.1941, about 840 men, women and children are buried here;

3) in the forest of Geruliai, about 10 km east from Telz, period 1-15.9.1941, about 1,580 men, women and children are buried here;

4) Viesvenai- a grove about 14 km from Telz, 2 km from Vishovian village in the direction of Luknik, 500 meters from the road, period - second half of 1941, 40 families are buried here.

In 1970 70 Jews lived in Telz, by 1979 – 44, and in 1989 - only 23.

זכר לקדושי עירנו
טעלז
עיר הישיבה הגדפורסמת מרכז רוחני דתי
של ייהדות ליטא
לזכר הורינו אחנו אחיותינו וילדיהם הי ד
שנהרגו נטבחו ונקברו חיים ע י הנאצים
הגרמנים והליטאים ימ ש בשנות השואה
תש א 41 זברם לא ימוש מקרבנו לנצחי
ימ הזברון כ א בתמוז ז באליול ז ב בטבת
ת נ צ ב ה   יוצאי טלז

After the war, memorial monuments were erected at the murder sites
and in the "Holocaust Cellar" on Mount Zion in Jerusalem, where a
tablet in memory of the Telz community was affixed.

Bibliography:

Yad-Vashem archives: M-9/15(6); TR-10/40; 0-3/640, 3217; 0-22/53, 55; 0-36/2/204-207

Koniukhovsky Collection 0-71, Files 34, 35, 37, 59

YIVO,NY, Collection of the Jewish Communities in Lithuania, Files 461-465, 1666

Elitsur (Ritov) Sarah, "Biyeri ubemistorim" (Hebrew), Tel Aviv, 1987

Gotlib, Ohalei Shem (Hebrew), page 350

Telsiai Book (Hebrew and Yiddish), editor Yitshak Alperovitz, Association of former Telz Jews in Israel, Tel Aviv, 1984

Janulaitis Augustinas. Zydai Lietuvoje (Jews in Lithuania), (Lithuanian) Kaunas 1923

Baltakevicius Juozas, Lietuvos Miestai (Lithuanian cities), Siauliai 1932

HaMeilitz (St. Petersburg) (Hebrew): 7.7.1869, 4.3.1879, 21.2.1882, 9.5.1882, 20.7.1883, 30.7.1883, 7.2.1893

Dos Vort, Kovno (Yiddish): 25.10.1934, 10.11.1934, 11.11.1934, 13.11.1934, 18.12.1934, 4.3.1935, 12.3.1935, 22.8.1935, 10.10.1935, 17.10.1935, 22.10.1935, 30.10.1935, 25.9.1938, 2.12.1938, 12.2.1939

Folksblat, Kovno (Yiddish): 18.8.1935, 20.8.1935, 26.8.1935, 14.10.1936, 24.5.1937, 11.7.1938, 28.7.1939, 29.11.1939, 3.11.1940, 19.11.1940

Di Yiddishe Shtime (The Jewish Voice) Kovno (Yiddish): 22.9.1920,
15.10.1920, 18.5.1922, 26.1.1923, 25.5.1923, 3.1.1928, 17.6.1928, 26.10.1928,
26.6.1929, 1.10.1929, 11.11.1929, 29.1.1930, 14.2.1930, 14.5.1930, 3.9.1930,
25.3.1931, 19.6.1931, 26.6.1931, 15.1.1932, 27.5.1932, 24.9.1935, 10.10.1935,
16.10.1935, 17.10.1935, 23.10.1935, 4.11.1935, 3.8.1936, 26.5.1937,
10.10.1937, 20.10.1937, 18.5.1938, 6.6.1938, 20.12.1939

Yiddisher Hantverker (Jewish Artisan) Kovno, (Yiddish): Nr.4, 1.11.1938.

Di Tsait (Time) (Yiddish), Kovno, 4.12.1933

Der Yiddisher Lebn (Jewish Life) (Yiddish) Kovno-Telz,15.7.1938

HaNe'eman (The trustee) (Hebrew) Telz, Nr. 21,1930

HaTsofeh (Observer) (Hebrew) Tel Aviv, 30.8.1940, 2.9.1940, 19.7.1946

Yiddishe Tsaitung (Jewish newspaper) (Yiddish), Landsberg, December 1947,
January-July1948

Tsait (Time) (Yiddish) Shavl, 12.6.1924

Folksshtime (Voice of the people) (Yiddish) 7.6.1958

Appendix 1 A partial list of Rabbis who officiated in Telz.

Ze'ev-Volf Lipkin (father of Yisrael Salanter), in Telz 1835-1858 (the year of
his death).

Yosef Rozin (Reizin), in Telz 1864-1873, died in 1885 in Slonim.

Yehoshua Heler (1814-1880), in Telz 1876-1880.

Eliezer Gordon (1840-1910), from 1874 in Telz, from 1884 headmaster of the
"Yeshivah".

Yosef-Leib Blokh (1849-1930), since 1884 headmaster of the "Yeshivah",
from 1911 Rabbi of Telz.

Avraham-Yitskhak Blokh (son of Yosef -Leib) (1891-1941), from 1930
Rabbi of Telz and spiritual leader of the "Yeshivah", member of "Moetseth
Gedolei HaTorah" (Council of Leading Rabbis), leader of "Agudath Yisrael"
and active in the "Yavneh" chain. Murdered on the 15th of July 1941.

**Appendix 2 A partial random list of Rabbis who studied at Telz
"Yeshivah" and their ultimate place of appointment.**

Avraham-Eliyahu Regensburg-Chicago; **Yom Tov Lipman Levin**-
Brooklyn; **Yitskhak Lax**- Bronx; **Shimon Grosbein**-Brooklyn; **Moshe
Shatskes**- headmaster at the "Yeshivah University" in New-York; **Robinson**-
Chicago; **Yosef David Fein**-Portland; **Eliezer Pupko**- Philadelphia; **Dov
Revel**-headmaster of the Yitskhak-Elkhanan Yeshivah in New-York; **Moshe
Ze'ev Cohen**-Chicago;   **Yisrael Lev**-Trenton, USA; **Barukh Rabinovitz**
Chicago; **Yitskhak Izik Fridman**-Nakhlath Yitskhak, Israel; **Eliezer
Pshedmesky**-Bronx; **Moshe Shimon Zivitz**-Pitsburg; **Mirvis**-Capetown, S.A.

Appendix 3   A partial list of personalities born in Telz

A.L.Esterman (1859-1944), graduate of Berlin University, active Zionist together with Dr. Leo Motskin, Shmeriyahu Levin and others, later judge in Tel-Aviv.

Ben-Shemuel Melamed (1869-?), one of the Zionist activists in Germany, established the "Young Yisrael' movement in Germany together with Dr.Leo Motskin.

Yehudah Zilbert, Rabbi in Novgorod -Russia for 37 years.

Yisrael-Aba Tsitron-Kitroni , member of the "Va'ad Leumi" and one of activists of the "Mizrakhi" party in Eretz-Yisrael, wrote articles on "Halakha" issues.

Avraham Zusman (1831-1915), lived in Jerusalem from 1856, one of the founders of the first public library in town and among the establishers of the newspaper "Ariel" which in 1877 united with "HaKhavatseleth", died in Jerusalem.

Moshe Krein (1892-1933), from 1920 in Johannesburg S.A., editor of the newspaper "Dos Neie Vort" (The New Word), wrote poems and articles, from 1930 high official of the Foreign Trade Ministry in Moscow, died in Berlin.

Ya'akov Rabinovitz (1909-?), journalist, secretary of the Z"S (Zionist Socialist) party in Lithuania, was imprisoned in Kovno ghetto, from 1948 in Montreal, published articles at "Dos Vort" Kovno, "Afrikaner Yiddishe "Canader Odler" etc.

Avraham-Aba Verner (1837-1911), Rabbi in Finland until 1891, later Rabbi for 20 years in London.

Yisrael Aharoni (Aharonovitz) (1882-1946), from 1901 in Eretz-Yisrael, pioneer of research of fauna of Eretz-Yisrael and neighboring countries, established the Zoological Museum at the Hebrew University in Jerusalem, lecturer on Zoology at the University.

Berl Cohen (1911-1993), general secretary of the Z"S party in Lithuania, deputy editor of the Yiddish daily "Dos Vort" in Kovno. In the years 1941-1943 was imprisoned in Kovno ghetto and survived thanks to a Lithuanian peasant who saved him. In 1950 immigrated to America and settled in Brooklyn, published several books in Yiddish, among them the extended book "Shtet, Shtetlakh un dorfishe Yishuvim in Lite bis 1918" (Cities, towns and villages in Lithuania until 1918), NY 1992.

Appendix 4   A partial list of the educational staff at the "Yeshivah"

Meir Atlas (1848-1925)

Shimon Shkop, teacher in Telz 1884-1902

Khayim Shalom Tuviyah Rabinovitz , teacher in Telz 1900-1931

Eliyahu Meir Blokh (1894-1955), teacher in Telz till 1940 when he went to America for collecting money for the Yeshivah, partner in establishing the Telz Yeshivah in Cleveland

Azriel Rabinovitz, teacher since 1931, murdered in the Holocaust

Yisrael Ordman, teacher, murdered in the Holocaust

Mordekhai Rabinovitz, teacher

Yehudah Leib Khasman (1869-1936), since 1896 spiritual director at the Yeshivah, since 1927 spiritual director at Khevron Yeshivah, died in Jerusalem

Pinkhas Moshe Gordon, spiritual director

Zalman Blokh (1886-1941), since 1924 spiritual director

Ya'akov Katz, spiritual director 1903-1908

Shemuel Fondiler, "Mashgiakh" (inspector), murdered in the Holocaust

Moshe Olshvang (1902-1941), inspector, murdered in the Holocaust

Appendix 5 Partial list of correspondents who wrote in the Hebrew newspapers:

"HaMeilitz": Avraham Dimant, Ze'ev Holtsberg, Levin, Shelomoh Fridman, Yehoshua-Heshl Kalman

"HaMagid": Eliezer Benyamin Dobkin, Yitskhak Markus, Meir Brik, Eidl Gordon

"HaTsefirah": Khayim Aharonson, Barukh Margalioth, Eliezer Benyamin Dobkin

"HaCarmel": Avraham Simkhah Mapu, Meir Eliyahu Shapira

Appendix 6 List of the teachers of the Hebrew "Yavneh" high school in Telz during all the years of its existence.   (*) murdered in the Holocaust:

Rabbi Dr.Borer *,	Gitah Gutman *,
Shapoznikov *,	Mrs. Pogramansky,
Mrs. G.R.Broide,	Dr.Imanuel Shereshevsky,
Rabbi Khayim Kron *,	Ya'akov Shereshevsky,
Rabbi Yitskhak Shmuelovitz *,	Yehudah Volgemut,
Mrs. Hindah Rabinovitz *,	Dr.Eliezer Blokh,
Mrs. Sarah-Leah Helfan *,	Mrs. Axelrod

For the Lists of:

Telz murdered Jews

Telz Jews who passed away after World War II

Telz men who fought during World War II in the ranks of the Red Army

Telz men who fell in battle fighting against the Nazis

Go to the Appendices in the Telz Shtetlinks page:

www.shtetlinks.jewishgen.org/telz/telzap1.html

Utena (Utyan)

Utyan (in Yiddish) is located in the northeastern part of Lithuania, near the Kaunas-Zarasai road, is situated between two lakes, with the stream Vyzuona, a tributary of the river Sventoji, flowing through its middle. Utyan was first mentioned in historical documents in 1261, when the Lithuanian Great Prince Mindaugas handed the town over to a confederate, the Magister of the Livonian Order. In 1599 King Zigmund Vaza granted Utyan the right to maintain a fair, but during the "Northern War" (1700-1721) the town was destroyed by the Swedes and did not recover for a long time.

Until 1795 Utyan was part of the Polish-Lithuanian Kingdom, when the third division of Poland by the three superpowers of those times - Russia, Prussia and Austria - caused Lithuania to become partly Russian and partly Prussian, so that the part of Lithuania which included Utyan fell under the rule of Czarist Russia. From 1802 it belonged to the Vilna province (Gubernia) and from 1843 became a part of the Kovno province.

The St. Petersburg-Warsaw road, which was constructed in the years 1830-1835, passed through Utyan, causing it to develop rapidly. And in 1899 a narrow gauge railway line, connecting Ponevezh-Utyan-Shventsian, was constructed.

At the end of the 19th century two large fires devastated the town, when, in 1879, two thirds of its houses were burnt down, and the second fire, in 1890, destroyed half the houses. However, after a short time Utyan was rebuilt, this time according to a plan, which dictated that many stone or brick houses were built instead of the previous wooden ones.

Germany occupied Utyan from 1915-1918, when it was developed by the forced mobilization of the local population. At the end of December 1918 the Bolsheviks took over, establishing harsh Soviet rule, but in June 1919 the Lithuanian army managed to expel them, and from then on Utyan became a district administrative capitol in independent Lithuania.

Jewish Settlement till after World War I
Society and Economy.

Jewish settlement in Utyan was among the oldest in Lithuania. In the old Jewish cemetery, located about three km from the town, there are headstones dating back to the 16th century. During the period of "Va'ad Medinath Lita" (The Autonomy Institution of Lithuanian Jews 1623-1764), the Utyan community was attached to the "Galil" (District) Vizhun. In 1665 there were 341 individual Jewish tax payers, which meant that the entire Jewish population counted at least 400 people, and then in 1765 the Jewish population of Utyan counted 565 people.

In 1846 Mosheh Montifiori (1784-1885), the well known lobbyist for Jewish affairs, came to Russia to meet Czar Nikolai I and his ministers, to try to improve aspects of Jewish life in Russia. Many Jewish communities presented memoranda to Montifiori, specifying their problems. Amongst them was an outstanding memorandum written by the Utyan-born young Rabbi Mordehai Gimpel Yofe, mentioning that during the last famine about 150 Utyan Jews, adults and children, died of hunger. He contradicted accusations by the government that Jews are idlers and did not want to work on the land, proving that thousands of Kovno Gubernia Jews had asked to be allocated land for agriculture, but that only 16 families had actually been permitted to engage in agriculture.

In 1847 there were 1,416 Jews in Utyan, and in 1897 - 2,405, this being 74% out of a total population of 3,250.

During the second Polish uprising in 1863, the Utyan Jewish community sent a telegram of loyalty to the Czar, and the town judge came to the synagogue and read out the Czar's reply.

In the 1860s the splendid synagogue and bath house were built, for the huge sum of 10,000 Rubles.

A cholera epidemic hit the town in 1866 and many people died. The wealthy Aryeh-Leib Mats established a committee to help victims and provide medication for the poor. The "Pristav" (representative of the government) helped with money, also allowing his horses to bring grain from the villages, as peasants were forbidden to enter the town at that time.

During the big fire of 1879 mainly Jewish homes were destroyed, as they were the majority. Many Jewish communities sent help, amongst them being the Moscow community where donations were collected at the initiative of the philanthropist Ze'ev-Klonimus Wissotsky (the founder of the tea firm). As a result of the fire, the authorities prohibited the building of new houses which were not in accordance with the plan of the town, however preparation of such a plan took a long time. Realizing this, the Gubernator allowed Jewish merchants to erect temporary wooden buildings for their shops. Five years later, despite their protests and court applications, forty Jewish shop owners were ordered to destroy their temporary buildings, and as a result they lost their livelihood. As it was recounted, the whole issue came to the fore because of an informer on a Jewish merchant who had built a three storey house near the wooden buildings and whose business had failed.

As mentioned above, the big fire of 1890 burnt down most of the Jewish houses and their shops, including their contents. The splendid Synagogue, the great Beth-Midrash, the "Minyan HaKhasidim" and the Klois, were all destroyed. The fire caused 300 families to become homeless and to live in great poverty. On the 7th of July 1890, the Hebrew newspaper "HaMeilitz" published an emotional appeal signed by local Rabbi Binyamin Aizenshtat, asking generous Jewish people to help, and thus save many souls.

As a consequence more and more brick and stone houses were built in Utyan, with many Jews volunteering to serve in the fire brigade, where a Jew (Aron Yosef fun Barg and later Meir Garber) was in charge for many years. The impact left by the fires was so strong, that for a long time the residents of Utyan would count the years according to them.

Utyan Jews made their living from commerce, shop keeping, crafts and peddling, the main economic activity taking place at the weekly market and at the four-yearly fairs. Utyan Jews also dealt in timber, money lending for interest as well as taverns, and later on they opened wholesale shops.

Among the Jewish craftsmen one could find builders, fishermen, tailors, carpenters, blacksmiths, shoemakers, felt boots makers, shingle makers, tinsmiths, painters etc. The peddlers would travel through the neighboring villages with their merchandize.

At the end of the 18th century there were some Jewish owners of sawmills, but in particular Jews concentrated in establishing small enterprises. Two local Jews established workshops for knitting socks, marketing their products mainly in Vilna, but also in other places. These workshops employed poor Jewish girls, whose families lived in the lower part of the town, which had suffered from floods and from what was called "Di Blote" (The swamp). Wealthier people lived in the upper part of the town, called "Barg" (Mountain).

Education.

The education of young children – the teaching of the alphabet and reading in the "Sidur" (Prayer book) - was carried out by special "Melamdim", such as Hayim-Leizer, Shabtai-Hone, Aizik the "Shamash", Aharon Ben-Zion (Are Benche), Hayim, the "nipper" and others. Higher level "Melamdim" at this time were Shemuel Yakobson, who was a specialist in Hebrew grammar, also Eliyahu Ber and Hayim Henakh, the latter being known as the best "Gemarah" (Talmud) teacher and from whom boys after Bar-Mitsvah from neighboring towns would also come to learn. At the Klois of "Iche-Yankel" (Yits'hak-Ya'akov) there was a Talmud-Torah, run by Melamed Mosheh-Nathan, where poor boys studied free of charge.

At the beginning of the 20th century a modern school, a Heder Metukan (Improved Heder) was opened in Utyan headed by Reuven Vainonsky, over the objections of the veteran Melamdim.

There were no educational institutions for girls, and parents who wanted to provide them with a regular education were forced to hire private teachers. Shortly before World War I an educator for small children was brought in from Vilna, a woman named Granakh, who opened a Hebrew Kindergarten.

Religion and Welfare.

Religious life, and in fact communal life, was focused around the prayer houses, which were partly located in the "Shulhoif" (the back yard of the prayer houses): the Great Synagogue, "the cold one", which was built in 1862 and was so called because it was not heated in winter; the Beth-Midrash and the Kloiz. Nearby was the "Minyan HaKhasidim". The prayer houses which were destroyed in the fire of 1890 were rebuilt as solid brick buildings, and were named after their builders: "Yitshak-Yakov's Shul" and "Pese-Yehudah's Kloiz". There was also another Synagogue named "Hayei-Adam". All prayer houses also served as places for studying Torah.

In 1865 many religious study societies already existed for the study of Bible, Mishnah, Talmud, Agadah and Halakhah. Later a society for "Remembering the Death of Mosheh" appeared, whose leader was Rabbi Shaul Getsl Tsin, later a well-known Rabbi in New Jersey, USA.

The "Hakhnasath-Orkhim" society established a house in Utyan in 1876, where travelers received three meals a day as well as some money, in order to prevent them from begging from door to door.

In lists of donors for starving Jewish communities in Persia in the years 1871 and 1872, many names of Utyan Jews are mentioned (see the list of 75 names published in the Hebrew newspaper "HaMagid" in 1872 at the Jewishgen.org. Web Site, Litvak SIG by Jeffrey Maynard).

*(For the Rabbis who served during the years in Utyan see **Appendix 1**).*

Zionist and other activities.

An affinity to Eretz-Yisrael was instilled among Utyan Jews, and some Utyan Jews immigrated to Eretz-Yisrael during this period: Yehudah Zarecher with his wife immigrated to Jerusalem in 1825; Rabbi Mordehai Gimpel Yofe settled in Yehudiyah near Petakh-Tikvah in 1888; Y.M.Lerinman came in 1905 and opened a wine store in Jaffa.

In the old Jewish cemetery in Jerusalem there are at least three headstones of Utyan Jews:

Nehamah bath Eliezer from Utyan (Wife of Tsevi from Utyan), died in 1867;

Esther (from Linkeve) bath Shelomoh HaCohen from Utyan, died in 1874;

Hirsh ben Avraham from Utyan, died in 1878.

Several families, among them the teacher Shemuel Yakobson, Dov Rubinstein and others were subscribers to the Hebrew periodical "HaTsefirah".

In lists of donors for the settlement of Eretz-Yisrael from the years 1898, 1900 and 1903 many Utyan Jews are mentioned (see list published at the Jewishgen.org. LitvakSIG by Jeffrey Maynard from "HaMelitz" 1893-1903, with 91 names). The fund raisers were Duber Rubinshtein, Shemuel Yakobson and Yisrael-Gershon Cohen.

In another list from 1909, 55 names of Utyan Jews were mentioned *(see Appendix 2)* The fund raisers were Shemuel Yakobson and Eliezer Helfer.

The Utyan correspondents of "Hameilitz" were: Shabtai-Zalman Margalith, Aharon-David HaCohen and Shemuel-Yakov Yakobson.

During the events of 1905 many Jewish youths were active in revolutionary movements, such as the "Bund" (Anti-Zionist workers organization) or the "Self Defense". Due to this latter activity there were no riots against Jews in Utyan and its surroundings.

In view of heavy pressure from the authorities, in particular against Jewish youth and because of difficult economic distress, many Utyan Jews immigrated to far-away countries.

(For personalities born in Utyan see **Appendix 3**).

A market day in Utyan

During World War I

At the beginning of World War I the Russian rulers did not exile Utyan Jews to Russia, as was the case with most of the Kovno Gubernia Jews. This may have been due to Governor Veriovkin, who had estates in the vicinity of Utyan. In spite of this, because of intensive military activity before the German occupation, many Jews left the town and stayed in Russia during the war, but before this occurred, they still managed to absorb refugees from other Lithuanian towns, among them 82 children from Ponevezh.

During the three years of German occupation - from September 1915 till 1918 - Utyan Jews, together with the other residents, suffered from harsh rules and regulations which the Germans had introduced in economic and social fields.

Many Jews were mobilized for forced labor, and the synagogue, which had been requisitioned during this period, housed the civil government.

Many Jewish children studied in government schools, where lessons had to be given in German, but because the teachers did not know German, the lessons were in Yiddish. The teachers were Reuven Vainonsky and Sarah Baron.

During the immediate period after the German retreat in 1918, the residents of Utyan were left without any rulers. The affairs of the Jewish population, the majority, were conducted by a public committee whose members were Miha Shohat, Mosheh Kopilovitz, Ben-Zion Berman, Yisrael Beker and Kalman Meir Goldfain.

During Independent Lithuania (1918-1940)
Society and Economy.

After World War I many Utyan Jews, who had stayed in Russia as refugees during the war, returned home. Jews from surrounding villages and even from Vilna also settled in Utyan.

According to the first census performed by the new Lithuanian government in 1923, there were 4,890 residents in Utyan, including 2,485 Jews (51%). This ratio of Jews to non-Jews was more or less constant during the period of independent Lithuania (1918-1940).

According to the autonomy law for minorities issued by the new Lithuanian government, the minister for Jewish affairs, Dr. Max Soloveitshik, ordered elections to be held in the summer of 1919 for Community Committees (Va'ad Kehilah) in all towns of the state. In Utyan a Committee was elected which collected taxes as required by law and was in charge of all aspects of community life. It was active till the end of 1925 when the autonomy law was annulled.

The first chairman of the Committee was the cloth merchant Yisrael Beker; later he immigrated to Argentina, and Nisan Latz replaced him. Zaideman was the secretary of the committee. When tax payers refused to pay the taxes the committee had imposed on them, the young new chairman suggested rebuilding the nearly ruined "Mikveh" with the money collected, and thus the problem was solved.

After the committee was dissolved, all its property was transferred to the Jewish Folksbank. From then on this institution became the central focus around which many social activities took place.

During many years there was a Jewish mayor in Utyan, Avraham Zhurat. In the municipal council elections in 1931, seven Jews out of 12 council members were elected: Eliyahu Cohen, Shalom Zalman, Dr.Avraham Etingof, Yisrael Tsigar, Shalom Lifshitz, Yosef Glikman, Shalom Gold. The Jewish magistrate Yerakhmiel Berman served the town for sixteen years, until his retirement in 1935.

A Street in Utyan

At the elections for the first Lithuanian Seimas (Parliament) in October 1922, Utyan Jews voted as follows: for the Zionist list - 1,717 people, for "Akhduth" (Agudath Yisrael) - 66, for the Democrats - 12. Lithuanian rule having been established, Utyan was declared a district administrative capitol, upon which the town's economy developed quickly, with Jews also enjoying its benefits, making their living mainly from trade, crafts and light industry. They traded in flax, leather, timber, fruit, eggs, bristles, which they would buy from peasants in the villages or in surrounding towns, and sell on market days and fairs. Merchandize was exported abroad through nearby Dvinsk in Latvia, or through Ponevezh, which was connected to Utyan by a narrow gauge railway.

However, the establishment of produce and marketing enterprises by Lithuanian cooperatives and governmental companies caused the elimination of Jews from the wholesale and export trade.

A street in Utyan

According to the 1931 government survey of shops in the state, Utyan had 97 shops, of which 84 were owned by Jews (87%). The type of business is classified in the table below:

Type of the business	Total	Owned by Jews
Groceries	12	12
Grains and Flax	14	14
Butcher's shops and Cattle Trade	10	8
Restaurants and Taverns	11	7
Food Products	1	1
Textile Products and Furs	10	10
Leather and Shoes	9	9
Haberdashery and Home Utensils	2	2
Medicine and Cosmetics	4	2
Watches, Jewels and Optics	3	3
Radio, Bicycles, Sewing Machines	2	1
Tools and Steel Products	9	9
Timber and Heating Materials	2	2
Stationary and Books	4	2
Miscellaneous	4	2

According to the same survey, there were in Utyan 41 light industry factories, 25 of them owned by Jews (61%), as can be seen in the following table:

Type of the Factory	Total	Jewish owned
Metal Workshops, Power Plants	4	2
Textile: Wool, Flax, Knitting, Dyeing Plants	7	7
Sawmills	2	2
Food Products: Mills, Bakeries	13	1
Dresses, Footwear, Hats	7	6
Leather Industry: Production, Cobbling	1	1
Barber Shops, Bristle processing and others	7	6

In 1937 Utyan had 150 Jewish artisans: 31 shoemakers and stitchers, 19 needle workers, 18 butchers, 17 metal workers (tinsmiths, blacksmiths, locksmiths), 13 bakers, 10 carpenters, 6 hatters, 6 barbers, 6 painters, 5 felt boots makers, 5 watchmakers, 4 knitters, 2 glaziers, 2 book binders, 2 photographers, 1 oven builder, 1 electrician, 1 printer and 1 saddler. Jews also produced vegetables and fruit on leased land. During this period there were 2 Jewish lawyers (out of 3 in the town), 3 dentists and 1 doctor (out of 3).

The Jewish Folksbank, established after the war with the help of the "Joint" organization, played an important role in the economic life of the town. It had 35 members in 1920, by 1929 there were 529 members, and in 1935 about 600. There was also the "Gemiluth Hesed" society, which gave small interest-free loans to anybody requiring such a loan. This society was headed by Shemuel

Lifshitz, Kathriel Finkel and Kalman Goldfain. There was also a branch of "The United Association for Credit for Jewish Agriculture in Lithuania", headquartered in Kovno.

Relations between Jews and Lithuanians were more or less normal till the beginning of the 1930s. Occasionally there were some acts committed by ruffians, for example in 1926 four hoodlums attacked Jews walking in the street and chased them to the J. S. C. (Jewish Sport Club) club, where they smashed the windows.

Even during the years of autonomy law, Jews did not have equal rights. In 1922, land in the new part of the town was re-parceled and hundreds of plots were divided among residents, but all Jewish requests to receive plots were denied.

Fragments of the governmental Survey of Shops in Utena District in 1931

Cloth

UTENOS APSKR.

Aizin Necha, Malėtai, Vilniaus g.
Azbandas Elija, Labanoras.
Bermanas Bencelis, Utena, Viešoji g. 7.
Binderaitė Pezė, Anykščiai, Baranausko g.
Buividiškienė Slovė, Malėtai, Vilniaus g.
Burginas Ruvelis, Malėtai.
Capienė Šeinė, Anykščiai.
Eidelmanas Faivis, Tauragnai.
Eidelmanas Ch., Reizė Chavė ir Kacienė Rocha, Tauragnai.
Genkinienė Chasė, Vyžuonos.
Groisas Nochimas, Anykščiai, Baranausko g.
Kaganas Abramas, Malėtai.
Kaganas Berelis, Anykščiai.
Kopelovičius Leiba, Utena, Utenio A. 58.
Levinienė Feiga, Malėtai, Vilniaus g.
Levinas Mauša, Utena.
Macas Berelis, Utena.
Macas Todres, Utena, Utenio g. 47.
Portnoje Jankelis, Tauragnai.
Ručienė Agnė, Anykščiai, Baranausko a.
Ruvinas Kabas, Utena, Utenio g. 3.
Sacharus Mauša, Utena, Utenio g. 46.

Candies

UTENOS APSKR.

Bakas J., Utena.
Kabas G., Utena, Daržų g. 12.
Segalis Efraimas, Utena, Siauroji skersg. 24.

Timber Trade

UTENOS APSKR.

Berolskis Leizeris, Utena, Tauragnų g. 9.
Dubovskis Nosimas, Anykščiai, Gedimino g. 3.
Feldmanas Abromas, Utena, Ladygos g. 10.
Feldmanas Icikas, Anykščiai, Valančiaus g.
Givatinas Išeras, Anykščiai, Piestupio g.
Petronis Petras, Malėtai, Rašos dv.

Cosmetics

UTENOS APSKR.

Aškenaži Liuba, Utena, Viešoji a. 7.
Brenezas Vulfas, Utena, Kudirkos g.

The situation of the Jews also began to deteriorate because of government intrigues, which pushed Jews out of the wholesale and export trades and imposed unreasonable taxes on them. There was also the influence of the Association of Lithuanian Merchants (*Verslas*), which spread propaganda to persuade people not to buy in Jewish shops. Another decree imposed on the Jews was to move market day to Sabbath, and there were other harsh measures. All these caused many Utyan Jews, mainly the youth, to look for their livelihood in the bigger towns of Lithuania or in far away countries. Many immigrated to South-Africa, America, Cuba and Argentina, some of them later supporting those relatives who had remained in Utyan.

We can learn from the deeds of a prominent member of the community, Berl Sher, with many children and who was for many years a member of the municipal council, about the harsh conditions of most of Utyan Jews, who had to change their occupation frequently in order to make a living. His main occupation was covering roofs with slate, but often he baked beigls, produced candies and knitted socks. In the summer he traded different berries and before Pesakh he supplied the community with Matzoth.

In 1939 there were 115 phones in Utyan, 32 of them belonging to Jews.

Education and Culture.

Utyan Jewish children studied in two schools which were opened in the beginning of 1920. There was the Hebrew school of the "Tarbuth" chain with four classes and one preparatory class in which an average of 150 pupils studied, among its teachers Zar, Binder, the couple Laikh, Zilber, the director Matityahu Berkal and others. The second was the Yiddish "Kultur Lige" (Cultural League) school, where about 80 pupils studied, mainly from the poorer areas. The parents committee of this school also cared for the clothing and feeding of the needy children. Among the teachers of this school were Naftali Shteiman, his wife Rachel, Dambe, Lafkovsky.

The "Tarbuth" school in 1924-25 *(Picture supplied by Hayim Kuritsky)*

Third line from below, from right: fourth - Dr. Etingof*; seventh-teacher Binder;

Second line from below, from right: second-Hayim Zak*: Zalman Ozer;

Fourth line from left: seventh-Yoheved Sharfshtein; ? Rapaport*

(*) murdered in Rashe forest

For several years an adult school was located in this school building, which in fact was like a popular university with leftist tendencies. During regular lectures about 50 people participated, but social and cultural events initiated by this institution, such as the drama circle, involved very many young people. After the fascist revolution in Lithuania in 1926, new rules discriminated more and more against this institution till it was closed. In the beginning of the 1930s the director of the Yiddish school was accused of communist activity, detained and expelled from Lithuania. So was the acting director, the teacher Yosef Gar who was close to the "Poalei-Zion-Smol" (Leftist Zionist Workers) party, who was also detained and exiled from Utyan to Shaki.

The "Tarbuth" school in 1932-33 *(Picture supplied by Hayim Kuritsky)*

First line from below, sitting from left: Vainer Nehemyah; Gurvitz Yitshak; Kushner Toibe-Reize*; -----; Rabin ?? *; Treivush Betsalel *;

Second line, sitting from left: Shapira Aba; Zak Rivkah *: Katz ? *; ----;------; Muler Rasha *; Shuster Pesia *; Katz Kalman *;

Third line from left: ---; Krom Sarah-Malkah; Zak Dinah; Person Havah *; Korb Freide *;

Fourth line from left: Vainerman Yitshak; Mandel Barukh *; ---;---; Gordon Braine *;

Fifth line from left: Katz Efraim; ---; Sadur Alte; ---; Ashkenaz ? ; ---; Director and teacher Matityahu Barkel;   (*) murdered in Rashe forest

Sixth line standing: ---; ---; ---; Shumakher Dov *; ---; ---; Latz Tsevi;

From 1923 a Hebrew pro-gymnasium with about 50 pupils operated in town, some of these pupils continuing their studies at the Hebrew high school "Or" (Light) in Vilkomir.

There were two public libraries: one of "Tarbuth" with about 100 Hebrew books and the second of the "Kultur Lige" with about 700 books, mostly in Yiddish. After the "Kultur-Lige" was closed by the government, the library was transferred to the "Libhober fun Visen" (Friends of Knowledge) society.

Teacher Couple Laikh

The Yiddish School 1934 (?)

The Hebrew Pro-Gymnasium

Religion and Welfare.

During this period most religious activity continued to be concentrated around the six prayer houses, one of them being the "Hasidim". The handful of Hasidim had been reconciled to the hegemony of the "Mithnagdim", but from time to time controversies did break out over different issues. The watchmaker Hayim Karpov, of Hasidic origin, initiated a campaign to eliminate the tax on yeast and to sell it at lower prices, in order to lighten the burden of poor women baking Haloth (Challas) for Shabath. However, as most of the public did not want to harm the Rabbi, whose salary largely depended on this tax, it was collected till the start of Soviet rule in 1940.

In several of the prayer houses societies for studying "Talmud", "Ein-Ya'akov", Mishnah and Tehilim were active. In 1920 a "Yeshivah Ketanah" was established, named "Atereth Binyamin" after Rabbi Binyamin Aizenshtat who had just died. The Yeshivah was headed by Meir-Yitshak Leib and David-Yitshak Traub, and later came under the patronage of the Telz Yeshivah.

Among the welfare institutions acting in Utyan were: "Lekhem Aniyim" (Bread for the poor), "Tsedakah Gedolah" (Charity), "Linath HaTsedek", "Bikur Kholim" (Help for the ill) and "Hakhnasath Kalah" (Help for poor brides). Every Utyan Jew could get medical treatment and hospitalization in the large Jewish hospital "Bikur-Kholim" in Kovno for a small monthly payment.

The Old Synagogue

The "Hasidim" prayer house (Shtibl)

Pese Yehuda's Kloiz

The "OZE" organization concentrated on preventive medicine among school children. It also organized summer camps for sickly children which about 40 to 50 children attended every year. The doctor was Kukliansky. Funding was a monthly member's fee of one Lit, and from time to time there were tag days for collecting money for this organization. For some time it also supported a clinic where the poor received free medical treatment.

Zionist and other activities.

Among Utyan Jews many belonged to the Zionist movement, and all Zionist parties were represented. There were also the religious anti-Zionist "Agudath-Yisrael" and the leftist anti-Zionist "Folkspartei" parties.

The Zionist youth organizations in Utyan were: "HaShomer-HaTsair", Betar and others, in addition to an urban Kibbutz of "HeKhalutz". Sports activities, mainly soccer, were performed in the local "Maccabi" branch, with an average of 115 members. There was also the Yiddishist sports club Y.S.C. with about 110 members in 1926.

(For a partial list of personalities born in Utyan see Appendix 3)

Utyan children at a summer camp on behalf of "OZE"

In the table below one can see how Utyan Zionists voted for the various parties at six Zionist Congresses:

Cong. Nr.	Year	Total Shek.	Total Voter	Labor Party		Rev.	Gen. Z.		Gros.	Miz.
				Z"S	Z"Z		A	B		
14	1925	20	----	---	----	---	---	----	---	----
15	1927	109	80	6	21	11	17	---	---	25
16	1929	165	78		20	19	22	---	---	13
17	1931	86	64	9	14	26	17	---		3
18	1933	----	338	244		52	23	---	6	13
19	1935	1,000	920	518		----	75	114	73	140

Cong.-Congress; Shek.-Shekalim; Rev.-Revisionists; Gen.Z.-General Zionists; Gros.Grosmanists; Miz.-Mizrahi

The fifth class of the Hebrew school with teacher Mina

(Picture supplied by Sarah Vais)

First line sitting from right: Ita Harit, Rivkah Levin

Second line from right; Rachel Slovo

Last line from left: Rivka Shub, --- Goldman

Utyan Jews at a vacation in the 1930s

(Picture supplied and identified by Hayim Kuritsky)

1. Hayah Kuritsky-Mazinter; 2. Zelda Volf-Shraiberg; 3. Etl Aizen; 4. Sarah Segal-Korin; 5. Sarah-Rachel Segal

During World War II and Afterwards.

World War II actually started on the 1st of September 1939, when the German army attacked Poland. A German-Soviet agreement of August 23rd 1939 had stipulated that Lithuania would be under German influence, but that same year, in September 1939, it was decided by Germany and the Soviet Union that Lithuania would come under Soviet influence. According to this agreement on October 10th 1939, the Soviet Union returned Vilna to Lithuania, after it had been occupied by Poland. This included an area of 9000 sq.km. around the city, and Soviet troops were allowed to establish bases all over Lithuania.

On June 15th 1940, Lithuania was forced to establish a regime friendly towards the Soviet Union, and after the new government headed by Justas Paleckis was installed, the Red Army took over Lithuania. President Smetona fled, Lithuanian leaders were exiled to Siberia, and political parties were dissolved. A popular Seimas was elected, 99% of its members being communists, and unanimously "decided" that Lithuania would join the Soviet Union.

Following new laws, the majority of factories and shops belonging to Jews of Utyan were nationalized and commissars were appointed to manage them. Most of the artisans were organized into cooperatives (Artels). Some flats and buildings were confiscated.

There had been a short period of business prosperity after the Vilna region was annexed to Lithuania, when many of Vilna's Jews came to Utyan to visit relatives and shop there.

Several Jewish men, previously active in the Communist underground, now became important personalities, one of them being Faivush Ozer who was appointed to take charge of propaganda in the regional council of the communist party. In this job he also directed propaganda during elections for the popular Seimas, which decided to annex Lithuania to the USSR. Another Jew, named Berman, had an important job in the party's regional executive.

After these events the supply of goods decreased and, as a result, prices soared. The middle class, mostly Jewish, bore most of the brunt, and the standard of living dropped gradually.

All Zionist parties and youth organizations were disbanded and the Hebrew "Tarbuth" school was closed. The Yiddish school was enlarged and became an official Soviet institution headed by teacher Fruma Bernshtein-Melamed.

After part of Poland was annexed to Russia at the end of 1939, the students of the Radin Yeshivah arrived in Utyan as refugees and were sheltered there with the help of special funds.

In spite of sharp anti-religious propaganda spread by the new rulers, synagogues continued to be active, but the number of worshipers diminished. The Polish Yeshivah students, who tried to maintain their daily activities as usual, were auspicious amongst them.

In the middle of June 1941 several tens of Jewish families and also some single people, branded as "disloyal elements" and "enemies of the nation", were exiled by Soviet edict to the Altai region in Russia. Among them were owners of properties which had been nationalized, Zionist activists and others. Some family heads who were imprisoned in labor camps, perished there.

With the outbreak of war between Germany and the USSR, many Utyan Jews tried to escape to Russia, some being killed on their way by German bombings. Many of those who managed to reach Russia were conscripted into the Red Army and in particular into the Lithuanian Division, of whom about 30 fell in battle. . *(For the list of Utyan men who fell in battle see **Appendix 4**)*

The German army entered Utyan on Wednesday, at 2 PM on the 25th of June, the fourth day of the war, after bombing the town, and destroying several Jewish homes. Even before the Germans entered the town, Lithuanian nationalists took over local rule, began to bully local Jews and refugees who were passing through, pretending to search for weapons in Jewish houses, during which several Jews were murdered. After the Germans entered Utyan, Jews were taken to locate bombs and mines the Soviets had left behind, which also caused their deaths. The Lithuanians marked Jewish houses with the word "Jude", led German soldiers to them, and together they maltreated, hit and tortured their residents.

A group of Utyan youth 1940

(Picture supplied and identified by Hayim Kuritsky)

1.Hayim Kuritsky; 2. ? Yakrin *; 3.Shimshon Katz; 4.Mina Shuster *; 5.Yehudah Katz; 6.Yom-Tov Yakrin; 7.Liuba Shuster; 8.Tsevi-Hirsh Sharfshtein; 9.Zelda Volf-Shraiberg; 10.Tsadok Shraiberg; 11.Shabtai Shuster *; 12.Mordehai Idels; 13.Meir Shuster; 14.Yekutiel Sheinis *; Hayim Burkan; (*) murdered in Rashe forest.

One day they burst into the synagogues at the "Shulhoif" and threw out Torah scrolls and other sacred objects. The Rabbi of Aran, Tsevi-Ya'akov Bleiman, in Utyan on a visit, was taken from a neighboring flat where he was staying and forced to sing and dance with a Torah scroll in his hands. They then set all the books on fire, shaved Rabbi Bleiman's beard, tortured and badly wounded him. Due to the treatment he received from his son-in-law, Dr.Yudelovitz, he quickly recovered.

Due to new orders, Jews now had to wear yellow patches in the form of a Magen David on their clothing, on the back and on the chest. They were forbidden to walk on sidewalks, to buy or sell anything to a non-Jew, and non-Jews were forbidden to have any contact with them.

The Lithuanians detained Jews whom they suspected of being communists, and the jail was filled with prisoners, including the two Jewish doctors Dr. Yudelovitz and Dr. Oks. The synagogues were used as jails for Jews, Russians and communists.

On the morning of the 14th of July 1941 notices signed by the town's mayor Dr. Stepanavicius and the military commander, were posted in the streets, announcing that all Utyan Jews must leave their houses by 12 PM on that day, take their identity cards and move in the direction of Maliat (Moletai). They were allowed to take what they wanted without any restrictions, but were forbidden to destroy remaining property. A warning was also published, saying that any Jew found in the town after the fixed time would be shot on the spot. **On that day Lithuanian newspapers published, with great satisfaction, that Utyan was the first town in Lithuania to be "cleansed of Jews" (Judenrein).**

Even before the allotted time, Lithuanians ousted all the Jews, including the old, the ill and the invalids from their houses, hitting and abusing them. The sight of about 2,000 Utyan Jews leaving was terrible. It took just a few hours for them to be uprooted from their homes, which they and their ancestors had built and developed for generations.

After the Jews left the town they were led to the nearby Shilali forest. There everybody had to appear before a special committee, whose members were from the town's intelligencia amongst them a woman who registered their names and took their valuables from them, in particular gold and money. Whoever refused was shot immediately.

The Jews were left in this forest for three weeks, surrounded by a heavy guard of Lithuanians. Due to rain and hunger many became ill, and also unable to receive medical help, because the doctors were in prison. Every morning the men were taken to work in town, where they saw Lithuanians and Germans removing Jewish property from their houses. The only food the people in the forest received was bread. The men returning from work sometimes managed to bring some food and milk, which was divided among the children and the sick. In these hard conditions there was friendship and comradeship among the Jews in the forest.

On the 31st of July 1941 (7th of Av 5701), Lithuanian guards compiled a list of all men and women aged 17-55. Some of them, thought to be about 500 men, amongst them the town's Rabbi Nakhman Hirshovitz, the former Mayor Avraham Zhurat and his two sons, the wealthy Levior, the Shohet (ritual butcher) Yehuda Shafshtein and other important men, were taken away. All were murdered on that same day in the Rashe forest, about two km north of Utyan, and buried in previously prepared pits in a sandy area surrounded by swamps. The Jews in the forest, hearing the shooting, thought that Russian troops were approaching and that these would soon rescue them. Nobody reckoned that Lithuanians or Germans could engage in planned murder of innocent people, as the Germans and Lithuanians had spread rumors, which the people believed, that the men were working on a road. If not for these rumors, it could be that many Jews, in particular the youth, would have taken some initiative to rescue themselves.

According to a German source, 235 men, 16 Jewish women, 4 Communists and 1 robber were shot at that place on that day.

In the morning of the 7th of August 1941, another large group of the " fit for work" was led from the forest to the prison yard, where their documents, overcoats and trouser belts were taken from them. Then they were ordered to form lines and were led, guarded by armed Lithuanians, among them students and high school pupils, in the direction of Rashe forest for "so-called" work. Near the forest they were ordered to run several km, urged on by hitting, after which they were ordered to prostrate themselves on the earth. The women who had walked ahead, were ordered to proceed, and were then shot. After several minutes, some of the men were ordered to stand up and to proceed too.

One of the survivors, probably the only one, recounted later that he saw long pits. A Lithuanian with a mask on his face stood by one of the pits, a whip in his hand and hit everyone who passed by. Fearing the whip, people run ahead to the pit, where a German stood and shot them with a machine gun. There was a car parked nearby, its passengers being the mayor, the district doctor and another person who, together with other Lithuanians, stood and watched the show.

After about three weeks, all Utyan Jews had been murdered in the same place and buried in the pits.

(For the partial list of murdered Utyan Jews see Appendix 5)

At the conclusion of the murders, the pits were covered with a layer of soil, later on covered with lime and then with another layer of earth.

According to the findings of a Soviet investigation committee after the war, 8 pits were found on this murder site: the largest was 100 meters long, 4 m wide and 3 m deep. Parallel to this pit there were 2 more pits, one 30 m long, the other 20 m long. Then 5 more pits were found. **"9,000 peaceful citizens, men, women, the old and children were buried in all these pits after having been shot, some of them still alive".** Scraps of clothing were found on the corpses, the men having worn 3-4 pairs of trousers and the women 3-4 dresses.

Jews from the towns of Ushpol (Uzpaliai), Avanaste, Inturik (Inturke), Dabeik (Dabeikiai), Vizhun (Vyzounos), Toragin (Tauragenai), Maliat (Moletai), Kuktishok (Kuktiskes), Radeik (Radeikiai), Shkumian (Skiemonys) were also murdered here.

A few Jews, wandering through villages and forests in the surroundings, were caught and murdered. Except for those who managed to escape to Russia or to the Kovno Ghetto, no Utyan Jew survived. Only Tsadok Bleiman-Avitar, then a visitor in Utyan, was a witness to the murder and being wounded, managed to escape from the pit and travel in Kovno. A girl named Feige Yofe was saved by the local priest and later became a Christian.

The names of the 35 Lithuanian murderers and their German commander are recorded in the archives of Yad Vashem, as are the names of the few Lithuanians who endangered their own lives and hid several Jews. One of the survivors of Utyan was Leib Sher, who fought as a partisan.

After Utyan was liberated by the Red Army in the summer of 1944, surviving Utyan Jews began to return home from the USSR as well as from the woods. They began to hunt the Lithuanian murderers, of whom one was discovered, brought to trial and sentenced to 25 years in prison, but after a short period was pardoned and returned to his home in Utyan. Nine murderers were sentenced to the death penalty and their property was confiscated by the high court of the Lithuanian Socialist Republic - "for crimes against mankind and humanity....the murderers did not only murder the people, but with terrible cynicism they robbed the dead, ripped golden teeth from their mouths, chopped off fingers with golden rings, raped women before their death....". According to the court's decision, the verdict was definite and no appeal possible, but it is not known whether they were executed.

The remnants of the community, headed by Kalman Goldshtein, established a public committee which initiated the erection of a monument in memory of those murdered in Rashe forest, and on it an inscription in Hebrew and Yiddish, the first in Lithuania A channel was dug around the mass graves, to prevent damage from cattle.

Every year survivors of the Utyan Jewish community would arrange a commemoration service there, also visiting the great Jewish cemetery. These visits saved the cemetery from destruction till 1965, when it was razed in accordance with the town's plan prepared by the Utyan municipality. The small Jewish cemetery was destroyed earlier and its headstones used by nearby residents as building material.

The mass graves and the monument in Rashe forest

During the following years the authorities began to plot the yearly commemoration arrangements and also demanded that the inscription on the monument be changed. Despite the objection of the Jews to having a Lithuanian inscription on the monument and the intercession at the central committee of the communist party and the government, the old tablet was removed and a new one, with inscriptions in Lithuanian, Russian and Yiddish, was fixed instead.

In August 1988 a large sculpture named "Pain" created by the Lithuanian artist Valentinas Simonelis was erected in Rashe forest.

At the beginning of the 1990s a monument in the shape of a three storey tower was erected at the murder site. The inscription on it, in Yiddish, says: **"In this place the Hitlerist murderers and their local helpers murdered about 8,000 Jews, men, women and children on the August 7, 1941".**

The mass graves and the monument in Rashe forest

The inscription in Yiddish and Lithuanian on the front side of the monument: "In this place the Hitlerist murderers and their local helpers in July-August 1941 murdered about 8,000 Jews, men, women, children"

The inscriptions in Yiddish and Lithuanian at the sides of the monument:
"Here the majority of Utyan Jews were murdered"

The first excavations of the murdered in Utyan by the Soviet government in 1944.

The sculpture "Pain" in Rashe forest

At the same time at the site of the old Jewish cemetery, a memorial was erected and on it the inscription in Yiddish and Lithuanian: "The old Jewish cemetery. Blessed is the memory of the deceased".

In 1970 the Utyan municipality destroyed the 200 year old synagogue "Di Shul", whose front wall had been decorated by the local artist Yitshak Yofe.

Most of the remaining Utyan Jews and their siblings immigrated to Israel. In 1970 there were 28 Jews in Utyan, in 1979 – 12, and by 1989 only 9 Jews remained.

At the list of mass graves of the book "Mass Murder in Lithuania" Vol. 2, the mass grave of Utyan Jews appears as follows: The site-Rashe forest, 2 km north of Utyan; time-31.7.1941, 7.8.41, 29.8.41; number of murdered-about 4,000 men, women and children.

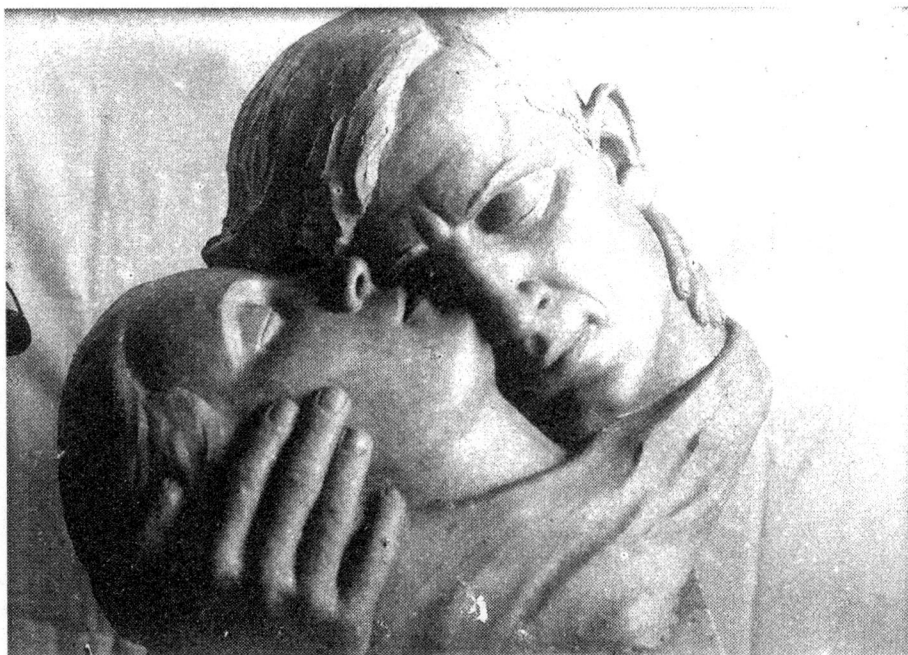

A sculpture of Yits'hak Jofe

According to the Jaeger report those murdered in Utyan included:

July 31, 1941- 235 Jewish men, 16 Jewish women and 4 Lithuanian communists.

August 8, 1941- 483 Jewish men, 87 Jewish women, and 1 Lithuanian who robbed the corpses of German soldiers.

August 29, 1941- in Utyan and Maliat- 582 Jewish men, 1,731 Jewish women and 1,469 Jewish children

All together 4,603 Jews.

A group of former Utyaner visiting Rashe forest in August 1997

Standing from right: Efraim and Taibe Katz, Frida Komeraz-Dragetsky, Leib Rozenberg (from Salok), his wife Zelda Komeraz, Hayah Kuritsky-Mazinter, Hayim Nir-Kushnir,

Above them: Mirah Kuritsky-Kremer and her son Dani Kremer. Below: Hayim Kuritsky and his wife Hayah Kaplan.

Sources

Yad-Vashem Archives: M-9/13 (2), 0-3/718; 0-53/21

YIVO, NY-Lithuanian Communities Collection, files 62-63; 1375; 1587; 1662

Report of the special government committee for investigation of the crimes committed by the Fascist-Germans and their helpers in Utyan district (Lithuanian).

Oshri, Hurban Lita (Hebrew), pages 159-194

Gar Yosef-Viderklangen (Yiddish), Vol. 1, Tel Aviv 1961, pages 159-184

Yizkor Bukh-Utyan un umgegend- Lite (Yiddish) (Yizkor Book: Utyan and Surroundings) Tel Aviv 5739 (1979)

Yerushalmi Eliezer, Pinkas Shavli (Hebrew) Jerusalem 5709 (1948), pages 335, 375, 420.

HaMeilitz (St. Petersburg) (Hebrew):16.3.1865; 5.8.1879; 30.11.1879; 21.11.1883; 8.3.1887; 8.4.1887; 21.4.1887; 27.4.1887; 12.5.1887; 7.10.1888; 22.6.1890; 25.6.1890; 10.5.1893

Dos Vort, Kovno (Yiddish): 26.11.1935

Folksblat, Kovno (Yiddish): 23.5.1935; 10.10.1935; 29.10.1935; 30.10.1935; 27.7.1938; 23.8.1938; 6.7.1939; 10.7.1939

Di Yiddishe Shtime, Kovno (Yiddish):28.7.1922; 1.11.1922; 26.4.1923

Kovner Tog (Yiddish)10.7.1926; 15.7.1926

Yiddisher Lebn ,Kovno (Yiddish): 15.7.1938

Naujienos - Chicago (Lithuanian) 1949

1941-1944 (Lithuanian).

Appendix 1
Partial list of Rabbis who served during the years in Utyan

Till the beginning of the 19th century the names of rabbis who served in Utyan (if there were some) are unknown.

Duber Yofe died in 1823

Avraham-Tsevi Aizenshtat (born in1813 in Byalistok. Died in 1865 in Koenigsberg when coming there for curing), grandfather of Leon Rabinovitz-redactor of "HaMeilitz"

Binyamin Aizenshtat (1846-1920) son of Avraham-Tsevi, served in Utyan for 52 years till his death.

Avraham-Tsevi Aizenshtat (1871-1939), son of Binyamin, born in Utyan where he served for 19 years till his death

Avraham-Aba Shlomovitz (1852-1906) in 1888 established a "Yeshivah" in Utyan

Nakhman Hirshovitz, the last Rabbi of Utyan, murdered by the Lithuanians in 1941

Left: Tombstone of Rabbi Binyamin Aizenshtat
Right: His son: Rabbi Avraham-Tsevi

Appendix 2

List of Utyan donors for the "Settlement of Eretz-Yisrael" in 1909

Lifshitz Tsadok, Rubinshtein Dov, Gordon Shimon-Leib, Brener Refael, Katz Yakov, Berkovitz Leib, Matz Alter, Tsin Shaul-Getsl, Gold Shalom-Heshl, Matz Tsevi, Vaininshker Reuven, Goldfain Hayim-Zalman, Shulman Zalman. Kraskin H., Druk Yehiel-Yosef, Levit Hayim, Bak Mendel, Katz Yisrael, Hayat Dov-Leib, Epshtein Aharon-Yosef, Lifshitz Ben-Zion, Kav Ben-Zion, Kav Yeshaya, Levin Monish-Yitshak, Ulfbelman Shemuel, Kantor Elhanan, Glikman Ben-Zion, Buz Barukh, Shapiro Aba-Leib, Sharfshtein Yosef, Peril Avraham-Dov, Miler Yerakhmiel, Katz Nahum, Shvabsky Aba-David, Shub Avraham-Mosheh, Finkel Yonah, Zak Eliyahu-Avraham, Polavnik Barukh, Hadav David, Meler Mendl, Aizenshtat Meir, Barilsky Hayim-Tsevi, Berlin Ze'ev, Haitovitz Tsevi, Bershtein Shelomoh-Yakov, Lifshitz Shneur-Zalman, Gilinsky Barukh, Katz Mosheh, Shadur Leib, Rufeil Yekutiel, Zurer Hayim-Shelomoh, Bak Betsalel-Nisan, Finkel Shimon, Azur Shimon.

Appendix 3

Partial list of personalities born in Utyan

Mordehai Gimpel Yofe (1820-1892), a well-known rabbi in his generation, one of the first rabbis helping the "Hovevei-Zion" movement. Died in Petakh-Tikvah.

Dov-Aryeh Hayat (1893-?), rabbi in Libau, later in Long Beach and Boston.

Matityahu Utyaner one of the important men of Vilna and one of the most learned men in Lithuania.

David-Nathan Brinker (Bar Yakar), public worker at the "Mizrahi" party in Eretz-Yisrael. Died in 1951 in Jerusalem.

Morris Kantorovitz (1881-1964) for many years member of South-Africa's parliament

Ze'ev Volf Shor (1844-1910), writer and journalist, in the 1870s. He described his travels through Africa, India, China, the Philippines and more in the Hebrew newspapers HaMeilitz, HaYom, HaShakhar. From 1888 in America, where he was among the pioneers of the Hebrew press and of the Zionist movement. He was a delegate to the fourth Zionist congress which took place in 1900 in London. He founded the Hebrew periodical "Hapisgah" in 1889 which became the central tribune of the Hebrew literature in America and East-Europe. He published several books. Died in Chicago.

Ya'akov-Meir Lerinman (1847-1929), from 1905 in Eretz-Yisrael, published articles in HaMeilitz, HaTsefirah etc. and one book. Died in Yafo.

Reuven Rubinshtein (1891-1967), delegate of the Lithuanian "Seimas", one of the leaders of Lithuanian Jewry, redactor of the largest Yiddish daily newspaper in Lithuania "Di Yiddishe Shtime", in 1940 exiled by the Soviets to Siberia, from 1948 in Israel. Member of the editorial board of the three volumes of "Yahaduth Lita". Died in Tel-Aviv.

Yisrael Hodosh (1908-1972), born in Vilna but as a small boy moved with his parents to Utyan. From 1934 in Eretz-Yisrael. One of the founders of the Yiddish newspapers in Tel-Aviv "Letste Naies" and "Yidishe Zeitung", from 1956 its redactor. Published in it articles and translations from Russian and French. Died in Tel-Aviv.

Aharon Brestovitsky (1916-1944), wrote articles in different Yiddish periodicals and in the newspaper "Vilner Tog". Perished in the Kloge forced labor camp in Estonia.

Appendix 4: Utyan men who fell in battle during World War II serving in the Red Army and at the Partisans.

Aizen Efraim;

Aizen Yitshak;

Ozur Feive;

Evenshtein Avinoam (IDF);

Bleiman Yitshak;

Goldfain Iser;

Gurvitz;

Gulinsky Yitshak;

Halbershtam Shimon;

Hamburg Zalman;

Zar David; Zar;

Zukher Zalman;

Zukher Pesakh;

Hadav (?) Nakhum-Leib;

Hayat Pesakh;

Yakrin Yosef;

Lifshitz Shneur;

Melamed Naftali;

Miler Faivush;

Markus Mote;

Nates Tsalel;

Elsberg Yehudah;

Fas Avraham;

Finkel Shaye;

Katz Shimon;

Katz Yitshak;

Kacherginsky Mosheh;

Kamraz Berl;

Renkovitsky Mosheh;

Ribnik;

Reznik;

Reznik;

Rokhman Leibe;

Shokhat Zalman;

Shvartz Motel;

Motie (son of Barukh Shvok);

Appendix 5

A partial list of Utyan Jews who were murdered by the Lithuanians in summer 1941

Ashkenazi Aba;

Mrs. Ashkenazi with 2 children;

Abramson and family;

Aizen Etie;

Brainin Shemuel;

Brainin Henakh;

Brainin Etel;

Brener Ahi Khanan and family;

Burkan Yosef; Burkan Hanah;

Burkan Perl; Brener Reuven and family;

Buslovitz David and family;

Bleiman Mosheh and family;

Bernshtein Meir-Yitshak;

Blokh Shimon;

Blokh Ovadyah;

Blokh Shabtai;

Britanishky Mosheh and family;

Belitsky and family;

Baralsky and family;

Fridman Montsik; Fridman Pesie;

Fridman Ben-Zion;

Finkel Batyah and family;

Finkel Katra and family;

Finkel Binyamin and family;

Fanger Yosef (Teacher) and family;

Finkel Yonah; Finkel Zalman;

Finkel Rachel;

Finkel Itse the musician;

Feldman David and family;

Feldman Haikel and family;

Feldman Avraham and family;

Fainblum and family;

Flat Aba and family;

Flekser Motl and family;

Goldfain Golde;

GoldfainAvraham;

Goldfain Golde and family;

Gurvitz Avraham;

Garber Yitshak;

Garber Hene;

Garber Sarah;

Grinblat (Dentist);

Garber Elkhanan and family;

Gordin Avraham;

Gordin Lina;

Gordin Bruna;

Dembo and family;

Hamburg Esther and family;

Handelson Mosheh;

Hayat Aba and family;

Hayat Hirshl and family;

Hayat Lerner and family;

Katz Reuven;

Katz Avigdor;

Katz Havah;

Katz Leibl;

Katz Yehudith; Katz David;

Katz Reizel;

Katz Mosheh;

Katz Rachel and her two sons;

Katz Eliezer, Yosef;

Katz Mihah;

Katz Yehudah;

Katz Meir-Yitshak (Pharmacist);

Katz David (Hotel owner);

Katz Yosef (in Kovno ghetto);

Katz Yosef (in Dvinsk ghetto);

Khor Shimon and family;

Kagan Yosef and family;

Kovalsky Golde;

Kovalsky Berl;

Kupeliovitz Mosheh;

Kupeliovitz Sarah;

Kupeliovitz Meir and wife;

Kupeliovitz Sarah-Feige;

Kupeliovitz Hayah;

Kupeliovitz Braine;

Kupeliovitz Shelomoh;

Kupeliovitz Shprintse;

Kupeliovitz Rachel;

Kuritsky Yeshayahu;

Kuritsky Mina and family;

Kuritsky Yerakhmiel and family (from Aniksht);

Klavin Idl and family;

Krasko Tsemakh and family;

Kavinsky Nahum and family;

Kofer Hayah;

Kofer Rachel;

Kutsgal Hayim-Yisrael;

Kutsgal Feige;

Kutsgal Shneur and family;

Kvores Zalman and family (from Alunta);

Kaufman Yakov and family;

Kacherginsky Shepsl and family;

Kab Yerakhmiel and family;

Kab Yakov-Note;

Kris Meir and family (in ghetto Dvinsk);

Kremerman Mantsik and family;

Kuznietz Leibl and family;

Kovolsky Tsirke and family;

Krevner Yakov and family;

Lifshitz Iser; Lifshitz Hayah;

Lifshitz Malkah;

Lifshitz Rachel;

Lifshitz Hanah;

Lifshitz Eliezer;

Lifshitz Dov;

Lifshitz Reizel;

Lifshitz Ben-Zion;

Laiftog Shelomoh-Dov;

Levin Motl and family;

Levin Yisrael and family;

Leibovitz Shemuel and family;

Lifshitz David and family;

Landau and family;

Lap Mosheh and family;

Latz Mendl and family;

Latz Nisan and family;

Luninsky Sasha and family;

Lishinsky Sasha and family;

Marantz Mosheh and family;

Markus Barukh and family;

Miler Hanah and family;

Miler Hayim Eliyahu and family;

Markus Hayim Leib;

Markus Elkhanan;

Markus Berl and family;

Minster Itsik and family;

Neimark Golde and family;

Nates Faivel and family;

Nathanson Barukh and family;

Person Hayah;

Person Havah;

Person Ida;

Person Mordehai;

Pikatkin Hinde;

Pakeltsik (tailor) and family;

Sadur Etl;

Sadur Hayim;

Sadur Berl;

Segal Eliyahu and family;

Segal Liova and family

Rokhman and family;

Rotenberg and family;

Rupeitz Mordehai (from Aniksht);

Ribnik Mihael and family;

Rabin Hirsh (kantor) and family;

Rudiatchevsky Hayim-Shelomoh and family;

Sheinis Ozer and family;

Sheinis Hirshe and family;

Shelkan Tanhum and family;

Shraiberg Abrasha and family;

Sharfshtein Yehoshua and family;

Shimonovitz Eliezer;

Shimonovitz Esther;

Shimonovitz Taibe;

Shimonovitz Beile;

Shimonovitz Yeshayahu;

Shuster Shabtai;

Shuster Meir and family;

Shohat Mikhl Tsadik and family.

Tsiger Yisrael;

Tsiger Sheine;

Tsiger Henekh;

Tsiger Taibe;

Tsesarek Hayim;

Troib Avraham and family;

Troib Nathan and family;

Treivish Yeshaya and family;

Treivish Hirsh and family;

Vainerman Leah;

Volf Iser;

Volf Mosheh;

Volf Etie;

Vaininsky Reuven and family;

Vainerman Mina;

Vainerman Aba and wife;

Yakrin and family;

Yofe Itsik and family;

Yofe Yitshak (Sculptor);

Yofe Avraham;

Zak Yosef and family;

Zak Shmerl and family;

Zaharik Aryeh;

Zaharik Eliyahu;

Zaharik Avraham,

Zaharik Reuven;

Ziskind Berl and Itsik;

Zilber More and family.

Varéna (Aran)

Varena - Aran in Yiddish - is located in the southeastern part of Lithuania, about 35 km distance from the district administrative center Alytus on the right bank of the river Merkys, at the confluence of the River Varene, this being the origin of the town's name.

Aran was established at the beginning of the 15th century by Grand Duke Vytautas, who had founded a hunting estate there.

Until 1795 Aran was part of the Polish-Lithuanian Kingdom, when the third division of Poland by the three superpowers of those times - Russia, Prussia and Austria – took place and Lithuania became partly Russian and partly Prussian. The part of the state which lay on the left side of the Nieman river (Nemunas) was handed over to Prussia, which ruled there during the years 1795-1807, while the other part, including Aran, became Russian.

After the defeat of Napoleon by the Russian army in 1812, all Lithuania including Aran, was annexed to Russia in 1815, first into the Vilna Gubernia and then from 1843 into the Kovno Gubernia.

In 1881 a large fire engulfed Aran. That same year the Russian rulers established a training camp and army barracks near the town, as a result of which Aran developed and several shops and barrooms were opened.

In 1847 only 158 Jews lived there, but by 1897 there were 1,473 Jews out of 2,624 residents.

In 1894 a railway line was constructed near Aran, and then connected to the Russian railway network. At the beginning of the 20th century Aran had several factories, producing cardboard, starch, tiles, bricks, lime and other items. At the end of the 19th century Aran became a county administrative center and was included in Vilna Gubernia.

During World War I the town was badly damaged. In 1915 it was occupied by the German army which ruled there till 1918, when the Lithuanian state was established. In 1920, when Poland occupied Vilna and its region, Aran became a border town, the river Merkys separating it from the region occupied by Poland. The railway track which traversed the town was ruined and only a road connected it with other parts of Lithuania, the barracks were now being used by the Lithuanian army.

The cardboard factory and two blacksmith workshops continued to work in Aran, and during the years 1926-1940 there were also two sanatoriums for tuberculosis patients.

Jewish Settlement till after World War I

Several Jews lived in Aran by in the middle of the 18th century, but their number increased with the development of the town's commerce, and in particular as a result of its connection to the railway network. Jews prospered especially from commerce: about 30 Jewish shops made a living from the tens of thousands of soldiers in the nearby barracks. The Jews owned also several factories: 2 cardboard factories, one for the production of starch, 2 flour mills and 1 saw mill.

Letters from 1905 report the improvement in the economic situation of Aran's Jews. Some brick buildings appeared, among them a new Beth-Midrash and a house for passers-by (Hakhnasath Orkhim).

In the summer of 1894 a large fire ravished most of the town, with only 10 houses and the prayer houses left intact. Four children perished in the fire and 200 Jewish families lost all their property, becoming homeless. The Hebrew newspaper "HaMelitz" reported that on that day three carts loaded with bread and another cart loaded with used clothes were sent by the Jewish community of Meretch to help the victims of the fire.

The local corespondents of "HaMelitz" were Shalom Shtern, Yehoshua Budzon, Tankhum Reizes.

The Rabbis who served in town during these years were:

Yoel-Zelig Zalkind (1839- ?), who officiated in Aran in the middle of the sixties of the 19th century;

Eliezer-Yehudah Berman, from about 1880 till 1899;

Matityahu-Gedalyah Kabatsnik, in Aran 1900-1902;

Shelomoh-Zusman Henin (1864-?), in Aran from 1903;

Tsevi Ya'akov Bleiman, the last Rabbi of Aran, who was murdered in Utyan in 1941.

Several welfare societies were active in Aran: Bikur Kholim (Sick Care), Gemiluth Khesed (Small Loans without Interest), Tomkhei Tsedakah (Charity), Lekhem Aniyim (Bread for the Poor).

The Zionist movement began to influence the local Jewish community when the first Zionist congresses assembled. In 1898 there was already a Zionist Society with 200 members. In 1899, towards the third Zionist Congress, a delegate from Aran participated in the regional conference of Russian Zionists, which took place in Vilna.

In 1898 the "Center of Correspondence" in Kishenev exchanged letters with 14 Zionist Societies of the Vilna Gubernia, including Aran.

Many names of Aran Jews appear in lists of donors for the settlement of Eretz-Yisrael from the years 1898, 1900 and 1903. "Hamelitz" (1902) names 17 Aran donors. A list from 1909 shows 29 donors: Mosheh Shumakher, Avraham-Mosheh Ruazanov, Mordehai Gordon, Hayim Kreiner, Yosef Yershansky, Shelomoh Khazanovitz, Hayim Tatelis, Avraham-Yehudah Veksler, Mosheh Frank, Y.P.Ingel, Yosef Vilkishky, Mosheh Blekharovitz, Eliezer Zusman, Eliyahu Rogovsky, Uriyah Festenstein, Ze'ev Elfman, Avraham Yezevsky, David Koran, Pesakh Khazanovitz, Kopl Galpern, Rehava'am Beker, David Gurshevsky, Hayim Mikhalovsky, A.D,Godak, Mordehai Levin, Aryeh Katz, Tsevi Lubetsky, Ya'akov Gurel, Simhah Golub.

World War I broke out in August 1914, and by the middle of April 1915 the Russian army began to retreat from Lithuania, after being defeated in the battles of Tannenberg and in the Mazurian lakes in Prussia. In the beginning of May of that year, the commander of the Russian army ordered all Jews exiled from the Kovno Gubernia into the Poltava and Yekaterinoslav Gubernias, on the pretext that the Jews were friends of the Germans and could be spying for them. For several days 120,000 Jews, amongst them Aran's Jewish population, were exiled in terrible conditions, during which they lost almost all their property.

During independent Lithuania (1918-1940).

Due to the occupation of the Vilna region by the Polish army in 1920, Aran became a border town and the river Merkys became the border between Poland and Lithuania. The Jewish community of Aran was also divided and 15 families remained on the Polish side of the town, but they managed to return to the Lithuanian side of the town later, and rebuilt their lives anew. During this period Aran was a county administrative center as before, in the Alytus district.

According to the autonomy law for minorities, issued by the new Lithuanian government, the Minister for Jewish affairs Dr. Max (Menakhem) Soloveitshik ordered elections to be held in the summer of 1919 for community committees in all towns of the state. In Aran a committee was elected, which collected taxes as required by law and which was in charge of most aspects of community life, acting till the end of 1925 when the autonomy was annulled.

A street in Aran

According to the first census carried out by the government in 1923, Aran had 399 Jews (180 men and 219 women). But the number of Jews diminished, many emigrated to America, Argentina, Uruguay and some of the youth to Eretz-Yisrael. One of them, Shelomoh Kaplan (1920-1948) was killed by a shell in Jerusalem in May 1948 when rushing to help a wounded woman.

At left: Stamp of the Minister for Jewish affairs.

At right: Stamp of the National Council of the Jews of Lithuania.

During the first years of independent Lithuania (1919-1920), Aran's Jews suffered from adverse economic conditions and received help from "YeKoPo" (Committee for Helping Jewish refugees) who provided remarkable sums of money for food, timber for heating, medical care, loans for artisans and for baking Matsoth for Pesakh.

During this period Aran's Jews made their living from commerce, crafts, agriculture, and in particular from the military camps in the vicinity as well as the weekly market day every Tuesday. Many Jewish laborers worked in the cardboard factory of David Yershansky. The timber trade which had developed before the war, suffered because Vilna and its region were now on the other side of the border.

The beautiful view and fresh air in Aran and its surroundings attracted many vacationers in the summer months, and this too added to the income of the town's Jews.

In 1937 28 Jewish artisans worked in the town: 5 tailors, 5 butchers, 4 shoemakers, 3 bakers, 3 stitchers, 2 blacksmiths, 1 hatter, 1 carpenter, 1 knitter, 1 barber, 1 photographer, 1 tinsmith. Meir Levin was the doctor and pharmacist.

The Folksbank, directed by Iser Veksler and with 99 members in 1927, played an important role in the economic life of Aran's Jews. But despite this the economic situation in town grew worse and many families left, in particular the youth, in order to search for a living elsewhere, with many moving to Kovno and others emigrating abroad.

Among the 13 telephone subscribers in 1939 there were no Jews.

Jewish children studied at the Hebrew school of the "Tarbuth" chain, with a complement of about 60 children in the twenties, decreasing to only 30 by1930. In the same year 25 boys studied at the local Talmud-Torah.

The "Talmud-Torah" of Aran 1930

Immediately after the war a library had been established, comprising about 1,500 books in 1937, half of them in Hebrew, which contributed much to the education of the youth. During these years literary and musical evenings were held, their income being donated to the library and to the "Literaten Farein" (Society of Literature), which was founded in 1937. In April of that year a party was arranged on the initiative of Ozer Ingel, who also delivered a lecture on " Yiddish literature in accordance with the jubilee of the writer Opatoshu", speaking Lithuanian because half the audience were Lithuanians. The artistic part of the evening was performed by Meir Levdon and Pesakh Tatarsky.

The stamp of the "Talmud-Torah" of Aran

Farewell from a family before its emigration to America

Many of Aran's Jews were members of the Zionist movement and in the elections for Zionist congresses they voted for most of the Zionist parties, as can be seen from the results enumerated in the table below:

Congr. Nr.	Year	Shekalim	Voter	Labor Party		Rev.	G.Z.		Gro	Miz.
				Z"S	Z"Z		A	B		
15	1927	15	11	2	5	1	3	--	--	--
16	1929	32	15	2	3	3	7	--	--	--
17	1931	97	78	39	8	24	7	--	--	--
18	1933	---	146	120		19	2	--	5	--
19	1935	---	154	132		--	3	4	14	1

Rev.-Revisionists; G.Z.-General Zionists; Gro.-Grosmanists; Miz.-Mizrahi

Fund raising for "Keren HaYesod", "Keren Kayemeth" and Kapa'i (Fund of Eretz-Yisrael workers) took place. The Zionist youth organizations active in Aran were "Gordonia", "HaShomer-HaTsair" and "Betar".

The Synagogue and the Beth-Midrash were the home for learning, for the "Shas" (Mishnah and Talmud) society as well as the "Tifereth Bakhurim" group for the youth.

Among the welfare societies there were "Gemiluth Khesed" and "Hakhnasath Kalah" (Support for poor brides) and the "Khevrah Kadisha" (Burial Society). In 1879 the "Gabaim" (Chairmen) of the "Shas" (Talmud) society were Yisrael Kaplansky (?) and Meir Kalvarisky, of the "Khevrah Kadisha" - Yosef Shlevin and Tsevi-Dov Levitan.

Among the personalities born in Aran were:

Shalom Cohen (1889-1955), who wrote many works of research on the history of Jewish doctors in the world, mostly written in English, some in Hebrew. He died in New York.

Avraham Blekharovitz, a known cantor, who at the age of 21 was the first soloist at the Riga State Theater. He was chief cantor in Buenos Aires in the fifties, and later on a concert-singer in New-York.

During World War II and Afterward

World War II broke out as result of the German invasion of Poland on the first of September 1939, and its consequences were felt several months later for Lithuanian Jews in general, and especially for Jews of the southern part of the state which bordered on Poland.

In agreement with the Ribbentrop-Molotov treaty on the division of occupied Poland, the Russians occupied the Suvalk region, but after the delineation of exact borders between Russia and Germany the Suvalk region fell into German hands. The retreating Russians allowed anyone who wanted to join them to move into their occupied territory, and indeed many young people left the area together with the Russians. The Germans drove the remaining Jews out of their homes in Suvalk and its vicinity, robbed them of their possessions, then directed them to the Lithuanian border, where they were left in dire poverty, as the Lithuanians did not allow them to enter Lithuania and the Germans did not allow them to return. Thus they stayed in this swampy area in cold and rain for several weeks, until Jewish youths from the towns and villages of this part of the state smuggled them into Lithuania by various routes, with much risk to themselves. Altogether about 2,400 refugees passed through the border or infiltrated on their own, and were then dispersed in the "Suvalkija" region (the part of Lithuania laying on the left side of the Nieman river).

In June 1940 Lithuania was annexed to the Soviet Union and became a Soviet Republic. Following new rules, the majority of the shops belonging to the Jews of Aran were nationalized.

All Zionist parties and youth organizations were disbanded and the Hebrew school was closed.

Supply of goods decreased and, as a result, prices soared. The middle class, mostly Jewish, bore most of the brunt, and the standard of living dropped gradually.

The Germans were in Aran by the 23rd of June 1941, the second day of the German army's invasion into the USSR. The fast advance of the Germans prevented the escape of the local Jews, and thus all remained in town.

The first days after the occupation passed relatively quietly. On the surface nothing changed and there were no offenses against Jews. But under the surface there was intensive activity among Lithuanians in order to integrate into the "new order" and to get rid of the Jews.

The "Activists", the local "intelligence" were headed by Adv. Minkunas, who was also the inspector of forests, as well as the secretary of the local court, post clerks and others. They now wore white stripes with swastikas on their sleeves and waited for a signal to act. And the signal was given on Friday night, the 28th of June, when all Aran's Jewish men were awoken and ordered to come to the police station in the morning with shovels in their hands. Seventy men presented themselves at the police station at five o'clock on that morning. The Lithuanian police chief delivered a venomous speech informing them that as from that day the life of Jews was not covered by law, and that they would have to work hard, because it was they who had brought disaster onto the Lithuanian people.

Amongst other things they were ordered to repair the roads which had been damaged during the fighting. The work was carried out under hard conditions, without food, without appropriate tools, and with much abuse by Lithuanian guards. In addition to the Jews being hit, they were robbed of their watches.

On the first of July Jewish youngsters who were members of the "Komsomol" (Communist youth) organization were taken to a nearby forest and shot. On the third of July the Jews were ordered to hand over their cows and bicycles. On the 10th of July a "Judenrat" of 12 members was established in order to act as liaison with the authorities and to ensure the execution of their orders.

On the 16th of the month the Jews were ordered to put a yellow "Magen-David" on their garments, with the letter "J" on the front and back of their clothes, and were also forbidden to have any contact with non Jews.

The former communists sympathizers, who by now had become policemen, Gestapo clerks etc. treated the Jews with special harshness and cruelty.

On the 12th of August 1941 Lithuanian policemen raided Jewish houses looking for young, strong men and for important and intelligent Jews. Ten men were taken and, under the pretext that they would be sent to work, were sent to Alytus, where they were murdered together with Jews brought from other small towns in the surroundings. In Aran people did not want to believe that they had been murdered, although no news was heard from them for a long time.

On the 17th of August Jews were forced from their homes and eleven young men were taken to an unknown place.

On the first of September 24 Jews, among them women and sick people, were taken out of the town and disappeared. Meanwhile the chief of the local police Sadauskas and the chairman of the county council Tarila extorted money and valuables from the Jews, making various empty promises.

There were Jews who managed to sneak out of the town and to escape to the nearby towns Vasilishok and Radin, which belonged to Belarus, as people then thought that these outrages happened only to the Lithuanian Jews.

On the fifth of September Jews were abducted again for so called work, but were murdered on the way. The saw mill owner Miler was brutally tortured, all his money stolen, and after his wife and his 15 years old daughter were raped in his presence, all were shot.

On Monday, the 8th of September 1941, the remainder of Aran's Jews, about 125 people, among them 70 children, were concentrated into the synagogue. Armed Lithuanians, including all the civil servants of Aran, guarded the Jews to prevent their escape. One 12 years old girl, Liba Yurkansky, managed to escape, but the Council Chairman Tarila chased her on horse back and brought her back.

Hundreds of Lithuanians from the nearby villages arrived on carts and with sacks, in order to rob Jewish property.

The next day, the 9th of September (17th of Elul 5701) all were brought to a forest not far from Aran, where they were murdered.

According to German sources 541 Jewish men, 141 women and 149 children, altogether 831 Jews, were murdered on that day.

According to the list of mass graves published in the book "Mass murder in Lithuania" vol. 2, the following are the mass graves of Aran:

> In a forest 1.5 km from Aran, 200 meters on the left on the road to Druckunai village, lie 831 victims.

> In Marcinkunai forest, between Lake Kastina and the railway station, some 200 meters from the station, lie about 200 victims.

The mass grave and the monument 1.5 km from Aran. The inscription in
Yiddish and Lithuanian: In this place the Hitler murderers and their local
helpers in 1941 murdered 300 Jews, men, women, children.

The inscription in Hebrew, Yiddish and Lithuanian:

"In this place the Nazi-murderers with their local helpers on the 2-nd of September 1942 murdered more than 600 Marcinkoniai Jews, children, women, men."

The mass grave and the monument at Marcinkoniai forest

Bibliography.

Yad-Vashem Archives-Files: M-1/E-63/19-1; 2215/2314; 0-3/640, 5760; TR-2/5096.

Koniukhovsky collection 0-71, files 34, 177.

YIVO, Lithuanian Communities Collection, file 105.

On the Ruines of Wars and Disturbances, Notebook of the regional "YeKoPo" committee 1919-1931 (Yiddish), editor Mosheh Shalit, Vilna 1931.

Gotlib, Ohalei Shem, page14.

Di Yiddishe Shtime (The Yiddish Voice) Kovno (Yiddish): 11.1.1931,

Folksblat, Kovno (Yiddish): 19.4.1937.

HaMeilitz (St. Petersburg) (Hebrew): 11.7.1894

Veisiejai (Vishey)

Vishey (in Yiddish) is situated in the southern part of Lithuania, close to the Polish border. The town was built along the shores of Lake Ancia (pronounced Ancha) where a bridge connects the two parts, with many woods and lakes in its surroundings. The district administrative capitol Lazdey is about 20 km distance from Vishey.

Vishey was founded during the first half of the sixteenth century near the estate of the Lithuanian Prince Glinsky, after King Zigmund "The Old" permitted the establishment of a bar room near the estate and to maintain markets.

Aerial photo from Vishey taken by the German Luftwaffe In 1944

Photo supplied by Barney Rubin

Vishey from the air

Until 1795 Vishey was part of the Polish-Lithuanian Kingdom, after which the third division of Poland by the three superpowers of those times - Russia, Prussia and Austria – resulted in Lithuania becoming partly Russian and partly Prussian. The part of the state which lay on the left side of the Nieman river (Nemunas), including Vishey, was handed over to Prussia which ruled there during the years 1795-1807, Vishey being a county administrative center during these years.

After Napoleon defeated Prussia and according to the Tilzit agreement of July 1807, Polish territories occupied by Prussia were transferred to what became known as the "The Great Dukedom of Warsaw", which was established at that time. The King of Saxony, Friedrich-August, was appointed Duke, and the Napoleonic code now became the constitution of the Dukedom, according to which everybody was equal before the law, except for the Jews who were not granted any civil rights.

During the years 1807-1813, Vishey belonged to the "Great Dukedom of Warsaw" and was part of the Bialystok district. The Napoleonic code was then introduced in this region, remaining in effect even during the Lithuanian period. In 1827 Vishey had a population of 737 people.

In 1815, after the defeat of Napoleon, all of Lithuania was annexed to Russia, as a result of which Vishey was included in the Augustowa Province (Gubernia), and in 1866 it became a part of the Suwalk Gubernia as a county administrative center.

Jewish Settlement till World War II.

Apparently Jews started to settle in Vishey in the middle of the eighteenth century after the Great Hetman Masalsky, the owner of the estate at this time, invited them there in order to promote commerce. Jewish merchants would buy grain and other agricultural products in the surroundings, transport them to Grodno and in return import industrial goods from there. A document of 1783 in possession of the Vishey church states that several tens of Jewish families were living there after getting permission to do so from Bishop Zienkewitz of Vilna in 1748. They had their synagogue and a "Kahal". In 1797 there were 518 people and 85 houses in Vishey.

In November 1811 the Russian finance minister Matushevitz invited Jewish representatives from all ten Gubernias of Poland to a meeting in order to discuss the issues of taxes and of military service of Jewish youth. The representative of Lomzha Gubernia was Sender Abramovitz from Vishey.

In the 1870s century many Lithuanian Jews immigrated to America. In a list of immigrants from 1869/70 the name of A.Miler from Vishey was found.

By 1897 the population of Vishey numbered 1,540 people, of whom 974 were Jews (63%), who made their living from commerce, crafts, fishing and agriculture, with several Jewish families owning great estates. In those days the economic situation of Vishey Jews was sound, but the large fire of 1872 badly affected the economy for many years to come. In this same year Vishey Jews donated money for the hungry, the collectors being Eliyahu Kaplovsky, Dr.Shemuel Kukliansky and Aba-Leib Tuman.

In 1891 a "School for Boys" was opened, supervised by the local Rabbi Nathan-Neta Kabak and the learned Ben-Zion Rastokhotsky. Russian was also taught and the teachers were M.P.Vainshtein and Sh.Izersky. Before World War I a "Kheder Metukan" (an improved Kheder) was established by David Boyarsky, one of its teachers being the known writer A.A.Kabak.

During 1886-87 Dr.Ludvig-Lazar Zamenhof lived there, where he worked professionally as an optometrist and created the International Language Esperanto.

"In this place stood the house in which in 1886-1887 lived and worked the creator of the Esperanto language Ludvig Zamenhof"

(In Lithuanian on the left and in Esperanto on the right)

The designer of this monument was V.Margelis

Long before the "Khibath Zion" movement spread among the Jewish communities of Russia, single Jews from Vishey immigrated to Eretz Yisrael. At least two tombstones of Vishey Jews were found in the old cemetery of Jerusalem: Etl daughter of Avraham, died in 1879, and Ya'akov-Yehoshua Beharav Tsevi grandson of "Peney Yehoshua" (the famous book of Rabbi Ya'akov-Yehoshua Falk, 1680-1756), who died in 1885.

Zionist activity started at the end of the nineteenth century when a "Zionist Association" was established. In 1899 Vishey Zionists were in contact with the Zionist Center in Kishinev, which was in touch with all "Zionist Associations" in Russia. In 1899 and 1903, lists of donors from Vishey for "The Settlement of Eretz Yisrael" were published in the Hebrew periodicals of these times. The collector was Dan Yeshaya Cohen. The "Bund" organization also held a strong position in the town till World War I.

During World War I, on the first of April 1915, Vishey Jews, numbering some 400, were exiled, at the order of the retreating Russian army. After the war and the establishment of the Lithuanian state, only half of them returned.

During the Period of Independent Lithuania (1918-1940).

After the war the returning Vishey Jews, who found their property plundered and most of their houses ruined, had to start life anew.

Z.Pitler from Vishey fought as a volunteer for the independence of Lithuania.

According to the Autonomy Law for minorities issued by the new Lithuanian government, the minister for Jewish affairs Dr. Max Soloveitshik ordered, in the summer of 1919, that elections be held for Community Committees in all towns of the state, and such a Committee was also elected in Vishey. It was active till the end of 1925 when the autonomy was annulled. During its existence the Committee collected taxes as required by law and was in charge of almost all aspects of community life, mainly the registration of births, marriages and deaths. These registration books were badly damaged in a fire in 1924, the remains being stored in the YIVO archives in N.Y. In this fire the synagogue, the school and many other buildings were ruined.

According to the first census performed by the Lithuanian government in 1923, Vishey had a population of 1,295 people, including 516 Jews (40%).

During this period Vishey Jews made their living from commerce, crafts, agriculture and fishing. According to the government survey of 1931 there were 15 shops, 12 of them owned by Jews (80%), consisting of 4 textile shops, 2 butchers, 2 restaurants, 1 shoe shop, 1 sewing machine shop, 1 iron and tools shop (Fridman) and 1 pharmacy (Shaul Kukliansky). There were about ten "shops of small goods" as written on the boards above the entrances. Since everybody had to work and earn money, these shops were managed by family members of the craftsmen, who sold kerosene, salt, sugar, flour, herring, haberdashery and other goods. The larger shops owned by Leib Flaxman, Benjamin Hasan and Mote Miller, sold manufactured articles.

According to the same survey there were 9 workshops, of them 7 in Jewish hands (78%): 2 bakeries, 1 brick factory, 1 saw mill, 1 flour mill and power station (M.Miller and son), 1 shoe factory. By 1939 only one of the 4 textile shops were still left and the iron and tools shop did not exist anymore.

In 1937, 23 Jewish artisans, members of the Artisans Association, still worked: 4 tailors (Hayim Doktorsky, Gershon Soloveichik, Mosheh Pshezhorsky), 3 shoemakers (Yankel Doktorsky and his son Faive, Alter Shneider, Shelomoh Levinsky), 3 butchers, 2 bakers (Binyamin Rude, Mikhael Rude), 3 blacksmiths (Leib Khmilevsky, Leizer Ofchinsky, Orchik Bereznitsky), 2 stitchers (Hirsh Zalman Kviatkovsky, Meir Yosef Ribak), 2 carpenters, 1 oven builder (Avraham Berkman), 1 cord maker (Borovsky), 1 knitter and 1 barber (Avraham Sheinkin). There was also a group of Jewish coachmen (Aharon-Hayim and Zelig Shultz, Yankel-Zalman Khmilevsky, Aizik Pitler, Hayim Baltler, Yerukham Milinarsky), who transported goods from Kovno and nearby towns to Vishey, and fish and agricultural products from it.

In addition to this there was the Zimenman family (Moshe, his son David-Elia and his grandson Aron), builders, who used to build log houses in the surrounding villages. They also rebuilt the synagogue burnt down in the fire of 1924. Yankel Kamerunsky and his son made caps, Velvel Fleisher and Dumblevsky caught fish all their lives, Elkhanan Fridkovsky and Hayim-Leib Pitler managed a fishing business. Motel Frank and Motel Arnberg bought agricultural products (each of them in different periods) for export, Nakhum Shneider made lemonade, and the Lozovskis and the Hofman's cultivated land. Some people used to rent their plots.

There were two Jewish doctors (Kopelman and Rik) and one medic (Berel Kukliansky), but in 1939 only one doctor was left.

Most Jews left agriculture, turning to commerce or crafts instead, but many continued to maintain a small auxiliary farm with a vegetable garden, some fruit trees, a cow or a goat and a chicken run beside their houses. Some continued to catch fish and lobsters from the lake.

A group of Vishey youth

The second from left in the first row-Shakhne Bereznitsky (living in Vilna), the sixth-Eliezer Peltin (died in 1999 in Kibbutz Mishmaroth).

The first from left in the second row-Zlate Milinarsky (murdered in Katkishke) *Photo supplied by Y .Bereznitsky*

The Jewish "Folksbank" played an important role in the economic life of the town. It had 116 members in 1929, but by 1939 only 70 remained. Katz was the first director of the bank, followed by Mrs. H.Presman-Bereznitsky. There was also a branch of "The United Company for Credit to Jewish Agrarians". Vishey had 11 phone owners in 1939, including 5 Jews.

During this period the number of Jews decreased, mainly for economic reasons. Most young people moved to the big cities of the state or immigrated abroad including Eretz Yisrael. The big fires of 1924 and 1929 added to the decrease of the Jewish community.

Jewish children received their elementary education at the Hebrew school of the "Tarbuth" chain, whose headmasters were Hayim Shultz and later Kaplan, with an average of 60 children studying there. Many of its graduates continued their studies at high schools, some of them at the Kovno University, and among them two who graduated with a M.D. degree, named M.Shnaider and Y.Levinson. The latter served as a battalion commander in the medical corps of the Red Army during the war, after which he became professor in the faculty of medicine in Kovno University.

The town had a library of about 700 books in Hebrew and Yiddish, as well as a dramatic circle under the guidance of the barber Avraham Sheinkin.

Vishey Jewish girls
First line from right: Leah Fridkovsky, Ida Peltin, Eli-Yitshak Frank
Second line from right: Hayah Iglovsky, Sarah-Leah Peltin, Sheine Bereznitsky, Hinde Arenberg, Rivkah Khmilevsky, Rivkah Frank.

Vishey Jewish girls

First line sitting from right: Rivkah Khmilevsky, Hayah Shimansky, Sarah Yedvabnitsky, Lozovsky

Second line from right: Haya Iglovsky, --------, Zlate Milinarsky.

Photo supplied by Y.Berznitsky

During this period many local Jews belonged to the Zionist movement and all Zionist parties had their adherents. This can be seen in the results of elections for Zionist congresses as detailed in the table below:

Congr. Nr.	Year	Total Shek.	Total Voter	Labor Party		Rev.	General Zionists		Gros.	Miz.
				Z"S	Z"Z		A	B		
16	1929	42	22	--	2	15	5	--	--	--
17	1931	--	25	4	6	11	4	--	--	--
18	1933	---	45	42		--	2	--	1	--
19	1935	---	58	57		--	1	--	--	--
21	1939	33	32	26		--	1	--	5	--

Cong.-Congress; Shek.-Shekalim; Rev.-Revisionists; Gros.-Grosmanists; Miz.-Mizrahi

From right: Esther-Zlate Berznitsky-actor of the Jewish popular theater, Leah Podgorsky   Photo supplied by Y. Bereznitsky

Collectors for the national funds (KKL and Keren Hayesod) would come from Kovno to Vishey from time to time and would be made very welcome.

Among the Zionist youth organizations were "Gordonia" with 40-50 members (one of the activists was Eliezer Peltin, later in Kibutz Mishmaroth in Israel), "Tseirei Zion", "HeKhalutz" and the sport organization "Maccabi".

In the fire of 1872 the "Beth Midrash" was ruined too, but it was rebuilt and served as the religious and public center. Vishey cantors with their choirs were famous in Lithuania and would perform in synagogues in nearby towns.

The fire of 1924 razed the "Beth-Midrash" again and Rabbi Yosef Goldin appealed to former Vishey inhabitants in America for urgent help to rebuild it.

Among the Rabbis who served in Vishey were: Eliyahu Margalioth; Nathan-Neta-Klonimus Kabak (1854-1913),in Vishey from 1890; Nakhman Kolyaditsky; Avraham Reznik, who was a delegate to the communities conference in 1920; Yosef Goldin, and the last Rabbi of Vishey was Yekhezkel Goldshlak. These last two were murdered in the Holocaust.

Vishey branch of "Gordonia"

Members of these organizations were helpful in collecting donations for KKL. There was a "Volunteer Fire Brigade", most of its members being Jewish, who also maintained a wind orchestra.

Benyamin Rud-commander of the Jewish Volunteer Fire Brigade and amateur actor .　　　　Photo supplied by Y. Bereznitsky

The Jewish wind band

First line below from right: Mikhal Rud, Yosef Upnitsky, Faivel Doktorsky

Second line from right: Alter Shliakhtsitz, Hirsh-Zalmen Kviatkovsky, Balkosatsky, Mosheh Shnaider, the conductor, -------, Podgorsky, Yakov Bereznitsky

Third line from right: -----, ------, -----, Mosheh Fridman, Avraham Pitler

Among the personalities who lived in Vishey were: Mordehai Smolnik, who served as the "Shamash" (synagogue beadle) and who was very conversant with the "Talmud"; Menakhem Diskin, philanthropist and public worker; Shlomo Hirshel, the veteran "Melamed" in town, and A.A.Kabak, (1883-1944) the son of the Rabbi. The latter, who lived in Eretz Yisrael from 1911, was a writer and translator, who published many novels and stories in Hebrew and translated novels from world literature into Hebrew.

During World War II and afterwards

World War II started with the German invasion of Poland on the 1st of September 1939, and its consequences for Lithuanian Jews in general and Vishey Jews in particular were felt several months later.

In agreement with the Ribbentrop-Molotov treaty on the division of occupied Poland, the Russians occupied the Suvalk region, but after delineation of exact borders between Russia and Germany the Suvalk region fell into German hands. The retreating Russians allowed anyone who wanted to join them to move into their occupied territory, and indeed many young people left the area together with the Russians. The Germans drove the remaining Jews out of their homes in Suvalk and its vicinity, robbed them of their possessions, then directed them to the Lithuanian border, where they were left in dire poverty. The Lithuanians did not allow them to enter Lithuania and the Germans did not allow them to return. Thus they stayed in this swampy area in cold and rain for several weeks, until Jewish youths from the border villages smuggled them into Lithuania by various routes, with much risk to themselves. Altogether about 2,400 refugees passed through the border or infiltrated on their own, and were then dispersed in the "Suvalkiya" region.

In 1940 Lithuania was annexed by the Soviet Union and became a Soviet Republic. Following new rules, all the Zionist parties and youth organizations were disbanded and Hebrew educational institutions were closed. Some Jews started to join the new ruling institutions. The local amateur troupe ("Artistic Brigade") established by the "Folks Hilf" (Red help-MOPR) performed plays in town and during the October celebrations in 1940 in Lazdey the play "Bar Kokhva" of Goldfaden was produced with the accompaniment of a local Jazz band.

Supply of goods decreased and, as a result, prices soared. The middle class, mostly Jewish, bore most of the brunt, and the standard of living dropped gradually.

On the 22nd of June 1941 the German army entered Vishey and Lithuanian gangs immediately started to rampage. They imprisoned the Jewish men in the synagogue and took them from there to forced labor such as cleaning the streets, destroying bunkers the Soviets had built and other types of works. The Jews were also woken at night and abused.

The German town mayor made efforts to save Vishey Jews and in particular a girl he loved, but the Lithuanians complained that he was a "Jews lover" and he was sent to the front line.

On the fifteenth of September 1941 all Vishey Jews were transferred under heavy guarding to Lazdey and put into the Ghetto that was established in Katkiske, about one and a half km from Lazdey. There the Jews from Lazdey, Rudamin, Vishey, Kopcheve and small settlements of the surroundings were concentrated. They were laced in the army barracks by family, and the entire area was surrounded by barbed wire and armed Lithuanian guards. Daily work groups were used for work outside die compound.

Initially, they gave each person 200 grams of unsalted bread and 300 grams of potatoes. Gradually the rations were cut down, and an epidemic of dysentery broke out. People suffered and starved. Some sneaked out and ran to nearby villages where they exchanged personal belonging for food or begged for food. A certain relief occurred when some of the local farmers were allowed to engage Jews as workers on their farms, provided that they would return them to the ghetto at night. Those who ate at the farms would give up their share of the food in the ghetto so that others could benefit from it.

The internal arrangements of the work schedule were conducted by the Jewish managed *Arbeits Amt* (Work Office). A special committee to manage all the affairs of the ghetto was created from representatives from all of the communities. The pharmacist Astromsky from Kopcheve was their leader. He did not do a thing without consulting with Rabbi Gershtein of Lazdey. A Jewish police force was organized in the ghetto but had very little authority

Every gentile was able to do whatever he pleased. Hardly a day passed without some torture or criminal act. For example, a Lithuanian policeman once took a liking to the boots of Yehoshua Vilensky from Rudamin. He called him over, shot him dead, and took his boots.

One day the ghetto was shocked by the secret news Sheina Idovitz and Golda Katorovsky related upon their return from work on Monday, October 27th. Every day they were taken to the town to work for the German commander. That day, they heard a conversation between the commandant of Mariampol who screamed at the commandant of Lazdey what a terrible shame it was that his Jews were still alive. The commandant from Lazdey apologized and explained that he needed the Jews who were doing necessary work and many of the essential crafts. The commandant from Mariampol screamed again, "You have to fulfill your task or otherwise you will be sent to the front" whereby the commandant of Lazdey replied, "I am a soldier and a man of war, and you won't scare me with this kind of a threat.'

The mood in the ghetto was electrified instantaneously. The sounds of the wings of death shook the people and scared them in anticipation of the following day. That night some people escaped from the ghetto and went looking for a hideout with the farmers or in the fields. A few days later, however, when no special events had occurred, everything returned to normal. They expected that the commandant would continue to protect the Jews under his control. By the end of October, most of the Jews throughout Lithuania were already murdered, while those of Lazdey were among some of the very few left alive.

On Thursday, October 30, 1941, the ghetto was sealed and nobody was taken out to work. They were able to see that the murderous Lithuanians were walking in the distance with spades in their hands. Upon asking the chief of the police as to the meaning of this scene, he responded nonchalantly, "They are going to dig pits for you. This will take a few days and that is exactly the length of time left for you to be alive." After that explanation, many attempted to run away even though the place was well guarded by armed guards. The following morning, escapees were returned to the camp, some wounded and some murdered, and the chief of police came to calm the Jews. He told them that running away does not make sense since everywhere the German foot steps the Jews get wiped off the face of the earth. He went on to say that a Jew can never find a hiding place from the bullet that is marked for him, and that very soon the end will come for all the Jews wherever they on might be.

The Lithuanians sealed all the windows and doors to the barracks with planks and metal bars, and the Jews stayed locked up without water or food. Despite all their efforts, 180 people managed to escape from the barracks in the first two nights.

On Monday, November 3, 1941 (the 13th of *Mar-Heshvan,* 5702), the Jews were taken naked from the barracks to the dug out pits about 300 meters away from the barracks and about 300 meters west of the forest. About 1600 souls were shot to death there. Not one person managed to escape. Although the Germans gave the orders for the 'operation,' they participated only as the observers at the scene of the crime. The actual executioners were Lithuanians. A gang of apparently experienced murderers from Mariampol also participated in the executions. This gang seemed experienced because of their actions and later, that they refused the Germans' offer to photograph them in order to "memorialize" their actions. Only in December of 1941 did the first signs of the German's retreat and defeat appear when the Germans were forced back into winter defensive positions. As mentioned earlier, many escaped before the slaughter. Some were badly wounded, caught, and brought back to the ghetto. On the day of the slaughter, they were dragged with the other sick and helpless to the pits. Many of the escapees were killed by the farmers. After a while, the Lithuanians stopped murdering the captured escapees and incarcerated them instead. When the number of the captured escapees reached 35, they took them to the mass graves and murdered them there.

From the entire 180 who escaped, only 6 survived the war: Rivkah (Gershtein) Mikhnovsky and her husband Ze'ev Mikhnovsky, Dov Zef, Miriam Kuleisky and her sisters Gita and Bath-Sheva Koifman-all from Lazdey; Khmilevsky from Vishey; Gedalya Cohen from Rudamin.

Vishey Jews together with those from Lazdey, Rudamin and Kopcheve (Kapciamiestis) who were imprisoned in Katkiske, were murdered on the 3rd of November 1941 (13th of Kheshvan 5702). According to Lithuanian sources 1,535 men, women and children are buried in the mass graves. A monument was built on these graves after the war and the inscription was replaced in the nineties.

Entrance gate and monument in the background of the mass graves in Lazdey *Photo taken by Ruth ben David*

The monument on the mass graves

The tablet of the monument with the inscription in Lithuanian and Yiddish: "Here the Hitlerist murderers and their local helpers at Nov. 3, 1941 murdered 1535 Jews from Lazdey district men, women, children."

Picture supplied by Ruth ben David

Road sign with the inscription: "Place of the mass murder of the Jews in 1941 in Katkishke"

The Fridkovsky sisters survived thanks to two Lithuanian peasants, Zharnauskas and Levulis. After the German retreat they were murdered by Lithuanian nationalists for saving the Jewish girls.

Fulgentas Luvelis and his daughter Nida - the son and granddaughter of the murdered savior of the Fridkovsky sisters at the Jewish cemetery in Kopcheve. Behind is them Yehudah Fridkovsky.

Photo supplied by Yehudah Fridkovsky

The pharmacist Shaul Kukliansky and family were saved too thanks to Lithuanian peasants of the surroundings. His son Shemuel became later professor of Law at the Vilna university. A native of Vishey, David Goldin, who was in the Kovno Ghetto, escaped to the partisans where he perished in 1944.

Vishey men who fought against the Nazis as soldiers of the Red Army were: S.Bereznitsky, H.Brazovsky, Y. and Y.Levinsons, Y.Milinarsky and B.Soloveichik who fell in battle.

After the war, Dr. Felix Zandman, whose grandmother Tema Freidovitz was from Vishey, established in USA a net of factories for production of electronic components named "Vishey". Branches of this net, "Vishey-Israel", were established in Holon, Dimonah and in Migdal-HaEmek.

The former Vishey Jews in Israel installed a Memorial Tablet for their community at the "Holocaust Cellar" at the Mount Zion in Jerusalem.

לְזֵכֶר עוֹלָם
לִקְדוֹשֵׁי עִירֵנוּ קְהִילַת
◈ וִישֵׁיי ♨
‹לִיטָא› הי"ד
שֶׁנִּרְצְחוּ וְנִסְפּוּ בִּשְׁנוֹת הַשּׁוֹאָה,
יוֹם הַזִּכָּרוֹן עֲשָׂרָה בְּטֵבֵת ‹וְיוֹם הַשּׁוֹאָה›
שְׂרִידֵי יוֹצְאֵי קְהִילַת וִישֵׁיי בְּיִשְׂרָאֵל וּבַתְּפוּצוֹת

**Tablet in remembrance of Vishey Community at the Holocaust
Cellar on Mount Zion in Jerusalem**

**According to the census of 1970, 1979 and 1989 there was no Jew in
Vishey.**

For a map of Vishey with the Jewish houses and a list of their inhabitants see
Appendix I.

A meeting of former Vishey'ers in Israel

Bibliography

Yad Vashem Archives: Koniuchovsky Collection 0-71, Files 131

YIVO, NY, Collection of Jewish Communities in Lithuania, Files 361-366

Gotlib. Ohalei Shem, (Hebrew) page 64.

Eliezer Peltin, Sipur Khayai (Story of my life) (Hebrew) Private edition 1996

HaMeilitz (St. Petersburg) (Hebrew): 30.1.1893

Folksblat, Kovno (Yiddish): 24.12.1935; 25.4.1939; 30.5.1939; 17.11.1940

Dzuku Zinios-(Lithuanian) Article of Yosif Levinson "Once there were Jews in Veisiejai"18.1.1992; 23.1.1992; 1.8.1992

Jerusalem of Lithuania. No.7(58), October 1995. Article of Yosif Levinson

Antanas Pupienis, Po Dzukijos dangumi (Under the Sky of Dzukija) (Lithuanian).

Valstybines Leidybos Centras. Vilnius 1996

Appendix I

Map and List of Vishey Jewish Families according to the Houses they lived in (submitted by Yosif Levinson)

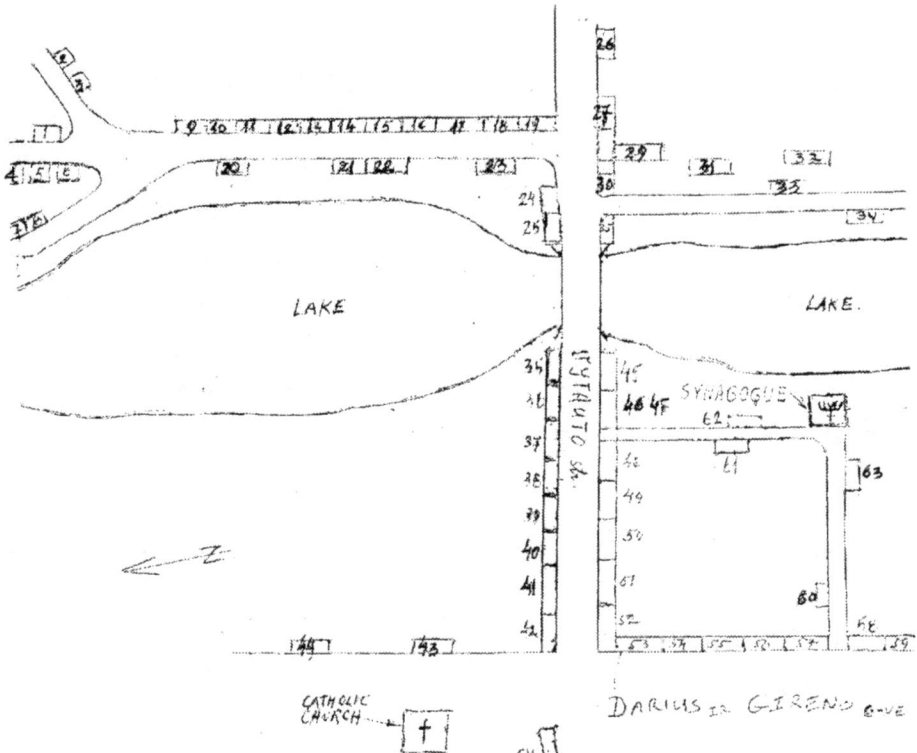

Vishey in 1941
(without scale)

☐ Jewish house

Compiled by Yosif Levinson

1. L.Khmilevsky	7. Levinson, Timiansky
2. Mosheh the fisherman	8. Shvartz
3. Shneider (the Shokhet)	9. Kamerunsky
4. I.Flaxman	10. Fridkovsky
5. -----------	11. M.Frank
6. Sh.Levinsky	12. Kh.Podgursky

13.-------------

14.J.Podgursky

15.H.Podgursky

16.Balkosatsky

17.M.Rud

18.M.Borovsky

19.Kh.Doktorsky

20.Vizhansky

21.H.Chesler

22.Alter the carpenter

23.J.Podgursky

24.M.Rud

25.Ts.Rud

26.Soloveichik

27.Brazovsky

28.Kh.Shultz

29.L.Ofchinky

30.A.Berkman

31.A.Tsimerman

32.M.Kapulsky

33.Dumblevsky

34.Lozovsky

35.Sh.Kukliansky

36.J.Khmilevsky

37.Fridkovsky

38.B.Rud

39.Fridman

40.----------

41.Kabrovsky

42.Solnitsky

43.Fainsod

44.I.Mlinarsky

45.J.Doktorsky, F.Doktorsky

46.J.Kukliansky

47.Z.Pitler

48.Z.Shultz

49.G.Kukliansky

50.J.Goldin

51.P.Yedvobnitsky

52.Ts.Rubin

53.L.Flaxman

54.N.Mlinarsky

55.J.Kukliansky

56.Kh.Yedvobnitsky

57.Kh.Iglovsky

58.Miler

59.Sheinkin, Yankovsky

60.Hofman

61.A.Shnaider, M.Shnaider

62.V.Fleisher

63.Sh.Fink

64.---------

65.Sh.Flaxman

66.Berznitsky

67.Kh.Pitler

68.A.Pitler

69.Berkman

70.Gail

71.Arnberg

72.Ribak

73.H.Khmilevsky

74.Peltin

75.M.Frank

Vilkaviškis (Vilkovishk)

Vilkovishk (in Yiddish) is located in the southwestern part of Lithuania on the shores of the river Seimena, a tributary of the river Sesupe, about 18 km from the border with Prussia (now Russia) and 3.5 km from the St. Petersburg-Berlin railway line. It was one of the oldest towns in Lithuania, when in 1660 King Jan Kazimir granted it the rights of a city (Magdeburg rights).

Until 1795 Vilkovishk was part of the Polish-Lithuanian Kingdom, when the third division of Poland by the three superpowers of those times - Russia, Prussia and Austria - caused Lithuania to become partly Russian and partly Prussian. The part of the state which lay on the left side of the Nieman river (Nemunas), including Vilkovishk, was handed over to Prussia who ruled it during the years 1795-1807.

Under Prussian rule the residents were encouraged to build stone or brick houses, instead of wooden ones, for which they were granted a third of the expenses. In those years the importance of Vilkovishk increased, it being a commercial center on the road from Kovno to Koenigsberg.

After Napoleon defeated Prussia and according to the Tilzit agreement of July1807, Polish territories occupied by Prussia were transferred to what became known as the "The Great Dukedom of Warsaw", which was established at that time. The king of Saxony, Friedrich-August, was appointed duke, and the Napoleonic code now became the constitution of the dukedom, according to which everybody was equal before the law. except for the Jews who were not granted any civil rights.

During the years 1807-1813, Vilkovishk belonged to the "Great Dukedom of Warsaw" and was part of the Bialystok district. The Napoleonic Codex was then introduced in this region, remaining in effect even during the Lithuanian period.

In the summer of 1812, Napoleon, with a huge army of about 250,000 soldiers, stayed there for 4 days, causing great damage to the residents of the town and its surroundings. Napoleon told a delegation of Vilkovishk Jews, who had approached him requesting that the army stationed there remove their horses from the synagogues - it being before "Tisha beAv" (9th of Av) and the Jews wanted to mourn the destruction of the Temple in Jerusalem, - that he had been in Palestine with his army in 1898-99, and that if he managed to conquer that land he would re-establish the Jewish Kingdom.

After the defeat of the French army in Russia many retreating soldiers were frozen to death and drowned in the lakes around Vilkovishk, and 80 French soldiers and 3 generals were buried in the vicinity of Vilkovishk. In 1815, after the defeat of Napoleon, all of Lithuania was annexed to Russia, as a result of which Vilkovishk was included in the Augustowa Province (Gubernia), and in 1866 it became a part of the Suwalk Gubernia as a district administrative capitol.

The Russians built large barracks near the town as well as several factories, one factory for producing spirits and a few large factories for extracting oil etc. They also built big storehouses where locally produced goods were stored together with imported ones, for distribution to neighboring towns.

Vilkovishk in these years was the center for processing pig bristles, and in 1900 about 1,000 workers were employed in this industry.

During the years1882, 1886 and 1895 the town suffered from extensive fires.

In 1915, during World War I, Vilkovishk was captured by the German army who ruled there till 1918, when the independent Lithuanian state was established. During the period of independent Lithuania (1918-1940) Vilkovishk was a district administrative capitol as it had been before and appropriate institutions, such as district offices and the regional court, were located there. There were also 3 hospitals (2 of them private), 4 pharmacies, 2 high schools, 3 elementary schools, one trade school, several libraries, 2 printing presses, 8 doctors, 8 dentists and 2 cinemas.

In the 1920s the railway line Kazlu-Ruda--Marijampole--Kalvarija--Alytus was constructed, resulting in the transfer of the regional commercial center to Marijampole.

During Soviet rule (1940-1941) Vilkovishk continued to serve as a district administrative capitol.

The invasion of Lithuania by the German army in June 1941 caused the destruction of most (about 90%) of the houses in Vilkovishk. During the first months of the German occupation (June-September 1941), they together with their local helpers murdered 3056 people, most of them Jewish. Vilkovishk was liberated from the Nazis by the Red Army on the 9th of August 1944.

Jewish Settlement till after World War 1.

According to tradition, Jews began to settle in Vilkovishk already in the 14th century, but in the old Jewish cemetery tombstones were found dating only from 1575. At the beginning of the 16th century Queen Bona (wife of King Zigmunt August the Second) donated timber to the citizens of Vilkovishk for building prayer houses. Jews too were among the beneficiaries and built their synagogue in 1545, which existed till World War II, having been renovated several times over the years. It contained a grandiose oak "Aron Kodesh" (Holy Ark), three stories high (11 meters), decorated with artistically engraved wooden ornaments, which housed several scrolls brought by those expelled from Spain as well as the usual Sifrey Torah (Scrolls of the Torah).

At the beginning of 18th century deceased Jews from Koenigsberg (Prussia) were brought to Vilkovishk for burial, because they were not allowed to build a cemetery for themselves.

The Old Synagogue

An old tombstone at the Vilkovishk cemetery

In the middle of the 18th century a cholera epidemic hit the town of Vizhan (Wizajny - now Poland) about 35 km south of Vilkovishk. Jewish refugees from there who were not allowed to enter Vilkovishk, settled in a forest nearby and the community of Vilkovishk supplied them with food. Many of them died and were buried near the forest. Descendants of these Jews later settled in Vilkovishk and lived there till the Holocaust.

A community committee consisting of the Rabbis and the respected personalities of the community administered public life. This committee managed all the religious, educational and welfare institutions. State rule in general did not intervene in internal issues of the Jews, thus the Rabbis were authorized to register births and deaths, to collect taxes for community needs and also to act as judges in conflicts among community members. The notebook (Pinkas) of the community from the years 1692-1833 is located in the Central Archives of the History of the Jewish People in Jerusalem.

During the 19th century the Jews were the majority of the entire population of Vilkovishk. In 1857, out of a total of 5,503 people in the town, 4,559 were Jews (83%), and by 1897 this had increased to 5,788 people, but included only 3,480 Jews (60%).

During the years 1869/70 Jewish immigration to America started. In a list of immigrants from Vilkovishk the following names appear: L. Aronberg, H. Volkovitz, A. Varshavsky, M. London, S. Levi, M. B. Likhtenstein, S. Neuman, T. Memlonusky, S. Karigarsky.

In the 1880s and 1890s Jews from Russia would arrive in Vilkovishk in order to cross the border to Germany without a passport, and from there to sail to America. This was attempted for mostly financial or political reasons, but sometimes the smugglers were caught by the Russian Border Guard, whereupon the Vilkovishk community was obliged to free these Jews from jail. In 1898 a warning was published in the Hebrew newspaper "HaTsefirah" (printed in Warsaw) against attempting to cross the border without a passport, signed on behalf of the community of Vilkovishk by: Rabbi Zvi Mah-Yafith, Rabiner (official Rabbi) Eliyahu Shereshevsky; Trustees: Sender Turberg, Efraim-Mendel Pustapedsky; Gabaim (honorary officers): Yekhezkel Yafe and Yehosua Lipman Yofe.

Over the years the Jews concentrated on trade in grains, timber and agricultural products designated for export to Germany. There were Jews in Vilkovishk who owned considerable fields (according to the Napoleon Code Jews could acquire land in this region), also growing vegetables and fruits. The fire of 1882 harmed 180 Jewish families, and in 1886 300 Jewish houses burnt down. The fire of 1905 destroyed many Jewish houses, resulting in help being supplied by the Jewish French "Alliance" association and Barons Rothschild and Hirsch.

There were many Jewish shopkeepers, various artisans and car and carriage owners who transported goods and passengers to the railway station and to neighboring towns. In particular the industry of processing pig bristles for the production of brushes was developed in Vilkovishk. There were 4 big factories of this kind – belonging to Sobolevitz, Rozin, Vilkovisky and Vindsberg - who employed more than 400 Jewish workers in addition to several smaller workshops. These workers were the first ones who organized and arranged strikes in order to improve their working conditions.

A page of the Pinkas

In 1896 a strike took place in Vindsberg's factory, organized by members of the "Bund" party from Vilna (Avraham Alexandrovitz and Ortshik), the workers demanding a reduction of daily working hours to 10, and they achieved their goal. At that time the "Union of the Brush Workers" was established, and in 1898 a proclamation "To the Jewish Brush Workers in Lithuania and Poland" concerning the struggle for workers rights was issued by this union. The "Bund" also organized illegal demonstrations causing conflicts with the police and some of the demonstrators were detained (the tailor Volokh, Shemuel Joffe, Eliyahu Slitovsky, Yisrael Kenigsberg). In 1911 about 1000 bristles workers, mostly Jewish, struck in order to establish an eight-hour working day and a supplement of 75 Kopeiki(100Kopeiki= 1Ruble) per week, thus becoming the first workers in Lithuania to benefit from an eight-hour day. The "Bund" organization fought not only for workers rights, but also propagated knowledge and Yiddish culture among the working classes.

There were many prayer houses in town: the old synagogue, the "Beth Midrash", four "Klois'es": the German, the French - where Napoleon's soldiers had lodged - the "Khevrah Kadisha" and the R' Ya'akov Yeshayahu, and one "Shtibl". The brush workers had their own prayer house which was called "Khevrath S"Kh (Hebrew initials of Pig Hair) This society (Khevrah) was established in 1875, initiated by the "Magid" from Kelem (Kelme) who taught those workers "Khayei Adam" and "Mishnah" (see the front page of the "Pinkas" of this society, below).

The "Beth Midrash"

A "Khevrah Kadisha" was also active, whose "Pinkas" (Notebook) existed from 1811 and "Khevrath Mishnah" whose "Pinkas" already existed in 1761.

Education of Jewish children was mainly in the hands of "Melamdim" (religious teachers), and at the end of the 19th century the "Melamed" Moshe Sudarsky, very beloved by his pupils and honored by the entire public, became famous in Vilkovishk. Many pupils of the "Khadarim" and "Talmud Torah" continued their studies in the "Yeshivoth" in town or in neighboring towns.

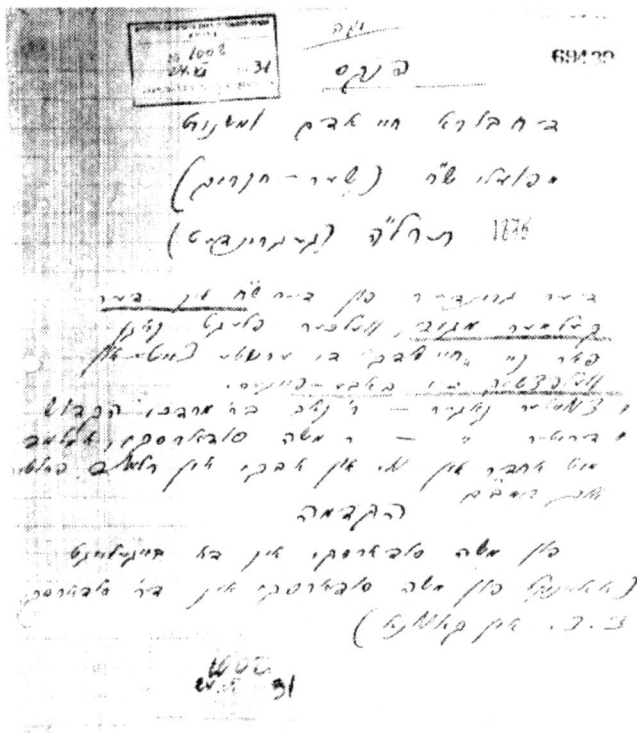

In 1867 there was a Russian-Jewish school, with one of its teachers being Nakhum-Tuviyah London, who immigrated to America in 1895, published articles in the Hebrew press there and also participated in the writing of the English Jewish Encyclopedia. In 1879 there was a school directed by Rabiner E.Shereshevsky, and in 1903 he established a school with three classes, in which religious and general subjects were taught.

Part of the youth were fluent in the Hebrew language and showed great interest in the origins of the new Hebrew literature. An association called the "Distributors of Knowledge" (among the Jews) in Russia sent Hebrew books and periodicals which were received with excitement, and letters of thanks were sent to the distributors.

In those years the "Sopher" (Scribe) Mosheh was famous in Vilkovishk and its surroundings, as a writer of Scriptures and as an artist who created more than 500 artistic "Mizrakh" signs indicating the east, the direction towards Jerusalem, which were fixed on the eastern walls of many Jewish homes, and many "L'Shanah Tovah" signs. The climax of his work was a "Sidur" (prayer book) written by hand and ornamented, which he prepared for the "Home for the Aged" in town.

Among the Rabbis who served in Vilkovishk during this period were: Eliezer Landa (1791-1886); Ya'akov David Vilevsky (1845-1914); Tsevi Hirsh Mah-Yafith (1840-1919).

Among the "Dayanim" (Religious Judges) were Ya'akov Rabinovitz; Ya'akov Shpaier; Yehudah Yitshak Segal; Elkhanan Haparush; Dov-Ber Kamaika; Khananyah Cohen.

Many welfare institutions were active in Vilkovishk: "Gemiluth Khasadim" (ran a "Pinkas" from 1800); "Maskil el Dal" (their "Pinkas" dates from1880) giving loans to the needy without interest and small payments for returning the money; "Mathan BeSeter" which helped people whose economic situation had deteriorated and who were embarrassed to ask for help; "Maoth Khitim" provided the needy with necessities for "Pesakh". In 1910 all four institutions were united into one big institution "Tsedaka Gedolah". "Hakhnasath Kalah" helped poor brides; "Linath haTsedek" supplied poor travelers with food and accommodation; "Bikur Kholim" helped needy patients and sent them doctors and medicines. There were also Jewish public baths and several "Mikveh". In 1912 the community built a magnificent "Home for the Aged" with a lovely garden.

Zionist activity had started in the 1890s, and expressed itself in publicity and fund raising for the settlement of Eretz-Yisrael. Yitshak Eliezer Izersky, a pharmacist, immigrated to Eretz-Yisrael in the 1870s and opened a shop of medicines in Yaffo. Vilkovishk Jews who immigrated to Eretz-Yisrael at that time were Rabbi Zevulun Kharlap (died in Jerusalem in 1898) and Adinah Kahansky (arrived in 1902), who opened a restaurant in Rishon leZion which became a meeting place for writers and workers' leaders. She published articles in the periodical "Hapoel HaTzair" and was a member of the local council.

In the old cemetery of Jerusalem there are three tombstones of Vilkovishk Jews: Ze'ev-Wolf son of David (died in1878); Yitshak son of Mosheh HaCohen (died in 1888); Tsevi son of Aharon HaCohen (died in1899).

The "Zion" society in town, headed by pharmacist Fainberg, had 400 members in 1899. At the regional conference of Zionist Societies, which took place in 1899 in Vilna, Rabbi Zvi Mah-Yafith participated as delegate from Vilkovishk. On "Khol HaMoed Succoth" 1903 the "Center of the Zionist Societies of Suvalk Gubernia" gathered in Vilkovishk and there drafted regulations for the societies' activities, which were adopted. In 1901-1902 about 200 "Shekalim" (membership cards of the Zionist organization) were sold in town. At that time 500 shares of the so-called "Colonial Bank" (The Jewish Colonial Trust Ltd., established by Dr.Herzl at the second Zionist Congress in 1899, the predecessor of the Anglo-Palestine Bank), each costing one pound, were sold in Vilkovishk. In the summer of 1913, before the 11th Zionist Congress, a conference of Zionist Societies, gathered in Suwalk with the participation of a delegate from Vilkovishk.

During these years the "Tseirei Zion" and "Poalei Zion-Smol" parties acted in town and were a counter weight to the anti-Zionist "Bund".

During World War I. Vilkovishk passed several times from one power to another, the Jews suffering from abuse and maltreatment by Russian soldiers, and many left. During the German occupation (1915-1918) the Jews, like every one else, suffered from the various restrictive edicts of occupation rule and Jewish community life was paralyzed. The Jewish Bendet Rabinovitz was the mayor of Vilkovishk during these years.

During the Period of Independent Lithuania (1918-1940).

Society and Economy.

When the German occupation ended after the war and the Lithuanian state was established, Jews of Vilkovishk started to return home. The economic situation of the returning residents was very bad and they needed help. A Jewish relief committee was established in Vilna which provided financial help to needy communities in Lithuania (see document below, written in German - Wladislawow is the old name of Kudirkos Naumiestis).

A view of Vilkovishk with the Old Synagogue in the background

The autonomy law issued by the government regarding minorities in Lithuania, including Jews, gave substantial encouragement to social and economic life. Elections for the Community Committee took place in 1919 and the two workers parties, "Poalei Zion" and the "Bund" won an absolute majority. The first meeting of the Committee took place on the 30th of December 1919, with Misler being elected chairman, and because the protocols were written both in Hebrew and in Yiddish, Bilotsky was elected as the Hebrew secretary and Guterman as the Yiddish secretary (see document below written in Hebrew).

During the years of its existence the Committee collected taxes as required by law and was in charge of all aspects of community life.

During the elections for the municipal council, which took place in 1921, 11 Jews out of 21 council members were elected, in the 1924 elections there were 12 Jews in a council of 24 members, and a Jew officiated as Chairman of the District Council. In 1931, 8 out of 12 council members elected were Jews: Avraham Liudvinovsky, Bendet Rabinovitz, Shelomoh Reizen, Ya'akov Rozenholtz, Reuven Haskel, Yosef Kabaker, Avraham Makovsky and Mordehai Zimansky. But in the 1934 election only 6 Jews were elected, out of 12 council members. Meir Varshavsky, the Deputy Mayor and treasurer of the municipality for many years, was also a Jew. In 1936 there were 7 Jews among the 19 employees of the municipality. Among 110 government officials there was only one Jew.

According to the first survey arranged in Lithuania in 1923, there were 7,263 people in Vilkovishk, including 3,206 Jews (44 %).

When conditions stabilized the Jews started to reestablish their businesses and to establish new enterprises, but the town did not return to the status it had before World War I. The brush industry, which had sustained hundreds of families, became more and more restricted, until by 1935 this branch only employed about 50 workers, who also suffered from labor conflicts with their employers. The reason for this crisis was the shortage of raw materials in Lithuania and the prohibition of export by the USSR, who was the main supplier of bristles.

פראטאקאל

The first page of the first meeting of the Community Committee

In these years the signs on Jewish shop were written in Lithuanian and Hebrew or Yiddish, but after a short time they were smeared all over with tar at night.

The committee was active until the end of 1925 when the autonomy was annulled by the nationalist government who took over the rule in the state.

Another reason for the deterioration of Vilkovishks economy was the construction of the railway line Kazlu Ruda-Marijampole-Kalvarija-Alytus, which transferred economic activity from Vilkovishk to Marijampole. The annulment of the autonomy and the seizure of rule by the Nationalist party in 1926 also caused a deterioration of conditions for Jews in Vilkovishk. The new rule encouraged the establishment of Lithuanian consumer cooperatives in order to compete with the Jewish merchants and also imposed heavy taxes on them. The total closure of the border with Poland cut off trade with this country and land reform which was carried out by the government took away part of Jewish owned land, adding to the worsening of economic conditions of Vilkovishks Jews.

Despite this the Jews established new enterprises, such as for the extraction of oil, for soap, cigarettes, a flour mill, a printing press etc., and with all the difficulties the number of Jews in Vilkovishk did not decrease. Only a part of the youth immigrated to Eretz Yisrael or moved to other towns in Lithuania.

According to the 1931 government survey of shops in the state, Vilkovishk had 154 shops, including 130 owned by Jews (84%). The partition according to the type of business is given in the table below:

Type of the business	Total	Owned by Jews
Groceries	14	13
Grains and Flax	11	10
Butcher's shops and Cattle Trade	17	12
Restaurants and Taverns	19	10
Food Products	9	9
Beverages	6	6
Textile Products and Furs	22	21
Leather and Shoes	9	9
Tobacco and Cigarettes	1	1
Haberdashery and Home Utensils	11	11
Medicine and Cosmetics	4	2
Watches, Jewels and Optics	3	3
Bicycles and Sewing Machines	2	1
Tools and Steel Products	6	6
Building Materials and Furniture	2	2
Heating Materials	8	8
Overland Transportation	3	2
Stationary and Books	2	1
Miscellaneous	5	3

According to the same survey Vilkovishk had 50 light industry factories, 42 of them owned by Jews (86%), as can be seen in the following table:

Type of the Factory	Total	JewishOwned
Metal Workshops, Power Plants	3	2
Headstones, Bricks	1	0
Chemical Industry: Spirits, Soaps	4	4
Textile: Wool, Flax, Knitting	2	2
Tar Industry	1	0
Paper Industry: Printing Presses	2	2
Beverage. Cigarettes	13	10
Dresses, Footwear	5	5
Leather Industry: Production, Cobbling	2	2

By 1937 Vilkovishk counted among its working population 87 Jewish artisans, as follows: 16 tailors, 11 bakers, 10 butchers, 10 barbers, 7 shoemakers, 4 hatters, 3 watchmakers, 2 seamstresses, 2 painters, 2 tinsmiths, 2 leatherworkers, 2 stitchers, 1 rope maker, 1 carpenter, 1 photographer, 1 oven builder, 1 glazier, 1 electrician and 10 others. Most of them were organized in "The Association of Jewish Artisans" which had a club and a loan fund.

In addition to the merchants, industrialists and artisans there were 35 families engaged in agriculture. There were also 7 buses, 3 of them owned by Jews, and out of the 4 taxis 1 belonged to a Jew (in 1935).

From 1926 the manager of the power station owned by the municipality was the Jew Meir Varshavsky, who was praised for his work, as well as a Jewish mechanic who worked in the station. At the end of 1935 both were dismissed, the employers using the excuse of "restrictions". The district engineer was also Jewish.

An important factor in the economic life of the town was the "Folksbank" established with the help of the "Joint" in 1928, when it had 718 members. By 1935 it had only 368 members: 79 shop owners, 56 artisans, 48 merchants, 37 workers, 32 free profession owners, 31 agrarians, 21 cart owners, 12 industrialists, 8 clerks and 44 miscellaneous members. The capital of the bank was 55,000 Litas (1$=6 Litas). Loans to the amount of 300,000 Litas were given and the total sum of deposits came to 170,000 Litas. Wholesalers used the services of the private bank of Yosef Sperling.

In 1939 there were 190 phone owners in town, 64 of them belonging to Jews and Jewish institutions.

Education and Culture.

Instead of the traditional educational system of "Khadarim" and "Talmud Torah" a modern Hebrew educational chain was established. It included a kindergarten, an elementary school of the "Tarbuth" network, a religious school of the "Yavneh" organization and a high school.

The high school was established in 1919 at the initiative of a founders committee whose members were intellectual Jewish merchants, advocates of the Hebrew language who cared for the education of their children. They were Ya'akov Khmilevsky, A.Zeiberg, A.Volberg, Ya'akov Solomin, Peretz Silver, Yosef Sperling, Shimshon Volovitzky, Neta Teitelbaum and Neta Matz.

In August 1919 hundreds of children started their studies in this high school, where all subjects were taught in Hebrew with Sephardi pronunciation. The first director was Dr. M.Cohen and after him came Dr.Tsemakh Feldstein, Dr.Yehoshua Fridman, Dr.Mosheh Yardeni, Shelomoh Trachtenberg, the last director being Shraga Halperin.

גמנסיון ראלי עברי.
חב"ד "יבנה וסדר"
וי עזישקי.

לכי

ה ז מ נ ה.

בזה מתכברים אני להזמין את כי להגיגת

יובל העשר לקיום הגמנסין הראלי העברי בוילקמישך

(תרע"ט-תרפ"ט)

והגחת אבן הפנה לבמסמין ובית ספר למכניה

שתהיה ביום ה' י"ב סן תרפ"ט ...שע"ו-88..

התחלה בשעה 5 בצהרים.

סדר החגיגה.

א) ארט חגיגי בגמנסין.

ב) הנחת אבן הפנה.

ג) סעודה ערבית.

בכבוד

ועד ההגיגה.

The invitation for the celebration of the tenth anniversary of the High School and the laying of the cornerstone for the new building of the High School and the Vocational School, June 20, 1929

Fragments of the governmental Survey of Shops in Vilkaviskis District in 1931

Cloth

VILKAVIŠKIO APSKR.

Blapaslovempiené S., Kybartai, žydų g. 5.
Berenšteinaité Chana, Pilviškiai, Turgavieté 2.
Blochas Ch., Kybartai, Sinagogos 7.
Černevskienė Chané, Vilkaviškis.
Eisikis Ch., Vilkaviškis, Gedimino g. 11.
Eisonas Monos, Pilviškiai, Turgaus g. 9.
Evizonas Mérianas, Virbalis, Vilniaus g. 45.
Fainbergiené Rocha, Vilkaviškis, Turgavie-
té 34.
Fainbergas Ch., Vilkaviškis, Gedimino g. 3.
Feinbergas Nochumas, Virbalis, Turgavieté 12.
Finkelšteiniené Ch., Pilviškiai, Turgavieté 16.
Fridmaniené Gitel, Vilkaviškis, Turgavieté.
Fridmanas Vulfas, Pilviškiai, Turgavieté 12.
Garbes Girėas, Virbalis, Vilniaus g. 53.
Geršteinas B., Pilviškiai, Turgavieté 22.
Gitelevičius Ieikas, Virbalis, Vilniaus g. 49.
Gochenbergas Samuelis, Virbalis, Vilniaus
g. 53.
Goldšteiniené Dvora, Virbalis, Vilniaus g. 44.
Gunterias J., Bartininkai.
Gurvičiené N., Vilkaviškis, Vytauto g. 17.
Chazonas Ovséjas, Vilkaviškis, Turgavieté 15
Ironiené D., Vilkaviškis, Turgavieté 1.
Jablonas Fišelis, Pilviškiai, Turgavieté 3.
Jasveniené Chaja ir Jasvenas, Kybartai, Sena-
pilés 55.
Kaplanni B. ir G., Vilkaviškis, Vytauto g. 7.
Kaplaniené Indė, Turgavieté 6.
Laksiené Jochveda, Vilkaviškis, Turgavieté 20.
Laprunakiené Riva, Vilkaviškis, Kestučio g. 5.
Levitas E., Kybartai, Vištyčio g. 5.
Lebertaritius Jonas, Gražiškiai.
Liphicos Abromas, Vilkaviškis, Turgavieté 17.
Mikliemskis Joselis, Vištytis, Baltyčios g. 13.
Mejerovičius Osvrio, Vilkaviškis, Kestučio 11.
Mileas S., Kybartai, Senapilés 50.
Otkeniekis S., Virbalis, Vilniaus g. 41.
Orlinskis J. D., Virbalis, Turgavieté 12a.

Petrulis V. ir Gripotas, Vilkaviškis, Gedimi-
no g. 8.
Ryckis A. ir Malmarvičius S., Virbalis, Tur-
gavieté 16.
Rubinoviené Dora, Vilkaviškis, Turgavieté 8.
Seinenakis, Kybartai, Senapilés g. 83.
Sluckis Aronas, Vilkaviškis, Turgavieté 7.
Svaroas Ickus, Pilviškiai, Turgavieté 8.
Trivalai Peša ir Aronas, Vilkaviškis, Turga-
vieté 18.
Vladislavorskiené C., Pilviškiai, Jurkšų g.
Volovickis Simsonas, Vilkaviškis, Kudirkos
g. 2.
Zedachiené Rachilé, Vilkaviškis, Vytauto g. 13.
Želko Juozas, Gražiškiai.

Grocery

VILKAVIŠKIO APSKR.

Aronpaszas Mordchelis, Vilkaviškis, Sinagogos
g. 5.
Balberiškis Abromas, Vilkaviškis, Vytauto g.
25.
Bergneris V., Kybartai, Senapilés g. 99.
Fainbergas Jakobas, Vilkaviškis, Vytauto g.
27.
Geležinas Juozas, Virbalis, Geležinkelio sto-
tis.
Ginsburgas J. ir Scarcas, Kybartai, Sinago-
gos g. 5.
Heimanas Tobijas, Kybartai, Senapilés gt.
Heimnnyté Ehana, Virbalis, Vilniaus g. 19.
Jurkšaitis M., Kybartai, Naujakuriu g. 54.
Lakouskis Sanderis, Virbalis, Vištyčio g. 19.
Levinsonas Girėas, Vilkaviškis, Kestučio g. 18
Levinsonas I., Vilkaviškis, V. Kudirkos g. 18.
Logmanas ir Grosbardas, Vilkaviškis, Kestučio
g. 30.
Norkelninas Vincas, Kybartai, Algimanto g.
Okrovskis Judelis, Virbalis, Gedimino g. 31.
Solekios Br. ir B-vé, Pilviškiai, Turgavieté 3.
Samenas Isakas, Virbalis, Vilniaus g. 11.
Vinkelšteinas Šliomas, Vilkaviškis, Vilniaus g.
23.
Volbergas Berelis, Vilkaviškis, Vytauto g. 30.

Candies and Chocolate

VILKAVIŠKIO APSKR.

Irmontas Abromas-Leizeris, Vilkaviškis, Vy-
tauto g. 16.
Kiterné Sora, Virbalis, Gedimino g. 1.
Peretunakis M., Vilkaviškis, Vytauto g. 46.
Sifororivičius Izaokas, Vilkaviškis, Gedimino
g. 16.
Treitelhanmas, Vilkaviškis, Žaliumynų g. 3.

Soap Factories

VILKAVIŠKIO APSKR.

„Jukaras", Zeibergas, A ir Zilberis P., Vilkaviškis, Kestučio g. 9.
Zilberis P., Vilkaviškis, Stotiés g. 11.

Among the teachers were M.J.Mendelson-Mishkutz, Dr.A.Rozenberg, B.Meshorer, Dr.Yehudah Holtzman-Etsyoni, J.Strelitzky, D.Zilberstein, A.M.Tshertok and others.

The teachers of the Hebrew High School

Sitting from right: B.Meshorer; Dr.Cohen; Dr.Tsemakh Feldstein; Dr.Y.Etsyoni; Lithuanian teacher.

Standing from right:Y.Zilberstein; -----; M.Y.Mendelson; -----; Shimon Zak; Hayim Vilkovishky.

The tenth anniversary of the Hebrew High School

Sitting from right: A.Volovitzky (delegate of the pupils); Dr. Cohen (Teacher of Science); Rabbi Grin; Dr.Sakenis (Education Minister); Head of the department of high schools in the ministry; Dr. Yardeni (headmaster); Y.M.Mendelson (lecturing).

The first graduation class completed its studies in 1921 and the Lithuanian government representative at the matriculation examinations was Dr.Yosef Berger (Harari), the director of the Education Department of the Jewish ministry. This was the only occasion during the Jewish autonomy in Lithuania when the government authorized a Jew to participate in the matriculation examinations and to sign matriculation certificates on its behalf.

The school was financed by tuition fees paid by the pupils, but due to the deterioration in the economic situation of Vilkovishk Jews many of them had difficulty in paying the high fees. For several years the Lithuanian government supported the school, and in 1929 the cornerstone for a new building of the High and the Vocational schools was laid (see the invitation for the celebration above). The building was erected thanks to donations of a Vilkovishk Jew who had immigrated to London named Krovelsky of the "Joint" organization, and of the Sobolevitz Brothers from Vilkovishk. The new building housed both the High and Vocational schools, where subjects of metal and electricity were taught. The vocational school was connected to the "ORT" network and teaching languages were Yiddish and Hebrew.

In the middle of the 1930s, after the Nazis seized power in Germany, a group of Jewish youths from Germany arrived at the school to learn a vocation prior to their "Aliyah" to Eretz Yisrael

A class of the high school 1926 or 1927

First line sitting from left: Nekhamah Openheim, Ya'akov Cohen, Rachel Mikhnotsly, Sheine Stalovsky, David Fainberg, Frida Melamdovitz

Second line sitting from left: Aryeh Balberishky, Shmeriyahu (Zunia) Pustopedsky, Nekhamah Rabinovitz, Teacher Mishkutz, Sarah Neishtot, Goldshmit, Imanuel Albom.

Third line standing from left: Shifrah Sider, Mordehai Shershenevsky,

Hayim Srolevitz, Yehudith Shperling, Alter Hayat, Frida Hayat, Reuven Levin, Hanah Tchernotzky, Meir Tabatchnik.

The director and teacher of this school was for several years (1929-1933) Aryeh Volovitzky, born in 1908 in Vilkovishk. He immigrated to Eretz-Yisrael, where he changed his name to Ankorion. He was a lawyer (Dr. Jur.) and worked in the public sector, later being elected to the "Kneseth" on behalf of the Israeli Labor party.

Many of the graduates of the high school continued their studies in the Lithuanian University in Kovno and also abroad. Some of them immigrated to Eretz Yisrael where they became doctors, lawyers, teachers, merchants, Kibutz members etc., all loyal to Jewish culture and to the spirit of Lithuanian Jewry.

In 1935 there were 120 pupils in the high school, its conditions worsened from year to year, but none the less it survived until Soviet rule in Lithuania in 1940.

In Vilkovishk two Hebrew books were printed: "Speak Hebrew - about the question of Speaking Hebrew", by M.Yardeni 1932, and "The History of the new Hebrew Literature, Vol. 1, the 'Haskalah' literature in Central Germany (1784-1829)" by H.N.Shapira, 1940, a lecturer of Judaica in the Lithuanian university, who was murdered by the Nazis in the Kovno Ghetto.

1931 High School Class with the gymnastics teacher Starkovsky

In the years 1918-1919, at the initiative of the "Bund" and "Poalei Zion-Smol" who dominated the community committee, many cultural institutions were established. They organized the "Kultur Lige" (League for Culture), a popular university, a Yiddish school, a consumer cooperative, the trade union of the brush workers, which became the center of all brush workers in Lithuania and also a sick fund. All these institutions existed till 1926, when they were closed together with the liquidation of autonomy, when the nationalist party began to rule in Lithuania.

In 1925 a branch of the association "Libhober fun Visen" (Supporters of Knowledge) was founded in Vilkovishk, which established a library with 1,500 books in Yiddish. Next to it was a reading room where lectures on different themes took place. There was also the Zionist-Socialist "Sirkin Society", which maintained a large library in Hebrew and Yiddish.

The Jewish theater from Kovno often presented its plays and so did the "Hebrew Studio", which existed for a only few years.

In March 1939 "The Artisans Association" arranged a big party in the big hall of the cinema, where the play "Two Kuni Lemel" was performed with great success.

There was also "The Society of Jewish ex-soldiers who fought for the independence of Lithuania" with its 25 members.

Zionist and Other Activities.

During the autonomy the workers parties "Bund" and "Poalei Zion" dominated the Jewish public. At the head of the "Poalei Zion" party stood Efraim Bruker and his wife Rashel, the accountant Album and Yisrael Nitzevitz.

A delegate from Vilkovishk participated in the regional conference of "Poalei-Zion" which took place in Suvalk in 1919.

The "Bund" was forced to stop its activities in 1921, where some of its members merged with the underground Communist party and others with the "Poalei Zion-Smol (Left)", which too was forced to disband after the nationalist party took over in Lithuania.

From the entire Yiddishists group in Vilkovishk there remained only the "Folkists" (populists), who stood for the use of the Yiddish language and opposed Zionism. Their organ of opinion was the daily newspaper "Folksblat" published in Kovno.

In those years the Zionist organization with all its nuances became the dominating movement among Vilkovishk Jews. All Zionist parties were active there: Z"S (Zionist-Socialist), Z"Z (Tseirei Zion) from the labor movement; the General Zionists; Mizrakhi; Revisionists; WIZO (Women International Zionist Organization). The Zionist youth organizations who were active were: HeKhalutz, HaShomer HaTsair, Betar.

One can judge the state of mind among Vilkovishk Jews according to the results of the elections for the first Lithuanian Seimas (Parliament) which took place in October 1922: Zionists received 609 votes, Akhduth (religious) 290 votes, and Democrats 92 votes. In the table below we can see how Vilkovishk Zionists voted for the different parties at six Zionist Congresses:

Vilkovishk

Cong. Nr.	Year	Total Shek.	Total Voter	Labor Party		Rev	G.Z.		Gros	Miz.
				Z"S	Z"Z		A	B		
14	1925	120	--	--	--	--	--	--	--	--
15	1927	264	170	44	27	16	75	--	--	8
16	1929	664	268	102	17	83	61	--	--	5
17	1931	351	268	138	16	60	46	--	--	8
18	1933	---	724	498		151	60	--	5	10
19	1935	1,001	896	596		--	56	109	97	38

Cong.-Congress; Shek.-Shekalim; Rev.-Revisionists; G.Z.-General Zionists; Gro.-Grosmanists; Miz.-Mizrahi

Meeting of the "General Zionist HeKhalutz" in Vilkovishk May 19, 1934
On the left side is the front of the Jewish "Home for the Aged"

Group "Pil" of "HaShomer HaTsair" 1925

The Z"S party, or as it was called later "The Eretz Yisrael Workers Movement" was very active in Vilkovishk in the thirties. The cultural and artistic parties this movement arranged would always attract large audiences. For example, in December 1934 in the hall of the Hebrew High School, a big party in honor of the "Histadruth" (Federation of Labor in Eretz-Yisrael) was arranged. The speakers on the history and the function of the "Histadruth" were: M.Varshavsky, M.Yarovsky, M.Karnovsky and Al.Varshavsky. Those who participated in the artistic part of the party were David Neishtot, Avraham Olvitzky and Y.Faktorovsky, and the organizer of the party was Avraham Vinderovitz. Among the excellent activists in Zionist and pubic work was Mrs. S.Litovitz, who immigrated to Eretz-Yisrael in the middle 1930s.

A group of "Khalutzim" from Germany with their local escorts at the Vilkovishk railway station before their departure to Eretz-Yisrael 1934

In those years two "Kibutzei Hakhsharah" (Training Kibutzim) on behalf of "HeKhalutz" and the General Zionists acted in Vilkovishk. Many of these "Khalutzim" made "Aliyah" and were among the founders of the Kibutzim Beth-Zera, Givath-Brener, Dafna, Yagur, Tel-Yosef etc.

Sport activities were carried out at "Maccabi" with its 168 members, "Bar-Kokhva", "HaPoel", "Betar", and the Yiddishists "Y.A.K", which included football, gymnastics, bicycle riding, swimming and table tennis.

Religion and Welfare.

The old synagogue and the other prayer houses which existed before the war, continued to fulfill their mission after most of Vilkovishk Jews returned home. All the societies for learning Judaism were active again as was the "Khevrah-Kadisha."

During all this period the Rabbi of the community was Eliyahu-Aharon Grin (1875-1941), who was murdered in the Holocaust.

After the disbanding of the Community Committee in the middle 1920s, the welfare activities were transferred to the "Ezrah" society, which together with the "Adath Yisrael" society had about 120 members who donated about 500 Litas per year. These societies helped the poor, arranged fund raisings (as for "Maoth Khitim" for Pesakh) and also initiated special welfare activities.

The pride of the community was its "Home for the Aged" which also had a nursing department. Its budget was covered by donations and by a regular allowance from the municipality (2,000 Lit. per year).

The "OZE" organization dealt mainly with Jewish school children, and its clinic was open twice a week. The municipality supported it with 2,400 Lit. per year (1932).

The welfare institution "Maskil El Dal" who gave interest free loans to the needy, renewed its activity in 1918 at the initiative of J.M.Levinovitz, its director for many years.

The Community also cared for the Jewish soldiers who served in the infantry regiment stationed in Vilkovishk for Kosher food, especially during the Jewish holidays

During World War II and afterwards.

World War II started with the German invasion of Poland on the first of September 1939 and its consequences for Lithuanian Jews in general and Vilkovishks Jews in particular were felt several months later.

In agreement with the Ribbentrop-Molotov treaty on the division of occupied Poland, the Russians occupied the Suwalk region, but after delineation of exact borders between Russia and Germany the Suwalk region fell into German hands. The retreating Russians allowed anyone who wanted to join them to move into their occupied territory, and indeed many young people left the area together with the Russians. The Germans drove the remaining Jews out of their homes in Suwalk and its vicinity, robbed them of their possessions, then directed them to the Lithuanian border, where they were left in dire poverty. The Lithuanians did not allow them to enter Lithuania and the Germans did not allow them to return. Thus they stayed in this swampy area in cold and rain for several weeks, until Jewish youths from the border villages smuggled them into Lithuania by various routes, with much risk to themselves. Altogether about 2,400 refugees passed through the border or infiltrated on their own, and were then dispersed in the Vilkovishk and Mariampol districts. Vilkovishk alone accommodated 300 refugees, among them tens of "Khalutzim", who received a warm welcome and loyal assistance for which Lithuanian Jews were famous. It should be mentioned that Vilkovishk Jews provided help to the refugees in spite of the fact that their own situation was continuously deteriorating.

In June 1940 Lithuania was annexed to the Soviet Union and became a Soviet Republic. Following new rules, the majority of the factories and shops belonging to the Jews of Vilkovishk' were nationalized and commissars appointed to manage them. All the Zionist parties and youth organizations were disbanded, several of the activists being detained and Hebrew educational institutions were closed. Supply of goods decreased and, as a result, prices soared. The middle class, mostly Jewish, bore most of the brunt and the standard of living dropped gradually. Five families and two bachelors were exiled to Siberia, the heads of these families being sentenced to 5-18 years of forced labour in the terrible Reshoti camps there. They were:

Uliamperl Yitzhak, with wife and son, blamed for being the owner of a nationalized factory, and who died in Reshoti;

Pustopedsky Shmeryahu (Zunia) with wife Liuba, blamed because he was a member of the Betar organization, survived Reshoti;

Zimansky Avraham (single), the same accusation, survived;

Starkovsky Ya'akov (single), the same accusation, died in Siberia;

Uliamperl Munia (with wife and two children), also blamed for being a Betar member, died in Reshoti;

Kovarsky Berl (with wife), accused of being a shop owner, died in Reshoti;

Goldberg Mosheh (with wife and son), blamed for possessing a farm, died in exile.

At dawn on the 22nd of June 1941, Vilkovishk was bombed by the German Air Force, the center of the town was destroyed, and most of the Jewish houses including the old synagogue went up in flames. This was the beginning of the German invasion of the USSR. Most of the Jews who had fled from the bombed town returned and crowded together into the remaining undamaged houses. The German army entered Vilkovishk on the first day of the invasion, but the Lithuanian nationalists did not wait for orders from the Germans and started plotting against the Jews immediately. They robbed Jewish houses, guided Germans into Jewish houses and told them to take anything they wanted. Two days later, on the 24th of June, all Jewish men were ordered to gather in the market place, from which they were sent in groups to various types of work, such as cleaning the streets of ruins, collecting dead Russian soldiers and burying them, and other duties for units of the German army. Some groups were sent to nationalized agricultural farms.

Because Vilkovishk was situated within 25 km of the German border, the decision on the fate of the Jews was handed over to the Gestapo in Tilzit, where an order was issued to clean the area of Jews and communists. Jews were ordered to wear a yellow patch on their garments and were forbidden to walk on sidewalks. Every day communists were hunted down, and this was used as a pretext to detain Jews, who had no contact with communist activities.

One night at the beginning of July, on orders from the Tilzit Gestapo, all Jewish men, except for the ill, were taken from their homes and led by Lithuanian policemen to the building of the Priests Seminar outside the town. There the policemen stood in two lines on both sides of the stairs, and the Jews had to walk between them where they were badly beaten with sticks and iron bars. Three men who tried to resist were killed immediately, one of them being Yosef Tchihak. They were buried in the yard of the Seminar.

After a week or so the men from the Seminar, which included the sick who had been left in town previously, were transferred to a barracks outside the town which was encircled with barbed wire and was proclaimed a Ghetto. A committee of four men was appointed - "The Committee of the Jews".

On the 27th of July 1941 the Ghetto was surrounded in force by Lithuanian guards. In order not to arouse panic and to prevent attempts to escape, the guards soothed the Jews, telling them that nothing bad would happen to them. The commander of the guard gathered 250 Jewish men, equipped them with spades, took them to the training yard of the barracks and ordered them to dig ditches. The explanation was that there was an urgent need to store oil tanks in the ground. The duplicity of this commander was so shocking that he summoned one of the Jewish men, who had once dealt with oil issues, and asked him if the ditches would be suitable for that purpose. All the men returned home that evening.

The next day, on the 28th of July (4th of Av 5701) 800 men, including 65 non-Jewish Communists were taken to this yard, where they were ordered to remove their clothes, after which they were shot and buried in the previously prepared ditches. Back in town people could not believe that the men had been killed, as rumours were spread that the men had been transferred to another working place. Those women who still lived in town and came to visit their husbands bringing food parcels, approached the German commander asking about the fate of the men. He soothed their fears and received money and valuables from them, promising to clarify the whereabouts of their menfolk.

On the first of August all the women and children who still lived in town were forced to move to the barracks. Everyone was allowed to take belongings of up to 25 kg and 250 . The women immediately discovered the mass graves, despite the fact that the yard had been leveled and there were no signs left. The Lithuanian guard forbade the women to approach the site. There were two ditches in the yard, one 20 meters long and 5 m wide and the other 14 m long and 3 m wide, and near them another empty ditch.

On the 24th of September 1941 (3rd of Tishrei 5702 - Tsom Gedalyah) the women and children were murdered too. Many escaped but were caught later. Only two young sisters, from the Faktorovsky family survived and were hidden by a Lithuanian woman (named Juziene) in a small village 9 km from Vilkovishk. This woman saved the sisters for humane motives only, and did not receive any reward for her deed.

According to official Soviet data, 3,056 people were murdered in Vilkovishk by the Germans and their local helpers during June-September 1941.

After the war, the few Vilkovishk survivors found the site of the mass graves deserted, with cows grazing on them, and grave robbers having ransacked the graves looking for gold teeth. After many requests the local Soviet authorities finally agreed to erect a fence around the graves. At the beginning of the 1990s a monument was erected on this site, with the following inscription in Yiddish and Lithuanian: **"Here the blood of about 7000 Jews (men, women and children), Lithuanians and war prisoners of various nationalities, was spilt, savagely murdered by the Nazi murderers and their local helpers in the 6th and 7th months of 1941".**

The Monument on the mass graves

The inscription in Yiddish

The inscription in Lithuanian

Picture supplied by Sh.Pustopedsky

In 1986, former Vilkovishk Jews in Israel erected a memorial monument for the community of Vilkovishk in the Holon cemetery. (See above)

Bibliography.

Yad-Vashem Archives: M-1/E-1250/1208; M-33/987; TR-2/154; 0-3/3770;

Koniukhovsky Collection 0-71, Files 130, 159, 160, 168.

YIVO, NY, Collection of the Jewish Communities in Lithuania, Files 210-301, 1381, 1515, 1663, 1664, 1682.

Shmeriyahu (Zunia) Pustopedsky - The Way from Lithuania to Siberia and Eretz Yisrael (Hebrew), Private Edition, Rekhovoth 1997.

Dr. Ari Ankorion-Pirkei Hayim (Chapters of Life) 1908-1986, Private Edition.

Zimrani A.- Vilkovishk (Manuscript),(Hebrew), Tel-Aviv 1987.

HaMeilitz (St. Petersburg) (Hebrew): 8.2.1881; 9.4.1883; 17.3.1884; 7.6.1886; 25.6.1887; 7.3.1891; 11.4.1896.

Dos Vort, Kovno (Yiddish): 24.10.1934; 26.12.1934.

Folksblat, Kovno (Yiddish): 27.2.1935; 3.7.1935; 5.7.1935; 8.7.1935; 30.8.1935; 28.1.1937; 5.3.1937; 29.3.1937; 16.3.1939.

Di Yiddishe Shtime (The Yiddish Voice) Kovno (Yiddish): 10.9.1920; 4.5.1932.

Yiddisher Hantverker (Jewish Artisan) Kovno, (Yiddish): Nr.3, 1938.

Funken -Kovno (Yiddish), Nr. 23-30, 1931.

Appendix I.   A partial List of Personalities born in Vilkovishk.

Zevulun Harlap (1840-1898) - immigrated as a young man to Eretz Yisrael, later a "Dayan" in Jerusalem;

Mosheh Leibovitz-Maimon (1860-?), a well known painter, graduated from the Art Academy of St.Petersburg in 1883, his famous two paintings are "The Anusim" (The Marranos) and "The Hashmonaim";

Miriam Mergel-Mozeson (Verzhbelovsky)(1841-1920) - writer and translator from English into Hebrew;

Gorge Margalith (1853-1924) - researcher of the Bible, orientalist in England;

Brothers Eliyahu (1863-1932) **and Levi** (1866-1938) sons of **Shemuel Levin-Epstein** - Zionist activists, publishers and printers in Eretz Yisrael;

Leon Kameika (1864-1957), son of the Rabbi of Vilkovishk Dov-Ber Kameika, journalist and publisher of many Yiddish newspaper in the USA, from 1904 one of the publishers of "Morgen Journal";

Yehudah Kenigsberg (1853-?) - in the USA from 1893, published many articles in the Yiddish and Hebrew press;

Dr. Eliyahu Sintovsky (1880-1943) - in the USA from 1914, journalist and writer, published articles in the "Bund" press in Vilna and New York;

Dr. Shemuel Levin (1883-1941) - Headmaster of the Yiddish high school in Kovno and one of the central personalities of the psychological-pedagogic division of YIVO, published articles on this subject in the Yiddish newspaper "Folksblat" of Kovno, murdered in Kovno Ghetto;

Dr. Shemuel Melamed (1885-1938), from 1914 in USA, journalist and writer, published books on philosophical themes in German, English, Hebrew and Yiddish;

Adv. Michael Gerber - was the president of the Zionist Organization of Canada;

Menakhem Krakovsky (1869-1930) - Rabbi, journalist and author of rabbinical literature;

Yosef Blokh (1871-1936) - socialist leader in Germany;

Ana Rosental (1872-1941) - of the leaders of "Bund";

Dr. Nakhman Rakhmilevitz (1876-1941) - active in "Agudath Yisrael" party, Deputy Minister for commerce and finance in the first Lithuanian government, active in the autonomy institutions, member of the Seimas and later consul of Lithuania in Tel-Aviv;

Dr. Ari Ankorion (Volovitzky) (1908-1986), teacher, journalist, lawyer, member of the 5th, 6th, 7th and 8th "Knesseth" on behalf of the Israeli Labor party.

Mordehai (Max) Pustopedsky (1899-1941) a well known figure in Vilkovishk, published a poem in Yiddish "Erev Pesakh in Vilkovishk" which made a great impression in town;

Dr. M. Dembovsky, murdered in Vilkovishk in1941, was a doctor in the cavalry of Budioni at the time of the Russian revolution, published his memoirs in Yiddish "Mit di Kozaken iber Bukovine un Galitzie" (With the Cossacks through Bukovina and Galitzia), Vilkovishk 1923;

Hayim Varshavsky (1907-1944), member of the center of the Zionist-Socialist party, murdered in Dachau;

A. M. Filipovsky publisher and editor of the periodicals "Di Velt" (The World), Vikovishk 1934, "Di Yiddishe Velt" (The Jewish World), Vilkovishk 1935.

Virbalis (Virbaln or Verzhbolov)

Virbaln (Virbalis in Lithuanian) can be found on the main road stretching from Kovno (Kaunas) to East Prussia (now under Russian rule), about 90 km south-west from Kovno and 4.5 km of the (former) German border, and the railway station with the same name (now Kybartai) which is on the railway route from St.Petersburg to Berlin.

The town Virbaln was founded in 1539-1540 on the initiative of the Queen Bona Sfortsa, the wife of King Zigmunt "The Old". The name was then Nova Volia. It is found in documents under this name until the 18th century, but in the 16th century it had a second name "Verbolov". In 1593 King Zigmunt Vaza granted it "The Privileges of a Town" (The Magdeburg Privilege). He also prohibited construction of synagogues and other non-Catholic praying houses in Virbaln. This "Privilege" was observed in Virbaln during the Lithuanian rule. There was a municipality and a mayor.

Until 1795 Virbaln was included in the Polish-Lithuanian Kingdom. The same year the third division of Poland by the three superpowers of those times - Russia, Prussia and Austria, divided Lithuania between Russia and Prussia. The part of the state that sprawled on the left side of the Nieman river (Nemunas) including Virbaln was handed over to Prussia. During the Prussian rule (1795-1807) Virbaln was named Wirballen.

According to the Tilzit agreement of 1807, Polish lands occupied by Prussia were taken away and "The Great Dukedom of Warsaw" was established on them. The King of Saxony Friedrich-August was appointed as the Duke. At the core of the Constitution of the Dukedom was the Napoleonic Code, according to which everybody was equal before the law, however the Jews were not granted any civil rights.

During the years 1807-1813 Virbaln belonged to the "Great Dukedom of Warsaw" and was included in the Bialystok District. In 1813, after the defeat of Napoleon, who's retreating troops passed through the town, all of Lithuania was annexed to Russia, and Virbaln was included in the Augustowa Region (Gubernia). In 1866 Virbaln was included in the Suwalk Gubernia. The construction of the main road in 1829 from St. Petersburg to Warsaw stretching through Virbaln, spurred the growth of the town.

The town developed fast and served as a connecting terminal for transfer of goods from Russia to Western Europe. During Russian rule (1813-1915) the town was renamed Verzhbolova boasting a grand railway terminal near the border with Prussia, built on the route from St.Petersburg to Berlin in the 1860s. The new town developing around the station - Kybartai - grew fast and in a few years overtook Virbaln.

At the beginning of World War I Virbaln burnt down in fires and was deserted by the majority of its population. In 1915 Germans occupied Virbaln and ruled in the area until 1919 followed by its transfer to the Independent Lithuanian State.

Gruss aus Wirballen
Привѣтъ изъ Вержболово

Marktleben

The Market Place, 1912

(Picture supplied by Martin Miller)

The Jewish Settlement before World War 1

Society and Economy

Apparently, Jews began to settle in Virbaln in the second half of the 17th century. In July 1669 an order of King Zigmunt the Third was issued prohibiting the Jews from building synagogues in Virbaln. Therefore a conclusion may be drawn that Jews lived in Virbaln as early as the period indicated above.

In the old Jewish cemetery there was a tombstone dating back to 1735, but it is known that in 1728-1729 there were Jewish leaseholders in Virbaln, as there is a record of complaints submitted to authorities against them at that time.

On the "Shavu'oth" holiday in 1790 a Virbaln Jew Elazar was executed in a "Blood Libel" against him. This happened during the rule of the cultured King Stanislaw Poniatowsky, who was against the verdict. Despite his effort, Elazar was executed. For many subsequent years his name would be mentioned on the day of "Mentioning of the Death" prayer .

The law of Czar Alexander the First, prohibiting the Jews from living within 50 miles (Russian) of the western border of the state was in effect until 1862. However, according to the 1885 year census, 1,253 Jews, lived in Virbaln making up 50% of the total population. During the years 1876-1879, when the Jew Gringard was in charge of community affairs, a bathhouse was built in town and the cemetery was fenced in. Members of the community committee were J.Skudsky and L.Markel.

In the middle of the 1870s and, in particular, in the 1880s, many of Virbaln Jews migrated abroad, mainly to America, South Africa, England, Ireland etc. The main reason for the migration was widespread incitement of anti-Semitism in the area. In the winter of 1883 the notorious anti-Semite of those days, Lotostansky passed through the railway station of Virbaln promoting his books among the officials of the station. His books were full of abuse and insults directed against Judaism and Jews. Among other issues, he promoted the idea that Jews were undoubtedly using Christian blood for their religious needs, aiming to impress the officials with his musings. The Jewish educated elite of Virbaln raised money and bought 11 books by Prof. Khvolson who refuted all Lotostansky's allegations. The books were distributed among the officials who read them after getting hold of Lotostansky's books.

The same year "haMeilitz" accused the Russian priest of Virbaln of preaching belief in Lotostansky's words. When the article was brought before him, he realized that it was a plot and demanded to clear his name. The incident was described at the weekly periodical by Avraham Landman from Virbaln and it was approved by prominent personalities of the town, such as Yehudah-Leib Freidenberg, Mosheh-Aharon Yakobi, Ya'akov-Aryeh Volpe, Shimon Frenkel, Yekhezkel-Tsevi Brode, Yisrael-Meir Volfovitz.

In 1886 there were 2,515 people in Virbaln, among them 1,253 Jews (50%).

Before World War I the economic situation of Virbaln Jews was quite stable. They made a living in commerce and agriculture. They grew vegetables, fruits and tobacco. Many of them earned a living by trading with Germany and providing different border services. As mentioned before, a considerable amount of Russian imports and exports passed through the railway station of Werzhbolova. Many Jews earned a living using the privilege granted to citizens of Virbaln to cross the border to the German town Eydtkuhnen, permitting them to buy a limited amount of goods and bringing it to Russia without paying customs. Goods beyond the permitted quota were smuggled into Russia and sold for profit.

Another source of income was smuggling immigrants over the border to Germany. There were cases of fraudulent "smugglers" who would cheat the emigrants by taking away various items belonging to them. On other instances "the smugglers" would keep them in the hostel longer than necessary in order to extort more money. Sometimes the smugglers would set their eyes on a young woman or a nice girl in the hostel and would detain her longer than necessary. In 1896 a young woman was shot to death trying to cross the border illegally. All this aroused fury in the community against the "smugglers".

However, thousands of Jews who arrived in America with the help of these smugglers remembered them favorably, despite the fact that they had not always been treated fairly.

At the end of the 19th century the industry of brushes manufactured from pig bristles developed in Virbaln, and hundreds of Jewish workers were engaged in the trade. They organized into a powerful vocational union with a membership of about 100 people. In the years 1893-1897 following its induction, the "Bund" (the Jewish anti-Zionist Workers' Organization) organized large strikes in the area. The goal of the strikers was to improve the working conditions. Consequently, a part of the demands of the Jewish workers were met due to these strikes.

In 1897 there were 3,293 people in Virbaln, among them 1,219 Jews (37%)

Education and Culture

Before the middle of the 1880s Jewish children in Virbaln were educated in the "Kheder's" (Khadarim), the "Talmud-Torah's" and in the "Yeshiva's" (Yeshivoth). Only a few studied in the Russian high schools in the big towns. In 1887 an order was published by the government for all the "Melamdim" to get a Teaching License granted by the Inspector of Education of the Suwalk Gubernia.

The licensure set conditions for the "Kheder" to be like a state school and include the Russian language in the curriculum. In cases where the "Melamed" didn't know Russian, he would be obliged to find a certified teacher. If such a teacher could not be found, children, ages seven and older would have to study two hours every day in a Russian school.

Another condition was that all the teaching materials should have the stamp of the Governmental Censor. There were cases when Bible books published in Berlin or Vienna were found in some "Kheders" without the stamp of the Censor. As a result the "Melamed" would lose his Teaching License.

In these years Avraham-Eliyahu Sandler established a "Kheder Metukan" in Virbaln (Improved Kheder). Hebrew, Russian, a Bible course with commentaries and Mathematics were taught. Many of Virbaln Jews were the students of Mr. Sandler who taught school for almost forty years. His students knew Hebrew and the Bible perfectly. The Hebrew weekly newspaper published in St.Petersburg "HaMeilitz" from April 1884 stated that even the women knew Hebrew. Esther Golda Goldberg and Beile Hayah Jakobi were mentioned as students who were cited as setting the best example.

One of the teachers of the school was the well-known commentator of the Bible Sh.L. Gordon (Shalag). Later, a couple by the name Hanah and Reuven Kaplan opened a modern "Kheder". There was another "Kheder" in Virbaln, namely that of Pinkhas Pintchuk, and a "Talmud-Torah" for the children of the poor. In both the Sandler and the Kaplan Kheders, boys and girls studied together, which was a novelty in those days.

Its worthwhile mentioning that the Hebrew weekly "HaMeilitz" published at least 31 articles dealing with life of the Virbaln Jews from the years 1879-1900. Most often the correspondents were M.A.Shaudinishky and A.E.Sandler.

Religion and Welfare

In 1770 a "Beth Midrash" was built in Virbaln. Through the years it became too small for all the people who came to pray. In 1864 a Synagogue was built, but in 1880 the issue of seats was not settled, causing conflicts in Virbaln

On the last day of "Pesakh" 5642 (1882) an argument broke out in the Synagogue on the subject of "Aliyoth laTorah" ending in clashes and police intervention. Another building for prayers was built in 1870.

At the end of the 19th century Virbaln had a "Talmud-Torah", a "Cheap Kitchen" (from 1877) and a "Home for the Aged" (from 1895). In 1907 "Aid Services for Immigrants" was established in Virbaln.

In the 1880s there were reports on Virbaln published in "haMeilitz" dealing with con artists who visited the town, trying to extort money from people under false pretenses.

There was a case of a young man who arrived to Virbaln, impressing people favorably. One of the residents was ready to make a match for his daughter. The Rabbi of Virbaln started to investigate the case, and found that the man had left a wife in Liverpool, married another wife in Raseiniai, then almost married a third woman in Virbaln. He was thrown out of the town in shame.

In 1879 two young people M.M.Mariampolsky and T.Yentelzon founded a group "Hakhnasath-Orkhim" to look after people who were traveling through Virbaln on their way to Prussia. The same year a few highly respected people of Virbaln founded an association "Gemiluth Khasadim" which was mandated to lend money for a period of six month in exchange for silver, gold and copper items. This method was strongly criticized by the public as, in fact, only the rich had silver and gold to exchange for loans.

In 1888 Yehudah-Leib Segalovsky founded the association "Somekh-Noflim" which gave out loans to the needy people in Virbaln in order to save them from hunger. The trustee of the association Shemuel-David Vishtinetsky was a prominent activist of the association.

The same year Rabbi Yitshak Blazer from Kovno purchased a farm near Virbaln for 75,000 Rubles – an enormous amount for those years- donated by the Lakhman Brothers from Berlin. He appointed a manager of the farm who had to run the farm according to the Laws of the Torah. The goal of the farm's management was to resolve the economic problems of "The Kolel Prushim" (a Yeshivah of Pharisees) established in Kovno.

One of the personalities acting for the good of the community was Eliyahu Varshavsky, the grandson of the Gaon from Vilna (GARA), who lived most of his life in Virbaln making his living by painting houses. He was also a teacher of "Torah" and was the head of the "Khevrah-Kadisha". Welfare issues and activities of other institutions were dealt with according to his advice. He died at the age of 64 on the first day of Succoth 5646 (1886).

Zionist Activities

Jews from Virbaln immigrated to Eretz-Israel even before the period of "Khibath-Zion". In the old cemetery in Jerusalem at least 5 tombstones of Virbaln Jews can be found: Yehudah ben Mosheh-Tsevi (child), died in 1873;

Meir-Avraham Sandler ben Yehezkel, 1874; Mosheh-Nahum ben Shaul, 1883; Barukh ben Avraham, 1890; Aharon ben Barukh, 1893.

The Association of "Khovevei Zion" (Fans of Zion) began to raise money for settlement in Eretz-Israel in 1884, but as early as 1880 a teacher Shlomsky collected 36 Rubles for the same goal. One of the ways to collect donations was by selling paintings of Moshe Montifiori. Another way was by selling "Aliyoth" in the synagogue. On the 1896 list of contributors for settlement in Eretz-Israel there were names of 13 Jews from Virbaln with Rabbi A.Lap topping the list. (See Appendix 1). The 1898 list carried the names of fundraisers Shaudinishky, pharmacist S.Vinsberg, Eliyahu Varshavsky and C.Z Dogilaitsky.

At the conference of "Khovevei-Zion" which took place in Vilna in 1889, the delegate from Virbaln was the local Rabbi David-Tevele Katsenelboigen.

Before the second Zionist Congress gathered in Warsaw in August 1898 a conference of the Zionists from Russia. Among the 160 delegates from 93 towns was also a delegate from Virbaln.

Before the third Zionist Congress a regional conference of the "Zionist Associations" from the Lithuanian "Gubernias" Kovno, Suwalk, Grodno and Vilna gathered in Vilna in the summer of 1899 represented by 71 from 51 towns. Rabbi Efraim Lap was a delegate from Virbaln.

Before the fourth Zionist Congress a conference of the "Zionist Associations" gathered in Vilna in 1900 with a total of 168 delegates, among them Rabbi Efraim Lap from Virbaln. At this conference he was elected as the Regional Deputy Representative of the Suwalk Gubernia. Before the fifth Zionist Congress between the July 1st, 1901 and July 1st, 1902, 200 "Shekalim" (membership cards of the Zionist organization) were sold in Virbaln

The local "Zionist Association" distributed "Shekalim" and sold shares of the "Otsar Hityashvuth Hayehudim" (The Jewish Colonial Trust), raising funds for "Keren Kayemeth Leyisrael" (KKL - Jewish National Fund) and collecting books for The National Library in Jerusalem. Among other things it was very active establishing the "Khadarim Metukanim" where education was pro-Zionist.

The educational and literary activity of Sh.L.Gordon and Ben Avigdor started in Virbaln. They married the two sisters of Shelomoh Blumgarten - Yeho'ash (1872-1927), who was a well-known writer and poet. A native of Virbaln, he worked on the great project of translating the Bible into Yiddish.

During World War I the town burnt down and was deserted by the majority of its population.

During the Period of Independent Lithuania

Public and Economic Life

With the establishment of the Lithuanian State in 1918, Virbaln citizens began to return to their town. After the eviction of the German army at the beginning of 1919, life in Virbaln returned to normal. Virbaln was included in the Vilkovishk (Vilkaviskis) district.

According to the Autonomy Law Regarding Minorities in Lithuania, elections for the Jewish Community Committee in Virbaln took place. Eleven members were elected: 2 from the list of "Tseirei Zion", 5 from "Mizrakhi", 2 artisans and 2 independents. The Committee was active until the end of 1925 when the Autonomy law was annulled. During the years of its existence the Committee collected taxes as required by law, sometimes with the help of the Police, and was in charge of all areas of community life.

According to the first census conducted by the Lithuanian Government in 1923 there were 4,018 people in Virbaln, among them 1,233 Jews (31%). During this period Virbaln Jews made their living in commerce, craft, agriculture and industry. The border between Lithuania and Germany remained the same as during the Czar's rule. Likewise, it was an important factor of the life of Virbaln Jews. The export of poultry, geese and other agricultural products provided a living for many families in town. In addition the town had 5 Jewish grocery shops, 7 butchers, 6 bakeries, 3 shops for tools and iron products, 5 shoemakers, 4 tailors, 2 glaziers, 2 tinsmiths, 2 hairdressers, 2 tombstone builders, 2 watchmakers, 1 photographer and one tavern owned by Jews.

Many of Virbaln Jews made their living in agriculture. Several Jews were owners of big fields in the vicinity and during agricultural season they employed hundreds of workers. Most of them cultivated grain crops but there were others who grew cucumbers, beetroot and fruits. (Fridlender, Vladislavovsky, Skudsky, Hilenberg, Gringard, Berezdovsky, and others).

Agronomist Ya'akov Filipovsky was respected and praised as the greatest specialist in cultivating species of fruit trees and berries in Lithuania. His nursery in Virbaln supplied seeds to most of the gardeners in Lithuania. Gardeners from all over Lithuania would come to his show garden to advance their knowledge. He also grew seeds of cucumbers and beets for fodder.

Jews Zerko and Kamber built a power station in Virbaln which supplied the town with electricity. Jews also owned a flourmill (Miler), a sawmill (Lakovsky), a few oil factories (Kagansky and Ridlitzky), a metal casting plant (Zerko) and chicory production (Kapushevsky). There was a Jewish doctor (L.Kagansky), a Jewish dentist (Mrs. Pauzisky) and a Jewish pharmacy (Ziman) in Virbaln.

The brushes industry acted like before the war and employed hundreds of workers.

In 1937 there were fifty two Jewish artisans in Virbaln: 10 butchers, 7 bakers, 7 shoemakers, 5 hairdressers, 4 tailors, 4 watchmakers, 3 stitchers, 3 painters, 3 tinsmiths, 2 hat makers, 2 cloth dyers, 2 photographers, 1 potter. In 1939 Virbaln had 41 telephone subscribers, among them 21 belonged to Jews (51%).

In the centre of economic life in Virbaln was the Jewish Folksbank with 320 members in 1927. In 1929 the number grew to 342.

There was also a branch of "The United Company for Financial Credit for Jewish Agrarians" in town.

Until 1934 there were 4 Jews in the Town Council among a total of 9 Council members (Leizer Kagansky, Joseph Pagramat, Mosheh Vishtinetsky, Volf Naishtot). However, only 3 Jews were elected (Kagansky, Vishtinetsky, Haimovitz) in the elections of 1934. For many years Virbaln had a Jewish Deputy Mayor.

The Volunteer Fire Brigade fulfilled an important role in town. Most of its members were Jews for many years working under the leadership of Gedalyah Abeloviz.

With the beginning of the Nazi rule in 1933 in Germany, trade with this country gradually diminished. Traffic through Kibart, the nearby border town decreased, and only a few Jews would pass through on their way to Eydtkuhnen - the German town on the other side of the border. This had a substantial influence on the economic situation, and many Jews left Virbaln, in particular the youth. Most of them moved to Kovno and a part immigrated abroad, or to Eretz-Yisrael.

Education

After the end of the War in 1918 children's education became an issue in Virbaln. A group of activists understood that the "Kheder Metukan" (Improved Kheder) no longer fulfilled the task of education under the new conditions. An idea was born to establish a Hebrew high school in town, preceded shortly by the founding of the first Hebrew high school of the Diaspora in Mariampol. It was clear to the initiators that a small community of only 1,200 people could not stand that heavy burden. They were faced with competition against schools in the nearby German towns, where Jewish children from Kibart were enrolled. Thus a decision was reached that the school would accept children from neighbouring towns, mainly Kibart, Vishtinetz and Naishtot-Shaki. Registration started at the 29th of Iyar 5679 (1919).

Until 1921 the school offered a program equivalent to half of high-school curriculum (pro gymnasium) but later it changed introducing a complete high school education. In 1929 the board of directors of the school acquired a two storey, red brick building on the main street, renovated and redesigned to suit the needs. Central heating was installed, a novelty in these days. The school had Physics and Nature Laboratories.

בפרוגמנסיון העברי בוויירבלן

(כאשר מטעם המפשלה הליטאית) הקים מחדש אייר תרע"ט

_____ מתקבלים תלמידים _____

1919 ביום א' לסדר נח, כ' חשון תר"פ 26 לחודש אקטאבר

בחינות הקבלה תתחלנה ביום ד' כ"א באייר. כ"ח תשרי תר"פ 22 לחודש אק־
1919. בשנת הלמודים דתרע"ט הפתיחה נב מחלקה: רביעית ורמישית. תלמ־
דים חדשים מתקבלים לשהי שבעות ולהשג המחלקות היסוריות.
ידיעות מפורטות אפשר להשיג בלשכת הפרוגמנסיון.
הכתבת:

Vedejui Virbalio Žydų progimnazijos Virbalis Vilkav. apskr.

Announcement (in Hebrew) in the Jewish press in Lithuania regarding the commencement of studies in the Hebrew High-School in Virbalis on the October 26, 1919

Students came from all walks of life. Some arrived from schools in Russia; others were from German schools operating under the jurisdiction of German occupation and still others came from "Khadarim" and "Yeshivoth". They were of different age groups and a varied elementary school background. Most of them did not have a proper knowledge of the Hebrew Language. There was no curriculum, textbooks or teaching materials.

The end of the first school year at the Hebrew pro-Gymnasium in Virbaln
17 Elul 5679 (September 1919)

Owing largely to the efforts of Virbaln and Kibart Jews who acted to assure a budget for the school and to the devotion of the teachers' team and their director Dr. Ya'akov Robinson a splendid institution was established. Dr. Ya'akov Robinson who was a native of Serey (Seirijai) and a graduate from Warsaw Law School returned to Lithuania to accomplish this difficult pioneering task. A known lawyer and public servant, he became later the advisor to the Lithuanian Foreign Ministry before World War II and later the legal adviser of the Israeli delegation to the UN.

1925 was the year of the first graduating class. Among its first teachers - Avraham Eliyahu Sandler, Mitkovsky, Masha Frenkel, Dudnik, Shilansky, Aharon Frank, Mosheh Frank, Fridman, Reizel Rozenblum (the daughter of A.E.Sandler), Geisinovitz (later known as Aba Akhimeir, one of the leaders of the Revisionist Party in Eretz-Yisrael), Sambursky, later professor of mathematics at the Hebrew University in Jerusalem, Ash-Bartana, subsequently a teacher of mathematics in the "Rehaviah" high school in Jerusalem. Reuven Kaplan was Secretary of the school throughout its existence.

In the middle of the twenties Director Dr. Robinson left the school, and Dr. Shnitzler was nominated as the incumbent. Later, Michael Bramson was appointed who was a tall, slender man, a former captain of the Lithuanian army, a strict disciplinarian, and thought to be among the best teachers of the Lithuanian language. During these years many teachers changed, among them the Bible teacher Mr. Salant who was popular with the students. He emigrated to Eretz-Israel and taught for many years at the Kibutz Ein-Harod. Nature was taught by Mr. Tzimbalist who subsequently immigrated to Eretz-Yisrael. The Lithuanian language teacher was Mr. Katz, while B.Shulgaser, an immensely popular amateur actor, taught English. His wife Mrs. Shohat-Shulgaser taught German. A strict disciplinarian, she appeared for her classes elegantly dressed and made up, which was unusual in those times. Mr. Kizel, a quiet and modest man, very popular with his students, taught Hebrew and literature in higher grades. Mr. Lifshitz was the teacher of drawing, but students holding the subject in low esteem, made him suffer. The teacher of mathematics was Tabakhovitz. and others included Averbukh and Jerushalmi.

In 1934 the government closed the high school, and a pro-gymnasium with four classes opened in place of the old school, with Tabakhovitz as director. A year later he was asked to take over the position of director of the Hebrew High School in Mariampol.

M.Bramson, the former director of the Virbalis High School, moved to Kovno where he subsequently founded the Jewish-Lithuanian High School.

The High School in Virbalis was closed because of low enrollment in the higher grades and a budget deficit. The pro-gymnasium was a private school and was administered by a special "Haskalah" Committee whose chairman was Michael Shadkhanovitz from Kibart. He often covered deficits with his own money. This school functioned until Lithuania became the Soviet Republic in the summer of 1940; It was then that the Hebrew Education Network, the pride of Lithuanian Jewry, was disband.

The Eighth Graduating Class of Virbaln Hebrew High-School (1933?)

The Teachers are in the rectangles. At the first row above from right: Salant, M.Bramson, and Dr.Y. Rabinson, Averbukh.

At the second row: ---, F.Shohat, Shulgaser, ---,Dr.A.Pozisky (?), --- , Linde

At the third row: D.Katz, Sh.Kizel, A.E.Sandler, R.Kaplan, Lifshitz, and L.Lakovsky.

In the rectangle below the building of the High-School

Elementary education for Jewish children was accessible through the Hebrew Kindergarten and the Hebrew school of the "Tarbuth" (Culture) Branch. There was also a governmental school where Yiddish was taught with no tuition fees required. A few dozen of poor children studied at the school.

Religion and Welfare

In Virbaln there were two big Synagogues and four or five "Kloisim" (small praying rooms). Many children on "Ben Zakai" fellowship studied "Gemara" in the evenings and "Agadah" (Fables) from Bialik and Ravnitzky "Sefer haAgadah" books before lunch on Saturdays. "Sha"s" (Mishnah) society was active in Virbaln as well.

The Rabbis of Virbaln were Yehudah Blumgard (from 1872), David-Tevele Katsenelboigen (1850-1931), Efraim Lap (1859-1926), also active in the "Zionist Association" and Yitshak Hirshovitz (1871-1941), the last Rabbi of Virbaln who was a member of the "Yavneh" centre (a chain of Religious-Zionist schools). He was murdered in the Holocaust.

The remains of the Jewish cemetery in Virbaln (1995)

During World War I, when refugees flocked into town a relief committee was formed in Virbaln to help the absorption and settlement of a large number of refugees.

Among its welfare institutions Virbaln had "Bikur Kholim", a Women Fellowship, "Gemiluth Khesed" established with the funds of Aba Vishtinetsky. In 1939 when refugees from Poland escaped to Lithuania, the National Committee, that was established for this purpose decided that Virbaln should absorb 100 refugees, and the community fulfilled that task.

Zionist Activity

Virbaln was known for its Zionist ambience. Many of its people spoke Hebrew acquired at the "Khadarim Metukanim" before the Hebrew High School was established. For many years Hebrew signs were displayed on Jewish stores, in spite of strict rules. The Hebrew elementary school and the Hebrew high school educated students promoting Aliyah to Eretz-Israel. Many graduates of that high school are presently residing in Israel.

The "HeKhalutz" movement can be traced back in Virbaln as early as 1919, when a group of Khalutsim (Pioneers) united under the name "Kheiruth" (Freedom). Having acquired training with Lithuanian peasants during a period of one-year ("Hakhsharah") the group immigrated to Eretz-Israel.

Another group "Akhvah" followed them. Many groups of "Khalutsim" got their training at the farm "Kibush" (Conquest) near Kibart and in other Lithuanian and Jewish farms in the vicinity (April, Shatenshtein, Rozenberg etc.) The Zionist circles in town and youth in particular ardently supported the training. In 1934 an urban Kibbutz of "HeKhaluts" was organized in the town itself.

A branch of "haShomer-haTsair" the first in Lithuania was established in Virbaln in 1921. There were about fifty members of different ages. A similar number of members could be found in the "Beitar" branch established some time later. There was also a branch of "Netsakh" (abbreviation of Zionist Pioneer Youth) in Virbaln.

"HaShomer HaTsa'ir" branch, 1924

Zionist ambience in town was evident in the elections to the first Lithuanian Seimas (Parliament) in October 1922. 324 votes were cast for the Zionist list, 128 for "Akhduth" (Agudath-Israel) and 36 for the Democrats. The number of votes for the Zionist Congresses increased from 36 in 1927 (the 16th Congress) to 278 in 1935 (the 19th Congress). In the table below results of the elections for the Zionist Congresses 15th-19th (1927-1935) in Virbaln are presented.

Cong. Nr	Year	Total Shek.	Total Voter	Labor Party Z"S	Z"Z	Rev.	G. Z. A	B	Gro	Miz.
14	1925	40	--	--	--	--	--	--	--	--
15	1927	60	36	4	5	--	14	--	--	13
16	1929	147	42	7	2	1	23	--	--	9
17	1931	81	63	22	4	6	26	--	--	5
18	1933	--	192	129		29	22	--	5	7
19	1935	300	278	206		--	5	27	7	33

Cong.-Congress; Shek.-Shekalim; Rev.-Revisionists; G.Z.-General Zionists; Gro.-Grosmanists; Miz.-Mizrahi.

Among the prominent personalities of Virbaln we find Kalev Blumgard (1808-1897), Barukh ben Shemuel Vizhansky (died 1899); Feivel Gringard (died 1951 in Tel-Aviv). They were the first Zionists in town. Another couple Mordehai and Sarah Hilenberg educated their children in Hebrew and offered their house as a meeting place for all Zionists. Mordehai Hilenberg together with Ridlitzky and Pargamut were among the founders of the Hebrew High School in Virbaln.

Among the natives of Virbaln were Nekhemyah Volpiansky (1877-1937), a writer, a musician and a chess player; Tsevi-Hirsh Filipovsky (1816-1872), a mathematician and an editor, Gregory Sanders - the son of A.E.Sandler – who was the first reporter from Canada for the Jewish newspaper "Der Freind" published in St. Petersburg, Masha Benia (Benyakonsky), a known popular singer of Yiddish and Hebrew songs in USA, Dr. Mendel Sudarsky, who spent his youth in Virbaln, and was the steering power behind many cultural institutions in Lithuania. He was the chairman of the management of "Ort" in Lithuania and a member its world center as well as of the "OZE" and "HIAS". He was the publisher and the editor of the Yiddish daily newspaper in Kovno "Folksblat". In 1937 he and his family immigrated to America where he continued to work for the Yiddish periodicals "Tog", "Forverts" and others. He was the publisher and editor of the two volumes of the book "Lite", the great remembrance project dedicated to Lithuanian Jewry, published in 1951 in New York.

During World War II and Afterwards

It should be mentioned that Virbaln Jews provided help to refugees from the Suwalk region at the end of 1939, in spite of the fact that their own situation was continuously deteriorating. According to the agreement in the Ribbentrop-Molotov treaty the Russians occupied the Suwalk region, but after delineation of exact borders between Poland, Russia and Germany the Suwalk region fell into German hands. The retreating Russians allowed anyone who wanted to join them to move into the occupied territory, and indeed many young people left the area together with the Russians. The Germans kicked out the Jews remaining in Suwalk and the vicinity from their homes; they were robbed of their possessions, then directed to the Lithuanian border, and left in dire poverty. The Lithuanians did not allow them to enter Lithuania and the Germans did not allow them to go back. Thus they stayed in this swampy area in cold and rain for several weeks, until Jewish youth from the border villages in Lithuania smuggled them into Lithuania by different routes, with much risk to themselves. Altogether about 2,400 refugees passed through or infiltrated on their own, and were then dispersed in the Vilkavishk and Mariampol districts. In Virbaln alone 100 refugees were accommodated, among them tens of "Khalutsim" in the Jewish farms in the vicinity, who got a warm welcome and loyal assistance for which Lithuanian Jews were famous.

In June 1940 Lithuania was annexed to the Soviet Union and became a Soviet Republic. Following the new rules, the majority of the factories and shops belonging to the Jews of Virbaln were nationalized. All the Zionist parties and youth organizations were dismissed, and several of the activists were detained. The "Comsomol" (The Communist Youth Organization) started to mobilize the youth into its ranks.

Hebrew educational institutions were closed and towards the 1940/1941 school year, the main language of instruction at the Hebrew School was changed to Yiddish. The supply of goods decreased and, as a result, prices soared. The middle class, mostly Jewish, was hit hard, and the standard of living dropped gradually. At the beginning of June seven families, the owners of nationalized factories and shops and Zionist activists were exiled deep into Russia. The others sat "on their suitcases" and awaited their turn.

Rumors added to the tension. It was feared that according to the Molotov-Ribbentrop treaty on the division of Poland, Lithuania would be divided as well, and Virbaln and surrounding areas would be handed over to Germany. This area was home to many Germans, who began to depart to Germany, adding to the tense atmosphere.

Before the war there were about 600 Jews in Virbaln.

At 5:30 in the morning on June 22nd, 1941, the German Army entered Virbaln encountering no resistance. All prisoners, including the prisoners of resistance to Soviet Rule, were immediately freed. These men started to organize local groups to take revenge on the Communists, and the Jews, and to help the Germans gain control and restore public life.

At the beginning the town was ruled by the military institutions, and no special measures were taken against the Jews. In a few days civil rule was restored. One of the first orders was to impose restrictions on Jews. They were forbidden to maintain any contacts with non-Jews, forced to wear yellow patches on their garments and had to hand over their radios. In addition, a curfew was imposed from 6 o'clock in the evening until 6 o'clock in the morning.

On the night of July 7th Lithuanian activists detained all the Jewish men who were 16 years of age and older, ordering them into a farm north of Virbaln and crowding them into a cellar. Women, children, the aged and the sick remained in their homes.

Between July 7th –July 10th the men were ordered out of the cellar to the fields, about two km north of the town. During the Soviet rule, anti-tank trenches were excavated, designed to stop the German invasion. These trenches were not deep enough, and the men were ordered to dig deeper.

On Thursday, July 10th, 1941 (the 15th of Tamuz 5701), the men were lined up in-groups of 15-20 people, with their backs towards the trenches. In this position they were shot. Prior to the shooting they were forced to undress and hand over their money and valuables. Most of the gunmen were Lithuanians.

After the murder of the men, the women, the aged and the children were forced into a Ghetto established on the almost empty streets where the repatriated Germans had once lived. The head of the Ghetto was the only dentist in town,

Mrs. Sheine Pauzisky, who used to socialize with Lithuanians who were also her patients. She had connections in state and municipal institutions. A special food shop was opened in the Ghetto. The shopkeeper was a Lithuanian, an honest man, who made sure supplies for the Ghetto residents lasted.

Women and children from Kibart were brought to the same ghetto. (among them were the mother of the author Hayah, his 16-year-old sister Tekhiyah, his aunt Sarah Leibovitz and his 13 years old cousin Tziporah).

All the young women and children aged 12-16 would take on different jobs in the town and the vicinity. A quasi-employment-bureau was established in the Ghetto where unemployed people would come to look for work, and the peasants of the surrounding areas would select women and teens for work. There were notorious and evil people among these employers who treated women and children very badly. However, there were also brave people who maintained contacts with Jews. There were some who hid 10 Jewish women when the murders began. Of these few, only Bela Mirbukh and her mother from Virbalis survived, hiding at the farm of a Lithuanian teacher for three years, near the town where Bela worked as an agricultural worker. Bela Rosenberg, the young daughter of nearby farm owners survived, hiding somewhere in the vicinity.

One night, at the end of July or at the beginning of August, all the older women, the sick and the unemployed were taken to the anti-tank trenches where they were shot and buried.

After this "action" the rulers promised that no more evil would happen to the Jews. The women were told that their husbands were working different jobs in the vicinity. All this time Lithuanians, acquaintances and strangers, would arrive to tell the women that they had seen their husbands who asked to deliver a message to their wives to send them money, valuables and clothes. The women responded positively because they trusted that that these messages were true, refusing to believe the women working outside who told them their men were murdered. Among the Lithuanian population rumors spread that the end of the Jews was close, but no one came to warn the Jews about the destiny awaiting them.

On the night of Thursday, September 11^t, 1941 (the 19th of Elul 5701) Lithuanians arrived in carts and ordered all the women and children to the anti-tank trenches where they cruelly murdered all.

Of all the Jewish Community of Virbaln only three women hidden by Lithuanian families managed to survive.

Such was the tragic end of the thriving Jewish Community of Virbaln that existed more than 300 years.

In 1970 there were 1,489 people in Virbaln, and not one Jew.

The names of the Lithuanian murderers and a list of the names of the rescuers are saved in the archives of Yad Vashem.

In the 1960s a monument was built on the mass graves.

רא איז פֿארגאסן געוואָרן
דאָס בלוט פֿון בערך 10,000
ייִדן (לידער, פֿרויען, מענער),
ליטווינער, קריגס-געפֿאַנגענע
פֿון פֿאַרשיידענע נאַציאָנאַליטעטן,
וועלכע די נאַצי-רוצחים און
זייערע מיטהעלפֿער
האָבן גרויזאַם דערמאָרדעט
אין 1941.VIII-VII

The monument on the mass graves near Virbalis established in 1991. The inscription in Lithuanian and Yiddish on the tables says:

Here was spilled the blood of about 10,000 Jews (Men, Women and Children), Lithuanians, War prisoners of different nationalities, who were cruelly murdered by the Nazi murderers and their helpers in July and August 1941.

(Among the victims there were the Author's Mother, sister, aunt and cousin)

In the Lithuanian plaque it is written "...by the Nazi murderers and their local helpers..."

In May 1987 the monument in memory of the communities of Kibart (Kybartai), Virbaln (Virbalis) and Pilvishok (Pilviskis) was unveiled at the cemetery in Holon.

The inscription (in Hebrew) says: Monument in memory of the martyrs who perished in the Holocaust in Av-Elul 5701, July - August 1941 from the Communities of Pilvishky, Kibart, Virbaln Lithuania

Bibliography

Yad-Vashem Archives:. JM / 1825; M-9 / 12(6); M-33 / 987, 995; TR-10 / 1096

Koniukhovsky Collection 0-71, Files 154, 157, 158

Akhsanyah shel Torah (Report of the Hebrew High-School in Virbaln 1919-1921), (Hebrew) Berlin-Virbaln 1921

Yaffe Mosheh - The Hebrew Pro Gymnasium in Virbalis: Bemisholei haHinuch (In the paths of education) Kovno (Hebrew), 1937

Lite, New-York 1951, volume 1 & 2 (Yiddish)

The Jewish Encyclopedia, St. Petersburg 1908-1913, (Russian), Vol. 5, pages 507-8

YIVO, NY, Collection of the Jewish Communities in Lithuania, Files 387-401; 1587,1665; pages 17,716-18,740

Oral testimony by Virbaln natives Z.Vladislavovsky and L.Lakovsky

HaMeilitz (St. Petersburg) (Hebrew): 2.9.1879; 23.10.1880; 5.11.1880; 19.7.1881; 20.9.1881; 16.5.1882; 22.3.1883; 2.7.1883; 23.7.1883; 3.8.1883; 20.8.1883; 31.10.1883; 21.4.1884; 20.6.1884; 1.1.1886; 3.5.1886; 11.7.1886; 13.8.1886; 14.7.1886; 4.11.1886; 19.11.1886; 13.6.1887; 20.7.1887; 19.1.1888; 6.2.1888; 23.1.1889; 6.3.1900; 8.5.1900.

Dos Vort, Kovno (Yiddish): 10.11.1934

Folksblat, Kovno (Yiddish): 25.4.1939

Di Yiddishe Shtime (The Yiddish Voice) Kovno (Yiddish): 6.7.1922; 19.6.1931

Appendix 1

List of Donors from Virbaln for the Settlement of Eretz-Israel in 1896

Beilak Yitzhak

Dogilaitzky Zelig

Goldshtein Tsevi

Gordon Shemuel-Leib (Shala"g)

Gringold Yehezkel

Hokhenberg Mosheh-Idl

Kaplan Reuven

Lam Mosheh

Lap Efraim-Dov haKohen , Rabbi

Sandler Avraham-Eliyahu

Verzhbelovsky Avraham

Vishtinetzky Shemuel-David

Vizhansky Barukh

Žeimelis (Zheiml)

Zheimel (Zeimelis in Lithuanian) is situated in the north central part of Lithuania four km. from the border of Latvia, its name having been mentioned in old manuscripts dating back to the 13th century. From the 14th century until the 18th centuries the Zheimel estate had been administered by German feudal lords, and the town of Zheimel which developed near the estate was the county administrative center from 1568 on. In 1613 King Zigmunt Vaza granted Zheimel the privilege of holding two fairs a year.

Until 1795 Zheimel was part of the Polish Kingdom, but at that time Poland was divided for the third time among the then three superpowers - Russia, Prussia and Austria - and most of Lithuania, including Zheimel, was apportioned to Russia.

During Russian rule (1795-1915) as well as during Lithuania's period of independence (1918-1940), Zheimel was again the county administrative center. During the German occupation in World War I, Zheimel was connected by a narrow gauge railway to Joniskis and before World War II a railway line was laid which led from Zheimel through Joniskelis to Panevezys.

Jewish Settlement until World War I.

Testimony to the fact that Jewish settlement in Zheimel was one of the oldest in Lithuania can be seen on tombstones dating back hundreds of years which were found in the old cemetery of the town, for example as the year of birth (1738) of the Jewish scholar Shelomoh Zalkind Horovitz, who was one of the students of Moses Mendelsohn and a member of the "Sanhedrin" during the time of Napoleon. Horovitz was an expert on oriental manuscripts in the National Library in Paris.

The Jews of Zheimel made their living from commerce and agriculture and almost every family had a small garden near their home. There were 753 Jews in the town in 1847.

In a news item which appeared in the newspaper "Ha Magid" in the year 1883, it was reported that a synagogue, one of the oldest in Lithuania and a study house (Beth Midrash) were built in 1862. In the 1880s, Zheimel gained publicity because of a dispute over the election of a Rabbi for the town. Two camps formed in Zheimel, each one wishing to impose their will on the other. As both sides were willing to use any means, such as informing the authorities, including violence, and smashing of windows, the authorities had to intervene.

The dispute in Zheimel lasted until Rabbi Abraham-Yitshak Hacohen Kook, who received his first appointment there, was elected Rabbi of Zheimel in 1887. Rabbi Kook officiated in the town for 7 years and managed to make real peace between the warring camps. During his tenure of office Rabbi Kook enriched the library of the Beth haMidrash and strengthened the welfare societies in the town, such as "Hakhnasath Orkhim", "Bikur Kholim", and "Gemiluth Khasadim." Owing to his efforts a bath house and a sauna were also built. In 1903 R. Kook immigrated (ascended) to Eretz Yisrael, becoming the Rabbi of Jaffa. From 1918 he officiated as the Chief Rabbi of Jerusalem, and from 1921 until his death in 1936 was the Chief Rabbi of Eretz Israel.

HaRav Kook

Rabbis who were appointed in Zheimel before and after Rabbi Kook were **Shelomoh** (from 1824 to 1864), **Benjamin-Dober Diamand** (from 1864), **Shalom Elkhanan Jaffe** (from 1883), who emigrated to the U.S. and served as a rabbi in St. Louis and Brooklyn, **Ya'acov-Dov Rapaport** (from 1896), who settled in Kefar Saba, Israel, in 1926, acquired a vineyard there and sent his son to cultivate it. R. Rapaport was the first Rabbi of Kefar Saba.

In 1891 a welfare society, "Lekhem Aniyim" - Bread for the Poor - was established with the assistance of the Mayor Prince Liven, who donated 35 pud of flour (570 kg), 50 funt of sugar (205 kg), and 3.5 kg tea to the society every 10th week. The Jewish benefactors were Tsevi Hirsch Abramovitz and Eliyahu-Matityahu Khayuth (Khayes). In the list of donors for the Yishuv (settlement) of Eretz Yisrael during the years 1900 and 1903 many of the people of Zheimel are mentioned.

In 1897 its population numbered 1266 people, among them 679 Jews (54%).

After World War I, Zheimel was cut off from its large rural hinterland, which was incorporated into Latvia. This fact and the policy of the Government of Lithuania, which strove to undermine the foundation of the Jewish economy, were the reasons for the decline of Zheimel's Jews fortunes, as a result of which many emigrated to South Africa, the United States, and Eretz Israel.

The Period of Lithuanian Independence.

Following the law of autonomies for minorities issued by the new Lithuanian government, the minister for Jewish affairs Dr. Menakhem (Max) Soloveitshik ordered elections to community committees (Va'ad Kehilah) to be held in the summer of 1919. In Zheimel a community committee of seven members was elected It was active in most spheres of Jewish life in the town for several years (1919-1925).

According to the first census carried out by the Lithuanian Government in 1923, there were then 1209 people in Zheimel, including 378 Jews (31%). The town was part of the Siauliai district.

During the years 1927-1928 Zheimel received much publicity because of a trial against five Jewish butchers who were accused of the murder of the local veterinary surgeon. The accused were each sentenced to five years in jail, but the Supreme Court reduced their sentence to only eight months. The Jews of Lithuania saw in this trial a Lithuanian version of the Beilis blood libel trial of 1913 in Russia. One of the defending counsels of the accused was the lawyer Dr. Ya'acov Robinson, previously the first director of the Hebrew high school in Virbalis. The well known lawyer A. Gruzenberg, the defending counsel in the Beilis trial, also advised the defense in this case.

During this period the Jews of Zheimel made their living mainly through commerce. There were merchants in the town who engaged in the export of flax, grain, etc., Zheimel being then a center for the export of flax. In the middle 1920s 250 wagons of flax seeds and about 200 wagons of flax would be exported from Zheimel during a season. Other Jews made their living as buyers in the villages, teamsters, packers and similar vocations.

During 1928 there was a severe crisis in Zheimel because the crops of flax and grain had failed, as a result of which many Jewish families had no means of support for their families, and thus a committee to help the destitute was established to provide bread and wood for heating for those in need. The Association of Zheimel Jews in America sent them $100, which was divided among 28 very needy families.

According to a government survey from 1931, there were 26 businessmen in Zheimel, 20 of whom were Jews, as detailed below:

Branch or sort of business	Total	Jewish Ownership
Grocery stores	3	2
Flax and Grain	7	7
Butcher shops & livestock trade	2	0
Restaurants & pubs	1	0
Clothes, furs, textiles	5	5
Shoes, leather, shoemaking	1	1
Medicines & cosmetics	1	1
Radios, sewing machines, electrical equipment	1	1
Work tools & iron implements		1
Paper, books & stationery	1	0
Miscellaneous	3	2

All the shops were concentrated around the market square from which four streets branched.

In 1937, 17 Jewish artisans worked in Zheimel: 9 tailors, 3 butchers, 2 bakers, 1 tinsmith, 1 photographer, and 1 barber, and in 1925 there were 2 Jewish physicians in the town. The Peoples Bank (Folksbank), which in 1927 had 118 members, played an important role in the town's economy. Out of 50 private and public telephone subscribers in 1939, 5 were Jewish.

From the mid-1930s the number of Jews in the town dwindled, due to the crisis in Lithuania and the overt propaganda by the Lithuanian merchant organization Verslas against buying from Jews. This caused many of them to seek their fortune elsewhere, and during those years many left the town, especially the young people who emigrated to Eretz Israel.

The primary education of the Jewish children of Zheimel was given at the Hebrew school belonging to the Tarbuth network, which had a special building of its own, built at the end of the 1920s. There was a library in Zheimel, and an amateur troupe which gave theater performances also in the surrounding towns.

Many of Zheimel's Jews belonged to the Zionist camp, almost all the Zionist parties were represented in the town and collections of donations were held for the National Funds "Keren Kayemeth", "Keren haYesod" and "Keren Tel-Hai". On the 26th of December 1934 a letter of one of the activists of "Keren Kayemeth" in Zheimel was published in the Yiddish daily newspaper "Dos Vort" in which he protested against "Keren Tel-Hai" of the Revisionists for distributing boxes of their fund to collect small donations similar to the popular blue box of "Keren Kayemeth".

The division of voters to the Zionist congresses during the 1930s is shown in the following table:

Cong. Nr.	Year	Shek.	Votes	Labor Party	Rev.	General Zionists		Grosmanists	Mizrahi
						A	B		
18	1933	----	108	66	36	4	----	1	1
19	1935	----	99	70	---	---	15	13	1
							National Block		
21*	1939	61	45	35	---	---	10		

Cong.-Congress; Shek.-Shekalim; Rev.-Revisionists;
  *The elections took place in the school building.

Zionist youth movements were active, among them Betar and HeKhalutz. Sports activities took place at the local Maccabi branch within whose framework a football team also functioned.

The "Maccabi" Soccer Team (?) of Zheimel

(Photo supplied and identified by Barry Mann)

Number	Name
1	- Unknown -
2	Moshe Yakushok
3	Ttzalel Marcunski
4	- Unknown -
5	Meyshke Gel
6	Meier Mann
7	- Unknown -
8	Herr (Herris)
9	Arke Yankelevich
10	Mateske Lakunishok
11	- Unknown -
12	Yerukham Mann
13	Benjamin Tarutz
14	Haike Israelson
15	Barukh Itkin
16	Hirshke Kremer
17	- Unknown -
18	Hirshke Tarutz
19	Hayimke Lakunishok
20	Feivel Zagorski

Zheimel "Maccabi" Branch, 1927

(Photo supplied and identified by Barry Mann)

Number Name	Number Name
1 Feivel Zagorski	20 Devorah Schneider
2 - Unknown -	(Synagogue Shamash's daughter)
3 Orke Gandz	21 - Unknown -
4 Meier Mann	22 Abke Herr
5 Itzke Burstein	23 Toybe Horovitz (Guta's sister)
6 Khilke Marcunski	24 Rivkah Singer
7 - Unknown -	25 His sister married Isser Israelson
8 - Unknown -	26 Aaron Mann
9 Matya Blume Lepar	27 Etka Kahn
10 Hanke Singer	28 Rohka Glezer
11 - Unknown -	29 Guta Horovitz
12 Benjamin or Dovidke Tarutz	30 Henokh Tarutz
13 Hirshke Kremer	31 Mateske Lakunishok
14 Tzemakh Yakushok	32 Mosheh Yakushok
15 Libe Dveire Mann	33 Shifrah Tabak
16 Zelda Lakunishok	34 Boska (Batya) Zagorski ?
17 Mosheh David Tarutz	35 Chilke Marcunski
18 Mosheh Gel	36 Stira Marcunski
19 Etke Burstein	37 Motka Yakushok
	38 Leyvi or Meyke Yakushok

The old synagogue and Bet Hamidrash were also the center of religious life in the town during this period. The Rabbis who officiated in Zheimel were R. Hayim-Zalman Kron, R. Yisrael Kravitz, R. Leib Siger, and R. Aryeh Leib Schneider, who were all murdered by the Lithuanians during the Holocaust.

Among the native born of Zheimel was the son of Rabbi Kook, by the name of R. Tsevi Yehudah son of R. Abraham-Yitshak Kook (born in 1821), in due course to be one of the principals of the "Merkaz Harav" Yeshivah in Jerusalem, who prepared to print and publish his father's writings. Others were Aharon Khayuth, who emigrated to Eretz Israel in the 1890s, built a flour mill in Tel Aviv and founded the Chamber of Commerce in Jerusalem. Also Nathan Rapaport, who emigrated to Eretz Israel in 1906 and was one of the first ten settlers in Kefar Saba, and was killed in 1921 while defending Petakh Tikvah against Arab marauders.

With the annexation of Lithuania by the USSR, and on becoming a Soviet Republic in 1940, part of the Jewish shops were nationalized, the Zionist political parties and youth movements were disbanded, and the Hebrew educational establishment closed. The supply of goods decreased, and as a result prices soared. The middle class, mostly Jewish, was hit hard, and the standard of living dropped gradually.

On the 22nd of June 1941 war broke out between Germany and the Soviet Union and the German army entered Zheimel at the end of the same month. Prior to that ten Jewish families had managed to escape to Russia.

During the first months of the Nazi German rule, the Jews did not suffer from any special oppression. But on the 8th of August 1941 (14th of Av 5701) the Lithuanian auxiliary police rounded up the Jews of Zheimel, transported them a distance of 2 km from the town into a forest and murdered them all by shooting.

In a document found in Zheimel after the war, an application by the local council to the district officer in Shavel is quoted as follows:

"In answer to your inquiry Number 962, we hereby inform you that in Zheimel there were a total of 205 Jews. 44 escaped to the Soviet Union, 160 were shot to death on the 8th of August 1941. At present there are 2 Jewish women here who tried to escape but returned, and they will be sent to Zagare (Zhager)."

According to Soviet sources, a mass grave was found after the war near the village of Veleisiai about 2 kilometers from Zheimel, where about 150 men, women and children are buried.

In 1959 there were 1,106 people in Zheimel and not one Jew!

The Mass Grave near the Village of Veleisiai.

The Old Jewish cemetery
The inscription in Hebrew, Yiddish and Lithuanian:
"The old Jewish cemetery, let the remembrance of the dead be sacred."

Barry Mann at his grandfather's house, 1999

Chamber of the Holocaust at Mount Zion in Jerusalem

(Photo supplied and identified by Barry Mann)

Number	Name
1	Esther Kremer
2	Basya Zagorski
3	- Unknown -
4	Shemuel Kremer
5	Evelyn (Buskin) Kremer
6	Zvi Kremer
7	Hana Gel (Wilk)
8	Berka Lakunishok
9	Frida Wilk, mother-in-law of Chana Gel
10	Dovydas Marcunski
11	Stira Marcunski
12	From Joniskis
13	From Joniskis
14	Minka Yankelevich

Bibliography:

Lite, New-York 1951, volume 1 & 2 (Yiddish).

Yad-Vashem archives, the Koniukhovsky collection 0-71, file 107.

YIVO, NY-Collection of the Jewish Communities of Lithuania, files 403-436, 1385,1587.

HaMeilitz- St. Petersburg, 21.11.1884; 15.5.1885; 5.6.1885; 9.3.1895.

Der Yiddisher Cooperator -Kovno, 1929 Nr.2-3.

Folksblat-Kovno16.10.1935.

Dos Vort-Kovno 26.12.1934.

Žemaičių Naumiestis (Naishtot-Tavrig)

Naishtot-Tavrig (in Yiddish) is situated in the Zemaitija region of Western Lithuania, near the Sustis River, about 2 kilometers from the border with East Prussia and 35 kilometers northwest of the district city of Tavrig (Taurage).

Until the First World War it was called "Naishtot Sugint" in Yiddish. Naishtot is mentioned in the official land registry in the year 1650, in 1750 the town being granted commercial privileges and in 1792 the right to self-government. After the third division of Poland in 1795, Naishtot became part of Russia, as did most of Lithuania, its name being changed to Aleksandrovsk having been annexed to the Vilna Gubernia (Province), and as from 1843 to the Kovno Gubernia. During the second half of the nineteenth century the town developed considerably, to the extent that there were 165 houses in 1860 with 1,600 people living there, the majority being Jews.

Its proximity to the German border and the existence of a customs office boosted its commerce. There were warehouses for merchandise, 30 shops and taverns, 3 flour-mills, 3 workshops for leather processing, a hospital, an elementary school, with two yearly fairs and two weekly markets being held in the town. By 1897 the population had increased to 2,445, including 1,438 Jews (59%).

When World War I broke out in 1914, most of Naishtot's houses were burned down, and being too near the front, its inhabitants evacuated to safer places. During the years 1914 - 1918 Naishtot was ruled by the German Army, and after the war, when independent Lithuania was established, the Germans returned the town to the new state. From the middle of the 1930s it was called Zemaiciu Naumiestis, the *"new town of the Zemaitija people."*

The Jewish Community until the end of World War I.

Jews settled in Naishtot at the beginning of the seventeenth century and made their living by trading, mainly grain and flax, with Memel, Koenigsberg and Hamburg. They also owned shops and a few families grew vegetables.

In due course the Jews built two synagogues - a Beth-Knesset and a Beth-Midrash. Among the Rabbis who served in Naishtot were Avraham ben Shelomoh-Zalman, (a brother of the Gaon of Vilna), the author of the book "Ma'aloth Hatorah" ("Steps of the Torah") published in Koenigsberg, 1851 (5611); his son Eliyahu ben Avraham; his son Shelomoh-Zalman ben Eliyahu; Ya'akov Bendetman who died in 1861 and whose book "Zikhron Ya'akov" was published by his grandson in Vilna in 1875 (5635); Eliezer Yehoshua Shapira (from 1898).

Zionist ideas began to find roots in Naishtot in the 1880s. On the occasion of Mosheh Montefiore's 100th birthday in 1884, a special prayer "Mi Shebeirah" was offered in his honor by Torah readers, and contributions were given for the settlement of Eretz-Israel. The money raised was sent to the editorial board of the Hebrew newspaper "HaMeilitz" in St. Petersburg in order to be transferred to Eretz-Israel. There were, however, many opponents to Zionism in Naishtot.

During those years, hundreds of Naishtot's Jews emigrated to South Africa, England and America. Some Jews returned to Naishtot after having lived in South Africa for a few years, bringing a lot of money with them. In 1884 about 200 young men emigrated to South Africa, of whom 10 returned home to Naishtot, after becoming wealthy. In those years there were families in Naishtot whose only income was the money sent to them by their relatives from South Africa.

In Naishtot, like in most of the Jewish communities, mutual aid funds existed. When a pogrom took place in the city of Nizhni-Novgorod in Russia in July 1884 and Jews were murdered, money was raised for the kinsmen of the victims. The emigrants from Naishtot in South Africa also raised a considerable sum of money, which was sent to its destination via the Rabbi of Kovno, Yitshak Elhanan Spector.

During this period a Jewish physician (Dr. Paul Valk) and a Jewish pharmacist (Julian Vainstein) were active in Naishtot and both were very devoted to helping the sick and poor of the town.

The German Army occupied Naishtot at the beginning of the First World War, as mentioned before. They transferred Jewish youth from Poland to Naishtot, placing them in the synagogues which had been turned into labor camps, surrounded by a wire fence, its inhabitants occupied in various tasks of forced labor and as conditions were very bad, hunger and sickness prevailed. Naishtot's Jews helped the imprisoned far beyond their ability, in spite of the fact that it was strictly forbidden to maintain any contact with the prisoners.

During the Period of Independent Lithuania.

At the beginning of the 1920s Naishtot elected a community committee of nine members, in accordance with the Autonomy Law for Jews. This committee acted via sub-committees in most spheres of Jewish life and existed until the end of 1925. The committee owned some agricultural land of a few hundred hectares outside the town, a part of which was sold to local Jews and another part was leased, this area being owned by the community until Lithuania became a Soviet Republic in 1940.

According to the first survey of the Lithuanian Government in 1923, there were 1,771 people, of them 664 Jews (37%), in the town.

The Jews made their living mainly from commerce, while some of them were craftsmen. The German border being near, the export of horses, geese, flax, eggs and other agricultural produce went by way of Naishtot, many Jewish families earning their livelihood from this trade, although the main exporters were local Germans.

According to the government survey of 1931, Naishtot had 33 shops, 22 (63%) of them owned by Jews according to the table below:

The type of the business	Total	In Jewish Ownership
Groceries	2	0
Butcher shops and meat trade	7	4
Restaurants and taverns	8	4
Textile products and furs	3	2
Leather and shoes	2	1
Haberdashery and cooking utensils	1	1
Drugs and cosmetics	1	1
Watches and jewelry	2	2
Others	9	7

According to the same survey the Jews in Naishtot owned a power station (S. Rabin), a wool combing workshop and a bakery. In 1937 there were 25 Jewish craftsmen: 6 tailors, 4 shoemakers, 4 butchers, 2 tinkers, 1 baker, 1 hatter, 1 carpenter, 1 barber, 1 watchmaker and 4 other tradesmen in the town.

The Market Place

The Folksbank, established in 1925 and claiming 102 members was accepted as a member of the Association of the Folksbanks in Lithuania in 1930 and contributed much to the economic life of the town. In 1939 there were 40 telephones, of which 10 belonged to Jews.

Jewish children were educated in the local Hebrew school established in 1920 and many of them continued their studies in the Hebrew High Schools and "Yeshivoth" of the state (Tavrig, Telsh, Kelm, Slobodka). There was also a "Heder" in Naishtot with very few pupils as well as a Jewish library with several hundred books in Hebrew and in Yiddish.

From time to time there were theatrical performances by local amateurs. The synagogue (shul) which was burned down in 1914, was rebuilt as a magnificent brick building thanks to the donation of 1,000 pounds from the former citizens of Naishtot, Sami Marx and the brothers Luis and Max Rothchild from South Africa. The initiative for this enterprise came from Rabbi Ya'akov Mosheh Lesin, who was also the last Rabbi of Naishtot **(see plaque on the synagogue below).**

This building still stands as can be seen in the photo above that was taken in 1996. In the "shul" prayers took place only during the summer, because it was too cold in the winter. In the other synagogue, the "Beth-Midrash", where most middle class people prayed, all were acquainted with the "Torah", they would study a page of the "Talmud" in the evenings. There was an additional house of prayer (Klois) for the craftsmen of Naishtot, which also served as their meeting place. In this "Klois", in addition to praying, they would learn a chapter of "Ein Ya'akov" (a collection of tales in the "Talmud"). Some boys of Naishtot were organized in "Tifereth-Bakhurim", an organization whose task it was to learn "Torah" and to be engaged in public and social activity.

Naishtot's welfare institutions consisted of "Linath Hatsedek" and "Gemiluth Hasidim", helping those in need, as well as the "Ezrah" and "Adath-Israel" societies, who competed with each other with regard to managing the community's affairs.

Many of Naishtot's Jews supported the Zionist idea and there were supporters of all the Zionist parties. In the elections to the first Lithuanian "Seim" (Parliament), which took place in October 1922, 161 Jews voted for the Zionist list, 105 - for "Akhduth" (Religious) and 3 for the Democrats.

Below are the results of the elections to the Zionist congresses in Naishtot:

Cong. Nr.	Year	Total Shek.	Total Voter	Labor Party		Rev.	G. Z.		Gr.	Miz.
				Z"S	Z"Z		A	B		
15	1927	---	24	14	2	---	2		---	---	6
16	1929	---	19	---	5	1	3		---	---	10
17	1931	---	34	17	3	5	1		---	---	8
18	1933	---	---		52	39	8		---	3	44
19	1935	---	246	112		----	1		16	13	104

Shek.-Shekalim; Rev.-Revisionists; G.Z.-General Zionists; Gr.-Grosmanists; Miz.-Mizrahi

"HeKhalutz"(established by the initiative of Avraham Benjaminovitz), "HeKhalutz-HaTzair" and "Beitar" were among the Zionist youth organizations. Members of these organizations would raise money for the Jewish National Funds, such as the Keren Kayemeth, Keren Hayesod and Keren Tel-Hai. There was also an "Urban Kibutz" of "HeKhalutz" in Naishtot in 1923.

Many of the youngsters were organized in "Maccabi", which had a football team and athletics classes.

**The Synagogue in Zemaiciu Naumiestis (Naishtot-Tavrig), Lithuania
April 1996**

The Plaque on the Synagogue

**" HERE UNTIL JUNE 22, 1941 WAS SYNAGOGUE WHICH WAS LED BY THE
WORLD FAMOUS RABBI J. M. LESINAS"** *(Rabbi Lesin in Yiddish)"*

(Photo and translation supplied by Gerrard Rudmin)

Family of Rabbi Lesin

(Photo courtesy of Dr. Ben Lesin – son of Rabbi Lesin)

On the whole, relations between the Jews and the Lithuanian majority were more or less correct. But in the middle of the 1930s a branch of the Lithuanian Merchants Association "Verslas" was established in Naishtot, whose task it was to expel the Jews from commerce. In March 1936 there was an attempt to stage a pogrom on Naishtot's Jews as a result of a blood libel, but the police crushed it before it began. In April 1939 two Lithuanians were caught trying to erase signs of Jewish shops.

On the third of May 1939, during a big market fair in Naishtot, violence broke out against the Jews, when windows of Jewish houses and of the Beth-Midrash as well as the schools were smashed. During those several hours when the crowds rampaged, the local police did not intervene, and only forces summoned from outside stopped the raging crowd.

During this "Pogrom" 1722 windows and much furniture in 62 Jewish houses were broken (A partial list of the Jews who were injured in this pogrom is given in Appendix 1). The estimate of the damage amounted to 8360 Lit (A worker earned 3-4 Lit per day).

The authorities intervened and 21 Lithuanians were punished in that same month: 18 were sent to a labor camp, the other three were fined. As a result of these and other events the number of the Jews in Naishtot decreased to 120 families, many Jews emigrating to South Africa and America, and the youth to Eretz-Yisrael.

Among the native sons of Naishtot there were Sami Marx, in due course a millionaire in South Africa, a senator and friend of the former President of South-Africa Paul Kruger; N.D. Hofman, a correspondent of "HaMeilitz" and later the pioneer of the Jewish press in South-Africa; Shemuel Talpiyoth, an educator in Montreal, who was a correspondent of the newspapers "HaMeilitz", "HaTzefira", "HaTzofeh" and "HaZeman" and published many articles in the "Kanader Adler"; Eliyahu Ragoler served as Rabbi in several communities in Lithuania, and also Shelomoh Zalman Abel, one of the founders of the famous Yeshivah of Telsh.

During World War II and Thereafter.

With the annexation of Lithuania to the Soviet Union in the summer of 1940, most of the industrial plants and big shops were nationalized. The supply of goods was reduced, and consequently prices rose. The middle class, mostly Jewish, was badly hurt, its standard of living reduced and several Jewish families were exiled to Russia. All Zionist parties and youth organizations were dispersed and Hebrew educational and cultural institutions were closed.

On the June 22, 1941, at 5 o'clock in the morning, the German Army entered Naishtot As a result of shooting from the dwellings of the Soviet officers, 14 German soldiers were killed, and in response the Germans arrested many Jewish men and imprisoned them in the local Lutheran Church. Only after the Lithuanian priest assured the Germans that the Jews were innocent, were they allowed to return to their homes. In the first weeks of the occupation the Jews were employed in various types of work, such as sweeping streets, repairing roads, and many Jews worked in a big German field bakery. They had to wear a yellow patch on their clothes and were forbidden to walk on the sidewalks.

At the beginning of July all the Jews were ordered to leave their houses and to concentrate in a few houses in the Pigs street, a derelict quarter near the Sustis River, which was the Ghetto of Naishtot's Jews.

Sometime in June the Jews were forced, by means of threats and beatings, to remove all the holy books, the "Torah Scrolls", the "Aron Kodesh" and even the benches from the synagogue, to take them to the yard and to burn them.

The Germans and the Lithuanians took five Jewish girls from the Ghetto, and what happened to them is not known. They were: Rivkah Lesin, Menuhah Volpert, Sheine Glat-Shor, Gisa Berelowitz, Hanah Shnaid and Rachel Lerman.

On Saturday, 24th of Tamuz 5701 (19.7.1941), all men 14 years old and above were ordered to assemble in the yard of the synagogue, where the old and the sick, about 70 people, were separated from them. Ten men were released in order to take care of the women and children in the Ghetto and the remaining 27 men were put on trucks, to be transferred in the direction of the German border. At their request, the S.S. men allowed them to take warm clothes from their homes. The same evening they arrived in Heidekrug, about 15 km from

Naishtot, where they were imprisoned in a labor camp. On that day all the old and the sick from Naishtot and the neighboring town Vainutas were forced to dig a big hole, after which they were made to take off their clothes and were then murdered by Lithuanian policemen in the valley of Siaudvyciai. Trucks of Jews from Pajuris, Shvekshna, Verzhan (Veivirzenai), Riteve (Rietava), Khveidan (Kvedarna) and Laukuva were brought to this place and all were shot and buried there. More Jews from other towns were brought to the Heidekrug camp, where Naishtot's Jews found many acquaintances and even friends with the S.S. and the foremen, but these people distanced themselves and behaved badly to them. The Jews in the camp worked very hard, suffering from hunger and abuse, and the women in the Ghetto were taken to work with peasants in the vicinity. One day, probably the 4th of Tishrei (September 25, 1941), the ten men, all the women and children were taken to Siaudvyciai and murdered there. The Jewish men were kept in the Heidekrug camp for more then two years, during which time some were murdered by the Germans, but at the end of July 1943 those still alive were transferred to Auschwitz. On their arrival there (the first of Av 5703) a selection took place and 99 of them, among them some of Naishtot's Jews, were sent to the crematorium. In October 1943 thousands of men, among them the survivors of Naishtot, were transferred to Warsaw, where they worked to clear the debris of the ruined Ghetto. Their material and sanitary conditions were so bad that typhus broke out and many of them died. When the battle front approached Warsaw in the summer of 1944, some of the forced laborers were sent to a camp near Dachau, others were left in the same place and worked in explosive blasting. Only a few of Naishtot's Jews who were left in Warsaw, were eventually freed by the Red Army, the others, who had been sent to Bavaria, were freed by the American Army. Of those Naishtot Jews who had been forcibly sent to the Heidekrug labor camp, only seven survived. The Berelovitz family, one of the few Jewish families who managed to escape to Russia at the beginning of the war, returned to Naishtot at the end of hostilities. During the night between the 11th and the 12th of May 1946 their houses were blown up by Lithuanian nationalists and the mother of the family Nekha Berelovitz, her daughter Hanah Berelowitz, her brother Asher Joselevitz and Mordehai Berelovitz were killed. Shelomoh Berelovitz, who fought with the Red Army in freeing Lithuania from the Nazis, was badly injured. In his trial the murderer testified that he killed the Jews because he could not tolerate the fact that Jews were returning to Naishtot and settling there again.

The survivors and a few other natives of Naishtot who returned from Russia managed, after great efforts, to set up a tombstone on the mass graves on which they wrote:" Here rest citizens of the Soviet Union who were murdered by the Nazis."

The mass graves near the village Siaudvyciai, 3 kilometers east of Naishtot-Tavrig where the Jews of this town, the town of Vainutas and the vicinity were murdered and buried.

לזכר עולם

לקדושי קהילת

נוישטאט

(ע"י טבריג ליטא) הי"ד

שנרצחו ונספו

ע"י הגרמנים והליטאים ימ"ש

בשנת תש"א 41.

יום הזכרון כ"ד תמוז

דמם הקדוש לא ימוש מקרבנו לנצח

ת' נ' צ' ב' ה'

יוצאי וזכרידי קהילת נוישטאט

בישראל ובתפוצות

להנצחה לקדושי נישטאט

באחרי הבואה בהר-ציון ירושלים

Plaque for Naishtot-Tavrig in the Holocaust Cellar at Mount Zion in Jerusalem

The translation of the plaque is:

In eternal memory of the Naishtot-Tavrig Martyrs who were murdered by the Germans and the Lithuanians in 5701-1941.

Memorial day is on the 24th of Tamuz.

We will remember them forever.

Former citizens of the Naishtot Community in Israel and in the Diaspora.

In "Martef Hashoah" (The Holocaust Cellar) on Mount Zion in Jerusalem, the former citizens of Naishtot in Israel erected a memorial plate for their community.

Sources:

Yad Vashem Archives, the Koniukhovsky Collection 0-71, files 4,16; M-1/E-1619

YIVO, Collection of the Lithuanian Jewish Communities, file 1532, pages 63819-815, 63797, 63804, 63808, 69607-610

Gotlib, Ohalei Shem, page 365

Our Town Naishtot, published by the Naishtot-Tavrig natives committee in Israel 5742-1982

Di Yiddishe Shtime (Kovno)- 13.1.1928, 28.3.1930, 3.3.1936, 4.3.1936, 5.5.1939, 8.5.1939, 12.5.1939, 16.5.1939

Dos Wort (Kovno) 5.5.1939

Volksblat (Kovno) 25.4.1939

Der Yiddisher Cooperator (Kovno) - Nr. 2-3, 10, 1930

Hameilitz (St, Peterburg) - 26.3.1883, 28.7.1884, 27.10.1884, 7.12.1884, 7.9.1886, 12.9.1886

Appendix I

A Partial List of the Jews of Naishtot-Tavrig Injured in the Pogrom of May 3, 1939

Berelovitz Hayah-Riva	Kruger Bliuma
Berelovitz Faivel	Lapin Leib
Birk Mosheh	Levenberg David
Blumberg Hene	Leizerovitz Shemuel
Blumberg Motel	Levi Salomon
Blumberg Shelomoh	Levin Hirsh
Braude Berl (Beth Hamidrash)	Levinzon Aba
Davidzon Motel	Lipshitz Hayim
Disler G. Dr.	Joselevitz Leib
Dubinsky Efraim	Joselevitz Stere
Elert Avraham	Nosel Sholem
Falt Eliyahu	Rabin Salomon
Girshovitz Faivel	Rabinzon Meir
Glat Eliyahu	Shulman David
Grosman Grisha	Shvartz David
Kalner Avraham	Shur Yisrael
Katz Shelomoh	Zaks Avraham

Appendix II

List of Naishtot-Tavrig Jews who fought with the Red Army during World War II

1.	Gold Izik	(Died in battle in 1943)
2.	Lasky Leib	(Died in battle in 1943)
3.	Kruger Izik	(Died in battle)
4.	Shnaid Avraham	(in Israel)
5.	Dubinsky Jeshayahu	(in Israel)
6.	Leibovitz Jeshayahu	(in Israel)
7.	Berelowitz Shelomoh	(in Israel)
8.	Troib Zalman	
9.	Berelovitz Mordehai	(killed in Naishtot 1946)
10.	Katz	(killed in Naishtot 1945)
11.	Joselevitz Asher	(killed in Naishtot 1946)
12.	Robinzon Benjamin	(in Israel)
13.	Kaganovitz Yisrael	(in Kovno)
14.	Kelner Dov	(in Israel)

Appendix III   List of Naishtot-Tavrig Jews Living in Israel

Abramovitz Elik
Adar- Lipshitz Hasiah
Abramovitz Meir
Aldema-Judelevitz Zehavah
Alexander-Reznik Liuba
Akravi-Rabinovitz Jonah
Avinokham-Judelevitz Tziporah
Elert David
Elert Yisrael
Blumberg Aharon
Berelowitz Shimon Aharon
Berlowitz Shelomoh
Brukman-Davidzon Eta
Bernshtein-Glukh Bela
Blumental-Abramovitz Hayah
Benjaminovitz Sarah & Yisrael
Ben Har (Blumberg) Betsalel
Cohen David
Columbus-Markus Tsesna
Davidzon Sarah
Dubinsky Jeshayahu
Disler-Robinzon Tzirl

Disler Shimon
Fayet Eliyahu
Filmeister-Kelner Sarah
Goldberg Jehoshua
Goldberg Malkah
Gershenovitz Batya & Mosheh
Gros-Jankelevitz Miryam
Glesner-Rodner Miryam
Glas Dov
Galperin-Elert Leah
Glik Azriel
Guselevitz Menakhem
Hirshfeld-Fayet Jonah
Hartuv-Rabinovitz Malkah
Hofman David
Ilan- Shavshevitz Tovah
Judelevitz-Nekhames Gita
Jafe Gita
Kadesh Shoshana & Yehudah
Zerakh
Kaplan Azriel
Kelner Dov

Kruger Mosheh
Kuperberg-Joselevitz Hana
Kurland-Berelovitz Gita
Lasky Refael
Leibovitz Shaya
Lesin Ya'akov Mosheh, Rabbi
Levitan-Givshon Fruma
Levitan-Lapin Sarah
Levinzon Gedalyahu
Levinzon Shoshana
Lifshitz Ya'akov
Lifshitz Shemuel
Lifshitz Ze'ev
Lipnitzky- Rodner Matla
Lokshen Tzirl
Lubin-Khaitovitz Pola
Lubinsky-Kelner Slava
Mendelson-Zakon Ida
Miler-Judelevitz Nekhamah
Milner Mosheh
Milshtein-Elert Nekhamah
Neuman-Reznik Batyah
Nusovsky Nekha
Peltz-Segal Gita
Perlshtein- Gordon Dinah
Priman-Levinson Slava
Rabinovitz-Kruger Rachel
Rapoport-Kaplan Hana
Rafaeli-Shlomovitz Bluma

Raikh-Gordon Fruma
Reznik Ber Hirsh, Rabbi
Reznik Hanah
Reznik Gita
Reznik Betsalel
Robinzon Benjamin
Robinzon-Kaplan Shoshana
Robinzon Betsalel
Rodner David
Rodner Akiva, Rabbi
Rodner Perl-Peninah
Rozman-Zakon Ela
Shalom-Reznik Jafah
Shavshevitz Yitshak
Solomovitz-Zaks Bluma
Shavit-Shavshevitz Rivkah
Shlapobersky-Fayet Eta
Shlapobersky-Shapiro Pesia
Shnaid Avraham
Shnaider-Berelowitz Jokheved
Shor Mosheh
Troib Asnath & Elkhanan
Troib Zalman
Troib Yosef
Veis-Grosman Sarah
Volpert Yitshak
Zaltzman-Volpert Bilhah
Zaks Aryeh

Appendix IV

List of Naishtot-Tavrig Jews Living Outside Israel

Beker Hasyah	South Africa
Beker Khiene	South Africa
Beker Leizer	South Africa
Beker Avraham	South Africa
Beker Betsalel	South Africa
Blumberg Frida	South Africa
Berend-Ziman Esther	South Africa
Bernshtein Ita	(of the family of Meir-Leib) U.S.A.
Bernshtein Ete	(of the family of Meir-Leib) U.S.A.
Bernshtein Sarah	(of the family of Meir-Leib) U.S.A.

Bernshtein Eidke	(of the family of Meir-Leib) U.S.A.
Bernshtein Yisrael	(of the family of Meir-Leib) U.S.A.
Gold Leizer	Germany
Goldberg Shabtai	U.S.A.
Elert (Eli) Heiny	South Africa, Johannesburg #
Fayet Aryeh-Leib	South Africa
Fayet-Berend Miryam	South Africa
Hofman Aryeh-Leib	South Africa
Jankelevitz Zelig	South Africa
Katsev Hanah Roise	U.S.A.
Katsev Meir	U.S.A.
Lapin Benjamin	U.S.A.
Lesin-Glat Malkah	U.S.A.
Lesin Meir-Yisrael, Rabi	U.S.A.
Lesin Etl	U.S.A.
Levinzon Ya'akov	U.S.A.
Mendes Motel	South Africa
Shnaid Tzipke	South Africa
Shnaid Mosheh	South Africa

 # Information supplied by his cousin Barry Mann, El Paso, Texas, USA

www.ingramcontent.com/pod-product-compliance
Lightning Source LLC
Chambersburg PA
CBHW071917160426
42814CB00042B/134